KARL MARX
FREDERICK ENGELS
COLLECTED WORKS
VOLUME
50

KARL MARX
FREDERICK ENGELS

COLLECTED
WORKS

INTERNATIONAL PUBLISHERS
NEW YORK

KARL MARX
FREDERICK ENGELS

Volume
50

ENGELS: 1892-95

INTERNATIONAL PUBLISHERS
NEW YORK

This volume has been prepared jointly by Lawrence & Wishart Ltd., London, International Publishers Co. Inc., New York, and Progress Publishing Group Corporation, Moscow, in collaboration with the Russian Independent Institute of Social and National Problems (former Institute of Marxism-Leninism), Moscow.

Editorial commissions:

GREAT BRITAIN: Eric Hobsbawm, John Hoffman, Nicholas Jacobs, Monty Johnstone, Jeff Skelley, Ernst Wangermann, Ben Fowkes.

USA: James E. Jackson, Victor Perlo, Betty Smith, Dirk J. Struik.

RUSSIA: for Progress Publishing Group Corporation— Yu. V. Semyonov, Ye. N. Vladimirova; for the Russian Independent Institute of Social and National Problems—L.I. Golman, M.P. Mchedlov, V.N. Pospelova, G.L. Smirnov.

Library of Congress Cataloging in Publication Data

Marx, Karl, 1818-1883.
    Karl Marx, Frederick Engels: collected works.
1. Socialism — Collected works. 2. Economics— Collected works. I. Engels, Friedrich, 1820-1895. Works. English. 1975. II. Title
HX 39. 5. A 16 1975 335.4 73-84671
ISBN 0-7178-0550-6 (v. 50)

Printed in the USA

Contents

FREDERICK ENGELS LETTERS
October 1892 to July 1895

1892

1893

vi

1895

xii

Supplementary Letters

Notes and Indexes

Illustrations

Engels in the vicinity of Zurich in September of 1893
(from left to right) Dr. Ferdinand Simon, Frieda Simon, Clara Zetkin, Engels, Julie and August Bebel, Ernst Schattner, Regina and Eduard Bernstein

PREFACE

The fiftieth and concluding volume of the English edition of the works of Marx and Engels contains letters written by Engels between October 1892 and July 1895.

In the last years of his life, Engels witnessed amazing changes in the politics and economics of contemporary society. Processes which began in the capitalist world in the 1870s had led, by the early 1890s, to major changes affecting every aspect of life, thereby exerting a direct impact on the working-class movement. The emergence of parliamentary government, the expansion of voting rights, the complete legalisation of trade unions and other worker organisations had created favourable conditions in which to campaign for a real improvement in the position of working people, for an increase of the influence of socialist parties and for the strengthening of their role in political life. There had also been changes in certain aspects of capitalist production, although these were not yet so obvious. As one might expect, Engels increasingly directed his thoughts to the prospects for and future of the struggle for working-class emancipation and to the ways and means of achieving its short-term and long-term goals; this is reflected in his numerous letters. His ideas on these issues were neither the result of abstract argument, nor were they the merely theoretical calculations of an academic isolated from the real world. To the end of his life, Engels maintained close contacts with the leaders of socialist parties in various European countries, with followers of Marx, with young scholars who showed an interest in his theoretical works and in Marxism, willingly sharing with them his views and ideas. A determined opponent of dogmatising, Engels revised many former concepts regarding forms and methods of proletarian struggle for workers' rights and a radical reformation of society in the light of history and the major changes taking place in his own day. Himself an eye-witness of the first steps taken by an independent working-class movement, and an active participant in this movement for almost fifty years, he was well positioned to appreciate the undoubted successes achieved by it. He saw their successes as visible proof of the validity of the Marxist theory on the historical role of the working class.

The early 1890s were, in this respect, a sign of things to come. By this time socialist parties had been set up in most European countries. They were winning ever-wider support, and held seats in the parliaments of a number of states. As a rule, their programmes were based on Marxist theory. The most powerful of these parties, the German Social-Democratic Party, whose success had led to the annulment of the Anti-Socialist law, was securing a growing number of votes at each successive election, and there seemed to be every reason to believe that it might soon become a decisive power in the Reichstag. When the English trade-union congress decided to include in its programme the demand for the nationalisation of the means of production, when the trade union representatives were sent to international socialist congresses, and the Independent Labour Party was set up in 1892, Engels began to anticipate the emergence in the near future of a mass political party of the English working class. The viability of the new International, which had emerged in the wake of the 1889 International Congress in Paris, had been proved by the enthusiastic response to its appeal for May Day demonstrations to campaign for an 8-hour working day. Hundreds of thousands of people were now taking part in these demonstrations every year.

All these events inspired Engels with optimism. If the working-class movement in the major countries of Europe continued to develop at this rate and along these same lines, then he believed this might accelerate the crisis of the capitalist system. 'The growth of the proletarian movement in all countries', he wrote to Bebel in October 1893, 'is about to precipitate a crisis ... which may not be upon us for some five or six years yet.' This optimism was further strengthened, as letters published in this volume (pp. 172-189) reveal, by his trip to Europe in the summer of 1893, in the course of which he visited Vienna, Berlin and Prague, and attended the final session of the International Socialist Congress in Zurich.

Engels's belief that the capitalist system—at least in Europe, to which his statements on this subject are invariably restricted—would collapse in the relatively near future was based not only on the success of the proletarian movement, but also on his theoretical analysis of new phenomena and trends in capitalist economics. In 1891, in his critique of the draft of the new programme of the German Social-Democratic Party, Engels noted that the creation of large joint-stock companies and trusts meant 'an end not only to *private production* but also to *planlessness*' (present edition, Vol. 27, p. 224). Further on he writes that 'the material and cultural conditions' for the transformation of capitalist production into socialist production 'on behalf of society as a whole and according to a preconceived plan' are being created by capitalist society itself (ibid.).

Subsequent events confirmed that Engels had correctly identified the trends appearing in the development of capitalist production. He believed, however, that these trends were leading, moreover in a relatively short historical period of time, to the collapse of the capitalist system. While appreciating that 'those economic consequences of the capitalist system, which must bring it up to the critical point, are only just now developing', he nonetheless considered it quite possible that this crisis in the capitalist system would occur quite soon as a result of events taking place in the major states of Europe (see this volume, pp. 59, 75-6, 273). In articles, and particularly in letters, Engels identified individual cases of corruption involving a number of prominent politicians in France, Italy and elsewhere as symptoms revealing the general inability of the bourgeois state to discharge its functions, as indications that the existing social order was on the verge of collapse. '... there is nothing stable about France ... a crisis of the first water in Italy...—he wrote to F. A. Sorge on January 16, 1895, 'in short, things are growing critical throughout the whole of Europe' (p. 424).

This crisis of bourgeois society, a crisis which Engels believed to be imminent, would also be the result, in his opinion, of the intensifying economic conflict among the major capitalist countries, caused in part by the emergence of the USA onto the world market. Developing this idea in a letter to N. F. Danielson, dated 24 February 1893, Engels wrote that economic rivalry between the USA on the one hand, and England, France and Germany on the other, could only mean that 'the crisis must come, *tout ce qu'il y a de plus fin de siecle*' (p. 111). Clearly Engels supposed that this rivalry would provoke an acute economic crisis which would spread to the political and social spheres, and that this might well create the prerequisite conditions for the collapse of the capitalist system, a collapse which, so he believed, would occur not automatically, but as a result of the energetic actions of the working class. In December 1894, he wrote to P. Lavrov, '... the whole of Europe is warming up, crises are brewing everywhere, particularly in Russia' (p. 389). Three months later, in a letter to Vaillant, he wrote: 'The end of the century is taking a decidedly revolutionary turn' (p. 455).

Pondering the various possible forms of that revolutionary crisis which might, in his view, create favourable conditions in which the proletariat could win political power in the countries of Europe, Engels's hopes turned in particular to Germany, which had the strongest socialist workers' movement and was suffering from acute internal conflicts. On 5 December 1892, he wrote to Laura Lafargue 'the next revolution ... is preparing in Germany with a consistency and steadiness unequalled anywhere else' (p. 59). He believed that the revolution, having begun in Germany or France, or possibly in some other country, for example in Austria or Russia, would inevitably spread to other countries. 'If France', he wrote to Lafargue on 27 June 1893, *'perhaps*, gives the signal, it will be in Germany—the country most profoundly influenced by socialism, and where the theory has the most deeply penetrated the masses—where the fight will be settled' (p. 157). At the same time he believed it very likely that 'if it does not bring the final victory, it will nevertheless make that victory a foregone conclusion' (p. 175).

As we now know, these prognostications were not fulfilled. However, this does not mean that they had no real basis. That his arguments were not groundless, and that he had accurately noted the trends is shown by the major events which marked the first decades of the 20th century. On 8 February 1895, Engels wrote to G. V. Plekhanov: 'And when the devil of the revolution has someone at his collar, then he has Nicholas II' (p. 440). Indeed, ten years later, a popular revolution developed in the Russian Empire, and if it was not then victorious, it nonetheless shook the foundations of the autocracy and made a profound impact on other countries, particularly in the East. Engels often expressed the idea that the approaching war would be pan-European, and twenty years later that war broke out. However, his main prognosis concerning the imminent collapse of capitalism proved invalid, and not only as regards the timing. Having recognised that his and Marx's hopes that the proletariat would be victorious as early as the mid-19th century (see present edition, Vol. 22, p. 533) were mistaken, Engels nonetheless remained captive to such illusions, believing that capitalism had already exhausted its potential by the end of the century, and that conditions were ripe for the emergence of new social relations. His postulates that the latest economic crisis would bring with it the collapse of bourgeois society, that capitalism had outlived itself and was at the time failing to stimulate the development of productive forces were proved mistaken by the subsequent course of history.

However, those same facts upon which Engels based himself when assessing the objective pre-conditions necessary for the victory of the new social order, for a socialist revolution, facts which, so it seemed to him, confirmed the inevitability of the emergence in the near future of the possibility of a radical reformation of society, were also the facts which prompted him to reassess concepts formulated in the wake of the revolutions of the 19th century as regards the ways and means by which the proletariat could achieve political power, a factor which he considered of major importance and a necessary prerequisite of any transition to new social relations

The letters published in this volume reveal the development of Engels' thoughts on the strategy and tactics of the emancipation struggle. He realised that the methods used in those revolutions in which he himself had been actively involved were no longer applicable: 'The era of barricades and street fighting has gone for good; *if the military fight*, resistance becomes madness. Hence the necessity to find new revolutionary tactics, (see this volume, p. 21) he wrote to Lafargue in November 1892. At the same time—and most importantly—by the 1890s the working class in the majority of European countries had much greater opportunity to use legal methods thanks to the emergence, albeit in differing forms, of parliamentary government. Here Engels attributed the main role to parliamentary activity by the socialists, and to universal suffrage. He did so basing himself on the experience of the German Social-Democratic Party, whose practical activity deeply influenced his thinking. A number of Engels's letters (to Victor Adler on 11 October, to August Bebel on 12 October, and on 18 October 1893) contain ideas which received their final formulation in Engels's last work, *Introduction to Karl Marx's 'The Class Struggles in France, 1848 to 1850'.* Emphasising the importance of the campaign for universal suffrage then being mounted in Belgium and Austria, he wrote to August Bebel: 'The suffrage movement won its first victory in Belgium, and now Austria is about to follow suit. At the outset this will ensure the *survival* of universal suffrage, but also encourage us to make further demands—in Germany no less than in France and Italy' (p. 206). In another letter to Bebel he again emphasises the importance of legal methods of proletarian struggle, arguing that 'governments are again coming under the control of a living political movement among the people ... it is *we* who determine it', its 'conquests in the libertarian sense, greater political power for the working man, the extension of his freedom of movement' (p. 219).

The letters published in this volume provide manifest evidence of the pleasure which Engels felt at the successes of the socialists and their increasing influence. This is clearly seen in a letter from Engels to Julia, Bebel's wife, about a meeting between Bebel, Lafargue and Burns at his flat: 'That such a meeting should be possible, a meeting at which the three leading parliaments of Europe, the three dominant nations of Europe, will be represented by three Socialist Party leaders, is in itself proof of what enormous advances we have made' (p. 131). A year later he expressed his confident belief that 'before long there will be no European parliament without labour representatives (ibid., p. 283). 'Today', he wrote to E. Vandervelde in October 1894, 'the socialist movement everywhere is more powerful than the so-called public force' (p. 357). These successes, achieved by using exclusively 'legal' methods, strengthened his view that universal suffrage and other legal methods now made it possible for the working class to win political power by peaceful means. He anticipated, however, preventive actions by reactionary forces. Such counter-measures must, in his opinion, inevitably involve the violation of constitutional rights and the open use of force. This, in its turn, might compel the masses to offer direct resistance, that is, to attempt to seize power by force, by the use of arms. In other words, Engels did not exclude the possibility of using such methods, but only in response to coercive action by the ruling circles. 'Where there is no reactionary power to be overthrown', he wrote to Bebel on 7 October 1892, 'there can be no question whatever of revolutionary power (p. 8). He developed this same idea further in a letter to Lafargue a month later: 'It's even ten to one that universal suffrage, intelligently used by the workers, will drive the rulers to overthrow legality, that is, to put us in the most favourable position to make the revolution' (p. 29). Nonetheless he continues to see any attempt at armed uprising as foredoomed if the ruling circles still command the armed forces. He did not, it is true, exclude the possibility that in Germany, the army might become '$1/3 - 2/5$ socialist' (p. 225) as a result of the growing influence of the Social-Democratic Party in the countryside, which provided the bulk of army recruits. However, as many of his letters show, he hoped in the main that the current situation would enable the socialists to become the parliamentary majority, and thus implement their immediate goals.

Such an outcome, however, in Engels' view, could only be achieved by expanding socialist influence to ever broader sections of working people, and above all, the working class. 'A revolution in the minds' of workers, he wrote, ' ... is a guarantee of a far mightier and more comprehensive revolution in the world'. (p. 296). He attached particular significance to socialist propaganda among the peasantry, 'without which we cannot expect to be victorious'.

In his letters, Engels devotes considerable space to his thoughts on specific events in the European proletarian movement, moreover not only in Germany, France and England, as in previous years, but also in Austria, Belgium and Italy, where this movement was rapidly gaining strength. An increasing number of letters pass between Engels and Victor Adler, Filippo Turati, Antonio Labriola (most of the letters addressed to Labriola have still not been found). New names also appeared, such as E. Vandervelde, leader of the Belgian socialists. Engels's attention was drawn in particular to facts demonstrating the success of the socialists and their practical activity, the struggle of the popular masses to extend democratic freedoms, strikes and other worker demonstrations in support of their economic demands. These letters illustrate Engels's deep interest in internal party issues, and especially in the larger and more influential parties. In Germany these issues concerned relations between the Marxist core of the party leadership and reformist elements, particularly in matters relating to the party programme, and also to parliamentary tactics; in France the main issues were solidarity among socialist forces, ways and means of creating a single socialist party, and the role and tactics of 'the workers' movement in this process; in England the issues were the creation of a mass independent party of the working class, the role of existing socialist organisations in this process, their mutual relations, and also the need to support the trade unions in their desire to take an active part in the international socialist workers' movement; in Italy the main issue was that of strengthening, both organisationally and ideologically, the young socialist party, etc.

In a number of letters Engels expressed his views on the state of and prospects for the socialist movement in the USA. He saw the sources of its weakness as lying not so much in the sectarian line being pursued by the Socialist workers' Party, the bulk of whose membership was made up of German immigrants, as in objective circumstances, which created 'considerable and peculiar difficulties to the *steady* growth of a labour party' (p. 236).

While criticising the reformist tendency which existed in some social-ist parties, Engels nonetheless considered that such differences of opinion should be solved primarily by internal party debate, but that 'to do away with every question involving genuine controversy', was impermissible (p. 376). Furthermore, as regards the various views among socialists on the ways and means of achieving their immediate goal—the political power of the proletariat—he wrote: 'Once we are agreed on that, differ-ences of opinion ... as to the ways and means of struggle are unlikely to give rise to a dispute over principles' (p. 119).

Engels's letters offer striking evidence of his desire to give every possible encouragement to contacts among leaders of socialist parties in different countries, and to inform his colleagues about the experience acquired in the course of the liberation struggle, about major events in the working-class movement, and about the state of affairs in socialist organisations. He informs the Lafargues in detail about the electoral successes of the German Social-Democrats (p. 154), about the state of affairs in English socialist organisations (pp. 342-44). He informs Bebel about the English miners' strike (pp. 204-5), with Sorge he shares his views on the activi-ties of the French Workers' Party (p. 249), on the political situation in England (pp. 81, 229), and on the battle among various trends within the German Social-Democratic Party (pp. 141-42). Almost every event of any significance in the European workers' movement between 1893 and 1895 is reflected to some degree or other in his letters of this period.

The material published in this volume shows that Engels continued his contacts with Russian socialists, revealing a lively interest in the situation in Russia. Having analysed the situation in the country, he posited that it might soon become the arena of revolutionary events. How well Engels knew the situation in Russia is revealed by his letter to N. F. Danielson, who translated *Das Kapital* into Russian and with whom he corresponded for many years, up to the end of his life. In a letter written on 24 February 1893, Engels noted the acute social contradictions, in this country with a huge peasant population, where, as a result of the rapid if belated, devel-opment of capitalism, the crisis might prove ... more powerful and acute than anywhere else (p. 112).

Together with an analysis of the current state of affairs in the prole-tarian liberation struggle in various countries and its future prospects, Engels's letters also contain his assessment of and ideas on the consolida-tion and development of international proletarian links, the activities of the new International, and relations among the socialist parties. In many cases where misunderstandings clouded these relations, Engels acted as an arbiter, seeking to mitigate the discord and to assist in finding a compromise solution. The position he adopted helped, for example, in resolving the conflict between the German Social-Democratic Party and socialists in a number of other countries over whether May 1 should be marked by ceasing work, or should be limited to demonstrations held in the evening (see volume 49, p. 115). On this issue Engels argued that every party must adhere to the international commitments it had assumed or, if that were not possible, reach agreement on its actions with the other parties to such commitments. Engels believed that complete equality and independence in resolving problems constituted the essential basis of relations among socialist parties, a belief he set out most clearly in a letter to Lafargue dated 3 January 1894: 'A certain manner of proceeding may be excellent for one country, and utterly impossible or even disastrous in another' (p. 254).

Engels supported the widest possible participation in international socialist congresses by working-class organisations, including those which did not pursue socialist aims. 'These groups', he wrote to Turati on 16 August 1894, 'by the very fact of attending our congresses, are unconsciously drawn into the socialist lap' (p. 341).

Not believing himself to have the right to interfere in the activities of socialist parties, Engels limited himself to advice and recommendations, and even these he sent only to those closest to him, to whom he was able to say unpalatable things with perfect frankness. To Bebel, Liebknecht, Kautsky, Paul and Laura Lafargue, Adler, Sorge and others with whom he regularly corresponded, he gave his evaluations and expressed his criticisms, occasionally in quite sharp, and in some cases perhaps not altogether objective terms. However, this was not intended for the eyes of others, nor, of course, was it seen by either writer or reader as some infallible truth. Indeed, many optimistic prognostications and hopes were not intended for publication at all, were often coloured with emotion, and in many cases cannot be viewed as the result of any precise or detailed analysis.

The case is very different when it comes to letters written to people with whom Engels was little acquainted, often in reply to direct theoretical questions, or containing theoretical criticism of a particular economic, philosophical or historical work, or outspoken polemics with their authors. Here Engels is always precise, his evaluations restrained, his conclusions argued and less categorical. Such, for example, are his letters to Franz Mehring (14 July 1893) and to Borgius (25 January 1894). which are de voted to clarifying a number of fundamental questions relating to the materialist concept of history, and which conclude, as it were, a cycle of letters dealing with this subject and published in Volume 49 of the present edition. Here he returns yet again to a criticism of the vulgar interpretation of historical materialism, which denies that ideological or other non-economic factors have any influence whatsoever on the historical process. 'An historical moment, once it is ushered into the world by other, ultimately economic, causes,' he wrote to Mehring, 'will react in its turn, and may exert a reciprocal influence on its environment, and even upon its own causes' (p. 165).

These letters may be grouped together with a number of others also devoted to theoretical and historical questions: to Robert Meyer, 19 July 1893; to W. Sombart, 11 March, and to Conrad Schmidt, 12 March 1895; and also to Hirsch, 19 March, to Paul Lafargue, 3 April, to Karl Kautsky, 21 May 1895, and a few others. Of particular interest here are comments of a methodological nature, still pertinent today. Engels once again warns against a dogmatic approach to Marxism. 'But Marx's whole way of thinking', he wrote to Sombart, 'is not so much a doctrine as a method. It provides not so much ready-made dogmas as aids to further investigation, and the method for such investigation' (p. 461). His thoughts on the objective nature of the historical process are very profound: 'As Marx sees it, the whole of past history, so far as major events are concerned, is an unconscious process, i.e., those events and the consequences thereof are not deliberate; either the supernumeraries of history have wanted something that was the diametrical opposite of what was achieved, or else that achievement entailed consequences quite other than those that had been foreseen' (ibid). Engels sets out his understanding of the dialectics of the necessary and the fortuitous, the concept and the phenomenon (p. 466), ideologies (p. 164), the role of the individual in history (p. 266), and also some ideas on the history of the Peasant War in Germany in the 16th century (p. ???), the communal form of ownership (pp. 214, 488) and other questions.

As in previous years, questions of foreign policy were often touched upon in Engels' correspondence, primarily in terms of ascertaining the position of the socialist parties with respect to the threat of war. Engels was more certain than ever that 'the next war, if it comes at all, will not permit of being localised in any way', that 'given the enormous armies of today and the appalling consequences for the vanquished, a localised war is no longer possible' (p. 100). He repeated again and again that the socialist workers' movement had no interest whatsoever in war. 'At the moment a war would be utterly useless to us; we have a sure means of making progress which a war could only disrupt', he wrote to Sorge, on 18 January 1893 (p. 84). In his letters there is a reference to a series of articles entitled 'Can Europe Disarm?', written with the aim of helping the German Social-Democratic Party determine its position on the draft new military law (p. 107). He also used these articles when the French socialists turned to him for advice during the drafting of a law to replace a standing army with a militia system (p. 253).

Right up to the end of 1894, Engels' letters reveal the enormous work he had to undertake in order to prepare for the press the manuscripts of the third volume of *Das Kapital*. Having returned to this work in the autumn of 1892, he continued it, with only brief interruptions, up to the publication of the book at the beginning of December 1894. Almost every letter during these years contains at least one brief reference to his work on the manuscript, and then on the proofs. 'I have been compelled to decline all outside work, though ever so tempting, unless absolutely necessary', he wrote in March 1893 (p. 123). More than a year later, having sent the last part of the manuscript to the printers, he summed up the situation in a letter to Nikolai Danielson: 'Everything not absolutely necessary had to be put back in order to finish Vol. 3rd' (p. 309).

Following the publication of the book, Engels immediately began to carry through his own plans. On 17 December 1894 he described to Laura Lafargue a detailed plan for re-editions and new works, a plan amazing in its scope. 'That is my position', he wrote, '74 years, which I am beginning to feel, and work enough for two men of 40 ... But as it is, all I can do is to work on with what is before me and get through it as far and as well as I can' (p. 387). He did not abandon the idea of new editions of the earlier works of Marx, which had become virtually unobtainable, and, as he wrote to R. Fischer on 15 April 1895, 'I have a scheme for again presenting Marx's and my lesser writings to the public in a complete edition' (p. 497). However he succeeded in carrying through only a small part of this project.

The contents of this volume reveal the attention which Engels gave, regardless of his occupation with other affairs, to new editions of Marx's works and of his own, and their translation into other languages. He wrote the introductions for new editions, edited or read through translations. He willingly assisted followers of Marx who published articles popularising Marx's theory and seeking to apply the materialist concept of history to the study of specific facts and events.

The volume contains a wealth of material revealing Engels's character, his responsiveness and willingness to reply to any question, provide any assistance not only to those close to him, but on occasion even to people he barely knew or did not know at all. His rigorous adherence to principle combined with a desire to listen to, understand and seek to convince his opponent, his readiness to engage in any discussion, but his intolerance of pretence and deliberate falsehood. Many of his letters are full of concern for Marx's daughters, his friends and supporters, in whose affairs he always took an active interest.

Special mention must be made of those of Engels's letters which speak about his trip to the continent in August-September 1893. In them he describes his impressions of what he saw and the changes that had taken place in Europe over the previous two decades, the state of affairs in the workers' movement in Germany and Austria, and his assessment of the International Socialist Congress in Zurich. Everything in these letters is of interest: the details of daily life noted by his sharp eye, his stories, full of humour and good will, about people he met, and his optimistic impressions of meetings with workers—members of the Social-Democratic Party.

Some of the letters contain references to the writing and publication of Engels' last works—*The Peasant Question in France and Germany* (pp. 367-68), and *Introduction to Karl Marx's 'The Class Struggles in France,* 1848 to 1850 (pp. 444; 457-58, 489-90), and to the polemics they provoked.

***

Volume 50 contains 320 of Engels's letters, of which 229 are here published in English for the first time. Of the 89 letters already published, 38 were previously printed in abridged form. Previous publications are indicated in the notes. This volume also includes the first publication in English of Engels's will and the supplements to it, and also five letters by Marx and Engels written between 1842 and 1859 but not included in the corresponding volumes of their correspondence.

Obvious slips of the pen in the texts of the letters have been corrected without indication. Abbreviated proper names, geographical names and individual words are given in full. Defects in the manuscript are indicated in footnotes, while lost or illegible passages of the text are indicated by omission points. If occasional reconstruction is possible it is given in square brackets. Any passages deleted by the author are reproduced at the bottom of the page in cases where there is a significant discrepancy. Rough drafts of letters or fragments reproduced in some other documents, etc., are indicated either in the text itself, or in the notes.

Foreign words and expressions in the text of the letters are left as given by the author, with a translation where necessary; Russian (cyrillic) words are noted but printed in English. English words and expressions used by Engels in text written in German and French are printed in small caps; (large caps if capitalized in original).

In the case of references to one and the same fact or event in the texts of different letters, the endnote number is duplicated.

The texts of the letters and notes were prepared by Oksana Matkovskaya (letters from October 1892 to August 1893), Yevgeniya Dakhina (letters from September 1893 to December 1894), and Natalia Kalennikova (letters from 1895 onwards and supplements). The Preface was written by Boris Tartakovsky. The volume was edited by Irina Shikanyan, Valerija Kunina and Boris Tartakovsky. The Name Index and the Index of Periodicals were prepared Vera Popova; index of quoted and mentioned literature by Alexander Panfilov (Russian Independent Institute of Social and National Problems).

This volume, including the Subject Index, was prepared for the press by International Publishers, New York, from the manuscript materials available.

To The Reader

Volume 50 completes the first and, as yet, the only edition of the works and correspondence of Karl Marx and Frederick Engels in English known as the *Collected Works*.

This edition of the works of Marx and Engels was undertaken on the request of Marxist scholars in England and the USA by the Institute of Marxism-Leninism (now the Russian Independent Institute of Social and National Problems, and is published jointly by Lawrence and Wishart (Great Britain), International Publishers (USA) and 'Progress' (now Progress Publishing Group Corporation), Moscow. The idea of publishing this unique English-language edition of the *Collected Works* of the founders of Marxism was supported by scholars not only in English-speaking countries, but also in a number of other countries in Europe and Asia. The high level of scholarship and the quality of the publication have repeatedly won commendation in the international press. The present edition is the most complete of all those issued to date. It offers the reader a comprehensive review of the written legacy of Marx and Engels, reveals the development of Marx's theory from the moment of its inception, and sets the works in their historical context.

This edition comprises 1,968 works, including those which remained unfinished, or which were not published during the lifetime of their authors, as well as other documents written by them. Approximately half of these (805) are here published in English for the first time. Thirteen volumes (volumes 38-50) are devoted to the enormous epistolary output of Marx and Engels—3,957 letters—of which most (2,283) have hitherto never been published in English.

This edition also offers English-speaking readers their first opportunity to acquaint themselves with a newly comprehensive way of publishing Marx's economic works, including the three volumes of *Capital* and two preparatory manuscripts (volumes 30-37).

Great changes have taken place since Marx and Engels wrote their works, changes which could not be anticipated in their day, and many postulates in their theory now inevitably require critical reassessment. One thing, however, remains indisputable, and that is the enormous contribution they made to the development of socialist thought. The unbiased reader can appreciate the scale of their intellectual influence.

There can be no doubt that the publication of the theoretical and epistolary work of Karl Marx and Frederick Engels has enriched man's scientific and cultural legacy.

The editors wish to express their thanks to subscribers and readers for their co-operation over a period of some 29 years (the first volume was published in 1975), during which they have expressed both criticism and unwavering interest, and also commendable patience in awaiting publication of the final volumes.

FREDERICK ENGELS

LETTERS

October 1892—July 1895

Frederick Engels, 1893

1892

1

ENGELS TO LUDWIG KUGELMANN

IN HANOVER

London, 4 October 1892

Dear Kugelmann,

Very many thanks for the little bit of Leibnitz.[1]

As regards *Herr Vogt*[a], please send one copy to Bebel and two to me, but if you yourself don't possess another, it goes without saying that you should keep one and send only one to me.[2]

As regards *The Knight of the Noble Consciousness* and *Palmerston, What Has He Done*, I have unearthed one more copy of each and these are enclosed herewith.

On the other hand I have only one copy of the *Neue Rheinische Zeitung*, but no loose issues, and only a few volumes of the *Revue*[c]; if I want a complete set I have to borrow it. You had better get Miquel to return you yours. After all *he* is the only one who might now be endangered by its possession and he'll be grateful to you for taking it off his hands. However Volume I as well as other individual volumes occasionally crop up in second-hand booksellers' catalogues.

For the rest, I am keeping tolerably well. But if you are expecting an exhaustive pathological discourse on my somewhat complicated and no doubt also somewhat obscure case, I'm afraid I cannot oblige you. I am in correspondence with many doctors in 5 or 6 countries and all of them

---

[a] K. Marx, *Herr Vogt*. – [b] K. Marx, *Der Ritter vom edelmütigen Bewusstsein*. – [c] *Neue Rheinische Zeitung Politische-ökonomische Revue*.

want the same sort of information. This would involve me in a medical correspondence more time consuming than my political correspondence, and that is absolutely out of the question. As it is, my work on Volume II[a] is being hampered by the business matters I have to attend to, of which there are more than enough. So do please excuse me. The whole thing is not at all serious, but merely an occasional nuisance.

With my best compliments to your wife and daughter.[b]

Your

F. Engels

First published in: Printed according to the original
Marx and Engels, *Works*,
First Russian Edition,   Published in English for the first time
Vol. XXIX, Moscow, 1946

2

ENGELS TO HUGO LINDEMANN AND CARL STEGMANN[3]

IN LONDON

122 Regent's Park Road, N.W.,
London, 6 October 1892

Dear Sirs,

In reply to your favour of 2.X, I have in the past frequently complied with requests of a similar nature from gentlemen who were quite unknown to me, but my experience in these cases has been such that unfortunately I have had to make up my mind to discontinue the practice.[4]

As a result of an indisposition, moreover, I expect to be tied to my sofa for a considerable time to come and hence am in no condition to go searching in my library for old, seldom used periodicals.

---

[a] of *Capital* – [b] Gertrud and Franziska Kugelmann

In the circumstances I regret that I cannot oblige you in the way you wish and remain,

Yours very truly,
F. Engels

First published in:
Marx and Engels, *Works*,
Second Russian Edition,
Vol. 38, Moscow, 1965   Printed according to the original

3

ENGELS TO AUGUST BEBEL

IN BERLIN

London, 7 October 1892

Dear August,

First to business.

Lafargue sent me a *France* with the enclosed notice of an interpellation by Millevoye,[5] a Boulangist.[6] He intends to make use of this opportunity to remind the Chamber of everything done by the German Socialists in 1871 and thereafter to maintain or restore good relations between France and Germany, and of what they have had to endure as a result. He would like to have:

les dates des protestations des socialistes allemands, les paroles prononcées au Reichstag et ailleurs, et les condamnations subies.[a]

Now since the things I have here are incomplete or only to be extracted with untold labour from collections of periodicals buried in numerous packing-cases, during which process I might easily overlook what is most important, you would greatly oblige me and the French if you would take out the most cogent items and send them to me together with dates and references (from the official stenographic report). That is,

---

[a] The dates of the protests by the German Socialists, the speeches made in the Reichstag and elsewhere, and the sentences served.

1. The statements which led to the incarceration of the Brunswick Executive in 1870 in Lötzen, along with date and period of detention.[7]

2. Your protest in the Reichstag against the annexation[8] and perhaps also one or two cogent passages from the *Volksstaat* attacking the war and the annexation;

3. A few trenchant excerpts from later Reichstag speeches by you and Liebknecht, along with dates and particulars of the subject of the debate in which they were made;

4. Anything else that seems to you important.

Not a great deal is needed. You will know roughly how much is needed for a speech and if you then add 1 or 2 spare quotations, that will do. I should be glad if you would also quote some of *your own* statements, lest the French should imagine that Liebknecht did it all himself or even say that Liebknecht was an exception and that the others thought differently.

Yesterday we sent you in the *Workman's Times* 2 French newspapers with reports on Liebknecht's speeches and also a piece by Guesde which will have pleased you.[a]

Lafargue will be drumming up support in Carmaux and other towns in the South until his return on the 16th or 17th of this month, That is when the Chamber reassembles, and he must have the material by then.[9]

He writes to say that the patriotic press, all of which, and particularly *La France*, is in the pay of Russia, has launched furious attacks on Liebknecht. The Russian embassy now pays the newspapers by the job—so much for each individual article accepted. Which is also a sign that the Russians are short of funds. There is no doubt that Liebknecht has raised a furore. I don't begrudge the old man his popularity and, in two respects, can only hope, 1. that it won't make him even more obstinate with regard to the editorship of the *Vorwärts* and, 2. that in the Reichstag the malicious sniping of the *German* patriots and accusations of high treason, etc., don't suddenly provoke him into maintaining the opposite, thereby landing not just himself in the cart but us as well. A reporter on the *Gaulois* quotes him as saying: 'Were Germany to declare a war of aggression on France, the German Socialists would declare war on their own government, et moi-même je prendrais un fusil pour

---

[a] J. Guesde, "Vive l'Internationale!" *Le Socialiste,* 16 October 1892.

défendre *l'intégrité du territoire français.*[a] When he corrects this obviously exaggerated report, it is not impossible that he will go to the opposite extreme, should the Junkers and bourgeois in the Reichstag work him up into a real passion.

Lafargue says that Loubet and the Minister for Public Works, Viette, would go to considerable lengths to bring about an acceptable settlement of the strike at Carmaux[10] and compel the company to climb down, but that Freycinet is against it. The latter has designs on the presidency of the Republic and therefore wants to keep in with the voters of the Right and the Centre.

Otherwise, Lafargue is very satisfied with the Congress.[11]

The 12 copies of the *Neue Zeit*[12] arrived here and were passed on to Tussy. The chaps ought to have sent them to *her* instead of to me, but as it was a day was lost. Unfortunately there has recently been a change of ownership at the *Pall Mall Gazette* and we don't yet know what prospects the paper will now hold out for us.

Your account of the movement among the miners tallies with our experience in this country; here, too, the chaps keep themselves very much apart from the other branches of labour and are progressing more slowly than the rest. But in our case, the fact that there is already a strong workers' party behind them will eventually see us through; the chaps are *bound* to join us, once the movement has taken a hold on them. On the other hand there are, both here and in Germany, bad and unreliable leaders who cannot be induced to trust the workers in other branches. In this country, moreover, the petty jealousies existing between the men of one coal-field and another have so far not even permitted the creation of a united guild comprising all mine workers.

I shall do my utmost to stop the French from dispensing with your contributions. It is vitally important that occasionally, at any rate, accurate reports on the German movement should appear in Paris and particularly that the public should be made aware of the general political situation in which you people have to carry on the fight. You alone can do that, nor is there any need at all for you to come into conflict with Liebknecht as a result, provided he doesn't regard contributions to the French paper[b] as his monopoly. That wouldn't do at all.

---

[a] and I myself would take up a musket in order to defend *the integrity of French territory.*
[b] *Le Socialiste*

You need have no fear that Burns is keeping too much in the background. The man's vanity is on a par with Lassalle's. But compared with the precipitate way in which K. Hardie thrusted himself to the fore to secure pride of place by resorting to little dodges, he was unquestionably right in adopting a non-committal attitude.

At the moment I am reading Hans Müller[a] and have not yet finished. It is all stale stuff and long familiar to us. The few bad speeches he quotes are not even skilfully chosen. Had I wanted to make out a case against the petty-bourgeois goings-on in the party or parliamentary group, I should have provided quite different material. The Steamship Subvention alone provides eight times as much as he does and of better quality.[13] He takes a speech made by Liebknecht in 1881[14] during the period of general confusion that followed the promulgation of the Anti-Socialist Law[15] instead of later ones when the political situation makes the pacific, philistine overtones seem far less excusable, and then goes so far as to assert that power is in all circumstances revolutionary and never reactionary. The jackass fails to notice that where there is no reactionary power to be overthrown there can be no question whatever of revolutionary power. After all, you cannot start a revolution against something that can be removed without the least effort.

If there is one thing that sends the self-opinionated students, the men of letters and the would-be literati of the working class into a state of impotent rage, it is the sight of our party calmly continuing along its victorious course without needing the help from these petty panjandrums. If mistakes are made, the party is strong enough to deal with them itself. Witness the undeniably tame philistinism of the majority of the parliamentary group at the time of the Steamship Subvention, witness the traditional tendency of the Party Executive, a tendency which continued to manifest itself for a short while *after* the Anti-Socialist Law had been repealed, to intervene in a dictatorial manner (and which, moreover, had its counterpart in an *identical* tendency among the executives of the previous Berlin organisation), etc., etc. Our Party is now so strong that it could, without risk of degeneration, digest not only a goodly number of petty bourgeois but also the "heddicated" and even the worthy Independents,[16] had not the latter given themselves their marching orders.

---

[a] H. Müller, *Der Klassenkampf in der deutschen Sozial Demokratie*

Time for the post. Regards to your wife[a] and yourself from Louise[b] and

Your

F. E.

First published in:
Marx and Engels, *Works*,
First Russian Edition,
Vol. XXIX, Moscow, 1946

Printed according to the original

Published in English for the first time

4

ENGELS TO LUDWIG KUGELMANN[17]

IN HANOVER

London, 10 October 1892

Dear Kugelmann,

Vogt received with thanks.[2]

If you send for second-hand booksellers' catalogues on jurisprudence, political science and modern German history, especially for the period round 1848, you will light on individual copies of the *Revue*[c] from time to time. I myself have acquired one or two copies in this way.

Have just finished Chapter 27 of the third volume[d]; 29-34 present the main difficulty.

Kindest regards to your wife and daughter.[e]

Your

F. E.

First published in:
Marx and Engels, *Works*,
First Russian Edition,
Vol. XXIX, Moscow, 1946

Printed according to the original

Published in English for the first time

---

[a] Julie Bebel – [b] Kautsky – [c] *Neue Rheinische Zeitung. Politisch-ökonomische Revue* – [d] of *Capital* – [e] Gertrud and Franziska Kugelmann

5

ENGELS TO LAURA LAFARGUE

AT LE PERREUX

London, 14 October 1892

My dear Löhr,

Thanks from Louise and myself for your letters this morning. Had one from Paul from Bordeaux last night.

Business first. Enclosed you find

1. Manifest des sozial demokratischen Ausschusses (Executive) Braunschweig 5. September 1870[a] with a letter from Mohr and myself[18] but which Paul better quote as from *Mohr*, who, I believe, signed it. *This is referred to in the MS. extracts under No. III* (on page 2).

2. First and Second Addresses of the General Council of the International on the War, July 23rd 1870 and Sept. 9th 1870.[b] With French translation *made, I believe, in Geneva;* it very likely requires revision both as to correctness and style.

3. A series of MS. extracts received from Bebel who with his wife[c] set to work at once to supply us with what we wanted.

I think this will be sufficient for Paul's speech, though I don't envy you the task of translating all these things, especially the rather lax style of our Reichstag orators.

Anyhow, now Paul is armed and need not depend upon Liebknecht's promises which are sooner made than kept, as a rule.

I am glad Paul is going to take part again in the debates of the Chambre,[d] and if he is wise, he will attend the Palais Bourbon[e] assiduously during this last session of the present Parliament. I have some notion that electors want to see and hear something of the parliamentary activity of their deputy, and if they do not, there may be a risk not only of losing his seat, but also of not so easily securing another. After all, as things are now, both in France and Germany, electoral success in many places at least, depends on the votes of a number of *hangers-on* of the party, men

---

[a] Manifesto of the Brunswick (Executive) Committee of September 5, 1870. – [b] See present edition, Vol. 22, pp. 3-8, 263-70. – [c] Julie Bebel – [d] Chamber – [e] The Bourbon Palace (housing the French Chamber of Deputies)

that are influenced by petty considerations, and whose simple abstention may lose the seat. Then, too, Paul's first speech[19] showed evident signs of *embarras*, caused by his not being used to the new atmosphere where he had to live, move and have his being; and the sooner and the more he gets used to that and to the parliamentary forms, standing orders, and business habits of the Chambre, the better. This time he will have to show them that their howlings and interruptions will not intimidate him, and if he only tries, I am sure he can do it. I don't know French Chambers, but it seems to me, in a similar case I should take no notice of interruptions, reply to none of them, and in the last extremity call upon the president to ensure to me my right of being heard. (Capital advice on the part of one who notoriously cannot keep his own temper!)

Arndt you describe quite correctly. I see from Liebknecht's report on his journey[a] that he gives Arndt a mild slap but a slap anyhow, and probably he will have been told, at Marseille, of the proceedings of Blanquists[20] and Allemanists.[21] Liebknecht seems quite intoxicated with his triumph and, for the moment, *plus français que les français eux-mêmes*.[b] Unfortunately he always deals in extremes, and I can only hope that he will not be goaded, by patriotic bullies in the Reichstag, into tumbling head over heels into the opposite extreme. So far, his attitude in his speeches in Mannheim[22] etc. has been all that could be desired.

I understand your news about Roubaix to this effect that the people there will ask Paul to stand for the *Chamber* next autumn. That would be very good, Roubaix would be a pretty safe seat, while Lille seems rather shaky, to be carried at a period of extra local excitement, but very uncertain, so far, at ordinary periods.

Anyhow, *ca marche en France*[c] (everything but the *Journal quotidien!*)[d] and Carmaux[10] shows not only the progress of our ideas among the working-class, but also the fact of the bourgeois and the government *knowing*, it. The self-contained attitude of the people there—*et encore des méridiouaux, des Gascons gasconnants!*[e]—and the quiet but determined way in which the socialist town-councils proceed without any possibilist weakness or concessions, show an immense progress. The more the French are coming to the front, the more I shall be glad. The Continental movement, to be victorious, must be neither all French nor all German,

---

[a] W. Liebknecht, 'Agitations bericht. Nach Marseille und zurück,' *Vorwärts*, 12 October 1892. – [b] more French than the French themselves – [c] everything is on the move – [d] daily paper – [e] And Southerners into the Bargain, bragging braggarts!

but franco-allemand. If the Germans taught the French how to use the suffrage and how to organise strongly, the French will have to penetrate the Germans with that revolutionary spirit which the history of a century has made traditional with them. The time has passed for ever where one nation can claim to lead all the rest.

The *Socialiste* does not contain, in its report, the resolution of the Congrès *syndical* of Marseille[23] with regard to the *Glasgow* affair,[24] nor any allusion to it. How is it that this business is enveloped in such mystery?

Aveling's article, of *The Pall Mall Gazette*,[a] is also published in the *Workman's Times. Do you still receive that paper?*

Love from Louise and Yours affectionately,

F. Engels

First published, in the language
of the original (English), in:
F. Engels, P. et L. Lafargue,
Correspondance, t. III, 1891-1895,
Paris, 1959

Reproduced from the original

6

ENGELS TO PASQUALE MARTIGNETTI

IN BENEVENTO

London, 18 October 1892

Dear Friend,

The business of the duchess[b] has been cleared up. I only knew the lady by her married name of Mrs Edgren and was unaware that her maiden name was Miss Leffler.

Unfortunately Mrs Aveling had lost the *duchessa*'s address and had some difficulty in getting hold of it. That too has now been sorted out. Mrs Aveling has written to her about you warmly recommending you, so

---

[a] E. Aveling, 'Discord in The International. Continental Opinion on the British Trades Unionists.' *The Pall Mall Gazette*, No. 8598, 11 October 1892 – [b] of Caianiello

all you have to do is hand over the enclosed note.[25] I wish you success!

I presume that it is you that I again have to thank for the translation of the last part of my German preface to the *Lage, etc.*[a]

I am working on Volume III of Marx's *Capital*, and have to devote every available moment to it—hence must be brief while remaining

Yours,
F. Engels

First published, in the language of the original (German), in: *La corrispondenza di Marx e Engels con italiani*, 1848-1895, Milano, 1964

Printed according to the original

Published in English for the first time

7

ENGELS TO LUDWIG SCHORLEMMER

IN DARMSTADT

London, 18 October 1892

My dear Schorlemmer,

I have your letters of 31 July and the 9th inst. It was my fault that Pumps forgot her *Schmollis*.[b] After so long an interval she no longer trusted herself to write in German off her own bat, and so I did it for her. Naturally I knew nothing of her tippling exploits in Darmstadt and put "*Sie*". Her husband[c] is not to blame, for he knows no German. Pumps is expecting a child any day, her fourth. Her second, a boy, unfortunately died, while her youngest, also a boy and really a very nice humorous little chap, is very delicate and at this moment far from well.

Because of what you said about Anschütz[26] I delayed writing this

---

[a] F. Engels, *The Condition of the Working Class in England*. – [b] A little ceremony in which the participants drink to the adoption of *Du* (thou), the intimate mode of address, *Sie* (you) being the formal term./Trans./ – [c] Percy Rosher

letter for several days in the hope of hearing from him. But up till now there has been nothing. The position is that I must know first of all how exhaustive the biography is to be, whether it is intended for a periodical and if so which, etc., etc. If the man proposes to deal with our Carl[a] merely *qua* chemist, all he needs are a few particulars that could serve as a framework. If, however, he intends to depict the *man* as he was, the question arises as to whether he is the most suitable candidate and whether one ought, without further inquiry, to place at his disposal the letters to and from Carl. Again, a chemist living in Germany would necessarily be unfamiliar with the circumstances of a man who had lived in England for 30 years and more, and this would involve me in work of a much more comprehensive nature. That would not deter me. I should gladly devote as much time to it as I could spare, once I had seen the back of Volume III of *Capital* to which I have now returned. But who will provide me with a guarantee that my information is used in the spirit in which it was given? When in our presence, and in fact he spent all his vacations here in London except when he went to Germany in the summer, Carl was first and foremost a Social Democrat and up till now Social Democrats have been somewhat thinly represented in the ranks of the chemists. It certainly wouldn't do if, in his biography, the biographer were, so to speak, to beg his readers' pardon because the man whose life he was depicting had had the misfortune to be a Social Democrat!

Anschütz was, if I'm not mistaken, for a time a pupil of Carl's in Manchester. As already mentioned; I shall be glad to be of service—in so far as I have the time—but first of all I must know what is required and what kind of biography it is to be.

The executors in Manchester[b] are right in wanting to wind up whatever can be wound up without going into the settlement of the copyright questions. That will take time if only because the publishers stand to gain from a certain delay and are therefore in no hurry. I have heard nothing from Roscoe either; doubtless he won't make a move until he can put forward and accept or reject specific proposals.

I hope your daughter continues to improve and that she has been able to leave her bed in the meantime.

Why the old man[c] didn't come to Darmstadt I don't know. Does his

---

[a] Carl Schorlemmer – [b] Philipp Klepsch and Ludwig Siebold – [c] Wilhelm Liebknecht

wife[a] still perhaps have relations there whom he would rather not see too often, while feeling reluctant actually to steer clear of them? As to the business of Müller's[b] adultery and whether he committed it or whether he didn't, not a word has so far penetrated to London.

Best compliments from Mrs Kautsky.

Yours,

F. Engels

First published in:
Marx and Engels, *Works*,
First Russian Edition,
Vol. XXIX, Moscow, 1946

Printed according to the original

Published in English for the first time

8

ENGELS TO CHARLES BONNIER

IN OXFORD

[*Draft*]

London, mid-October 1892

My dear Bonnier,

I have received Protot[c]—thank you. First of all, however, a correction. You say:

'whereas the French socialists are protesting against the Russian alliance and do not wish to hear about a war with Germany, Bebel in particular and you yourself are quite willing to accept the idea of a defensive war against France and Russia in which the German socialists would take part', and that 'these accusations, which are well received in France, irritate Guesde'.

If the French socialists are not expressly discussing the case of a defensive war in which they would be willing to repel an attack by the Emperor William,[d] this is because it is well known, recognised and accepted that

---

[a] Natalie Liebknecht [b] Hans Müller – [c] E. Protot, *Chauvins et réacteurs*. – [d] William II

there is no need to talk about it. There is not a single socialist in Germany who doubts that in such a case the French socialists would only be doing their duty in defending their national independence; there is not one who would hold it against them; on the contrary, they would applaud them, That is precisely the point of view in my article.[a] If I were not proceeding from the view that, should there be a foreign attack, the French socialists would take up arms to defend their homes, the whole of my article would be absurd. What I am requesting is the benefit of the same principle for the German socialists in the case of a Russian attack, even if it is supported by official France. The same holds true for Bebel's speeches. The people in France who use this as a basis for accusations against us belong to that kind who say: *quod licet Jovi gallici non licet bovi Germanici*[b]; to make them see reason is, it seems to me, the task of the French socialists, and presents no great difficulty.[c]

I would also warn you that what M. Protot cites from my article is nothing but gross falsehood.

You say that the brochure is well done. I find it very weak; the end, where this joker poses as an economist is more than grotesque. If he has a strong point, it is the royal disdain which he pours out on his readers. Indeed, one must assume that one's readers are incurable idiots in order to dare to offer them such a collection of palpable falsehoods (in which you see only snippets) and lies contradicting one another. Is it then sufficient to put on a masque of Déroulède in order to persuade those who create public opinion in Paris to swallow anything one wishes. Has Boulangism[6] survived Boulanger to the point of being more powerful than during Boulanger's lifetime?

Such a collection of lies and falsehoods is, in fact, irrefutable. It would require 3,200 pages to reassert the truth against these 32 pages. There is not a single quotation of any significance which is not shamelessly distorted; it was only after comparing several texts that I had the measure of M. Protot's affrontery.

As for the literary style, I find it lamentable, in striking contrast to the assiduity with which he has collected his material. Clearly another

---

[a] F. Engels, *Socialism in Germany.* – [b] what is acceptable for the French is not acceptable for the German – [c] The following phrases are crossed out in the draft letter: 'That such chauvinist stupidities irritate Guesde I can well believe, but that is not my fault, nor that of Bebel. As for the rest, when I sent my article to Paris, I warned my friends of the danger, expressing my fears due to national susceptibilities; but I was told that, on the contrary, this was just what was needed'.

hand was at work here. Certainly not Protot.

Nor is it, as *Vorwärts* believes, one of the *Unabhängiger*.[a][16] Their manifesto (Hans Müller's *Klassenkampf*)[b] is characterised by the lack of care he has taken in selecting his supporting texts.

Nor is it the French police; one senses that they have had a hand in it, but they are not the ones who have so interested themselves in the foreign policy of the Romanian socialists.

If M. Protot accuses the latter of being the enemies of Holy Rus, if he twice quotes the Bucharest *Munca* (Labour), and divulges that Nadejde de Jassi is 'Zingaro',[c] it is because he is acting in the interests of the Russian embassy, which must have supplied this information, and probably also the information on the German socialists, collected in Berlin by some attaché there.

Thus Protot's lampoon is not only in the interests of the police, but also in the interests of Russia; it is part and parcel of those frantic efforts that Russia is making to ensure a French alliance. It is Russia, in fact, which needs France. She is so completely exhausted by the social disorganisation caused by the economic transformation that she has been experiencing since 1861, by the ravages of deforestation, by the ruination of agriculture and the cottage industry, by famine and cholera, that she could not wage a war through to the end. Her finances and her credit are in a state of collapse reminiscent of France in 1788; if the western public continues to keep its purse closed, there remain only three alternatives: 1) bankruptcy, 2) the convening of a national assembly to sanction a new loan, which then might succeed in the west; 3) war as a measure of desperation—*and in that last case France is necessary*: once war were declared, the French army engaged, ten against one, the Tsar[d] would reach an agreement with William[e] and Francis Joseph,[f] who would hasten to meet him, and la belle France would pay the expenses of the banquet of reconciliation.

First published in:
Marx and Engels, *Works*,
First Russian Edition,
Vol. XXIX, Moscow, 1946

Printed according to the original

Translated from the French

Published in English for the first time

---

[a] the Independents – [b] H. Müller, *Der Klassenkampf in der deutschen Sozialdemokratie*. – [c] a gipsy – [d] Alexander III – [e] William II – [f] Francis Joseph I

9

ENGELS TO VICTOR ADLER

IN VIENNA

London, 23 October 1892

Dear Victor,

There is no need for you to worry about the Trades Unions' International Congress.[24] In the first place the whole business was probably only a device for getting the anti-Zurich resolution[27] accepted and might well not even be raised by the Parliamentary Committee.[28] Secondly, the attendance of individual Continentals is neither here nor there, seeing that even the Paris *bourse du travail*[29]—still, if no longer altogether, dominated by the Possibilists[30]—resolved that the Trades Unions be asked to abandon their plan. So who else might one expect to go? Maybe Mr Gilles, as representative of the German Independents[16]?!

It would be a *great* help if the Austrian Trades Unions[31] were to send their resolution to the Parliamentary Committee. I shall ask Aveling for the address which I cannot find.

Yesterday I walked up Primrose Hill for the first time and, provided I'm careful, think I shall have made some slight progress by the end of the week. I shall make a note of MacEwen. He is at any rate a CONSULTING SURGEON which means that he can only advise *other doctors* and not the public direct. But I shall find that out. You have no idea of the extent to which everything here, including medicine, is governed by etiquette and how one breach of that etiquette is infinitely more frowned upon than ten of the sexual code. I recall a dictum of the Mancunian Medico-Ethical Society which sat in judgement over my friend Gumpert in Manchester. While paying a visit of condolence (this was around 1866-67) to a family who were *not* his patients, he had expressed slight misgivings about their family doctor's having permitted other children to approach the bodies of two children who had died of scarlet fever. The other doctor lodged a complaint and the verdict was: THAT DR GUMPERT HAD COMMITTED A BREACH OF MEDICAL ETIQUETTE, THOUGH HE WAS MORALLY RIGHT! Well, again my best thanks—I shall follow your advice.

Tomorrow I shall again write to Stepniak about his work[32]. If you haven't had anything by the end of the fortnight, by 7 or 8 November say, please write to me again, then I'll send him a reminder. It's the only way you can get anything out of a Russian.

I am now on Volume III of *Capital*. If, just once during the past four years, I had been able to see three clear months ahead of me, it would have been finished long ago. But I never had any such luck. On this occasion I am making time for it by forcibly suppressing and by totally neglecting all my correspondence and other concerns. I found that I had made very good headway with the most difficult passage the last time I tackled it and up till now it's been going pretty smoothly, though admittedly I have now come up against the chief obstacle which has long been standing in my way.[33] But I work with a will and, so far, with undiminished vigour and doubtless something will come of it this time.

Herewith a document typical of anarchists of Czech nationality. The gentlemen are beginning to bludgeon one another with the principle that voting is a revolutionary act. I am prepared to excuse its deficiencies on the grounds that, not being Germans, the louts were not altogether aware of the full impact their rhetorical flourishes would have on a German.

We were all absolutely delighted by the good news about your wife.[a] We hope the improvement will continue and that before long you will be able to send us further glad tidings.

Warm regards from Louise.[b] to you, your wife and your children, and the same also from

Your

F. Engels

Add. of the Parliamentary Committee,
C. Fenwick, Esq., M.P.,
12, Buckingham Street, Strand,
London, W.C.

First published in: Victor Adler, *Aufsätze, Reden und Briefe.* Erstes Heft: *Victor Adler und Friedrich Engels*, Wien, 1922

Printed according to the book

Published in English for the first time

---

[a] Emma Adler – [b] Kautsky

10

ENGELS TO CHARLES BONNIER

IN OXFORD

[Draft]

London, 24 October 1892

My dear Bonnier,

In *Le Figaro* Guesde says:

> 'Just as Liebknecht stated that, in the case of aggression by France, he would be obliged to remember that he is German, we would remind the workers' party, in the case of German aggression, that we are French'.

Thus Guesde and myself are in perfect agreement, and it is with him that you should settle matters.

You speak of an *unfortunate* phrase by Bebel—which one? You reproach him with so many! If it is the one in *Figaro* that he would fire at Guesde, it belongs to M. Huret; Bebel writes that it existed only in this gentleman's fantasy.

You talk of preventing war, and you boast of having voted for Domela[34]— with his plan you would crush all the socialist parties in Europe.

It is all very fine to speak of preventing a war, from whichever side it might come. But why allow yourself to believe in illusions. Do the French socialists have some means of preventing the young William[a] from declaring war in a moment of madness? Can the German socialists forbid Carnot or some patriotic ministry to commit a similar folly? Furthermore, if it were William or the street-corner revanchists who were the real danger; it is the Russian government which is pulling the strings of these puppets, these by hopes, those by fears. So now prevent it from inciting war!

If war breaks out, *those who are defeated* will have the opportunity and the duty to bring about a revolution—and that's that.

First published in:
 Marx and Engels, *Works*,
First Russian Edition,
Vol. XXIX, Moscow, 1946

Printed according to the original

Translated from the French

Published in English for the first time

---

[a] William II

11

ENGELS TO PAUL LAFARGUE[35]

AT LE PERREUX

London, 3 November 1892

My dear Lafargue,

I am plunged up to the eyes in the 3rd Volume of *Capital* which must be completed once and for all. I am working on the least edited and most difficult part: banks, credit, etc.[33] I cannot interrupt the work for anything whatsoever, otherwise I should have to start from the beginning all over again. Hence all my correspondence is interrupted and I can write you only a few words.

It is most unfortunate that you believed in Millevoye's promises, who flouted you like a good politician[36]— in future you will know that in politics such people pass for GENTLEMEN. I get letter after letter from Germany in which they complain about your absence at the critical moment and I warn you that it will be difficult to have our people undertake work for debates from which the principal speaker for whom the work is done absents himself. Publication in pamphlet form[9] will not have a hundredth part of the effect of a parliamentary speech; that's a matter on which our Berlin people are well qualified by experience to pronounce.

The least you might do would be to send a delegate to Berlin on the 14th,[37] that would enable you to have it out with our people over there. So do try to send someone; it's an expedition that will pay.

You will have seen the reports in the papers of the ghastly effects, in Dahomey, of the new projectiles.[38] A young Viennese doctor[a] who has just arrived here (ex-assistant to Nothnagel) saw the wounds made by the Austrian projectiles in the Nürmitz strike, and he tells us the same thing. There's no doubt that people in danger of being shot to bits in this manner will want to know why. It's a capital thing for maintaining peace, but also for curbing the so-called revolutionary inclinations, on whose outbursts our governments count. The era of barricades and street fighting has gone for good; *if the military fight*, resistance becomes madness.

---

[a] Ludwig Freiberger

Hence the necessity to find new revolutionary tactics. I have pondered over this for some time and am not yet settled in my mind.

I am beginning to go out again a bit. I had nearly three months as a prisoner at home; now I am starting to walk, but little and slowly; but at least I realise that it will soon be over. And about time, as I feel that the lack of exercise in the open air must come to an end. And when I am completely restored, we can, I hope, arrange things so that you and Laura give us the pleasure of spending a few weeks with us. We have so many things to discuss, and it is time Laura saw London again.

Love from Mme Kautsky.

Ever yours,

F. Engels

First published in:
F. Engels, P. et L. Lafargue,
Correspondance, t. III, 1891-1894,
Paris, 1959

Printed according to the original

Translated from the French

12

ENGELS TO LAURA LAFARGUE

AT LE PERREUX

London, 4 November 1892

My dear Löhr,

This morning Meissner sends a remittance for £38—one-third of which £12.13.4d., covers your share and is settled by enclosed cheque which please acknowledge. There are about 400 copies left of Vol. II[a] and the second edition is in preparation. Fourth edition of Vol. I[a] is out, and 460 copies sold, which wipe off the greater part of the printing etc. cost; only 886 Marks remain to be covered and all the receipts beyond that will be profits to be divided with Meissner.

Third Volume[a] well in hand and will not leave off until finished. This can-

---

[a] of Marx's *Capital*

not be done unless I neglect correspondence, so you must excuse my brevity.

Now you ought to take seriously into consideration your impending visit to London; we have talked so much about it that at last it ought to be put into execution. We all should be so glad to see you here again once more.

I am in daily expectation of news that Pumps has had another baby. It's fully due if not overdue, she herself expected it a month ago, but she is always out of her reckoning.

I wonder whether Jack Burns did say the nonsense about the foreign working men, Huret puts into his mouth in the *Figaro*.[39]

Now then, to work again! The day I finish that section on Banks and Credit,[33] which has been my stumbling block for 4-5 Years (because under 3 months of *absolutely free* time it can't be done and these 3 months I could not get)—the day I finish that, there will be some consumption of alcohol—you bet!

Love from Louise.

Ever yours,
F. Engels

First published, in the language of the original (English), in:
F. Engels, P. et L. Lafargue, *Correspondance*, t. III, 1891-1895, Paris, 1959

Reproduced from the original

13

ENGELS TO FRIEDRICH ADOLPH SORGE[40]

IN HOBOKEN

London, 5 November 1892

Dear Sorge,

You must forgive my laziness about writing; I have got to finish Volume III[a] this winter; it *must* be completed and this won't be possible unless I

---

[a] of *Capital*

set *all* my correspondence aside. I have been at it for 3 weeks and can only tell you that the work is going more smoothly than I could have hoped; the last time I had to break off, I had made good headway and now it's paying dividends. But there still remains a mass of work to do, though I am far enough advanced to be able to see the end of it. And nobody is more glad of that than I; this piece of work has been a burden on my conscience. I have forced myself to make time for it since it couldn't be done in less than 4 months of complete freedom from all other jobs; I know that, unless I do it now, it will never be done, for we are entering a period of rebellion and war. But like everyone else you will have to suffer for it pro tem—so please forgive me!

Your
F. E.

First published in *Briefe und Auszüge aus Briefen von Joh. Phil. Becker, Jos, Dietzgen, Friedrich Engels, Karl Marx u. A. an F. A. Sorge und Andere,* Stuttgart, 1906

Printed according to the original

Published in English for the first time

14

ENGELS TO SERGEI KRAVCHINSKY (STEPNIAK)

IN LONDON

London, 5 November 1892
122 Regent's Park Road, N.W.

My dear Stepniak

Thanks for your letter of the 25th October.[41] I find that Adler's letter to you was left here and has not yet been returned to you, so I enclose it now.

Kind regards to Mrs. Stepniak from Mrs. Kautsky and

Yours faithfully
F. Engels

First published in:
Marx and Engels, *Works*.
Second Russian Edition,
Vol. 38, Moscow, 1965

Reproduced from the original

Published in English for the first time

15

ENGELS TO AUGUST BEBEL

IN BERLIN

London, 6 November 1892

Dear August,

All this time I have been slaving away dutifully at Volume III[a] and not, I'm glad to say, without success. Today I may already be said to be fairly past the main obstacle, the credit system—upon which nothing remains to be done but the technical editing—which, however, is of a complex and time-consuming nature.[33] I have greatly enjoyed the work, firstly because I have discovered so many brilliant new sides to it—ask Louise,[b] to whom I have read quite a lot of it out loud—and secondly because it has also shown me that, when all's said and done, my old noddle is still up to the mark, even where relatively difficult things are concerned. The worst havoc the years have wrought is in the sphere of memory whose doors are no longer so easy to find or to open, which means a general slowing down. This is something I can very well put up with, however.

But though I may have broken the back of the work, it's very far from finished. Besides this section there still remain the two last ones (rather less than $1/3$ of the whole) which I haven't so much as looked at yet, and then comes the final, technical editing of the whole which, while not difficult, is all the more tedious and wearisome for that. It will probably take me the whole of the winter—and then there'll be the proofs—coinciding with those of the 2nd ed., Vol. II.[a]

I have made time for it by forcibly suppressing in all my correspon-

---

[a] of *Capital* – [b] Kautsky

dence in so far as it wasn't absolutely vital. Not my correspondence with you, however, although I cannot reply so promptly or in as much detail as I should like. Well, you won't, I suppose, have any objection if it means that the Witch[a] takes up her pen rather more often instead of me.

Lafargue has still to learn that, amongst bourgeois politicians, promises are made only to be broken.[36] In any case his intentions would have been frustrated by Standing Orders which preclude debate on such questions. He is still rather too much of a tyro on the floor of the Chamber; however he has promised to frequent it more regularly in future. They now want to publish the documents in pamphlet form.[9]

I expressed myself badly in speaking of Hans Müller.[b] I didn't mean that you, as the Party Executive, should take any notice of his concoction and still less that you should do so in the manner suggested by me. But *if* a polemic against the angry young man was embarked upon under your aegis, *then*, etc. it seems to me absolutely essential that the party should criticise its own antecedents on such occasions and thereby learn to do better. True, the blunders committed at the time of the Steamship Subvention,[13] etc., are over and done with, but the same people are still around and some, at least, are capable of acting as before. It all the blunders perpetrated by the parliamentary group and by some of its members are to be concealed under a mantle of love, this would, in my opinion, be tantamount to breeding Independents.[16] Messrs Frohme, Blos, etc., should acquire a thicker skin. Am I wrong in attributing certain motions redolent of 'Independence', tabled at the Party Congress by the Solingen people, to the latter's opposition to Schumacher's bourgeoisification and philistinisation?[42] A touch of retrospective veracity in the *Neue Zeit* would do no harm and you, with your tact and expertise, would be the right man for the job—but whether, of course, your position on the Executive doesn't make this inadvisable is another matter. One way or the other, however, such criticism must eventually be expressed.

It was with pleasure that I read the report of your Executive last night.[c] Very good. Calm, objective, adhering to the facts which are allowed to speak for themselves and only at the end a few necessary brief words denoting proud self-confidence. We shall have to see if Aveling can't get some extracts from it into the press. But over here you are virtually boy-

---

[a] Jocular name for Louise Kautsky – [b] See this volume, p. 8 – [c] 'Bericht des Partei-Vorstandes an den Parteitag, zu Berlin 1892', *Vorwärts*, No. 259, 4 November 1892.

cotted out of *sheer English chauvinism.* The existence in Germany of a labour movement with procedures so different from those of the British movement and which, though contemptuous of the TRADES UNION and politico-parliamentary rules here considered sacrosanct, nevertheless goes on from strength to strength, is exceedingly galling to people in this country. And I don't mean the middle classes. The old Trades Unions regard each of your victories as a defeat for themselves and their own methods. The Fabians[43] are riled at your forging ahead *despite* your having declared war upon all bourgeois radicals. The leaders of the SOCIAL DEMOCRATIC FEDERATION[44] detest you for refusing either to have secret dealings with them or to join the mutual admiration society which *Justice* has long been trying to make you accept, now by dangling a carrot, now by cracking a whip. Because of the vast ignorance of the English masses in regard to foreign affairs and their hereditary arrogance which leads them to look on a foreigner as a second-rate human being and everything occurring abroad as of little account, a conspiracy of silence is easily imposed. The *Chronicle*[a] is in the hands of the Fabians where labour matters are concerned, *Justice* has been led by Hyndman to espouse the cause of that rotter Gilles, the *Workman's Times* likewise believes that nothing's any good unless based on a big English-style TRADES UNION organisation—so where are we to get the thing published? Only in the bourgeois press, as a news item of general interest. If, for the space of no more than a year, we could find a paper willing to open its pages to straightforward accounts of the German movement, the whole business would come to an end. For there is enough latent internationalism, if nurtured, to put paid to the stupid arrogance of the British, at least in the majority of cases. But as it is...!

The *Workman's Times* is threatening to close down. There's more to this than meets the eye and we're trying to find out what. Nothing like that happens over here without jiggery-pokery of some sort.

Now *ad vocem*[b] Vollmar. As I see it, the man was attacked most ineptly. The pitfall in this case was the phrase state socialism. That phrase does not express any clear-cut concept but, like 'social question', etc., is simply journalese, a mere cliché from which anything or nothing may be interred. To contest the true meaning of such a word is sheer waste of time;

---

[a] *Daily Chronicle* – [b] as regards

for its true meaning consists precisely in its not having any. It would have been difficult to avoid examining this supposed concept in the *Neue Zeit* and what K. Kautsky has to say about it is, in fact, very good (except that he too supposes that the thing has absolutely got to have a *true meaning*).[45] But it is doing Vollmar an immense and quite unnecessary favour to contend with him in political debate about *what* state socialism is or is not—there's no end to such pointless political palaver. As I see it, what ought to be said at the Party Congress is this: 'My dear Vollmar, what you imagine state socialism to be is all one to us, but on various occasions you have said such and such about the government and our attitude towards it, and that's where we have got you; what you have said runs just as much counter to the tactics of the party as do the pronouncements of the Independents, and *it is for this you have got to answer.'* Only on the score of his unashamed arse-crawling to William[a] and Caprivi is he vulnerable, indeed very much so, and it was to this particular point I wished to draw your attention before the Party Congress.

Enclosure from the Witch.[b]

Cordial regards to your wife and yourself. We are glad to hear that there's an early prospect of your visiting us. Could be MOST BENEFICIAL politically over here; we shall do the necessary spadework. We *quite agree with you* about a weekly.[46] It would be tremendously effective abroad where we still very much feel the loss of the *Sozialdemokrat*; a good weekly survey of party events would be invaluable abroad.

First published in:
Marx and Engels, *Works,*
First Russian Edition, Vol. XXIX,
Moscow, 1946

Printed according to the original

Published in English for the first time

---

[a] William II – [b] Louise Kautsky

16

ENGELS TO PAUL LAFARGUE[35]

AT LE PERREUX

London, 12 November 1892

My dear Lafargue,

You do not tell me where I should address my reply, and so I am sending it to Le Perreux.

Herewith I append a cheque for £20 which you have asked, but I must warn you that in the future it will be *absolutely impossible* for me to make good the shortages of funds, let alone the peculations that might occur within the French party. Each national party ought to see to its own expenses, and one should not hear—in France, above all—this constant complaint that 'the fees are not remitted'. Such kind of things would never take place if there is just a bit of order; a cashier ought to be subject to some kind of control, and when he falls ill, he is to be replaced, and he is accountable for receipts and expenditures. If some inevitable misfortune assailed you—all right, let it be; but paying for such negligence of *responsible agents* of the party, that's tough indeed!

But, after all, the fat is in the fire—so much for that!

I have explained to Bebel the entire affair of Millevoye's[a]; it seems as if they are calming down on this account; your success at Carmaux and elsewhere must have contributed to that. The fruits of your peregrinations through France begin to ripen, and all of us are pleased to see the progress made in France. Do you realise now what a splendid weapon you in France have had in your hands for forty years in universal suffrage; if only people had known how to use it! It's slower and more boring than the call to revolution, but it's ten times more sure, and what is even better, it indicates with the most perfect accuracy the day when a call to armed revolution has to be made; it's even ten to one that universal suffrage, intelligently used by the workers, will drive the rulers to overthrow legality, that is, to put us in the most favourable position to make the revolution. We should reach a new stage in the 1893 elections, and then there will

---

[a] See this volume, p. 5

be that union between Socialists of different shades of opinions of which Liebknecht never stops talking. That union will come about as soon as there is a score of Socialists in the Chamber; if our people have—as I hope—a majority, they will be able to dictate terms. In the meantime, go on with your 'victories and conquests', and you will find that it is the Germans who will applaud you the most warmly.

Have you received the report of the German Executive Committee to the Berlin Congress[a]? It's magnificent—and it's war.[47]

The paper—oh the paper[48]! If the French bourgeoisie makes the same amount of difficulty before it lends money to the Russian tsar, that would, at least to some extent, make up for the cheated hopes this journal has aroused in us.

Kiss Laura,
Kind regards from Mrs Kautsky.

Ever yours,
F. Engels

First published in: Printed according to the original
F. Engels, P. et L. Lafargue,
Correspondance, t. III,   Translated from the French
1891-1895, Paris, 1959

17

ENGELS TO AUGUST BEBEL

IN BERLIN

London, 15 November 1892

Dear August,

Now you see how my work gets interrupted! These absurd *Tribüne* articles have *forced* me to intervene. Could you please ensure that the article

---

[a] 'Bericht des Partei-Vorstandes an den Parteitag zu Berlin 1892', *Vorwärts*, No. 259, 4 November 1892.

appears in the next number of the *Tribüne*—it's already too late for this week's.[49]

Can you send me *another copy of those collected articles on Bakunin?* Since *my* copy is regularly sent to Sorge, I no longer have them here, but it might be necessary for me to refer to them. Instead of working, I have had to look out the old stuff, but it was out of the question to let this tissue of lies go unchallenged. Can you find out who its author was?

Regards to Victor.[a] Louise will today be sending an account of Trafalgar Square to Vienna.[50]

Cordial regards to Mrs Julie,

Your
F.E.

[Postscript from Louise Kautsky]

Warm regards to Julie, Victor, Popp and the proper hunter before the Lord.[b] Have received the *Sozialist*. Many thanks.

Good luck with your work.

Love
Louise

First published in:
Marx and Engels, *Works*,
First Russian Edition,
Vol. XXIX, Moscow, 1946

Printed according to the original

Published in English for the first time

---

[a] Adler – [b] August Bebel

18

ENGELS TO SERGEI KRAVCHINSKY (STEPNIAK)

IN LONDON

London, 15 November 1892
122 Regent's Park Road, N.W.

My dear Stepniak,

Suppose you and Mrs Stepniak, Volkhovsky and his little girl all come on *Thursday*[a] and have dinner with us. If you come about 3.30 to 4, we can talk matters over and have dinner at 5. You know it is a long way from your place to this, and unless we arrange as above, you might easily miss your own dinner at home.

Kind regards to Mrs Stepniak from Mrs Kautsky and

Yours faithfully,
F. Engels

First published in: Marx and Engels,   Reproduced from the original
Works, Second Russian Edition, Vol. 38,
Moscow, 1965   Published in English for the first time

19

ENGELS TO AUGUST BEBEL
IN BERLIN

London, 19 November 1892

Dear August,

This time your Party Congress[51] didn't go off as brilliantly as it did on the last occasion. The debate on the question of salary leaves a very

---

[a] 17 November

nasty taste in one's mouth—not that I think the English or French would have done any better in *that* respect—though Louise refuses to admit as much. As I know from long experience, what we are up against here is one of the limitations imposed upon the outlook of working men by the conditions under which they have lived hitherto. The same people who think it perfectly natural for their idol Lassalle to have a private income and live the life of a consummate sybarite are denouncing Liebknecht for wanting, as their paid editor, barely one-third of that sum, although the paper yields them five or six times as much.[52] To be dependent, even on a labour party, is a hard lot. And, quite aside from the question of money, it's a most otiose position for anyone with any initiative to be editor of a paper belonging to the party. Marx and I were always agreed that we would *never* accept such a position and that the only paper we could have was one that was not financially dependent even on the party itself.

If taken too far, your 'nationalisation' of the press[53] would have very material drawbacks. It's absolutely *essential* for you to have a press in the party which is not *directly* dependent on the Executive or even the Party Congress, i.e. which is in a position unreservedly to oppose individual party measures *within* the programme and accepted tactics, and freely to criticise that programme and those tactics, within the limits of party decorum. As the Party Executive, you people ought to encourage a press of this nature—indeed initiate it, for you would then exert far more moral sway over it than if it were to come into being partly *against* your will. The party is outstripping the strict discipline of earlier days; with 2 or 3 millions and an influx of 'heddicated' elements, more latitude is needed than what has hitherto not only sufficed but actually proved a useful restraint. The sooner you people adapt yourselves and the party to this changed situation the better. And the first step is a *formally* independent party press. It is bound to come about but it would be better if you were to allow it to come about in such a way that it remains under your moral sway from the outset and does not arise in opposition to yourselves.

You people blundered badly—not in Berlin but at Brussels[54]— over the question of the May Day celebrations. You must have known at the time what you could promise and perform, and yet you went and promised more than you are now able to perform. I consider your own speech on the subject no whit inferior to Victor's and readily believe that a stoppage of work in Germany would demand sacrifices out of all proportion to victories and gains.[55] But when the strongest party in the world suddenly sounds a retreat in this way, the general impression this produces is *very bad. Noblesse oblige.* You are the fighting force, the *corps de bataille* of the modern labour movement and, what you promised in Brussels, you were morally bound to do. Now, while it is undoubtedly better not to follow up one stupidity with another, far greater one—granted the crucial importance just now is not to interrupt the German party's victorious progress—you should nevertheless consider what kind of impression this Berlin resolution is going to make on the world at large. The affair would also seem to have aroused indignation in France and the chaps there will doubtless be giving you a piece of their mind. You cannot afford to inflict such moral injury upon yourselves again—so *in Zurich* you must have the courage of your convictions and declare outright that you cannot commit yourselves to a stoppage of work; then, though people may be angry with you, they will not be able to reproach you with breaking your word and beating a retreat.[56] It is nonsensical to try and organise the movement uniformly in each individual country. The Austrians, to whom a stoppage of work on May Day is necessary, and who are accordingly prepared to make those very sacrifices which you rightly repudiated in your particular circumstances, are as justified in acting as they do as you were; now, however, they can make reproaches to which you can offer no answer. For by *their* very conduct they have proved that the *impossibility* clause laid down at Brussels does not apply.

We over here have not yet had the state socialism debate.

I must congratulate you on your resolutions. They are really first-rate and I know of only one person who could have improved on them, namely Marx. The resolution on state socialism, like that on anti-Semitism, hits the nail on the head. And it is precisely resolutions of this kind that have in the past been the Achilles' heel of the German movement; they have been sloppy, indeterminate, nebulous and cliché-ridden—in short, for the most part a disgrace. Fortunately they are so untranslatable that anyone translating them into a foreign language is compelled to read into them a meaning which they themselves do not possess.

Below is a theatre drawn by Louise or Aveling. For the past week the page thus embellished has been repeatedly placed amongst my writing paper, which is why it now has the honour of finding its way to you.[57]

Enclosed you will find[a] the twaddle talked by the seven Swabians[58]

---

[a] The enclosed text is missing.

of London—the Fabians[43] of the *Chronicle*[a]—about the Party Congress. The poor souls are in a mess. The great Shaw, having in May urged upon you the necessity of collusion with the Liberals and demonstrated that, failing such a policy, nothing could result but defeat and disgrace[59], now admits in a speech to the Democratic Club that they have been scandalously done in the eye by the Liberals and that all they had reaped on the occasion of the elections was—defeat and disgrace; also that the Liberals, together with the Tories, are now out to do the workers in the eye! And these are the people who propose to teach you 'practical politics'! In fact he now actually says that the two old parties have but *one and the same policy* and that, barring them, there is nothing but—Social Democracy! This will, I think, have the effect of a cold douche on our good Ede.[b] Cordial regards to your wife and all the friends.

Your

F. E. (in the stage box)

[*Postscript from Louise Kautsky*]

Love from the Witch herself; my enthusiasm for May Day isn't quite so extreme.

First published in: Marx and Engels, *Works*, First Russian Edition, Vol. XXIX, Moscow, 1946	Printed according to the original Published in English for the first time

20

ENGELS TO PAUL LAFARGLUE[35]

AT LE PERREUX

London, 22 November 1892

My dear Lafargue,

Thanks for the papers. The Panama business,[60] circumstances aiding and abetting, could well become for the bourgeois republic the Pandora's

---

[a] *Daily Chronicle* – [b] Eduard Bernstein

box that Emile de Girardin's file of dossiers, from which issued 'a scandal a day', was for the July Monarchy.[61] As long as this goes on, I think your place is in Paris, in the Chamber, at the centre of the news, to put yourself, and keep yourself, in touch with what is happening and in particular with what emerges from one day to the next. Every fresh piece of scandal which is brought to light will be a weapon for us. It's time I was done with the 3rd volume,[a] the close of the century is more and more charged with electricity. I'm glad to say it's going passably well (I mean the work on the 3rd volume) and I hope to finish it during the winter. The greatest difficulty has been overcome.

Sam Moore has just left us. He is going to spend the greater part of his leave in the country with his parents and will be back in January. We shall see him again next Sunday.[b]

If I am not mistaken I have already told you that Pumps had a little girl on the 13th—both are doing well.

For the last few days I have been well enough again to go out for a quarter of an hour; I hope this will help to restore me altogether.

The Germans have committed a fine blunder over May Day; not in Berlin, but in Brussels.[54] They ought to have reserved the right, at the International Congress, to celebrate the day in *their own way* and according to circumstances. Their withdrawal creates a deplorable impression and should you give them a good wigging, you'll be doing no more than your duty. Any other party could have allowed itself this retrogressive move; they, in their position as the main body of the European army, could not make it without great prejudice to the movement as a whole. I entirely approve the reasons which decided them in Berlin: the harm, to them, of a stoppage of work would have been out of all proportion to the advantages *to them*; but that should have been foreseen, and they should have had the courage at Brussels *not to vote for a stoppage*.

And what of Laura? When do we see her here? Kiss her for me.

Kindest regards from Louise.

Ever yours,
F. E.

Please keep me posted about the Panama affair with newspapers, it's

---

[a] of Marx's *Capital* – [b] 27 November

so important. We shall find that Wilson was only a tiny bit of a swindler compared with Reinach & Co.

First published in:
F. Engels, P. et L. Lafargue,
Correspondance, t. III, 1891-1895,
Paris, 1959

Printed according to the original

Translated from the French

21

ENGELS TO JULIE BEBEL

IN BERLIN

London, 29 November 1892

Dear Mrs Bebel,

Of all the letters I got on my birthday, yours is the first I feel impelled to answer. My most sincere thanks. I spent the day 'in the best of health', for, even though I am not in full control of my movements and cannot walk as much as I should like to, I nevertheless feel quite robust and everyone says I look very well. This time we turned my birthday into an English May Day celebration, i.e. we brought it forward from the Monday to the previous Sunday.[a] Louise felt that, as I couldn't fail to tipple somewhat on an occasion like this, one day would be enough and two days too many. We had a real houseful, our African, Sam Moore, also Bax, the Avelings, Bernsteins, Mottelers, the Russian Volkhovsky, and two working men from the Society[62]; that, I think, was all. No. I nearly forgot little Inka[b] who has really filled out on the food she gets in Berlin and whose plumpness suits her very well—now I have tangible proof that people have learned how to eat their fill in Berlin and let no one speak to me in future about starving Berlin!

We still had a small supply of dried woodruff and so Louise and I concocted a May cup with the aid of Moselle, red wine and champagne—at this foggy time of year it would hardly be possible to imagine, let alone

---

[a] 27 November – [b] Inka Fischer

brew, anything better. Since one and all had laid a good foundation in the shape of a cold meal, the said cup was valiantly attacked, not least by Your Humble Servant, the Narrator and, strictly between ourselves, several of the gentlemen, among them—I was about to say it but shall stop before it's too late—became somewhat the worse for wear. Julius[a] was in great form; he sang various songs and told funny stories though, with his customary obstinacy, indulged in nothing but water or coffee. In short, we were all very jolly until past midnight, which is saying a great deal, considering the distances here in London and the fact that all railway and omnibus services close down after 11 o'clock on Sunday night. And so I was able to retire to bed secure in the knowledge that I had entered my 73rd year in a worthy fashion. However I hope that my health will allow me to do even better next year. Then my birthday falls on a Tuesday, and so we shall again be able to make a start on Sunday, though in that case I should like to carry on carousing until Tuesday night.

I should like to have attended that beanfeast in Berlin. Inka tells me that she could not get through to you and Bebel because of the crush so there must have been an enormous number present.[63] Still, I don't doubt that I'll witness something of that kind again, if not this year then the next, provided that is, you come over and fetch us. The little Fischer girl sees in you so great a mental affinity with my dear good Lenchen that I can be doubly confident in placing myself in your charge.

As August left only *one* measly page for your use, I shall reverse the position and he will get only one from me.

With warm regards

Yours,
F. Engels

First published in: Marx and Engels, *Works,* First Russian Edition, Vol.XXIX, Moscow, 1946

Printed according to the original

Published in English for the first time

---

[a] Motteler

22

ENGELS TO AUGUST BEBEL

IN BERLIN

London, 29 November 1892

Dear August,

Many thanks for your good wishes—I stood the whole thing very well and without any evil after-effects whatever, nor should I be in any way averse to celebrating yet another birthday tomorrow—but so strict a watch is kept on me that I should never be allowed to indulge in such excesses! Your Prussian police are as nothing by comparison with a medical Witch[a] like this. But I always keep wondering what good it will do and what are the sins that have earned me such conscientious surveillance. Being unable to rid myself of a silly superstitious belief in 'equalising justice', I am drinking mineral water and lemonade and doing penance for the aforesaid sins without knowing whether I have actually committed them. More about politics in my next—in a day or two[b]—but I must see to it that I finish Volume III.[c] In France things look remarkably tempestuous; *c'est le commencement de la fin*[d]! The time will again come when the French will have an opportunity to show their *good* qualities.

Warm regards.

Your
F. E.

Thank you so much for the fine gluepot; it will be pressed into service straight away for Volume III.

First published in: Marx and Engels, *Works*, First Russian Edition, Vol. XXIX Moscow, 1946

Printed according to the original

Published in English for the first time

---

[a] Louise Kautsky – [b] See this volume, p. 48 – [c] of *Capital* – [d] it is the beginning of the end

23

ENGELS TO AN UNKNOWN CORRESPONDENT[64]

London, 29 November 1892
122 Regent's Park Road, N. W.

My dear Charlie,

Thank you very much for your nice letter and good wishes which I hope may all be fulfilled and as you have done me the honour of being born on the same day as myself, please accept my best congratulations on *your* birthday and the wish that you may live to be twice as old as I am now. Then you are sure to see something very grand and, worth seeing, and then perhaps you will now and then think of me as one who tried his best to bring about such a change.

With kind regards to your parents and brothers and sisters

Yours faithfully,
F. Engels

First published in: Marx and Engels, *Works*, First Russian Edition, Vol. XXIX, Moscow, 1946

Reproduced from the original

Published in English for the first time

24

ENGELS TO THE SOCIAL DEMOCRATIC PARTY SECRETARIAT[65]

IN BERLIN

London, 29 November 1892

Dear Party Secretariat,

This comes with my sincere thanks for your kind good wishes.[66]

My request to you, my dear Fischer, is that you also convey these thanks to your people.

While you, my dear Auer, must submit to my insisting that you now adopt in the personal sense the *Du* with which you, as the first half of the Secretariat, have hitherto been addressing me solely in a collective sense, it being understood that next year we shall make up for our failure to celebrate the solemn rite of *Schmollis*.

As the Hyena has also been brought into this affair, I shall give her the floor.

Your

F. Engels

[Postscript from Louise Kautsky]

It will be difficult, generally speaking, to give Bamberger the floor in London. Press Hyena's note.[67]

[Postscript from Engels]

Yes, but who in fact is the Hyena?

First published in: Marx and Engels, *Works*, Second Russian Edition, Vol. 38, Moscow, 1965

Printed according to original

Published in English for the first time

25

ENGELS TO PAUL STUMPF

IN MAINZ

London, 30 November 1892

My dear old Stumpf,

You could have given me no greater pleasure on my seventy-second birthday than by sending me the Ultramontanist[68] confirmation of our victory in the Mainz elections.[69] You Mainz people sometimes tend to be gas-bags—born wine salesmen—but when it comes to the point you can also buckle to and move mountains, and it will always be remembered in your favour that Mainz was the only German city to play an honourable role during the great revolution.[70] Nature gave you the gift of the gab which is just what is wanted when it comes to working on the peasants, the more so in that you have in the wine growers round about you a great quantity of material to work on. If you address yourself energetically to the task, you will be able to achieve something and show the Cologne people how it's done. From Mainz to Cologne and down to Cleve there's still many a poor soul to be snatched away from the priests and still many a constituency to be won, and this is precisely the moment when the gentlemen of the Centre[71] are on the point either of thoroughly compromising themselves over the military question or of leading the entire Centre up the garden path.

Apart from that, I should like to send you my best thanks and to say how glad I am that you had been keeping well and have been feeling even 'better' since. I too am keeping well. We had the whole Brimstone Gang[72] here on Sunday and a few more besides, all of whom vigorously addressed themselves to the wine cup.[a]

If we have a few more of these scandals in Paris[60], we may soon be able to re-enact the old comedy of autumn '47 in Brussels; the world is beginning to look shaky.

Your old
F. Engels

First published in: Marx and Engels, *Works*, First Russian Edition, Vol. XXIX, Moscow, 1946

Printed according to the original

Published in English for the first time

---

[a] See this volume, pp. 37-38

26

ENGELS TO NATALIE AND WILHELM LIEBKNECHT
IN BERLIN

London, 1 December 1892

Dear Mrs Liebknecht,

My best thanks for your kind note and good wishes for my seventy-second birthday which we celebrated last Sunday amidst the usual circle of friends,[a] all of whom remained until the 28th had actually dawned! Winter seems to have set in really early over there if you have already been blessed with snow and a temperature of 10 degrees R. We don't have such extremes, but rather content ourselves with a pleasing alternation of rain and fog, getting more of both than we should like.

Unfortunately it was not possible to send off this letter in time to give your Willy[b] my greetings on his birthday. I trust you will be so good as to accept these belated wishes. I thought it probable that your Theodor[c] to whom, as also to Karl,[d] please convey my sincere thanks for the good wishes, would be able to take a break from his tedious week in Mittenwald by spending a Sunday with you, and I'm glad to see that this was in fact so. The best of luck to your Karl with his exams.[73] I, who never passed an exam in my life, can nevertheless well imagine how a young man must feel three months before such an event.

The Stadthagen affair has shown that they are still perfectly capable of persecuting us even without the Anti-Socialist Law.[15] That the debate on salary at the Party Congress[52] has caused your family great annoyance I can well believe, but that kind of thing is inevitable in public life. Not everyone is as eager as the German Reichstag to vote grants; in other countries even ministers and, on occasion, crowned heads no less, must expose themselves to unpleasantnesses of this kind. It is a case of everyone trying to prove that 'where money begins, benevolence ends'.[74] On the other hand, Liebknecht enjoyed a well-earned triumph with the Ems Despatch,[75] which makes up for a good deal, and then again his trip to Marseilles was an ovation from start to finish.[5]

---

[a] See this volume, pp. 37-38 – [b] Wilhelm Liebknecht jun. – [c] Theodor K. Liebknecht – [d] Karl Liebknecht

Pumps felt impelled to show the world that, despite her prematurely grey hair, she is still a young woman and therefore presented her husband with a baby girl a little more than a fortnight ago. Both are doing very well under the circumstances. I too am keeping pretty well on the whole but am still not yet mobile enough. However when one looks out of the window at the persistent downpour, one is less inclined to make a fuss about it.

Take good care of yourself; with best wishes to you and all your family.

Yours,
F. Engels

Dear Liebknecht,

You will have to wait a little while for the sequel to this, as Volume III[a] admits of no delay. In France it almost seems as though we are back in '47, and Panama[60] could well put paid to all the bourgeois *cochonnerie*.[b] The scandals of 1847 and of the Second Empire are trivial by comparison. Do write and tell your Paris correspondents to keep you informed about it and to send you the *material* in newspapers—these are matters you must pursue *in person*.

Your old
F. E.

First published in: Marx and Engels, *Works,* First Russian Edition, Vol. XXIX, Moscow, 1946

Printed according to the original

Published in English for the first time

---

[a] of Capital – [b] beastliness

27

ENGELS TO LUDWIG SCHORLEMMER

IN DARMSTADT

London, 1 December 1892

My dear Schorlemmer,

My sincere thanks for your kind good wishes for a day that was happily spent.[a] Though I may not actually be fit for active service in the 'glorious army' as I enter on another year of my life, I am nevertheless in good health and, on the whole, robust and I think you are right in saying that for the time being I shall continue to pull my weight.

To go by your latest information on Anschütz, it would certainly be best if we were to hear no more of him. Old Pflüger—a nephew of mine used to work in his laboratory—is, so far as I can judge, a real philistine and if, on top of that, Anschütz's father was a Prussian officer, that makes matters even worse, The fact is that it will be difficult to find the right man for Carl's[b] biography, one who is not only a chemist but also a Social Democrat, and not only a Social Democrat but also a chemist and, what's more, a chemist who has made a close study of the history of his discipline since Liebig's day. Presumably we shall have to wait and see whether we can find that man or whether we must content ourselves with the two aspects of Carl being treated separately. I myself must above all else finally complete Volume III of *Capital* and cannot see how I could break off just now—and on top of that there are also the proofs of the 2nd edition of Volume II!

And then, too, we live in very turbulent times, what with the military affair,[76] the impending crisis in Germany, the Panama scandals[60] and the crisis that has already set in in France as well as the crisis over Ireland that will almost certainly occur over here next spring.[77] In times like these my correspondence increases twofold and threefold and if, on top of everything else, one is forbidden on account of one's eyes to wield a pen by lamplight, how can one possibly manage? And as for daylight here in London in winter! We're glad if we get four or five hours of it and often there's none at all—gaslight all day because of the fog.

---

[a] See this volume, pp. 37-38 – [b] Carl Schorlemmer; see also this volume, p. 14

But it can't be helped and so long as things keep moving ahead in the outside world, one mustn't complain.

With my best compliments to your family,

Yours,
F. Engels

Best wishes from Mrs Kautsky.

I almost forgot to tell you that Pumps gave birth to a baby girl a fortnight ago last Sunday; both are doing well.

First published in: Marx and Engels, *Works*, First Russian Edition, Vol. XXIX, Moscow, 1946

Printed according to the original

Published in English for the first time

28

ENGELS TO CHARLES BONNIER[78]

IN OXFORD

[Draft]

[London, 3 December 1892]

My dear Bonnier,

Es wird nichts so heiss gegessen, wie es gekocht wird.[a] You have the admirable habit of serving warm, very warm, but would I not sometimes risk burning my lips? The newspaper, as you know, is not yet being published.[48]

You ask me to convey to the Germans a kind of ultimatum from the French. If I undertake to do so, will you guarantee that, in reply to a direct query by Berlin to Paris, Paris without disavowing me entirely would not say that I had exaggerated.

---

[a] If you don't cool it, you'll not be able to drink it.

As to the core of your ultimatum:

1) let us first see what will happen here between now and 1st May, and what will happen this 1st May.

2) Between May and August a number of things might happen before Zurich[56] which cannot today be anticipated,

3) and, all the more so, between August 1893 and May 1894.

With the military question in Germany,[76] with Panama[60] in France, with the Irish complication in England[77]—three acute imminent political crises—with an industrial crisis everywhere, it seems to me that we could put our time to better use than quarrelling over how to mark 1st May, 1894, a day on which, perhaps, we will have better things to do than 'demonstrate'!

As for your perennial Protot, I couldn't care less about him, any more than about his fellows, the agents-provocateurs of the German police. When will you adopt a similar attitude?

In any case, it seems to me rather odd that you are prepared to allow the English to disregard the resolutions of Brussels[54] but them alone.[79] What will French logic say to that?[a]

As for the rest I know only one party which has the right to reproach the Berlin Congress.[51] That is the Austrian party.[81] Until now 1st May in Berlin has been worth far more than those in Paris.

I am writing today to Bebel.[b] I will tell him of your ultimatum, but for the moment only as your personal opinion.

First published in: Marx and Engels, *Works*, First Russian Edition, Vol. XXIX, Moscow, 1946

Printed according to the original
Translated from the French
Published in English for the first time

---

[a] The following sentence is crossed out in the draft: 'The article by Bebel[80] has probably gone to press already, if in Paris they wanted to prevent it.' – [b] See next letter.

29

ENGELS TO AUGUST BEBEL

IN BERLIN

London, 3 December 1892

Dear August,

I was delighted by what you said in your letter of the 22nd about the disinclination you people feel for any further 'nationalisation' of the party press.[82] So there's no need to waste any more words on the subject.

As regards the May Day celebrations, I concede that you were perfectly right so far as the *Berlin* resolution was concerned. But the fact remains that the general impression you produced in Brussels was that in future you too would celebrate on 1 May and not invoke the permission not to do so that was granted *purely by way of an exception.*[54] So you shouldn't be surprised by the hullabaloo to which the Berlin resolution has given rise. But your intention of getting Congress to settle on Sunday as the day on which celebrations should be held in future is likely to hit on some snags. Except for the English everyone will be against it, many of the smaller parties out of sheer bravado. It would be a sorry retreat and *the last people to join in its* official *proclamation* would be those who secretly reserve the right *to do likewise,* whether it was proclaimed or not.

Well, yesterday evening I got a rabid letter from Bonnier (he never writes any other kind) in which, having read your article in the *Neue Zeit,*[83] he declares in the name of the French that, if the first Sunday in May were to be adopted, they would drop the whole business of May Day. *'Jamais,'* he writes, *'notre parti n'acceptera (le dimanche) et nous sommes bien décidés à tenir ferme.'*[a] And he believes you people are playing with fire.

I wrote and told him[b] 1. that things are never as black as he paints them, 2. asking who had authorised him to speak in the name of the French party, 3. that before May 1893, and between then and August '93 in Zurich[56] and between then and *May '94* much might happen

---

[a] Our party would never agree (to the Sunday) and we are fully determined to stand firm.
– [b] See this volume, Letter 28

that we didn't expect and that, with 3 acute political crises in the offing (Army in Germany,[76] Panama in France[60] Ireland in England[77]) and a general industrial crisis, we probably had better things to do than bicker about how best to demonstrate on 1 May '94, when we might have work of a very different nature to do; 4. how his proposal to allow the *English*, and *them only*, to celebrate on the Sunday chimed in with French logic; 5. that I knew of only one party—the Austrian[81]—which had any right to reproach the Germans, that the May Day celebrations in Berlin more than made amends for those in Paris and 6. that I had passed on his ultimatum to you, but purely *as his own private opinion*.

The man is consumed by an irrepressible urge to be up and doing but, such being the case, he shouldn't have gone to Oxford where he is all on his own with red Wolff[a] who is completely out of everything. It's a priceless idea, wanting to direct the European labour movement from Oxford—the last genuine remnant of the Middle Ages still to be found in Europe—but for us it makes an infuriating amount of unnecessary work and I shall protest in no mean terms to Paris about this go-between. The really unfortunate thing is that he's the only person who understands German save for Laura, and she lives out of town.

For the rest, the Party Congress went off quite well, but subscribing to the resolution[84] despite the sundry rubbish it contains, must have been a bitter pill for Vollmar to swallow.

Ede came to see me, bringing with him a whole bunch of letters from K. Kautsky—who had also written to me—all of them concerned with the *Neue Zeit*, and wanting me to add my mite. My opinion is that, if you accept the change proposed by Dietz, you should think it out and prepare for it properly, and not go ahead till January, otherwise it will be altogether premature.[85] But speaking generally, I should say that, since becoming a weekly, the *Neue Zeit* has to some extent relinquished its *old* character in favour of a new one which it has not been completely successful in assuming. The paper is now being written for two sets of readers and cannot do full justice to either.

If it is to become a popular, part-political, part-literary and artistic and part-learned journal, *à la Nation, then it will have to move to Berlin*. The political section of a weekly must be written at the hub of things, *on the eve of publication*, otherwise it will always be lagging behind. And,

---

[a] Ferdinand Wolff

save for the correspondents, those working on the political section must always be *in the same place*. The idea of editing a review in Berlin and London and publishing it in Stuckert[a] doesn't seem feasible to me. In any case there would be a 20 or 30 per cent difference in subscriptions between a Berlin and a Stuttgart weekly. I am regarding this simply from a bookselling point of view, having no more than a nodding acquaintance with the other aspects that need to be considered and about which you out there will be better informed than I.

But if the *Neue Zeit* undergoes these changes, it will appeal to only one *section* of its former public and will have to be organised *solely* for their benefit. It would then no longer be open to those articles from which it has hitherto derived its greatest and most enduring value—the longer, learned papers which run on through 3 to 6 numbers. Hence, alongside the *Neue Zeit* there would have to be a predominantly learned monthly—if necessary even quarterly—journal with a correspondingly restricted circle of subscribers, and this would have to be offset by *raising the price* if the paper was to be kept going.

Indeed, it seems to me altogether necessary, if the party publishers wish increasingly to secure a monopoly of party publications, including learned ones, that they should not aim at bulk sales for everything, whether suitable for that purpose or not. An original paper on political economy is bound to be primarily a detailed treatise, nor can it be expected to sell in bulk. Similarly, a genuine historical work, the outcome of independent research, does not lend itself to publication by installments. In short, I think there should be two separate departments, one for bulk sales, the other for ordinary, slower-moving sales through booksellers, in smaller quantities and at a correspondingly higher price.

What happens when an attempt is made to boost sales beyond the limits called for by the nature of the case is something I have learned from my own experience. Though written as popularly as possible, my *Anti-Dühring* is by no means a book to suit *every* working man. But along comes Dietz, takes over part of the Zurich edition and then tries to boost sales by remaindering the thing at a reduced price with 11 assorted booksellers. This is not at all to my liking and next time I shall be on my guard. It is the only longer work I have written since 1845 and, whichever

---

[a] Stuttgart

way one looks at it, it is degrading to see it treated in that way. By the by, there's no need to say anything to Dietz about this—the thing is over and done with and cannot be altered, nor would I have mentioned it to you had it not provided an apt illustration of what I mean by the wrong way of selling books.

For the rest, times are growing critical. Every morning when I read the *Daily News* and such French papers as have arrived, it takes me right back to '47. At that time, too, one expected some further scandalous revelations each morning and one was seldom disappointed. The Panama affair[60] beats everything that went on in the way of corruption under Louis-Philippe and under Bonaparte III. The initial outlay, including bonifications to the press and Parliament, amounted to *83 million francs.* This will be the ruin of the bourgeois republic, for the Radicals[86] are as deeply implicated as the Opportunists.[87] On every side attempts are being made to hush things up, of course, but the more they are hushed up the worse they get. Once the revelations were under way and a few people had become irretrievably implicated in the scandal, these had perforce to cover themselves by betraying their accomplices and showing that they had only been swimming with the stream. Already the committee is in possession of such enormously compromising statements that there's no holding back; a *few* may slip through the net, but large numbers have already been named and, of course, the fewer the *names* that are compromised the greater the odium that attaches to the bourgeois republic. Though much may still happen in the meantime, this is nevertheless the beginning of the end. Fortunately all the monarchist parties are completely done for, nor will it be at all easy to find another Boulanger.[6]

Herewith an extract from Lafargue's letter for the *Vorwärts*—but do ensure that the paper *gives no indication whatsoever that the letter emanated from a deputy.*[88]

What Liebknecht entirely overlooked in the matter of Bismarck's Ems forgery was that that's the sort of thing diplomats *do* in secret but never boast about.[75] But if one of them does happen to boast about it, the breach of etiquette is such *as to render him persona non grata.* After this it will never again be possible to appoint Mr Bismarck Imperial Chancellor, otherwise any foreign government could refuse to enter into negotiations with a man who not only is not above using such methods, but actually boasts of having used them. The Imperial Government would risk incurring a general international boycott were Bismarck to become Chancellor again. I believe it would do a lot of good if this were said on the floor of the Reichstag.

Many regards to your wife.[a]

Your
F. E.

[Postscript from Louise Kautsky]

Dear August,

It seems to be my fate that my space should be rationed because I once overstepped the mark and wrote a leader, so rather than look at your last letter, I shall look instead at the pretty inkstand that invites kind, happy thoughts and was inaugurated with the proofs of the second volume of *Capital*. Thank you very much for it—how good you both are; now that I'm equipped, I am, it seems, likely to run on and to be rapped over the knuckles for so doing. Well, that isn't what I was intending to write about—all I meant to say was that not once this week have I been able to get round to writing, there having been, alas, so much to prevent me—glassworkers, transport workers, Reumann, Victor,[b] meeting of the unemployed and, last but not least, the Jews. They are not getting the *Vorwärts*, August, so could you please make inquiries? Then, some time ago, I asked if you could let me have another copy of the *Vorwärts'* report on the Congress, but you probably forgot—I'd like two if at all possible, otherwise one; it's the report on the Party Conference I want, not the one made by you people at the Conference. Victor enjoyed the time he spent with you and wrote saying that to him it seemed as though the poor Austrians were standing guard in the wet and the cold, whereas you people were sitting snug in your encampment, despite the struggle and the fighting. Then there's another thing—I still have two English reports on the International Glassworkers' Congress[89] to spare. Would you like one? It's very interesting, but you would have to write a few lines about it by way of justification and send a sample copy, and would you please ask Fischer if he might perhaps write something for a Bavarian paper, in which case I would send him the other copy. I would, of course, send them without any strings attached but I feel responsible because it's the English who have to pay for the whole thing, so I'd be grateful if you'd let me know. I must close, so more anon; it's time for the post and I must close.

With loving kisses to you and Julie,

the Witch

[Postscript from Engels]

Please convey my most sincere thanks to the parliamentary group for their kind telegram last Sunday.[90]

---

[a] Julie Bebel – [b] Adler

First published in:
Marx and Engels, *Works*,
First Russian Edition,
Vol. XXIX, Moscow, 1946

Printed according to the original

Published in English for the first time

30

ENGELS TO KARL KAUTSKY

IN STUTTGART

London, 4 December 1892

Dear Baron,

My best thanks for your good wishes in respect of a day that was spent very happily. Alas, tippling still does not agree with me and I shall have to atone for it by abstaining for the next few weeks.

Thank you, too, for sending the prospectus for the new journal—do you know the chaps[91]? I have never heard of any of them.

I haven't yet been able so much as to look at Schmidt's latest on the rate of profit[a] since, until Volume III[b] is finished, I shall have to fend off everything that might entail extra work—there being far too many inter-ruptions as it is.

As for the *Neue Zeit*, 85 Ede[c] and I have discussed it at length, and yesterday I wrote a long letter[d] to August on the subject.

It is my opinion that if, as proposed by Dietz and August, the *Neue Zeit* is to be given a lighter, more popular tone and made 'more interest-ing' from a literary point of view, it will have to *move to Berlin*. For only there can a political review covering all events up *to the eve of publication* be catered for on the spot and only there can a wealth of artistic and literary work, which would otherwise come a week too late, be produced

---

[a] C. Schmidt, 'Die Durchschnittsprofitrate und das Marx'sche Wertgesetz,' *Die Neue Zeit*, 1892/93, Vol. I, Nos. 3 and 4. – [b] of *Capital* – [c] Eduard Bernstein – [d] See this vol-ume, Letter 29

with speed and 'immediacy'. This and other circumstances would mean that a Berlin edition would have 20 or 30 per cent more subscribers than a Stuttgart one.

But in that case the *Neue Zeit* would have to sacrifice the better part of its contents—and the latter would call for a monthly or quarterly of a more rigorously learned nature than hitherto and which, because intended for a smaller public, would have to be sold at a *higher price*.

But what if neither is feasible? In that case—and this has only just occurred to me—it might perhaps be better to turn the *Neue Zeit* back into a monthly but with the same capacity as at present, i.e. 104 sheets a year and 8-9 a month. The longer articles could then appear in one, or at most 2, numbers and would, in the second case, have to be subdivided into I, II or I, II, III, IV installments which would be conducive to their general intelligibility. With 2 sheets a month it's *impossible* to break off longer articles at the point the sense requires, since this would almost invariably be precluded by considerations of space and diversity. But in this way you could train your contributors to divide up their things *themselves* into 2 installments. And then there could be 'something for everyone' in every number. But here again, you would have to reckon on a reduced circulation, and hence be obliged to raise the price—or so at least it seems to me.

At all events, before making any experiments you should consider the matter carefully. Once made, a false step is difficult to reverse.

If the weekly *Neue Zeit* were to move to Berlin it would, in many respects, replace the weekly central organ which might otherwise hold out for another year. Between now and then a great deal may happen. Things are livening up. It looks as though the Panama scandal[60] might mark a turning-point so far as the development of France is concerned. You should pester Lafargue about collecting material for a longish essay on the subject, or supplying you with articles as each particular phase of the scandal reaches its climax. With that sort of material the *Neue Zeit* would be able to outstrip the dailies even in the matter of factual news.

As for the *Vorwärts*—the less said the better!

Your
F. Engels

Herewith a trifle for the *Neue Zeit*. If you think Sternberg's report is too long, condense it; having once got going I translated the whole thing.[92]

First published in:
*Aus der Frühzeit des Marxismus,
Engels Briefwechsel mit Kautsky,*
Prague, 1935

Printed according to the original

Published in English for the first time

31

ENGELS TO PAUL LAFARGUE[35]

AT LE PERREUX

London, 5 December 1892

My dear Lafargue,

Your remarks concerning Bebel compel me to refer back to your letter from Lille.[93] What you say about him is unfair in the extreme. Far from Liebknecht correcting Bebel on any matter whatsoever (an amusing idea to anyone who understands the situation), it's precisely the contrary that is taking place. It is Liebknecht who is promising wonders, and if the whole thing doesn't collapse and dissolve, it's thanks to the work Bebel is doing. If Liebknecht said only agreeable things to you at Marseilles, don't forget that this is how he behaves with everyone;[5] that he always acts on the impulse of the moment and that consequently he says white here today, but tomorrow somewhere else he will say black, and he will maintain in all good faith that he has not contradicted himself. You complain about the Berlin resolution concerning May 1st,[54] well and good, according to our German press, Liebknecht is reported to have said that at Marseilles he explained the position to you, including the impossibility for the Germans to stop work on May 1st; and that 'the French' had fully acknowledged the force of his arguments. If that is true, by what right do you complain of the Berlin resolution? If Liebknecht has erred (for he believes what he says), what have you to say of the man who, according to you, 'corrects' Bebel?

I fear that behind all this lies the dissatisfaction of our Oxford hermit.[a] If his impulsive nature makes him unjust to Bebel, who is an ironic and *business-like* character, the heat he is generating during his compulsory activity in the heart of the only city in the world where the Middle Ages continue in full swing, will drive this aversion to the point of hatred. As it is, I never get a letter from him which does not teem with abuse of Bebel. I grant all that, I give full recognition to the hermit's good faith and goodwill, but firstly an enthusiast of that kind is a dangerous guide in matters of practical life, particularly when he lives in the isolation of Oxford, consumed by the desire to do something for the movement. And it's not just something to do that he needs, but positively something important and decisive. You know how he pestered us over the paper.[48] The day before yesterday he sent me a veritable ultimatum in the name of the French Party (he always speaks in its collective name) addressed to the German Party: if the Germans at Zurich propose the postponing of the May celebrations to the first Sunday, the French will withdraw from the demonstration altogether, and there will be, if not war, at least something like the breaking off of diplomatic relations—and goodness knows what else. Anyhow he warns the Germans 'that they are playing with fire'. However, his French logic allows him to add that if the English insist on demonstrating on the Sunday, the French would see no harm in it!

I answered him fairly ironically that I would communicate his ultimatum to Bebel, but only as his personal opinion.[b]

Naturally I don't take Bonnier's explosions for the attitude of the French Party; on the contrary, even if you authorised him I should not do so; I know him to be quite incapable—with the best will in the world—of expressing other people's ideas and words without putting in his own. He can't help it; like Liebknecht, he only knows two shades, black and white; he either loves or hates; and as he cannot love Bebel, he needs must hate him. But you would be monstrously wrong to form your view of the German movement according to his. Laura being in the country cannot gainsay all the gossip about the Germans, and it's a great pity that he is the only one of you all who understands German.

---

[a] Charles Bonnier – [b] See this volume, pp.46-47

Have you seen his 'Moment'? There are poems in it (Heine's *Poesiemusik,*[a] *die Instrumental- und Vokalpoesie die keine Musik ist*[b]), poems on Germany; that 'unfathomable' and extremely chaotic Germany which has never existed outside Victor Hugo's imagination. The Germany which was supposed to be preoccupied only with music, dreams and clouds, and which left the care of matters here below to the French bourgeois and journalists. This good fellow would but speak of oaks, of forests, of students with scars on the face, of Gretchen and other playthings—and this after having lived in a country which is today the most prosaic and workaday in the world. Do read all that, and if then you believe a single word of what he has to say about Germany, it will be your fault.

Besides, you may remember that recently, as you needed documents with respect to Liebknecht, it was Bebel who immediately set himself to work for you, while Liebknecht—though it concerned him closely—would but confine himself to sending several newspapers to you.

Enough of that. Had it not been to destroy the false judgements about the most perspicacious, the most sensible and the most energetic man in the German party, I would not have written to you at such length. I wanted to write about Panama,[60] but here is the bottom of the 4th page—and so I shall write about that to Laura.[c]

Ever yours,
F. Engels

First published in:
F. Engels, P. et L. Lafargue,
Correspondance, t. 111, 1891-1895,
Paris, 1959

Printed according to the original

Translated from the French

---

[a] poetry-music – [b] instrumental and vocal poetry which is not music – [c] See next letter.

32

ENGELS TO LAURA LAFARGUE

AT LE PERREUX

London, 5 December 1892

My dear Löhr,

It's a long time yet till April, but if it cannot be managed otherwise, well then we must submit and only consider the matter finally settled, *affaire bâclée*, that you celebrate, both of you, your silver wedding here. And maybe you may manage a few days with us in the meantime, at all events we will consider that an open question still.

If you do not receive this week the *Arbeiterinnenzeitung* please let us know; Louise will write again. The paper having been handed over to the women altogether has probably caused some irregularities which will soon be set right.

Ah le Panama[60]! I can tell you I am 45 years younger again, and living through a second '47. Then *La Presse* (Girardin's) brought every day a fresh revelation about some scandal.[61] or some other paper brought a reply to some charge of his; and this went on till it killed Louis Philippe. But those scandals, and even those of the Second Empire dwindle into nothingness compared with this Grand National Steeplechase of Scandals. Louis Bonaparte took jolly good care, when he coaxed the peasants' money out of their buried hoards, to do so for the benefit of his State loans, which were safe; but here the savings of the small tradesman, the peasant, the domestic servant and above all of the *petit rentier*,[a] the loudest howler of all, have gone into irretrievable ruin, and the miracle has been performed of transforming a canal which has *not* been dug out, into an unfathomable abyss. 1,500 million francs, 60 million pounds sterling, all gone, gone for ever, except what has found its way into the pockets of swindlers, politicians and journalists; and the money got together by swindles and corrupt dodges unequalled even in America. What a base of operations for a Socialistic campaign!

The thing has evidently been based upon its own immensity.

---

[a] small rentier

Everybody considered himself safe because everybody else was as deeply in it. But that is just what now makes hushing up impossible; partial disclosures having set in, the innumerable receivers of 'boodle' (for here American is the only possible language) are by their very numbers debarred from common and concerted action, everybody fights on his own hook and as best he can, and no talking and preaching can prevent a general *sauve qui peut*.[a] That the *police* have placed themselves at the disposal of the Committee after the strike of the courts of law, shows that confidence in the stability of swindle is broken, and that it is considered safe to keep well with the 'financial purity' side.

To my mind *c'est le commencement de la fin*.[b] The bourgeois republic and its politicians can hardly outlive this unparalleled exposure. There are but three possibilities: an attempt at monarchy, another Boulanger,[6] or socialism. The first and the second, if attempted, could only lead to the third, and thus we may be called upon, long before we in consequence of our own action had a right to expect it, to enter upon a career of immense responsibility. I should be glad of it, if it does not come too soon and too suddenly. It will do our Germans good to see that the French have not lost their historical initiative. A country cannot pass through 200 years like what 1648-1848 were for Germany without leaving a small impression of the philistine even on the working class. Our revolution of 48/49 was too short and too incomplete to wipe that out altogether. Of course, the next revolution which is preparing in Germany with a consistency and steadiness unequalled anywhere else, would come of itself in time, say 1898-1904; but revolutionary times, preparing a thoroughgoing crisis, in France, would hasten that process, and moreover, if the thing breaks out in France first, say 1894, then Germany follows suit at once and then the Franco-German Proletarian Alliance forces the hands of England and smashes up in one blow both the triple and the Franco-Russian conspiracies; then we have a revolutionary war against Russia—if not even a revolutionary echo from Russia—*vogue la Galère!*[c]

Love from Louise who is at a meeting of actors and dramatists for the foundation of a freie Bühne or *théâtre libre*[d] or what not.[94]

---

[a] panic – [b] this is the beginning of the end – [c] be that as it may – [d] free stage or free theatre

My respectful salutes as well of those of our tom-cat Felix to your animals.

Ever yours,
F. E.

Mendelsons were here last night, spoke a good deal of their visit to Le Perreux.

First published, in the language of the original (English), in: F. Engels, P. et L. Lafargue, *Correspondance*, t. III, 1891-1895, Paris, 1959

Reproduced from the original

33

ENGELS TO MRS STEPNIAK (KRAVCHINSKY)

IN LONDON

London, 6 December 1892
122 Regent's Park Road, N.W.

Dear Mrs Stepniak,

Mrs Kautsky showed me your note in which you are kind enough to ask me to spend next Saturday evening with you. I should do so with the greatest pleasure, but unfortunately my locomotive capabilities are still too limited to enable me to undertake such distant expeditions.

I am at present practically confined to the neighbourhood of Primrose Hill, and Mrs Kautsky will be able to tell you that I have been obliged to decline invitations besides yours.

Kind regards to Stepniak from

Yours sincerely,
F. Engels

First published in: Marx and Engels,
Works, Second Russian Edition, Vol. 38,
Moscow, 1965

Reproduced from the original

Published in English for the first time

34

ENGELS TO WILHELM ELLENBOGEN[95]

IN VIENNA

London, 7 December 1892
122 Regent's Park Road, N.W.

Esteemed Comrade,

Many thanks for kindly sending your *Geschichte des Arbeiter-Bildungsvereins.*[a] I regard the publication of studies on the history of the Austrian labour movement as a highly rewarding task, the more so since in our fast-moving time some moments, important in themselves, are lost to posterity as they only live on in the memory of the participants and have never been recorded in writing. I, for my part, am again working diligently on Volume 3,[b] a bit of news which will probably compensate you for my not answering your kind letter in person.

Yours faithfully[c]
F. Engels

[*From Louise Kautsky*]

Dear Comrade,

I enjoyed reading your correction in the latest issue of the *Arbeiterzeitung.* For that devilish misprint had accused you of bigamy too, something you had completely overlooked in your eagerness to exculpate yourself in the eyes of the female comrades. Also going off today will be the report of the International Glass-Workers Congress,[89] which will surely be of great interest to you. Many

---

[a] by Wilhelm Ellenbogen – [b] of Marx's *Capital* – [c] in Engels' handwriting

thanks for sending your pamphlet. With warm greetings,

Your

Louise Kautsky

First published in *Novaya i noveishaya istoriya*, No. 6, Moscow, 1980

Printed according to the original
Published in English for the first time

35

ENGELS TO PYOTR LAVROV[96]

IN PARIS

London, 14 December 1892

My dear Lavrov,

I do not see why I would oppose the publication of the letter from Lopatin about a conversation that he had with me.[97] Therefore do as you like.

I was pleased to learn from Mendelson that you are well. As for me, I have no reason to complain—quite the contrary. For three months now I have been working on the 3rd volume of *Capital*, and although there is still a great deal to do, this time I have grounds to hope that I will finish it.

As for the Berlin resolution, I am of the opinion that the Germans committed at *Brussels* the mistake of promising—although indirectly—more than they can fulfil.[54] The 1st May 1890 and '91 has shown that in Germany a strike is impractical; the sacrifices were not worth the possible gains. At Hamburg alone the attempt cost more than 100,000 marks.[98] The coincidence that 1st May 1892 was a Sunday led them to forget in Brussels that real world to which the crisis—more acute this time in Germany than elsewhere—has sharply returned them.

The strike on 1st May '93 could cost us too dear—in Germany, and, by reaction, elsewhere. A strike in Germany would dry up both funds and financial credit of the party for more than a year. And that at a time of military crisis and the possible dissolution of the Reichstag,[76] with elections in May or June.

It is the law of the development of parties that a party which has achieved a certain degree of power finds that the very demonstrations which it could not do without in its early days have become impractical.

For the rest, as for the forms, one could have shown a little more regard for the susceptibilities of others. However, what will you—these are the *grobe Deutsche*[a] who do not know how to sugar the pill.

As regards the rest, it seems to me that Panama[60] is more important than 1ˢᵗ May, given the times. Panama puts me in mind of 1847, when every day one could expect some new scandal.[61] 1847 dug the grave of the July Monarchy, and what will 1892 bring?

Yours,
F. Engels

First published, in Russian,
in *Voprosy istorii KPSS*,
No. 7, Moscow, 1965

Printed according to the original
Translated from the French
Published in English for the first time

36

ENGELS TO LAURA LAFARGUE

AT LE PERREUX

London, 20 December 1892

My dear Löhr,

Yesterday we forwarded by Van Oppen and Co's Express (they have an office in Paris too, but I did unfortunately not note the address) the box with pudding and cake, and hope it will arrive safe (directed to you, Le

---

[a] unpolished Germans

Perreux). The pudding is not quite boiled out, our copper would not heat last Saturday and so, instead of twelve hours' boiling, the unfortunate pudding only got about nine or ten, But if you give it two to three hours' boiling before serving, it will be all right.

Before crossing the Channel, the Oxford sage[a] gave us a call here. I hope I quietened his anxiety about the first of May[b] to some extent, The attempt, in 1890, to *chômer*[c] at Hamburg alone cost the party above 100,000 marks[98], and in my opinion it would never do to allow the bourgeois to bleed the German party's cash and credit *'à blanc'* just at the moment when a dissolution of the Reichstag[76] is in the air, and when every farthing would be wanted.

Panama is delightful,[60] The papers you so kindly send me, and old Mother Crawford's letters—though awfully cut down by the respectable people of the *Daily News*—form already a pretty comprehensive dossier which I intend to complete up to the—I hope—*bitter* end. Respectability here, of course, triumphs.

Wenn sich das französische Laster erbricht, setzt sich die englische Tugend zu Tisch[d]—and I'll be damned if I do not prefer a thousand times that plain open outright French vice to this hypocritical British virtue. Here corruption has been brought into a system and has been endowed with a complete code of étiquette which you have only to keep within, in order to be perfectly bullet-proof against all charges of *undue* corruption. In France no man would stand a chance in a popular constituency, a town especially, who openly wanted to get into Parliament for the purpose of furthering his own interests; here, anybody who wanted to get in for any other purpose would be considered a fool and a Don Quixote. The English Panama is called Building Society and has more than one head— the savings of the small people have been eaten up in these societies by wholesale, and no great fuss about it.[e] One M.P. is in here too, Spencer Balfour—he will take the Chiltern Hundreds and retire into private life—while lots of M.P.'s make money by selling their names as directors of all sorts of swindling companies, which is considered perfectly fair so long as it is not pushed to excess.

On Friday[f] we expect Pumps and her family here, as we have not room

---

[a] Charles Bonnier – [b] See this volume, pp. 46-47 – [c] strike – [d] When French vice fails, British virtue sits down to a meal – [e] See this volume, p. 75 – [f] 23 December

enough in the house we have taken lodgings next door but one—the old Marquis's house is now a lodging house! I think I wrote to you that on November 13th Pumps had a little girl.

Shall write to Paul after the first rush of the holidays is over.

Ever yours,
F. Engels

[Postscript from Louise Kautsky][a]

My dear Laura,

Should I do penance, in sackcloth and ashes? But I'd rather not for I regret all my misdeeds as it is. Because of my not writing I suffer more than you do. After my return the General[b] was no longer his old self and I had hardly any time of my own, but when I did have time I was in no mood for writing. Yet now and again everything turned out very well. I look forward to the spring when we'll be able to talk to our hearts content. My best regards to the M.P.[c]

With love and kisses

Your

Louisa

First published, in the language of the original (English), in: F. Engels, P. et L. Lafargue, *Correspondance*, t. III, 1891-1895, Paris, 1959

Reproduced from the original

---

[a] written in German – [b] Engels' nickname – [c] Paul Lafargue

37

ENGELS TO AUGUST BEBEL

IN BERLIN

London, 22 December 1892

Dear August,

We recently had the pleasure of seeing Cato Censorius Bonnier here while in transit from Oxford to Paris. I think I made some impression on him by pointing out that 1. his manner of giving ultimatums[a] is hardly calculated to promote mutual understanding and 2. that it really might be better if the German party were to preserve its funds and its credit for the eventuality of a dissolution and future elections rather than dissipate both on a stoppage of work on May Day. It's unfortunate for both French and Germans that this chap should be an indispensable middle-man between the two, since Guesde seems reluctant to make use of any one else. But thwarted as it is by the isolation and inactivity of Oxford, his enthusiasm plus his intense urge to be up and doing serves to evoke discord rather than collaboration. And in the present state of Europe what is called for above all else is precisely the harmonious collaboration of Germans and French.

Many thanks for the Reichstag stenographic reports. I shall not be able to read your big speech about the Army until tonight, but I was delighted by what you said about Heinze's law.[99] So long as prostitution cannot be wholly eradicated, our first bid ought, I think, to be the girls' total exemption from any kind of extraordinary legislation. Here in England this is more or less the case; there are no 'morality police', and no controls or medical examinations, but the police still have tremendous power because it is a punishable offence to keep *a disorderly house*, and every house in which a girl lives and receives visitors can be treated as such. But although this law is enforced only on rare occasions, the girls are none the less exposed to frightful extortion on the part of policemen. This relative freedom from degrading police restrictions enables the girls to preserve an independent and self-respecting character in a way that

---

[a] See this volume, pp. 46-47

would hardly be possible on the Continent. They look upon their situation as an unavoidable evil to which, since it has befallen them, they must resign themselves, but which otherwise need in no way affect their character or self-esteem and, given the chance to get out of their profession, they seize upon it, as a rule, successfully. In Manchester there were whole colonies of young men—bourgeois or clerks—who lived with girls of this kind, being in many cases legally married to them and treating them at least as well as a bourgeois would a woman of his own class. The fact that now and then one of these girls might take to the bottle in no way distinguished them from their middle-class counterparts over here, themselves no strangers to the habit. Indeed, some of these married girls, having moved to another town where there was no fear of their running into 'old acquaintances', have been introduced into respectable middle-class society and even into the squirarchy—squires being the English equivalent of country Junkers—without anyone's noticing anything in the least objectionable about them.

It is my belief that, in dealing with this matter, we should above all consider the interests of the girls themselves as victims of the present social order, and protect them as far as possible against ending up in the gutter—or at least not actually force them into the gutter by means of legislation and police skulduggery as happens throughout the Continent. In this country the same thing was attempted in a number of garrison towns where controls and medical examinations were introduced, but it didn't last long; the only good thing the *social purity* people have done has been to agitate against this.

Medical examinations are absolutely worthless. Wherever they were introduced here, syphilis and gonorrhoea increased. I am convinced that a police surgeon's instruments are exceedingly effective in transmitting venereal disease, since he would be unlikely to spend time or trouble on disinfecting them. Free courses on venereal disease should be made available to the girls, then most of them would probably take precautions themselves. Blaschko has sent us an article on medical controls[a] in which he is forced to admit that these are absolutely useless; if he were to draw the logical conclusion from his own assumptions, he would be bound to conclude that prostitution must be freed from all restrictions and the girls be protected

---

[a] A. Blaschko, 'Die moderne Prostitution', *Die Neue Zeit*, Stuttgart, 1891-1892, Vol. II, Nos. 27, 32.

against exploitation, but in Germany that would seem utterly utopian.

I hope that Kneipp treatment is doing Dietz good; at all events Naso[a] maintains that the crack-brained parson made him astoundingly healthy. By completely changing the habits of people the routine of whose urban professional lives has made them a bit rigid and set in their ways, and by forcing them to take exercise in the open air, the said cure may, from what I have heard, do them a certain amount of good or, indeed, harm—according to the nature of the case—just as does the 'water cure' when it is not as a rule the mineral water that does the trick, but rather the change of routine and the strict diet. But otherwise you are right; amongst our people there is many a one who deems it his duty fervently to embrace any and every new 'ism' and, likewise, any disgruntled bourgeois or bureaucratic malcontent, any obscure literary or artistic genius. He may equally well set himself up as the protector of all victims of persecution and injustice, and discover in every ism a theory of world redemption hitherto suppressed by the wicked capitalist world order. It is an excellent way of turning to account and putting on display the very things one has *not* learnt. One has only to look at what the late-lamented *Volksstaat* achieved in that sphere!

The Panama business[60] gets nicer every day. As so often in France the affair is taking a quite dramatically exaggerated course. At any moment, or so it seems, the efforts to thrust it out of sight are going to succeed, and then up it springs again where least expected and more vigorously than ever before. Now the situation is such that no hushing up will avail. First the affair was to be hushed up in the courts, whereupon fresh revelations necessitated the setting up of a committee of inquiry; then it was the latter that was to be hamstrung, an attempt that was only partially successful and only to the extent that further legal proceedings of a more serious nature were instituted. And now there's a spate of fresh revelations and prosecutions of deputies and senators. The ball has been set rolling and is very far from coming to a stop. Standing in the wings are 1. Constans, who knows that he is played out and is anxious to avenge himself, 2. Rochefort and the Boulangists,[6] who also know a great deal, 3. the Orléans family, who would like to make use of all this farcical business to attempt a restoration. All these people know a great deal and can to a large extent prove it. And if the worst comes to the worst, Ch.

---

[a] Leonhard Tauscher

de Lesseps and Rouvier will avenge themselves by compromising as many people as possible and involving them in their fall. Rothschild summed up the situation in the words:

> 'I need the monarchy and shall buy it once and for all; the Republic costs me too much, since every few years I have to buy yet another ravenous crew.'

What wouldn't that jackass Boulanger give for that now if he hadn't shot himself! He'd be in clover; indeed, I shouldn't be surprised if an attempt were made to find another Boulanger. Fortunately this would not be at all easy. The monarchy, too, is down on its luck—the Right voted as one man for the Panama lottery[100] and, what is worse, made propaganda for it in the rural areas, thus landing philistines and peasants in the cart. The 1,700 million francs that were swallowed up consisted to a very large extent of *the savings of little men* (over 800,000 are said to be involved!), hence the wave of indignation, while the Right (Clerical Monarchists) who at first rejoiced over the Panama scandal, are now turning coy.

How it will all end is obvious—ultimately in *our* favour. But in a country as incalculable as France it is difficult to predict what intermediate stages there will be. Several, at any rate, before our people really take possession of the stage. Only if there were to be revolution in Paris would the Socialists come to power; for in Paris—cf. the Commune—*every* revolution is automatically socialist. But Paris is less turbulent than the provinces and that is a good thing, Paris is blasé, not least because the workers, disunited, confused and patriotic (in so far as they sense that Paris is—wrongly, or so they feel—*no longer the political hub of the world*), can see no way out. Should the scandals continue, there might be a presidential crisis—Carnot has at least *connived* at a lot of dirty work—and whatever happens there will be parliamentary elections next year. Also a good many municipal elections in Paris. All this will provide more than enough legal loopholes. On the other hand, uncertainty as to the reliability of the army (which is new to general military service and not so hardened to it as Prussia) is a safeguard against coups d' état, as is the unarmed state of the masses (who this time could not, as always before, turn to the National Guard for guns and ammunition) against attempted uprisings. It therefore seems very probable that the crisis will take a peaceful course. It's just what we need, however, if we are to have time to reap the benefits of Panama—no violent upheavals and time for the ferment to take effect throughout the country. In the provinces the Marxists have virtually no rivals; in Paris it is, for the time being, quite a good thing if Blanquists,[20] Allemanists[21] and Broussists[30] should wear each other out.

At all events, *internal* developments in France have again become of paramount importance and we shall soon see to what extent the chaps are equal to the tasks by which they are confronted. I must say that, where major crises such as this one are concerned, I have considerable confidence in them. Not in their ability to win instant and striking victories—there may yet be short-lived episodes of a horribly reactionary nature—but in their ability eventually to emerge with honour. Nor, from our point of view, should things happen too quickly. We too require time for growth.

Quite between ourselves, I am over the worst so far as Volume III[a] is concerned. The difficulties in the most difficult section have been surmounted.[33] But until I have been through the last two sections I can say nothing definite about the date of completion. There may still turn out to be individual difficulties that will take some time. But I have sighted land and the worse and most time-consuming part is behind me; this time I shall finish. When you come over here I shall show it to you.

You would in any case do better to come via Calais; it's hardly any further from Stuttgart and maybe even somewhat nearer than via Ostend.—Cordial regards to you, your wife[b] and your children and a Happy Christmas to you.

Auf Wiedersehen,

Your

F. E.

First published in:
Marx and Engels, *Works*,
First Russian Edition,
Vol. XXIX, Moscow, 1946

Printed according to the original

Published in English for the first time

---

[a] of *Capital* – [b] Julie Bebel

38

ENGELS TO KARL KAUTSKY[101]

IN STUTTGART

London, 24 December 1892

Dear Baron,

I have been trying to persuade August to cross the Channel this winter, if only for a few days, and am not without hope of his concurring. Should he do so, and since he will in any case have to travel via Stuckert,[a] I should be obliged if you could give him Marx's old Ms., together with such parts of the Ms. as you may have already completed.[102] The rest we shall settle at some future date. For now that there is every prospect of Volume III's long gestation period at last drawing to its close, it's important that I should have the material for Volume IV at my disposal.

You shall have a more detailed reply to your letter shortly—in the meantime a Happy Christmas and cordial regards from

Your
F. Engels

First published in:
Aus der Frühzeit des Marxismus.
Engels Briefwechsel mit Kautsky,
Prague, 1935

Printed according to the original

Published in English for the first time

---

[a] Stuttgart

39

ENGELS TO WILHELM LIEBKNECHT

IN BERLIN

London, 28 December 1892

Dear Liebknecht,

A Happy New Year to you, your wife[a] and your children.

As regards the French, I pointed out to Lafargue more than a week ago that now's the time.[b] However, it's quite possible that the chaps don't want to expend their powder too soon. To begin with, the Panama affair[60] is still in its early stages, the more important revelations won't come till after the New Year, and so far nothing serious has been *proven*, legally speaking, against any living parliamentarian; in January, both Radicals[86] and Monarchists may find themselves well and truly in the soup and then it will be possible to speak up far more effectually. Secondly, there are, in the Chamber, not only Marxists but also Blanquists,[20] Allemanists[21] and free lances *à la* Cluseret—not to mention complete reprobates such as Lachize and Thivrier who have latched on to our coat-tails—and, with the socialist groups in Parliament differing as they do, it would be easy for the others to give them as good as they got, so to speak. Now an attempt is being made to find a common basis for action. If this succeeds, as seems probable, it will be easier to get something done.

I tender this merely as a possible explanation for the chaps' silence.

In this country we have long had to contend with Bonnier's enthusiasm. He fairly peppered us with shot over the May Day business.[54] I drew his attention to your statement in the *Vorwärts* in which you said that at Marseilles you had given the chaps advance notice of what the Germans' attitude would be on 1 May '93, and that they had declared themselves satisfied.[c]

So they have no right to complain. I then went on to tell him that, what with Panama in Paris, the military business in Berlin[76] and a general industrial crisis into the bargain, there might be something better for us

---

[a] Natalie Liebknecht – [b] See this volume, pp. 58-59 – [c] W. Liebknecht, 'Agitationsbericht Nach Marseille und zurück', *Vorwärts*, No. 239, 12 October 1892.

to do on 1 May than demonstrate.[a] Indeed, in Paris he would subsequently seem to have realised as much. The man has the best of intentions, but anyone wanting to have a finger in the pie of the labour movement of three countries has no business to live in Oxford.

Cordial regards to you all,

Your
F. E.

[Postscript from Louise Kautsky]

Dear Mrs Natalie,

May I associate myself with the General's[b] letter and his good wishes. Having myself answered the question in the affirmative, I wish you, your dear husband, and your children a very Happy New Year.

Sincerely yours,
Louise Kautsky

First published in:
Wilhelm Liebknecht, *Briefwechsel mit Karl Marx und Friedrich Engels*, The Hague, 1963

Printed according to the original

Published in English for the first time

40

ENGELS TO FRIEDRICH ADOLPH SORGE[103]

IN HOBOKEN

London, 31 December 1892

Dear Sorge,

Just a line or two before the year ends. Your letters of 18 November and 16 December received—many thanks. Did you get the parcel of books I posted to you in September, containing the *Condition of the Working*

---

[a] See this volume, p. 47 – [b] F. Engels' nickname

Class, new edition, and *Socialism: Utopian and Scientific*,[a] translated by Aveling with an introduction by me? If not I shall send you another parcel by registered mail.

Here, in old Europe, things are proceeding at a somewhat livelier pace than in your 'youthful' country which still can't quite extricate itself from the hobbledehoy stage. It is remarkable, though perfectly natural, that in so young a country, which has never known feudalism and has from the outset grown up upon a bourgeois basis, bourgeois prejudices should be so firmly entrenched even in the working class. Indeed it is precisely his opposition to a mother country still garbed in feudalism that leads the American working man to suppose the traditional bourgeois economic system he has inherited to be by its nature something immutably superior and progressive, a *non plus ultra*. Just as in New England, where puritanism, precisely because it is the *raison d' être* of the whole colony, has become a traditional heirloom and all but indistinguishable from local patriotism. However much the Americans may twist and turn, they cannot simply discount, as if it were a bill, what is beyond doubt a tremendous future, but will have to wait until it falls due; and precisely *because* that future is so great, their present must be largely taken up with preparations for it, a task which, as in any young country, is chiefly of a material nature and calls for a degree of conservative thinking, a clinging to traditions connected with the founding of the new nationality. The Anglo-Saxon race—those damned Schleswig-Holsteiners as Marx always called them—is in any case slow in the uptake, a trait its history both in Europe and in America (economic success and, on the whole, peaceful political evolution) has tended to foster. Here momentous events alone can be of any avail and if, in addition to the transfer—now almost complete—of state-owned lands into private hands, industry were to expand under a somewhat less hare-brained tariff policy and foreign markets be conquered, things might also go well for you people. In this country, too, the class struggles were more violent during the *period of growth* of large-scale industry and petered out precisely at the time of Britain's undisputed industrial domination in the world; similarly in Germany the growth of large-scale industry since 1850 has coincided with the rise of the socialist movement, and in America things are not likely to turn out any differently. It is the revolutionising of all time-honoured conditions

---

[a] Both works were written by F. Engels. See vols. 4 and 25 of this edition.

by the *growth* of industry which likewise revolutionises men's minds.

Furthermore, the Americans have long provided the European world with proof of the fact that the bourgeois republic is the republic of capitalist businessmen in which politics is merely a business transaction like any other—something which the ruling bourgeois politicians in France have long known and practiced on the quiet, and whose truth is at last being brought home to the French on a national scale by the Panama scandal.[60] Not that the constitutional monarchies can preen themselves on their virtue, for each has its own little Panama; England, the *building society scandals* of which one, 'the Liberator', has conscientiously 'liberated' vast numbers of small depositors of savings amounting to some £8 million[104]; Germany, the Baare scandals and Löwe's "Jewish rifles'[105] (which prove that the Prussian officer is, now as always, a thief, but in a very, very small way—the one thing that is modest about him); Italy, the Banca Romana, already an approximation of Panama, which has bought some 150 deputies and senators[106] and concerning which, so I am told, documents are shortly to be published in Switzerland; Schlüter should keep an eye out for anything about the Banca Romana that appears in the press. And in Holy Russia the Russian Prince Meshchersky waxes indignant over the indifference with which the Panama revelations are received in Russia, the only explanation for this being, he says, that Russian virtue has been corrupted by the example of the French, and that 'we ourselves have more than one Panama here at home'.

However, the Panama affair is the beginning of the end of the bourgeois republic and may soon place us in some very responsible positions. The *whole* of the opportunist[87] and the better part of the Radical gang[86] are compromised up to the hilt; the government is seeking to hush things up but that is no longer possible, for documentary evidence is in the hands of people who *wish* to overturn those now in power: 1. The Orléans, 2. the former minister Constans, now out of the running because of revelations about his scandalous past, 3. Rochefort and the Boulangists,[6] 4. Cornelius Herz who, being himself deeply involved in all manner of frauds, has plainly taken refuge in London merely in order to buy his way out by compromising his fellows. All these people have more than enough evidence against this thieving crew, but are holding back, firstly and more generally, so as not to expend all their powder at one go and, secondly, in order to give the government and the *courts of law* time to become hopelessly compromised. This is all grist to our mill; enough information gradually leaks out not only to keep the pot on the boil and run the *dirigeants*[a] increasingly onto the rocks, but also to allow time for the scandal and the revelations to do their work in the remotest parts of the country before the inevitable dissolution of the Chamber and the general elections which, however, ought *not* to come *too soon*.

That things have very nearly got to the point at which our chaps in France will be the only possible rulers of the state is evident. But it mustn't happen too quickly, our people in France being by no means ripe for leadership. As things are now, it is absolutely impossible to say what intermediate stages there will be in the meantime. The old Republican parties are compromised down to the last man, while the Royalists and Clericals, having sold Panama lottery tickets[100] on a vast scale, have identified themselves with that affair—if that idiot Boulanger hadn't shot himself, he would now be cock of the walk. I should be curious to know whether the old unconscious logic of French history will again assert itself on this occasion. There are going to be a great many surprises. If only during the interval in which the air is being cleared, some general or other doesn't seize power and foment a war; that is the only danger.

In Germany the party's undeviating, irresistible advance proceeds at a steady pace. Everywhere small successes provide proof of progress. If the Army Bill[76] is adopted more or less as it stands, there'll be a new floodtide of malcontents coming to join our ranks. If the bill is thrown out, there'll be a dissolution, a general election, and we shall get at least fifty seats in the Reichstag which, in a conflict, might often give us the deciding vote. At all events the struggle, while it may, perhaps, also break out in France, can only be fought to a finish in Germany. But it's a good thing that Volume III[b] is now at last to be completed—not that I can say when that will be. Times are growing unsettled and the wind is rising.

A very Happy New Year from myself and Mrs Kautsky to you and your wife,[c]

Your

F. Engels

First published in: *Briefe und Auszüge aus Briefen von Joh. Phil. Becker, Jos. Dietzgen, Friedrich Engels, Karl Marx u. A. an F. A. Sorge und Andere*, Stuttgart, 1906

Printed according to the original

Published in English in full for the first time

---

[a] leaders – [b] of *Capital* – [c] Katharina Sorge

41

ENGELS TO KARL HENCKELL[107]

IN ZURICH

[London, end of 1892]

The Song of Steam, typical of an early, if past, phase of the Labour movement and one which Germany has also experienced.

First published in: *Buch der Freiheit.*
Gesammelt und herausgegeben von
Karl Henckell, Berlin, 1893

Printed according to the original

Published in English for the first time

1893

42

ENGELS TO FILIPPO TURATI

IN MILAN

[London,] 7 January 1893

Dear citizen Turati,

I was very pleased to see the translation of the *Manifesto* in the *Lotta di classe* but I am so overloaded with work that I have not been able to compare it with the original. In a few days I will send you a copy of the most recent German edition (London), with the complete prefaces, for your pamphlet edition.

As for my writing a preface, here is my position. Another Italian friend, whom you no doubt know, is preparing a translation, and perhaps a lengthier work on this writing.[a] As he told me of his intention before the publication of the first issue of *Lotta di classe* I feel I must consult him before giving you a definitive answer.[108] Moreover, I am beginning to find these prefaces an embarrassment. Only recently I had to write one for a Polish translation. I really have nothing new left to say.

Best wishes to yourself and Mme Kulisbov from Mme Kautsky, from Bebel, who is with us at the moment,[109] and from myself, *insieme coi nostri auguri il nuovo anno.*[b]

Sempre vostro[c]
F. Engels

---

[a] A. Labriola, *In memoria del Manifesto dei comunisti* – [b] accept also our Happy New Year greetings and best wishes – [c] Ever yours

First published, in the language
of the original (French), in:
K. Marx, P. Engels, *Scritti italiani*,
Milano-Roma, 1955

Printed according the original
Translated from the French
Published in English for the first time

43

ENGELS TO MARIA MENDELSON[110]

IN LONDON

[London,] 10 January 1893

Dear Mme Mendelson

Thank you for your letter. I immediately wrote a short article on the arrests in Paris which left for Berlin that same evening—you will probably see it in *Vorwärts* in a few days.[111]

Ever yours,
F. E.

Bebel has left this afternoon.
Greetings from Mme Kautsky.

First published in:
Marx and Engels, *Works*,
First Russian Edition,
Vol. XXIX, Moscow, 1946

Printed according to the original

Translated from the French

Published in English for the first time

44

ENGELS TO PHILIPP PAULI

IN FRANKFURT AM MAIN

London, 11 January 1893

Dear Pauli,

I entirely agree that we should each of us send a contribution to Perkin for the Schorlemmer LABORATORY[112] as you suggest; but not by any means that I should decide upon the sum without any prior agreement or knowledge of the actual circumstances. What we should offer depends on altogether too many circumstances of which I am completely ignorant. The *comité* in Manchester will surely be sending, or have sent out, some sort of appeal indicating roughly the amount to be raised, and an initial list of the first subscriptions, etc., etc. After all, one has got to know all this if one is to have any idea how high or low one should, or alternately should not, go.

Would you therefore be so good as to inquire from Perkin what has been done in this respect and, if you think fit, ask him to inform me of it so that we have some kind of yardstick to go by.

It's a disgrace that these university chaps should be such jackasses! I even had to put pressure on Roscoe to get him to write the article for *Nature*.[a] And the Germans—how proud they could be of Schorlemmer! But he didn't belong to the you-scratch-my-back-I-scratch-yours clique and that's why, now he's dead, he has to suffer for the fact that he was no Panamite of academic learning. Panama left, right and centre, nothing but Panama,[60] even in academic chemistry!

Cordial regards to your wife and children, and likewise to yourself, from

Your old friend,

F. Engels

Pumps and her family came to stay over Christmas and the New Year; the new baby is a very delicate little thing yet, despite the cold, they all got back safe and sound to Ryde.

First published abridgedin:
G. Mayer, *Friedrich Engels
Eine Biographie,* Bd. II,
The Hague, 1934 and in full in:
Marx and Engels, *Works,*
First Russian Edition,
Vol. XXIX, Moscow, 1946

Printed according to the original

Published in English for the first time

---

[a] H. E. Roscoe, 'Carl Schorlemmer', *Nature,* Vol. XLVI, 25 August 1892.

45

ENGELS TO MARIA MENDELSON

IN LONDON

[London,] 16 January 1893

Dear Mme Mendelson,

The article in *Vorwärts* of which you speak was written in Paris.[a] It seems that the author was told that the 5 arrested Poles belonged to the same socialist school as, among the Russians, Plekhanov and his friends; and the correspondent has thus committed the *quid pro quo* that we have all sadly read.

The article which I sent to *Vorwärts* is in the following issue (No. II, 13th January).[111]

Let us congratulate ourselves nonetheless that this latest base action by the French government has only led to an expulsion.

Mme Kautsky joins her greetings to those of your devoted

F. Engels

First published in:
Marx and Engels, *Works*,
First Russian Edition,
Vol. XXIX, Moscow, 1946

Printed according to the original
Translated from the French
Published in English in full
for the first time

46

ENGELS TO FRIEDRICH ADOLPH SORGE[113]

IN HOBOKEN

London, 18 January 1893

Dear Sorge,

Today I am sending you two old numbers of the defunct *Berliner Volks-Tribüne*, the others having got mislaid in the turmoil of Christmas; if I

---

[a] 'Russische Polizei-Allmacht in Frankreich', *Vorwärts*, No. 10, 12 January 1893 (in the running headline 'Politische Uebersicht').

find them I shall send them on to you. The reason for my failure to put them in the post was the Bakunin article which in the end I felt bound to answer, and that meant keeping the numbers here in case of possible controversy. In the last (13th)[a] article, which has unfortunately been mislaid—we have just realised that it has meanwhile been sent to you by Mrs Kautsky[b]—there is yet another batch of rubbishy anarchist lies. The author, who gives his name—one Héritier (a young Genevese, nurtured in the bosom of old J. Ph. Becker) tries to justify himself even after my answer—mendaciously. Since he has written to me, I shall reply,[c] notifying him that, if be does the same sort of thing in his proposed opus, I shall rap him severely over the knuckles for it.[49]

Over here the Independent Labour Party,[114] about which you will have read in the *Workman's Times*, has held a conference in Bradford. Owing to their sectarian attitude the Social Democratic Federation,[44] on the one hand, and the Fabians,[43] on the other, have been unable to absorb the socialist accretions in the provinces, so that the setting up of a third party was no bad thing. But now, such is the extent of those accretions—especially in the industrial districts of the North—that even at this, the first congress, the new party was more strongly represented than either the Social Democratic Federation or the Fabians, if not more strongly than both put together. And since the *bulk* of its members are undoubtedly first class, since its centre of gravity lies in the provinces rather than in that hive of intrigue, London, and its programme is substantially the same as our own, Aveling did right in joining it and in accepting a position on the Executive. If the petty private ambitions and intrigues of the London panjandrums can be kept under some control, and its tactics are not *too* misguided, the Independent Labour Party may succeed in enticing away the masses, not only from the Social Democratic Federation but, in the provinces, also from the Fabians, and thus enforcing unity.

The Social Democratic Federation has pushed Hyndman completely into the background. It did so badly as a result of his policy of intrigue that—thanks to the provincial delegates—Hyndman has been utterly discredited in the eyes of his own people. An attempt to regain his popularity on the Unemployed Committee—on which other people sat too—by means of revolutionary ranting (his personal cowardice being

---

[a] 12th in the Ms. – [b] Engels inserted this afterwards, in the margin. – [c] See this volume, pp. 85-86

a byword among his best friends), merely resulted in an increase of the influence wielded by Tussy and Aveling on that Committee. The only thing the Social Democratic Federation insists upon is its seniority as the *oldest* socialist organisation over here but in other respects it has grown far more tolerant of others, has ceased to inveigh against them and is on the whole appreciably more aware of being what it is, namely far smaller than it made itself out to be.

Here in London the Fabians are a bunch of careerists who have sense enough to recognise the inevitability of a social upheaval but are quite incapable of entrusting this gigantic task solely to the untutored proletariat and are therefore accustomed to take the lead; fear of revolution is their guiding principle. They are the 'heddicated' par excellence. Their socialism is municipal socialism; it is the *commune* not the nation, which, at any rate to start off with, is to be the owner of the means of production. They then proceed to propound this, their socialism, as the extreme but inevitable consequence of bourgeois liberalism—hence their tactics of not directly confronting the Liberals as opponents but of inducing them to draw socialist conclusions, *ergo* they cheat them in order to PERMEATE LIBERALISM WITH SOCIALISM and do not put up socialist candidates against the Liberals, but rather foist the former on them by force if not by false pretences. That in so doing they are either betraying and hoodwinking themselves, or else are hoodwinking socialism, they do not, of course, realise.

With great assiduity they have produced, along with all manner of trash, a number of good propaganda pieces—the best of this kind, in fact, the English have produced. But the moment they come to their own brand of tactics and gloss over the class struggle, the rot sets in. Hence, too, their fanatical hatred of Marx and all the rest of us—because of the class struggle.

Needless to say, the chaps have a big middle-class following and therefore funds and, in the provinces, they have many dependable working men who refuse to have anything to do with the Social Democratic Federation. But 5/6 of their provincial members see more or less eye to eye with us and, when it comes to the point, they will definitely desert. In Bradford—where they are represented—they have several times voiced unqualified opposition to the Fabians' London Executive.

As you see, it is a critical juncture so far as the movement over here is concerned, and something may come of the new organisation. For a short while it looked as though it might come under the wing of

Champion who, whether consciously or unconsciously, is working for the Tories just as are the Fabians for the Liberals—under the wing of Champion, then, and of his ally Maltman Barry, whom you will remember from The Hague[115] (Barry is now by his own admission *an agent* in the regular pay of the Tories and MANAGER OF THE SOCIALISTIC WING OF THE CONSERVATIVES!)[116]—see *Workman's Times* of November and December—but in the end Champion thought it best to resume his editorship of the *Labour Elector* and has thus taken up the cudgels against the *Workman's Times* and the new party.

It was a shrewd stroke on Keir Hardie's part to place himself at the head of this new party and yet another blunder on the part of John Burns to remain aloof on this occasion as well, having already done himself a great deal of harm by his total inertia outside of his own constituency. I am afraid be may land himself in an impossible situation.

It goes without saying that, in this instance too, personal ambition is causing men like Keir Hardie, Shaw Maxwell and others to pursue sundry ulterior aims. But the danger inherent in this diminishes in proportion as the party itself grows in strength and numbers, and has, indeed, already receded because of the necessity of not leaving any loopholes for competing sects. In recent years socialism has made enormous headway among the masses in the industrial districts, and I look to those masses to keep the leaders properly in order. Of course there will be blunders and to spare, and also jiggery-pokery of every description; let us only hope we are able to keep them within proper bounds!

At worst the setting up of a new organisation may be regarded as an advantage in that it is easier to achieve unity when there are *three* competing sects than when there are two which are diametrically opposed to one another.

As regards what you wrote about Poland on 23 December, since the time of Kronstadt the Prussians have been prepared to go to war with Russia and are therefore *pro*-Polish (indeed have provided proof of this).[117] The said Poles will have sought to exploit this *to provoke a war whereby they hope to be liberated with Germany's help.* But that is *not at all* what Berlin wants and, should they pull off their coup, Caprivi will undoubtedly leave them in the lurch. At the moment a war would be utterly useless to *us*; we have a sure means of making progress which a war could only disrupt.

Warm regards to your wife and yourself. Mrs Kautsky, who wrote to

you on Saturday, though unfortunately too late to catch the post, also
sends her regards.

Your

F. E.

First published abridged in:
*Briefe und Auszüge aus Briefen
von Joh. Phil. Becker Jos. Dietzgen,
Friedriech Engels Karl Marx u. A.
an F. A. Sorge und Andere*, Stuttgart,
1906 and in full in:
Marx and Engels, *Works*,
First Russian Edition,
Vol. XXIX, Moscow, 1946

Printed according the original

Published in English
in full for the first time

47

ENGELS TO LOUIS HÉRITIER

IN GENEVA

[Draft]

[London,] 20 January 1893

Dear citizen,

It is with sincere satisfaction that I see from your letter of 25 December
that the passage taken from your article on Becker[a] was distorted in translation.[49] Indeed, I was amazed when I saw your name at the end of the
article. I had heard you spoken of with truly paternal affection, and the
expressions used in your article on Becker constituted a far too painful
contrast. Unfortunately, you still let the public believe them to be yours,
as the rest of the article also.

As for what you have to say in the *Volks-Tribüne* concerning my observations, this in no way changes my opinion. You must know that MM.
the anarchists invented the slander about the conference held in Marx's
house[118] with the sole purpose of proving that Marx wished to secure his
own preponderance by any means, fair or foul. You say that this is his
domination over the delegates. For you this alleged fact is worth being

---

[a] Johann Philipp Becker

told. However, when I prove that it is false, you say that is a mere detail of no importance whatsoever.

I have proved the falsehood of your assertion. You said that the London conference placed the Jurassians *under the command of the Geneva Federal Council*. I find that to be the opposite of the truth. You reply: 'What I said seems to me today *to be the absolute truth.*' You remind me of good manners, though I do not know in what respect: do you wish me to remind you of sincerity?

Your No. XII[a] proves once again that you know almost nothing about what happened outside the anarchist milieu. Judging by your observations concerning the Geneva internationals, it would seem to me impossible that you have seen a complete collection of the *Egalité de Genève*. If the Geneva internationals were *to some extent* infected by petty-bourgeois ideas, they shared this defect with their adversaries, the anarchists, whom you prefer, yet who offer only the reverse of the petty-bourgeois coin, and with almost all the French and Belgian internationals—Proudhonists with few exceptions. Of all the groups of the Romance languages, only those among the Spanish supporters of the General Council were Social-Democrats in the present sense of that term. As for the rest, have those of Geneva proved today that they are worth more than their predecessors?

In the same No. XII,[a] you reproduce a large number of anarchist errors and lies, and you accord them a faith which, after my warning, should have lost some of its original naïvety. You promise a second work on this same topic. I hope that, before engaging upon the matter, you will obtain some documents which shed light on the assertions and machinations of the anarchists, and which will certainly enable you to judge impartially. Otherwise you will oblige me to reply again. It is of little importance what the bourgeois newspapers have to say about the old International, but when its history is distorted even in party organs this is quite a different matter. All that I ask of you is that you should not write about a subject without having studied both sides, the documents on this side and on that. Our worker public has to snatch from its meals and its sleep the few hours that it can devote to reading: it therefore has the right to ask that everything we present should be the result of conscientious work, and not lead to futile controversies that it is impossible to follow.

---

[a] A mistake in the original. Should read 'XIII'. The reference is to article XIII.

First published in:
Marx and Engels, *Works*
First Russian Edition,
Vol. XXIX, Moscow, 1946

Printed according to the original

Translated from the French

Published in English for the first time

48

ENGELS TO AUGUST BEBEL[119]

IN BERLIN

London, 24 January 1893

Dear August,

I continue. Aveling's verbal accounts have reinforced a suspicion previously entertained by me, namely that Keir Hardie nurtures the secret wish to lead the new party[114] in the same dictatorial fashion as Parnell led the Irish, and that his sympathies incline more towards the Conservative than towards the Liberal opposition party. He has said openly that, come the next elections, there should be a repetition of Parnell's experiment whereby he forced Gladstone to toe the line and that where no Labour candidate can be put up, people should vote Conservative by way of giving the Liberals a taste of their power.[120] Now this is a policy which, in certain circumstances, I myself have demanded of the English, but to proclaim something of this sort in advance, not as a possible tactical measure, but as tactics to be pursued *no matter what the circumstances* smacks strongly of Champion. Especially when, at the same time, Keir Hardie refers disparagingly to the extension of the suffrage and other reforms, which alone might be expected to give reality to working-class suffrage over here, as purely *political* matters which must take second place after social demands—eight hours, industrial safety, etc. Though, renouncing as he does their *enforcement* by Labour M.P.s, he fails to explain how these social demands are to be implemented unless by grace of the middle classes, or else by means of indirect pressure exerted by Labour's casting vote in the elections. I draw your attention to this knotty point in order that you may be informed should occasion arise. For the time being I do not attach any particular importance to the matter since at the very worst Keir Hardie is likely to err gravely in his estimate of the workers in the industrial districts of the North of England, who are not a flock of sheep, and since he will, in any case, encounter opposition enough in the Executive. But a tendency of this kind ought not to be completely ignored.

I look forward very much to seeing the stenographic report of Singer's speech about the Stock Exchange; in the *Vorwärts* it read quite excellently.[a] But in dealing with this subject there is one point which all our chaps tend to overlook. The Stock Exchange is an institution in which the bourgeois exploit, not the workers, but *one another*; the surplus value that changes hands on the Stock Exchange is already *extant* surplus value, the product of *past* exploitation of labour. Only when that process is complete can it serve the hanky-panky on the Stock Exchange. To begin with, the Stock Exchange is merely of indirect interest to us, in the same way as its influence and its repercussions on the capitalist exploitation of labour are merely indirect and exerted in a devious way. To suggest that the workers should take a direct interest in, and wax indignant over, the fleecing on the 'Change of the Junkers, manufacturers and petty bourgeois is to suggest that the workers should resort to arms to protect the possession by their own immediate exploiters of the surplus value they have filched from those self-same workers. What an idea! But as the finest fruit of bourgeois society, as the breeding ground of extreme corruption, as the forcing house of the Panama[60] and other scandals—and hence, too, as a first-class means for the concentration of capitals, for the disintegration and dissolution of the last remnants of natural cohesion in bourgeois society and, at the same time, for the destruction of all obligatory moral concepts and their inversion into their opposite—as an incomparable element of destruction, as the most powerful accelerator of impending revolution—in this historical sense the Stock Exchange is indeed of immediate interest to us.

I see the Centre[71] has moved that there be a stay of prescription for the period in which the Reichstag suspends prosecutions. Since the Centre is the dominant party the motion seems likely to be carried.[121] *Should* this happen, it would seem to me inappropriate to make the government a gratuitous present of the above limitation of *parliamentary* rights without any *quid pro quo*. The *quid pro quo* should consist in the express acknowl-

---

[a] *Vorwärts*, No. 17, 20 January 1893

edgement that the Reichstag's right of suspension is also applicable to penal *detention*. Otherwise the Reichstag would again be beating a retreat—whatever legal plausibility the measure might seem to possess.

The bogey of war has again raised its head. Herewith Dalziel's despatch from today's *Daily Chronicle*—as a youthful competitor of Reuter, Wolff and Havas, Dalziel is more readily open to such reptilian manoeuvres.[122] The affair as such is absurd. The Russians are simply not prepared for war and would have to be quite off their heads to embark on one now. There is, of course, a possibility that, after the failure of the last Parisian loan,[123] they would only be able to obtain money in Paris if war were really imminent or had already broken out—but that would be a counsel of despair. What cannot be completely ruled out is the possibility that the Opportunists[87] and Radicals[86] in France will *seek* to save themselves from Panama by means of a war or at any rate have this at the back of their minds as a last recourse. But where could they find the pretext that would justify them in the eyes of the world? As I have said before, in the next war England will play a dominant role on account of its naval supremacy.[124] And as it happens, England has just played a nasty trick on the French in Egypt.[125] To gain England's support, in the present state of tension between the two governments, there would have to be a *casus belli* which, even to *your* philistine, would seem a gross provocation, and this Caprivi will not provide.

The more information I gather on this point, the more I am struck by the fact that Bismarck formed the Austrian *resp.* Triple Alliance.[126] simply in order that he might, on the eve of the now inevitable war, give Austria to Russia in exchange for France: Leave me France and I'll leave you Austria and Turkey and, what's more, unleash Italy against Austria via Trieste and Trient.[a] And he clearly imagined he would pull it off. Reflect for a while on the course of history since 1878[127] and you will, I believe, come round to my view.

To me Tutzauer's hire-purchase speech in the Reichstag Report (*Vorwärts*) of the 21st is quite incomprehensible. He wasn't speaking as a *Social Democrat* but as a furniture salesman.[128] How could this have happened? The Young[129] will be overjoyed.

Last night there was a concert and ball for the benefit of the Society.[62] I stayed until 11 o'clock and shall now presumably be exempted for a while

---

[a] Modern name: Trento.

from such obligations; Louise[a] had to stay at home because of neuralgia in her side. She is a bit better, but still suffers a lot of pain which, Freyberger says, will persist for another day or two. Otherwise her cold is on the mend and her voice and general condition have also improved. She sends you and your wife her warmest regards, as does

Your

F. E.

First published abridged in:
F. Engels, *Politisches Vermächtni.*
Aus unveröffentlichen Briefen,
Berlin, 1920 and in full in:
Marx and Engels, *Works,*
First Russian Edition,
Vol. XXIX, Moscow, 1946

Printed according to the original

Published in English in full
for the first time

49

ENGELS TO MARIA MENDELSON

IN LONDON

[London,] 24 January 1893
122 Regent's Park Road, N. W.

Dear Mme Mendelson,

Would you be so kind as to send me another half-dozen copies of the circular in reply to the one issued by Free Russia? I would like to send it to my friends in Germany and elsewhere; perhaps you would be so good as to tell me if it has been sent to Bebel and *Vorwärts*.

Is there a printing error on page 1, line 4? Is Dragomanov recommending the *Po*lonisation of Lithuania, or its *co*lonisation (by Russian colonists)?

Friendly greetings from myself and Mme Kautsky.

Sincerely yours,

F. Engels

Mme Kautsky is suffering from a cold and an attack of neuralgia, oth-

---

[a] Kautsky

erwise she would already have called to see you.

First published in:
Marx and Engels, *Works*,
First Russian Edition,
Vol. XXIX, Moscow, 1946

Printed according to the original

Translated from the French

Published in English for the first time

50

ENGELS TO KARL KAUTSKY

IN STUTTGART

London, 26 January 1893

Dear Baron,

Gine has just told me that you are awaiting an answer from me about Marx's biography.[130] It had in fact escaped my mind that this was urgent. Please accept my apologies.

I wouldn't know what to add to the material you mentioned—unless perhaps one or two bits from the sketch[a] in the *Handwörterbuch der Staatswissenschaften* that was sent to you. Elster—a cousin of Conrad Schmidt's who referred him to me—asked me to write something for him, which I did, wholly from our own standpoint, all unsuspecting that be would print it—after he had deleted a few excessively unbourgeois passages. Well, it's all one to me.

The matter of the *Neue Zeit* has, of course, been shelved for the time being on account of Dietz's treatment, apart from the fact of your having spoken to August.[b] He says it is impossible to revert to a monthly. In which case the *external* arrangements will doubtless remain pretty well unaltered—and it is up to the editors to make the paper more meaty and more amusing for its readers. At all events it seems to me that any drastic change will have to be put off until Dietz is fit for work again. And you yourself will in any case be swamped with a superfluity of good and well-

---

[a] F. Engels, *Marx, Heinrich Karl.* – [b] See this volume, pp 49-50, 53-54

meaning advice regarding your own department, so I shall spare you that.

Tussy is tremendously busy agitating; she has been in the Midlands, Edinburgh and Aberdeen and is supposed to be coming here today. When I see her, I shall ask her for some personal reminiscences about Moor.[131]

I gave Ede the Brazilian paper,[132] though I told him that the importance of these South American parties is always in inverse proportion to the grandiosity of their programmes.

Ede is gradually recovering from his neurasthenia; he has likewise regained his old sprightliness, as is evident from his personal behaviour and also from his article on Wolf to whom he does *too much* honour.[a] I believe that what he now needs most of all is something to liven and cheer him up in order that his soundness of judgement may once more gain complete control over his still somewhat excessive aspirations after justice.

Nothing fresh to report otherwise.—Also and, belatedly, a Happy New Year to you.

Your
F. E.

First published in:
*Aus der Frühzeit des
Marxismus. Engels Briefwechsel
mit Kautsky*, Prague, 1935

Printed according to the original

Published in English for the first time

51

ENGELS TO HERMANN ENGELS

IN BARMEN

London, 26 January 1893

Dear Hermann,

What the deuce is going on? Yesterday there was first of all a telegram from Vienna, then one from Dresden, then, at five o'clock this morning, one from New York and, at 11 this morning, your own—all inquiring

---

[a] E. Bernstein, 'Der neueste Vernichter des Sozialismus', *Die Neue Zeit*, Vol. I, Nos. 16, 17, Stuttgart, 1892/93.

after my health. Well, I haven't felt better for a long time, I can again walk an English mile, I over- rather than under-indulged in good things at Christmastime, am game for anything and perfectly fit for work and now all of a sudden I'm supposed to be seriously ill!

I telegraphed back to you immediately.[133] saying I was perfectly hale and hearty, and this I hereby confirm. Next summer I hope I shall be able to give all of you visual proof of the fact.

My love to all the relatives, also to Emma[a] and your children and grandchildren and, finally, to you yourself from

Your old
Friedrich

First published in
Deutsche Revue, Jg. 46,
Bd. 111, 1921

Printed according to the original

Published in English for the first time

52

ENGELS TO WILHELM LIEBKNECHT

IN BERLIN

London, 29 January 1893

Dear Liebknecht,

Herewith a small token of my 'serious loss of strength' on the evidence of which you will, I trust, 'hourly await my demise'.[b] Where did this nonsense originate? I should like to discover who the scoundrel is!

I have so arranged the article[c] as to enable you to publish it either in three numbers[d] or in a supplement; the latter might perhaps be best. I haven't signed it, for otherwise I should inevitably put the chaps in Rome onto the track of my Italian source.[e] The man has been insufficiently cautious in his conduct of the correspondence which has evidently been

---

[a] Emma Engels – [b] See this volume, p. 107 – [c] F. Engels, 'Vom italienischen Panama – [d] of the *Vorwärts* – [e] Antonio Labriola

subject to rigorous surveillance. Moreover I still don't know whether the relevant documents are in a safe place abroad and so it is essential to avoid doing anything that might deliver them up into the hands of the Italian government.

I have mentioned names only where the facts relating to them have already appeared in the Italian press and could therefore be produced as supporting evidence. The only exceptions are the *two* names *Arbib* and *Martini* on p. 3; I could provide no supporting evidence for these, so if you have misgivings delete them.

The bearer of the revered name is Menotti Garibaldi, a lad who has already been hard at work for *years past* founding all sorts of things.[134]

Not long ago the *Vorwärts* alluded to Bonghi the *Republican*[a]—the man is an arch-reactionary and an ex-minister of the *Right*. All in all, the *Vorwärts* has been notable for such mistakes regarding foreign countries, *not least England!*

Give my regards to your wife and children.

Your
F. E.

First published in:
"Marx and Engels, *Works*,
First Russian Edition,
Vol. XXIX, Moscow, 1946

Printed according to the original

Published in English for the first time

53

ENGELS TO FILIPPO TURATI[135]

IN MILAN

London, 30 January 1893

Dear citizen Turati,

You will have a few words of introduction tomorrow, if possible.[b] However, I would ask you not to attach to the 1848 Manifesto the 1884

---

[a] 'Das italienische Panama', *Vorwärts*, No. 22, 25 January 1893. – [b] F. Engels, 'To the Italian Reader'.

programme of the English Socialist League.[136] The Manifesto is a historic document, *sui generis*.[a] and if you attach to it a document dated forty years later, you will give the latter a special character.[108] Moreover, I cannot at the moment find the English original for comparison, because I have not seen it since it first appeared, and I know nothing about the programmes and other publications of the Socialist League, a society which has rapidly become anarchist, so that all those members who did not want to take part in this change of front (the Avelings, Bax, etc.) have withdrawn. As a result the League that has been dead for some time is now only referred to here as an *anarchist* society. You can imagine, therefore, to what *quid pro quo* a reprint of the original programme together with the 1848 Manifesto might lead.

Greetings to Mme Kulishov and yourself from Mme Kautsky and yours truly,

F. Engels

First published, in the language of the original (French), in:
K. Marx, F. Engels, *Scritti italiani*, Milano-Roma, 1955

Printed according to the original

Translated from the French

Published in English for the first time

54

ENGELS TO FILIPPO TURATI

IN MILAN

[London, 1 February 1893]

Dear citizen Turati,

Here is the preface.[b]

You are going too quickly for me in Italy. Your Panamino,[106] which threatens to become a Panamone, is undergoing evolutions and vicissitudes at such a rate that we here in London cannot keep up with events in Rome. Therefore I have refrained from speaking about them, for fear

---

[a] unique of its kind – [b] F. Engels, 'To the Italian Reader', see also Note 108.

of being outdated the very next day. This should explain why what I have written is not particularly topical.

But where on earth were the socialist, deputies during these decisive days? Ours in Germany would never be forgiven if they had not been present at the Colajanni meeting—it would have cost them their mandates!

Yours,

F. E.

First published, in the language
of the original (French), in:
*Filippo Turati attraverso le lettere di
corrispondenti (1880-1925),*
Bari, 1947

Printed according to the original

Translated from the French

Published in English for the first time

55

ENGELS TO MARIA MENDELSON

LONDON

[London,] 7 February 1893
122 Regent's Park Road, N. W.

Dear Madame Mendelson,

A thousand thanks for the trouble you have taken to translate the two articles for me.[137] As for the *warning—ostrzezenie—*I had already deciphered it with the help of a Polish dictionary that I inherited from Marx. And the *Gazeta Robotnicza* has really been of unexpected assistance in my Polish studies—you say that the Polish in this newssheet is too German. Then it is like the Russian of Lavrov, and that explains why the Russian of the one and the Polish of the other present me with so few difficulties. I am indeed making progress, and if I had time to apply myself seriously to it for three months, I would venture to garble in Polish.

I will try to make use of your manuscripts—in the meantime I would ask you to let me know if I may publish the facts contained in your letter on the Moscow students and Russian officers—without, of course, revealing the source of my information.[138]

Kind regards from Mme Kautsky.

Yours,
F. Engels

First published in:
Marx and Engels, *Works*,
First Russian Edition,
Vol. XXIX, Moscow, 1946

Printed according to the original

Translated from the French

Published in English for the first time

56

ENGELS TO VLADIMIR SHMUILOV[40]

IN DRESDEN

[Copy]

London, 7 February 1893
122 Regent's Park Road, N. W.

Dear Comrade,

My best thanks for your kind hope that I should attain my nineties. If I remained as I am now, I should have no objection but were I, like so many, to degenerate physically and mentally as well, I would really rather not. Were that the case, I should prefer to be counted out.

As to your requests regarding Marx's biography,[140] I am afraid that there is little I can do to meet them. Moreover I lack the time, being engaged on the 3rd volume of *Capital* and unable to take time off from it.

Ad[a] I. There is nothing I can recommend over and above the biographical material already in your possession. Nothing reliable, at any rate.

Ad II. Marx's practical activities between 1844 and 1849 were in part devoted to the working men's associations, especially the Brussels association between 1846 and 1848, and to the League.[141] It is only on these last that you will find anything in print, namely in our prefaces to the *Manifesto* (LATEST Berlin edition, 1892) and in the *Revelations Concerning the Communist Trial* along with my introduction[a] thereto, Zurich edition,

---

[a] as to

1885.—As regards the International, Eichhoff *ALONE* is reliable,[b] for he worked from Marx's notes; all the rest from Fribourg,[c] to Laveleye[d] and Zacher,[e] are a source of nothing but *LIES AND MYTHS*. Here it would be more a case of writing a fat book to set matters right than of sending material for a third party to work on. I can, however, send you two publications issued by the General Council (*Prétendues Scissions* and *L'Alliance de la Démocratie Socialiste*)[f] for the decisive struggle with Bakunin.—Héritier's offering in the *Berliner Volks-Tribüne* on the subject of the *Jura Federation and M. Bakunin*[49] betrays unexampled naïveté in its blind faith in the anarchists' inventions and, from what Héritier writes and tells me, his translator has vitiated it still further in the anarchist sense. (In which case, by the way, the Russian censor will, with his excisions, guard you against a good many mistakes.)

Ad III. You will have to get hold of *The Holy Family* by fair means or foul. In no circumstances will I let my own copy out of my hands and to supply particulars of the contents is an impossible task. Nor would it do any good to write out for you the main passages. You must be familiar with the *whole*. It surely ought to be possible to pick one up in Berlin.

As to the *genesis* of historical materialism, you will, in my opinion, find everything you want in my *Feuerbach* (*Ludwig Feuerbach and the End of Classical German Philosophy*)—the appendix by Marx *is*, of course, itself the genesis! Also in the prefaces to the *Manifesto* (new Berlin edition, 1892) and to the *Revelations Concerning the Communist Trial*.

Marx quietly elaborated the theory of surplus value in the fifties, all on his own, and resolutely refused to publish anything on the subject until he was in absolutely no doubt about each of his conclusions. Hence the non-appearance of the 2nd and subsequent instalments of *A Contribution to the Critique of Political Economy*.[142]

I am sending you the *Splits* and *Alliance* by post and hope these will suffice. Unfortunately that is all I can do for you.

Kindest regards to Gnardnauer and all the comrades over there.

---

[a] F. Engels, *On the History of the Communist League.* – [b] W. Eichhoff, *Die Internationale Arbeiterassociation. Ihre Gründung, Organization, politisch-sociale Thätigkeit und Aus breitung.* – [c] E. E. Fribourg, *L'Association internationale des travailleurs.* – [d] É. de Laveleye, *Le Socialisme contemporain.* – [e] [J.] Zacher, Die Rothe Internationale. – [f] K. Marx and F. Engels, *Fictitious Splits in the International* and *The Alliance of Socialist Democracy and the International Working Men's Association.*

Ever yours,
F. Engels

First published in:
Marx and Engels, *Works*,
First Russian Edition,
Vol. XXIX, Moscow, 1946

Printed according to the copy
written by Shmuilov

Published in English in full
for the first time

57

ENGELS TO AUGUST BEBEL

IN BERLIN

London, 9 February 1893

Dear August,

First of all my congratulations on your magnificent speech of 3 February which had already given us enormous pleasure in the *Vorwärts*[a] excerpt but came out even better in the stenographic report. It is a master-piece, in no way impaired by one or two minor theoretical inaccuracies, these being inevitable in verbal delivery. You are quite right to arrange for copies of the speech to be distributed in their hundreds of thousands,[b] notwithstanding and in addition to the distribution of the whole debate in pamphlet form.[c]

This debate, in which the worthy bourgeois sought to dispel the te-dium of sittings that had grown arid—thanks to their intrigues behind the scenes—and also, whenever chance offered, to lead us nicely up the garden path, has turned out to be a truly colossal victory for us. And that they themselves sense this is borne out by the fact that after Liebknecht's speech they had had enough and indicated as much—through Stoecker![143] So now at last the gentlemen have realised that if a parliament devotes it-

---

[a] No. 30 of 4 February 1893 – [b] A. Bebel, *Zukunftsstaat und Sozialdemokratie. Eine Rede des Reichstagsabgeordneten August Bebel in der Sitzung des deutschen Reichstags vom 3. Februar 1893.* – [c] *'Der sozialdemokratische 'Zukunftsstaat'. Verhandlungen des deutschen Reichstags am 31. Januar, 3., 4., 6. und 7. Februar 1893, veröffentlicht nach dem offiziellen stenographischen Bericht.*

self for five days on end to social reorganisation in our own sense of the term and if, on top of that, the said parliament is the German Reichstag, this is a milestone symbolising yet another victory for the workers' party. This latter circumstance has given proof to the whole world, friend and foe alike, of the triumphant position won by the German party. If things go on like this, we shall soon be able to exist at no cost of effort to ourselves, on the stupidity of our opponents alone.

It was obvious that you would have to bear the brunt of the debate. So far as I can judge, Frohme's speech did indeed provide some pretext for the victorious hullabaloo from Richter and Bachem and Hitze, and the business of Thomas Aquinas and Aristotle ought to be carefully investigated. If what Hitze asserted is correct, Frohme lacked the competence to quote from them, but if not, he ought to have made a personal statement in self-vindication.[144] Otherwise everything went off beautifully and Liebknecht's concluding speech, though indifferent in content, was nevertheless 'trenchant' and good polemically. In short, it has been a triumph. The Witch[a] was so overjoyed that yesterday she called me Agnes Pinchpenny, whereupon I drew her attention to the fact that she was a proper Fidgety Ann, as anyone who knows her will confirm. She is even worse than the latter, for its not so much her legs that are fidgety but her brain.[145]

There is much to be said for your suggestions as to what the best plan for the Russians would be in case of war.[146] But don't forget that if the overthrow of France would be intolerable to Russia, the suppression of Germany would be no less so to Italy and England. *Every localised war* is more or less subject to control by the neutrals. The next war, if it comes at all, will not permit of being localised in any way. They—the Continentals at any rate—would all be drawn in during the first months, it would automatically begin in the Balkans and England at most might be able to remain neutral for a time. Your Russian plan, however, presupposes a localised war and that, given the enormous armies of today and the appalling consequences for the vanquished, I no longer regard as possible.

In Egypt it is simply a case of the Russians (the French are mere puppets on strings) making things difficult for the English, and thereby tying up their troops and fleet as much as possible. If war broke out, Russia would then have something to offer the English in return for an alliance

---

[a] jocular name for Louise Kautsky

or at least their neutrality and at such a juncture the French would be delighted to exchange Egypt for Alsace. Meanwhile the Russians are up to the same game in Central Asia on the Indian border where it will be years before they are strong enough to mount serious attacks and where the ground is very far from being prepared for this purpose. Incidentally, in connection with Egypt, Turkey should also fall to Russia.

(Have just had another Russian visitor who has held me up for over an hour, the result being that it is now 4 o'clock and in consequence this will have to be a shorter letter.)

I see that on your Military Committee you also have a Major Wachs. If he is the same man as a cousin of Dr Gumpert's of Manchester, I met him there some 25 years ago, At that time he had joined the Prussians as a former lieutenant in the service of Hesse-Cassel and was much disappointed to find amongst his victors of 1866 the same preoccupation with spit and polish as had, or so he thought, been the cause of Hesse-Cassel's defeat.[147] I gave him some encouragement, saying that if he would only go ahead and stick it out with the Prussians, he would probably discover that the army also had its good sides. Later on, at Spichern,[148] when in command of a company, he greatly distinguished himself by occupying on his own initiative a railway tunnel *in defiance of his major*. In the General Staff's history[a] he is mentioned in most glowing terms—one of the very few lieutenants of whom it makes any mention at all. Since then I have read various strategic-political essays of his—most of them on the East—in which there are some very good things along with others (political) with which I don't agree. At all events he is an efficient officer—if it's the same man.

By the way, a compromise seems more probable than ever. Even the Free Thinkers[149] and the Centre[71] are prepared to supply 28,000 men, while Bennigsen is offering 40,000. No doubt so many will fall by the wayside that the government will get 50,000 rather than the 60,000 it wanted (perhaps also just a few more, provided it doesn't waver)[76] and the bourgeois fatherland will once again be saved from dissolution and conflict.

The 'ball' was thought up by our charming Witch's fidgety brain. The 'Society'[62] gave a concert which was followed by a ball. At 11 o'clock the *first* part of the concert ended, whereupon I obediently took my leave,

---

[a] *Der deutsch-französische Krieg 1870-71*. Redigirt von der Kriegsgeschichtlichen Abteilung des Großen Generalstabes. Part 1, Vol. 1, p. 341, Berlin, 1874.

so the dancing cannot have started before 1 o'clock. She herself always speaks of dancing with a condescension more appropriate to someone many years her senior, and if she is to dance a waltz you yourself will doubtless have to lead her onto the floor. In which case I'm by no means so certain that her Viennese blood might not reassert its rights.

In the next (February) No., now at the printers, the Polish *Przedswit*, which comes out here, will contain the following item:[150] At Grajewo, on the East Prussian border, there is a junior Russian official by the name of Spatzek, a Bohemian by birth, who is employed on translating way-bills. Despite his wretched wage he makes long journeys, some of them as far as Constantinople, leads a fast life, frequently enters Prussian territory on the pretext of hunting and is very friendly with Landrat von der Gröbben of Lyck who provides him with a vast quantity of hunting and other travel permits. When the frontier was closed on account of cholera, nobody was allowed across, but Mr Spatzek along with his wife and H-n, another Russian official suspected of spying, were able to travel to Königsberg without hindrance. In the opinion of people on the far side of the border this gadding about on German territory is purely and simply for the purpose of spying out the outer forts sited between the East Prussian lakes, on which occasions our overwise Prussian Landrat is only too pleased to be made use of by his Russo-Bohemian friend. The arrogant Prussian bureaucrats are everywhere easily taken in.

Moreover the Russian troops on the border were not long ago the recipients of a whole load of literature, to wit numerous copies of a pamphlet by Alexandrov, a lieutenant in the artillery in Tashkent, *On the causes and necessity of the impending war.*[a] One copy has been issued to each company in order that the officers may duly enlighten their men.

Perhaps you might be able to make use of this information in your private conversations with the people on the Military Committee.

Over here Keir Hardie has moved an amendment on the subject of unemployment[151] to the Address (Reply to the Speech from the Throne[b]) in Parliament. In itself this was quite a good thing. But Keir Hardie committed two colossal blunders. 1. The amendment was formulated quite unnecessarily as *a direct vote of censure* on the government, so that its acceptance would have forced the government to resign and thus the whole thing was tantamount to a Tory manoeuvre, 2. he chose to be seconded by

---

[a] A. H. Aleksandrov, [original text in Russian]. – [b] by Queen Victoria

the Tory Howard Vincent, a Protectionist, rather than by a Labour member, thereby completing the picture of a Tory manoeuvre and of *himself* as a Tory puppet. Moreover 102 Tories voted in his favour and only 2 Liberal-Radicals,[152] not one Labour member. Burns was agitating in Yorkshire. As I have already written you,[a] his manoeuvrings and pronouncements since Bradford[153] have more than once been suggestive of Champion's influence; this has now become more than a suspicion. The source of his means of subsistence is unknown, and over the past two years he has spent a great deal of money on travelling. Where does it come from? The English working-man demands of his parliamentary representatives and other leaders that they devote all their time to the movement. But if he won't pay them, he himself is to blame if they accept money from other parties as a means of support and for electoral purposes. So long as this goes on, there will always be Panamites[154] amongst the labour leaders over here.

Incidentally, if Mr Keir Hardie continues to be allowed to behave in this way, he will soon be laid low. The working men of Lancashire and Yorkshire are not the sort of people to attach themselves to conservative leading-strings or to pluck the Tories' chestnuts out of the fire for them. Just give K. Hardie enough time and the consequences of his policy will rebound on him personally and become evident to all.

Burns has gone to Halifax to agitate in connection with the elections and consequently did not vote on Keir Hardie's motion.

For it is by-election time in Huddersfield and Halifax, two manufacturing towns in Yorkshire, each of more than 100,000 inhabitants. The Independent Labour Party has put up a candidate[b] in Halifax, as have the other two parties. Then it made the following offer to the Liberals: If you withdraw your candidate in Halifax[c] so that we only have the Tory[d] to contend with, we'll vote for you in Huddersfield. The Liberals refused. Whereupon the LIBERAL WAS DEFEATED LAST TUESDAY IN HUDDERSFIELD[e] by the Tory[f]—as a result of the Independent Labour Party's abstention, Again, at another by-election in Burnley, Lancashire, not far from Halifax, the Liberals polled 750 fewer votes than in the previous election—also as a result of our abstention. The poll in Halifax is being held today and the Tory will probably be elected. That would bring Gladstone's majority, now 36, down to 34. Events such as these are

---

– [a] See this volume, p. 87 – [b] John Lister – [c] William Rawson Shaw – [d] Alfred Arnold – [e] Joseph Woodhead – [f] Joseph Crosland

making things hotter each day for the Liberals. Up till now progress has been splendid and Gladstone will have to capitulate to the workers. Most important of all are the political measures, namely the extension of the franchise for working men by implementing what is presently on paper and which would increase the Labour vote by 50 per cent, the curtailment of the duration of Parliament (now seven years!) and the payment of electoral expenses and M.P.'s salaries out of public funds.

Meanwhile these fresh successes scored by an independent policy are bound to increase the working man's self-esteem and tell him that virtually everywhere the fate of the elections, and hence of each government, lies in his hands. That is the most important part: self-confidence and self-reliance on the part of the class. It will also tide them over all the miserable little intrigues which are simply the result of the masses' lack of confidence in themselves. Once we have a body of working men that really moves en masse, the crafty manoeuvrings of those worthies the leaders will cease, for they will do them more harm than good.

Louise's letter went off at 5.30 p.m. by the night boat. This is going off at 9 p.m., i.e. by the first day boat. Perhaps you would tell us at what time each of them arrives so that we know which post is the best.

Once again warm regards to your wife and yourself from Louise and

Your
F. E.

First published in:
Marx and Engels, *Works*,
First Russian Edition,
Vol. XXIX, 1946

Printed according to the original

Published in English for the first time

58

ENGELS TO LAURA LAFARGUE

AT LE PERREUX

London, 12 February 1893

My dear Löhr,

Glad indeed I was to see your handwriting otherwise than outside an *Intransigeant* or a *Figaro*, and I reply at once, as today Sunday I have a few minutes free and tomorrow I shall have to rush off again into the jungle of Banks, Credit, moneyed capital, rate of interest, in order to finish off *Das Kapital*, book III, chapters 30-36. It is—this section V—as good as finished as far as real difficulties are concerned, but it wants a good deal of 'finishing' in the literary sense: arranging, weeding out repetitions etc.[33] This I hope to settle in 8-10 days, then come Sections VI and VII, and then—the end. My correspondence in the meantime is suspended and my rack is full, cram-full of unanswered letters from all quarters, reaching from Rome to New York and from Petersburg to Texas; so if I snatch a moment to write to you, it's only because *it's you* and no one else.

Louise[a] sent you a letter of *seven pages* rather more than a week ago—have you really never received that? Please inquire, we will do the same here.

Yes, the *Arbeiterinnen-Zeitung* you will like. It has a healthy proletarian character in it—including the literary imperfections—which contrasts very agreeably with all the rest of the women's papers. And you may well be proud of it, for you too are one of its Mamas!

I am sorry to hear about Paul's continued unsatisfactory health—has he not yet got rid of that infernal taenia? Surely there is plenty of *Filix Mas* or *Kousso*[b] to be had in Paris to drive it out, even without a regular siege. Of course as long as he nurses it, he will not get well, the beast will eat him up. And why in the name of goodness *does* he *travel* thus? Nobody out of France can make it out that he and others allow this splendid opportunity to slip out of their hands.[155] I can very well understand that the harum-scarum lot of so-called Socialist deputies does not want him to speak, they all pull in different directions and play each his own game, and they know that Paul, once in the tribune, would be unaccountable and incon-

---

[a] Kautsky – [b] medicinal herbs

trollable by them, but from our point of view that is the very reason why he *should* speak. Are the Socialists, just before the elections,[156] by their silence to create the suspicion that they are no better than the Panamitards and have reasons of their own to screen them and to hush the whole thing up? In Italy that is the case, the couple of men elected in the Romagna (as Socialists) are in the hands of the government through the *subventions paid by the latter to the so-called cooperative societies directed by the former*, and which subventions as likely as not come out of the coffers of the Banca Romana. That accounts for their silence.[106] But in France!?! I can assure you, this unaccountable silence has not raised the respect in which the French Socialists are held abroad. Of course, Brousse and Co. have had their share out of the secret funds furnished by Panama—but is not that a *reason more* for our people to speak out? Formerly *à la guerre comme à la guerre* was a *French* proverb, is it still so?

According to Mother Crawford, the severe sentences on the Lesseps and Co. are mere dust thrown into the eyes of the *gogos*[a]—the Court of Cassation will quench them,[157] on the ground that the Prinet instruction did not interrupt prescription, and that therefore the *délits en question sont préscrits*.[b] If that turns out to be the case, then it means that the 'knowing ones', *ceux qui ont touché*[c] are bold enough to tell all France that she is a *gogo* all over. That would be *se moquer du monde*[d] with a vengeance.

Well, I hope the popular wrath *will be roused* at last, and vengeance taken. It's getting time.

Bebel shall send you his speech of the 3rd February in the stenogramm. It is really splendid, and you may find it very useful for the *Socialiste*.[158] Our people have had the Reichstag all to themselves for a fortnight. First the *Notstandsdebatte*,[e] *3 days*, and all parties, from the government downwards, imploring our men to use their power to smooth matters down with the striking colliers, etc.[159] Then the colossal blunder of the bourgeois to provoke our people to a debate on the future organisation of society—this lasted *five* days[143]!—the first time the subject as been discussed in *any* parliament. And only three speakers on our side at all—Bebel spoke twice, Frohme and Liebknecht—and the bourgeois had to leave us the *last word* and give it up in despair (for we could stop the *clôture*[f] by a simple count out, there never being the quorum of 201 present).

---

[a] simpletons – [b] misdemeanours in question are prescribed – [c] those who made something out of it – [d] to cock a snook at public opinion – [e] emergency debate – [f] closure

While you were flooded I was 'dying'—according to the papers. Last Tuesday week[a] a telegram from Vienna: was I actually off? Then one from Dresden; at 5 in the morning, knock up, one from New York. This went on for a couple of days more until we found out that almost all Berlin papers had a paragraph, I was *in einem so hochgradigen Kräfteverlust, dass mein Ableben stündlich erwartet wurde.*[b] Who invented this rubbish I can't make out. Anyhow, he be damned.

Love from Louise, and from

Ever yours,
F. Engels

To Paul: *Exeat taenia*[c]!
Sam Moore left again for the Niger 28th January.

First published, in the language
of the original (English), in:
F. Engels, P. et L. Lafargue,
Correspondance, t. III, Paris, 1959

Reproduced from the original

59

ENGELS TO AUGUST BEBEL

IN BERLIN

[London,] 24 February 1893

Dear August,

You will have received the document I sent off by registered mail yesterday. A word or two more on the subject.

I had envisaged its being published in 8 articles in 8 successive numbers of the *Vorwärts*. But some other method may seem better to you, in which case feel free.

I do not much like the title *Can Europe Disarm?* And yet I cannot think

---

[a] See this volume, pp. 92-93 – [b] in such an extreme state of failing strength that my demise was hourly awaited – [c] Out taenia go!

of anything better.[160] You couldn't very well call it a *Social-Democratic Military Bill*, though this might do at a pinch if you were to adopt the proposal *en bloc*.

I sent the thing to you rather than to Liebknecht because you are a member of the Military Committee and asked me for a 'lecture'. That will exonerate me so far as he is concerned. Also because I would sooner entrust you than him with such alterations as may be demanded by the Press Laws, and, in general, because the article is the concern not merely of the *Vorwärts*, but of you all, and you might have your own individual opinions as to the best method and time of publication—at any rate *before* the matter is again debated in plenary session.

As you will have seen from the *Workman's Times*, the English working man is, thanks to the Avelings, now kept better informed about party affairs on the Continent,[158] especially those in Germany.[161]

After what happened in the last elections, the Liberal government has had to stir its stumps a bit. True, the measures are 'Liberal' but at any rate better than might have been expected. The new Bill re electoral registers,[162] if it should go through, will 1. strengthen the Labour vote by at least 20 to 30 per cent and give the workers an absolute majority in another 40 or 50 constituencies, and 2. save the candidates a considerable outlay every year; the latter have *themselves* been responsible for getting their voters placed on the register, and that's a very expensive business over here. This can pass muster.—Salaries for M.P.s are very much on the cards and should materialise, if not in this session, then almost certainly in the next one. Gladstone has accepted them *in principle*. Again, it's a great advantage that there should be only *one* electoral register, i.e. only *one* suffrage, for all public elections, and the importance of this is enhanced by the fact that there is another Bill in sight for the setting up of Parish (over here rural parishes) Councils[163] which will eliminate the last traces of what has hitherto been a semi-feudal system in country districts. If all this goes through and becomes law during this session, the political position of the working class will be materially improved, which is in itself an added incentive for the chaps to make the most of that new position. However many intrigues and blunders there may be over here, and these will be legion, there can be no doubt that tremendous progress is being made, and in a few years' time you may already find cause for surprise in the English.

I don't see why you shouldn't give a straight account of the Spatzek business. Come to that, it has been published in Polish in the February issue of *Przedswit*.ᵃ

If Wachs is *tall*, he's not the right chap. He was, so far as I can remember, about the same size as yourself, with brown hair. But where all these waxen majors come from, I cannot conceive.ᵇ

The Witchᶜ has just finished, so I must fall in and await orders—warm regards to your wife and yourself,

Your

F. E.

First published in:
Marx and Engels, *Works*,
First Russian Edition,
Vol. XXIX, Moscow, 1946

Printed according to the original

Published in English for the first time

60

ENGELS TO NIKOLAI DANIELSON[164]

IN ST. PETERSBURG

London, 24 February 1893

My dear Sir,

Pardon my long silence. It was not voluntary, I have to make an effort—a supreme effort—to finish Vol. IIIᵈ this winter and spring. In order to attain that, I have to forbid myself all extra-work and even all correspondence that is not absolutely necessary. Otherwise nothing would have detained me from continuing with you the discussion of our highly interesting and important problem.[165]

I have now finished—all but a few formal matters—the *rédaction*ᵉ of Section V (Banks and Credit), the most difficult of all, both from the state of the subject and *from the state of* the manuscript. Now remain but two sections—1/3 of the whole—of these the one—rent of land—is

---

ᵃ See this volume, p. 102 – ᵇ A play of words in the original: the name Wachs is derived from the word 'wächsern' meaning 'waxen'. See this volume, p. 101 – ᶜ jocular name for Louise Kautsky – ᵈ of Marx's *Capital* – ᵉ editing

upon a very difficult subject too, but as far as I recollect the Ms.[a] is far more finished than that of Section V. So that I still hope to be able to complete my task in the allotted time. The great difficulty was, to get 3-5 months absolute freedom from all interruption, so as to devote the whole time to Section V, and that is now fortunately done. In working, I have often thought of the immense pleasure this volume will give to you when it appears. I shall send you advance-sheets as I did for Vol. II.

Maintenant revenons à nos moutons.[b]

We seem to be agreed upon all points except one, which you tackle in both your letters of 3d October and 27 January, though in each from a different point of view.

In the first you ask: was the economic change, which after 1854 had become unavoidable,[166] of such a nature that it must, instead of developing the historical institutions of Russia, on the contrary attack them in their root? In other words, could not the rural commune be taken for the basis of the new economic development?

And, January 27th, you express the same idea in this form: the *grande industrie*[c] had become a necessity for Russia, but was it unavoidable that it was developed in a capitalistic form?

Well, in, or about, 1854 Russia started with the commune on the one hand, and the necessity of the *grande industrie* on the other. Now, if you take the whole state of your country into account, as it was at that date, do you see any possibility of the *grande industrie* being grafted on the peasants' commune in a form which would, on the one hand, make the development of that *grande industrie* possible, and on the other hand raise the primitive commune to the rank of a social institution superior to anything the world has yet seen? And that while the whole Occident[d] was still living under the capitalist *régime*? It strikes me that such an evolution, which would have surpassed anything known in history, required other economical, political and intellectual conditions than were present at that time in Russia.

No doubt the commune and to a certain extent the artel, contained germs which under certain conditions might have developed and saved Russia the necessity of passing through the torments of the capitalistic *ré-*

---

[a] of Section VI (see present edition, Vol. 37) – [b] Literally: let's return to our muttons; an expression from the French medieval farce, meaning: let's return to the subject of our conversation. – [c] large-scale industry – [d] West

gime. I fully subscribe to our author's letter about Zhukovsky.[a] But in his, as well as in my opinion, the first condition required to bring this about, was the *impulse from without*, the change of economic system in the Occident of Europe, the destruction of the capitalist system in the countries where it had originated. Our author said in a certain preface to a certain old manifesto, in January 1882, replying to the question whether the Russian commune might not be the starting-point of a higher social development[b]: if the change of economic system in Russia coincides with a change of economic system in the West—so that the two complement each other, the present Russian common ownership of land may serve as the starting-point for communist development.[c]

If we in the West had been quicker in our own economic development, if we had been able to upset the capitalistic regime some ten or twenty years ago, there might have been time yet for Russia to cut short the tendency of her own evolution towards capitalism. Unfortunately we are too slow, and those economic consequences of the capitalistic system which must bring it up to the critical point, are only just now developing in the various countries about us: while England is fast losing her industrial monopoly, France and Germany are approaching the industrial level of England, and America bids fair to drive them all out of the world's market both for industrial and for agricultural produce. The introduction of an, at least relative, free trade policy in America is sure to complete the ruin of England's industrial monopoly, and to destroy, at the same time, the industrial export trade of Germany and France; then the crisis must come, *tout ce qu'il y a de plus fin de siécle.*[d] But in the meantime, with you, the commune fades away, and we can only hope that the change to a better system, with us, may come soon enough to save, at least in some of the remoter portions of your country, institutions which may, under these circumstances, be called upon to fulfil a great future, But facts are facts, and we must not forget that these chances are getting less and less every year.

For the rest I grant you that the circumstance of Russia being the *last* country seized upon by the *grande* capitalist *grande industrie*, and at the

---

[a] The reference is to the letter Marx wrote to the editors of the *Otechestvenniye Zapiski* (see present edition, Vol. 24, pp. 196-201). – [b] K. Marx and F. Engels, 'Preface to the Second Russian Edition of the *Manifesto of the Communist Party*' (see present edition, Vol. 24, p. 426). – [c] Phrase in Russian in the original. – [d] which signifies better than anything else *the end of the world*

same time the country *with by far the largest peasant population*, are such as must render the *bouleversement*[a] caused by this economic change, more acute than it has been anywhere else. The process of replacing some 500,000 landowners[b] and some 80 million peasants by a new class of *bourgeois* landed proprietors cannot be carried out but under fearful sufferings and convulsions. But history is about the most cruel of all goddesses,[b] and she leads her triumphal car over heaps of corpses, not only in war, but also in 'peaceful' economic development. And we men and women are unfortunately so stupid that we never can pluck up courage to a real progress unless urged to it by sufferings that seem almost out of proportion.

> Always yours
> P. W. R.[167]

Address *Mrs Kautsky*, please, not Mrs Roscher.

First published in Russian, in
Minuvshiye gody, No. 2,
St. Petersburg, 1908

Reproduced from the original

61

ENGELS TO PAUL LAFARGUE[35]

AT LE PERREUX

London, 25 February 1893

My dear Lafargue,

How time passes! Old Harney reminds me this morning that yesterday was the anniversary of the February revolution. 'Long Live the Republic!' Lord, we have so many other anniversaries to celebrate now that one forgets these semi-bourgeois occasions. And to think that in five years it will be a half century since that one took place. At the time we were all en-

---

[a] overthrow – [b] word in Russian in original

thusiasm for the republic—with a small r; since it has been written with a capital R, it seems worthless, save as an almost obsolete historical stage.

Your speech was very good and I regret only one thing: that it was not delivered two months ago.[168] But better late than never.[a] It doesn't surprise me that the Chamber and the press found it ill-timed; if we were to wait upon their *placet*[b] we should never open our mouths. As for the Millerand & Co. Radical Socialists, it is absolutely essential that the alliance with them should be based on the fact that our Party is a separate Party, and that they recognise that.[169] Which in no way rules out joint action in the forthcoming elections, provided that the distribution of seats to be jointly contested is made in accordance with the actual state of the respective forces; those gentlemen are in the habit of claiming the lion's share.

Do not let the fact that your speeches in the Chamber do not create as much stir as formerly discourage you. Look at our people in Germany: they were booed for years on end, and now the 36 dominate the Reichstag. Bebel writes saying: if we were eighty or a hundred (out of 400 members), the Reichstag would become an impossibility. There is not a debate, no matter what the subject, in which we do not intervene and we are listened to by all the parties. The debate on the socialist organisation of the future lasted five days,[143] and Bebel's speech[c] was wanted in *three and a half million copies*. Now they are having the whole debate published in pamphlets[d] at five sous, and the effect, already tremendous, will be doubled!

You are absolutely right to prepare for the elections. We ought to conquer at least 20 seats. You have the immense advantage of knowing, from the municipal elections, the *minimum* extent of your strength in each locality; for I am sure that, since last May, you have appreciably increased it.[170] That will help you greatly in distributing candidatures between yourselves and the Radical Socialists. But possibly you would prefer to put up your candidates wherever you stand a chance, with the proviso to withdraw them, if necessary, in favour of the Radicals, for the second ballot, in the event of the latter having polled more votes.

The most important thing in the elections is to establish once and for

---

[a] See this volume, pp.105-06 – [b] invitation – [c] A. Bebel, *Zukunftsstaad und Sozialdemokratie. Eine Rede des Reichstagsabgeordneten August Bebel in der Sitzung des deutschen Reichstags vom 3. Februar, 1893.* – [d] *Der sozialdemokratische 'Zukunftsstaat' Verhandlungen des Deutschen Reichstags am 31. Januar, 3., 4., 6. und 7. Februar 1893 Veröffentlicht nach dem offiziellen stenographischen bericht.*

all that it is our Party which represents socialism in France, and that all
the other more or less socialist fractions—Broussists,[30] Allemanists,[21] and
pure or impure Blanquists[20]—have been able to play a part beside us only
by virtue of the dissensions incidental to the more or less infantile phase
of the proletarian movement; but that now the stage of *infantile* disorders
is over, and the French proletariat has reached full consciousness of its
historic position. Should we win 20 seats, all the others combined will
not have as many, since they are more likely to lose some than to gain
any. In which case things will go forward. In the meantime, *nurse your
re-election*: I have a feeling that your absences from the Chamber have
not contributed any too much to ensure it.

Panama[60] is not finished, not by a long chalk. And it is a disgrace
that the trouble and honour of making disclosures should be left to the
Royalists and their dubious allies. They could not have a better battle cry
than: Down with the robbers, and if the great mass of the *stupid* countryside takes their part against the Republicans, it is to the cowardice of the
Radical Republicans[86] that they will owe this triumph. You say that the
republic is not in danger, that the deputies have returned from the recess
with this certainty; well, then, they should strike for all they are worth
and not let themselves be confused with the robbers by their silence. You
are quite right: the political ineptitude of the whole bourgeoisie defies the
imagination.

The only country where the bourgeoisie still has a little common
sense is England. Here the formation of the Independent Labour Party[114]
(though still in embryo) and its conduct in the Lancashire and Yorkshire
elections[a] have put a match to the government's backside; it is stirring itself, doing things unheard-of for a Liberal Government. The Registration
Bill[162] unifies the suffrage for all parliamentary, municipal, etc., elections,
2) adds at least 20 to 30 per cent to the working-class vote, 3) removes
the cost of election expenses from the candidates' shoulders and places
it on those of the government. The payment of an honorarium to M.P.s
is promised for the next session; and there are also a whole number of
juridical and economic measures for the benefit of workers. In short, the
Liberals recognise that, to make sure of governing at the present time,
they can do nothing but increase the political power of the working class
who will naturally kick them out afterwards.

---

[a] See this volume, pp.82-3, 87

The Tories, on the other hand, are behaving at the moment with unbounded stupidity. But once Home Rule[171] is on the Statute Book, they will realise that there is nothing for it but to enter the lists to gain power, and to that end there remains but one means: to win the working-class vote by political or economic concessions; thus Liberals and Conservatives cannot help extending the power of the working class, and hastening the time which will eliminate both the one and the other.

Amongst the workers here, things are going well. They begin to realise their strength more and more, and that there is only one way of using it, namely, by forming an independent party.

At the same time international feeling gains ground. In short, things are going well everywhere.

In Germany the dissolution of the Reichstag is always a possibility[76]; however, it lacks probability; everyone, apart from us, is afraid of it. We should win 50 to 60 seats.

On March 26th there will be an international conference at Brussels for the Zurich Congress.[172] Shall you go to it?

GOOD RIDDANCE TO YOUR TAENIA, and look after your bowels; I was going to make AN IRISH BULL by saying: they are the sinews of war!

Ever Yours,
F. Engels

First published in:
Cahiers internationaux,
No. 78, Paris, 1956

Printed according to the original

Translated from the French

62

ENGELS TO LAURA LAFARGUE[173]

AT LE PERREUX

London, 25 February 1893

My dear Laura,

You know the saying that the most important part of a woman's letter always is the postscript. But it's an infernal calumny, and I am going to prove it. In my last letter I not only did not put the principal subject in the body of the letter, but not even in the postscript, and have now to send it in a separate note.

And this is, about your silver wedding here on the 2nd of April. You know you have promised, and I keep you to your word. Now as it is as likely as not, or rather more likely, that Paul will have to go to the Brussels Conference, March 26th,[172] would it not be the best if you came direct from Paris about the same time he goes to Brussels and left him to come over from thence? Unless you prefer going with him and having a look at your native place which I am told has much improved in order to show itself worthy of the honour you conferred on it.

Anyhow it seems to me that it is getting time to make some preparations for the happy event, and so, not being able, or rather having forgotten to add this postscript to my last letter to you, I now tack it to the letter for Paul and hope you will take it into your most serious consideration and let us know your pleasure as soon as may be convenient.

Love from Louise and

Your ancient admirer
F. Engels

First published in
Cahiers initernationaux,
No. 78, Paris, 1956

Reproduced from the original

63

ENGELS TO THOMAS COOK AND SON[174]

IN LONDON

[Eastbourne], after 3 March 1893

Dear Sirs,

Your letter of the 3rd has been forwarded to me here.[175] The gentleman in question[a] is a young physician and member of the University of Vienna, Austria, where he graduated and practised with distinction.

---

[a] Ludwig Freyberger

He has been highly recommended to me by a prominent member of the Austrian Parliament,[a] and I have no doubt that you will find him a very desirable customer.

First published in:
Marx and Engels, *Works*,
Second Russian Edition,
Vol. 39, Moscow, 1966

Reproduced from the original

Published in English for the first time

64

ENGELS TO WILHELM LIEBKNECHT[176]

IN CHARLOTTENBURG—BERLIN

Eastbourne, 7 March 1893
28 Marine Parade

Would you send 6 or, if possible, *12 copies* of the article[b] to me in *London*. I have been in Eastbourne for the past few days so as to get a breath of fresh air[175]; peculiar climate—sometimes you can sit out very comfortably in the open and then it turns cold and windy again; so far, luckily, it hasn't rained much.

Kind regards to your family,

Your
F. E.

First published in:
Marx and Engels, *Works*,
First Russian Editition
Vol. XXIX, Moscow, 1946

Printed according to the original

Published in English for the first time

---

[a] Engelbert Pernerstorfer – [b] F. Engels, 'Can Europe Disarm?'

65

ENGELS TO FILIPPO TURATI[177]

IN MILAN

[Eastbourne,] 12 March 1893

Dear Citizen Turati,

I am sending you the proofs, though I have not been able to examine them in depth in the little time you gave me.[178] I am staying at the sea coast for a few days,[175] and the packet was sent to me here, which was a further loss of time.

You are free to add the programme of the International—that is, the Statutes and Preamble,[a] or the Inaugural Address of 1864,[b] as I do not have here a copy of the Russian edition of the Manifesto. I do not know exactly what it is you are talking of.

Thank you for the two brochures, which I shall read with great interest.

Mme Kulishov has probably received a letter from Mme Kautsky by now.

Greetings to Mme Kulishov and to yourself from Mme Kautsky and yours truly,

F. E.

First published, in the language of the original (French), in: *Annali*, an. I. Milano, 1958

Printed according to the original

Translated from the French

Published in English for the first time

---

[a] K. Marx, 'General Rules and Administrative Regulations of the International Working Men's Association'. – [b] K. Marx, 'Inaugural Address of the Working Men's International Association'.

66

ENGELS TO F. WIESEN[179]

IN BAIRD (TEXAS)

London,[180] 14 March 1893
122 Regent's Park Road, N. W.

Dear Comrade,

An accumulation of work has prevented me from replying any sooner to your note of 29 January.

I don't see why it should necessarily represent an infringement of the Social-Democratic principle if *a man* puts up candidates for some political office for which election is required and if *he* votes for those candidates, even *if he* is engaged in an attempt to abolish that office.

One might consider that the best way to abolish the Presidency and the Senate in America would be to elect to those posts men who had pledged themselves to bring about their abolition; it would then be logical for one to act accordingly. Others might consider this method to be inexpedient; it's a debatable point. There could be circumstances in which such a mode of action might also involve a denial of the revolutionary principle; why it should always and invariably be so, I entirely fail to see.

For the first objective of the labour movement is the conquest of political power for and by the working class. Once we are agreed on that, differences of opinion between upright men, in full command of their wits, as to the ways and means of struggle are unlikely to give rise to a dispute over principles.

In my view the best tactics in any given country are those which lead most quickly and surely to the goal. But in America in particular that goal is still a very long way off, and I believe I would not be wrong in attributing to this very circumstance the importance which is still sometimes attached to such academic issues over there.

I authorise you to publish these lines—unabridged.

Very sincerely yours,

F. Engels

First published, slightly abridged, in: *Briefe und Auszüge aus Briefen von Joh. Phil. Becker, Jos. Dietzgen, Friedrich Engels, Karl Marx u. A. an*

F. A. Sorge und Andere, Stuttgart, 1906 and in full (in English) in *Science and Society*, Vol. 11, No. 3, New York, 1938 Printed according to the original

67

ENGELS TO LAURA LAFARGUE[173]

AT LE PERREUX

Eastbourne,[175] 14th March 1893
28 Marine Parade

My dear Laura,

Well, that was a pleasant letter of yours. So we expect you as early as possible[a] in the course of next week, and once here, we shall not let you cross the Channel again under, *at least*, a fortnight or three weeks; even if the 'honourable member'[b] could not be spared from his agitating tour for so long.

We shall return on Friday[c] to London. On Saturday Louise and I have both promised to speak at the joint Commune Celebration of the Verein[62] and Bloomsbury Society[181]—a *joint* festival, though I'd rather have a good butcher's joint. The Sunday following is the Brussels Conference[172]—that is to say the *second* Sunday following, viz. the 26th; you do not say whether Paul will be there though it would be *very* important, on account of certain intrigues carried on by the old clique Hyndman-Brousse-Allemane, supported, for the time being, by Seidel, the secretary of the Zurich Committee[182] ; evidently a last attempt is going to be made by this brokendown lot to prepare for themselves a more favourable position at the Congress. From Brussels, Bebel[183] is almost certain to come to London for a few days and maybe Liebknecht too.

Now I should be uncommonly glad to have Paul and Bebel here together for a few days in order to do away once for all with certain French prejudices against Bebel who is by far the best man we have in Germany, in spite of what the French may consider his Teutonic rudeness. So you see I have a special interest of a political character, besides the personal one, in your showing up here early in the week.

I do not at all object to a *tour de France*[d] made by Paul in an organised electoral campaign; on the contrary I consider it a capital move. But a

---

[a] See this volume, p. 116 – [b] Paul Lafargue – [c] 17 March – [d] journey in France –

deputy after all has certain duties in the Chamber, especially in this Panama[60] time, and as every election depends, after all, on the votes of a goodly number of *plus ou moins indifferent*[a] philistines, it struck me that his re-election might be put in jeopardy by his neglect of his parliamentary functions. Indeed I have heard something to that effect hinted at. And when I saw his continued absence during some very important moments of the Panama crisis, I could not help thinking that he was losing some very important chances, and that all this could be brought up against him. *Après tout*,[b] it would be too much generosity on his part to prepare seats for others and lose his own. If you were as strong in France as our people in Germany, where above twenty seats belong to us almost *et par droit de conquête et par droit de naissance*,[c] then it would be different, but then such violent campaigns would not be required either.

To-day is Mohr's dying day, and just the tenth anniversary. Well, in strict confidence I can tell you, that the 3rd volume[d] is as good as ready. The most difficult section, Banks and Credit,[33] is finished; only two more sections remain, of which only one (Rent of Land)[e] may offer some *formal* difficulties. But all that remains to be done is mere child's play to what I had to do. Now I need no longer fear interruptions. What I had not been able to get before this last winter, was 4-5 months clear of such interruptions; now I've had them and the thing is as good as done. Only don't tell anyone, as I cannot yet fix the time, within a couple of months, when the Manuscript can go to the printer's.

As to what you say of Jaurès, that fills me with terror. *Normalien et ami, sinon protégé, de Malon*[f]—which of the two is worse? And yet, neither of them is a qualification equal to the superiority of a man who can write in Latin on the origin of German Socialism.[g]

Now then I must close. The sooner we hear from you in London about the day of your arrival and the earlier you fix that date, the better. *Ainsi donc, au revoir*,[h] from Louise and

your old

F. Engels

---

[a] more or less apathetic – [b] after all – [c] both by right of conquest and by birthright – [d] of *Capital* – [e] Section VI (see present edition, Vol. 37) – [f] Malon's fellow-student and friend, if not protégé – [g] J. Jaurès, *De primis socialismi germanici lineamentis apud Lutherum, Kant, Fichte et Hegel.* – [h] Thus, till we meet.

Of course I shall send you a bit of a compromising document—a trifle of a ... chèque, saving your presence! I have not got any here with me, else it would follow herewith.

First published in
Cahiers internationaux,
No. 78, Paris, 1956

Reproduced from the original

68

ENGELS TO MARIA MENDELSON

IN LONDON

Eastbourne,[175] 15 March 1893
28 Marine Parade

My dear Mme Mendelson,

I could not describe the joy with which Mme Kautsky and I received this morning the news that St.[a] is once more out of danger—we talked of him yesterday evening with some anxiety. All's well that ends well, and I cannot wait to see him again on Saturday[b] evening—in any case, we hope to have the pleasure of seeing both of you on Sunday at our place.

We have been here for a fortnight, and we are returning to London the day after tomorrow. The weather is wonderful, and the sea breezes have done us a great deal of good.

Au revoir! Very best wishes from Mme Kautsky.

Your devoted friend,
F. Engels

We are expecting Bebel on Monday or Tuesday,[183] and M. and Mme Lafargue a few days later.

First Published in:
Marx and Engels, *Works*,
First Russian Edition
Vol. XXIX, Moscow, 1946

Printed according to the original

Translated from the French
Published in English for the first time

---

[a] Stanislaw Mendelson – [b] 18 March

69

ENGELS TO HENRY DEMAREST LLOYD[184]

IN CHICAGO

[Draft]

Eastbourne, middle of March 1893

Dear Sir,

I have duly received your two favors of 3/2 and 9/3 with enclosures. I very much regret that I shall not be able either to assist personally at your Congresses[185] or to supply the papers you ask me for. I should send them to you with the greatest pleasure, were it not that all my time is at present taken up with the manuscript of the third book of my late friend Karl Marx's great work on Capital, which I am preparing for publication. This third book ought to have been out years ago; but never until now could I secure that continued freedom from interruption which alone will enable me to finish my task. I have been compelled to decline all outside work, though ever so tempting, unless absolutely necessary. By the time your congress meets, the MS ought to go to press, but this could not be, were I to accede to your request. For the work you ask me to do ought not to be journalistic commonplace; it ought to be the very best I can furnish, it would require mature study and thought; and that means a considerable amount of time, which for the reasons given, I am not in a position to sacrifice.

I have, however, forwarded you per bookpost a copy of the English edition of the *Communist Manifesto* of 1848 (by K. Marx and myself) and another of my *Socialism: Utopian and Scientific*[a] published a few months ago, as a small tribute which I hope may prove of interest to some members of your Labor Congress.

First published in:
Marx and Engels, *Works*,
First Russian Edition,
Vol. XXIX, Moscow, 1946

Reproduced from the original

---

[a] translated by E. Aveling and published in London in 1892

70

ENGELS TO FRIEDRICH ADOLPH SORGE[186]

IN HOBOKEN

London, 18 March 1893

Dear Sorge,

We have just spent a fortnight by the sea at Eastbourne[175] where we had magnificent weather and whence we have returned greatly refreshed. Now we can get down to work again. But in fact the visiting season is once more upon us—next Sunday (tomorrow week) there's the Brussels Conference on the Zurich Congress,[172] when Bebel will nip over here for a few days[183] the Lafargues will be coming at the same time and I am glad to have again inveigled the young man over here so that he and I can discuss French affairs at some length. All the same I ought still to have enough time left to finish off Volume III[a] since I am now over the worst.

The matter of the *Socialiste* has now been settled.

It would seem that a crash is the only solution to the silver business in America.[187] For Cleveland does not, it seems, have either the strength or the courage to smash this vicious circle of corruption. And it really would be a good thing if there were to be a crisis. A nation—a *young* nation—so proud of its 'practice' and at the same time so frightfully bone-headed in the matter of theory as America can only eradicate so ingrained an idée fixe at the cost of damage to itself. The plausible idea that, if one has no money when one needs it, this is because there is not enough money in the world at large, is a childish notion common both to the PAPER CURRENCY nonsense à la Kellogg and to the silver nonsense, and the surest cure for it is experimentation and bankruptcy which last might also prove quite beneficial to ourselves in other respects. Provided only some sort of tariff reform is achieved this autumn, there will be no need for you to repine, for the rest will surely follow. The main thing is that American industry is becoming capable of competing on the world market.

Over here things are going *very well*. The masses are undoubtedly on the move, and of this you will find details in Aveling's admittedly somewhat long-winded reports in the *Volkszeitung.* The best evidence of this

---

[a] of *Capital*

is the fact that the old sects are losing ground and having to fall into line, The *Social Democratic Federation*[44] has actually deposed Mr Hyndman; every so often he is allowed to do a little grumbling and grousing about international politics in *Justice*, but he is finished, HIS OWN PEOPLE HAVE FOUND HIM OUT. For the space of ten years the man lost no opportunity of provoking me personally and politically, and I never did him the honour of replying, in the conviction that he himself was man enough to effect his own ruin; eventually I was proved right. After a whole decade of carping they recently invited Tussy to write reports on the international movement for *Justice*, an invitation she naturally declined pending the public retraction of the infamous calumnies of herself and Aveling which *Justice* has for years been the vehicle.

The same thing is happening where the Fabians[43] are concerned. As in the case of the Social Democratic Federation, their own branches in the provinces have outgrown them; in this, as in the Chartist movement, Lancashire and Yorkshire are again taking the lead. Men like Sidney Webb, Bernard Shaw, etc., who WANTED TO PERMEATE THE LIBERALS WITH SOCIALISM, must now submit to being permeated BY THE SPIRIT OF THE WORKINGMEN MEMBERS OF THEIR OWN SOCIETY. They fret and fume but IT'S NO USE—either they remain on their own, officers without soldiers, or they conform. The first seems more likely and is also more desirable.

The Independent Labour Party[114]—as the latest arrival—has brought with it fewer ingrained prejudices, contains good elements, the working men of the North being the arbiters, and to that extent is the most genuine expression of the present movement, True, there are amongst the leaders all kinds of odd individuals and even many of the best, as in America where you are, have acquired the parliamentary system's deplorable habit of cliquism, but they have the support of the masses who will either teach them how to behave or throw them overboard. They still make blunders and plenty of them, but the worst perils are over and I now look for rapid progress which will not be without its repercussions in America.

In Germany the situation has almost reached crisis point. According to the last reports on the sessions of the Military Committee a compromise would hardly seem possible.[76] The government is making it impossible for the gentlemen of the Centre[71] and the Free Thinkers[149] to change sides,[a] and a majority cannot be obtained without 40 or 50 of their number. So

---

[a] See this volume, p. 101

there'll be a dissolution and new elections. *If all goes well*, I reckon that we shall get 2 1/2 million votes, for our numbers have grown like mad. Bebel's estimate is 50 or 60 seats, for the geography of the constituencies is not in our favour and all the others band together against us so that, in the second ballot, we cannot convert even substantial minorities into majorities. I would rather that things carried on as they are until 1895 when we should be able to make an impact of a very different order, but no matter what happens everything, from Richter to Little Willy,[a] must needs help us on our way.

A young man from Texas, F. Wiesen of Baird, wanted me to make a statement deploring the nomination of candidates 'for President' as a denial of the revolutionary principle, since the intention was to abolish the Presidency, I sent him the enclosed answer.[b] Should a *garbled* version be made public, be so good as to get the *Volkszeitung* to print this.

I trust you and your wife are now enjoying better health. Warm regards to you both from Mrs Kautsky and

Your

F. Engels

We have sent you the debate on the future organization of society.[143] Newspapers may have been somewhat irregular while we were away, but should be complete.

First published, slightly abridged, in: *Briefe und Auszüge aus Briefen von Joh. Phil. Becker, Jos. Dietzgen, Friedrich Engels, Karl Marx u. A. an F. A. Sorge und Andere,*

Stuttgart, 1906 and, in full, in English, in *Science and Society*, Vol. II, No. 3, New York, 1938

Printed according to the original

---

[a] William II – [b] See this volume, p. 119

71

ENGELS TO KARL KAUTSKY

IN STUTTGART

London, 20 March 1893

Dear Baron,

Lessner's article[a] reads very well though it certainly cost Ede a vast amount of work to lick it into some sort of literary shape. As to the *Neue Rheinische Zeitung*'s review, I once remarked—the notion suddenly came into my head—that it would be by no means a bad idea if the whole thing were to be reprinted *en bloc* and that this might be suggested to Dietz. On further consideration I realised, of course, that there were sundry snags and that it would saddle me with more work than I could properly take on until Volume III[b] was finished, so I thought no more about it. But Lessner seems to throw himself into literature with the same impetuosity as once he did into painting.

As a matter of principle I have ceased to read anything further on the rate of profit, not having read either little Schmidt's second article[c] or that by Landé.[d] These must wait until I get to the preface to Vol. III. In the meantime your irrepressible private adversary, Stiebeling, has again sent me his latest opus,[e] hoping—though probably in vain—that I shall accord it a kindly notice.

As to the source of the nonsensical report about my illness, I am completely in the dark, but there was not the least occasion for it. Nor can I discover where it first appeared or in what paper, so I have no clue whatever to go by. Still, we have cracked divers bottles in honour of my serious loss of strength and my hourly awaited demise.[f]

Five of the seven sections of Vol. III have been finished but for the—formal—final editing; the main difficulty, the section on credit,[33] has

---

[a] F. Leßner, 'Erinnerungen eines Arbeiters an Karl Marx. Zu dessen zehnjährigem Todestage, 14. März 1893', *Die Neue Zeit*, No, 24, Stuttgart, 1892/93. – [b] of *Capital* – [c] C. Schmidt, 'Die Durchschnittsprofitrate und das Marx'sche Werthgesetz', *Die Neue Zeit*, Nos. 3, 4, Stuttgart, 1892/93. – [d] H. Landé, 'Mehrwerth und Profit. Ein ökonomischer Versuch', *Die Neue Zeit*, Nos. 19, 20, Stuttgart, 1892/93. – [e] G. Stiebeling, *Das Problem der Durchschnitts=Profitrate. Kritik einer Kritik mit einem Nachtrag.* – [f] See this volume, pp. 92-93, 107

been overcome. I am now on rent[a] which may take up yet more time, so I still can't say *when*. This is *between ourselves*.

Had I known that you were still prepared to continue working on the *Theories of Surplus Value*,[102] I should have let you keep it, but having heard nothing for years and as I need the Ms. occasionally for purposes of comparison in connection with Vol. III, I wrote asking you for it. In view of your other activities there would, after all, have probably been considerable uncertainty about when you might be done with this and subsequent instalments.[b] We shall settle this account shortly.

The manifold plans regarding the *Neue Zeit* would seem to have been consigned to oblivion—let us hope it will carry on, even without such violent revolutions, But it still seems to me that the fundamental shortcoming lies in the fact that the contents are aimed at *one* kind of reader, while the price is based on *another*.[c]

Over here the movement is making excellent progress. The danger of sectarianism—presented both by the Social Democratic Federation[44] and by the Fabians[43]—has been largely averted; the Independent Labour Party[114] will either absorb them or spur them on and get rid of their useless leaders. The masses, especially in the North, in the industrial areas, are finally and indubitably on the move. Blunders and dirty tricks there will still be in plenty, but that can be dealt with. The day before yesterday Aveling was in Manchester where the Executive of the Independent Labour Party were holding their first meeting. The resolutions were quite satisfactory. Aveling was chosen to represent it in Brussels[172] and later also in Zurich,[56] along with Keir Hardie and Shaw Maxwell. No doubt you will be hearing more from Ede. (This is in confidence, of course; I don't know what the chaps intend to publish.)

Kindest regards.

Your
F. E.

First published in: Printed according to the original
Aus der Frühzeit des Marxismus.
Engels Briefwechsel mit Kautskys,   Published in English for the first time
Prag, 1935

---

[a] Section VI, *Capital*, Vol. III (see present edition, Vol. 37) – [b] See Engels, letter to K. Kautsky of 24 December 1892 (present edition, Vol. 49) and this volume, p. 71 – [c] See this volume, p. 50

72

ENGELS TO LAURA LAFARGUE

AT LE PERREUX

London, 21 March 1893

My dear Löhr,

I hope you had my letter from Eastbourne.[175] We returned here on Friday all the better for our holiday.[a]

Today I have a letter from that eternal bore Argyriades (*zu deutsch Silbermannssohn*,[b] and quite as depreciated as the metal he takes his name from) asking me for an 'article' (*rien que ça!*)[c] for his *numéro unique*[d] of his May Journal; and that in the name of the *Commission d'organisation de la Manifestation du 1-r mai—cet Argyriades argenté n'est pas l'homme aux trois cheveux comme Cadet Rousselle, mais bien l'homme aux trois adresses*[e]: 1) Question Sociale, 5 Boulevard S. Michel, in a red flag over the left; 2) Commission d'organisation, 108 rue du Temple, in a timber over the right, and 3) P. Argyriades himself, 49 rue de Rivoli over the leaf at the bottom.

Well, as I am quite in the dark about the ins and outs, the *amitiés, inimitiés et neutralités*[f] the various sets in Paris, I don't know what to reply and should be glad if you would kindly tell me how our friends are placed with regard to the *Commission d'organisation* in general and the silvery Grec and his Blanquist friends in particular and what I had better do? As to an article, that is out of the question, at the very outside I should send him what the Yankees call a 'sentiment'.

And perhaps you can tell us at the same time when we may expect you here? which question reminds me of something else, namely of the necessity of not forgetting to enclose the cheque for ten pounds with which I remain, with love from Louise

Yours affectionately,
F. Engels

---

[a] See this volume, pp. 117-123 – [b] in German Silbermannssohn (Silvermanson) – [c] nothing less – [d] unique number – [e] Organising Commission of the May Day Demonstration—this silvery Argyriades is not like Cadet Rousselle, a man with three hairs, but a man with three addresses. – [f] friendships, enmities and neutralities

First published, in the language
of the original (English), in:
F. Engels, P. et L. Lafargue,
Correspondance, t. III, 1891-1895,
Paris, 1959

Reproduced from the original

73

ENGELS TO AUGUST RADIMSKY

IN VIENNA

London, 21 March 1893

Dear Comrade Radimsky,

In reply to your esteemed note of the 18th inst., I can only tell you how glad I am that the *Communist Manifesto* will be appearing in Czech translation as well.[188] It goes without saying that, so far as I am concerned, there is absolutely no objection at all; on the contrary, it will give not only me but also Marx's daughters the utmost pleasure.

But if Adler told you that I have a 'command' of the Czech language, he was, so far as I am concerned, pitching it a bit high. I am happy if, with much toil and the help of a dictionary, I can understand one column in a newspaper. Nevertheless I much look forward to the numbers of the *Délnické Listy* you have been so kind as to promise me. They'll help me to keep my hand in rather better.

With cordial regards to the Czech comrades and to you yourself.

Yours truly,
F. Engels

First published, slightly abridged,
in: *Karel Marx a Bedrich Engels,*
Komunisticky manifest, Vidén, 1893
and, in full, in the book: *Victor Adlers
Aufsätze Reden und Briefe.*
Erstes Heft: *Victor Adler und*

Friedrich Engels, Wien, 1922

Printed according to the text of the book

Published in English the first time

74

ENGELS TO JULIE BEBEL

IN BERLIN

London, 31 March 1893

Dear Mrs Bebel,

August's presence[183] has made me conscious of the shameful fact that I have long owed you an answer to your kind letter, so I have at once taken up my pen lest you should continue to have cause to resent my tardiness. August, I can assure you, is exceptionally well and takes his raw eggs in brandy with admirable punctuality. The fact that his stomach is in excellent fettle was proved conclusively last evening at the Mendelsons and still more so later on at home, for after that good but truly enormous supper he slept more soundly than any of us.

We are expecting Burns here today and thus, for the first time in history, three Socialist members of parliament from Germany, France[a] and England will come together. That such a meeting should be possible, a meeting of the three deputies of the three leading parliaments of Europe—three Socialist Party leaders representing the three dominant nations of Europe—is in itself proof of what enormous advances we have made. I only wish that Marx were alive to witness it.

Well, now it is also time to remind you of your promise to visit us here in the summer and take me back with you to Germany.[189] True, August is afraid that a possible dissolution of the Reichstag might upset everything, but that is something I cannot see, for if there is in fact a dissolution, it will happen this month, i.e. in April (which will be upon us tomorrow), while the elections will be held in June at the latest,[76] in which case a holiday will be more necessary than ever—for August as well as for yourself—and if you were to see the fine weather we have here and all the greenness of spring which also brings with it a mass of flowers that lasts until the end of June, you would assuredly come, dissolutions and fresh elections or not. So, as always, I shall count on your keeping your word and shall also accompany you to Berlin, for since last autumn our respective trips have been indissolubly linked.

---

[a] Paul Lafargue

And now for yet another matter. August had taken it into his head to return on Monday.[a] But over the past ten years or so Easter Monday has become a proper holiday over here—one of the four so-called Bank Holidays.[190] It is a real popular festival. That being the case, all the railways are busy with extra trains and excursion parties, all the stations are filled to overflowing and all the regular trains are neglected by the management, since what matters is the extra profit. These Bank Holidays are the only days in the year when it is somewhat dangerous to travel on English trains, and consequently no one travels on those days unless he has to. We therefore implored August to abandon his plan and not leave until Tuesday, which he has promised to do. I am positive you will agree that he shouldn't travel on a day when arrivals and departures are never punctual and when all the accidents that didn't occur during the previous three months have a habit of occurring all on one day.

And now I shall take a hearty swig in honour of your coming visit—for we are at this moment enjoying our morning glass of ale.

With warm regards,

Yours,

F. Engels

First published in: Printed according to the original
Marx and Engels, *Works*,
First Russian Edition,   Published in English for the first time
Vol. XXIX, Moscow, 1946

75

ENGELS TO M. R. COTAR[191]

IN PARIS

[Draft]

[London,] 8 April 1893[b]

Dear Comrade,

I have kept your letter of 21/3 on one side for some time. Lafargue and Mrs Lafargue were on the point of coming over here and I therefore

---

[a] 3 April – [b] 1892 in the Ms.

wished to take the opportunity of consulting *both* Marx's daughters personally about your inquiry.

You are totally unknown not only to me but also to the Lafargues, and you will understand that it wouldn't do to entrust a total stranger with a matter as important and as difficult as the French translation of Volume II of *Capital*.

Apart from a thorough knowledge of the German language, it also calls for an equally thorough grounding in economics, and this, unfortunately, is to be found only very rarely amongst young socialists. That is something that would also have to be discussed beforehand.

Next, you seek my collaboration—and on this score all I can say to you is that for years to come my time will be fully occupied with projects that are of at least equal importance.

Most important of all, however, and this alone might give actuality to your inquiry, is that there should be a publisher for the translation. If you have one, that and nothing else would repay the trouble involved in taking the other questions into consideration.

Yours very truly

First published in:
Marx and Engels, *Works*,
First Russian Edition,
Vol. XXIX, Moscow, 1946

Printed according to the original

Published in English for the first time

76

ENGELS TO GEORGE WILLIAM LAMPLUGH[192]

IN PORT ERIN (ISLE OF MAN)

London, 11th April 1893
122 Regent's Park Road, N. W.

My dear Lamplugh,

Thank you for dropping the formalities. I, as you see, do the same. We should have been very glad to see you and your wife and children here, but I know what London is to a man who visits it with his complete family and so we'll excuse you this time, but this is the last time we do excuse you.

I am glad your life as a surveyor suits you so very well. It must be a great relief to you after the boring work in the office and in the corn exchange of East Riding. I would like it for a short time too, but only for a short time. In the long run, I couldn't live without the hum of a big town. I have always lived in big cities. Nature is wonderful. I have always liked going back to her as a change from the movement of history, but History, after all, seems even more wonderful than Nature to me. It took Nature millions of years to produce conscious beings and now it takes these conscious beings thousands of years to act together consciously; conscious not only of their actions as individuals, but also of their actions as a mass; acting together, and effecting in common a common purpose, willed by them in advance. That end we are now on the point of attaining. And to watch this process, this approaching accomplishment of a thing never before attained in the history of our earth, seems to me a spectacle worth looking at, and for the whole of my past life I have been unable to turn my eyes away from it. However, it is tiring, especially if you believe you are called upon to co-operate in the process; and then the study of Nature comes in as a grand relief and remedy. For after all, Nature and History are the two components in which we live, move and have our being.

Kind remembrance from all friends here.

Ever yours
F. Engels

First published in
Letopisi marksizma, Book I,
Moscow-Leningrad, 1926

Reproduced from the original

First written in English

77

ENGELS TO FRANZ MEHRING[193]

IN BERLIN

London, 11 April 1893

Dear Mr Mehring,

Naturally I have not the slightest objection to your printing the passage from my letter of 28 September you copied out and sent me. All I would ask is that you make one change in the final sentence:

'while the Lavergne-Peguilhenian generalisation would be reduced to its true content, namely that feudal society engenders a feudal world order'.[194]

The original wording is really too slipshod.

I look forward to seeing the *Lessing-Legende* published on its own. That kind of thing is greatly impaired if brought out piecemeal. It was very meritorious of you to work your way through the tangled mass of Prussian history and to establish the correct correlations therein. The Prussia of today makes this absolutely essential, however disagreeable the work as such may be. There are various points, especially in this or that passage where you retrace the links with the preceding period, on which I do not entirely see eye to eye with you, but that does not prevent me from saying that yours is by far the best work that exists on this period of German history.

Yours very truly,
F. Engels

First published in:
Marx and Engels, *Works*,
First Russian Edition,
Vol. XXIX, Moscow, 1946

Printed according to a handwritten
copy by Franz Mehring

Published in English for the first time

78

ENGELS TO JULES GUESDE

IN PARIS

[London], 14 April 1893

My dear Guesde,

I am sending you my short piece[a] for your May number.[b]

Lafargue has told me that you are ill. I wish you a rapid and total recovery.

We indeed have need of you as our Roubaix deputy. This time we must

---

[a] F. Engels – [b] *Le Socialiste*

succeed in getting a small, compact column[156] into the Palais Bourbon which will establish once and for all, and without any possibility of misunderstanding, the nature of French socialism, so that all the disparate elements are obliged to rally around it.

Only then will the French socialists be able to recover throughout the world the standing that is theirs by right, and the important position that they must occupy in the general interest.

Yours sincerely,
F. Engels

First published in:
A. Zévaès, *De l'introduction du marxisme en France*,
Paris, 1947

Printed according to the book

Translated from the French

Published in English for the first time

79

ENGELS TO LAURA LAFARGUE

AT LE PERREUX

London, 25 April 1893

My dear Laura,

As for the last few days we have neither heard from you nor seen any papers with your handwriting on them, we are beginning to be anxious about your health, and the enclosed letter from Ravé with the influenza atmosphere it breathes, is not encouraging either. It is this letter which puts the pen into my hands to-day. I don't know anything about any of the points he mentions.[195] At all events, I do not want to write to him anything which may interfere with what you have been good enough to do in the matter. Therefore

1. Herewith a portrait—but could they not secure the cliché[a] of the one which appeared in the *Illustration*[196] (believe) about last May? that would be cheaper.

---

[a] negative

2. The title I have no objection to, not knowing what you may have proposed or might prefer. I leave that, like the rest, entirely in your hands.

3. The proof-sheets are no use to me. I write to him[25] that I sent his letter to you, to settle all points, and that I shall be quite satisfied if he sends the proofs to you.

I returned last night from Manchester, where I assisted at the funeral of poor Gumpert (he was cremated). He fell ill, as you heard while here, last December of angina pectoris, which, brought on embolism of the brain with partial paralysis, and succumbed last Thursday[a] to a fresh attack, after fearful sufferings.

May Day here is as confused as in Paris. The Eight Hours Committee and the Trades Council[197] are sure to have a separate demonstration each. And in this critical period Aveling falls ill, the Hull Dock Strike[198] intervenes and may lead to a general Dock and Shipping Strike all over the kingdom, giving Tussy more to do than she can manage—so that nobody knows how matters will go.

I hope you received Louise's[b] letter sent on Saturday,[c] and I hope moreover soon to learn that you have got over your fit of influenza.

Salut au citoyen Représentant,[d] if he is about.

Love from Louise and from

Yours affectionately
F. Engels

First published, in the language of the original (English), in: F. Engels, P. et L. Lafargue, *Correspondance*, t. III, 1891-1895, Paris, 1959

Reproduced from the original

---

[a] 20 April – [b] Kautsky – [c] 22 April – [d] Greetings to the citizen deputy (Paul Lafargue)

80

ENGELS TO LUDWIG SCHORLEMMER

IN DARMSTADT

London, 29 April 1893

My dear Schorlemmer,

I got your letter of 22 March and then the notification of your daughter's death. Please accept my heartfelt condolences. Your earlier letters had already prepared me for it and from what you had said it was hardly to be expected that she would survive the spring. And if, as in your case, one is constantly a witness to the suffering caused by illness, while knowing that no remedy exists, one is bound in the end to resign oneself more readily to the final deliverance. Mrs Kautsky also asks me to convey to you her sincere condolences.

Death has also claimed its victims over here. Last December Dr Gumpert suddenly went down with an incurable heart complaint and on the 20th of this month he died of it. Last Monday[a] I attended the burial, or rather cremation, in Manchester. Unfortunately I had to get back the same day and thus missed the chance of looking up Siebold or Klepsch and could not therefore glean any further information on the subject of the estate. This is another matter that will be adversely affected by Gumpert's death. He was an energetic man who, especially in the case of the ailing Siebold, managed successfully to hurry things on, and, in view of the friendly relations we had enjoyed for many years, was glad to be of help. I have heard absolutely nothing more about the manuscripts and publisher's contracts. If you are unable to tell me anything about this, I shall write to Siebold again shortly.[199]

I recall having seen Dr Spiegel on one occasion over here years ago. I think he will make a thoroughly good job of Carl's career and attainments as a chemist.[200] Unfortunately it wouldn't do to publish anything more than that in a scientific journal.

Your hopes for a dissolution of the Reichstag[76] will in all likelihood be fulfilled within the next week or fortnight. Caprivi has got himself into such a fix that he probably cannot concede as much as the gentle-

---

[a] 24 April

men of the Centre[71] and the Free Thinkers[149]—who are bent on compromise—could consent to without imperilling the existence of their
parties. I would rather that the dissolution were postponed until 1895;
by that time we shall occupy a very different position and may become
the crucial party in the Reichstag. One way or the other, we're bound to
benefit by it.

At Easter, or rather on Good Friday,[a] a German member of the
Reichstag—Bebel—a French deputy—Lafargue—and an English member of parliament—Burns—Socialists all three—met for the first time at
my house. A historical milestone too.

With sincere regards from Mrs Kautsky and myself

Yours,

F. Engels

First published in:
Marx and Engels, *Works*,
First Russian Edition,
Vol. XXIX, Moscow, 1946

Printed according to the original

Published in English for the firs time

81

ENGELS TO PABLO IGLESIAS

IN MADRID

[Draft]

London, April 1893

Dear friend Iglesias,

I cannot answer your letter without first complaining of your addressing me formally with *usted*. I don't think I have deserved this. We are old
members of the International and have been fighting side by side, for over
twenty years in the same battles. When I was your Secretary for Spain,
your people did me the honour of addressing me informally with *tú*,[b] and
so I ask you to go on in the same way.

Enclosed herewith are a few lines[c] for your May issue,[d] I have written

---

[a] 31 March – [b] an equivalent of French vous and tu – [c] F. Engels, 'To the Spanish Workers
—on the First of May 1893'. – [d] *El Socialista*

to Eleanor Marx-Aveling and to Bebel, asking them to contribute their share.

Regards and revolution,
Yours

First published in:
Marx and Engels, *Works*,
First Russian Edition,
Vol. XXIX, Moscow, 1946

Printed according to the original

Translated from the Spanish

Published in English for the first time

82

ENGELS TO FRIEDRICH ADOLPH SORGE[186]

IN HOBOKEN

London, 17 May 1893

Dear Sorge,

The Lincoln affair happened while I was still in Manchester—at the end of 1864—but I have no more than a hazy recollection of it, nor, amongst Marx's and my papers, have I ever set eyes on Lincoln's reply.[201] Maybe I shall come upon it tucked away somewhere, if ever I get round to sorting out and classifying the chaotic mass of stuff, but of that there can be no question unless I have three or four weeks to devote to it. All I can find is in Eichhoff's pamphlet on the International, Berlin, 1868 (based on notes and material of Marx's); p. 53 reads:

'Lincoln's re-election on 8 November 1864 was an occasion for the General Council to send him an address with its best wishes. At the same time, it called mass meetings in support of the Union's cause. That was why Lincoln, in his message of reply, expressly acknowledged the services of the International Working Men's Association for the good cause.'[a]

In short, all I can say is that such material as I have on the International

---

[a] W. Eichhoff, *Die Internationale Arbeiterassociation...* (see present edition, Vol. 21, pp. 361-62).

Working Men's Association *before 1870* is very incomplete—some of the General Council's minutes, Marx's and Lessner's, and also partly Becker's[a] collections of newspaper cuttings and, finally, Marx's letters to myself. I haven't even got a complete set of the General Council's official documents, proclamations, etc., let alone the correspondence of the secretaries who retained virtually all of it. There are no official Congress minutes at all. Nevertheless, it's far better than anything anyone else has got, and I shall classify it as soon as I can. But when?

Volume III[b] is progressing steadily. I have reached the two final sections[c] and here too, I think, the worst is now behind me. But there's still several weeks' work to be done on them, after which I shall proceed to the final editing. I should like to send part of it to press before the summer holidays but don't know whether I shall manage this. The final editing can be done while printing is actually in progress. And the matter is becoming urgent, for it looks as though we in Germany are about to enter a period of great turmoil and struggle which means that the thing has got to be finished before then.

What my views are concerning German affairs you can see from the interview in *Le Figaro*[d] which I am sending you by the same post as this. As in all interviews, the text has in parts become somewhat insipid and the thread sometimes gets lost, but otherwise it has been correctly reported. The morale of our people in Germany is altogether excellent; so far as they are concerned, the election campaign is a real boon and they revel in it, despite all the trouble and effort it costs them. Bebel, who spent a week here at Eastertime[183]—after the Brussels Conference[172]—is a new man and writes to say that; in addition to Hamburg, he has been asked to stand for Strasbourg in Alsace where in 1890 we had 4,800 votes as against 8,200, and where a lot of the Francophils will vote for him. There are between a hundred and a hundred and ten constituencies in which we shall be kicking off with more than one third of the total poll (to go by the 1890 results) and in some eighty of the constituencies we shall, I think, either get in straight away or else in the second ballot. How many will fall by the wayside in the latter depends on the opposition candidate. Against Conservatives[202] or National Liberals[203] our chances are very good, less so against Freisinnige[149] and still less so against the Centre

---

[a] Johann Philipp Becker – [b] of *Capital* – [c] Sections VI and VII (see present edition, Vol. 37) – [d] Interview of Frederick Engels to the correspondent of *Le Figaro* on 11 May 1893

supposing our opponents' candidate sticks to his guns over the military question.[76] Bebel hopes for 50 or 60 seats in all.[204]

The atmosphere in Germany has changed a lot and, though the bourgeois press may still vociferate as loudly as ever, the respect our people now command in the Reichstag has gained for them a position very different from before. Nor is it possible for anyone to turn a blind eye to the ever-growing might of the party. If, at the next elections, we again show a marked increase, respect may grow on the one hand but so, on the other, will fear. And the latter will drive the worthy philistines of one accord into the government camp.

The May Day celebrations over here were very nice, but although they only happen once a year, they are already becoming almost a routine affair; they have lost their first bloom. Once again the narrow outlook of the Trades Council[197] and of the socialist sects—Fabians[43] and Social Democratic Federation[44]—has led to our having two demonstrations. But everything went according to plan and we—the Eight Hour Day Committee—drew a far bigger crowd than the combined opposition. Our international platform,[205] in particular, was very well attended. I would estimate that there were in all 240,000 people in the park, of whom we had 140,000 and the opposition 100,000 at the outside.

Champion, with his TORY and LIBERAL UNIONIST funds[206] (allegedly £100 for each of the 100 working-class candidates agreeing to stand in hopeless constituencies merely in order to deprive the Liberals of votes), has been made a thorough fool of by our old friend Maltman Barry. This blockhead, if Scottish speculator, has joined the Tories of whom, by his own admission,[a] he is the paid agent, and would seem to have been planted alongside Champion, whom the fund-dispensing Tories do not altogether trust, as a sleeping partner and watchdog—what the Jesuits call a *socius*. Thus, during Champion's illness, he was sole editor of the *Labour Elector*, and told such improbable tales *out of school* that he quite spoiled his own little game, thus temporarily saving the Independent Labour Party[114] from becoming the pawn of the aforesaid gentry. Unfortunately Aveling has been seriously ill for a month now; in view of the constant caballing that goes on here, he cannot well be spared. He has gone to Hastings[207] to recuperate for a while.

If we should poll a considerably larger number of votes in Germany, this

---

[a] See this Volume, p. 84

will have a favourable effect on the elections this autumn in France.[208] If our people there get a dozen men into the Chamber (they are counting on getting four seats in the Département du Nord alone), it will mean they'll have a nucleus there that will be strong enough to compel the Blanquists[20] and Allemanists[21] to join forces with them.

I am glad that your wife and you are better again. Warm regards to her and to yourself from L. Kautsky and

Your

F. Engels

First published in:
*Briefe und Auszüge aus
Briefen von Joh. Phil. Becker,
Jos. Dietzgen, Friedrich Engels,
Karl Marx u. A, an F. A. Sorge
und Andere,* Stuttgart, 1906

Printed according to the original

83

ENGELS TO PYOTR LAVROV

IN PARIS

London, 21 May 1893

My dear Lavrov,

The day before yesterday I sent you by post a book by N. F. Danielsont: *Ocherki Nashego Poreformennogo Khozyaistva.*[a]

He also informed me that the parents of our friend H. Lopatin have had news of him, and that he is well.[209]

You promised to send me a copy of the brochure in which you were going to publish a letter of Lopatin in which I am mentioned—I still have not received it.[97] As I have been told that it has appeared, the packet must have gone astray in the post. Could you send me another copy?

---

[a] The title of the book, *Outlines of Our Post-Reform Economy,* is written by Engels in Russian.

I hope you are keeping well—just as I am, with no reason to complain.

Yours truly,
F. Engels

First published in:
Marx and Engels, *Works*,
First Russian Edition,
Vol. XXIX, Moscow, 1946

Printed according to the original

Translated from the French

Published in English for the first time

84

ENGELS TO ISAAC A. HOURWICH[184]

IN CHICAGO

London, 27 May 1893
122 Regent's Park Road, N. W.

Dr. Isaac A. Hourwich
Dear Sir,

Many thanks for your interesting study on the Economics of the Russian Village,[a] which I read, I hope, not without profit.

As to the burning questions of the Russian revolutionary movement, the part which the peasantry may be effected to take in it, these are subjects on which I could not conscientiously state an opinion for publication without previously studying over again the whole subject and completing my very imperfect knowledge of the facts of the case by bringing it up to date.[210] But for that I am sorry to say I have not at present the time. And then, I have every reason to doubt whether such a public statement by me would have the effect you expect of it. I know from my own experience of 1849-52 how unavoidably a political emigration splits itself up into a number of divergent factions, so long as the mother-country remains quiet. The burning desire to act, face to face with the impossibility of

---

[a] I. A. Hourwich, *The Economics of the Russian Village*.

doing anything effective, causes in many intelligent and energetic heads an over-active mental speculation, an attempt at discovering or inventing new and almost miraculous means of action. The word of an outsider would have but a trifling, and at best a passing effect. If you have followed the Russian emigration literature of the last decade, you will yourself know how, for instance, passages from Marx's writings and correspondence have been interpreted in the most contradictory ways, exactly as if they had been texts from the Classics or from the New Testament, by various sections of Russian emigrants. Whatever I might say on the subject you mention, would probably share the same fate, if any attention was paid to it. And so from all these various reasons, I think it best for all whom it may concern, including myself, to abstain.

Yours very truly
F. Engels

First published, abridged, in:
G. Mayer, *Friedrich Engels. Eine Biographieg*, Bd. II, Haag, 1934, and in full in:
Marx and Engels, *Works*, First Russian Edition, Vol. XXIX, Moscow, 1946

Reproduced from the copy of the original

85

ENGELS TO HENRY DEMAREST LLOYD

IN CHICAGO

London, 27 May 1893
122 Regent's Park Road, N. W.

Dear Sir,

I beg to acknowledge receipt of your book *A Strike of Millionaires against Miners,* 2nd ed., for which please accept my best thanks.[211] I shall read it with great interest. Here in England modern capitalism, during the century and a half of its full development, has lost much of its original brutal energy and moves onwards with a moderated step; even in France and Germany, this is to a certain degree the case also; it is only in industrially young countries like America and Russia, that capital gives full fling to the recklessness of its greed. The consolation, however, lies in this: that by this very recklessness it hurries on the development of the immense resources of these young countries, and thereby prepares the period when a better system of production will be able to take the place of the old.

In America, at least, I am strongly inclined to believe that the fatal hour of capitalism will have struck as soon as a native American working class will have replaced a working class composed in its majority by foreign immigrants.

Yours very faithfully
Fred. Engels

First published, in the language   Reproduced from the original
of the original (English), in:
Henry Demarest Lloyd,
A Biography by Caro Lloyd,
Volume One, New York and London, 1912

86

ENGELS TO KARL KAUTSKY[193]

IN STUTTGART

London, 1 June 1893

Dear Baron,

Many thanks for drawing my attention to Brentano.[212] The man has evidently not forgiven me for having once again nailed him down with regard to the old *Concordia* business, No doubt he wishes to participate in A. Mülberger's life-long hostility to me.[213] Not that I greatly care. But all the same, I should like to make the gentleman's acquaintance in this new sphere. He seems to me very much the sort of person who would make a splendid ass of himself in prehistory. However, I'm not quite sure whether you mean Vol. 1 or Vol. 3 of the journal; please let me know by postcard and also whether it is to be had *separately,* in which case I should order it. The very fact of his defending Westermarck[a] is enough; the latter is a duffer par excellence, exceedingly diligent but no less superficial and muddle-headed for all that.

I have just read Elie Reclus' PRIMITIVE FOLK—what it is called in French I don't know.[b] Here again, unparalleled muddleheadedness and pragmatism; moreover, his material is appallingly jumbled up so that one is often at a loss to know what tribes and peoples he is talking about; such material as might be of value is absolutely useless in the absence of an accurate comparison with sources. Add to that the anti-theological prejudice of an anarchist who, on top of that, is a son of a Protestant clergyman. There is an occasional good, cynical observation. Valuable to Englishmen in so far as it flies in the face of their respectable preconceived ideas.

The elections brought joy only to ourselves and to Caprivi. It's too funny for words to see how the Centre[71] and the Free Thinkers,[149] the two parties most anxious to avoid a dissolution[76] because they were most afraid of the electorate, should now, *after* dissolution, be on the whole more afraid of the government and the possibility of conflict than they are of the electorate—so afraid, in fact, that, even before the elections, they have split into two sides of which one has come out squarely in favour of the government while the other still continues to vacillate. I must say, I had never imagined that progress towards the 'one reactionary mass'[214] would be so rapid. The resistance put up by the Richters and Liebers is, in fact, a very half-hearted and ineffectual affair and, should we gain the victories—in numbers of votes polled, seats being of lesser importance—which this disarray seems to promise, that resistance might collapse altogether. In which case we shall be the only opposition party, and then the fun can begin.

It is strange how circumscribed all these 'heddicated classes' are by their social milieu. Such gasbags of the Centre and the Free Thinker Party as still remain in opposition represent farmers and lower middle-class, if not actually working-class people of whose fury at the ever-increasing burden of taxation and the impressment of recruits there can be little doubt. Yet that popular fury is transmitted to their honourable deputies through heddicated organs, lawyers, merchants, parsons, schoolmasters, doctors, etc., men who, because of their more general education, see a little bit further than the party masses and who have learnt enough to know that,

---

[a] E. Westermarck, *The History of Human Marriage.* – [b] É. Reclus, *Les primitifs....*

in a major conflict, they would be crushed between the government and ourselves. Hence they seek to avoid such a conflict and transmit the fury of the populace in muted form to the men in the Reichstag—let there only be compromise! Needless to say, they fail to see that *this* method of postponing the conflict propels the masses on to *our* side, i.e. gives us the strength, when the conflict comes, to fight it out to the finish. I expect to see a significant advance on the occasion of these elections—$2^1/_4$ million votes, maybe more[204]—but *many more still* the next time!

Caprivi's joy, by the way, will be short-lived. If, as seems probable, his demand goes through, the masses will be driven over to us from the other side. And for a couple of years Germany will doubtless be able to stand the strain of additional taxation, but this demand will not be the last. In a couple of years Russia may give the *appearance* of having recovered a little, whereupon the more will have to be demanded again and in that case even the one reactionary mass may be driven to seek another dissolution. All over Europe we are again coming into the revolutionary mainstream—*vive la fin de siècle*[a]!

Bax's sketches[215] are certain to cause you trouble. Though they have their moments, these are becoming increasingly rare and the style as a whole is tailored to a local and, what's more, pretty narrow readership consisting of Fabian[43] and other intellectuals.

Your Berlin correspondent[b] has a pronounced subjective streak, but he can write, and has a good command of the materialist view of historical—though not, perhaps, always of current-events. His *Lessing-Legende* was quite excellent, although there are one or two points on which I would place a different interpretation.

You can manage the Zurich Congress on your own.[56] My plans are not yet settled, but I shall most certainly go to Zurich in the middle of August and hope to meet you there.[189] For the rest, I hope you will keep fit and well.

Your

F. E.

First at published in:
Aus der Frühzeit des Marxismus.
Engels-Briefwechsel mit Kautsky,
Prague, 1935

Printed according to the original

---

[a] Long live the end of the century! – [b] Franz Mehring

87

ENGELS TO HERMANN BAHR

IN LONDON

[*Draft*]

[London, beginning of June 1893]

Dear Sir,

I regret that I am unable to comply with your request.[216]

In the first place, it so happens that my party comrades in Germany are conducting an election campaign against, among others, anti-Semitic candidates,[217] which means that at this juncture party interests preclude my expressing an impartial opinion about anti-Semitism.

In the second place, I believe that my party comrades in Vienna and in Austria generally would never forgive me were I to allow myself to be interviewed for the *Deutsche Zeitung.*

I remain, Sir, etc.

First published in:
Marx and Engels, *Works*,
First Russian Edition,
Vol. XXIX, Moscow, 1946

Printed according to the original

Published in English for the first time

88

ENGELS TO FILIPPO TURATI

IN MILAN

London, 6 June 1893

Dear citizen Turati,

Thank you very much for the information you were good enough to send me on the subject of the Domanico project.[218] I would very much like to reply to him as a young girl in Bellagio[219] replied to me more than fifty years ago when I said to her: '*Bella tosa, damm un basi'*—'*domani!*'ᵃ Unfortunately that is impossible. He knows perfectly well that I am legally impotent in his case; he is not asking me for any authorisation, but simply suggesting that I associate myself in some way with his quite disinterested undertaking. As it is quite impossible for me to take on the revision of the translation (even if Domanico was willing to do it), I have no means of exerting pressure on him; I thought it was better for the moment to gain time and ask him for information; you will find at the end of this letter a copy of my reply to him.ᵇ

Is the edition of *Capital* in the Economist's Library in Turin to which you refer an Italian edition? I would be very interested in it, since that is something of which I have been unaware up till now; would you be so kind as to let me have the full title? and the name of the translator and the editor? so that I can get hold of a copy of this translation in order to say a few words about it in a new German edition or in the preface to the 3ʳᵈ volume.

As for Deville's résumé, I have reviewed the first part, but not the second half, the editor was too rushed. That is why Deville has sometimes presented as *absolute* theses of Marx which he had posited only as *relative*, as valid on certain conditions or with certain restrictions. However, that is the only fault I can find.[220]

The second edition of the 2ⁿᵈ volume of *Capital* will soon appear. I am reading the proofs of the last part, and it will not be long before it is published. There are only the printing errors to be corrected, but in a book of this kind that is always important.

Thank you for the translation of the *Manifesto*.[108]

Best regards to Mme Kulishov and to yourself from Mme Kautsky and yours truly,

                                          F. Engels

First published in the language   Printed according to the original
of the original (French), in
Annali, an. I, Milano, 1958   Translated from the French

                                         Published in English for the first time

---

ᵃ 'Kiss me, my sweetheart'—'tomorrow'. A play on words: 'domani' means 'tomorrow' and Domanico is a surname. – ᵇ See next letter.

89

ENGELS TO GIOVANNI DOMANICO

IN PRATO (TOSCANA)

[Draft]

[London,] 7 June 1893

Dear citizen,[a]

In reply to your kind letter of the 2nd of this month, I wish to thank you for letting me know of your intention to publish an Italian edition of Marx's *Capital*.[218]

But before answering your various questions, I have to know who is going to make translation and how, as this work is very difficult and demands of the translator both a profound knowledge of the German and of political economy.

The translation from the French edition alone wouldn't be perfect as the Italian suits more the philosophic style of the author.

I believe that the necessary means will be found to complete the work of such great importance and to publish a new edition that would be up to the contents of the book.

Sincerely

Yours,

F. E.

Copy to Turati 6/6/93

First published in:
Marx and Engels, *Works*,
First Russian Edition,
Vol. XXIX, Moscow, 1946

Translated from the Italian

Published in English for the first time

---

[a] In Engels' draft this phrase is missing. He inserted it in the copy of this letter intended for Turati (see previous letter).

90

ENGELS TO STOJAN NOKOFF[221]

IN GENEVA

London, 9 June 1893
122 Regent's Park Road, N. W.

Dear citizen Nokoff,

A thousand thanks for the trouble you have taken in being the intermediary between the editorial board and myself, and dispatching No. 2 of the Bulgarian *Social-Demokrat*. I, for my part, dare to count on your good will in asking you to forward the lines enclosed to his address.ª If it is not too much to ask, I would be grateful if you would let me know, merely by postcard, whether I am mistaken in identifying Sevlievoᵇ as the town otherwise known as Philippopolis? I do not have a Bulgarian dictionary, my Serbian dictionary offers no clarification, but I have the vague impression of having read somewhere that this was the Bulgarian name of this town.[222] If I am correct, you need not reply.

Yours sincerely,
F. Engels

First published in:
Letopisi marksizma,
Book I, Moscow, 1926

Printed according to the original

Translated from the French

Published in English for the first time

ª F. Engels, 'To the Editorial Board of the Bulgarian *Social-Demokrat*'. – ᵇ Sevlievo is written by Engels in Bulgarian.

91

ENGELS TO PYOTR LAVROV

IN PARIS

London, 13 June 1893

Dear Lavrov,

Tomorrow will be your seventieth birthday. I hope you will permit us to tender you our most sincere congratulations on this occasion. May you live to see the day when the Russian social-revolutionary movement, to which you have selflessly dedicated the whole of your life, will triumphantly plant its flag on the ruins of Tsarism.

Your sincere friends
Friedrich Engels

Louise Kautsky
Eleanor Marx-Aveling
Edward Aveling

First published in
Istoriya SSSR, No. 5,
Moscow, 1965

Printed according to the original

Published in English for the first time

92

ENGELS TO LAURA LAFARGUE

AT LE PERREUX

London, 20 June 1893

My dear Löhr,

I was glad to conclude from your letter that there was still time to insert, in your *Ravé amendé et corrigé*,[a] such of my suggested alterations

---

[a] amended and corrected

as you approve of.[195] That was one of the reasons why I did not lay great weight on having the proofs here: once the matter *mise en page*,[a] it is difficult to insert alterations which necessitate either the cutting out, or the putting in, of a line or a few lines; at least in Germany I have had many a hard fight about the extra expence arising therefrom, and Mister Sonnenschein is careful to insert, in the agreement, a precise limit of what such alterations may cost extra. As to your two objects: to have a faithful translation, and one that should read as an original work, you have certainly attained them both and I am longing to read myself—without keeping one eye constantly on misprints and formal matters—again in your French: when I read it I said to Louise there is only one man in and about Paris that knows French, and that one is neither French nor a man but Laura.

As to the Alsatian Ravé I'll forgive him his Alsatianism in consideration of his working-class countrymen; the 12,000 Mühausen[b] votes for Bueb, the 6,200 Strasburg ones for Bebel (who is almost sure to get in there) and the 3,200 Metz ones for Liebknecht, besides odds and ends all over the country. Bebel who has been there several times lately is quite in love with the Alsatian working men and with the country altogether, although at Strasburg last Sunday fortnight they nearly smothered him bodily with their enthusiasm in Hammerle's beer-garden.

Our elections went off glorious.[204] In 1890—20 seats, now 24 carried at the first assault; in 1890—about 60 ballottages, this time 85. Of seats we lost two and gained six new ones; of the 85 ballots, there are 38 in which, in 1890, we did not get into the ballot (only the two candidates with the highest number of votes are admitted to ballot); and of the 85, there are also 38 in which we have chances (in the remaining 47 we are in a hopeless minority, unless miracles happen) and out of these 38 we may reasonably expect 25 successful elections. But the gap caused by the complete break-up of the Radical (Freisinnige) Partei[223] has created such a state of confusion that we must be prepared for a series of surprises; amongst the Radicals, party discipline has ceased to exist and the people in each locality will just act as they think fit. By bringing up our full strength at second ballot by the assistance of the bourgeois democrats in South Germany and of the mutual jealousies and bickerings of the other parties, we shall be able to come up again to the old complement of 36,

---

[a] is set up – [b] French name: Mulhouse

so that only for an increase above that number we shall be dependent on the active assistance of Radicals, Anti-Semites[217] and Catholics,[71] that is to say upon the strong anti-military current which pervades the peasantry and petty-bourgeois class.

But the number of seats is a very secondary consideration. The principal one is the increase of votes, and that is sure to be considerable. Only we shall not know it until the full official returns are placed before the Reichstag; the most important part of that increase will consist in the— relatively small—number of votes cast in entirely *new*, remote country places, showing the hold we are beginning to take of those rural districts which were hitherto inaccessible to us and without which we cannot expect to be victorious. When they are all counted up, I still believe we shall have something like $2^{1}/_{4}$ million votes, more than has ever been cast for any other party in Germany.

Altogether, the effect has been stunning upon the whole of the German and English bourgeois press. And well it may be. Such a steady, unbroken, resistless progress of a party has never been seen in any country. And the best of it is that our increase of 1893 involves—by the extent and variety of the newly broken ground it shows—the certain promise of a far greater increase at the next general election.

The new departure of the *parti ouvrier*[a] with regard to 'patriotism' is very rational in itself[b]; international union can exist only between *nations*, whose existence, autonomy and independence as to internal matters is therefore included in the very term of internationality. And the pressure of the pseudo-patriots, sooner or later, was certain to provoke an utterance of this kind, even without the alliance with Millerand and Jaurès[169] who no doubt have also urged the necessity of such an act. Guesde's interview in the *Figaro*[224] is excellent, not a word to be said against it. The address of the Conseil—here I am interrupted. I shall have to go to the railway station. Mrs. Gumpert (you know Dr. Gumpert died a short time ago) is going to Germany and on the way going to stay a few days with us, and I must fetch her from the train. So I must say good-bye for a day or two, my observations on the address being of no great importance and no hurry whatever about them. Good luck to the everlasting traveller.[c] What a change has come over poor Clémenceau that even a Déroulède

---

[a] workers' party; reference to the French Workers' Party – [b] See next letter – [c] Paul Lafargue

can bull-bait him![225] *Sic transit gloria mundi.*[a] The anti-Semite patriotic bullies seem to have it all their own way both in France and Germany as far as the bourgeois are concerned!

Love from Louise and your old

General[b]

First published, in the language (English), in: F. Engels, P. et L. Lafargue, *Correspondance*, t. III, 1891-1895, Paris, 1959

Reproduced from of the original

93

ENGELS TO PAUL LAFARGUE[35]

AT LE PERREUX

London, 27 June 1893

My dear Lafargue,

You were absolutely right to protest against the imbecilities of the anarchists and Boulangeo-Jingoes[226]; even though Millerand and Jaurès (who certainly preceded you in this matter) contributed to this that does not matter. Particularly on the eve of a general election[156] it is impossible to leave the field wide open to slander. So we are agreed on this point; the Germans have done as much on more than one occasion, to the great distress of Bonnier who moves in an idealistic anti-patriotic sphere (though mainly anti-patriotic for others, since no one wishes more than he that 'France should take the lead in the movement'). And here is the National Council uncompromisingly declaring itself patriotic—and at the very moment when the elections in Germany[204] quite as uncompromisingly prove that it is not France which is taking the lead at present—poor Bonnier, he was here on Sunday, and looked quite abashed.

Your declaration will have its effect in France, I hope, and I hope with

---

[a] A phrase from the ceremonial speech during the election of the Pope – [b] jocular name for Engels

equal fervour that it will go unnoticed in Germany. This is why: they are not grave matters, but I believe I should draw your attention to them to make sure you avoid them next time.

I don't want to speak of your use of the word patriot, of what you define as the only 'true' patriots.

That word has a limited meaning—or else such a vague one, depending on circumstances—that for my part I should never dare to apply that title to myself. I have spoken to non-Germans as a German, in the same way as I speak to Germans as a pure Internationalist; I think you could have achieved a greater effect if you had simply called yourself French—which is a statement of *fact*, a fact including the logical consequences which flow from it. But no matter, it's a question of style.

You are again perfectly right in extolling France's revolutionary past, and to believe that its revolutionary past will find response in its socialist future. But it seems to me that, having reached that point, you incline a little too far towards Blanquism, i.e., towards the theory that France is destined to play the same role in the proletarian revolution (not merely that of *initiator* but also that of *leader*) as it played in the bourgeois revolution of 1789-98. This is contrary to the economic and political facts of today. The industrial development of France has lagged behind that of England; at this juncture it is behind that of Germany which has made giant strides since 1860; the working-class movement in France today cannot be compared to that of Germany. But it is not the French, nor the Germans, nor the British who, by themselves, will win the glory of having crushed capitalism; if France—PERHAPS—gives the signal, it will be in Germany, the country most profoundly influenced by socialism and where the theory has the most deeply penetrated the masses—where the fight will be settled, and even then neither France nor Germany will ensure final victory so long as England remains in the hands of the bourgeoisie. Proletarian emancipation can be only an international deed; if you try to turn it into a purely French deed you are making it impossible. The exclusively French leadership of the bourgeois revolution—albeit inevitable, thanks to the stupidity and cowardice of the other nations—led to—do you know what?—to Napoleon, to conquest, to the invasion of the Holy Alliance. To try and assign the same role to France in the future is to distort the international proletarian movement, as, indeed, the Blanquists do, and make France look ridiculous, for beyond your frontiers such pretensions are made fun of.

And look where this leads you. You speak of

> France, at ITS immortal Paris Congress in 1889,[227] raised the banner, etc., etc.

How you in Paris would laugh if the Belgians spoke of Belgium at ITS immortal Brussels Congress of 1891,[228] or Switzerland at ITS immortal Zurich Congress[229]! Furthermore, the actions of these congresses are actions neither French, Belgian nor yet Swiss, but international.

Then you say:

> the French Workers' Party[11] is at one with German Social-Democracy against the German Empire, with the Belgian Workers' Party[230] against the Cobourg monarchy, with the Italians against the Savoy monarchy, etc., etc.

There would be nothing against all that if you had added: *and all these parties are at one with us against the bourgeois Republic which oppresses us, Panamises us and ties us to the Russian tsar.* After all, your Republic was made by old William[a] and Bismarck; it is quite as bourgeois as any of our monarchist governments, and you mustn't suppose that with the cry of 'Long live the Republic' on the day after Panama,[60] you will find a single supporter in the whole of Europe. The republican form is no more than the simple negation of monarchy—and the overthrow of the monarchy will be accomplished simply as a corollary to revolution; in Germany the bourgeois parties are so bankrupt that we shall pass at once from monarchy to the *social* republic. Hence you cannot go on opposing your bourgeois republic to the monarchies as something to which other nations should aspire. Your republic and our monarchies are all one in relation to the proletariat[b]; if you help us against *our* monarchist bourgeois, we shall help you against your republican bourgeois. *It's a case of reciprocity and by no means the deliverance of the downtrodden Monarchists by the great-hearted French Republicans*; this doesn't tally with the international outlook and even less with the historical situation which has brought your republic to the feet of the tsar. Don't forget that, if France makes war on Germany in the interests and with the help of the tsar, it is Germany which will be the revolutionary centre.

But there is another very regrettable affair. You are

> 'at one with German Social-Democracy against the German Empire'.

---

[a] William I – [b] The following phrase is crossed out in the manuscript: 'and if one is to speak about alliance and international unity, it is necessary for this...'

This has been translated in the bourgeois press as *'gegen das deutsche Reich'*.[a] And that is what everybody will see in it. For Empire means 'Reich' as well as 'Kaisertum' (imperial regime); but in 'Reich' the emphasis is laid on the central power as representing *national unity*, and for this, the political condition of their existence, the German Socialists would fight to the end. *Never* would we wish to reduce Germany to the pre-1866 state of division and impotence. Had you said against the emperor, or against the imperial regime, no one could have said much, although poor William[b] is hardly of a stature to deserve being honoured in this way; it is the owning class, landlords and capitalists, which is the enemy; and that is so clearly understood in Germany that our workmen will not understand the meaning of your offer to help them to defeat the crackpot of Berlin.

So I have asked Liebknecht not to mention your declaration insofar as the bourgeois papers do not do so; but if, based upon this unfortunate expression, there were attacks on our people as traitors, it would give rise to a rather painful argument.

To sum up: a little more reciprocity could do no harm—equality between nations is as necessary as that between individuals.

On the other hand, your manner of speaking of the republic as a desirable thing in itself for the proletariat, and of France as the chosen people, prevents you mentioning the—unpleasant but undeniable—fact of the Russian alliance, or rather the Russian vassalage.

Well, that's enough, I think. I hope I have convinced you that in the first flush of your renascent patriotism you have overshot the mark a little. Not that it is very important and I hope the thing will go by without raising a dust, but should it recur it might lead to unpleasant controversies. Your published documents, though intended for France, must also PASS MUSTER abroad. If it comes to that, our worthy Germans have not always been correct either, in all their expressions.

As for the German elections, I am prouder of the defeats than of the successes. We have lost Stuttgart by a minority of 128 votes out of 31,000 electors, Lubeck by 154 out of 20,000, and so on. On this occasion all the parties formed a coalition against us; even the democrats of the South, who left us in the lurch at Stuttgart, at Mannheim, at Pforzheim, at Speyer and voted for us only in Frankfurt. What we won we owe—for the first time—entirely to our own strength. Consequently the 44 seats are worth ten times

---

[a] against the German Reich – [b] William II

more than 100 won with the help of the liberals and democrats.

Liberalism has completely abdicated in Germany. There is no real opposition outside our Party. William will have his soldiers, his taxes and—his Socialists in the army and outside the army, in ever-growing numbers. The final figure of the socialist votes will not be known for 10-15 days; Bebel thinks it will not be above 2 million; the season was against us, many workers are scattered in the countryside during the summer and omitted from the register, he estimates the resulting deficit for us at more than 100,000 votes.

The Amiens, *amende honorable* is splendid! There's no one like the French for these strokes of genius against obsolete laws.[231]

Love to Laura and to you from Louise. Kiss Laura for me.

Ever yours,
F. E.

First published in:
Cahiers internationaux,
No. 78, Paris, 1956

Printed according to the original

Translated from the French

94

ENGELS TO PAUL LAFARGUE[35]

AT LE PERREUX

London, 29 June 1893

My dear Lafargue,

I am writing to Bebel and explaining the situation to him[25]; there are certainly many reasons in favour of a postponement of the Congress to a later date.[232] But

1. November is out of the question, nobody goes to Zurich in winter when it is raining and cold. Further, your Chamber, the Reichstag and the British Parliament will be in session then. So give up that date. Another can be settled later.

2. It would be regrettable if the French *Marxists* and the Germans, and they alone, proposed an adjournment. But it would be quite another mat-

ter if *all the French socialist fractions* unanimously made this request. See what can be done in this regard, but *do it quickly*, for

3. The Swiss will have to submit your request to the others and take their advice—at any rate they will plead that necessity, seeing that Seidel, the secretary of the committee,[27] is a fanatical anti-Marxist and intrigues with all our opponents here and in France.

You will have some difficulty in persuading the Blanquists[20] and the two kinds of Possibilists[30] to support your motion, but it is very important. If the others are satisfied with the dates 6-12 August, you are hardly likely to succeed on your own.

Ever yours, in haste,
F. Engels

First published in:
F. Engels, P. et L. Lafargue,
Correspondance, t. III, 1891-1895,
Paris, 1959

Printed according to the original

Translated from the French

95

ENGELS TO FILIPPO TURATI

IN MILAN

London, 12 July 1893

Dear citizen Turati,

On Saturday[a] sent back to you, by registered mail, the Italian *Capital*.[b] Thank you. I have compared some passages, particularly in the 1st and penultimate chapters (general tendency of capitalist accumulation). As you say, it is translated entirely from the French text, which continues to be more popular than the German. The passages I compared were translated fairly accurately, which is not very difficult given that the two languages are so closely related, and the greater freedom of movement offered by Italian in comparison to French.

---

[a] 8 July – [b] See this volume, pp. 149-151

I noticed that the reverse of the title page carries the legend: *proprietà letteraria*,[a] which will prevent Domanico from using this translation as it stands.[218] I still have not received any reply from him, perhaps he is beginning to realise the difficulties involved in his undertaking.

The 'last part' of which I spoke in my letter[b] is, of course, from the 2nd volume, 2nd edition, which will appear closer to September. The 3rd volume is still giving me trouble, but happily the end is in sight. However, I have not achieved my goal of finishing this work before my summer holidays. And that may cause a further delay of several months.

As for the French edition of the 2nd and 3rd volumes, it would be rather difficult to find the translator they require. It's a job which a few people would be willing and capable and persevering to bring to completion. The 2nd has 500 pages, and the 3rd will have 1,100-1,200.

Poor Martignetti! Is there no way of rescuing him from this *benedetto*[c] hole of Benevento, and finding him some occupation in a place where he could also learn the literary language of his country? He displays extraordinary assiduity and willingness. He translates for me with a fanaticism worthy of a better cause; but it seems he has little success in business affairs, and an unlucky star has followed him everywhere.

Will we see each other in Zurich?[189] Good Lord, if all goes well I might be able to be in Zurich at least for the last day of the Congress; that is my plan; however, as it does not entirely depend on me but on a combination of more or less fortuitous circumstances, it is very uncertain, and we would both probably do well not to speak of it. If there is something which frightens me, it is your threat to speak to me *en Meneghino*.[d] In 1841 I spoke it passably well, and understood it perfectly.[219] However, when, about thirty years later, I found myself at Como[233] for a day or two, I did not understand a single word; my ear had completely lost the habit. Thus I can say in all truth that I still speak a few words of your so very expressive dialect, but I understand nothing at all. As for your French, it is still better than mine, and in any case nothing prevents you from writing to me in Italian.

Do you read English? If you do, I could send you a newspaper from time to time.

Salut cordial[e]

Yours,

F. Engels

---

[a] copyright – [b] See this volume, p. 151 – [c] damn – [d] Milan dialect – [e] Heartfelt greetings

Greetings to Mme Kulishov from Mme Kautsky and myself.

First published abridged,
in the language of the original
language (French), in:
*Filippo Turati attraverso le
lettere di corrispondenti (1880-1925)*,
Bari, 1947 and in full in:
Annali, an. I, Milano, 1958

Printed according to the original

Translated from the French

Published in English for the first time

96

ENGELS TO FRANZ MEHRING[234]

IN BERLIN

London, 14 July 1893

Dear Mr Mehring,

It has taken until today to get round to thank you for the *Lessing-Legende* you were so kind as to send me. I did not wish merely to send you a formal note acknowledging receipt of the book, but also and at the same time to say something about it—its contents. Hence the delay.

Let me begin at the end—with the appendix, 'Über den historischen Materialismus'[a] in which you have brilliantly collated the essentials in a manner that must convince any impartial reader. If I have any criticism to make, it is that you accord me more merit than I deserve, even if one takes account of what I may, perhaps, have found out for myself—in course of time—but which Marx, with his swifter *coup d'oeil*[b] and greater discernment, discovered much more quickly. If one has been fortunate enough to spend forty years collaborating with a man like Marx, one tends, during one's lifetime, to receive less recognition than one feels is due to one; when the greater man dies, however, the lesser may easily come to be overrated—and that is exactly what seems to have happened in my case; all this will eventually be put right by history, and by then one will be safely out of the way and know nothing at all about it.

---

[a] 'On Historical Materialism' – [b] insight

Otherwise only one point has been omitted, a point which, however, was never given sufficient weight by Marx and myself in our work, and in regard to which we are all equally at fault. For we all of us began, as *we were bound to do*, by placing the main emphasis on the *derivation* of political, legal and other ideological conceptions, as of the actions induced by those conceptions, from economic fundamentals. In so doing we neglected the formal in favour of the substantial aspect, i.e. the manner in which the said conceptions, etc., arise. This provided our opponents with a welcome pretext for misinterpretation, not to say distortion, Paul Barth being a notable case in point.[a]

Ideology is a process which is, it is true, carried out consciously by what we call a thinker, but with a consciousness that is spurious. The actual motives by which he is impelled remain hidden from him, for otherwise it would not be an ideological process. Hence the motives he supposes himself to have are either spurious or illusory. Because it is a mental process, he sees both its substance and its form as deriving solely from thought—either his own or that of his predecessors. He works solely with conceptual material which he automatically assumes to have been engendered by thought without inquiring whether it might not have some more remote origin unconnected therewith; indeed, he takes this for granted since, to him, all action is *induced* by thought, and therefore appears in the final analysis, to be *motivated*, by thought.

The historical ideologist (here historical is used as an omnibus term for political, legal, philosophical, theological, in short, for all spheres appertaining to *society* and not merely to nature)—the historical ideologist, then, possesses in every sphere of science a material which has originated independently in the thought of previous generations and has undergone an independent course of development of its own in the brains of these successive generations. True, external facts appertaining to one sphere or another may also have helped to determine that development but according to what has been tacitly assumed, those facts, themselves are merely the fruits of a mental process, and thus we still find ourselves in the realm of pure thought which would appear to have succeeded in assimilating even the most recalcitrant facts.

What has above all deluded the majority of people is this semblance of

---

[a] P. Barth, *Die Geschichtsphilosphie Hegel's und der Hegelianer bis auf Marx und Hartmann*. Ein Kritischer Versuch.

an independent history of political constitutions, legal systems and ideological conceptions in each individual sphere. When Luther and Calvin 'overcome' the official Catholic faith, when Hegel 'overcomes' Fichte and Kant, or when, with his republican *Contrat social*, Rousseau indirectly 'overcomes' the constitutionalist Montesquieu, the process is one which remains within the confines of theology, philosophy and political science, which represents a stage in the history of these spheres of thought and never emerges from the sphere of thought. And since the advent of the bourgeois illusion of the eternity and ultimacy of capitalist production, even the overcoming of the Mercantilists by the Physiocrats and Adam Smith has come to be regarded merely as a victory of the concept, not as the conceptual reflection of changed economic facts, but as the correct perception, now at last achieved, of actual conditions as they have always and everywhere existed. If Richard Coeur-de-Lion and Philip Augustus had introduced free trade instead of becoming involved in the Crusades, we should have been spared five hundred years of misery and folly.

We have all, I believe, neglected this aspect of the matter, which I can only touch on here, to a greater extent than it deserves. It's the same old story—initially, form is always neglected in favour of substance. As I have said, I, too, have done this, never realising my mistake until after the event. Far be it from me, therefore, to reproach you on that score—as the senior culprit I am in no way entitled to do so, quite the contrary—but rather I would draw your attention to this point with a view to future occasions.

Hand in hand with this goes the ideologists' fatuous conception that, because we deny independent historical development to the various ideological spheres which play a role in history, we also deny them any *historical efficacy*. Underlying this is the ordinary, undialectical conception of cause and effect as rigidly opposite poles, quite regardless of any interaction. The gentlemen forget, often almost deliberately, that an historical element, once it is ushered into the world by other, ultimately economic, causes, will react in its turn, and may exert a reciprocal influence on its environment and even upon its own causes. Cf. Barth, for example, on the priestly caste and religion, your p. 475. 1 was delighted by the way you dismissed this quite incredibly superficial johnnie. And they go and make the chap professor of history at Leipzig! Old Wachsmuth used also to be there; he too was not a little shallow-pated but he had a tremendous feeling for facts—a very different sort of chap.

For the rest I can only remark of this book what I said more than once about the articles when they appeared in the *Neue Zeit*, namely that it is by far the best account of the genesis of the Prussian state that exists, indeed I might even say the only good one, being in most cases an accurate and minutely detailed exposition of correlations. One can only regret that, while you were about it, you did not feel able to include the whole course of events up till Bismarck; nor can one help hoping that you may some day do so and present the whole picture, from the Elector Frederick William to old William,[a] in context. You have, after all, already done the preliminary studies which you have all but completed at any rate so far as the essentials are concerned. And, after all, it has got to be done some time, before the rickety contraption collapses. The exploding of the monarchist-patriotic myths, if not exactly a necessary prerequisite for the elimination of that bulwark of class rule, the monarchy (a *purely* bourgeois republic in Germany having already become an anachronism before it has ever existed) is nevertheless one of the most effective means to that end.

You would then also be better off as regards space and opportunity when you come to depict local Prussian history as part of the whole German *misère*. This is a matter upon which my views differ here and there from your own, notably as regards the conditions responsible for the dismemberment of Germany and the failure of the German bourgeois revolution in the 16th century. If I get round to revising the introduction to my *Peasant War*, as I hope to do next winter, I shall be able to enlarge on the points in question.[235] Not that I consider those you adduce to be incorrect, but I should include some others and marshal them rather differently.

I have always found, when studying German history—which is one long, continuous *misère*—that a true perspective can only be obtained by comparing it with the same periods in France, because what happens there is the exact opposite of what happens in Germany. There we have the establishment of the national state from the *disjecta membra*[b] of the feudal state at the very time of our worst decline. There, a rare kind of objective logic permeates the whole course of events; in our case, a barren and ever more barren haphazardness. There, the English conqueror of the Middle Ages, who intervenes in favour of the Provençal nationality as opposed to North French nationality, represents foreign intervention; the English wars are, as it were, the equivalent of the Thirty Years' War

---

[a] William I – [b] scattered members

which, however, ended with the ejection of foreign intervention and the subjection of the South by the North. Next comes the struggle between the central power and its Burgundian vassal,[a] supported by his foreign possessions and playing the part of Brandenburg-Prussia, a struggle which, however, ends in victory for the central power and puts the seal on the establishment of the national state.[236] And at the selfsame time in Germany, the national state (in so far as the 'German Kingdom' within the Holy Roman Empire can be called a national state) collapses completely, and the wholesale plundering of German territory begins. It is a comparison that is exceedingly humiliating to Germans, but all the more instructive for that, and now that our working men have again placed Germany in the van of the historical movement, it may be somewhat easier for us to swallow the ignominy of the past.

But what is of particular significance so far as developments in Germany are concerned is the fact that the two member states, which eventually partitioned the whole of the country between them, were neither of them purely German but were colonies on captured Slav territory—Austria a Bavarian, and Brandenburg a Saxon, colony; also the fact that they acquired power *in* Germany only with the support of foreign, non-German possessions—Austria with that of Hungary (not to mention Bohemia), Brandenburg with that of Prussia. Nothing of the kind happened on the western frontier, more at risk than anywhere else; on the northern frontier it was left to the Danes to protect Germany against the Danes, while in the South there was so little to protect that the frontier guards, the Swiss, were actually able to detach themselves from Germany!

But I am divagating—my loquacity can, at any rate, serve you as proof of the extent to which your book has stimulated me.

Once again, many thanks and warm regards from

Yours,

F. Engels

First published abridged in:
F. Mehring, *Geschichte der Deutschen Sozialdemokratie*, Bd. III, Th. II, Stuttgart, 1898 and in full in: Marx and Engels, *Works*,

First Russian Edition Vol. XXIX, Moscow, 1946

Printed according to the original

---

[a] Charles the Bold

97

ENGELS TO RUDOLPH MEYER[237]

IN PRUHONICE NEAR PRAGUE[139]

London, 19 July 1893

Dear Mr Meyer,

It is, I agree, quite interesting that those worthies the Conservatives should believe (desire) that Caprivi might destroy Social-Democracy.[238] Just let him try. A new Anti-Socialist Law[15] can only strengthen the party in proportion to the individual existences it destroys. Anyone who has got the better of Bismarck need have no fear of his successor. Any attempt to abolish or tamper with universal suffrage will revive the old oracle: 'If you cross the Halys, Croesus, you will destroy a great empire.' If Caprivi does away with universal suffrage he will destroy a great empire, namely that of the Hohenzollerns.

So you have found violations of the theory and practice of agriculture in Bebel's *Frau*[a]? Well, it is scarcely possible to provide a critique of to-day's wasteful and generally uneconomic management of agriculture and industry, along with tips as to how, given the social order that automatically arises out of economic conditions, this could be done differently and better, and at the same time as to how, given shorter working-hours for each individual, production could be significantly increased—all this, I say, is scarcely possible without exposing oneself to attack by people with a practical knowledge of one branch or another. Hence Bebel is obviously either expressing himself badly or has failed to understand his authority when he says that the yield of a cornfield can be increased threefold or more by fully exploiting the protein content of gluten. There can be no question of that. I could point to a dozen or more minor inaccuracies of a like nature, but they don't affect the main issue.

Similarly in the case of the transport of meat from regions overseas. Hitherto enough has been available for shipment in one form or another to Europe. But with growing demand and a growing tendency to change over from pasture-land to arable—in those regions too—this is *bound* to

---

[a] A . Bebel, *Die Frau und der Sozialismus*, Chapter 22.

reach a peak before long and then decline. Whether it comes about a few decades sooner or later is largely immaterial.

However, the main objection you raise is that work on the land cannot be done by industrial labour and that in agriculture the reduction of the working-day to a uniform period throughout the year is impossible. Here you have misunderstood Bebel the turner.

So far as hours of work are concerned, there is nothing to prevent us from taking on at seed or harvest time, or whenever a quick supply of extra labour is needed, as many workers as may be required. Assuming an eight-hour day, we can put on two, even three, shifts a day, Even if each man were to work only two hours a day—in this special employment—eight, nine or ten shifts could be put on in succession, once we had a sufficiency of people trained in the work. And that and nothing else is what Bebel is saying. Similarly, in industry one wouldn't be so thick-headed, assuming a two-hour shift engaged, say, in spinning, as to keep increasing the number of spindles until each spindle produced what was required of it when run for two hours. Rather, one would keep the spindles running for between ten and twelve hours, while the operatives would only work for two, a new shift being put on every two hours.

Now as to your objection about the poor town dwellers who are spoiled for agricultural work for life, you may very well be right. I readily admit my inability to plough, sow, reap, or even lift potatoes, but luckily we have in Germany so huge a rural population that by intelligent management we could without more ado drastically reduce each man's working hours and still retain supernumeraries. Supposing we turned the whole of Germany over to farms of between 2,000 and 3,000 morgens[a]—more or less, depending upon natural conditions—and introduced machinery and every modern improvement, would we not then have more than enough skilled labour amongst the agricultural population? But obviously there is not enough work on the land to keep that population busy throughout the year. Large numbers would idle away much of their time if we didn't employ them in industry, just as Our industrial workers would waste away physically if they were denied the opportunity of working in the open air and particularly on the land. I agree that the present grown-up generation may not be up to it. But we can train young people to that end. If, for several successive years, the lads and lasses were to go into the

---

[a] 0,25 ha

country in summer when there is something for them to do, how many terms would they have to spend cramming before being awarded their doctorates in ploughing, harvesting, etc.? You are surely not suggesting that a man should spend his whole life doing nothing else, that, like our peasants, he should work himself silly before he acquires some useful knowledge of agriculture? And that and that alone is what I infer from Bebel's book when he says

> that production itself, as also a person's training, both physical and mental, can be brought to its highest level only when the old division of labour between town and country, between agriculture and industry, has been done away with.

Now as to the question of the profitability of the large estate as against that of the small farm, this can, in my view, be simply explained by the fact that in the long run the large estate engenders the small farm just as much and just as inevitably as the latter, in its turn, engenders the former. In precisely the same way as cut-throat competition gives rise to a monopoly and vice versa. This cycle is, however, inextricably bound up with crises, with acute as well as chronic distress, with the periodically recurring ruin of whole sections of the population, and likewise with the vast dissipation both of the means of production and of what is produced. And since we have now fortunately reached a stage at which we can dispense with these worthies the big landowners no less than with the landed peasants, and agriculture, no less than industry, has likewise now reached a stage of development which, in our view, not only admits of, but demands, its appropriation *en bloc* by society, it is up to us to break the *circulus vitiosus*.ᵃ To that end the big farms and large manorial estates provide us with a much better opportunity than the small farms, just as in industry large factories are more readily suited to that purpose than small workshops. And this is reflected in the political sphere in that the rural proletarians on the big estates become Social-Democrats, just like the urban proletarians, once the latter are able to exert pressure on them, whereas the unsuccessful farmer and urban artisan arrive at Social-Democracy only by the devious route of anti-Semitism.[217]

To say that the owner of a manorial estate—LORD or SQUIRE—who has emerged from feudalism, will ever learn to run his affairs as would a bourgeois and, like the latter, be capable of regarding it as his first duty, come what may, to capitalise each year a proportion of the surplus value

---

ᵃ vicious circle

secured—such a statement runs counter to all experience in all previously feudal countries. When you say that these gentlemen are compelled by necessity to stint themselves of much that goes with the way of life appropriate to their station, I quite believe you. But that they can ever learn TO LIVE WITHIN THEIR INCOMES AND LAY BEYOND SOMETHING FOR A RAINY DAY is quite outside my experience. It has never yet happened, or at most by way of an exception, and certainly not in the case of the class as such. After all, these people have existed for the past two hundred years thanks solely to the assistance of the state which has seen them through every crisis...

Yours,
Friedrich Engels

First published in *Monatsschrift für Christliche Social-Reform*, Heft 3, Vienna-Leipzig, 1897

Printed according to the magazine

Published in English in full for the first time

98

ENGELS TO LAURA LAFARGUE

AT LE PERREUX

London, 20 July 1893

My dear Löhr,

D'abord[a] thanks for translation of the *Chronicle* Interview—though it was hardly worth while.[239] And then an inquiry.

Some time ago Bonnier sent me a letter from a Diamandy (Roumanian) asking me to write for a new Review[b] of his and announcing me that they had anticipated my permission and translated for the 1st No., *which they would send*, the chapter on Barbarism and Civilisation.[240] I waited but received nothing. Then, a few days ago, I wrote, saying that I had not had the review[25] but anyhow had no time to write for him.

---

[a] First of all – [b] L'Ere nouvelle

After that they send *to me* a *Separatabdruck*[a] of that chapter stating on the cover that they intended publishing the whole first in the review and then in book-shape. But the review they did not send to me, but to *Tussy*. From her I got it this afternoon and see that I am quoted as a regular contributor along with Kautsky, Paul, and others who perhaps were not asked any more than myself—that however articles by Guesde and Paul are promised and Paul's essay on Mohr's Materialism[b] is re-printed in part.—The translation of my chapter seems to be Roy's. Now, all that, along with Léo Frankel as administrateur, opens out before my bewildered eyes such a vista of possibilities and impossibilities that before taking another step in the matter I must seek information and advice at your door. Paris is *unberechenbar*,[c] but Paris *doublé de* Bucarest becomes a mystery in the third power, and I give it up.

What funny people the French government and Parliament are! Panama[60] passes off with a fizz instead of an explosion, the *coup d'état* against the *bourse du travail*[d] leaves the workpeople *blasés* and passes off quietly, but the Siamese humbug sends the very same parliamentary patriots off in a blaze of enthusiasm for Colonial Conquest—the same men who a few years ago almost killed Ferry 'the Tonkinois' because he tried to engage them on the same line[241]! Verily the bourgeoisie has outlived itself everywhere.

To-morrow Louise and I are going, for a week, to Eastbourne (address as before, 28 Marine Parade), as I feel the want of a little recruiting of strength before undertaking my trip to Germany.[189] Last year's disap-pointment has made me careful; I don't want to be laid up again lame in an armchair for six weeks. We leave Eastbourne Friday 28th July and London for Continent 1st August—meet Bebel and wife in Cologne and go via Strasburg to Switzerland where I shall meet my brother[e] and expect to be in Zürich for close of Congress 12th or 13th August. Thence with Bebel to Vienna and Berlin.

Will Paul and you be in Zürich? The Swiss got letters from other Parisian organisations, that the elections very likely would *not* be in August, in spite of all newspaper reports, but only in September[156]; that and the English objections decided against the application for adjournment.[232]

Post-time—9 o'clock, though perhaps this will not reach you till Saturday morning!

---

[a] off-print – [b] Lafargue, *Le matérialisme économique de Karl Marx.* – [c] unpredictable – [d] Labour Exchange[29] – [e] Hermann Engels

Love from Louise and your
   ever thankful 'Translated-one'.

                                        F. Engels

First published, in the language   Reproduced from the original
of the original (English), in:
F. Engels, P. et L. Lafargue,
Correspondance, t. III, 1891-1895,
Paris, 1959

99

ENGELS TO FILIPPO TURATI[242]

IN MILAN

                                        London, 20 July 1893
Dear citizen Turati,

I hasten to reply to your letter of 17th, which I received yesterday evening.

Mme Marx-Aveling is executor under Marx's will; as for the literary part of the inheritance, I am responsible. Neither of us has ever heard talk of any Unione tipografica-editrice of Turin, and even less have we ever sold to this society 'property rights for the works of Marx' which (fortunately) belong to us entirely to this day. Not a single soldo of money from this Union has ever touched our hands.[243]

As regards the 1st volume of *Capital*, these property rights include the German and French editions. In accord with the relevant international treaties, everyone is now free to do any translations; we cannot oppose this. If anyone asks for our authorisation, this is a purely voluntary act on their part.

It is not altogether impossible that the Union has entered into some kind of contract with the editor of the French edition, M. Lachâtre, but it is highly unlikely. I know nothing of it. However, even if this is the case, M. Lachâtre could only sell that which is his property, and at the very most that was the French edition. Thus the Union could do no more than oppose an Italian translation from the French.

However, now the book by Deville has been published and is freely circulating in France. If *in France* no one has attempted to bring a charge of infringement of copyright against this book, then there is even less chance of anyone trying something of the kind.

Thus it is ridiculous, unless the legislation in Italy is wholly out of line. However, as the Code Napoléon has served as the basis for civil legislation in almost the whole of Western Europe, I do not think I am mistaken to see the case from this point of view.

What is amusing is the affrontery of these gentlemen: 'we purchased from the heirs to this property, etc.' Clearly they have succeeded in this on other occasions.

As for Zurich, the situation is still as it was when I last wrote to you[a]; let us all hope for the best!

Greetings to Mme Anna and yourself from Mme Kautsky and from yours truly,

F. Engels

First published, in the language of the the original original (French), in: *Annali*, an. I, Milano, 1958 Published in English for the first time

Printed according

Translated from the French

100

ENGELS TO WILHELM LIEBKNECHT

IN BERLIN

Eastbourne, 27 July 1893

Dear Liebknecht,

The day after tomorrow, i.e. the 30th of this month, is your and your wife's Silver Wedding and so I am writing to send you my very best wishes on this joyous occasion. May it find you both in excellent shape and be a day of unalloyed pleasure and may you be granted a life of health and happiness for the 25 years that remain until your Golden Wedding.

Whenever a festive occasion of this kind comes the way of one of us old

---

[a] See this volume, p. 162

comrades in arms, it takes our thoughts back to the old days, to the old battles and assaults, to the defeats at the beginning and the eventual victories we have experienced together, and we rejoice that in our advancing years we have not been destined to remain in the self-same breach—after all, we have long since gone over from the defence to a general attack—but rather to advance together in the same line of battle. Yes, old man, many are the assaults we have been in together and I hope we'll be in more of them to come including, if all goes well, the one which, if it does not bring the final victory, will nevertheless make that victory a foregone conclusion. Fortunately both of us can keep our spirit up and both of us are spry for our age, so why shouldn't we manage to do so?

Bebel will be giving you and your wife on our behalf—Louise Kautsky's and mine—a small memento of your celebration, which I trust you will kindly accept and remember us by.

With cordial regards and good wishes from

Your

F. Engels

First published in:
Marx and Engels, *Works*,
First Russian Edition,
Vol. XXIX, Moscow, 1946

Printed according to the original

Published in English for the first time

101

ENGELS TO NATALIE LIEBKNECHT

IN BERLIN

Eastbourne, 27 July 1893

Dear Mrs Liebknecht,

I was delighted to receive the picture of the house in Bruch where I was born and spent my childhood.[244] The photograph is a very good one and shows every detail with which so many of my memories are associated. It was very nice of Liebknecht to have it taken, and I would ask you to thank him most kindly on my behalf.

Provided there are no upsets I shall be visiting Berlin in September for a couple of days when I shall have the pleasure of greeting all of you again. In order to fortify myself somewhat for the long journey,[189] have been spending a few days here by the sea,[245] greatly to the benefit of Mrs Kautsky and myself. We return tomorrow.

It is typical of the Prussians to persecute your Karl in this way; the bureaucrats are incapable of forgiving him his father.[246]

And now once again my hearty congratulations on your Silver Wedding and warm regards to you and your sons.[a]

Yours ever,
F. Engels

[*Postscript from Louise Kautsky*]

In company with the Avelings and other friends we shall drink a toast to you both with a '68 port next Sunday.[b] Your very good health!!

From your
Louise Kautsky

First published in:
Marx and Engels, *Works*,
First Russian Edition,
Vol. XXIX, Moscow, 1946

Printed according to the original

Published in English for the first time

---

[a] Karl and Theodor – [b] 23 July

102

ENGELS TO NICOLAS PETERSEN

IN COPENHAGEN

London, 31 July 1893
122 Regent's Park Road, N. W.

Dear Mr Petersen,

I am prevented from answering your letter of the 3rd inst. in detail since I will be leaving for the Continent tomorrow.[189] After my return I will try and go into the questions you raise. Meanwhile thank you for sending those very interesting statistics. Warmest greetings,

Your
F. Engels

First published, in the language of the original (German), in: *Meddelelser om Forskning i Arbejderbevaegelsens Historie*, No. 11, Copenhagen, October 1973

Printed according to the original

Published in English for the first time

103

ENGELS TO LUDWIG SCHORLEMMER

IN DARMSTADT

London, 31 July 1893

My dear Schorlemmer,

I do not wish to set off on my trip to the Continent,[189] which begins tomorrow, without replying to your letter of the 27th.

Unfortunately there will not be time to see you in Darmstadt, as I shall be traveling straight through to Switzerland and Austria.

Nothing definite from Siebold. He too has been sent to Switzerland for the Alpine climate and won't be back for some time. Nothing can be done about the matter until I return.[199]

That is all. I must close, for there were visitors between 10 and 4 and I didn't have a minute to myself.

Many regards to you and your family.

Yours,

F. Engels

First published in:
Marx and Engels, *Works*,
Second Russian Edition,
Vol. 39, Moscow, 1966

Printed according to the original

Published in English for the first time

104

ENGELS TO HERMANN ENGELS

IN THUSIS (GRAUBÜNDEN)

6 Merkurstrasse, Hottingen-Zürich
16 August 1893

Dear Hermann,

I have been staying with Anna Beust since yesterday and am at last sufficiently far removed from the turmoil to be able to write to you.[189] I had quite a nice journey. There were some highly diverting dust storms to begin with, followed by just enough rain to make the dust stick to one's clothing. In Zürich they took me to the Hotel Baur en ville where I was very well accommodated but never felt at home. Then, finally on Saturday evening, with the most difficult part accomplished, a moderate carousal gradually got under way (I say moderate advisedly; only *half* litres were served) combined with excursions on the lake. Tell Elsbeth[a] that people here have already discovered how talented I am at growling. The other day Bebel remarked in a postcard that I had done nothing the whole evening but growl with contentment.

Zurich has come on a great deal and outdoes even Barmen. There ev-

---

[a] Elsbeth Engels

ery third house used to be an 'inn'; here, however, there are three inns to every two houses. The Beusts live in very pleasing style with a wonderful view from a gigantic balcony big enough to hold a ball on. Anna Beust is very well preserved and one of the most beautiful old women in existence, besides being witty and vivacious, clever, energetic and resolute; it is a pleasure to be with her. Her son Fritz is in charge of the school, while the other, Adolf, has a very good medical practice; both have nice wives and two noisy, lively boys apiece. Adolf lives at home and Fritz close by in a house he has built.

Next week I shall probably go into the mountains for a while with Bebel. However I shall be back in about a week or so, and round about the 3rd, 4th or 5th of September we are leaving for Munich and Vienna.

At the Congress[56] there were three or four Russian women with really lovely eyes, somewhat reminiscent of your sister-in-law Berta's[a] when I saw her in Altenahr years ago. But my real sweetheart was a truly delightful Viennese factory girl,[b] charming of countenance and engaging of manner, such as one rarely comes across. I shall never forgive Bismarck for having excluded Austria from Germany, if only because of the Viennese women.

From what they tell me here, the Hotel Bellevue is not one of the best. I hope it nevertheless suited you all right. Let me know sometime how you got on. With much love to Emma,[c] Elsbeth, Walter[d] and you yourself from your old 'weed that never dies'.

Friedrich

By the way, you might also pay a call on Anna Beust. She has not set eyes on or heard from you for ages.

First published in
Deutsche Revue, Jg. 46,
Bd. III, Stuttgart-Leipzig, 1921

Printed according to the original

Published in English for the first time

---

[a] Berta Croon – [b] Adelheid Dworak – [c] Emma Engels – [d] Walter Engels

105

ENGELS TO LAURA LAFARGUE

AT LE PERREUX

Merkurstr. 6, Zürich-Höttingen
21 August 1893

My dear Löhr,
I have been in Switzerland for some weeks.[189] Louise, Dr. Freyberger and I left August 1st via Hook of Holland, met Bebel and his wife at Cologne, passed one night at Mainz, the next at Strasburg, the third at Zürich. Thence I went to Thusis in Graubünden where I met my brother[a] and family and stayed a week, returned to Zürich just in time for the closing of the congress and am now staying with my cousin Mrs. Beust.

As to the elections of yesterday,[208] we are in complete uncertainty and shall be so until this afternoon—no papers being published in Zürich on Monday mornings. So anything to be said on that subject must be delayed until end of this letter.

I found Germany completely metamorphosed. Steam chimneys all over the country, but where I passed, not numerous enough over a small district, to create a nuisance by their smoke. Cologne and Mainz are transformed. The old town is there still where it was, but around or aside of it has arisen a larger and newer town with splendid buildings disposed according to a well-arranged plan, and with large industrial establishments occupying distinct quarters so as not to interfere with the aspect or the comfort of the rest. Cologne has made most progress, having nearly trebled its inhabitants—the Ring is a splendid street, there is nothing equal to it in all England. Mainz is growing, but at a slower rate. In Strasburg you see too distinctly the separation between the old town and the new district formed by university and government buildings, an external addition, not a natural growth.

Paul naturally will be most curious to hear about Alsace. Well, the French may rest satisfied. In Strasburg, to my astonishment, I heard nothing but German spoken. Only once, two girls, Jewesses, who passed me,

---

[a] Hermann Engels

spoke French. But this is very deceptive. A very intelligent young Socialist, who lives there, told me that as soon as you go outside the city gates, the people speak, and purposely, nothing but French. In Mülhausen[a] too, he said, ⁴/₅ths of the population, working men and all, speak French. Now this was not the case before the annexation.[247] Since the railways were opened, the French language began to spread in the country districts, but even now the French they speak is to a great extent of their own manufacture. But anyhow it is French, and shows what the people want. When the annexation took place, I once said to Mohr: the consequence of all these attempts at regermanisation will be that more French will be spoken in Alsace than ever before. And so it has turned out. The peasant and workman stuck to their German dialect as long as they were Frenchmen; now they do their utmost to shake it off and speak French instead.

Such arrant fools as these Prussians you never saw. They flattered the nobility and bourgeois who, they ought to have known, were hopelessly frenchified, and bullied the peasants and workmen, who, at least in language, had retained some remnant of German nationality. The country is under the thumb of maires,[**] gendarmes, tax-gatherers, appointed by the central government and mostly imported from abroad, who do as they like and live among themselves, separated from and detested by the people.

All the old oppressive laws of the French Second Empire[248] are scrupulously maintained and enforced, and sometimes even improved upon by old ordinances dating from the ancien régime and unearthed by learned functionaries who have discovered that the revolution has forgotten to state expressly that they are repealed! Moreover, all the chicanery innate to Prussian officials, is imported and improved upon. The consequences are natural. When I asked my friend: then, evidently, if the French by some chance or other were to return, nine-tenths of the people would receive them with open arms, he said that was so.

In Strasburg the old bourgeoisie keep quite to themselves and do not mix in any way with the intruders. With the rest of the people, Bebel is very popular, wherever he was recognised, they came to the shop doors and saluted him. You may be sure he will bring the state of things in Alsace before the Reichstag in a fashion different from that of those asses of protestataires who seem to rejoice in every fresh measure of oppression,

---

[a] Modern name: Mulhouse. [**] Chief executives, Mayors

for fear the people *might* get reconciled with the new régime, and who consequently have lost the best part of their hold on the population. In this case as in every other, it will turn out that our party is the only one that can and will do what is really wanted.

(This moment a telegram from Roubaix to Greulich's house that Guesde is elected. Hurrah! Hope to hear this afternoon about Paul' s victory.[249]

As to the Congress[229] it was a pity that our people had not at least 5-6 men here.[250] The one effect has been obtained: Blanquists[20] and Allemanists[21] have made themselves eternally ridiculous and contemptible *devant le monde socialiste.*[a] But now *this falls on French socialism generally*; now the others speak simply of 'the French', and that is very unlucky indeed. Had there been even a small minority of Marxists, that would not be the case. But if you find in English and continental socialist papers the French Socialists treated as a set of chaps who do not know their own minds for two minutes together, and who will vote by acclamation the greatest piece of nonsense if thereby they think they can aggravate *'les allemands',*[b] You need not be astonished. I have heard Swiss Socialists (and the *German* Swiss have very strong *French* sympathies) declare that now it was evident that chauvinism was ineradicable in the French mind, and I had to tell them what things—gall and wormwood to every *chauvin*[c]—I had been able to say in French in your Almanac,[d] without any bad results anywhere. So you see the fiasco of these spouters falls upon all France, our people included. And Jaclard with his peevish articles in *Justice* makes it worse still. Well, I hope the elections will put us in a position to show to all Europe that Jaclard and Allemane *ne sont pas la France.*[e] And yet I believe Jaclard voted in very many cases with Bonnier and the small vanishing minority.

The women were splendidly represented. Besides Louise, Austria sent little Dworzak, a charming little girl in every respect; I fell quite in love with her and whenever Labriola[f] gave me a chance, eloped with her from the entanglements of his ponderous conversation. These *Viennoises sont des Parisiennesnées, mais des Parisiennes d'il y a cinquante ans.*[g] Regular grisettes. Then the Russian women, there were four or five with wonderfully beautiful *leuchtende Augen,*[h] and there were besides Vera Zasulich and Anna Kulischoff. Then Clara Zetkin with her enormous capacity for

---

[a] in the eyes of the socialist world – [b] the Germans – [c] chauvinist – [d] F. Engels, 'Socialism in Germany'. – [e] are not France – [f] Antonio Labriola – [g] Viennese women are born Parisians, but the Parisians of 50 years ago – [h] shining eyes

work and her slightly hysterical enthusiasm, but I like her very much. She has ascended the Glärnisch, a mountain full of glaciers, a very severe effort for a woman of her constitution. Altogether I had the happy lot to fall from the arms of one into those of the next and so on; Bebel got quite jealous— he, the man of the 'Frau',[a] thought he alone was entitled to their kisses!

Now I leave a bit of room for this afternoon's news. The Beust boys wish to be remembered. Louise is in Austria, Bebel and Bernstein are still here. By 4th September Bebel and I are off to Vienna, up to then the above address holds good.

Good luck to Paul!

Ever your old
General[b]

4 p.m. News that Paul is *en ballottage*[c]—please say how the chances stand— and that Ferroul is beaten, and Jourde in ballot. A few lines on the results generally will be gladly received as bourgeois papers are not to be trusted.

First published in the language of the original (English), in: F. Engels, P. et L. Lafargue, *Correspondance*, t. III, 1891-1895, Paris, 1959

Reproduced from the original

106

ENGELS TO EMMA ENGELS[251]

IN ST. MORITZ

Alpnachstadt, 23 August 1893

Dear Emma,

I am here today and will be in the Bernese Alps tomorrow. A week from now I will be back in Zurich.[189] hope the Engadin is doing all of you

---

[a] 'Woman'; an allusion to A. Bebel's work *Die Frau und der Sozialismus* – [b] jocular name for Engels – [c] is to stand second ballot

good. Greetings to everybody from

Your
Friedrich

First published in *Beiträge*   Printed according to the original
zur Geschichte der Arbeiter-
bewegung, No. 1, Berlin, 1979   Published in English for the first time

107

ENGELS TO LAURA LAFARGUE

AT LE PERREUX

Zürich, 31 August 1893

My dear Löhr,

Thanks for your letter and the papers which came to hand yesterday. I had been for 6 days in the Berner Oberland with August and St. Mendelson—fine weather and splendid scenery.[189] The Jungfrau had put on an extra clean white night-dress for us. Jungfrau, Mont Blanc and Monte Rosa are the three finest *massifs* of the whole Alps.

Yesterday we were on the Uetliberg, a hill close to Zurich. with a fine though rather distant view of the snowy chain. When, after 1870, old Thiers was here with his lot, he at once explained the whole to them; pointing at the Glärnisch (due South-East of the Uetli) he said that was the Mont Blanc. The landlord of the hôtel at the top, a perfect connoisseur of the whole range, ventured to suggest that this was the Glärnisch, and that the Mont Blanc was in a nearly opposite direction, and invisible from that point—but the little man replied: *Monsieur, je suis Adolphe Thiers, et je dois savoir cela! C'est bien là le Mont Blanc!*[a]

I am glad you consider the result of the elections of the 20th a victory. Let us hope this will be confirmed next Sunday by the return of Paul and Delcluze besides some others. Otherwise I am afraid our party will not be able to play the part in the Palais Bourbon[156] which I and many others wish it to play. If

---

[a] Sir, I am Adolphe Thiers and I should know this! I can assure you that is Mont Blanc!

we have 8-10 men there, they will form a nucleus strong enough to force the Blanquists,[20] Possibilists[30] and Independent Socialists to group themselves around it and thus to prepare a united party. But if we are only 3 or 4, the other fractions will each be about as strong, and unification will not only be more difficult, but also have more of the character of a compromise. Therefore I hope we may enter the Palais Bourbon in full force.

I hope the *Socialiste* will not bring Guesde's letter to his electors.[a] Whatever may be thought of it in France, outside the border it would sound simply grotesque. To declare his election a revolution, by which socialism *fait son entrée au Palais Bourbon,*[b] and from which a new era dates for the world in general, is coming it rather too strong for ordinary mortals.

I enclose a German five mark note, to enable you to telegraph to us the result of the poll next Sunday.[208] August and I are leaving here on Monday morning[c] for Munich and shall stay there over Tuesday. Now by Monday evening or Tuesday morning at latest we suppose you will have all the results as far as they interest us. As soon as you can, but not later than Tuesday afternoon, *please telegraph the names of our men and the places for which they have been returned*, and if the money goes so far, any further information of interest. The telegram to be addressed in German:

Bebel, Hotel Deutscher Kaisert Munich:

but the rest had perhaps better be in French, so as to secure correct sending off.

On Tuesday evening or Wednesday we shall go on to Salzburg, thence to Vienna where we stay for a few days, and then to Berlin. If you will be good enough to send some further information by letter to Vienna (where it can be used for the *Arbeiterzeitung*) please address to Frau L. Kautsky, Hirschengasse 46, Oberöbling, Vienna, Austria. (An inner cover is unnecessary as she will know it is for me.)

And now good luck to all our candidates and to Paul especially! I put little trust in the promises of opportunists,[87] but I hope that in *his* case they may turn out true for once.[252]

What benefit has the Millerand-Jaurès alliance[169] brought to us in this campaign? I am utterly unable here to form a judgment.

Love from yours ever,

F. E.

---

[a] J. Guesde, Letter to the Electors of the 7th Electoral District, *Le Socialiste*, 26 August 1893. – [b] makes its entry into the Palais Bourbon – [c] 4 September

First published in French,
Abridged in *Cahiers du communisme*,
No. 11, Paris, 1955 and in full, in the
language of the original (English), in:
F. Engels, P. et L. Lafargue,
Correspondance, t. III, 1891-1895,
Paris, 1959

Reproduced from the original

108

ENGELS TO LAURA LAFARGUE[253]

AT LE PERREUX

Berlin W., den 18 September 1893
Grossgörschen-Strasse 22 a.

My dear Löhr,

Enfin![a] Arrived here Saturday night, after 6 days in Vienna and 1 in Prague[189] (where we met your old adorer Rudolf Meyer). Vienna is an extremely beautiful town, with glorious boulevards (Ringstrasse), and the immense square between Rathhaus and—vis-à-vis—new Burgtheater, with Parliament to the right and University to the left, is unequalled in the world. But Vienna is too big for its people, they are only beginning to *learn* the use of these boulevards; in about 10 years everything will be ten times finer, because 10 times more alive with people.

Altogether the Continent has undergone a complete revolution since I last saw it.[254] Everywhere life, activity, development, compared to which England appears stationary. Of Berlin I have not seen much (not a square foot as yet of the Berlin I left in 1842,[255] as what I have seen so far, is all new addition) but it is indeed externally splendid, though, I fear, internally full of discomfort. Bebel (where Louise and I are staying) has a very pretty and comfortable floor, but Library[b] where we spent last evening lives in a set of apartments so awfully arranged by the builder that it horrified me. Here in Berlin they have invented the 'Berliner Zimmer', a room with hardly a trace of a window, and that is where the Berliners

---

[a] At last! – [b] jocular name for W. Liebknecht given to him by Marx's daughters

spend almost all their time, To the front is the dining-room (best, reserved for swell occasions) and the salon (even more select and reserved), then the 'Berliner' *Spelunke*[a]; next a dark corridor, a few bedrooms *donnant sur la cour*,[b] and a kitchen. A sprawling unhomely arrangement, specifically Berlinerisch (that is *bourgeois*-berlinerisch): show and even splendour in front, darkness, discomfort and bad arrangement behind, the front for show only, the discomfort to be lived in. At all events that is my impression *at present*; let us hope it may get mended.

Yesterday we were in the Freie Volksbühne[256]—the Lessing Theater, one of the nicest and best of Berlin had been hired for the occasion. The seats are drawn for as in a lottery by the subscribers and you see working men and girls in the stalls and boxes, while bourgeois may be relegated to the gods. The public is of an attention, a devotion, I might say, an enthusiasm *sans égale*.[c] Not a sign of applause until the curtain falls—then a veritable storm. But in pathetic scenes—torrents of tears. No wonder the actors prefer this public to any other. The piece was rather good and the acting far superior to what I had expected. The *Kleinbürgerei*[d] of old has disappeared from the German stage, both in the acting and in the character of the pieces. I will send you a short review of the latter.

In Vienna I had to appear twice before the 'party'.[257] I am quite enchanted with them. As lively and as sanguine as the French, but slightly more solid. The women especially are charming and enthusiastic; they work very hard, thanks, to a very great extent, to Louise. Adler has done wonders; the tact, the constant vigilance and activity, with which he holds the party together (not an easy thing with such lively people as the Viennese), are beyond praise, and if you consider moreover the difficulties of his private position—a wife ill with nervous ailments, three children and interminable pecuniary difficulties arising therefrom—it is almost inconceivable how he can keep his head above water. And these Austrians—a mixture of all races, Celtic, Teutonic, Slavonic—are far less manageable than our North Germans.

Library looks very well, collecting the elements of a paunch; his wife made a Bowle for us with wine and fruit; there was a rather numerous company. He lives *au quatrième*[e] and outside Berlin proper, in Charlottenburg, but his apartment costs him some 1,800 Marks = 2,250 fr.

---

[a] squalid hole – [b] overlooking the courtyard – [c] without its equal – [d] provincialism – [e] on the fourth floor

As to your elections I hope Paul's hopes may be verified.[252] As most of the men elected are utterly unknown to me, I have no means to form a judgment. Vaillant's letter in the *Petite République Française*[a] looks promising, let us hope that circumstances may tend to keep him in the right direction. If *our 12 men* are really *ours* and not like Thivrier and Lachizeq then a good nucleus may be formed.

When we came to Prague, there was the little *état de siège*[b] in force there. *Nobody in our hotel ever thought of asking for our names! Voilà ce que c'est que l'Autriche: Despotismus gemildert durch Schlamperei.*[c]

Amitiés à[d] Paul. Ever yours,

F. Engels

Louise, Bebel *und Frau grüssen euch beide herzlichst.*[e]

Your copy of Paul's article and Paul's letter we gave to Adler who used them for his very good article in the *Arbeiter Zeitung.*[259]

First published, in the language of the original (English) in: F. Engels, P. et L. Lafargue, *Correspondance*, t. III, 1891-1895, Paris, 1959

Reproduced from he original

109

ENGELS TO KARL KAUTSKY

IN STUTTGART

Berlin, 25 September 1893

Dear Baron,

I cannot *possibly* allow the letter in question to be launched upon the world without an introduction.[260] Our opponents would at once gleefully

---

[a] E. Vaillant, Unité socialiste' in *La Petite République Française*, 10 September 1893. – [b] state of siege – [c] That's Austria all over: despotism mitigated by slovenliness. – [d] Regards to – [e] and his wife send you both warmest greetings

set about both writer[a] and recipient[b] and it's going to cause enough of a scandal as it is. But not having the letter here, I cannot write an introduction. You people ought to have seen to this beforehand; I shall not be able to do anything about it before the 30th or the 1st of October.

Regards,

Your
F. E.

First published in
*Aus der Frühzeit des Marxismus.
Engels Briefwechsel mit Kautsky*,
Prague, 1935

Printed according to the original

Published in English for the first time

110

ENGELS TO LAURA LAFARGUE

AT LE PERREUX

London, 30 September 1893

My dear Löhr,

We arrived here all right yesterday morning[189] and my first and agreeable duty is to remit to you one third of Meissner's remittance for 1892/93 of £60. = 20.—and one fifth of Sonnenschein's ditto of £5.10.5. (²/₅ go to the translator and ³/₅ to the heirs[261]) — thus £1.2.1

£21.2.1

for which the cheque is enclosed. Please inform me of its safe receipt.

You may have seen in the papers how I was drawn out of my reserve— first at Zurich, then at Vienna[257] and finally at Berlin.[262] I fought as hard as I could but it was no use, they must have me out. Well it will be the last time, I have informed them I will not go there again except under a written engagement that I shall be allowed to travel as a private individual. Anyhow they everywhere received me more than splendidly, far more so than I did, or had a right to, expect.

---

[a] Heinrich Heine – [b] Karl Marx

As to the movement in Austria and Germany, it has exceeded my most extravagant expectations. Our French friends will have to bestir themselves if they will not be left behind. There is a power there, and both our men and their opponents know it.

At Vienna I was at a meeting of some 6,000, and at the Konimers in Berlin they honoured me with, there were 4,000 present—only the representative men and women of the party—and I can assure you it was a pleasure to see and hear this people. When you come from England with this distracted and disunited working class we have here, when you have heard for years nothing but bickering and squabbles from France, from Italy, from America, and then go amongst these people—the German-speaking ones—and see the unity of purpose, the splendid organisation, the enthusiasm, the *unverwüstliche Humor, der aus der Siegesgewissheit quillt,*[a] you cannot help being carried away and saying: this is the centre of gravity of the working class movement. And if our French friends do not care, the Austrians may take the wind out of their sails. They are a mixed race—Germans grafted upon a Celtic (Noric)[263] stock and getting strongly mixed with a Slavonic element—thus combining the three chief European races in their blood. Their temper is very much like the French—more lively and sanguine than the less mixed Germans, and more capable of initiative by impulse. Unless Paris minds its p's and q's, Vienna may give the signal of the next revolution. I like the people very much, and the Viennese women remind me very much of the French working women of 40 years ago; of course they are oversanguine of success just like the French, but I think they are a deal clearer headed than those Parisians who fell in love with Boulanger—must close—company arriving.

Kind regards to Paul

Ever yours
General[b]

Louise *grüsst herzlich.*[c]

First published in:
Marx and Engels, *Works*,
Second Russian Edition,
Vol. 39, Moscow, 1966111

Reproduced from the original

Published in English for the first time

---

[a] inexhaustible humour arising from the confidence in victory – [b] jocular name for Engels – [c] cordial regards from Louise

111

ENGELS TO JULIE BEBEL

IN BERLIN

London, 3 October 1893

Dear Julie,

You and August will have got our postcard of Friday's date.[264] I found a colossal pile of work waiting for me and, with the help of Louise who is still up to her eyes in printed matter, have now toiled and moiled my way through what was the most urgent, and am thus able to drop you a couple of lines.

Well, after our departure on Thursday,[189] we saw Adolf Braun for a moment at the Zoologischer Garten Station and then continued on our way. In our compartment there were two shabby looking johnnies who turned out to be something of a nuisance; luckily one of them, an Englishman, was completely drunk by ten o'clock, after which they spent the rest of the day in the corridor.

In Hanover we had a meal consisting of soup and meat during the course of which we were joined by good old Kugelmann and his daughter[a], who is far nicer than he is. He again treated me to a whole catalogue of medical precepts for the governance of my life, but also to a little basket containing meat sandwiches, apples and half a bottle of wine. The sight of it sent us into transports—red wine! But alas, it was so-called 'red port', a sweetish concoction which we bestowed upon the ticket collector in return for his kindness.

Soon after this there arose a lively debate between the ticket collector and some of the passengers on the question of whether those bound for the Hook of Holland ought not to change at Löhne and travel via Rheine-Salzbergen. We stuck firmly to Oberhausen, since Louise's ticket did not leave us any other alternative. At Minden, however, the train was already half an hour late and, since we had only 17 minutes at Oberhausen in which to make the connection, there was every prospect that we should miss it. It was here that the time-table August had given me in the morning really came in handy. We took the old Cologne-Minden railway

---

[a] Franziska Kugelmann

which I knew to be one of the most soundly built in Germany. As we passed these stretches, we could see that we were making up for quite a bit of lost time, and in this way we arrived punctually at Oberhausen.

The mining district between Hamm and Oberhausen is just like a piece of the English black country. The atmosphere and the towns just as smoky and black as in England, and the houses, because mostly painted in light colour, even more unpleasantly blackened than the bare English brick.

In Holland we again heard passengers and ticket collectors drop all kinds of dark hints about missed connections, but nevertheless we arrived at Rotterdam at 8.42 Dutch, i.e. 9.42 German time. That hour's difference had made everything all right (it hadn't been quite clear to us from August's time-table exactly where the change of time became operative and hence we had been in a state of *uncertainty*).

And though in Rotterdam we had to walk from one station to the other—about 10 minutes away—we still had some time in hand and arrived there before those who had travelled via Löhne-Rheine-Salzbergen.

Aside from a little of Kugelmann's fare, Louise had taken only one bowl of soup at Arnheim and another at Rotterdam, whereas I had subsisted on Kugelmann's fare and beer. It was blowing quite nicely when we left. I soon turned in and was quite pleasantly rocked to sleep, but didn't suspect there was anything amiss until I woke up in broad daylight after 8 hours, when we should long since have been in Harwich! I got up—I had the cabin all to myself—no one on board was stirring. I went up on deck to find it completely empty—everywhere wet decks and signs of its having been a rough night. At last a young German came along and confided to me that we had been through a frightful storm. Soon after, a few damsels appeared, and then Louise; the poor thing had been closeted in a small cabin with five others and had heroically survived the worst, despite her hysterical and sea-sick entourage. Eventually, however, when the big rollers were succeeded by a choppy sea, she too momentarily succumbed to the importunities of old Neptune.

We arrived two hours late in London—the Avelings were at the station—found everything in excellent order and attacked our work with the recklessness customary in those who have heroically weathered a slight storm. Nothing much would seem to have happened here, and it is only by degrees that we shall be able to find out about the little comings and goings of the local movement.

Apropos, Ede Bernstein maintains that Paul Singer has totally misunderstood his article.[a] He never said that one should compromise, according to circumstances, with Conservatives,[202] National Liberals,[203] Ultramontanes,[68] etc.; *all he had in mind was the Freethinking People's Party.*[223] I told him that I for one could not have deduced that from his article; at all events, the latter possibility is one he has also left open.

But now, dear Julie, I must thank you and August once again for all the kindness and friendship you showed me, not only in Berlin but also in Zurich—and which August showed me throughout our trip; I can but remind you of your promise to pay us a visit here in the spring so that we for our part can show you London. Cordial regards to you both and to all our friends,

Your

F. Engels

[Postscript from Louise Kautsky]

Dearest Julie,

I really am more than up to my eyes in work and as yet can see no way out of it, not even for writing letters. The General[b] who is settling down to his writing, has told you how we fared on the journey, but forgotten to say that he monopolised the sandwiches you gave us. All went very well with him on the trip, he was always cheerful and in good spirits, always worried about missing our connections, and full of beans. On Sunday I myself at once fell back into my former, housekeeping role. But our guests treated me indulgently. Please tell August that I have not yet been able to find out anything definite about the second English edition;[265] I wish to see the book myself and shall get someone to buy it for me, but Reeves certainly wouldn't sell it to me direct.

I add my warmest thanks to those of the General. I have not had time to reflect upon all that I have experienced, and am living as if in a dream, a dream interspersed with work. And you, poor tormented souls, how are you? Love and kisses to you and August from

Your

Louise

First published in Russian
in: Marx and Engels, *Works*,
First Russian Edition,
Vol. XXIX, Moscow, 1946

Printed according to the manuscript

Published in English for the first time

---

[a] E. Bernstein, 'Die preussischen Landtagswahlen und die Sozial-demokratie. Ein Vorschlag zur Diskussion'. In: *Die Neue Zeit*. No. 52, 1892-93, Vol. II. – [b] jocular name for Engels

112

ENGELS TO HERMANN BLOCHER

IN BASLE

London, 3 October 1893
122 Regent's Park Road, N. W.

Dear Sir,

Not until today, immediately after my return to this country,[189] have I been able to reply to your letter of 11 August.[266]

There are several copies of *The Holy Family*[a] in Berlin, while in Switzerland Dr Conrad Schmidt, lecturer at Zurich University, Klus-Hegibachstrasse, Hirslanden, might be able to help you get hold of one.

As regards Bruno Bauer's career up till 1843, his fortunes and opinions, you might find some information in Ruge's *Hallische*, subsequently *Deutsche Jahrbücher*; likewise in Bruno's own writings. Also, in regard to the years 1844-46, in his works and his *Allgemeine Literatur-Zeitung*. After 1843 both Marx and I completely lost touch with the Bauers who didn't come to London until some time towards the end of the 50s— Edgar for a prolonged stay, Bruno for a visit, at which time Marx saw them again. However, so far as I know, Bruno never had anything to do with either the materialist view of history or scientific socialism, but if he ever had, this could only be discovered from Bruno's later writings, those of the '50s and '60s. It could hardly be denied that Marx's views exerted a certain amount of influence upon Bruno's subsequent works on early Christianity, but on the whole Bruno's conception of historical causation remained primarily idealistic.

It is my opinion that no one could successfully write a book about Bruno without spending a long time in Berlin where all the material has accumulated.

Very sincerely yours,
F. Engels

---

[a] K. Marx and F. Engels, *The Holy Family, or Critique of Critical Criticism. Against Bruno Bauer and Company.*

First published in Russian in:
K. Marx and F. Engels, *Works,*
First Russian Edition,
Vol. XXIX, Moscow, 1946

Printed according to the original

Published in English for the first time

113

ENGELS TO JOHN B. SHIPLEY

IN LONDON

[*Draft*]

[London], 3 October 1893

Dear Sir,

On my return from abroad[189] I find your letter of Aug. 10th. I am afraid I cannot be of any use to you in your dispute with your family. Even were your *legal* right to the money a good deal clearer to me than it is, I could only say that you, as a poor man, would hardly have the ghost of a chance, in English law courts, against wealthy people who moreover could fight you with your own money. But supposing you had the money to fight, my advice would still be: keep it rather than waste it on law.

As to a lawyer such as you describe and who would be willing to undertake your lawsuit, you will not be astonished if I tell you I do not know such a one.

Regretting I cannot give you a more comforting reply

I remain etc.

First published in Russian
in: K. Marx and F. Engels, *Works,*
First Russian Edition,
Vol. XXIX, Idoscow, 1946

Reproduced from the original

Published in English for the first time

114

ENGELS TO FRIEDRICH ADOLPH SORGE[184]

IN HOBOKEN

London, 7 October 1893

Dear Sorge,

We returned here on Friday 29 September and soon afterwards received your letter of the 22nd. I have been away for two months.[189] Louise Kautsky and I travelled to Cologne where we met Bebel and his wife and from there we all went on together via Mainz and Strasburg to Zurich, whence I slipped off for a week to Graubünden where I met one of my brothers.[a] But I had had to promise to be back for the end of the Congress on which occasion they induced me, *malgré moi*,[b] to join in the finale about which you will have read.[267] But that set the tone for the entire trip and completely put the lid on my intention of travelling purely as a private individual. I stayed another fortnight in Switzerland, after which Bebel and I travelled via Munich and Salzburg to Vienna. There the whole business of placing myself on display began all over again. First I had to attend a beano at which, however, there was room for only about 600, and the others also wanted to see me; so on the last evening there was another mass meeting at which I had to say a word or two.[257] Thence via Prague to Berlin where, having protested vehemently against a mass meeting they had planned, I got away with a beano at which 3,000 or 4,000 people gathered.[262] The chaps meant all this very kindly, but it isn't my cup of tea and I'm glad that it is over; next time I shall demand a written agreement to the effect that I shall not have to display myself before the public but shall be travelling as a private individual on private business. I was, and still am, astounded at the magnificence of the reception I was given, but I would sooner leave such things to members of parliament and public speakers; for *them* it's all part of the job, but has little to do with my kind of work.

But in other respects, after 17 years of absence,[254] I found Germany completely revolutionised—industry enormously advanced as compared with before, agriculture—large- and small-scale—*very much* improved,

---

[a] Hermann Engels senior – [b] willy-nilly

and hence our movement making capital progress. Such little freedom as our people possess, they have had to win for themselves—wresting it more especially from the police and the *Landräte after* the relevant laws had already been promulgated in writing. And hence you find an assured, confident demeanour such as has never been evinced by the German bourgeoisie. Needless to say, they are also open to criticism on a number of individual counts—for instance, the party press, notably in Berlin, is not abreast of the party—but the masses are first-rate and better as a rule than the leaders, or at any rate than many who have come to occupy leading roles. With such chaps, nothing is impossible—they are really happy only in the midst of the struggle, they live for the struggle alone and are bored if their opponents do *not* provide them with work to do. It is an actual fact that another Anti-Socialist Law[15] would be greeted by most of them with sardonic laughter if not with positive glee—it would, after all, again give them something new to do each day!

But alongside the Germans of Germany we should not forget the Austrians. By and large, they are not as advanced as these Germans, but they are more vivacious, more French, more easily carried away into performing great deeds, but also into perpetrating blunders. Seen individually, I prefer the average Austrian to the average German, the average Viennese working man to his fellow in Berlin and, so far as the women are concerned, I infinitely prefer the Viennese working woman; she possesses a naïve spontaneity beside which the studied precocity of her Berlin counterpart appears insufferable. If *messieurs les Français* don't look out and make haste to resume their erstwhile tradition of revolutionary initiative, then it might happen that the Austrians will take the wind out of their sails and seize on the first opportunity to get things going.

Incidentally, Berlin and Vienna, together with Paris, are now the most beautiful cities in the world, London and New York being filthy holes by comparison, especially London which has seemed quite strange to us since our return.

In November *messieurs les Français* will have to show what they are capable of.[268] Twelve Marxists and four Blanquists,[20] five Allemanists[21] and two Broussists,[30] along with a few Independents and some twenty-four *socialistes radicaux*[86] *à la* Millerand in the Chamber constitute a goodish lump of leaven and should produce a nice state of fermentation *provided* they stick together. But will they? The 12 Marxists are, by and large, completely unknown quantities; Lafargue is missing, while Guesde, who *is a member*, is an infinitely more capable speaker but also an infinitely more gullible optimist. I am racked with curiosity. Even before the election our Marxists had already concluded a sort of pact with Millerand & Co.[169] which the Blanquists, and in particular Vaillant, would appear to have associated themselves with by contributing to Millerand's *Petite République française*. Again, the Blanquists are taking a very firm stand against the Russian alliance just now. But I have received no direct news about the present state of the various parties, probably because they are not yet clear about it themselves.

I trust you and your wife are in good health. Cordial regards to you both from

Your
F. Engels

I met De Leon and Sanial in Zurich. Was not impressed.

[*Postscript from Louise Kautsky*]

Dear Mr Sorge,

May I pester you again by asking whether it would be possible for you to send me two copies of the *Woman's Journal*, or do you think I should do better to order it direct on behalf of a woman friend of mine in Vienna? If so, what is the best way of paying the Americans and to whom do I address myself? But that's not all. Please could I have a three cent Columbus stamp, if this isn't asking too much of you. I am besieged by so many stamp collectors who want it. Many thanks in advance and my most cordial regards to you and your wife,

Yours,
L. Kautsky

First published, abridged,
in the book: *Briefe und Auszttge
aus Briefen von Joh. Phil. Becker, Jos.
Dietzgen, Friedrich Eggels, Karl Marx*

u. A. an F. A. Sorge und Andere,
Stuttgart, 1906

Printed according to the original

115

ENGELS TO VICTOR ADLER

IN VIENNA

London, 11 October 1893

Dear Victor,

We arrived back here on 29 September[189] with mounting recklessness, attacked the pile of work we found waiting for us.

Though I was unable to discover Comrade Höger's 'whole series of boulevards' in Berlin, there can be no doubt that, so far as appearances go, it is a very fine city; even in working-class districts all one sees are palatial façades. But what lies behind those façades is better passed over in silence. The poverty of working-class districts is, of course, universal, but what I found particularly overwhelming was the 'Berlin living-room',[a] a place unimaginable anywhere else in the world, a refuge of darkness and stale air as also of your Berlin philistine who feels perfectly at home there. Golly! There was nothing of the kind in August's apartment, which was the only one I liked, but in any of the others I'd go off my head.

However in writing this letter it was not my object to send you the above *cri de cœur*, but rather to congratulate you and the Viennese.

First, your Schwender speech[269] which shows once again how sure is your grasp of the difficult and complex conditions in Austria, and how firm a hold you keep on the clue in the labyrinth. And at this particular juncture that is of the utmost importance.

In the second place I must especially congratulate you and the Austrians generally on the resounding victory won as a result of your agitation for suffrage, namely Taaffe's Electoral Reform Bill.[270] And here I must enlarge somewhat.

Having taken a look at your country, people and government I have come to realise ever more clearly that really outstanding victories are within our grasp there. An industry that is growing rapidly but which, because of years of high protective tariffs, still largely continues to operate

---

[a] See this volume, p. 187

with outmoded productive forces (the equipment I saw in the Bohemian factories proved as much); the industrialists themselves. I mean the bigger ones—the majority of whom are as closely involved in the Stock Exchange as in industry proper; in the towns, philistines who are more or less indifferent to politics, have abandoned themselves to sybaritism,[271] and desire above all to be left to pursue their pleasures in peace; in the country, either a rapid slide into debt or the swallowing up of small properties; the real ruling classes are the big landowners who, however, are quite content with their political position whereby they are assured of a rather indirect domination; also the upper middle class and a scattering of haute finance[a] closely linked with the big industrialists whose political power is *much less immediately* in evidence but who are also quite content with this state of affairs; among the propertied classes, i.e. the grandees, there is no desire to turn indirect into direct, constitutional rule, while among the small fry no serious effort is made toward true participation in political power; the result is indifference and stagnation, punctuated only by the feuding over nationalities between various members of the aristocracy and the bourgeoisie, and by the events arising out of the union with Hungary.

Above all this there hovers a government whose absolutist proclivities are subject to few formal, and these for the most part only fictive, restraints; nor, in practice, does it encounter many obstacles. For it is by its nature conservative and so, too, is your aristocrat, your bourgeois and your philistine bon vivant. The peasant, however, in his rural isolation, cannot achieve any organised opposition. What is wanted of the government is that it should *live and let live*, and this is something at which the Austrian government has always been adept. Hence the fabrication—explicable also on other grounds—of laws and regulations that exist only on paper, hence, too, the extremes to which that process is taken, its elevation into a principle and the astonishing administrative slipperiness which, I must say, exceeded anything I could have imagined.

Well then, in a stagnant political situation such as this, one in which the government, despite its extraordinarily advantageous position vis-à-vis the individual *classes*, is nevertheless perpetually getting into hot water: 1. because those classes are split up into umpteen nationalities and hence, contrary to all the rules of strategy, march united (against the workers) but fight divided (i.e., against one another), 2. because of

---

[a] high financiers

perpetual money troubles, 3. because of Hungary, 4. because of involvements abroad—in short in a situation like this, I told myself, a worker's party with its own programme and tactics, which knows what it wants and how to get it, has sufficient will-power to do so, and is, moreover, thanks to a happy miscegenation of Celts, Slavs and Germans, in which the latter element predominates, possessed of a gay, mercurial temperament—that party need only develop its capabilities enough to score quite outstanding successes. With none of the other parties knowing what they want and a government which likewise does not know what it wants, but lives from hand to mouth, a party which knows what it wants and wants it with tenacity and singleness of purpose, is bound to win in the end. And all the more so in that everything the Austrian Workers' Party[272] wants and *could* want is no more than is also demanded by the country's progressive economic development.

Here, therefore, we have a situation more propitious to rapid success than in any other country, even in Germany where, though development has been more rapid and the party is stronger, yet resistance is far more determined. Add to that the fact that Austria, a great power in decline, still feels ill at ease in Europe, a feeling that has always been foreign to Prussia, a small power in the ascendant. And, having joined the ranks of the 'modern' states in 1866, Austria also feels ashamed of *internal* weaknesses—which it need not have done when still an avowedly reactionary state. Indeed, the less a country wants to be a genuinely modern state, the greater will be its desire to be regarded as such, and the more strongly reaction rears its head in Prussia—where it is under far greater restraint than in Austria—the more liberal will be the attitude adopted by Austria out of malicious glee.

Now, the situation in Europe—I mean the *internal* situation of the individual states—is approximating ever more closely to that of 1845. The proletariat is increasingly coming to hold the same position as the bourgeoisie did then. At that time it was Switzerland and Italy who set things off; Switzerland with her internal strife between democratic and Catholic cantons which came to a head in the Sonderbund War[273]; Italy with Pio Nono's[274] liberal endeavours and the liberal-nationalist changes in Tuscany, the small duchies, Piedmont, Naples and Sicily. The Sonderbund War and the bombardment of Palermo[275] were, as everyone knows, the immediate precursors of the February revolution of 1848 in Paris.

Today, when the crisis might come to a head only five or six years hence, Belgium would seem to be taking over the role of Switzerland,

Austria that of Italy, and Germany that of France. The struggle for suffrage began in Belgium[276] and is being taken up on an impressive scale in Austria. And there can be no question of a settlement being reached on the basis of some sort of half-baked electoral reform. Once the ball is rolling, the impulsion will communicate itself to all around it, and thus one country will immediately affect its neighbour, So besides the possibility of your scoring great victories there is the opportunity, i.e. hence also the likelihood, of your doing so.

Such, more or less, is the tenor of what I expounded to Louise yesterday afternoon as my view of Austria's immediate mission. And at 8 p.m. the *Evening Standard* brought the news—still in rather indefinite terms—of Taaffe's capitulation,[a] while today we are given the Bill, at any rate in very general outline. Well, now the ball really *has* got rolling, and you people will see to it that it doesn't stop. I don't want to say anything about the Bill until I am rather better informed, but of one thing I feel sure, namely that Taaffe would like, *à la* Bismarck, to split the now undivided urban Liberal vote and play off the workers against the bourgeoisie. Not that we have any objection; the Liberal and other bourgeois parties will try and restrict enfranchisement still further, and you might thus find yourselves in the pleasant position of supporting the worthy Taaffe against his parliament. At all events, it's a bonus that is not to be sneezed at and, before I come back, you will doubtless be duly installed as a deputy in the Diet. The *Daily Chronicle* is already talking of 20 *safe* seats for Labour. With 20, or even less than 20, the Diet will be a very different kind of body from what it has been hitherto, and the gentlemen will be amazed at the life that this will inject into the ramshackle old place. And if a few Czechs should happen to get in alongside our German chaps, it will put something of a damper on the squabbling over nationalities, and enable Young Czechs and Old Czechs[277] and German Nationals to see each other in an altogether new light. And here one might say that the entry of the first social-Democrats into the Diet, will mark the beginning of a new era in Austria.

And it is you people who have brought this about and, because of the dawning of this new era, we all of us rejoice that we shall have in the Diet a man with so incisive an intellect as yourself.

Warm regards from Louise and

Your

---

[a] 10 October 1893

F. Engels

Regards from Louise to yourself and also from me to Popp, Reumann, Adelheid, Ulbing and tutti quanti.

First published in *Arbeiter-Zeitung*, No. 327, October 28, 1920

Printed according to the book: *Victor Adlers Aufsätze, Reden und Briefe*. Erstes Heft: *Victor Adler und Friedrich Engels*, Wien, 1922

Published in English for the first time

116

ENGELS TO AUGUST BEBEL

IN BERLIN'

London, 12 October 1893

Dear August,

We are sending you Reeves's edition of *Woman*.[265] In my view the *legal* position (upon which the whole thing turns when you're dealing with a chap like Reeves) is as follows:

1. So far as the translator is concerned, international copyright provides protection for three years from the publication of the original, but only if during the *first* year the *first* part of a translation authorised by the author has actually appeared in print. Accordingly you would have absolutely no claim unless Walther's[a] translation had appeared within one year of the publication of a new German edition containing *substantial* alterations and additions not contained in the earlier one; this was hardly the case.

2. There remains Mrs Adams Walther's claim. Whether she has any depends on whether, upon the publication of the first English edition, she reserved the Copyright or whether she expressly or tacitly assigned it to the publishers, the Modern Press. This should be ascertained. If she did not expressly reserve it then, legislation over here being what it is, it is ten

---

[a] Adams Walther

to one that it was tacitly assigned to the publisher and that consequently she too no longer has any claim.

3. So far as I know, the latter, one Foulger, had long since had to wind up his business and was no doubt glad to come to any sort of agreement with Reeves.

Accordingly it is almost certain that you cannot do anything in the legal line, nor is it at all likely that Mrs Adams Walther can do anything either, but this should be ascertained. If you could procure me a copy of the agreement between Mrs Walther and the Modern Press I could, if necessary, consult a lawyer. But unless everything is *absolutely cut-and-dried* there's nothing to be done with a laddie like Reeves; in his speculative enterprises he is as unscrupulous as they come, and getting money out of him is a virtual impossibility; I, too, have unfortunately had dealings with him, and not even the threat of a lawsuit is of any real avail. In cases such as these, laddies of his stamp generally make over everything to their wives or concoct a BILL OF SALE (assigning their stock, etc., to a fictitious or genuine creditor).

Yesterday we got two splendid bits of news.

First, the beginning of the end of the pit strike. After the lock-out of the workers, engineered by the *big* colliery owners on 28 July: 1. in order to raise prices and curtail production, 2. so that ruinous contracts, carelessly entered into, for a year's supply of coal to gasworks and other municipal undertakings *could be broken with impunity* because, in all such contracts, *strikes provide indemnity against breach of contract*, 3. to depress wages and 4. to ruin the small mining companies and buy them up at knock-down prices—this is coming increasingly to be the permanent motive behind all big LOCK-OUTS—well then, after the said lock-out had been going on for over two months and public opinion among the middle classes, who had been hit by the coal shortage, had also begun to turn—against the mine owners, things came to a head. During the first week of October the agreement expired whereby the mine owners had undertaken, on pain of a £1,000 fine, to re-open their pits, but only if wages were reduced by a full 25 per cent (of the former wage plus the 40 per cent increase gained after 1889, i.e. at the 1889 wage plus 15 per cent), and on condition of the strike's being called off by the miners' committee. A number of the smaller collieries immediately defected and resumed work at the *pre*-July wage (i.e. at the 1889 wage, plus the 40 per cent increase). The mayors of the larger towns in the Yorkshire and Midlands mining districts then foregathered and proposed a settlement which, in fact, boiled down to a 10 per cent reduction in wages. Had the masters accepted, this could have been dangerous as it might have placed the workers on the horns of a dilemma—either they, too, accepted or they risked turning against themselves a public opinion that is always fickle and ready to applaud any kind of compromise. But luckily the MASTERS—the big ones in the lead—were deluded enough to refuse forthwith, and within twenty-four hours the collapse of their ring was manifest to all. As from yesterday some thirty or forty thousand miners have returned to work at the *pre-July* wage, which means that the masters have totally renounced their demands and the hash of the colliery-owners' ring has been well and truly settled. This is the first instance in which a big strike, set on foot by the masters themselves at a time of their own choosing, has gone so completely awry, and therein lies its significance. It will be some time before they try the same thing again, but the workers have themselves suffered so much and endured such poverty that they, too, are unlikely to have much stomach left for a 'general strike'.

(Have just got yours and Julie's letter.)

The second piece of news was about the new Austrian Electoral Reform Bill.[270] It is a resounding victory for our people and I hastened to congratulate Victor upon it.[a] The *Daily News* thinks that the number of voters in Vienna will rise from 80,000 to 350,000, while the *Chronicle* estimates the number for Austria as a whole at three million—these estimates come, of course, from Viennese sources. At all events it's a bonus that is not to be sneezed at. The bourgeois in Vienna are already thinking in terms of twenty Social Democrat deputies.

It's more than probable that Taaffe is counting on his Bill being changed for the worse by Parliament, but it's a long shot and our chaps will see that he doesn't get away with it. What a delicious quirk of history if it should so turn out that our chaps have to protect the Prime Minister against his Parliament and against his own secret self! The main thing is that the ball has at last started rolling and in Austria our movement is powerful enough to prevent its being brought to a halt. And Taaffe cannot very well suppress demonstrations *in support* of his Bill.

From my general impression of Austria, I should say that that country will give us much cause for rejoicing in the immediate future. What with

---

[a] See previous letter.

the general prostration of all the parties, the general perplexity, the feuding over nationalities, what with a government that never knows what it wants and lives only from hand to mouth, what with laws that exist for the most part only on paper and the general sloppiness of the administration—of which I have, from my own observation, only recently got any real idea—what with all these things, a party which knows what it wants and how to get it, which genuinely wants it and is possessed of the required tenacity, is bound in the long run to prove invincible especially when, as in this instance, all its demands follow the same trend as the economic development of the country as such and are no more than the political expression of that development. Our party in Austria[272] is the only living force in the field of politics; otherwise there is nothing but passive resistance or new ventures that never come to anything, and this places us in an exceptionally favourable position in Austria. Furthermore, the changes that occur in the grouping of the bourgeois parties sometimes make it impossible for the government to be Conservative and, when it ceases to be Conservative, it simply becomes unpredictable, if only by reason of the fact that the party groupings of which it has to take account are likewise unpredictable. And again, the Austrian government is that of a great power which, though in decline, is nevertheless still a great power and, as compared with Prussia, a small power in the ascendant, is still capable of remarkable initiatives at such times as conservatism, sheer clinging to the status quo, ceases to be possible. That is my explanation for Mr Taaffe's 'leap in the dark'.

Another fact to be considered is that the growth of the proletarian movement in all countries is about to precipitate a crisis and that in consequence any successes *one* country may achieve will react powerfully upon all the others. The suffrage movement won its first victory in Belgium[276] and now Austria is about to follow suit. At the outset this will ensure the *survival* of universal suffrage, but also encourage us to make further demands—in Germany no less than in France and Italy. The way was paved for the February Revolution[a] by Switzerland's internal struggles and the constitutional upheavals in Italy. Again, the Sonderbund War[273] and the bombardment of Messina[b] by the Neapolitans[275] (Feb. 1848) were the immediate signal for the outbreak of revolution in Paris. Maybe the crisis will not be upon us for some five or six years yet, but I should say that the

---

[a] of 1848 in France – [b] a slip of the pen in the original; it should read Palermo

preparatory role will this time fall to Belgium and, in particular, Austria, while the dénouement will take place in Germany.

There is no fear that the cause will ever again be dropped in Austria; our people in that country will see to that. The Austrian Diet is an infinitely more stagnant froggery than the German Reichstag or even the Saxon or the Bavarian Chamber. The presence of a dozen Socialist deputies will have a far more galvanic effect there than it would in our case, and we are exceptionally lucky in having in Victor a chap who has so clear a conception of the complexities of conditions in Austria and is able to subject them to so incisive an analysis. His speech in the last *Arbeiter-Zeitung* is a real tour de force.[a]

Ede and Gina were here this morning. He isn't yet at all as he should be, has a mania for splitting hairs and increasingly recalls the sagacity of his *Volks-Zeitung* uncle; I often get the impression that old Aaron[b] in person is standing before me. It was he who spoilt things for himself in Switzerland. Having been told in Berne that one of them but not both at once would be admitted, he should have realised that the best policy would be to give precedence to Julius, as an invalid and, banking on this, to return six months later, *when they* could hardly refuse him admittance, at least for any length of time. But this his impatience would not brook. The best of it is that he now sometimes avers *he* would prefer to stay here and that it's Gina who wants to go to Switzerland. His dream is, as it always will be, to go back to Berlin. He really imagines this to be possible and is always consulting lawyers about it. Remains to be seen!

If Schlüter has any sense he will do himself and his wife the kindness of starting divorce proceedings. A suit of this kind against an *absent* wife for deliberate desertion has few disadvantages for either party, and after all he too must wish for complete freedom. This is not, of course, to say that he hasn't in any case been accustomed to enjoying that freedom whenever opportunity arose. It is always satisfactory, by the way, to hear that a woman one knows is plucking up the courage to make herself independent. The decision to part from her Hermann for good may have cost her many a mental struggle and she may thus at one time have given the impression of being by nature irresolute. What an expenditure of energy bourgeois marriage demands—first until one has got to that stage, then for so long as the nonsense lasts and then until one is finally done with it.

---

[a] fine specimen – [b] Aaron Bernstein

We have just come back from a walk in the park—glorious autumn weather, a pretty sunset in a cloudless sky and beautifully coloured foliage. Downstairs the table is being laid; we are having Welsh mutton dressed as venison, accompanied by good old noodles. So I must hurry up and finish this. Louise and I thank Julie for her kind letters and are saving up our answers for next time. Warm regards from us both to both of you, likewise to Singer and his sister, to the Liebknechts and all our dear friends whose names I cannot list if the joint is not to grow cold.

Yours,
F. Engels

First published, in Russian,
in: Marx and Engels, *Works*,
First Russian Edition, Vol. XXIX,
Moscow, 1946

Printed according to the original

Published in English for the first time

117

ENGELS TO PAUL LAFARGUE[35]

AT LE PERREUX

London, 13 October 1893

My dear Lafargue,

Is the Paris letter in today's *Vorwärts* from you? This is why I am asking.

When I was in Berlin,[189] Liebknecht said he was arranging to take you on as correspondent for *Vorwärts*, but that the money had still to be voted by the Party Committee; in the meantime he asked me to tell you that it was a matter of regular work, of letters to be sent at stated intervals, once a week or a fortnight, for example, something which so far he had not been able to get from his French correspondents. I promised I would write to you about it as soon as he let me know that the matter had been clinched between you two.

I used the opportunity to reproach him for setting such store by any anti-Russian article of Vaillant's,[a] which he always faithfully reprints, whereas far more robust anti-Russian articles, published by *Le Socialiste* over a long period, have been passed over almost unnoticed by him. He apologised and promised to do better.

But he has not written a word about the matter of your correspondence, and he goes on translating and making much of Blanquist statements, even translating the *Chauvière*.[b]

He has, moreover, reprinted an article by young *Arndt*,[c] although this chap voted all the time with Argyriadès & Co. against the Germans at Zurich.[250] And Arndt is on the Blanquist revolutionary Central Committee.

So as you see Liebknecht leans very strongly towards the Blanquists. I'm not looking for reasons, I simply state the fact. Hence it is important that you should do everything, in despite of him, to maintain the position you have always held in relation to the German party: that of its main allies in France, who have first claim to be taken into consideration in relations between the German party and the French Socialists in general. And, to this end, you must be represented on *Vorwärts*, so that the Paris correspondence should be, at least to some extent, in your hands.

Of course the decision does not rest solely with the editorial board. The Executive Committee has something to say. And I am convinced that you will find support there, if it is needed. It goes without saying that I shall do my utmost to ensure the continuation of a close alliance between the German party and your party in France (which will not commit you to taking their money, that can always go to the Blanquists, if you don't want any more of it,[278] as you say; they will be delighted to take it). So let me know how far you have got with Liebknecht concerning your appointment as regular *Vorwärts* correspondent; and without delay, for, if there are difficulties, I must be able to take steps *before* the Cologne Congress on the 22nd of the month.[279]

Going by *Le Socialiste*, I counted on our having twelve deputies. It is true that, knowing no more than half of them even by name, I had my doubts about their reliability. But, according to your letter, you do not seem to know so far as half of them are concerned whether they are our people or not. Very unfortunate. With 12 sound chaps, led by Guesde, we

---

[a] Vaillant, "Zarismus und Republikanismus", *Vorwärts*, No. 222, 21 September 1893 – [b] E. Chauvière, Die französische Russenseuche", *Vorwärts*, No. 238, 10 October 1893. – [c] P. Arndt [Letter], *Vorwärts*, No. 221, 20 September 1893.

should soon have been able to compel the Blanquists,[20] Allemanists,[21] etc. to fall in with us. But if we can look to only half-a-dozen reliable people, we shall have to treat with these gentlemen on a more or less equal footing, in which case the old divisions may continue, or else, if there is unity, it will be achieved at the price of sacrifices in matters of principle.

Certainly Vaillant seems very much more sensible since his election than he was six months ago, but will he always be sure of a majority on his Central Committee? Or else, to make sure of it, may he not have to sacrifice his personal opinion on matters of substance to the prejudices of those silly conspirators?

It is sad that you were beaten at Lille.[252] You sacrificed yourself for the party: instead of nursing your constituents by assiduous parliamentary activity, you travelled about and collected votes *for others*. But the fact remains we need you in the Chamber too; and I hope you will get the first vacant seat.

The new paper will not—like the last one—be advertised 'to appear in October', I hope?[280] Will not *La Petite République Française* bar the way? This is another outcome of the Millerand-Goblet alliance[169]; you gave them far more help than they gave you in return. It's one thing for Millerand, but Goblet! an ex-Minister and candidate for the premiership!

Tomorrow I shall write a few words to Laura *on business*—I cannot manage it today, I have been interrupted all the afternoon and it is now past 5 o'clock. In the meantime, kiss her for me.

Greetings from Louise.

Ever yours,
F. E.

First published in:
F. Engels, P. et L. Lafargue,
Correspondance, t. III, Paris, 1959

Printed according to the original

Translated from the French

118

ENGELS TO LAURA LAFARGUE

AT LE PERREUX

London, 14 October 1893

My dear Löhr,

I have received 3 copies of the French *Origine de la famille* etc. To my surprise the words *'entièrement revue par M-me Laura Lafargue'*[a] which were on the proof of the title, do not appear there now. Is this, as I suppose, a little treachery of Ravé? If so I shall protest.

Voilà Fortin of Beauvais who informs me that he intends translating.

1. The *Kritik der Hegelschen Rechtsphilosophie* in the *Deutsch-Französische Jahrbücher* (by Mohr, 1844) and

2. the 3 Chapters *Gewaltstheorie*[b] of my *Anti-Dühring.*

I have absolutely no time to revise his work—and No. 1 is immensely difficult. And rather than revise Fortin's work (which you know from experience) maybe you'd rather do the whole thing yourself. The first— Mohrs epigrammatic style—I consider him uncommonly unfit to render. Nobody but you could do that.

He intends publishing them in the *Ere Nouvelle.*

What do you think I had better say to him?

Glorious victory in Austria. Taaffe proposes an electoral law[270] which is tantamount to universal suffrage at least in towns and industrial districts—so says Adler. Taaffe's policy is to break the power of the German Liberal Party (representing the German and Jewish bourgeoisie) and probably, too, to let as many Socialists replace Liberal Bourgeois as may be necessary to drive the other parties to a closer union and thus to give to him a working majority. The Lower House in Austria is composed of 85 representatives of the large landed proprietors, 21 of the Chamber of Commerce (these 106 are not affected by the new bill), 97 of the towns and 150 of the country districts (both of these will be elected according to the new bill).

For the present the country districts will send about the same Catholic

---

[a] 'completely revised by Mme Laura Lafargue' – [b] Theory of Force.

and Conservative members as hitherto, and the exclusion of analphabetes will here considerably restrict the suffrage; but in the industrial centres of the West and North (Vorarlberg, Austria proper, Bohemia, Moravia, perhaps Steiermark) the new bill will practically establish a very near approach to universal suffrage. It is calculated by bourgeois papers that the number of voters will be 5,200,000 instead of 1,770,000, and the number of socialist seats are estimated at from 20 to 60! Give us 20 to 24 (this is the number of signatures required for a motion to be discussed) and we shall upset the whole of this old-fashioned assembly. It is a complete revolution, our people in Vienna are jubilant, although', of course they insist upon *full* universal suffrage, direct elections, and abolition of the 106 privileged members.

Kind regards from Louise.

Ever yours

F. E.

First published, in the language of the original (English), in: F. Engels, P. et L. Lafargue, *Correspondance*, t. III, 1891-1895, Paris, 1959

Reproduced from the original

119

ENGELS TO NIKOLAI DANIELSON[281]

IN ST. PETERSBURG

London, 17 October 1893

My dear Sir,

When I received your letter of July 26th announcing your return home, I was on the point myself of going abroad for two months and am only just returned.[189] This is the reason of my long silence.

Many thanks for the copies of the *Outlines*[a] three of which I have for-

---

[a] Outlines of Our Post-Reform Economy (1893). [Written in Russian in original.]

warded to appreciative friends. The book, I am glad to see, has caused considerable stir and indeed sensation, as it well merited. Among the Russians I have met, it was the chief subject of conversation. Only yesterday one of them[a] writes:

'we in Russia are arguing over the 'fate of capitalism here'.[b]

In the Berlin *Sozialpolitische Centralblatt*[1] a Mr. P. v. Struve has a long article on your book.[c] I must agree with him in this one point, that for me, too, the present capitalistic phase of development in Russia appears an unavoidable consequence of the historical conditions as created by the Crimean War, the way in which the change of 1861 in agrarian conditions was accomplished, and the political stagnation in Europe generally. Where he is decidedly wrong, is in comparing the present state of Russia with that of the United States, in order to refute what he calls your pessimistic views of the future. He says, the evil consequences of modern capitalism in Russia will be as easily overcome as they are in the United States. There he quite forgets that the United States are modern, bourgeois, from the very origin; that they were founded by petits bourgeois and peasants who ran away from European feudalism in order to establish a purely bourgeois society. Whereas in Russia, we have a groundwork of a primitive communistic character, a pre-civilisation *Gentilgesellsehaft*,[d] crumbling to ruins, it is true, but still serving as the groundwork, the material upon *which* the capitalistic revolution (for it is a real social revolution) acts and operates. In America, *Geldwirthschaft*[e] has been fully established for more than a century, in Russia, *Naturalwirthschaft*[f] was all but exclusively the rule. Therefore it stands to reason that the change, in Russia, must be far more violent, far more incisive, and accompanied by immensely greater sufferings than it can be in America.

But for all that it still seems to me that you take a gloomier view of the case than the facts justify. No doubt, the passage from primitive agrarian communism to capitalistic industrialism cannot take place without terrible dislocation of society, without the disappearance of whole classes and their transformation into other classes; and what enormous suffering, and waste of human lives and productive forces that necessarily implies,

---

[a] Josif Goldenberg – [b] [phrase in Russian], III. Jobrgang, No. 1, Oct. 2, 1893. [Note by Engels, in the original, Oct. 1, which is a misprint.] – [c] P. Struve, 'Zur Beurtheilung der Kapitalistischen Entwickelung Russlands', *Sozialpolitisches Centralblatt*, No. 1, 2 October, 1893. – [d] gentile society – [e] money economy – [f] natural economy

we have seen—on a smaller scale—in Western Europe. But from that to the complete ruin of a great and highly I gifted nation there is still a long way. The rapid increase of population to which you have been accustomed, may be checked; the reckless deforestation combined with the expropriation of the old landlords[a] as well as the peasants, may cause a colossal waste of productive forces; but after all, a population of more than a hundred million will finally furnish a very considerable home market for a very respectable *grande industrie,* and with you, as elsewhere, things will end by finding their own level—if capitalism lasts long enough in Western Europe.

You yourself admit that

> 'the social conditions in Russia after the Crimean War were not favorable to the development of the form of production inherited by us from our past history'.

I would go further, and say, that no more in Russia than anywhere else would it have been possible to develop a higher social form out of primitive agrarian communism unless that higher form was *already in existence* in another country, so as to serve as a model. That higher form being, wherever it is historically possible, the necessary consequence of the capitalistic form of production and of the social dualistic antagonism created by it, it could not be developed directly out of the agrarian commune, unless in imitation of an example already in existence somewhere else. Had the West of Europe been ripe, 1860-70, for such a transformation, had that transformation then been taken in hand in England, France etc., then the Russians would have been called upon to show what could have been made out of their Commune, which was then more or less intact. But the West remained stagnant, no such transformation was attempted, and capitalism was more and more rapidly developed. And as Russia had no choice but this: either to develop the Commune into a form of Production, from which it was separated by a number of historical stages, and for which not even in the West the conditions were then ripe—evidently an impossible task—or else to develop into Capitalism, what remained to her but the latter chance?

As to the Commune, it is only possible so long as the differences of wealth among its members are but trifling. As soon as these differences become great, as soon as some of its members become the debt-slaves of the richer members, it can no longer live. The big peasants and village exploiters[b]

---

[a] [In Russian] – [b] [In Russian]

of Athens, before Solon, have destroyed the Athenian *gens* with the same implacability with which those of your country destroy the Commune. I am afraid that institution is doomed. But on the other hand, Capitalism opens out new views and new hopes. Look at what it has done and is doing in the West. A great nation like yours outlives every crisis. There is no great historical evil without a compensating historical progress. Only the *modus operandi* is changed. *Que les destinées s'accomplissent!*[a]

Yours ever

When Vol. III[b] in the press, will take care to send you advance sheets.

First published, in Russian,
in *Minuvshiye gody*, No. 2,
St. Petersburg, 1908

Reproduced from the original

120

ENGELS TO LAURA LAFARGUE

AT LE PERREUX

London, 18 October 1893

My dear Löhr,

Liebknecht informs me that the honorarium for Paul's letters having to be voted by the *Parteivorstand*,[c] he is as yet not in a position to reply. This is excusable. When we left Berlin, the *Parteivorstand*[c] was overwhelmed with very important business; then Liebknecht and Bebel had to leave for agitating tournées in Saxony where to-morrow the elections for the Saxon Landtag take place. Immediately upon that follows the Cologne Parteitag,[279] again taking the members of the *Vorstand* away from their regular activity.

---

[a] May destiny take its course! – [b] of *Capital* – [c] Party Executive Committee

Talking of the *Parteitag*,[a] at Cologne, Bonnier writes to say *il est possible que nous n'irons pas à Cologne, n'ayant pas reçu d'adresse du parti allemand.*[b] The address is everyday in the *Vorwärts*: '*Das Zentral-Empfangsbureau befindet sich: Hotel Durst (nomen est omen!), früher Gasthof zur Post. Marzellenstr. 5, in der Nähe des Zentralbahnhofs und des Doms*'.[c] The address of the paper *Rheinische Zeitung* is Grosser Griechenmarkt 115.

To Fortin I write[25] saying that he has to keep his hands off *Dühring*, and that the article of Mohr's is almost impossible to be translated, and moreover that I cannot undertake to revise his work.[d] I told him you were 'in possession' of *Dühring*[e] and that you had revised Ravé! I further told him you did not know the article of Mohr, perhaps he might let you have his copy to look it over; but nothing more; no hopes that you would or *might* do the work of revision for him.

I am very sorry you deleted your name from that title-page.[f] It would be a capital handle to work in connection with getting publishers, and *paying ones*, for your other translations. You have no business to be ashamed of your own good work, or to allow Ravé to adorn himself with other bird's feathers. There is no reason whatever for you to 'keep in the background'. And this kind of work nowadays ought to bring in money to you—surely *Ravé* is paid, and paid handsomely for his bad work which has to be licked into decent shape by you—and I do not see why you should not reap where you have sown.

Love from Louise
Ever yours
F. Engels

First published, in the language of the original (English), in: F. Engels, P. et L. Lafargue, *Correspondance*, t. III, 1891-1895, Paris, 1959

Reproduced from the original

---

[a] Party Congress – [b] we may not go to Cologne, not having received the address of the German Party – [c] The Central Reception Office is at: Hotel Durst (thirst—the name is an omen!)—formerly Gasthof zur Post, Marzellenstrasse 5, near the central railway station and the Cathedral. – [d] See this volume, p. 221 – [e] F. Engels, *Anti-Dühring* – [f] See this volume, p. 211

121

ENGELS TO AUGUST BEBEL

IN COLOGNE

London, 18 October 1393

Dear August,

I have just received notification from the publishers of the *Vorwärts*, etc., that they 'plan' to re-issue the *Anti-Dühring* and that all they require of me is to append a few brief remarks to the new edition. What I myself might perhaps 'plan' no one bothered to ask.

Now you will recall that during our trip[189] we agreed to give the *Anti-Dühring* to Dietz and, in lieu thereof, the shorter, more popular stuff to the *Vorwärts*. I shall therefore provisionally acquaint the gentlemen in Berlin of that fact, lest they should delude themselves further. I am sending this straight to Cologne, as I understand from Louise that you will be going from there to Stuttgart and will thus be able to discuss the matter with Dietz. The following are my terms for an edition of a size he can determine himself but of which he must also notify me:

1. A fee of 15% of the retail price, i.e. 15 Pfg. per mark. That is what we get here in England for *translations* of my stuff. Since the book does not, after all, lend itself to bulk sales except in a limited degree, he can fix the price accordingly.

2. The fee to be paid to Dr Victor Adler of Vienna.[282]

3. Dietz to undertake not to reduce the price either of the whole or of part without my written consent. This is to prevent the book from being used, as has happened before, to help shift certain slow-moving stock.

That is all.

As you know, Liebknecht (on that Sunday in Grunewald) tackled me with a view to my reminding Lafargue about regular work as a correspondent. This I promised to do as soon as he let me know that the Executive had approved Lafargue's fee. A report of the Paris Marxist Congress[283] from a Paris correspondent then appeared in the *Vorwärts*. I inquired of Lafargue[a] (having heard nothing from Liebknecht) whether it was by

---

[a] See this volume, pp. 208-09

him, to which he replied in the *negative*. Whereupon I asked Liebknecht[25] how the matter stood and have now received the following answer:

> 'Before leaving for Saxony, whence I have just returned, I wrote to August asking him to settle the matter with Lafargue. I am dependent on the Executive in all questions involving extraordinary expenditure.'

So it seems that you are once again to be held responsible for the omissions of others. Now admittedly the Executive has of late been absolutely overwhelmed with work, but I would venture to point out that the engagement of a newspaper correspondent could be attended to in a matter of minutes. It almost seems to me as though Liebknecht, with his growing predilection for Vaillant, had no particular desire to fix things up with Lafargue, otherwise he would no doubt have settled the matter *before* the Paris Congress and in that case would also have received the *authentic* report of it (the French did not admit reporters or members of the public).

Over here all is bustle. The day before yesterday we had Lehmann and Mrs Adams Walther and today we have Shmuilov, who proposes to marry here. I asked Mrs. Adams Walther about her arrangements with Foulger. She knew nothing definite, but will make inquiries from the friend who saw to the matter and will let me know the result. From what she was able to say, it seems highly probable that the copyright has been tacitly assigned to Foulger, and in that case absolutely no action whatever can be taken against Reeves other than by inserting an announcement in the papers to the effect that the said text has long been out of date.[265]

I intended to send you the 20 marks I borrowed on the last day but have not got round to going into town and collecting German notes. You shall have it next time. Should there be a further amount owing to you, as is quite possible, perhaps you would remind me in your next.

Tussy has got Lassalle's letters and will copy them out on her typewriter.[284] She will charge you the usual rate and I shall pay her. But what are you giving the heirs in the way of a fee? The handwriting is such that I still can't tell how much it will be.

21 Oct. Yesterday this letter was laid aside yet again, as I had to take Shmuilov to the registry office and help him deal with the preliminary formalities, he being unfamiliar with English and I being unable to find anyone else. It will be a month before the actual joining together in matrimony can take place.

In Austria the cause is doing splendidly. The general disorientation of the parties, the Emperor's[a] vacillation and the virtual certainty of a dissolution and new elections will provide occasion for the most splendid agitation on the part of our chaps and for creating a thorough commotion in the old morass. The various aristocratic and bourgeois parties are scuttling about in all directions like ants in the ruins of an antheap. The old order, shaky as it was, has now gone for good and all we have to do is see to it that things don't calm down again. And that won't be difficult.

Obviously there will be repercussions in Germany. Just as in 1848 when Vienna kicked off on 13 March, thereby compelling Berlin to follow suit on the 18th. Brussels[276] Vienna[270]—Berlin—is now the natural 'alphabetical order'. Prussian and other forms of local suffrage, the Constitution of Hamburg, etc., will doubtless each in turn have to swallow it. The period of stagnation and reaction in the legislative field that began in 1870 is over. Governments are again coming under the control of a living political movement among the people and it is we who are at the back of that movement, it is *we* who determine it, now negatively, now positively. We are now what the Liberals were before 1848, and our victories in the Belgian and Austrian elections have shown that the ferment we provide is strong enough to complete the process of fermentation now begun. But the process will be neither smooth nor rapid until we have also won direct or indirect victories in Germany—conquests in the libertarian sense, greater political power for the working man, the extension of his freedom of movement. And that too will come.

If you make use of the passages from Miquel's letters, don't expend all your powder at one go. Remember that hardly have the things *come out* than the effect is lost and cannot be repeated—unless, that is, we still have some ammunition in reserve.

There was a *very real* risk of a general strike in Austria and one cannot yet rule out the possibility of its being set in train *for the benefit of* Taaffe's ministry and his electoral reforms,[270] which would certainly be the height of historical irony. When the English miners were locked out,[b] it was clear how bemusing such a muddle-headed notion could be. The basic idea is to force the hand of the bourgeoisie by means of a general shortage of coal. This has its points if the workers take the offensive, i.e. do so when business is good. When business is depressed, on the other hand, industrialists find themselves with excessive stocks and collieries

---

[a] Francis Joseph I – [b] See this volume, p. 204

with more coal than they can sell. It is then that the capitalists seize the initiative, the aim being to cut down production by means of lock-outs, and to depress wages at the same time—in such a case a general strike is grist to the capitalists' mill, since it is in *their* interest that the production of coal be curtailed. What the English ought to have done was to advise the Continental miners *not* to strike on any account, so that if possible coal might be brought from the Continent to England. But everywhere people's heads were turned by the catchword 'general strike', the lockout in England was followed by the Belgian and French strikes[285] and such effect as these had in England could only have been of benefit to the capitalists.

Whereas the big colliery owners are still putting up a fight, more and more of the smaller ones are knuckling under. Some 80,000 men are back at work but about 200,000 are still out. The big ones are threatening the workers with the ultimate sanction, namely eviction from colliery-owned dwellings. If there were strike breakers ready and willing to move into these houses, the collieries would unquestionably see to it that this was done and would receive military aid to that end. Such, however, is not the case, and for the sake of a purely arbitrary act, the sole purpose of which would be to deposit the workers without shelter outside houses that would *remain empty,* the government will be unlikely to expose itself once again to the unpopularity it would attract as a result of a fusillade, as recently at Featherstone.[286] If it happens nevertheless, much blood will be spilt. This is an ultimate sanction the workers won't submit to.

The Avelings will be coming shortly, having just announced themselves for a meal. This house is like a dovecote. So good-bye and my regards to everyone, including Dietz and K. Kautsky and wife[a] when you get to Stuttgart.

Yours,
F. E.

First published, in Russian, in: Marx and Engels, *Works,* First Russian Edition, Vol. XXIX, Moscow, 1946

Printed according to the original and, partly, according to the book: *August Bebels Briefwechsel mit Friedrich Engels,* London-The Hague-Paris, 1965

Published in English for the first time

---

[a] Luise Kautsky

122

ENGELS TO LAURA LAFARGUE

AT LE PERREUX

London, 27 October 1893

My dear Löhr,

Though Fortin is a business-man, yet with the help of a Roumanian (with business habits partly of a Polish Jew, partly of a spendthrift boyar) he succeeds in creating a very fair muddle.

I wrote to Fortin[25] that you did not know the *Kritik der Rechtsphilosophie*[a] but if he thought proper, he *might send you his copy* of the *Deutsch-Französische Jahrbücher* so that you might read it and form an idea as to the advisability—both an to contents and to form—of its being submitted to the French working people. Diamandy, in his eagerness to get stuff for his review,[b] rushes at you and transforms, moreover, the one article into *plusieurs*[c] (business principles of the Polish Jew, to ask much so as to be able to rebate) as for instance:

— *Was kostet die Elle von dem Stoff?*

— *Fünfzehn Groschen.*

— *Fünfzehn sagt er, zwölfeinenhalben meint er, zehn wird er nehmen, sieben und einen halben ist die Sache werth, fünf möcht ich ihm geben, werd' ich ihm bieten zwei und einen halben Groschen!*[d]

Voilà ce que c'est.[e] Let Fortin first send you his copy and then you will see what you will see.

As to the *Gewalttheorie*,[f] not a line in Fortin's letter led me to conclude that the thing had *been* already *done* and I don't believe it either. To make you believe that you are *en face d'un fait accompli*, is another of these Oriental tricks which they consider perfectly justifiable in the service of the

---

[a] See this volume, p. 211 – [b] *L'Ere nouvelle* – [c] several
– [d] 'How much is a yard of that stuff?'
  'Fifteen pence.'
  'He says fifteen, he means twelve-and-a-half, he would take ten, the thing's worth seven-and-a-half, I'd be prepared to give him five, so I'll offer him tuppence ha' penny!'
– [e] This is the thing. – [f] 'Theory of Force' (see F. Engels, *Anti-Dühring*, present edition, Vol. 25, pp. 146-71).

cause. You will never arrive at the facts, much less at any practical conclusion, until you have eliminated Diamandy and deal direct with Fortin.

Diamandy served me exactly the same with regard to the translation of the *Ursprung*[a] for the *Ère Nouvelle*.

I had a few lines from Bebel to-day about Paul's affair.[b] The delay was caused by 1. the Saxon elections; 2. the Cologne Congress[279] which prevented full meetings of the Executives, and overwhelmed them with business. As soon as both Bebel and Liebknecht shall have returned to Berlins, the matter will be settled. But Bebel says at the same time, there is a great distrust of Paris correspondents of French nationality, as hitherto everyone of them has ceased to write reports at the very moment when French affairs became highly interesting—they then looked after their own business and left the *Vorwärts* to shift for themselves. I shall do my best to persuade them that now Paul has no longer a free pass an the railways, this will cease as far as *he* is concerned, but I do hope that our Paris friends will at last learn to treat business as business and engagements as things to be fulfilled—at least *as a rule*.

Kind regards from Louise.

Ever yours,
F. Engels

First published, it the language
of the original (English): in: F. Engels,
P. et L. Lafargue, *Correspondance*,
t. III, 1891-1895, Paris, 1959

Reproduced from the original

123

ENGELS TO FERDINAND WOLFF[287]

IN OXFORD

[*Draft*]

[London,] end of October 1893

You write to say that 'I have disclosed...'. I do not know what hoary piece of gossip you are referring to and indeed this is a matter of the

---

[a] *Origin*, see this volume, pp. 211 – [b] See this volume, pp. 208-9, 215

utmost indifference to me. But when you start talking pompously about your 'silence', it evidently implies the threat that you might now break that silence. In which case you have met your match. If it really is your intention to threaten me, I have only one answer and that is: 'do your worst'. I don't care two hoots whether you speak or hold your tongue. But what I cannot understand at all in how you came to write me such an inane letter. I can find me explanation for it other than the state of nervous tension you are in. Otherwise you would realise that such conduct would debar me absolutely from having any further contact with you until you have rehabilitated yourself in my eyes.[a]

First published, in Russian,
in: Marx and Engels, *Works*,
Second Russian Edition,
Vol. 39, Moscow, 1966

Printed according to the original

Published in English for the first time

124

ENGELS TO KARL KAUTSKY

IN STUTTGART

London, 3 November 1893

Dear Baron,

1. Howell. His book *Conflicts*, etc., is a fat compendium of 536 pages and would in my opinion find few buyers in Germany, especially since all the earlier history and some of the later stuff is cribbed from Brentano.[b] Howell's *Trades Unionism New and Old*, 235 pp., is a shorter excerpt which appeared it 1891 and is also a year more up to date in regard to facts. If it was checked, provided with notes and translated in abbreviated form, it might possibly find buyers.

But Dietz must not allow himself to be cheated again as he was by

---

[a] See this volume, p. 243 – [b] L. Brentano, *Die Arbeitergilden den Gegenwart*. Bd. 1-2, Leipzig, 1871-72.

Sonnenschein through Stepniak[288] over the £25, which was just money thrown down the drain and which, besides, gives English publishers a false impression of their German colleagues business acumen. One ought not to make oneself an object of derision to such people. The only way to impress Englishmen is to insist on one's rights.

Well then, if one is to protect one's translation rights, the first part of the translation must, in accordance with international law, be published one year after the appearance of the original. In that case one is protected for three years in the country and language concerned, Otherwise not. According to this, neither Howell nor his publisher[a] have a claim to anything, legally speaking. Only considerations of decency could come into it. If Dietz is willing to conduct negotiations with Howell via Aveling (who is well acquainted with such matters) on a verbal basis and authorise him to offer, say, £2.10 = 50 marks, if pushed. Howell would probably consent to the translation *absolutely gratis*. I don't see why one should needlessly stuff money down the throats of the supercilious English so that they can brag to us Continentals about the commercial value of their books not only here but over there, while we poor devils are expected to be grateful when they do us the honour of translating us, even though we haven't been asked. And that blackguard Howell, to boot!

2. I can understand that you should wish to go to Vienna.[289] Austria is now the most important country in Europe, at any rate for the moment. It is here that the initiative lies, which in a year or two will have its repercussions in Germany and other countries. The good Taafe has set the ball rolling and it won't come to a halt so very soon.[270] Such being the case, it is only natural that every Austrian should wish to co-operate, for there's going to be enough to do. I was delighted with the Viennese; they are splendid fellows if sanguine, sanguine to a degree, no Frenchman could do better, and that means that they should not be spurred on but rather reined in, lest the fruits of long years of work be dissipated in a single day. Last night Ede read out to me what you had written to him about an article on the strike as a political weapon. I firmly advised *him* against writing the article.[290] To my mind the affair of the three-class electorate[291] has already earned him quite enough of a reputation as a man who has lost touch with the masses and who, from without, from his writing-desk, discourses in doctrinaire fashion on questions of immediate practical

---

[a] Frederick Orridge Macmillan

moment.[a] But I am also generally of the opinion that the effect of such an article could not be other than extremely harmful at this particular juncture. However cautious it might be, and however impartial and considered the language in which it was couched, the Vienna *Volkstribüne* would pick out the passages that *suited* its own book, reprint them in bold type and use them to scare off those who have enough trouble as it is in restraining the Viennese from embarking on hare-brained escapades. You say yourself that barricades are out of date (though they might come in handy again as soon as a third or two-fifths of the army had turned socialist and it was imperative that they be given an opportunity of changing sides), but a political strike must either score an immediate victory—simply by means of a threat (as in Belgium[276] where the army was *very shaky*)—or else end in a colossal fiasco or, finally, *lead direct to barricades*. And this in Vienna where you could be shot down without more ado by Czechs, Croats, Ruthenians,[292] etc. Once this business in Vienna has been settled one way or the other, either with or without a political general strike, the question will still be topical enough for the Neue Zeit. But just now a public discussion of the general theoretical pros and cons of this weapon could only be grist to the mill of the FIREBRANDS in Vienna. I know how difficult it is for Victor to counteract the magic power exerted on the Viennese masses by the catchword 'general strike' and how happy he will be if only he can put off the day of reckoning. That being so we ought, in my opinion, to take the utmost care not to do or say anything that might encourage the impetuous elements.

The Viennese working men should wait until the suffrage has given them the means to *take stock* of themselves and of their friends in the provinces; they will then be appraised of their strength and of how it compares with that of their opponents.

Incidentally, things might get to the stage when a general strike would be carried out under the aegis and more or less for the benefit of Electoral Reform Minister Taaffe. That would be the height of irony.

3. Once again my thanks for the *Parlamentarismus*[b] which you presented to me personally in Zurich.

4. As regards Heine's letter,[260] Tussy tells me she will give you her per-

---

[a] E. Bernstein, 'Die preussischen Landtagswahlen und die Sozial-demokratie. Ein Vorschlag zur Diskussion', *Die Neue Zeit*, No. 52, 1892-93. – [b] K. Kautsky, *Der Parlamentarismus, die Volksgesetzgebung und die Sozialdemokratie*, Stuttgart, 1893.

mission provided that Laura also agrees. I have hardly seen anything of Tussy lately—since I got back[189]—and then only for an odd moment or so. Both of them are tremendously busy and, because of meetings, they hardly ever put in an appearance on Sundays. However I should like to take another look at the letter before I say anything definite. The matter is open to considerable misinterpretation and must be given *much* thought.

5. Volume III.[a] Fair sheets. When the time comes I shall see to it that these sheets are placed at your or Ede's disposal *section by section*, provided, that is, I can get them out of Meissner. For I already need another copy for the Russian translation and Meissner is growing old and is no longer so accommodating as in the past. However I shall do my best. There are six sections in all, each of which I shall send you separately after it has come off the press.

Since returning I haven't done a stroke of work on the above but next week I hope finally to buckle to again.

6. The thing by Guillaumin and V. Pareto has just been sent to me by Lafargue—extracts were made by Lafargue; the introduction was evidently written by a bogus vulgar economist.[293]

To come back to the general strike, you ought not to forget that nobody was more delighted than the Belgian leaders that the affair should have turned out so well. They have had an anxious enough time and might have been forced to implement their threat; they themselves knew only too well how little they could accomplish. And this in a primarily *industrial* country with a thoroughly shaky and ill-disciplined militia-style army. But if, in such a country, there was nevertheless a chance of achieving something with this weapon,[276] what hope could there be in Austria where the peasant predominates, industry is sparse and relatively weak, the big towns are few and far between, the nationalities have been set at odds with one another and the socialists make up less than ten per cent of the total population (of adult males, naturally)! So for heaven's sake let us avoid taking any step that might tempt the working men, who are in any case impatient and thirsting for action, to stake their all on one card—and, what's more, at a time when the government wants this and could use provocation to bring it about.

The *Vorwärts* will always remain the same old *Vorwärts*. Of that I was left in no doubt while in Berlin. So I'm glad that the weekly[b] is to come

---

[a] of *Capital* – [b] *Der Sozialdemokrat*

out, for it will give the party an opportunity of appearing, at least in foreign eyes, in a form it need not be ashamed of. The *Vorwärts* comes out in Berlin, is read almost exclusively in Berlin (nine-tenths of sales) and, as a product of Berlin, is always viewed with indulgence. The weekly will also act as a counterweight to the *Vorwärts* influence on the rest of the party press. How things will work out as regards the mutual relationship of the two organs remains to be seen. I don't imagine that they will come to blows. The *Vorwärts'* subsidiary title of 'Central Organ' is of no importance whatever. They are welcome to the catchword.

At any rate, all kinds of changes are taking place in our party press, I am curious to know what will become of the *Neue Zeit*[85]; its reversion to a monthly was at all events a bold move. I don't believe that *in the long run* the weekly will prove a serious competitor.

So the best of luck when you visit Vienna. When you get there you might pay my respects to the Lowenbräu next to the Burgtheater; it used to be our midday headquarters.

With regards from household to household.

Your,
F. E.

First published in the book:
*Aus der Frühzeit des Marxismus.
Engels Briefwechsel mit Kautsky,*
Prague, 1935

Printed according to the original

Published in English for the first time

125

ENGELS TO VICTOR ADLER

IN VIENNA

London, 10 November 1893

Dear Victor,

I am sending you herewith part of a letter from August. I do not share his misgivings, for it seems to me that such possibilities are too remote and by now may to some extent be excluded. Make sure that the letter is destroyed as requested.

My letter of 11 October[a] crossed with yours of the same date. You will have seen that we are fully in agreement as regards our general view of the situation in Austria, a situation that seems to me rather more favourable now than it was then. Electoral reform, taking Taaffe's Bill as the minimum, will no longer be relegated to the background in Vienna. The Emperor[b] has approved it and the Emperor cannot back down. He, however, is far more representative of Austria than the Diet. It would seem that the new-born coalition goverment is already expiring, but even if this is not the case, it will come to grief at the first sign of positive action. Even if, as August supposes, it were to marshall the forces of Baernreitherism,[294] that would be no more than a very temporary expedient and would not prevent a collapse, should the question of action arise in some other quarter. This much is certain; Austria is now in the van of the European political movement, while we others limp along behind—even those countries that already have universal suffrage will not be able to elude the impulse provided by Austria. At Ronacher they *wanted* a set-to.[295] If you succeed it keeping the chaps on a tight rein, you can't go wrong. The one thing that might bring Windischgrätz, Plener and Jaworski together would be a set-to in Vienna and a victory combined with a fusillade.

Over here we're doing very nicely, In matters of serious reform the Liberal government is proving an abject failure. Even the Fabian society[43] has foresworn its allegiance and disavowed its whole policy of permeation. See the article by Autolycus (Burgess) on page one of the *Workman's Times*[c] on the Fabian manifesto which appeared in the *Fortnightly Review*.[d] If the Liberals can't do any better, there'll be a mass of Labour candidates come the next elections, and between thirty and forty will probably get in. In the municipal elections on 1 November the working men of the North began to take stock of themselves and scored a good many successes.

Regards from Louise and yours,

F. E.

---

[a] 10 Oct. in the original, which is a misprint, see this volume, p. 199 – [b] Francis Joseph I – [c] [J. Burgess] Autolycus, 'In a White Sheet', *Workman's Times*, 11 November 1893. – [d] 'To Your Tents, oh Israel!', *The Fortnightly Review*, No. 323, New Series, 1 November 1893.

First published in the book:
*Victor Adlers Aufadtze, Reden
und Briefe. Erstes Heft: Victor
Adler und Friedrich Engels,*
Wien, 1922

Printed according to the book

Published in English for the first time

126

ENGELS TO FRIEDRICH ADOLPH SORGE[43]

IN HOBOKEN

London, November 11, 1893

Dear Sorge,

Herewith a letter to Mrs Kelley (ex-Wischnewetzky) which I would ask you kindly to forward to her.[a] As soon as you know her present *correct* address, perhaps you would also be so good as to forward her the enclosed cheque for £1.12.11 of the Union Bank of London.

You should read the article by Autolycus[b] (Burgess)[43] on page 1 of today's *Workman's Times* on the Fabians' manifesto.[c] These gentlemen, who for years have declared that the emancipation of the working class can only be accomplished through the Great Liberal Party, who have loudly proclaimed that during elections any independent action by the workers vis-à-vis other candidates, Liberals included, is covert Toryism, who have let it be known that the permeation of the liberal party by socialist principles is the sole object in life for a Socialist,[59] now declare that the Liberals are traitors, that it is impossible to deal with them and that in the next elections the workers should, without regard for Liberals or Tories, put up their own candidates with the help of £30,000 which are meanwhile to be found by the Trades Unions—assuming that the latter do the Fabians this favour, which they assuredly won't. It is an outright *paterpeccati*[d] by these supercilious bourgeois who would graciously condescend to liberate the proletariat from above, provided only that the latter were sensible enough to realise that such a raw, uneducated mass could

---

[a] See this volume, p. 230 – [b] [J. Burgess] Autolycus, 'In a White Sheet', *Workman's Times*, 11 November 1893. – [c] 'To Your Tents, oh Israel!', The *Fortnightly Review*, No. 323, New Series, 1 November 1893. – [d] confession of guilt

not liberate itself and would come to nothing save by the grace of these canny advocates, literati and sentimental old women. And now the first attempt by these gentlemen, an attempt heralded by drums and trumpets as a worldshaking event, has gone so splendidly awry that they themselves must admit as much. That is what's so funny about the affair.

Warm regards to you and your wife. I hope you will both get through this winter better than the last. Over here it is already starting to turn wintry.

Yours,

F. E.

First published abridged in
Briefe und Auszüge aus Briefen
von Joh. Phil. Becker, Jos. Dietzgen,
Friedrich Engels, Karl Marx u. A. an
F. A. Sorge und Andere, Stuttgart, 1906
and in full, in Russian, in:
Marx and Engels, *Works,*

First Russian Edition,
Vol. XXIX, Moscow, 1946

Printed according to the original

Published in English in full for the
first time

127

ENGELS TO FLORENCE KELLEY-WISCHNEWETZKY[296]

IN CHICAGO

London 11 November 1893
122 Regent's Park Road, N. W.

Dear Mrs Kelley,

I have received from Swan Sonnenschein a/c Sales[a] for July 92—June 93 as follows:

Regular Sales 50 (plus 4 — 13 Copies) 3/6. — £8.l5.
Special Sales 51 (one copy to America!) *4.8.9*

£13.3.9 3

12½% of which = *£1.12.11*

As I am not certain whether your last address (Hull House, 335 s. Halsted St. Chicago) still holds good, I think it safer to send the cheque

---

[a] of the 2nd English edition of Engels' *The Condition of the Working Class in England*

to our friend Mr Sorge of Hoboken who will forward it to you as soon as you let him know that you have received this note.

We now and then see short reports of your activity in the papers, among others your speech in the Labor Congress, and are glad to find that you have found congenial work. With kind regards from Mrs Kautsky and myself

I remain Yours very truly

F. Engels

First published, in Russian,
in: Marx and Engels, *Works*,
Second Russian Edition,
Vol. 50, Moscow, 1981

Reproduced from the original

Published in English for the first time

128

ENGELS TO PAUL LAFARGUE

AT LE PERREUX

London, 19 November 1893

My dear Lafargue,

Liebknecht will have written telling you that they want to take you on as correspondent for *Vorwärts* and the Hamburg *Echo*, one letter a week, identical and sent simultaneously to the two journals, but they want it in German and suggest that Laura should translate it.

Herein the reason why they want it in German, and it is a very important one. The two papers could publish the identical report *on the same day*, so that it would be an original article in each of them. If publication is not simultaneous, if one of the two papers prints it a day later, it will be suspected of having taken the article from the previous day's issue of the other, like so many other news items taken from that issue.

Now there might be someone in Hamburg who would translate you—don't ask me how!—but in Berlin! There Liebknecht has established the custom of all translations being done by Mme Liebknecht or by one of his sons. The manuscript goes to Charlottenburg and into Liebknecht's house and God alone knows when the translation reaches the newspaper office. So there would be perpetual delays and, what is worse, delays of unpredictable length.

Therefore, the possibility of using your letters for the two papers and paying you a correspondent' salary depends entirely on your letters being sent in German. Furthermore this would safeguard you against editorial criticism; Bonnier tells me that Liebknecht rather overdid it with Guesde, which is what finally sickened him. The Hamburg editorial board, being entirely independent and, what is more, not knowing what goes on in Berlin and vice versa, your articles would be printed without being cut either in the one or the other paper, or, which is most likely, in both.

The question now is, will Laura be willing to do the translation? I hope so; that would enable you to clinch the matter at once. I am sure that with a little practice she would write as well in German as in English and French.

But, if this fails, would there be no way of having the translation done? Is there nobody who, in consideration of a small share of your fees, would do this job for you? Let us say 10 francs a letter for the translation and two copies, which would leave you 40 francs a letter, and would still provide an incentive to the translator. What about Frankel? But perhaps he himself is a *Vorwärts* correspondent (I have no idea at all who provides the Paris letters which I see in it from time to time). Anyway, think about it and try to arrange something. You realise that our Berlin people are doing their utmost, try to facilitate the business for them. And don't forget that this will enable you to speak to 60,000-70,000 subscribers, i.e., at least 250,000 readers without counting the readers of other papers who borrow their articles from these two organs, the most important ones that our Party in Germany has.

In any case, make a start with *Vorwärts* and leave the arrangements for the *Echo* and the translation for later. But it would be wise not to lose time over it. And further: Bebel as well as Liebknecht insist upon a *regular* contribution which will give them the outstanding events and your reflections and reports on the general situation. One letter a week, and on a fixed day, determined by yourself (I do not think they will lay down the day for you).

My love to Laura from whom I am still awaiting adamant[a] and other news.

---

[a] A play on words: *adamantin*—adamant, *diamanti*—a diamond, Diamandy—a surname (see this volume, pp. 221-22)

Greetings from Louise.

Ever yours,
F. E.

First published in:
F. Engels, P. et L. Lafargue,
Correspondance, t. III, Paris, 1959

Printed according to the original

Translated from the French

129

ENGELS TO NATALIE LIEBKNECHT[297]

IN BERLIN

London, 1 December 1893
122 Regent's Park Road, N. W.

Dear Mrs Liebknecht,

Thank you very much for your letter and kind good wishes for my 73rd birthday which I passed in the best of health and spirits. The Avelings and Bernsteins spent the evening with us, and empty bottles bore testimony to our good humour and general sense of well-being. If things go on like this there will, so far as I am concerned, be no reason why I should not repeat my visit to Berlin,[189] in which case we could again take coffee in the Zoological Gardens and comment upon the four-legged and two-legged, winged and wingless, roaring and talking zoological specimens on display, whether in captivity or at large.

Poor Gizycki! He's unable to walk as it is, and now they are also trying to prevent him from talking, and this, because he illicitly consorts with Social Democrats. Prussia is indeed not only a civilised state, but also a state of illuminati!

I am very sorry that your Karl should have acquired fibrositis while on His Majesty's service but let us hope he will soon get over it. At all events the best thing to do, once one finds oneself in those circumstances, is to carry out one's duties properly. I can readily imagine that *messieurs les officiers* will take care not to compromise themselves in the eyes of your sons,[a] those two sappers being uncomfortably close to the portals of the

---

[a] Karl and Theodor Liebknecht

Reichstag, for they are reluctant to figure personally in the debates there, no matter what the Minister of War[a] may say. And if in addition your sons, as used to be demanded of us volunteers[255] by my erstwhile captain, set 'an example to the company' then, their father notwithstanding, they cannot fail to gain promotion to non-commissioned rank. And that would be only right and proper. If Bebel is the son of an N.C.O., why should not Liebknecht be the father of one or more N.C.O.s? You've no idea how much nicer a uniform looks, with lace on, and, it would seem, that in Berlin the fair sex is far more susceptible to Moloch thus adorned. Nor is that by any means all, for as Heine says:

> But still more charming than all else
> Are Caesar's golden epaulettes[b]

However, we are unlikely to rise to such heights as that.

Well, the year of mourning in uniform will soon be over and then Karl will go to Hamm[298] which is also a very nice spot—or used to be; it was my mother's birthplace and I often used to go there as a child, but now everything has changed and it's a smoky, industrial sort of hole, though quite tolerable to live in.

Well, goodbye now, and please give my warm regards to Liebknecht and your children. We shall hold Liebknecht to his promise of coming here after the New Year. Mrs Kautsky also sends you all her warmest regards.

Ever yours,
F. Engels

First published, in Russian,
in: Marx and Engels, *Works*,
First Russian Edition,
Vol. XXIX, Moscow, 1946

Printed according to the original

Published in English for the first time

---

[a] Walter Bronsart von Schellendorff – [b] Heinrich Heine, *Himmelsbräute* (from 'Romanzero')

130

ENGELS TO FRIEDRICH ADOLPH SORGE[184]

IN HOBOKEN

London, 2 December 1893
122 Regent's Park Road, N. W.

Dear Sorge,

Many thanks to you and your wife for your good wishes and for your letter of 19 November.

I am very sorry to hear that you are suffering from gout and hope that it will recede as time goes on; it's an insidious complaint.

The repeal of the silver purchase law[187] has saved America from a serious financial crisis and will help to promote an industrial recovery. But I am not sure whether it might not have been better had there really been a crash. The phrase 'cheap money' seems to be deeply engraved in the minds of your Western farmers. In the first place, when they suppose that, if there be ample means of circulation in a country, the rate of interest must fall, they are confusing means of circulation with disposable money capital, a matter upon which considerable light will be shed in Volume III.[a] And, secondly, all debtors find it convenient to incur debts in good currency and subsequently pay them off in depreciated currency. Hence every indebted Prussian Junker clamours for bimetallism[299] that would rid him of his debts in disguised, Solonic fashion.[300] Had it been possible to postpone silver reform in the United States until there had been time for the consequences of this foolishness to redound on the farmers also, it would have dinned some sense into many a thick skull.

Tariff reform,[301] however slowly it may be put into operation, would already seem to have given rise to a kind of panic among the manufacturers of New England. I have learnt—both from private sources and the newspapers—that large numbers of workers are being laid off. But all this will die down the moment the Bill goes through and puts an end to the uncertainty. I am convinced that, in all the larger branches of industry, America can boldly go into competition with England.

As regards the German Socialists in America, things are pretty dire.

---

[a] K. Marx, *Capital*, Vol. III, Chapters XXIX-XXXIV.

The chaps you get from Germany are not as a rule the best—these stay over here—and are not in any case a fair sample of the German party. And, like everywhere else, every new arrival at once feels impelled to destroy and refashion everything that already exists so that a new era may be seen as having started with him. Moreover, the majority of these greenhorns remain stuck in New York for a long time if not for life, they are constantly being reinforced by new importations and are thus relieved of the necessity of learning the language of the country or acquiring a proper knowledge of American conditions. All this does a great deal of harm no doubt, but on the other hand there is no denying that conditions in America present considerable and peculiar difficulties to the *steady* growth of a labour party.

In the first place the constitution, based as in England on party government, whereby any vote not given to a candidate put up by one of the two government parties is regarded as *lost*. And neither an American nor an Englishman, since he wishes to influence the body politic, will throw away his vote.

Then, and more especially, immigration, which splits the workers into two groups, native-born and foreign, and the latter again into 1. Irish, 2. Germans, 3. a number of smaller groups, each speaking only its own language—Czechs, Poles, Italians, Scandinavians, etc. And, in addition, the negroes. To form a party of one's own out of all these calls for exceptionally strong incentives. Every now and again a powerful élan may suddenly make itself felt, but all the bourgeoisie has to do is to stick it out passively, whereupon the dissimilar working-class elements will disintegrate again.

3. Finally, the protective tariff system and the steady growth of the domestic market must have exposed the workers to a prosperity unlike anything that has been experienced for many years in Europe, (with the exception of Russia where, however, it is not the workers who reap the benefit but the middle classes).

A country like America, when really ripe for a socialist labour party, is certainly not going to be deterred by a handful of German socialist doctrinaires.

Part I of Vol. III (246 ms. pages out of approx. 1855) is ready for press.[a] *This is between ourselves.* Progress will, I hope, now be rapid.

---

[a] K. Marx, *Capital*, Vol. III, Book III, Chapters I-VII.

Cordial regards to you and your wife, and best wishes for your recovery from L. Kautsky and

Yours,

F. Engels

L. Kautsky, who will reply shortly, thanks you for your kindness, and has already written re the *Arbeiter-Zeitung* (Vienna); the *Pionierkalender* has *not* arrived.

First published, abridged in
*Briefe und Auszüge aus
Briefen von Joh. Phil. Becker, Jos.
Dietzgen, Friedrich Engels, Karl Marx
u. A. an F. A. Sorge und Andere*,
Stuttgart 1906 and in full, in
Russian, in: Marx and Engels,

Works, First Russian Edition,
Vol. XXIX, Moscow, 1946

Printed according to the original

Published in English in full
for the first time

131

ENGELS TO HERMANN SCHLÜTER[302]

IN HOBOKEN

No. 1

[London], 2 December 1893

Dear Schlüter,

Many thanks for your good wishes and for *Census Compendium I* which was most welcome and of which No. II will be more welcome still.[a] So the Americans are no longer as liberal as they used to be, and even a big journal does not get such things merely for the asking! All is well over here; I am once more at work on Vol. III[b] and it is with pleasure that I look back on the trip I made this summer.[189] You people are now at last about to rid yourselves of bimetallism[299] and the McKinley tariff[301] and this should give a considerable boost to progress over there. Although a thorough-going collapse of silver[187] might have gone a long way towards

---

[a] Department of the Interior, Census Office. Compendium of the *Eleventh Census: 1890*, Parts I-II, Washington, 1892-1894. – [b] of *Capital*

enlightening your remarkably stupid American farmer in regard to his cheap money. Regards from Mrs Kautsky.

Yours,

F. E.

Census book—see second postcard.

First published abridged in
*Briefe und Auszüge aus Briefen
von Joh. Phil. Becker, Jos. Dietzgen,
Friedrich Engels, Karl Marx u. A. an
F. A. Sorge und Andere*, Stuttgart, 1906
and in full, in Russian, in: Marx
and Engels, *Works*, First Russian Edition,
Vol. XXIX, Moscow, 1946

Printed according to the original

Published in English in full
for the first time

132

ENGELS TO HERMANN SCHLÜTER[302]

IN HOBOKEN

No. 2!!

[London,] 2 December 1893

Dear Schlüter

As regards *Census* I,[a] I first got a letter from the General Post Office, Washington, saying that, because of the way it was packed, the book must be paid for *as a letter*. I must either send $10.36c. for this purpose or let them have the sender's address (I didn't know either what was in it or who had sent it), or else say whether I wanted it sent *per express*. I asked for further details, at the same time saying they were at liberty to send it *per express*, which they did, and I got it ON PAYMENT OF 6/–. When sending me things in future, would you be so good as to put *your address*

---

[a] *Department of the Interior, Census Office. Compendium of the Eleventh Census: 1890*, Parts I-II, Washington, 1892-1894

on the outside in order that delays of this kind may be avoided or dealt with direct over there. I could not quite gather from the Washington General Post Office's letter why they didn't send the thing—whether because of the way it was packed or perhaps because it was inadequately stamped for book-post. Thanks again.

Yours,

F. E.

First published, in Russian,
in: Marx and Engels, *Works*,
First Russian Edition,
Vol. XXIX, Moscow, 1946

Printed according to the original

Published in English for the first time

133

ENGELS TO KARL KAUTSKY

IN STUTTGART

London, 4 December 1893
122 Regent's Park Road, N. W.

Dear Baron,

First of all my warmest thanks for your good wishes on my 73rd birthday which has left me fit and well.

Either you misinterpreted my remarks about the 'publisher' or I expressed myself badly.[a] It never occurred to me to lay the blame on *Dietz* or, indeed, any one individual, in as much as I was not sufficiently au fait with what had happened *over there* in regard to the Stepniak business[288] before this had come to my notice. I merely adduced it as an awful example that ought not to be followed. And in view of the position occupied by publishers in this country, there could be no doubt that the German *publisher* had gratuitously presented Sonnenschein (or so it must seem to him) with £25, which could not but give him, Sonnenschein, a somewhat indifferent idea of the business efficiency of German publishers. Nor can

---

[a] See this volume, pp. 223-24

you Stuttgarters contest this. And as the surest way of obviating anything of that kind, I drew your attention to the fact that, in this country, the consent of the author is not *in itself,* a safeguard since, in nine cases out of ten, the English *publisher* has the final say, for as a rule he has been assigned the copyright, including right of translation (this is *actually* stated *in print* in, for instance, every one of Sonnenschein's contract forms, or else he stipulates that he should have some say in the matter. So please tell Dietz that it never even crossed my mind to cast any aspersion whatsoever on *his* efficiency as a business man.

As regards international contracts, Sam Moore [originally] looked this up in PARLIAMENTARY PUBLICATIONS from which he made extracts, and the information about one year and three years was certainly correct *at that time.* I know nothing about the Berne Convention[303] and its ten-year term of copyright *for translations* and I should be grateful if you would let me know the date of the said Convention, in which case I could procure the copy made for Parliament.

Victor writes to say that the general strike in Austria is dead as a door nail; so a discussion of it would not be likely to do any harm.[a] But at the same time we have had inquiries from the Austrian *provinces* as to what we in this country think of a general strike.

I still believe that electoral reform, *at least* in the form hatched up by Taaffe and Franz Joseph, is a foregone conclusion in Austria.[270] Even if the coalition ministry succeeds in tabling and gaining acceptance for a Bill for the extension of the parliamentary franchise without, as it must, foundering in consequence, or in consequence of something else in the meantime, the matter will by no means be settled. In a country as artificially equilibrated as Austria, a stable balance, once destroyed, can be restored only with difficulty, maybe by force alone, and the government is only too well aware that even this will be effective only for a while and will leave the state weaker than it was before. And the fact that Franz Joseph has given his blessing to *this* particular piece of electoral reform which he has, indeed, declared to be his very own work, rules out once and for all the possibility of Austria continuing *as before.* Now it's

Humptius in muro sedebat, Dumptius alto,
Humptius de muro Dumptius, heu! cecidit

---

[a] See this volume, p. 257

Nec equites regis, nee agmina cuncta tyranni
Humpti te Dumpti restituere queunt.

Or:

HUMPTY DUMPTY SAT ON A WALL,
HUMPTY DUMPTY HAD A GREAT FALL,
ALL THE KING'S HORSES AND ALL THE KING'S MEN,
CANNOT PUT HUMPTY DUMPTY TOGETHER AGAIN.[304]

In all probability Taaffe will return to office after a certain interval; he would seem to have taken the Disraeli of 1867 for his model.[305] At the moment this caricature of an artful dodger, along with the irresolute Franz Joseph, is involuntarily engaged in making Austria the spearhead of the political movement in Europe, as Pius IX made Italy in 1846.[274]

You are right in leaving the *Neue Zeit* as it is for the time being.[85] In such a case one shouldn't mess about with something like this unless absolutely necessary. Since it is a weekly, then let it so remain unless really compelled to make a change.

Don't worry about Volume III.[a] Come what may, we shall see that you are in a position to do a review of it to coincide with the book's appearance.

Love from one household to the other.

Yours,
F. E.

First published in the book:
Aus der Frühzeit des Marxismus.
Engels Briefwechsel mit Kautsky,
Prag, 1935

Printed according to the original

Published in English for the first time

---

[a] of *Capital*

134

ENGELS TO PAUL ARNDT

IN LOUDON

[*Draft*]

[London,] 5 December 1893

Dear Mr Arndt,

I, too, can understand that you should have preferred not to call on me on a Sunday since, in view of various things that have happened in the meantime, I cannot possibly consort with you on the same easy footing as hitherto.

However, if you wish to speak to me, I shall be at home the day after tomorrow, Thursday, from 8 pm. onwards.

Yours faithfully,
F. E.

First published, in Russian, in: Marx and Engels, *Works*, Second Russian Edition, Vol. 39, Moscow, 1966

Printed from the original

Published in English for the first time

135

ENGELS TO LAURA LAFARGUE

AT LE PERREUX

London, 19 December 1893
122 Regent's Park Road, N. W.

My dear Löhr,

If I have not before replied to your letter of just a month ago, there were 2 causes for it:

1) because I was bound to finish, before Christmas, the final *redaction*[a]

---

[a] editing

of Section I-IV of Vol. III,[a] so as to be able to go to press at once after the new year. That is now done. By Easter I hope to have the whole of the Manuscript (2/3rds are still to be *finally* looked over) in the printer's hands, to be published in September.

2) because I had submitted to Bebel another plan[25] for the German translation, etc. of Paul's articles,[b] and was waiting for a reply. Nothing however has come of it and so, *vogue la galère*[c] on the present tack, which, as far as I can hear, has taken something like a final shape, and so it may be as well to leave things alone. Liebknecht is rather a queer customer to deal with in these matters of his *redaction*. We expect him here after the new year.

Now then, *ein anderes Bild*.[d] Yesterday we forwarded to you a box with the pudding, Paul's cake etc., *grande vitesse*[e] to be there about Wednesday or Thursday—Continental Daily Parcels Express, carriage paid, which, we hope, will arrive safely and suit your tastes. Bonnier ought to have a slice of the pudding for he came in for the stirring and he did stir it with might and main. He is improving vastly, shaking off his Germanisms and becoming actually French. Some time ago I went over to Oxford for a day, to look at the place and also at poor old Rote[f] *Wolff*[g]—your earliest admirer, for he admired you before you were 2 years old in Brussels. Poor devil, he is quite cracked again. He had written something about Bucher in the *Neue Zeit*,[h] and since then whenever a Wolf or Wolff (and you know they are as plentiful as the Smiths and Jones's) is alluded to, he imagines that this is meant for him, and so he makes it out that there is a complete conspiracy to pretend that he does not know Latin—and you know, not to know Latin is the awfullest crime a man can be guilty of in Oxford. But is it not a melancholy irony of fate, that one of the most *spirituel*[i] of men should end his career in the belief that he is the Massmann, not of a Heine, but of an imaginary conspiracy of second and third rate German literati! Then he is 81 years old—so, apart from other considerations, hardly any hope of recovery from this fixed idea which nobody can root out of his mind.

Your description of Guesde's elated status amused me very much.[307] I had seen something of it from the pompous proclamations he had issued from his new Jerusalem of the North, and was only glad they were not

---

[a] of *Capital* – [b] See this volume, pp. 231-32 – [c] *let's chance it* – [d] a different story – [e] express – [f] Red – [g] See this volume, pp. 222-23 – [h] F. Wolff, 'Bucher, Bismarck und v. Poschinger', *Die Neue Zeit*, Nos. 42 and 43, Vol. II – [i] witty

noticed by the bourgeois press abroad; contrasted with the part played by the French delegation at Zürich,[250] they might have served as groundwork for a lot of bad jokes. But *le bon sens français quel quefois n'a pas le sens commun,*[a] and that is just the beauty of it. Look at the *parti socialiste* in the Chamber. How long ago is it that Clara Zetkin in the *Neue Zeit*[b] made out 24 *élus*[c] ± socialistes, and that of the 12 elected on the Marxist program Paul did not know how many would turn up all right; and now, lo and behold, a parliamentary party of 54 socialist deputies which dashes into the majority like a brigade of cavalry, upsets one ministry and nearly dislocates another,[308] until this victorious career is all of a sudden, by Vaillant's bomb,[309] changed into a concentration to the rear, and the new members of the majority deprived of all the idealistic delusions they had brought with them from the provinces and turned into docile panamitard opportunists.[60]

Upon the whole I think it is rather useful to us. I cannot help imagining that amongst these 54 who have been many of them suddenly converted to what they call socialism, there cannot be that cohesion which is wanted for a serious fight. Let alone the old dissensions between the *real* old socialists '*de la veille*'[d] within the group, dissensions which it will take some time to overcome once for all. If this heterogeneous lot of 54 had been kept in the front rank of the chambre for any length of time, it must, either have split up, or else the old Radical wing—Millerand and Co.—must have become the determining element. As it is, time will be given to the various components of the group to make closer acquaintance with each other, to consolidate the group, and to eliminate, if necessary, one after another those elements which really have joined the group only by mistake. At all events, in the Dupuy—Casimir Périer campaign Millerand and Jaurès took the lead entirely, and that will never do in the long run, though I fully approve of Guesde and Vaillant having, *so far*, and under the present circumstances, kept in the background.

Paul's letters to the *Vorwärts* so far are very good, we look for them every week. And they are not *quite* so badly germanised as I have seen others done.

That *Feuerbach* must have given you a deal of trouble.[310] But from what I have seen of your work, I feel certain you have 'taken' all obstacles 'fly-

---

[a] sometimes French good sense has no common sense – [b] C. Zetkin , 'Die Wahlen in Frankreich', *Die Neue Zeit*, No. 52, 1892-93, Vol. II – [c] elected – [d] of yesterday

ing', to use a bit of hunting language. Have you got a publisher for it?

Will you accept the enclosed cheque £5.– for a Christmas box?

Louise is out shopping in a steady rain—that Christmas will cost her dear in colds and toothache.

Love from her and yours ever

F. E.

Kind regards to Paul who I suppose is happy to be *out* of parliament again.

First published, in the language of the original (English), in: F. Engels, P. et

L. Lafargue, *Correspondance*, t. III, 1891-1895, Paris, 1959

Reproduced from the original

136

ENGELS TO LUDWIG SCHORLEMMER

IN STUTTGART

London, 19 December 1893
122 Regent's Park Road, N. W.

My dear Schorlemmer,

If I have not written before now to thank you for your good wishes on my seventy-third birthday, you can blame it on Volume III of *Capital*. This must now be finished once and for all and consequently I have had to put the whole of my correspondence on one side without compunction or remorse. I have now one section left to be done and shall be able to use the few days remaining before the festive season to catch up.

I only passed through Darmstadt[189]—Mrs Kautsky, Bebel and wife, a Viennese doctor[a] resident over here and I were unable to ascertain the train in advance, which in any case only stopped for ten minutes or so, otherwise I should have telegraphed you. Otherwise the trip was very pleasant—apart from the tub-thumping I had to do, having once let my-

---

[a] Ludwig Freyberger

self in for it in Zurich. I travelled with Bebel to Salzburg, Vienna, Prague and Berlin and was away from home for a full two months, which did me a power of good. To observe the progress made in Germany both by industry and by the labour movement was in itself worthwhile, and to see our Viennese at work was also a pleasure.

As regards Carl's estate,[199] I have heard very little from Siebold and absolutely nothing about what has happened to the manuscripts and what contracts have been concluded with the publishers. Three matters are involved here:

1. The big work by Roscoe and Schorlemmer in an English and a German edition.[311]

2. Carl's own Manual of the Chemistry of the Carbon Compounds,[a] new edition of which was in course of preparation.

3. His manuscripts on the *early* history of chemistry[312] (according to what Spiegel says in the obituary, Siebold intends to publish this himself).

The English edition of Carl's *Ursprung und Entwicklung der organischen Chemie*[b][313] will be handled in London by one of his pupils, now a professor there.[c]

But with regard to the above three points Siebold says little or nothing, Before I write to him again, I should like to ask you whether *he* has told *you* anything about the matter and if so *what*, and whether it is agreeable to you if I ask him for further information. For I have no right whatever, legally speaking, to intervene and would not like Siebold to refer to or even so much as hint at this. If, however, I go and ask him for information for which *you* have appealed to me, that is rather a different matter and puts me in an altogether different position.

Siebold is an absolutely sterling chap but by nature not over-energetic and in recent years he has been weakened by illness. In which case a little bit of extra help can do no harm.

I hope you are safely rid of your influenza and your wife of the after-effects of pneumonia and are in a condition to face up to the coming festive season with strength, fortitude and cheerfulness.

With kindest regards.

Yours,

F. Engels

---

[a] *Lehrbuch der Kohlenst of fverbindungen oder der organischen Chemie* – [b] *Rise and Development of Organic Chemistry* – [c] Arthur Smithells

First published, in Russian,
in: Marx and Engels, *Works*,
First Russian Edition,
Vol. XXIX, Moscow, 1946

Printed according to the original

Published in English for the first time

137

ENGELS TO ADELHEID DWORAK

IN VIENNA

London, 21 December 1893
122 Regent's Park Road, N. W.

[*Copy*]

Dear Adelheid,

I still owe you my thanks for your kind congratulations on my 73rd birthday[314] and am sending them today in order to use the occasion for wishing you a very nice holiday. I hope that the vacation from oratory arranged for you during our stay in Vienna[257] has done you good and you are again as fit and full of fighting spirit as we all wish you to be. Unless I misread all the signs, you are in for eventful times and lengthy battles in Austria. May the workers there prove that, along with the necessary audacity, they possess the patience, calm, judgement and discipline which alone can lead to victory.

Cordial greetings to you and all comrades, Your old

F. Engels

Take it from me, I will still claim that '*kiss*' some day.

First published in: *Friedrich Engels
1820-1970. Referate. Diskussionen.
Dokumente*, Hanover, 1971

Printed according to the original

Published in English for the first time

138

ENGELS TO WILHELM LIEBKNECHT

IN BERLIN

London, 21 December 1893

Dear Liebknecht,

Yesterday evening I sent you an article on Italy. *I would ask you* NOT *to print it until further notice.* I fear I have misinterpreted the permission given me to publish it, which, apparently, does NOT extend to the stuff about the privy purse. Since the matters in question could land my source[a] in a most serious predicament and might deprive me of the source itself, I am also sending you a telegram. If you receive no further word from me, you can bring the ms. back with you in January and we shall then re-edit it.

Once again my kindest regards to you all.

Yours,

F. E.

First published, in Russian,
in: Marx and Engels, *Works*,
First Russian Edition,
Vol. XXIX, Moscow, 1946

Printed according to the original

Published in English for the first time

139

ENGELS TO FRIEDRICH ADOLPH SORGE

IN HOBOKEN

London, 30 December 1893
122 Regent's Park Road, N. W.

Dear Sorge,

Your postcards of 29 November and 17 December received with

---

[a] Antonio Labriola

thanks. First of all a Happy New Year to you and your wife from Louise Kautsky and myself.

You will have noticed, not without some surprise, that a Socialist group of between fifty-four and sixty men (they themselves don't seem to know exactly how many) has established itself in the French Chamber. Immediately after the elections[208] they numbered, at a *generous* count, twenty-four, twelve of whom had been elected on the strength of the Marxist platform. However, of these only six presented themselves at the Paris Party Congress and hitherto only four have *agreed*, in accordance with the congress resolution, to pay a part of their parliamentary salary into the party treasury.[283] (Which is not yet the same thing as actually paying it in—in France it was being said as early as 1870 that *les cotisations ne rentrent pas!*[a]) Well, thanks to the adhesion of the *radicaux socialistes*[b] of the Millerand-Jaurès group, there are now all of a sudden nearly sixty who have resolved to include the socialisation of the means of production as one of the aims—more immediate for some, for others, however, very remote—of their programme. Concentration is now the battle-cry in France. If in the past this meant a *concentration républicaine* (i.e. the subordination of *all* Republicans to the *right* wing, the Opportunists[87]), it now means a *concentration socialiste* and I only hope this does not mean the subordination of all Socialists to the Millerandists whose *practical* programme is assuredly more radical than socialist.

The first result of this alliance is that our people have as good as lost the chance of acquiring a daily of their own. Millerand's *Petite République Française* already occupies that position, so it will be difficult to produce an organ to compete with it—finance is more difficult to obtain and the others would complain that it would mean splitting the party! The more so as the *Petite République Française* is crafty enough to open its columns to *any* socialist group.

The second is that in the group's meetings the Millerandists command an absolute majority (ca. 30 against 24 at the most—Marxists (12), Allemanists[21] (3-5), Broussists[30] (2) and Blanquists[20] (4-6)).

Nevertheless *messieurs les Français*, intoxicated once again by victory, are crowing away for the benefit of all and sundry and would like to resume their place at the forefront of the movement. They have tabled a motion demanding that the standing army be changed into an army of

---

[a] contributions are not paid – [b] Radical Socialists

militia (Vaillant), while Guesde intends to table one on a European disarmament congress.[a] The plan is that the Germans and Italians shall table similar motions in their own parliaments, thereby naturally giving the impression that they are following in the footsteps of their French 'leaders'. What the handful of Italians—and an exceptionally muddle-headed handful at that—may do is of no consequence, but whether our Germans will consent without more ado to be taken in tow by the French seems doubtful to me. If, after twenty-five years of hard struggle, you have won for yourself a position of power and have two million voters behind you, you are entitled to take a closer look at the scratch lot who propose all of a sudden to assume command. The more so as *messieurs les Français* get exceedingly touchy the moment anyone commits the slightest breach of etiquette in respect of themselves.

Well, we shall have to wait and see. With these unpredictable Frenchmen it is always possible that lasting progress will result from this sudden and momentary success. But it would really be better for us to wait and see.

Next, I have to tell you—*but this is strictly between ourselves*—that yesterday the first third of the ms. of Volume III[b] was packed in strong oil-cloth (as was in its day that notorious forgery, the Cologne minute-book[315]) and will shortly be sent to the printers. The last two-thirds are still in need of the final—mostly technical—editing. If all goes well the book will come out in September.

Now for something else. Prof. Labriola[c] of Rome, with whom I have corresponded for several years and whom I met in Zurich,[189] is giving a course of lectures at the university there on the genesis of Marxist theory. He is a strict Marxist. To this end he has procured all the necessary literature but has never managed to set eyes on the *Holy Family*, although he has advertised in the Leipzig *Buchhändlerblatt*[d] and elsewhere to the effect that he will pay 'any price' for it. There was some prospect of his getting a copy on loan from Switzerland, but its owner[e] has suddenly vanished and is said to be travelling in Hungary. He is now urging me to do whatever I can to procure him a copy for three or four weeks. But I myself have only one and if that is lost it will be absolutely impossible for me to arrange for the inclusion of the new, later edition in the projected *Collected Works*.[316]

---

[a] See next letter. – [b] of *Capital* – [c] Antonio Labriola – [d] *Börsenblatt für den Deutschen Buchhandel und die mit ihm verwandten Geschäftszweige* – [e] Paul Ernst

Hence I cannot, on any account, let this one and only copy out of my hands. Now, a few years back, I sent you my spare copy. Would you be so good as to lend it to me for the above purpose for five or six weeks? You could send it to me as a BOOK-PACKET by *registered post* or, if you prefer, through an express agency *insured* for any sum you choose, and I should return it by whichever medium you may direct. I would, if that could somehow be arranged, send it to Rome through an agency, heavily insured (for 410 say) or, if that is not possible, by *registered post*. It should be stipulated that Labriola might have the use of it for *a maximum of four weeks*. I need hardly tell you that without a knowledge of this book he will be unable to hold the proposed course of lectures, still less realise his intention of publishing them at a later date. There are fewer than six copies in the whole of the German party and who has them I don't know. So please think the matter over.

My *Feuerbach* is being translated into French by Laura Lafargue and will shortly be coming out in Paris.[310]

Warm regards to your wife and you from Louise Kautsky and yours,

F. E.

I hope your health has improved. Louise Kautsky asks me to say that the paper[a] you send to Vienna arrives regularly.

Thank you for the greetings card.

First published, abridged, in
*Briefe und Auszüge aus Briefen
von Joh. Phil. Becker, Jos. Dietz
Friedrich Engels, Karl Marx u. A. an
F. A. Sorge und Andere*, Stuttgart,
1906 and in full, in Russian, in:
Marx and Engels, *Works*, First Russian
Edition, Vol. XXIX, Moscow, 1946

Printed according to the original

Published in English for the first time

---

[a] *Woman's Journal*

1894

140

ENGELS TO PAUL LAFARGUE

AT LE PERREUX

London, 3 January 1894
122 Regent's Park Road, N. W.

My dear Lafargue,

First, seasonal greetings to Laura and you from Louise and myself.

And now for your disarmament plan. I saw the Vaillant motion in *Le Parti Socialiste*, I did not have it from Laura.[317] Neither this paper nor your letter tells me whether it has already been tabled or if that is still to come.

The Germans have been demanding for years that the standing army should be turned into a militia, this is repeated in all their Reichstag speeches on militarism, the war budget, etc., repeated *ad nauseam*. I fail to see that the formal tabling of a Bill could add anything to it. Nevertheless, they will look into it.

As for the proposal to be made concerning a disarmament congress, that would be—like Vaillant's motion also—*a matter to be settled by a conference of delegates from the three parliaments*: French, German and Italian. One delegate from each nation would be enough. Any international action must have as a necessary premise a previous agreement both as to the basis and as to the form. It strikes me as inadmissible that one nationality should take the initiative publicly and then invite the others to fall in. The French, themselves pretty punctilious at times on matters of etiquette, should for their part observe democratic considerations. I shall not call the Germans' attention to this point, but I should not be surprised if this rather naïve invitation, to follow in the footsteps of the

French party, which has only just got into Parliament and is made up of such diverse and in some respects such little known elements, is not immediately accepted.

Now for the substance.

The Vaillant motion will be opposed by the military on the ground that militias on the Swiss model, possibly good enough for a mountainous country, lack the stability needed for a large army that has to operate on every kind of terrain. And there they will be right. To build a good militia army the foundation must be laid by the athletic and military training of the young; so it's a thing which would take from five to eight years; you would not have this militia until about the end of the century. Therefore if there is to be a Bill against which the bourgeois and the military cannot raise valid objections, this fact must be taken into account.

That is what I tried to do in the articles which appeared last year in *Vorwärts* and which I sent you.[a] I am sending you a further copy today. Here I am proposing an international agreement for the reduction—simultaneous and agreed jointly in advance—of the period of military service. To meet the usual prejudices as far as possible, I am proposing for a start a period of two years' enlistment, to be reduced as soon as possible to 18 months (two summers and the winter between), and then to one year and so on, until a class of young men have reached military age who shall have been through that athletic and military instruction which shall have fitted them to bear arms without further training. And then there would be a militia that would require no more than large-scale manoeuvres every 2 or 3 years to find its feet and to learn how to operate in large formations.

Now that the two-year period is already generally recognised one could demand 18 months at once, and reduction to 1 year in 2 or 3 years; during that time, the athletic and military training of young men between 15 and 18 could be set going, not forgetting that of boys between 10 and 15.

Vaillant's Bill has great need for revision by someone who knows what's what in military affairs, it contains things written in haste on which we could not stand up to serious argument. According to art. 9 (*all the children* of the country), the girls, too, are to be put through "all the evolu-

---

[a] F. Engels, "Can Europe Disarm?"

tions of the infantry, cavalry and artillery", etc., etc.

I am sending a copy of my articles to Vaillant, too.

Now then, if you could reach agreement with the Germans and the Italians for tabling a motion aimed at calling for a congress on disarmament and the transition—by simultaneous stages laid down in advance—to a militia system, that would be a splendid thing and have a big effect. But for mercy's sake don't spoil it by openly taking the initiative without preliminary consultation with the others. The conditions of internal policy as well as those governing each parliament are so different from each other that a certain manner of proceeding may be excellent for one country and utterly impossible or even disastrous in another.

The anarchist bomb[309] will become a thing of the past as have the glorious 2,500 francs of the Germans.[278] This will have an effect vis-à-vis the police; look at the Madrid verdict in the Muñoz case where the police was found guilty, too[318]; and in France it risks being openly implicated in the affair of bombs; if it slips off this time, it might be glad. This pitcher has been going to the well long enough, and it is about to be broken at last.

I hope that Laura has received her manuscript.[310]

Kiss Laura on my behalf. Greetings from Louise.

Ever yours,
F. Engels

First published in:
F. Engels, P. et L. Lafargue,
Correspondance, t. III, Paris, 1959

Printed according to the original

Translated from the French

141

ENGELS TO PYOTR LAVROV

IN PARIS

London, 4 January 1894
122 Regent's Park Road, N. W.

My dear Lavrov,

Thank you for your card—please accept my best wishes for the New

Year.

It would seem that, despite the harmony between Carnot and the tsar,[a] it will be the French, and not the outlawed Russians who will suffer persecutions and tribulations, the inevitable effect of anarcho-police bombs.[319] So much the better. After all, there are signs that even the Parisian *philistine* would seem to be feeling just a little shame for his hysterical actions of last October.

Could you let me have the address of Mr. Rapoport, who has just returned to Switzerland?

Best regards from
F. Engels

There is finally some hope that you will receive the 3rd volume of *Capital* before the end of the year. The Russian translation will be done as for the 2nd volume. I will send the proofs to Danielson.

First published in Russian
in: Marx and Engels, *Works*,
First Russian Edition,
Vol. XXIX, Moscow, 1946

Printed according to the original

Translated from the French

Published in English for the first time

142

ENGELS TO GIUSEPPE CANEPA

IN DIANO MARINA

[Draft]

[London, 9 January 1894]

Dear citizen,

Please excuse me for writing to you in French. Over the last twenty years I have lost whatever little ability I had in the use of Italian.

I have tried to find a short epigraph of the kind you wish[320] from the

---

[a] Alexander III

works of Marx, whom alone of the modern socialists, it would seem, is able to stand on a par with the great Florentine.[a] However, I have found nothing except the following passage taken from the *Communist Manifesto* (Italian edition of *Critica Sociale*, p. 35): "Al posto della vecchia società borghese divisa in class; cozzanti fra loro, subenta un'associazione, nella quale il libero sviluppo di ciascumo è la condizione per il libero sviluppo di tutti".[b]

It is almost impossible to sum up the spirit of the new age of the future in just a few words without lapsing into either utopianism or empty words.

Please accept my apologies if the quotation I offer is not wholly satisfactory. However, as you must be ready for the 21 (a date that augurs well, the execution of citizen Louis Capet), there is no time to lose.

E con distinti saluti

Suo[c]

First published, abridged, in Italian in a weekly *L'Era nuova* No. 1, 4 March 1894 and in full in Russian in: Marx and Engels, *Works*, First Russian Edition, Vol. XXIX, Moscow, 1946

Printed according to the draft manuscript collated with the text in the weekly reprinted in the book: K. Marx, F. Engels, *Scriti italiani*, Milano-Roma, 1955

Translated from the French

Published in English for the first time

---

[a] Dante – [b] "In place of the old bourgeois society, with its classes and class antagonisms, we shall have an association, in which the free development of each is the condition for the free development of all" (K. Marx and F. Engels, *Manifesto of the Communist Party*, this edition, Vol. 6, p. 506). – [c] Respectfully yours

143

ENGELS TO KARL KAUTSKY

IN STUTTGART

London, 9 January 1894
122 Regent's Park Road, N. W.

Dear Baron,

Ede has doubtless already told you of the despatch of part of the ms. of Volume III (approx. 1/3 of a cubic foot). Now that it has safely arrived in Hamburg, I am able to give you a short review of it for the *Neue Zeit* and this I enclose.[a] Please send a copy with *the article side-lined* to Otto Meissner's Verlag, Hamburg.

Work is continuing on the second third which I hope will soon be ready.

Your good wishes for Xmas as well as for the New Year were gratefully reciprocated in thought if not in words.

I shall now probably be able to get hold of the Berne Convention.[b][303]

I am anxious to see Cunow's book.[c] The man has done a great deal of swotting in his field and keeps his eyes open.

Dietz will be interested to hear that Laura Lafargue is translating my *Feuerbach* into French for the *Ère nouvelle*[310] and subsequent publication as an off-print. I have already looked over the first part. She translates deftly and conscientiously.

Ravé, who is less deserving of such praise, has again written to me; he has had a go at your *Thomas Morus*,[d] *mais c'est bien indigeste!*[e] For the man does not, in fact, possess an adequate knowledge of German, although he is an Alsatian and by rights should probably be called Rawe.

I'm glad that Victor should have promptly extracted the best bits from your latest article and made them available to the Viennese.[321] They were quite admirably suited to the situation there. According to Victor's last letter, all danger of anything silly being done is now past. In fact both the Czech and the trades union congresses have shelved the question of a GENERAL STRIKE[322] until the Party Conference[323] and Victor will

---

[a] *On the Contents of the Third Volume of 'Capital'.* – [b] See this volume, p. 240 – [c] H. Cunow, *Die Verwandtschafts-Organisationen der Australneger*, Stuttgart, 1894 – [d] K. Kautsky, *Thomas More und seine Utopie*, Stuttgart, 1888 – [e] but it's pretty heavy!

doubtless make sure that it is shelved yet again.

That's all for today—masses of letters still to attend to. Regards from one household to the other.

Yours,
F. E.

First published in the book:
Aus der Frühzeit des Marxismus,
Engels Briefwechsel mit Kautsky,
Prag, 1935

Printed according to the original

Published in English for the first time

144

ENGELS TO PYOTR LAVROV

IN PARIS

London, 10 January 1894
122 Regent's Park Road, N. W.

My dear Lavrov,

Thank you for your card of the 6th. The enclosed letter[25] contains a personal communication which I believe to be important, and therefore would not like to go astray. Would you be so kind as to send it to Mr. Rapoport as soon as you know his address. There is no particular urgency, a week will make no difference.

The first third of the manuscript of the 3rd volume[a] is at the printer's (20 chapters). I am busy with the final editing of the rest. If all goes well, we will appear in September,

If, as I hope, your health is no worse than mine, we shall neither of us have anything to complain of.

Your devoted friend,
F. Engels

First published in Russian
in: Marx and Engels, *Works,*
Second Russian Edition,
Vol. 39, Moscow, 1966

Printed according to the original

Translated from the French

Published in English for the first time

---

[a] K. Marx, *Capital*

145

ENGELS TO GEORGE WILLIAM LAMPLUGH, G. W.[324]

IN LONDON

London, 10 January 1894
122 Regent's Park Road, N. W.

My dear Lamplugh,

Your parcel was an agreeable surprise indeed. Many thanks! I am almost ashamed to confess that in my ignorance I had fancied the *Anatomy of Melancholy* to be one of the serious psychological disquisitions of the 18th century, which I hold in horror. Now I find that it, too, is a product of the grandest epoch of English literature, the beginning of the 17th century. I turn to it with pleasure, and have already seen enough to assure me that it will prove a constant source of enjoyment.

This reminds me that I have forgotten to let you have the only two works of mine that have been published in English[a]—I have made free to send them, to you by post and hope you will do me the favour of accepting them.

Dakyns told me on Sunday you were afraid of your little boy getting the influenza. Although there is more about of this beastly complaint than is desirable, I hope the danger has blown over.

Reciprocating your kind wishes for the New Year and with kind regards to Mrs Lamplugh.

I remain yours faithfully
F. Engels

First published in Russian, in, *Letopisi marksizma*, Book I, 1926

Reproduced from the original

Published in English for the first time

---

[a] F. Engels, *The Condition of the Working-Class in England*; *Socialism: Utopian and Scientific*

146

ENGELS TO HENRI RAVÉ[326]

IN POITIERS

[*Draft*]   [London], 10 January 1894

Dear citizen,

A thousand thanks for your good wishes for the New Year, which, I hope, will bring you good fortune also!

The translation of my book,[195] as it is at present, seems to me to be very good. As for the rest, since I edited the proofs, I also bear my share of the responsibility.

The style of Thomas Morus[a] will really seem rather heavy to the French public, but there are some good points, and the historical estimates have a more than transitory value.

At the moment I have no book I can offer you for translation, but if I find something, I shall let you know.

                                        Yours respectfully.

First published in Russian
in: Marx and Engels, *Works*,
First Russian Edition,
Vol. XXIX, Moscow, 1946

Printed according to the original

Translated from the French

Published in English for the first time

147

ENGELS TO VICTOR ADLER

IN VIENNA

                                        London, 11 January 1894

Dear Victor,

First, my thanks to you all, and especially to yourself, your wife and

---

[a] See this volume, p. 257

family, for your good wishes which I heartily reciprocate, and thanks also for the League tie-pin which I shall sport as soon as I have a suitable neck-tie to wear it with—I intend to buy one specially for the purpose.

That there is a great deal to be done over there I can readily believe and none of us can imagine how you are able to manage it all, and under the most difficult circumstances at that. We admire and envy you your tenacity. What particularly pleased me, however, was your assurance that an end *has* been put to the foolishness you had been fearing over there.[a] I have since received reports on the two Congresses[323] and have been able to discover at least some of the particulars therefrom. Things couldn't in fact have gone off better in regard to this crucial matter.

So far as the healthy development of the movement is concerned, it was a real blessing that the perspicacious Höger should have declared suffrage to be a bourgeois racket and not something to go on strike for,[327] and that the miners should, after their own fashion, have declared themselves opposed to any strike that did not also support the eight-hour day. And at Budweis the Czechs have also helped us by making admission condi-tional on recognition of the programme and tactics (à la Zurich[229]) and by shelving the general strike, which seemed more pervasive there than anywhere else, until the Party Conference,[323] when it will probably be shelved again.

K. Kautsky's article which you reprinted[321] will be of great help to your people. But it's indicative of the extent to which its author has lost touch with the living party movement. A few months ago he showed an inconceivable want of tact in proposing to sling a purely academic discussion of the general strike *in abstracto*, and of its pros and cons generally, into the midst of a movement engaged in a life and death struggle against slogans advocating such a strike.[290] And now comes this article which, at any rate in the passages you cite, hits the nail on the head quite admirably.

Anyhow, come next month and the Electoral Reform Bill, and you people will (be able to) start agitating again with a will. It was quite a good thing that the first high fever should have had a chance to run its course, for now the chaps will take a rather calmer view of things. Whichever way it goes, the government and the Diet are *bound* to place new weapons in your hands and next year there will be several score if

---

[a] See this volume, p. 257

not a whole crowd of you in parliament. Proletarians in that anachronistic assembly with its class hierarchies! Those chaps will show the French that the proletariat is not *le quatrième état*[a] as, by false analogy, they are so fond of describing it, but an utterly modern, youthful class incompatible with all that old nonsense of estates which it must disrupt *before* getting to the stage at which it can embark on its own particular task, the disruption of the bourgeoisie. I am already looking forward to the day when the first of our chaps sets foot in the Diet.

All the same, I still take the view that the coalition government will collapse the moment it tries to act in real earnest. I should say that in Austria the time has not yet come for the one reactionary mass[214]—not, at any rate, for its formation on a *lasting* basis. And even if the leaders in the Cabinet were to unite, the small fry in parliament would not succeed in doing so; and if, behind all this, you have a Franz Joseph yearning to get his Taaffe back, it seems to me that the days of Windischgrätz are numbered. And *in practice* Taaffe now stands for universal suffrage.

I am curious to see how the sixty so-called Socialists in the French Assembly will make out.[b] They are a mixed bunch, even some of the *socialistes de la veille*[c] being of a very indeterminate nature and also, despite their desire for fusion, encumbered with all manner of old and ugly memories; on top of that, however, all of these put together are in a minority as compared with the Millerand-Jaurès majority consisting of *socialistes du lendemain*[d] Indeed, the French preserve an obstinate silence in the face of any inquiry as to the nature of their group. On Sunday Bonnier will be passing through London on his way back from Paris; I shall question him and, no doubt, succeed in finding something out.

Volume III[e] is at last being printed. The first twenty chapters (664 pp. out of approx. 1870 ms. pp.) have already gone to press, I am working on the next third which only requires a final editing, and then it will soon be the turn of the last third which will probably call for rather more work. We shall be appearing in September, I think.

But now I must return to my beloved Chapter 23. Unfortunately a frightful lot of time was lost over the festive season.

Warm regards to your wife and children, Popp. Ulbing, Pernerstorfer,

---

[a] the fourth estate – [b] See this volume, p. 249 – [c] Socialists of yesterday – [d] Socialists of tomorrow – [e] of *Capital*

Reumann, Schrammel, Adelheid, little Ryba and tutti quanti,[a] but in particular to you yourself from

Yours,
F. Engels

First published in the book:
Victor Adlers Aufsätze, Reden und Briefe. Erstes Heft: *Victor Adler und Friedrich Engels,* Wien, 1922

Printed according to the book

Published in English for the first time

148

ENGELS TO GEORGE WILLIAM LAMPLUGH

IN LONDON

[London] 12 January 1894
122 Regent's Park Road, N. W.

My dear Lamplugh,

I had a dim recollection of having given you the *Socialism*[b] before, but was not sure. My memory for this sort of thing is getting awfully senile. Please dispose of the odd copy to your friend, as you propose, and I only hope he will find it digestible.

Compliments to Mrs Lamplugh.

Yours faithfully
F. Engels

The weather may now by and by permit of your visit to the Zoo, so when it comes off please drop us a postcard and say about what time after having seen the wild beasts you will be likely to look in here with your family.

---

[a] all the rest – [b] F. Engels, *Socialism: Utopian and Scientific*

First published, in Russian,
in *Letopisi marksizma*, Book I,
1926

Reproduced from the original

Published in English for the first time

149

ENGELS TO ALBERT DELON[328]

IN NIMES

[*Note*]

London, about 21 January 1894

Should first read the second volume and then refer back. To go by his letter to Diamandi, his German still isn't perfect but he's still working at it, in particular the terminology of political economy.

First published, in Russian,
in: Marx and Engels, *Works*,
Second Russian Edition,
Vol. 39, Moscow, 1966

Printed according to the original

Published in English for the first time

150

ENGELS TO W. BORGIUS[329]

IN BRESLAU[a]

London, 25 January 1894
122 Regent's Park Road, N. W.

Dear Sir,

Herewith the answers to your questions.

1. By economic relations, considered by us to be the determinant upon which the history of society is based, we understand the manner in which men of a certain society produce the necessities of life, and exchange

---

[a] Now Wroclaw

those products among themselves (in so far as division of labour exists). Thus they comprise the *entire technology* of production and transport. As we see it, that technology also determines the manner of exchange, likewise the distribution of products and hence, following the dissolution of gentile society, also the division into classes, hence the relations of rulers and subjects, and hence the state, politics, the law, etc. Economic relations further comprise the *geographical basis* on which these are enacted, and, indeed, the inherited remnants of earlier stages of economic development, remnants which often owe their survival only to tradition or *vis inertiae*[a] they also, of course, comprise the external environment by which this form of society is encompassed.

If, as you say, technology is indeed largely dependent on the state of science, then how much more is not the latter dependent on the *state* and the *requirements* of technology? If society has a technological requirement, the latter will do more to promote science than ten universities. Hydrostatics (Torricelli, etc.) owes its existence solely to the need to regulate mountain streams in Italy in the sixteenth and seventeenth centuries. Only since the discovery of its technological uses have we known anything rational about electricity. Unfortunately historiographers in Germany have got into the habit of writing about the sciences as though they had appeared out of the blue.

2. We see economic conditions as that which, in the final analysis, determines historical development. But the human race is itself an economic factor. Here, however, there are two points which should not be overlooked:

a) Political, juridical, philosophical, religious, literary, artistic, etc., development is based on economic development. But each of these also reacts upon the others and upon the economic basis. This is not to say that the economic situation is the *cause* and that it *alone* is *active* while everything else is mere passive effect, but rather that there is reciprocal action based, *in the final analysis*, on economic necessity which invariably prevails. The state, for instance, exerts its influence through protective tariffs, free trade, good or bad fiscal systems, and even your German philistine's mortal weariness and impotence, consequent upon Germany's impoverished economic condition between 1648 and 1830, and expressing itself first in Pietism and then in sentimentality and cringing servility

---

[a] the force of inertia

to princes and nobles, even this was not without economic effect. It was one of the greatest obstacles to recovery and was not removed until chronic poverty became acute as a result of the revolutionary and Napoleonic wars. Thus the effect of the economic situation is not, as is sometimes conveniently supposed, automatic; rather, men make their own history, but in a given environment by which they are conditioned, and on the basis of extant and actual relations of which economic relations, no matter how much they may be influenced by others of a political and ideological nature, are ultimately the determining factor and represent the unbroken clue which alone can lead to comprehension.

b) While men may make their own history, they have not hitherto done so with a concerted will in accordance with a concerted plan, not even in a given and clearly delimited society. Their aspirations are at variance, which is why all such societies are governed by *necessity* of which the counterpart and manifestation is *chance*. The necessity which here invariably prevails over chance is again ultimately economic. This brings us to the question of what are known as great men. The fact that such and such a man, and he alone, should arise at a particular time in any given country, is, of course, purely fortuitous. But if we eliminate him, a replacement will be called for and such a replacement will be found—*tant bien que mal*,[a] but found he will ultimately be. That Napoleon, this particular Corsican, was the military dictator rendered necessary by a French Republic bled white by her own wars, was fortuitous; but that, in the absence of a Napoleon, someone else would have taken his place is proved by the fact that the moment someone becomes necessary—Caesar, Augustus, Cromwell, etc.—he invariably turns up. If it was Marx who discovered the materialist view of history, the work of Thierry, Mignett Guizot and every English historiographer prior to 1850 goes to show that efforts were being made in that direction, while the discovery of the same view by Morgan shows that the time was ripe for it and that it was *bound* to be discovered.

The same thing applies to all fortuitous and seemingly fortuitous events in history. The further removed is the sphere we happen to be investigating from the economic sphere and the closer to the purely abstract, ideological sphere, the more likely shall we be to find evidence of the fortuitous in its development, and the more irregular will be the curve

---

[a] for better or for worse

it describes. But if you draw the mean axis of the curve, you will find that the longer the period under consideration and the larger the area thus surveyed, the more approximately parallel will this axis be to the axis of economic development.

In Germany the greatest obstacle to accurate interpretation is the irresponsible neglect of economic history in literature. It is so difficult, not only to rid oneself of the historical ideas drummed into one at school, but actually to get together the material necessary for the purpose. Who, for instance, has so much as read old G. von Gülich whose dry catalogue of material[a] nevertheless contains so much that throws light on innumerable political facts!

Come to that, I believe that the fine example provided by Marx in the *18. Brumaire*[b] should, precisely because it is a practical example, go a long way towards answering your questions. I also think that I touched on most of these points in the *Anti-Dühring*[c] Chapters 9-11 and II, 2-4, also III, and in the introduction, and again in the final section of the *Feuerbach*.[d]

Please do not take every word I have said above for gospel, but rather consider them in their general context; I am sorry not to have had the time to write to you in such careful detail as I should have had to do for publication.

Would you kindly convey my compliments to Mr ...[e] and thank him for sending me the ...[e] which greatly amused me.

Yours very sincerely,
F. Engels

First published in the magazine
Der Sozialistische Akademiker,
No. 20, 1895

Printed according to the magazine

Published in English for the first time

---

[a] G. von Gülich, *Geschichtliche Darstellung des Handels, der Gewerbe und des Ackerbaus handeltreibenden Staaten unsrer Zeit,* Bd. 1-5, Jena, 1830-1845 – [b] K. Marx, *The Eighteenth Brumaire of Louis Bonaparte.* – [c] F. Engels, *Anti-Dühring. Herr Eugen Dühring's Revolution in Science.* – [d] F. Engels, *Ludwig Feuerbach and the End of Classical German Philosophy* – [e] omitted in MS.

151

ENGELS TO RICHARD FISCHER

IN BERLIN

London, 1 February 1894
122 Regent's Park Road, N. W.

Dear Fischer,

Discussed the matter with Aveling yesterday.[330] After the Erfurt Party Conference,[331] and armed with the documents provided by you, Aveling again went to the *Daily Chronicle* and notified them of the facts (he had already been there once before and denounced Reuss as a spy, whereupon they had said they would get rid of him). But now all of a sudden the story was that the proprietor of the paper *wished* to keep Reuss on and so there was nothing they could do about it. But if Reuss nevertheless asserts that he gave notice himself on 9. Nov. 1891, i.e. immediately afterwards, it shows that, as a result of what Aveling had told them, they treated him in such a manner as to *force* him to give notice—the fact remains that he was made to go.

However you cannot publicly ventilate any of these matters because you would risk a public denial by the *Chronicle* people, since etiquette in this country strictly precludes publication of a newspaper's internal affairs and the chaps can thus tell any lies they choose and do so with complete impunity. If I were you I should drop the matter altogether since it is no longer of any importance whatever. The very most you could say would be that the Erfurt Conference took place in October 1891, immediately after which the information about Reuss was sent to London and that, as early as *9 November* Reuss had, by his own admission, found it necessary to give notice—and let the reader draw his own conclusions. Should you venture one step further, the *Chronicle* will state that, so far as it is concerned, the thing simply is not true, and neither it nor any other London paper will print a line of rectification from you. Such is the etiquette of the press over here.

We know nothing about Reuss being pilloried for the second time in the *Vorwärts*; you will have to look for it yourselves.

Would you pay my fee[332] to the party treasurer who can receipt it in the monthly account with the initials F. E. in L.

First published, in Russian,
Marx and Engels, *Works,*
First Russian Edition, Vol. XXIX,
Moscow, 1946

Printed according in: to the original

Published in English for the first time

152

ENGELS TO KARL KAUTSKY

IN STUTTGART

[Eastbourne], 13 February 1894

Dear Baron,

Am back in Eastbourne[333] again because of my usual lame leg, but it's already on the mend. Shall remain here until at least the 23rd of this month; if you should write, the address will be 28, Marine Parade, Eastbourne. Victor has snatched the *Critica Sociale* article away from under your nose and is translating it.[334] At the moment I've got no time at all since I am having to proof correct the whole of the rest of Volume III,[a] and page proofs rain down on me as inexorably as blows in the Cameroons.[335]

Ask Dietz to send the 8 marks with the next larger consignment to Vienna.[282]

I do not consider the term 'communism' suitable for *general* use today; rather it should be reserved for cases in which a *more exact* description is required, and even then it would call for an explanatory note, having virtually fallen out of use for the past thirty years.[336]

At the moment I consider Burns to be better and Jaurès to be less important than commonly made out to be.

Warm regards from one household to the other.

Yours,
F. E.

First published in:
*Aus der Frühzeit des
Marxismus. Engels Briefwechsel
mit Kautsky*, Prague, 1935

Printed according to the original

Published in English for the first time

---

[a] of *Capital*

153

ENGELS TO GEORG VON GIZYCKI[337]

IN BERLIN

[*Draft*]

Eastbourne[333], 17 February 1894
28, Marine Parade

Dear Sir,

In thanking you for your esteemed note of the 14th of this month, I can only say that for a long time to come I shall be so overwhelmed with work as to be unable to undertake any work even for the periodical press of my own party. It would be all the less admissible if I were to contribute to journals which, however genuine and honourable the views they represent, are none the less further removed from my own immediate standpoint.

For this and other reasons I must regretfully refuse your kind invitation, while remaining

Yours very sincerely,
F. E.

First published, in Russian,
in: Marx and Engels, *Works*,
First Russian Edition,
Vol. XXIX, Moscow, 1946

Printed according to the original

Published in English for the first time

---

[a] Deleted in the draft: If I were to let you have an article on the subject you propose (which, I must confess, I do not know very much about) or on some other subject, this would in all likelihood involve me in a debate concerning my materialist point of departure.

154

ENGELS TO EDUARD BERNSTEIN[338]

IN LONDON

[Eastbourne,][333] 22 February 1894

Dear Ede,

Thank you for your letter and for the offer of G. Bruno.[339] But just now I am busy with Chapter 41[a] (ground rent) and hope to polish off a few more chapters before my return on Thursday, a week today. So I should like to save up the book until I come back, when I should certainly be glad to read it. We have been sent the *Frankfurter Zeitung* feuilleton, 'Bebel und Vollmar'.[b] The weather here is unfortunately too cold for me to be able to *sit* out of doors very much and I am not yet really in a condition to do any walking. Until next week, then.

Kindest regards to Gine, Käte[c] and yourself.

Yours
F. E.

First published, in Russian,
in: Marx-Engels *Archives*, Vol. I,
1924

Printed according to the original

Published in English for the first time

155

ENGELS TO FRIEDRICH ADOLPH SORGE[113]

IN HOBOKEN

Eastbourne, 23 February 1894

Dear Sorge,

Because of temporary lameness I am again spending a few weeks

---

[a] Of the third volume of *Capital* (see Vol. 25 of this edition, pp. 698-705). – [b] G. Brandes, 'Bebel und Vollmar', *Frankfurter Zeitung*, 4 February 1894 – [c] Regina Bernstein and Käte Schattner

here—shall be back in London in six days' time.[333]

You will have received the card announcing Louise's marriage. Her husband, Dr Freyberger, is a young Viennese doctor who gave up his career at Vienna University because they refused to let him tell the workers about the *social* causes of their illnesses; he has now established himself here and has already shown the English that more medicine is to be learned on the Continent than in this country. For the time being we shall all continue to live together at Regent's Park Road.

The *Holy Family* has arrived safely in Rome and will be returned to me in the middle of March, when it will at once be sent on to you.[a]

Our strange socialist group in the French Chamber is still something of a mystery. It is not yet very clear how many of them there are or what their standpoint is. Guesde tables vast numbers of Bills none of which, needless to say, goes through. Jaurès is unlikely to see a repetition of his first sensational victories, since the immediate effect of the anarchist gentry's bombing exploits[309] has been to provide the Ministry and the cause of law and order with a solid majority.

In this country the official politicians, both Liberal and Conservative, are in a state of complete disarray. The Liberals can maintain their position only by making fresh political and social concessions to the workers, for which, however, they lack the courage. Thus, they are trying to do so with an election cry against the house of lords instead of proposing payment of members, payment of election expenses by the government, and second ballot. I.e. instead of offering the workers more power vis-à-vis the Commons *and* the lords, all they want is to give the Commons more power vis-à-vis the lords, and that is something the workers are no longer prepared to swallow. But in any case there will be a general election here this summer and, unless the Liberals *really* take their courage in both hands and make *genuine* concessions to the workers, they will suffer defeat and go to pieces; at present they are held together only by Gladstone who might kick the bucket any day. Then there will be a middle-class democratic party with pro-Labour tendencies, and what is left of the Liberals will go over to Chamberlain. And all this has come about simply as a result of pressure from a working class that is still disunited and only partially conscious. If, in due course, it attains full consciousness, things will take an altogether different turn.

---

[a] See this volume, pp. 250, 282, 299

In Italy something violent might happen any day now. The middle classes have retained all the abominations of a feudalism in decay and used them as an excuse for their own infamies and tyrannies. The country is at the end of its tether, there has got to be a change there, but the Socialist Party[340] is still *very* weak and *very* muddle-headed, although among its number it can boast some really capable Marxists.

In Austria, too, something is to be anticipated. The funny part of it is that Socialists there are looking for support to the Emperor[a] who, by giving his blessing to Taaffe's proposal for electoral reform,[270] has declared himself in favour of something that comes close to universal suffrage, in the genuine belief that this is a necessary counterpart to general conscription. The coalition government won't succeed in doing anything or, if it does succeed in enacting an electoral Bill, this will be regarded simply as a bonus, while the movement, with the Emperor's tacit consent, will proceed on its way at any rate until such time as Taaffe's reform is put through. And then our chaps will see to the rest.

In short things are proceeding very merrily everywhere, and prospects for the *fin de siècle*[b] look better every day.

To judge by appearances, the *Workman's Times* is at the point of death. Nor is the INDEPENDENT LABOUR PARTY[114] very much more lively; it's strange how slow and circuitously everything proceeds over here.

Many regards to you and your wife from the two Freybergers and

Yours,
F. Engels

First published abridged in
*Briefe und Auszüge aus
Briefen von Joh. Phil. Becker,
Jos. Dietzgen, Friedrich Engels,
Karl Marx u. A. an F. A. Sorge
und Andere*, Stuttgart, 1906
and in full, in Russian, in:
Marx and Engels, *Works*,
First Russian Edition, Vol. XXIX,
Moscow, 1946

Printed according to the original

Published in English in full
for the first time

---

[a] Franz Joseph I – [b] end of the century

156

ENGELS TO ADELHEID DWORAK AND JULIUS POPP

IN VIENNA

[London, February 1894]

Cordial congratulations[341] from me too, dear Adelheid and Popp. Good examples are, as it were, raining round us thick and fast, and were I not so old and lame a horse, who knows—I might still decide to go into harness again.

Your old
F. Engels

First published in: *Friedrich Engels 1820-1970. Referate. Diskussionen. Dokumente*, Hanover, 1971

Printed according to the original

Published in English for the first time

157

ENGELS TO PAUL LAFARGUE[35]

AT LE PERREUX

London, 6 March 1894
122 Regent's Park Road, N. W.

My dear Lafargue,

I have just read Jaurès' and Guesde's speeches on the corn tariffs. I must say Jaures' speech is astounding, and it seems to me regrettable that he was allowed to put forward his amendment in the name of the Party.[342] I don't wish to speak of his proposal that the State should hold the price of corn at a minimum of 25 francs, which is out and out protectionism, and purely to the advantage of the big landowners into the bargain, since the small ones *have no corn to sell*, their produce not even sufficing for their own consumption. Guesde certainly said that, but *after* Léon Say, whereas we should have been the first to proclaim it loudly, instead of following in the footsteps of Mr Say. And it was Jaurès' phrase-mongering which prevented us.

But just take the proposal to make the State responsible for corn imports. Jaurès wants to prevent speculation. So what does he do? He makes the government responsible for the purchase of foreign corn. The government is the executive committee of the *majority in the Chamber*, and the *majority in the Chamber* represents as fully as possible these very speculators in corn, in shares, in government stocks, etc. It's like the last Chamber, where they made the Panamists responsible for the Panama investigation! And these Panamists, re-elected last August, are the people you want to make responsible for the suppression of speculation! It's not enough for you that they rob France by means of the annual Budget and the Stock Exchange—where at least they use their own capital and their own credit—you want to present them with several thousand millions and the national credit, so that they can clean out other people's pockets more thoroughly by means of *state socialism*!

Further, Jaurès fancies he has made an altogether new and unheard-of proposal. But the *petty-bourgeois* Socialists in the canton of Zurich got in first; for years past they have been asking for state monopoly in the corn trade; *their state*, I may say, is a great deal more democratic than the French Republic, it can even treat itself to a chief of police who is a petty-bourgeois Socialist (Mr Vogelsanger) and knows nothing of omnipotent chief commissioners; and, besides, it is so small that it can afford many absurdities which mean nothing there, whereas a great nation cannot go in for such puerilities with impunity.

Guesde's speech naturally suffered by having to support, at least for the sake of appearances, some of Jaurès' proposals. Fortunately his audience drew him into the field of general principles; that saved us; he was able to limit himself to touching lightly on Jaurès' motion. Speaking for myself, I should have preferred to see Guesde make his formal contributions independently of Jaurès and as the mouthpiece of our group. However, he did what he could.

All this is the upshot of the alliance with the ex-Radicals whom we are forced to endure.[a] In the first place, why did Jaurès make promises to the radical voters which he knew he could not keep? A radical custom,[86] but in no wise socialist and one that we should do well not to adopt.

---

[a] See this volume, pp. 249, 262

Then your Mr Jaurès, this doctrinaire professor, who is nevertheless ignorant, above all, of political economy, and of essentially superficial talents, misuses his gift of the gab to push himself to the fore and pose as the mouthpiece of socialism, which he does not so much as understand. Otherwise he would never have dared to put forward *state socialism* which represents one of the *infantile diseases* of proletarian socialism, a disease which they went through in Germany, for example, more than a dozen years ago, under the regime of the Anti-Socialist Laws,[15] *when that was the only form tolerated by the government* (and even protected by it). And even then only a negligible minority of the Party was caught in that snare for a short while; after the Wyden Congress[343] the whole thing petered out completely.

Ah, yes, but we have a republic in France, the ex-Radicals will say to you; it's quite another matter in our case, we can use the government to introduce socialist measures! A republic, in relation to the proletariat, differs from a monarchy only in that it is the *ready-made* political form for the future rule of the proletariat. You have the advantage of us in that it is already in being; we, for our part, shall have to waste 24 hours creating it. But a republic, like any other form of government, is determined by what composes it; so long as it is the form of *bourgeois* rule, it is quite as hostile to us as any monarchy whatsoever (save in the *forms* of that hostility). Hence it is a gratuitous illusion to treat it as an essentially socialist form; to entrust it, whilst it is dominated by the bourgeoisie, with socialist tasks. We can wring concessions from it, but never look to it to carry out our job. Even if we were able to control it by a minority so strong that it could become a majority from one day to the next.

However, what's done can't be undone. There will be other opportunities when our people will be able to come to the fore and proclaim their own tendencies, by means of Bills.

So you were surprised by Louise's marriage? It has been brewing for some months. Freyberger has left Vienna and given up a brilliant university career because they forbade him to enlighten the workers, in his lectures, on the social causes of their ills. So he came here, and he has found very good openings in the hospitals here. Once that was settled, there was no further reason for delaying the wedding. While waiting for his expectations to materialise he came to join his wife here. you can see that it is an entirely matriarchal marriage, the husband is his wife's boarder!

That reminds me of my own matriarchal studies and the translation of them that Laura was good enough to do.[195] I hope she approved of the few small alterations I suggested, and that you have told her how charmed I was by the translation of that 3rd and 4th part. I kiss her by your proxy.

Yours very truly,
F. E.

First published in part in: Printed according to the original
Le Socialiste, No. 115,
24 November 1900 and in full in: Translated from the French
F. Engels, P. et L. Lafargue,
Correspondance, t. III, Paris, 1959

158

ENGELS TO AUGUST MOMBERGER

IN WIESBADEN

London, 9 March 1894
122 Regent's Park Road, N. W.

Dear Sir,

My reply to your esteemed letter of 26.2 has been somewhat delayed[344] by my absence from London.[333]

Things do not look very bright so far as English socialist literature is concerned. The leading publisher of books of this nature is Sonnenschein (W. Swan Sonnenschein & Co., Paternoster Square). While there is a lot of inferior stuff amongst his SOCIAL SCIENCE SERIES, it also contains the following:

W. Morris and E. B. Bax, *Socialism, its Growth and Outcome*;

E. B. Bax, *The Religion of Socialism*;

    do., *The Ethics of Socialism*;

Aveling, E. AND E. M[arx-Aveling], *The Working Class Movement in America*;

Lafargue, *The Evolution of Property*;

E. B. Bax, *Outlooks from the New Standpoint*;

Hyndman, *Commercial Panics of the l9th Century*;

Engels, *The Condition of the Working Class in England in 1844*;
  do., *Socialism, Scientific and Utopian*
etc. Again, the value of these things varies greatly.

There is also a multitude of shorter propaganda pamphlets of *very* varied quality, some being really good, some deplorably bad; none are easily obtainable through book shops. Most were published by the SOCIAL DEMOCRATIC FEDERATION[44] and the FABIAN SOCIETY.[43]

There is no journal similar to the *Neue Zeit* in this country. The socialist weeklies are:

Justice (organ of the SOCIAL DEMOCRATIC FEDERATION), publisher H. Quelch, 37a, Clerkenwell Green, London, E. C.

Workman's Times, 59, Tile St., Manchester (MANCHESTER LABOUR PRESS SOCIETY).

That is about all the information I can give you. I fear, however, that the sort of Englishmen you meet in Wiesbaden will be unlikely to provide many suitable candidates for our party.

Yours very truly,
F. Engels

First published, in Russian,
in: Marx and Engels, *Works*,
First Russian Edition.
Vol. XXIX, Moscow, 1946

Printed according to the original

Published in English for the first time

159

ENGELS TO VICTOR ADLER

IN VIENNA

London, 20 March 1894

Dear Victor,

A short while ago you asked me about translating the article in the *Critica Sociale* on the position, etc., of Italy.[334] Louise at once wrote a postcard on my behalf saying THAT YOU WERE WELCOME TO IT and I confirmed this a day or two later in a letter to you.[25] Soon afterwards an inquiry arrived from K. Kautsky who wanted to know if I would let him have the thing for the *Neue Zeit*. In my reply I told him that you had already snaffled it.[a]

But the article has *not*, in the meantime, appeared in the *Arbeiter-Zeitung*, and that puts me in an awkward position vis-à-vis K. Kautsky. So could you please let me know what is happening about it? I must say this makes me feel like the English landlady who, having on the one hand a nubile daughter and, on the other, a susceptible German lodger, demanded of the latter at the first sign of a flirtation: "WHAT ARE YOUR INTENTIONS WITH REGARD TO MY DAUGHTER?" But the fact that K. Kautsky has entered into competition with you will doubtless exonerate me.

Over here things are tending towards a general election[345] and everything that happens is done by way of preparation for it. The Liberals are as craven as ever. They must know that they can only retain their position by increasing the political power of the workers and yet they hesitate and flounder about nervously. Neither a cut-and-dried extension of the suffrage, nor the elimination of a property qualification which consists in burdening the candidate with *all* the election expenses while failing to give him a salary, nor any provision in the shape of a second ballot for the putting up of a *third* candidate (alongside those of the two official parties). At the same time they want to abolish the house of lords but don't lift a finger to produce a Lower House with the courage and ability to do this. The Tories for their part are making mistake after mistake. For two years they have been turning Parliament into a complete farce on the pretext of smashing HOME RULE[171]; with the Liberals, who took this lying down, they have played, and continue to play, Old Harry, as Randy Churchill demonstrated last night,[346] although, with elections in the offing, this is a risky business and might seriously shake the peace-loving [?][b] British philistine's faith in the Conservatives. Furthermore, Salisbury attempted to make the PARISH COUNCILS BILL[163] an occasion for playing a dirty trick on his Liberal Unionist allies,[206] Devonshire and Chamberlain, and exploiting them for purely TORY ends, so that the said alliance is no longer as steadfast as heretofore. In short, things are getting into a frightful tangle, and at the moment it is difficult to guess what the outcome will be.

My congratulations on the way you lulled the general strike to sleep

---

[a] See this volume, p. 269 – [b] *sic* in printed text

and likewise on your articles on the coalition government's electoral reform[347] and on the situation generally in Austria. The one in the issue of the sixth of this month was particularly brilliant. Not for a moment do I doubt that your party conference[323] will go off splendidly. My regards to all our friends and also to August and Paul Singer and Gerisch, if they attend the same.

Louise sends much love, as does

Yours,
F. E.

First published in: *Victor Adlers Aufsätze, Reden und Briefe Erstes Heft: Victor Adler und Friedrich Engels*, Vienna, 1922

Printed according to the book

Published in English for the first time

160

ENGELS TO NIKOLAI DANIELSON

IN ST. PETERSBURG

London, 20 March 1894
122 Regent's Park Road, N. W.

My dear Sir,

Today I forwarded to you, *registered*, sheets No. 1-6 (up to page 96) of Vol. III[a] containing the greater part of Section 1. The continuation will follow as it reaches me.

Your letters of 4th and 23rd XI and 24/II to hand, I shall reply as soon as possible.

Yours very faithfully
L. K.[b]

First published, in Russian, in *Minuvshiye gody*, No. 2, 1908 Published in English for the first time

Reproduced from the original

---

[a] of *Capital* — [b] Engels' pen name derived from Louise Kautsky's initials

161

ENGELS TO PANAIT MUSOIU[348]

IN BUCHAREST

London, 20 March 1894
122 Regent's Park Road, N. W.

Dear Comrade,

Owing to my absence from London[333] I have been prevented from answering your letter of 24 February any earlier. This I duly received as well as the *Manifestul comunist* and *Socialism utopic si socialism stiintific*^a for which very many thanks. Unfortunately I am not yet sufficiently versed in Romanian to be able to give an opinion on the merits of your translation. But I would caution you against taking the French translation as a basis when working on a German book.

Unfortunately time does not permit me to comply with your request that I write a preface to the new edition. I am busy putting the finishing touches to Volume III of Marx's *Capital* and, since printing is going rapidly ahead, I must devote all my time to the completion of the rest of the manuscript in order that no hold-ups should occur.

With kindest regards,

F. Engels

First published, in Russian,
in: Marx and Engels, *Works*,
First Russian Edition,
Vol. XXIX, Moscow, 1946

Printed according to the original

Published in English for the first time

---

^a K. Marx and F. Engels, *Manifesto of the Communist Party*; F. Engels, *Socialism: Utopian and Scientific*

162

ENGELS TO FRIEDRICH ADOLPH SORGE[113]

IN HOBOKEN

London, 21 March 1894
122 Regent's Park Road, N. W.

Dear Sorge,

I have today sent back to you with many thanks *The Holy Family* by BOOK POST, REGISTERED, following its safe return from the trip to Rome.[a]

Immediately after Easter I shall send you a parcel containing the Bax-Morris book[b] and Bernstein's Berlin Complete Edition of Lassalle Works.[c]

Auntie Motteler has just been here in company with Gertrud Liebknecht. Apparently the latter wants to move in temporarily with the former. What Liebknecht intends to do about her (she says he wants her to go back) remains a secret—doubtless also to himself. His eldest daughter, Mrs Geiser, is living in the worst possible circumstances and his wife and Gertrud are at daggers drawn. I don't in fact believe *he* has actually insisted that she return.

Have you seen the novel *Helena* by old Mother Kautsky in the *Vorwärts*? She has peopled her stage with a crowd of living party members, including Motteler and his wife. It is a poor imitation of the popular novels of Gregor Samarow[d] (Spy Meding). I shall be interested to see whether it is passed over in silence and am somewhat surprised that the *Vorwärts* should have taken it. The paper's feuilleton is censored by Mother Natalie Liebknecht.

The *Pionierkalender* received with thanks.

Over here the dissolution of Parliament draws on apace. At the new elections[345] more Labour candidates will be put up than ever before, though not nearly enough, and I'm not sure whether a whole crowd of them won't

---

[a] See this volume, p. 272 – [b] W. Morris and E. B. Bax, *Socialism, its Growth and Outcome*, London, New York, 1893 – [c] F. Lassalle, *Reden und Schriften*, Berlin, 1892-1893 – [d] Samarin in the MS

again be put up with the help of TORY money. The Liberals, like the TORIES, are both of them firm supporters of the indirect property qualification which consists in the candidate's being burdened with the entire costs of the election—ranging from 4100 minimum up to between £400 and £600 and even more for the *official* expenses alone, e.g. POLLING PLACES, etc. So if the working men fall into the clutches of Champion, who is offering 4100 per constituency (he got the money from Hudson, the soap manufacturer), the Liberals will have no cause for complaint. All in all their approach to the elections is characterised by a curiously obstinate refusal to face the facts. They act as though they wish to abolish the *Upper House* but refuse to remodel the *Lower House* (by increasing the power of the workers) in such a way that it would be capable of tackling something of the kind on its own. The TORIES, on the other hand, are more stupid than they ever were and that is saying a good deal. For the past couple of years they have been playing Old Harry with the Liberal government in the Upper and the Lower House. To this the Liberals have calmly submitted, while the philistines, who have been turning Conservative in droves, have rejoiced, since it was done on the pretext of removing the treasonable, anti-Empire HOME RULE BILL[171] HOME RULE Government. Now, however, that serious domestic legislation is on the agenda, they are continuing to play the same game, and that might be rather too much of a good thing for your peace-loving philistine. So things remain very uncertain and the new elections will at all events produce some surprising results. Whatever happens, Labour will be strengthened and the Liberals will be compelled to make further concessions to the working man.

In Austria, Belgium and Holland electoral reform has also been the order of the day. Before long there will be no European parliament without labour representatives. In Austria the cause is progressing very well. Adler is leading the movement with quite outstanding address and the Party Conference on Sunday [323] will also help.

Once the tariff business[301] has to some extent been sorted out on your side of the Atlantic and the duty on raw materials been abolished, the crisis will probably recede and the superiority of American industry over that of Europe will undoubtedly make itself felt. Only then will matters take a serious turn here in England, but then they will go with a bang.

I finished the first two thirds of Volume III[a] sooner than I had expected

---

[a] of *Capital*

and, since printing was rapidly forging ahead (twelve proof-sheets have already come back), I was compelled to make a brief announcement.[a] The final editing of the final third is not yet quite done, but next week I shall be getting down to it again.

Louise Kautsky has told you of her marriage to Dr L. Freyberger from Vienna. He is a young physician who in my opinion has a major scientific career ahead of him. He is practising in hospitals here and has since moved in with us. Apart from the name, therefore, Louise's address is unchanged.

Yours,
F. Engels

Warm regards to you and your wife from Louise and myself. I trust your health has improved.

First published abridged in:
Briefe und Auszüge aus Briefen von Joh. Phil. Becker, Jos. Dietzgen, Friedrich Engels, Karl Marx u. A. an F. A. Sorge und Andere, Stuttgart, 1906 and in full, in Russian, in: Marx and Engels, *Works*,

First Russian Edition, Vol. XXIX, Moscow, 1946

Printed according to the original

Published in English in full for the first time

163

ENGELS TO VICTOR ADLER

IN VIENNA

London, 22 March 1894

Dear Victor,

I wrote to you the day before yesterday,[b] and yesterday Louise wrote to you at the Köpernikusgasse by 'registered' mail.

Your report on the state of affairs over there gave us great pleasure. Less so the prospect of your spending your summer holidays in 'durance vile',[349] concerning which we had already seen something in *the Arbeiter-*

---

[a] F. Engels, *The Third Volume of Karl Marx's 'Capital', On the Contents of the Third Volume of 'Capital'*. – [b] See Letter 159

innen-Zeitung (as distinct from the *Arbeiter-Zeitung*). I wrote to you day before yesterday about conditions over here.[350]

But the disappearance of our letters to you is really getting beyond a joke. After Louise had written to you yesterday we tried as best as we could to reconstruct from memory the letters she had written. These were as follows:

1. In the middle of December she sent Adelheid (Dworak) an article on Female Factory Inspectors,[a] along with various notes for the *Arbeiter Zeitung*—Adelheid has written to say that she never got the letter.

2. Shortly before Christmas Louise wrote to *you* asking for some information about the doctor you had recommended to Tussy.

3. In January again to you asking *you*, amongst other things, to convey my apologies to your wife and saying I was indisposed.

4. Towards the end of January, when Lafargue was here and Burns met him at our house, an account of the latter's visit and conditions in England generally—the letter was from Louise to *you*.

5. In February she wrote to *you* urging you to use my article in the *Critica Sociale*.[334]

6 and 7. Two letters from her to you from Eastbourne between 9 February and 1 March.

8. She wrote to *Schacherl* at the *Arbeiter-Zeitung* saying she was unable to send the article[b] straight away.

9. On 4 March she wrote asking you to send the *Arbeiterinnen-Zeitung* to Dr Bonnier, 19 Regent St, Oxford and also gave some information about Jaurès and the Socialist group in the French Chamber.

Some of these letters were sent to you at the editorial office of the *Arbeiter-Zeitung*, some to your private address and both lots seem to have been disappearing with equal regularity. On the other hand the rest of Louise's letters to Vienna, including those to the gas-workers, have been arriving no less regularly, as have the replies.

Your eight-page letter to Louise has likewise *not* arrived.

So we shall now experiment for a time with *registered* letters. A cover address in Vienna might perhaps be a good idea.

Herewith what you wanted[c] for the Party Conference.[323]

---

[a] [L. Freyberger,] 'Weibliche Fabriks-Inspektoren,' *Arbeiterinnen-Zeitung*, Nos. 1 and 2, 5 and 19 January 1894 [b] [L. Freyberger] 'Zum 13 März', *Arbeiter-Zeitung*, No. 21, 13 March 1894 – [c] F. Engels, *To the Fourth Austrian Party Congress.*

Please give my kindest regards to all comrades including the Berliners. Louise and Freyberger send you their cordial regards, as does

Yours,

F. E.

First published in:
Victor Adlers Aufsäze, Reden und Briefe.
Erstes Heft: *Victor Adler und
Friedrich Engels,* Vienna, 1922

Printed according to the book

Published in English for the first time

164

ENGELS TO PABLO IGLESIAS

IN MADRID

[Draft]

[London, 26 March, 1894]

My dear friend Iglesias!

I duly received your letter dated 24 November, and I begin my reply by stating that this letter will be the last, if you persist in addressing me as 'usted'. Indeed, I have reason to feel offended by the fact that you refuse to address me in the manner customary among old members of the International and comrades-in-arms, the form of address which Anselmo Lorenzo, and many other comrades, old and young[a] accorded me as far back as 1872. So. let us please address each other as 'tu'!

I shall continue in French: I have not written in Spanish for more than twenty years now, and it would take me all day to write a letter in Spanish. Please forgive me![b]

Well now. I am very sorry that I missed the opportunity to see you in Zurich.[189] When I arrived at the Tonhalle[c] on the Saturday morning, many friends came to talk with me in the restaurant before going in to

---

[a] The following words are crossed out by Engels: 'French, German, Austrian, Swiss and others'. – [b] This part of the letter is written in Spanish, then follows the French text. – [c] The meeting-place of the Congress.

the meeting: I asked almost all of them to go and find the Spanish delegation, and to tell you that I was waiting for you; however, no one came. After the congress ended, I was told that I would certainly see you in the afternoon, on the steamboat. However, I looked for you in vain, and now I know what had happened. On the Sunday, no one was able to tell me where you were staying. I was told time and again that you had left, and I lost all hope of meeting you. I was extremely sorry, since one of the reasons, and not the least, why I came to Zurich was the hope of seeing my old friend Iglesias face to face and shaking his hand.

Thank you for sending me regularly *El Socialistae*, which I read with great pleasure every Saturday evening, and from which I have the satisfaction of seeing that you are gradually spreading across the whole of Spain, that socialism is being established on the ruins of Carlism[352] in the Basque countries, and that far away provinces of Galicia and Asturia are beginning to join the movement. Good luck!

As for the anarchists, they are perhaps on the verge of killing themselves. This fever of violence, this volley of assassinations, senseless and, in the final analysis, paid for and incited by the police, cannot but open the eyes of the bourgeoisie to the nature of this propaganda of madmen and agents provocateurs.[353] Even the bourgeoisie will realise in the end that it is absurd to pay the police, and through the police the anarchists, to blow up the very bourgeois who pay them. And if now we also risk suffering from the bourgeois reaction, we shall benefit in the long run because this time we shall succeed in proving to everyone that there is a world of difference between ourselves and the anarchists.

Over here the movement is progressing quite slowly. There is certainly a strong tendency towards socialism among the working masses. However, the historical conditions in England are such that this tendency in the masses produces, among the leaders, a host of different cross-currents which even fight against each other. Here, as in France, there will only be unity when there are some socialists in parliament. Today there are only two—which is one too many, or at least, too few.

In Italy the situation is becoming critical and revolutionary. I am sending you the *Critica Sociale* with an article which I have written on the request of my friends from Milan.[334]

In Germany we are continuing as usual. It is a well-organised and well-disciplined army which is growing every day, and which is advancing towards its goal with a sure and implacable step. In Germany we can almost calculate the day when[a] state power will fall into our hands.

In the meantime, I draw your attention to Austria. There a great battle is in the making. The ruling classes, the feudal nobility and the bourgeoisie, have exhausted their resources. An electoral reform is now inevitable. They are trying to arrange things so that the working class will not have too many representatives in parliament. But the workers are determined, they are forcing the bourgeois to retreat step by step, until they concede universal suffrage. After Zurich I visited Vienna; judging by what I saw there, the Austrian socialists have a great future.[b]

When I had reached this point, I received your letter dated 22 March. Unfortunately I am unable to send you a few lines for 1st May, since I have to finish the final editing of the third volume of *Das Kapital*, and am obliged to refuse *any kind* of collaboration, be it in connection with 18th March, or with 1st May. And what I have refused to the French, the Germans, the Austrians and others, I also cannot do for you.

Affectionately yours.

First published in Russian in:
Marx and Engels, *Works*,
First Russian Edition,
Vol. XXIX, Moscow, 1946

Printed according to the original

Translated from the
French and the Spanish

Published in full in English
for the first time

165

ENGELS TO BENNO KARPELES

IN VIENNA

London, 29 March 1894
122 Regent's Park Road, N. W.

Dear Sir,

I am in receipt of your esteemed note of the 19th inst. (postmarked Rome) and have also just received the first half volume of your book[354]

---

[a] The following phrase "we are the only party capable..." is crossed out by Engels. – [b] The text that follows is in Spanish.

from Vienna. I am most grateful to you for having sent it to me.

The extent to which both science and events have progressed since the appearance in 1845 of that early work of mine[a]—a work to which you accord such honourable mention but which in my view is much over-rated—cannot be better demonstrated than by the plan you were able to draw up for the elaboration of your book. The very fact that it was possible to tackle such an inquiry, embracing as it does every detail, even those which seem least significant, that might have a bearing on the point at issue within the field of investigation, and this by a simple layman, is an enormous advance in itself. May you succeed in completing your work exactly in accordance with your plan, thereby presenting us with a picture such as we have not possessed hitherto of the general situation of a large and highly interesting working-class community.

> I am Sir,
> Yours faithfully,
> F. Engels

First published, in Russian, in: Marx and Engels, *Works*, Second Russian Edition, Vol. 39, Moscow, 1966

Printed according to the original

Published in English for the first time

166

ENGELS TO HUNTER WATTS

IN LONDON

[Draft]

[London,] 3 April 1894

Dear Comrade,

I am very much obliged to you and the comrades of the S.D.F.[44] whose feelings you express for the honour you do me by asking me to lecture at your hall. But I am afraid I must decline. My work for our common cause lies in another branch of activity, where I believe I can be more useful,

---

[a] F. Engels, *The Condition of the Working Class in England*

and where I find full occupation for all the time at my command. Were I once to begin lecturing, at which trade moreover I am but a poor hand, I should no longer have a valid plea for resisting other invitations, and then I should have entirely to give up my present class of work. For this reason I have regularly declined all similar calls from the Fabian Society,[43] the I.L.P.,[114] and other bodies, with the exception made this year of the old Communist Verein,[a] where they claimed a fifty years' hold upon me.[62]

But then, as far as the S.D.F. is concerned, there is another question to consider. You cannot but be aware that for years, up to a comparatively recent period, *Justice*, the official organ of the S.D.F., has been in the habit of charging me with all sorts of offences. These charges, mostly vague insinuations of mysterious crimes, *Justice* has never specified, never attempted to provide, and yet never withdrew.[b]

First published, in Russian,
in: Marx and Engels, *Works*,
First Russian Edition,
Vol. XXIX, Moscow, 1946

Reproduced from the original

Published in English for the first time

167

ENGELS TO LAURA LAFARGUE

AT LE PERREUX

London, 11 April 1894
122 Regent's Park Road, N. W.

My dear Löhr,

Your agreeable letter comes just in time. I was on the point of writing to Paul this morning, and so I have a good pretext of changing the address of my letter. I had just read your translation in the *Ere Nouvelle* and was quite charmed by it.[310] It reads better than the original, there are only

---

[a] Society – [b] Then there follows a number of unfinished and crossed out phrases which amount to the following: 'I am therefore compelled to consider whether under these circumstances I do not owe it to myself for the present to refrain from presenting myself as a speaker in the hall of the S.D.F., And further, whether my appearance in that capacity would not be unwelcome to a large portion, perhaps even a majority, of those to whom the hall belongs.'

two or three slight alterations I would suggest for a possible reprint.

This leads me at once to the *libertaire*, alas not *libertin!* Dühring.[355] dear girl, vous avez fait vos preuves[a]! You arrange yourself with Bonnet as most convenient. Provided *the Manuscript passes through your hands*, it's all right and I will gladly look it over—within the limits of my time, *cela s'entend*,[b] which limits I am sorry to say are very narrow and don't look as if they were going to expand, on the contrary!

But I do wish you could use your talents and energies for some other kind of work which, besides credit, would also bring cash into the pocket of the worker. Could no arrangement be made with Carré for something of that sort?

I send you a No. of the *Rheinische Zeitung*, edited, as maybe you are aware, by the grand Karl Hirsch (since the 1st April). It is not, however, in order to give you a specimen of his elucubrations that I send it to you, but because it gives a report of the motion brought out in the Reichstag by Count Kanitz,[356] one of the most shining lights amongst those Prussian Junkers who are, according to Hermann Wagener, their theoretical champion, either *Ochsen von Geburt oder Ochsen aus Prinzip*.[c] This motion, made in the interest of the landed aristocracy of Eastern Germany, is almost literally the proposition [made by] *Jaurès*[d] which was to show the way to the socialist world how to use their parliamentary position in the interest of the working class and the peasantry. The same Count Kanitz has, the other day, proclaimed a new way to pay old debts, for the benefit of the German Empire: sell all your gold coin and replace it by about 4 milliards silver coin, which will leave 2 milliards clear profit (silver being bought at 28 pence the ounce and being turned into money at 60 pence an ounce) wherewith to wipe out the Imperial debt. Now if I wanted to be malicious, I might ask M. Jaurès whether, in return for Kanitz's acceptance of his corn motion, he would not accept Kanitz's silver motion which looks equally socialistic, and which, from an economic standpoint, is not a bit more objectionable. But I will be generous, even with Jaurès, and leave him alone; our French comrades, however, I cannot refrain from observing, ought really to look a little closer into the proposals of their ex-radical allies,[e] before they accept them blindfolded. A few more such escapades, and their reputation as political economists will be in great danger.

---

[a] you have proved yourself! – [b] be it understood – [c] oxen by birth or oxen on principle – [d] See this volume, p. 275 – [e] Ibid., p. 276

Of the *Discours sur le libre échange*[a] there exists but *one* copy which I by some accident got hold of through a second-hand catalogue. If that were to get lost, the whole thing, in the French original at least, would be lost *for ever,* I cannot send it unless there are strong guarantees against loss. I expect to-night a new *Postal guide* containing the latest information as to the international postal insurance arrangements; if these are satisfactory I will forward the thing to you at once, otherwise try some other means. Anyhow a reprint would be in every respect highly desirable.[357] In the meantime I will send you another copy of the English translation published in Boston.[358]

Sorel's *Métaphysique*[b] I really have not had time to read. I am awfully busy; deep in the Rent of Land (Vol. III[c]) which causes me a deal of trouble by Mohr's tables being almost without exception miscalculated—you know what a genius he was for figures!—and having to be recast. And 15 sheets are already printed so that there is no time to be lost with the remainder of the Manuscript. And then the hot weather—just as you have it at Le Perreux. In there anything *in* that Sorel's study?

Louise thanks you for your letter and will soon write to you; sends her kindest regards. Her husband is getting quite a reputation here as an anatomical preparator; he works a good deal for the anatomical Museum at Middlesex Hospital; the clumsy people here cannot come up to the Vienna standard in these delicate matters.

We have Gertrud Liebknecht here, back from America, but hardly much improved there.

Just read Paul's letter in the *Vorwärts*—capital.[d] So good that even Berlin translations cannot spoil it.

Ever your old
F. Engels

First published, in the language
of the original (English), in: F. Engels,
P. et L. Lafargue, *Correspondance*,
t. III, 1891-1895, Paris, 1959

Reproduced from the original

---

[a] *Speech on Free Trade* – [b] G. Sorel, 'L'ancienne et la nouvelle métaphysique', *L'Ère nouvelle*, None 3, 4, 5 and 6, March, April, May and June 1894 – [c] of *Capital* – [d] [P. Lafargue] Gallus, 'Die Heldenthaten der französischen Polizei', *Vorwärts*, No. 82, 10 April 1894

168

ENGELS TO FILIPPO TURATI[359]

IN MILAN

London, 12 April 1894
122 Regent's Park Road, N. W.

Dear Turati,

I am sending you by post the Anglo-American edition (*Discourse on Free Trade*.[358] K. Marx) of your discourse, and the German translation of *The Poverty of Philosophy*, where you will find this speech in the appendix.[a] As for the French text, this is to be reprinted in the Paris *L'Ère Nouvelle*.[357] There is only one copy of the French text, namely mine, and if it is lost there will be no way to replace it. I therefore still do not know how to send it to Paris, for if I have a copy made here, this will mean loss of time, and I have too much experience of the post to entrust the original to it.

The 2nd volume of *Capital* came but in Hamburg, published by *Otto Meissner*, as the 1st was, in 1893 (2nd edition). If I am not mistaken, the price is 6 marks. The same publishers are to issue the 3rd volume in September, to the great pleasure of the illustrious Achille Loria, a charlatan who warned everyone that Marx had never written this 3rd volume, but was always referring the reader to it simply to make a fool of him.[360]

Kindest regards from myself and Mme Freyberger (ex Kautsky, she has just married a young Austrian doctor living here) to Mme Kulishov.

Yours,
F. Engels

First published in the
language of the original
(French) in: *Annali*, an. 19
Milano, 1958

Printed according to the original

Translated from the French

Published in English for the first time

---

[a] K. Marx, *The Poverty of Philosophy*.

169

ENGELS TO HENRY WILLIAM LEE

IN LONDON

[London], 16 April 1894
H. W. Lee. Secretary
Social Democratic Federation

Dear Comrade,

Both you and the party who suggested to you the idea of my lecturing for you,[361] must have been aware that I have so far made it a rule not to lecture anywhere. But apart from that, I find myself in a peculiar position with regard to you, that is, if I rightly understand your letter, the Social Democratic Federation.[44]

You cannot ignore that for a long series of years and up to a comparatively recent period, *Justice*, the organ of the S.D.F., has constantly attacked me and brought all sorts of charges against me. While no attempt has ever been made to prove these charges, they have never been withdrawn. Nor has the S.D.F. ever disclaimed any responsibility for what *Justice* wrote. In consequence I have been compelled to keep entirely aloof from the S.D.F. and do not see how I can change my attitude unless that difficulty is entirely removed.

Yours faithfully,
F. E.

First published, in Russian,
in: Marx and Engels, *Works*,
First Russian Edition,
Vol. XXIX, Moscow, 1946

Reproduced from the original

Published in English for the first time

170

ENGELS TO THE EDITORIAL BOARD OF
A FRENCH SOCIALIST NEWSPAPER[362]

[*Draft*]

London, 24 April 1894
122 Regent's Park Road, N. W.

Dear citizen,

I have received your letter dated 20th of this month, but unfortunately I am quite unable to provide an article for the 1st May issue of your newspaper.

To begin with, I am unwell at the moment. However, even if I were in the best of health, the urgent work that I am presently engaged in (the publication of the 3rd volume of *Capital* by Marx) and that I cannot lay aside makes it impossible for me to undertake any other literary work. I have already warned those of our friends with whom I corresponded, and asked them to excuse me. You can well understand that I cannot now do for you that which I have officially refused to do for our friends in Spain, Austria and other countries.

I wish your newspaper every success, and send my fraternal greetings to the editorial committee.

Yours sincerely,
F. E.

First published in Russian
in: Marx and Engels, *Works*,
First Russian Edition,
Vol. XXIX, Moscow, 1946

Printed according to the original

Translated from the French

171

ENGELS TO CARL EBERLE

IN BARREN

London, 24 April 1894
122 Regent's Park Road, N. W.

Dear Comrade,

Your letter of 21 March arrived a day or two ago as did the album of Barmen you so very kindly sent me, and I should like to say how very grateful I am to the Social Democratic Club in Barmen and, in particular, to the compiler of the album, for this kind and for me both flattering and agreeable gift. Indeed it was an unexpected pleasure to be able to see the enormous changes that have taken place in Barmen during the twenty years that I have been away. I feel completely lost. Other than by the station and on one, the older, side of the Werther Bollwerk, I can no longer tell where I am from the pictures. Even the view taken on the Neuenweg, which surely cannot be more than a few minutes walk from the Bruch, is utterly strange to me. Only our old house remains unaltered.

Though it is cheering to see these signs of an upheaval that has changed the Barmen of my youth from a small philistine backwater into a large industrial town, what nevertheless pleases me most is the fact that people there have also experienced a significant change for the better. Had that not been the case, Barmen would even now be represented in the Reichstag by an out-and-out Conservative, some thoroughly sanctimonious 'swell', nor could there be any question of a Social Democratic Club in Barmen, while the last thing that would have occurred to Barmen's working men would have been to honour me with an album. Fortunately, however, the revolution in the appearance of the town is attended by a revolution in the minds of its working men and for us that is a guarantee of a far mightier and more comprehensive revolution in the world as presently constituted. With sincere regards,

Yours,
F. Engels

First published, in Russian,
in: Marx and Engels, *Works*,
First Russian Edition,
Vol. XXIX, Moscow, 1946

Printed according to the original

Published in English for the first time

172

ENGELS TO LAURA LAFARGUE

AT LE PERREUX

London, 11 May 1894
122 Regent's Park Road, N. W.

My dear Laura,

Just two lines.

Have the proofs of the *Discours sur le libre échange*[363] gone to Milan? If not, do please see that they are sent *at once*. Turati has published in the *Critica Sociale* a text which is a *traduction*[a] from the Russian of something made out of something in German,[364] and moreover so abbreviated that it is anything but Mohr. Now they threaten to publish this *en brochure*. And unless they get the French text soon, I shall not even be able to haul them over the coals for it, as they are doing 'their text'!

Surely it will be possible to make our French friends to treat business as business for once!

Just come back from town where we sent off the *last* of the Manuscript of Vol. III,[b]

If you get the *Neue Welt* with the *Vorwärts* or some other German paper, look at 'Aus finsteren Zeiten'[c] in No. 18. You will find there your grand-parents and Mohr transmogrified into a romance and I wish you may relish it.

Kind regards from Louise. Monsieur Guesde neither turned up nor wrote a line of excuse, *Les français sont si polis*![d]

Ever yours
F. E.

---

[a] translation – [b] of *Capital* – [c] 'Aus finsteren Zeiten', *Die Neue Welt*, Nos. 18 and 19, 1894
– [d] The French are so polite.

The *lazy woman*[a] says she is just writing 30 letters to Trades Unions and others anent an Austrian strike, and says she should be very glad of your assistance if she could have it.

Avvocato F. Turati
Portíci Galleria, V. E. 23
Milano, Italia

First published, in Russian,
in: Marx and Engels, *Works*,
Second Russian Edition,
Vol. 39, Moscow, 1966

Reproduced from the original

Published in English for the first time

173

ENGELS TO FILIPPO TURATI

IN MILAN

London, 11 May 1894
122 Regent's Park Road, N. W.

My dear Turati,

I am returning to you, *registered Post*, the proofs of *Libero Scambio, etc.*, together with the English edition,[358] which I would ask you to keep. The translation of my introduction is very good, except for a few points that are technically difficult—you will find the appropriate indications. However, Marx's speech, which is published in the *Critica Sociale*, is not a translation but a *summary*[364] that I despair of setting in order. I have written again to Paris[25] to ask them to send you the French original. In the meantime please compare with the English text. If you publish the text according to *Critica Sociale*, you will receive complaints that this is not the author's text, that this is to take liberties which are tantamount to *forgery*, etc., and unfortunately I will find it impossible to come to your aid, It would be better to rewrite it—it is not very long—than to expose oneself to such complaints.

---

[a] Louise Freyberger

Yours,

Engels

Greetings to Mme Anna Kulishov and you from Louise Kautsky-Freyberger and myself.

First published, in the language of the original (French), in: *Annali*, an. I, Milano, 1958

Printed according to the original

Translated from the French

Published in English for the first time

174

ENGELS TO FRIEDRICH ADOLPH SORGE[366]

IN HOBOKEN

London, 12 May 1894
122 Regent's Park Road, N. W.

Dear Sorge,

Yesterday we sent to you through G.W. Wheatley & Co (New York ADDRESS, U.S. Express Co., 49, Broadway) a parcel containing Morris-Bax and the Berlin Lassalle in fifty parts,[a] which I trust will reach you before long. CARRIAGE PAID. On the same day the remainder of the ms. of Volume III[b] went off to Hamburg, thereby removing a heavy load from my mind. The two final sections made me 'sweat good and proper'.[c] There will be sixty sheets of which twenty have already been set up in type.

I was greatly relieved to hear that the *Holy Family* had safely returned into your keeping after its strange Odyssey.[d] On the other hand the news about your eyes is most distressing. I hope you will consult a good specialist, for a lot can be done if steps are taken in good time. For the past fifteen years I too have had trouble with my eyes off and on. Having taken medical

---

[a] W. Morris and E. B. Bax, *Socialism, its Growth and Outcome*, London, New York, 1893; F. Lassalle, *Reden und Schriften*, Bd. 1-3, Berlin, 1892-1893 – [b] of *Capital* – [c] See K. Marx, *Capital*, Vol. III, Ch. 37-42 and 48-52 – [d] See this volume, pp. 250, 272, 282

advice I have again reached the stage at which the thing no longer bothers me at all, provided only that I don't write too much by lamplight.

Not long ago I caught a cold, which left me in no doubt that I am now an old man at last. On this occasion, what I had previously been able to treat as a minor annoyance, pretty well laid me low for a week and kept me under draconian medical supervision for a whole fortnight after that. Even now, I am expected to take care of myself for another fortnight, no less. It was a mild form of bronchitis which is not to be taken lightly in the case of the elderly, especially when, like myself, they have continued to tipple away merrily. Needless to say, I find this business of taking care of myself thoroughly distasteful, but Freyberger was, after all, quite right to prescribe it for me and, as to seeing that I carry it out, that is the province of Argus-eyed Louise who has doubled and tripled her vigilance. I think I have already written and told you [a] that we left our domestic arrangements as little changed as possible when we took in the young husband as a boards and lodger. All very nice and jolly, it is true, but only, alas, so long as one is in good health. Never in my born days have I been so plagued with medical attention as during this past month and I can only console myself with the thought that it was all done for my own good.

Dietzgen and wife were here for an hour or two on Sunday afternoon but unfortunately missed Tussy. I have given him recommendations to Bebel and Kautsky. They were very nice people.

I hope that your son[b] has since found a situation. With his knowledge of business, and having by now doubtless rid himself of a good many illusions as a result of practical experience, a bright young man like that should always fall on his feet in America.

Things are little changed over here. There is no chance of achieving any kind of unity amongst the labour leaders. But the *masses* are nevertheless moving ahead, Slowly it is true, and only now striving to acquire consciousness, yet the process is unmistakeable. It will be the same here as in France and, before that, in Germany: Unification will be forced upon them as soon as a number of independent working men (especially those who have been elected without the help of the Liberals) secure seats in Parliament. This the Liberals are doing their utmost to prevent. They are not 1. extending the franchise to the people who—*on paper*—already have it, but are, on the contrary, 2. ensuring that the registers of electors

---

[a] See this volume, p. 284 – [b] Adolph Sorge

will involve the *candidates* in greater expense than hitherto, since they are now to be compiled twice a year, the cost of compiling a *correct* register being borne by the candidates or the representatives of the political *parties* and not by the state. They have categorically rejected the principle of 3. electoral expenses being borne by the state or the municipality, also 4. of parliamentary salaries and 5. of second ballots. The retention of all these old abuses amounts to the outright disqualification of the labour candidates in at least three-quarters of the constituencies. Parliament is to remain a *rich man's club*. And this at a time when the rich, because content with the status quo, are all turning Conservative, while the Liberal Party is *slowly dying*, and becoming ever more dependent on the Labour vote. The Liberals, however, insist that the working man should only vote for a bourgeois and not for a working man, let alone an independent working man.

This will be the undoing of the Liberals. Their lack of courage is alienating the country's Labour voters, dissipating their small majority in Parliament, and, unless they make some *very bold* moves at the eleventh hour, they will probably be done for. Thereupon the Tories will take the helm and *carry out* what the Liberals intended—not merely to promise—actually to do. And in that case an independent Labour party is pretty well assured.

The Social Democratic Federation[44] over here and your German-American Socialists[367] share the distinction of being the only parties that have contrived to reduce Marx's theory of development to a rigid orthodoxy which the working man is not expected to arrive at by virtue of his own class consciousness; rather it is to be promptly and without preparation rammed down his throat as an article of faith. Hence they have both remained mere sects, having come, as Hegel puts it, from nothing by way of nothing to nothing.[a] I have not yet had time to read Schlüter's controversy with your Germans, but shall tackle it tomorrow. Judging by the *Volkszeitung*'s earlier articles, it would seem that the right note has been struck.

Give my warm regards to your wife and let us have some better news from you soon. Warm regards.

Yours,

F. E.

---

[a] G. W. F. Hegel, *Wissenschaft der Logik*

Warm regards from Louise.

First published abridged
in: *Briefe und Auszüge aus Briefen
von Joh. Phil. Becker, Jos. Dietzgen,
Friedrich Engels, Karl Marx u. A.
an F. A. Sorge und Andere*, Stuttgart, 1906
and in full, in Russian, in:
Marx and Engels, *Works*,

First Russian Edition,
Vol. XXIX, Moscow, 1946

Printed according to the original

Published in English in full
for the first time

175

ENGELS TO BORIS KRICHEVSKY

IN WEGGIS

[*Draft*]

[London,] 20 May 1894

Dear Sir,

I note from your letter of the 10th inst. that you have made and already sent to the printers a Russian translation of my works on Russia which recently appeared in Berlin, just as you did previously in the case of other writings by Marx and myself.[368]

I must needs draw your attention to the fact that, in accordance with the Berne Convention[303] *Introduction to Wage Labour and Capital* by Marx (1891) as well as the above-mentioned works are my literary property and that translations of them into foreign languages may not be published in the countries of the Union without my permission. Even though the matter of fees may play only a subordinate or no role at all in cases such as these, or where genuine party undertakings are concerned, I am nevertheless obliged to assert my rights in the interests of the cause, for otherwise it would mean my assuming joint responsibility for the publication of translations by unqualified or otherwise incompetent persons. And since I have already committed myself to a third party, I am under a twofold obligation.

So far as I am aware, it has hitherto been customary in the party, even in the case of translations of works unprotected by the Berne Convention, to show consideration for the writer by applying to him for authorisation.

When, however, a work falls within the terms of the Berne Convention, this is not simply a polite formality but the translator's bounden duty. You have chosen to ignore this. I hereby protest against your conduct and reserve all my rights.

My objection to the publication of an unauthorised Russian translation of my works on Russia from *Internationales aus dem 'Volksstaat'* is all the greater in that I have already made over the translation rights in the Russian language for these and other works, namely to Mrs Vera Zasulich.

This disposes once and for all with your inquiry regarding my preface.

Yours very truly

First published, in Russian,
in: Marx and Engels, *Works*,
Second Russian Edition,
Vol. 39, Moscow, 1966

Printed according to the original

Published in English for the first time

176

ENGELS TO GEORGI PLEKHANOV[369]

IN MORNEX (France)

London, 21 May, 1894

My dear Plekhanov,

First of all, please spare me 'mentor'—my name is simply Engels.

Next, thank you for your information. I have sent a registered letter to M. Krichevsky to say that the introduction to *Wage Labour and Capital*,[a] and also the articles on Russia in *Articles on International Themes from the Newspaper 'Volksstaat'* [370] are, according to the Berne Convention,[303] my literary property, and that any translation requires my consent; that I am obliged, in the interests of the cause, to stand upon my rights in order to prevent translations by incapable or otherwise incompetent[b] (or

---

[a] These words are written by Engels in Russian. See previous letter. – [b] A German word as given in parenthesis *'unbefungt'* (meaning unauthorised).

unauthorised) individuals; that therefore it was simply his duty to request my permission beforehand, which he did not do; that as a result *I would enter a formal protest against his actions, and reserve all my rights*; that, as regards the articles on Russia, I protested all the more since I had already committed myself, having granted authorisation for a Russian translation of these and other works to Madame Vera Zasulich.

If he now persists in publishing, we shall see; in any case, please let me know if it appears, and send me a copy.

As he also announces a translation of Kautsky's *Erfurt Programme*,[a] I felt obliged to warn the latter of the methods being used in my regard.[25] I told him nothing of what you wrote to me, but I told him that dishonesty was involved, and that he should get in touch with you to learn more.

I hoped to see Mendelson yesterday evening, but I hear that his wife is ill. If I can, I shall go to see him this week.

Thank you in advance for the copy of your Chernyshevsky.[b] I await it impatiently.

Here things are moving, albeit slowly and in zigzags. Take, for example, Mawdsley, the leader of the Lancashire textile workers. He is a *Tory*, a conservative in politics, and a pious believer in religion. Three years ago, these people were furious over the 8 hours day, and now they themselves insist on it. In a recent manifesto, Mawdsley, who a year ago was a vehement opponent of any separate politics by the working class, declares that the textile workers should think about direct representation in parliament, and a workers' newspaper in Manchester calculates that the textile workers in the county of Lancashire alone would control twelve seats in parliament. You will see: it is the trade-unions that will enter parliament; it is not the class but the branch of industry which is asking to be represented. But that is also a step forward. First let us break the subordination of the workers to the two large bourgeois parties by having textile workers in parliament, as we already have miners. When there are a dozen branches of industry represented, class consciousness will explode of its own accord.

To complete the comedy, in this same manifesto Mawdsley requests bimetallism[299] in order to preserve the supremacy of English cotton fabrics on the Indian market!

---

[a] phrase in Russian – [b] G. W. Plekhanov, *N. G. Tschernyschewski. Eine literar-historische Studie*, Stuttgart, 1894.

One can only despair at these English workers with their sense of imaginary national superiority, their essentially bourgeois ideas and opinions, their narrow 'practical' viewpoint, and the rampant parliamentary corruption which has infected their leaders. Yet things are moving nonetheless. Only the 'practical' English will arrive the last, but when they arrive, they will put a very heavy weight on the scales.

My greetings to Axelrod and his family,

Yours,

F. Engels

First published in Russian
in a collection *Gruppa
'Osvobozhdeniye truda'*, No. 2,
1924

Printed according to the original

Translated from the French
Published in English in full
for the first time

177

ENGELS TO STANISLAV MENDELSON

IN LONDON

[London,] 22 May 1894
122 Regent's Park Road, N. W.

My dear Mendelson,

I have received a long letter from Georgi Plekhanov which contains many things with regard to you and the Polish movement. I intended to read it to you last Sunday, but I have learned that Mme Mendelson was taken ill and that therefore you had to stay at home. If this be convenient to you, I shall come to see you the day after tomorrow, Thursday, from 2 to 2.30 in the afternoon, together with Mme Freyberger, who would like to see how Mme Mendelson is feeling.

Yours truly,
F. Engels

Our compliments to Mme Mendelson, who, we hope, is doing better.

First published in
Marx and Engels, *Works*,
First Russian Edition,
Vol. XXIX, Moscow, 1946

Printed according to the original

Translated from the French

Published in English for the first time

178

ENGELS TO GEORGI PLEKHANOV

IN MORNEX (France)

London, 22 May 1894
122 Regent's Park Road, N. W.

My dear Plekhanov,

Yesterday, shortly after my letter to you had left, Bernstein and Kautsky arrived at my house. That has inevitably changed my plans. I thought that I ought—even without waiting for your express permission—to read them your letter, and put them both in a position to judge for themselves of the Krichevsky business. The impression this created on them will, I believe, be everything you could have desired. Indeed, however much one might wish to remain neutral in issues and disputes within the Russian émigré community, one cannot excuse the behaviour of Krichevsky as regards the translation of the *Soziales aus Russland*[368] after learning about the translation undertaken by Vera Zasulich.[a] As for the rest, these gentlemen knew Karl Kautsky had given his consent to the translation of his Erfurt Programme[b]; however, he thought that it was to be printed in Russia, or at least, he had not the slightest idea that it would be published in Switzerland.

Ignatiev[c] is, so Kautsky told me, the pseudonym of Helfond (or some name similar to that), who is in Stuttgart. You probably know him. However, as I do not have Kautsky's authorisation to use this information, I would ask you to treat it as strictly confidential. According to Kautsky and Bernstein, it would seem that Helfond is an honourable fellow who has fallen into Jogiches' trap by accident rather than malicious intent.

---

[a] See this volume, p. 303 – [b] in Russian – [c] in Russian in the original.

Yours,

F. E.

First published in
Russian in: *Gruppa
'Osvobozhdeniye Truda'*,
No. 2, 1924

Printed according to the original

Translated from the French

Published in English for the first time

179

ENGELS TO BORIS KRICHEVSKY

IN WEGGIS

[*Draft*]

London, 31 May 1894

Dr B. Krichevsky, Weggis[a]

You have my permission to sell off the copies already in print of your Russian edition of *Wage Labour and Capital* along with my introduction, and I note with satisfaction that you will refrain from publishing my other works.[368]

Apart from that, I thank you for your letter of the 25th which I look upon as a most valuable contribution to the characterisation of certain trends amongst the Russian émigrés. Any inclination I might have to discuss its contents is tempered by the consideration that you yourself probably do not expect to impress anybody with these time-worn catchphrases à la Nechayev, since you yourself are doubtless aware how ludicrous it is to seek to act the Social Democrat while behaving like an anarchist.

But when you say 'that we could have had *no inkling* that you had already made over the translation rights to someone else', you might really have spared yourself that downright falsehood. You knew long before you wrote your letter of the 10th of May that V. Zasulich and Plekhanov were preparing a Russlan translation of 'On Social Relations in Russia'. In view of the character of these people and the friendly relationship I have enjoyed with them for many years, it goes without saying that they would

---

[a] See also this volume, p. 302

not have done so without my consent, and of this you quite definitely had more than an 'inkling'.

First published, in Russian,
in: Marx and Engels, *Works*,
First Russian Edition,
Vol. XXIX, Moscow, 1946

Printed according to the original

Published in English for the first time

180

ENGELS TO NIKOLAI DANIELSON

IN ST. PETERSBURG

London, 1 June 1894

My dear Sir,

Last week I forwarded to you sheets 7 to 16 incl. of Vol. III[a] and hope you have received them. They were *registered*, and my name as sender at the back (L. K.[b]).[371]

I am glad to learn of the success of the 'Essays'.[c] I hope a new edition is in the press. I should be very glad if I could find a German translator for the book, unfortunately most of the translation work from Russian into German is done by ladies, generally not well prepared for economic work.

With many thanks I received the Russian *'Origin'* etc.,[372] the translation, as far as I have read, seems to me very well done, and on the whole the censorship seems to have dealt leniently with the book.

The sheets were sent rather late, but it was the fault of the publisher who delayed them a long time. It is very hard work reading the proofsheets of a book like this. You will find in the sheets sent the solution of the question how the different rates of surplus value are equalised into one and the same average rate of profits, the law of the tendency of that rate of profits constantly to fall, and the mode in which commercial capital participates in the distribution of surplus value. This comes to a conclusion in Sheet

---

[a] of *Capital* – [b] Louise Kautsky – [c] Nikolai-on. [Danielson], *Outlines of our Post-Reform National Economy*, 1893 [title in Russian]

21, in which the 5ᵗʰ Section opens: the splitting up of profits into interest and 'profits of enterprise' (*Zins und Unternehmergewinn*), moneyed capital generally, banking and credit. This section fills up *a whole third* of the book; it has cost me more trouble than all the rest. — The last third consists of section VI: Rent of Land, and VII: the three kinds of revenue: Rent, profits (interest), wages.

The last of the Manuscript is in the printer's hands. But I only now find what an enormous amount of arrears of work I have on my hands, as everything not absolutely necessary had to be put back in order to finish Vol. 3ʳᵈ. This must be my excuse if I do not now recur to some of the economic questions previously discussed between us. As it is, I think we both have plenty of work on our hands and better leave that discussion for another time.

Yours very sincerely

L. K.

The volumes on industrial and agricultural development of Russia (Chicago Exhibition)[373] have reached me. Please accept my hearty thanks. They are very useful indeed, especially when compared with the 'Essays'.

First published, in Russian,
in *Minuvshiye gody*, No. 2, 1908

Reproduced from the original

Published in English for the first time

181

ENGELS TO PAUL LAFARGUE[35]

AT LE PERREUX

London, 2 June 1894

My dear Lafargue,

Herewith the cheque for £20. Please acknowledge receipt.

The last bit of the manuscript of Vol. IIIᵃ is at the printer's. What a

---

ᵃ K. Marx, *Capital*

relief! But the proof-sheets are giving me a rough time; they need close, unremitting attention, it's wearisome! And Meissner employs a rather careless printer, which makes my job twice as hard. Add to this that Dietz is printing the 3rd edition of my *Anti-Dühring* and you can take my word for it when I say that I am literally overwhelmed by proof-sheets.

Your description of fashionable socialism in France gave me a good laugh. But it could turn out to be a serious matter. If you had a strong, steady army like the two million German voters, well and good; that would control the heterogeneous mass of newcomers. But with a Party split into Marxists, Blanquists,[20] Allemanists,[21] Broussists[30], and several other ists, not to mention the ex-Radicals[86] of the Millerand stamp who boss all the others in the Chamber, it is very hard to say where this new fashion is going to lead you. You compare it to Boulangism[6]: Boulangism, after a few months' spree, ended in the mire and in ignominy. In a movement of this kind it is pretty well certain that phrase-mongers like Jaurès, who already arrogate to themselves the sole right to speak for you all in the Chamber, will boss things.

Today they have the ear of the House where they silence our people, tomorrow they will have the ear of the nation.

It is always on the cards that the whole thing will not turn out too badly, and even well; but, in the meantime, you will go through some curious experiences, and I am glad for us all that there is a solid combat corps in Germany whose actions will decide the battle. This socialist mania which is emerging in your country may lead to a decisive struggle in which you will win the first victories; the revolutionary traditions of the country and of the capital, the character of your army, reorganised since 1870 on a far more popular basis—all this makes such an eventuality possible. But to ensure victory, to destroy the foundations of capitalist society, you will need the active support of a much stronger, more numerous, more tried and more conscious socialist party than you have at your command. It would mean the achievement of what we have foreseen and predicted for many years. The French give the signal, open fire, and the Germans decide the battle.

In the meantime, we are nowhere near that and I am very curious to see how the confused enthusiasm surrounding you will resolve itself.

Even Carl Hirsch noted in the *Rheinische Zeitung* that behind all this noise over Turpin[374] there are but bourse speculators. It is only the English press that is forbidden to say this and consequently, it pretends to see in that an affair of high and low politics. Here one is sure that behind

any great political affair there must be the bourse and the smart opera-
tors, and this is why it is strictly forbidden to speak of that. Protestant
bourgeois hypocrisy! Look at Jabez Balfour and at Mundella who has just
resigned from his ministry and for good reason; look at Sir J. Ferguson
and Sir J. Gorst, who are also implicated and who probably have made
themselves ineligible for any future Tory ministry.[375]

The other day Kautsky came to us—he has been four times to us.
Louise and her husband received him in the most amiable manner; if
someone was embarrassed, it was not they.

As to your medallion (that is to say, mine), this will make difficulties.
Once I was foolish enough to have myself photographed in profile, but
this will never happen to me again. I have such a foolish look that I would
rather not have my portrait in profile go down to posterity. However, I
would be pleased to see the medallion of Marx (send it also for Tussy,
please!), and I am quite curious if your artist has succeeded in reproduc-
ing the nose which, in profile, has really impossible lines.

Kiss Laura on my behalf!

Greetings from Louise and Ludwig. The latter continues trying to get
English physicians to see how much their colleagues on the continent are
superior in real science, anatomy, physiology, pathology, etc.

Cordially yours,

F. Engels

First published in part in:
Le Socialiste, No. 115, 24 November
1900 and in full in: F. Engels,
P. et L. Lafargue, *Correspondance*,
t. III, Paris, 1959

Printed according to the original

Translated from the French

182

ENGELS TO WITOLD JODKO-NARKEVICH

IN LONDON

[London,] 5 June 1894
122 Regent's Park Road, N. W.

My dear Jodko,

I cannot recall exactly whether you have translated and published in Przedswit my article Eine polnische *Proklamation* (Internationales, aus dem 'Volksstaat'[370]). If you have, please send me another copy of *Przedswit* with this article; some Polish students from Vienna have asked me for permission to translate it.[a]

Yours

F. Engels

First published, in the language of the original (French), in the magazine *Z pola walki*, No. 4 (12), 1960

Printed according to the original

Translated from the French

Published in English for the first time

183

ENGELS TO STANISLAW ZABLOCKI

IN VIENNA

[*Draft*]

[London,] 7 June 1894

Dear Sir,

As you will see from the enclosed, the article in question[376] has already been published in Polish here, first in the London journal *Przedswit*, nos. 1-3. March 1894; it is now about to appear in pamphlet form also, together with two other pieces of mine, 'The Bakuninists at Work' and 'On Social Relations in Russia'. Since this pamphlet will soon be coming out—in an easily smuggled pocket edition—it would hardly seem worthwhile your making a new translation.

The editors of the *Przedswit* (Al. Debski), 7 Beaumont Square, Mile End, London, E., will be very glad to furnish you with any further particulars.

Yours very truly

I am sending you *Przedswit* by book post.[b]

---

[a] See next letter. – [b] See previous letter

First published, in Russian,
in: Marx and Engels, *Works*,
First Russian Edition,
Vol. XXIX, Moscow, 1946

Printed according to the original

Published in English for the first time

184

ENGELS TO KARL KAUTSKY

IN STUTTGART

London, 19 June 1894
122 Regent's Park Road, N. W.

Dear Baron,

If you would like to have two chapters from Volume III[a] for the *Neue Zeit*:

1. Interest and Profit of Enterprise (Chap. XXIII)
2. Externalisation of the Relations of Capital in the Form of Interest-Bearing Capital (Chap. XXIV),

I shall gladly place them at your disposal. Their content lends itself very well to this type of publication, while at the same time they do not contain any of the major solutions which should only appear in context and, for that very reason, should be reserved for publication in toto. No. 2 contains amongst other things the story of Dr Price, Mr Pitt, and the compound interest hocus-pocus[b]. If you would like to have them, I shall delete such notes, etc., as are not required from the first proof-sheets and send them to you as soon as I have got the revises, in about eight or sixteen days' time.

I have also routed out the old article *von den letzten Dingen*[c] which I am at last licking into shape for you (I resume after having been interrupted for two and a half hours by Liebknecht and Julius,[d] who have just left), but am changing it and giving it a different title[e]; since the time I began it I have been able to study many new things, some of them in the field of early Christianity.

---

[a] of *Capital* – [b] A reference to Richard Price's pamphlet, *Appeal to the Public on the Subject of the National Debt* (1771) and its supposed influence on Pitt's policy. – [c] *of Last Things*. – [d] Motteler – [e] *On the History of Early Christianity*.

But if I am to complete the aforesaid work, I must conclude this letter from which you will, I hope, see that my thoughts revert to the *Neue Zeit* whenever Old Father Time allows.[a]

Many regards from one household to another,

Yours,

F. Engels

First published in:
*Aus der Frühzeit des
Marxismus. Engels
Briefwechsel mit Kautsky*,
Prag, 1935

Printed according to the original

Published in English for the first time

185

ENGELS TO KARL KAUTSKY

IN STUTTGART

London, 26 June 1894
122 Regent's Park Road, N. W.

Dear Baron,

Marx's two chapters[b] despatched by registered mail at the same time as this. You might entitle them: 'From Book III of *Capital* by K. Marx'—I and II, and indicate in a note that these are Chapters XXIII and XXIV, taken from Part V, 'Division of Profit into Interest and Profit of Enterprise. Interest-bearing Capital'. The titles of the chapters must be retained in each case. In order to simplify things I have deleted the Greek, also all the notes save one important one.

The article 'On the History of Early Christianity'—that is what I shall probably call the thing—is in hand and, WELL ADVANCED. But yesterday there was a Händel festival at the Crystal Palace and Louise, I and the Avelings went to hear *The Messiah*. Today I have got to deal with my let-

---

[a] A play of words in the original: *Neue Zeit* (New Times) and 'alte Zeit'—old time. – [b] See previous letter.

ters and tomorrow I shall probably buckle to again, but Liebknecht is here and we are having a heat-wave.

Thank you for the bit of the *Volksanwalt*. As regards the thing from the *Critica Sociale*,[334] Victor has really been leading me up the garden path. After I had agreed to let him have it, he simply dropped the thing altogether and now proposes to await the moment when it 'becomes topical' again. Next time I shall be more wary; he treats his contributors in a very odd way. Well, I look forward keenly to seeing what the fate of your daily will be.[377] Not, I hope, that of Guesde's and Lafargue's *Socialiste* quotidien '*pour paraître en octobre*'[280]; only yesterday we were chaffing poor Bonnier about it when he passed this way.

So Carnot has been stabbed to death. A poor, stupid, boring fellow—the first Frenchman to rise to the top through being a bore—and *in France* too! But now Alexander III will repudiate the French alliance. 'Merci,' he will say, 'there's plenty of that sort of thing to be had at home and at less expense!' Incidentally, there might be a certain element of vengeance for Aiguesmortes in this.[378] I shall be curious to see how the sixty self-styled 'Socialists' in the Chamber will now behave.[a] That the affair will be exploited *à la* Hödel there can be no doubt, but on the other hand the sixty will weigh heavily in the scales at the presidential elections next Wednesday.[b]

Kindest regards from one household to the other.

Yours,

F. E.

27 June. Left unfinished yesterday,

Benno Karpeles intervened. During the past three days there has been 1. One Hellmut von Gerlach of Berlin, 2. Liebknecht, 3. Karpeles and, today, 4. Prof. Tönnies of Kiel—not to mention the Händel Festival the day before yesterday—so how can a man be expected to work?

First published in: Printed according to the original
Aus der Frühzeit des Marxismus,
Engels Briefwechsel mit Kautsky,   Published in English for the first time
Prag, 1935

---

[a] See this volume, p. 262 – [b] 27 June

186

ENGELS TO OTTO WACHS[379]

IN BERLIN

[*Draft*]

[London, end of June-beginning of July 1894]

To Major Wachs

Unfortunately, as things are in the Party today, I was obliged to maintain a certain reserve in view of the fact that he[a] contributes to *Das Volk*. Not because of the paper's standpoint which would have counted for little in a purely personal relationship, but until very recently its editor-in-chief, Mr Oberwinder, played a role in, and on the periphery of, the Social Democratic Party such as to make it absolutely imperative that we also observe a certain reticence vis-à-vis his colleagues.[380] Needless to say, it would never occur to me to ask of these, Mr Oberwinder's colleagues—as to whose good faith I am not in doubt—that they should believe what we know about him. As you are aware, every social group has its own *point d'honneur*[b] and that is what is at stake in this instance amongst us Social Democrats.

First published, in Russian, in: Marx and Engels, *Works*, Second Russian Edition, Vol. 39, Moscow, 1966

Printed according to the original

Published in English for the first time

187

ENGELS TO BORIS KRICHEVSKY

IN WEGGIS

[*Draft*]

[London, July 1894]

Dr Krichevsky—Weggis

1. You say: 'V. Zasulich's and Plekhanov's intention was, it is true,

---

[a] Hellmut von Gerlach – [b] sense of honour

known to us long before the 10th of May, but only at third hand'. The said third hand was that of Mr J. Blumenfeld, whose address, 3 Ch. de la Roseraie, Genève, is the *only* one supplied on the jacket of your edition of [K. Marx, *Wage Labour and Capital*][a]. According to the self-same advice, even subscriptions to Kautsky's work,[b] are to be sent to the same address (*no other being supplied*). If, therefore, V. Zasulich and Plekhanov sent the information in question to what was your Library's sole official address, this was perfectly adequate and it is puerile, anarchistic casuistry to describe it as information at third hand.

2. The moment you were in receipt of that information you were more than ever bounden to address yourself to *me* as the only person having the right to decide between the two claimants in this case. You did not do so because you already knew what my answer would be, because you wished to steal a march on V. Zasulich and Plekhanov in a dishonourable manner, and were counting on my bowing to a fait accompli. You were totally mistaken, because generally mistaken, in regard to the times, imagining that, at the present state of development both of the European and of the Russian socialist movement, it would be possible to revert to the old prevarications and impertinencies of a Bakunin or a Nechayev and this time, what's more, with success.

First published in Russian,
in: Marx and Engels, *Works*,
First Russian Edition,
Vol. XXIX, Moscow, 1946

Printed according to the original

Published in English for the first time

188

ENGELS TO LAURA LAFARGUE

AT LE PERREUX

London, 4 July 1894
122 Regent's Park Road, N. W.

My dear Löhr,

Tussy writes to say that the heat in Paris interferes with the free action of her intellect and in proof encloses 4 stamps 25 centimes each—I could

---

[a] Title in Russian – [b] Erfurt Programme [title in Russian]

have believed it without that! Anyhow I return the stamps to you as she may be leaving before they arrive.

I told Liebknecht Paul's letters were *das beste im ganzen 'Vorwärts'*[a] but he won't believe it—it's true all the same; his letter today about Carnot[b] is very good again, calm and clear judgment, none of the spasmodic paragraphs which the *Vorwärts* is so fond of launching on English and French politics.

Cannot you send me a few *Petite Républiques*? Just now the Jaures and Millerands are *on their trial*, and I am very much interested in seeing how they behave.[c] My confidence in their political and economical intellect does not exactly increase; but I shall only be too glad if they could prove me in the wrong.

Liebknecht left on Monday evening, had to speak at Aix la Chapelle on Tuesday.

Yesterday 10 sheets 3rd Vol. *Capital* which we had forwarded to Petersburg for translation were returned: *'Défendu'*![d]

I must close—another proof-sheet to be got ready and then I have to go to town.

Love to you all
Ever yours
F. Engels

First published, in the
language of the original
(English), in: F. Engels, P. et
L. Lafargue, *Correspondance*,

t. III, 1891-1895. Paris, 1959

Reproduced from the original

189

ENGELS TO LUDWIG SCHORLEMMER

IN DARMSTADT

London, 5 July 1894
122 Regent's Park Road, N. W.

My Dear Schorlemmer,

Now that the final manuscript of Volume III of *Capital* is in the print-

---

[a] the best thing in the whole of *Vorwärts* – [b] [P. Lafargue,] Gallus, 'Präsident Carnot', *Vorwärts*, No. 151, 3 July 1894 – [c] See this volume, p. 262 – [d] Prohibited

ers' hands, I am once again able to turn my attention to your affairs,[199] and can let you have the much delayed reply to your note of 25.4.

There are certain snags about the continuation of Carl's major work, brought out by the Vieweg Verlag, and this also applies to all the rest of his other stuff held by that firm. When I went down to Manchester I took a look at the contracts which stipulate that if, for instance, Carl were to die before completion of the whole, Vieweg might have the work completed *by a person of his own choosing*. This is the reason for his silence and also for his failure to publish the work left behind by Carl; he obviously wishes to retain a completely free hand. Nor can he be expected to pay any further royalties. For 1. by the terms of the contract, he will pay only for mos. that are *ready for press*, i.e. no unfinished stuff, and 2. will pay no royalties in respect of new editions to which *no changes have been made*.

In short, Vieweg can do exactly as he likes and will, if he is to bring out Vol. V, in any case have to find another author for the German edition.[311]

As regards Carl's work on the history of chemistry, Siebold has written to tell me that, because of constant illness, he has not yet been able to prepare the ms. for press, nor has he yet completed his English translation.[313] The poor devil has had rotten luck with his health, his nerves being again in a very poor state, and will need a long rest and plenty of fresh air if he is to recover. As far as money matters are concerned there is no need for you to worry; they are in good hands and, as things are now, Roscoe is also in control of this aspect so that ultimately one must content oneself with the particulars he supplies in respect of payments made for work such as revision, etc. It is possible that Roscoe's task has been made somewhat easier by his having dealt with Siebold direct instead of with myself as promised, but it won't make much difference since I should in any case have had to refer him to Siebold and Klepsch in respect of all settlements and should, in the end, have had to make do with his assurances. A vital factor here is that, with the rapid advances made in chemistry, any textbook becomes out of date within a year unless constantly revised and thus, where this sort of literature is concerned, only a living author can keep his end up vis-à-vis either publishers or readers.

I had hoped I might again visit Germany this summer but shall not be able to, the reason being that precisely during the summer months and because of matters connected with my lease I must remain in the vicinity of London so as to be able to return there at any moment should need arise; indeed, I don't even know when, if at all, I shall be able to repair to the seaside. I really ought to have got all this settled last year but I missed the opportunity while on the Continent[189] and, by the time I got back, it was too late.

You will shortly be able to read two chapters from Vol. III of *Capital*[a] in the *Neue Zeit*, and possibly something of mine as well.[b]

Liebknecht left on Monday, having been here for over a week.

It is tremendously hot as it is no doubt where you are. In Paris the heat is said to be intolerable.

Many regards from

Yours,

F. Engels

First published, in Russian,   Printed according to the original
in: Marx and Engels, *Works*,
First Russian Edition,   Published in English for the first time
Vol. XXIX, Moscow, 1946

190

ENGELS TO THE EDITOR OF THE *NEUE ZEIT*

IN STUTTGART

[London,] 9 July 1894

At the request of Mr K. Kautsky and in reply to his inquiry from Hirsau on 7.7.94, I beg to inform you that Chapter of *Das Kapital*, p. 359, lines 9 and 10 from the top, should read: '*Welchen Rohprofit es ihm als fungierendes—Kapital... abwirft*' ['what gross profit it yields to him as function*ing* capital'.] Likewise, on p. 368, line 3 from the top, the expression '*fungierendes Kapital*' ['functioning capital'] is correct.

Further, on p. 363, line 14 from the top, a comma may, in fact, be inserted after '*desselben*' ['of it'] in the sentence: '*in Form von denen das gesamte Kapital, abgesehen von dem in Geld existierenden relativ kleinen*

---

[a] See this volume, p. 314 – [b] F. Engels, *On the History of Early Christianity*.

Teil desselben, vorhanden ist' ['which make up the total capital outside of a relatively small portion of it, existing in money'], as this brings out the meaning better.[381]

I am *very pleased* about the discovery of the printing error on P. 359, namely *fungierendem* in place of *fungierendes*, for which kindly convey my best thanks to K. Kautsky,

Yours very faithfully,
F. Engels

First published in:
*Aus der Frühzeit des
Marxismus. Engels Briefwechsel
mit Kautsky*, Prag, 1935

Printed according to the original

Published in English for the first time

191

ENGELS TO KARL KAUTSKY

IN STUTTGART

London, 16 July 1894
122 Regent' a Park Road, N. W.

Dear Baron,

My article on early Christianity[a] goes off by registered mail today to the Editor, *Neue Zeit*, Furthbachatr. 12, as does this letter, since I have not got your exact address in Hirsau and do not know how long you will be staying there.

Since the ms. is barely legible and contains many corrections, I should be glad if you could send me the galley proofs. No doubt minor amendments and additions would be admissible in the case of such comprehensive material.

There was indeed a slip of the pen in the passage from *Das Kapital*, Chapter 23, and you did me a real service in pointing it out.[b]

Because of sundry business matters I cannot go away at the moment. At the beginning of August I hope to be able to go to the seaside. Nothing

---

[a] F. Engels, *On the History of Early Christianity.* – [b] See previous letter.

will come of a trip to the Continent this year. At this precise moment it is raining cats and dog.

Kindest regards from one household to the other.

Yours,

F. E.

First published in:
Aus der Frühzeit des Marxismus.
Engels Briefwechsel mit Kautsky,
Prag, 1935

Printed according to the original

Published in English for the first time

192

ENGELS TO VICTOR ADLER

IN VIENNA

London, 17 July 1894

Dear Victor,

I am glad that those few marks should have arrived so opportunely and trust you will use them to treat yourself to the rest and recuperation out in the country which are so absolutely essential to you. You simply *must* go away; what you need more than anything else is to recover from the wear and tear of your time in prison.[349] You yourself say you feel done in and that, if truth be told, is not surprising, so the moment you are released, out into the country with you! This would also be the best way of ensuring your wife's complete recovery.

The additional chapter (it is only the enlargement of an already extant one) in *Anti-Dühring* is by Marx, so the only work I had to do on it consisted in copying and editing.[382]

About 36 sheets of Volume III[a] have been set up and there will probably be more than 50 all told. Since it is wholly in Meissner's interest to get the thing out by September, it will doubtless be ready by then.

I wish your daily paper well and am already looking forward to seeing it.[377] It is really essential to set the insufferable *Vorwärts* an example of

---

[a] of *Capital*

'how things are done'. The chaps can hardly fail to follow it. However, when you are in jug, one sometimes becomes aware that the *Arbeiter Zeitung*, too, has men who are unsuitable and who push themselves to the fore where they have no business to be. But once the daily is in existence, your activities as a speaker will automatically be confined to a few occasions of crucial importance, and this will mean your spending less time in jug, while a dummy editor is in any case indispensable to the paper as such, if only as the sacrificial lamb who takes upon himself the sins of the editorial department.

And again, in Vienna, you have just now a soil more favourable to a daily than that proffered by Berlin. The political movement to which you belong is in the ascendant; you are assured of getting electoral reform[270] and the very fact of fighting for a goal such as this, for an immediate political advance is of tremendous advantage to your paper. Electoral reform, however, is no more than the impulse that will set the ball rolling and will necessarily entail other concessions relating to the press, association, assembly, legal practices, etc. In short, you are engaged in an offensive and one, which, to begin with at any rate, is assured of victory. In France, Germany and Italy, on the other hand, our people are engaged in what is a by no means always promising defensive action and have to withstand the onslaught of a reaction constantly reinforced by the adherence of the most disparate parties. It is proof that—in Germany, at least,—our people have really become a power in the land, while in France, a country riddled with revolution, it is proof that our people are at least *looked upon* as a power. But none the less you are, at the moment, in a better position to fight—you are attacking, gaining ground step by step, and every fresh bit of ground you seize and occupy not only strengthens your position but brings you vast numbers of fresh reinforcements. Your primitive constitutionalism is such that there are still at least a few positions for the workers to capture, and by lawful means at that, i.e. means whereby they themselves will be politically educated—positions which *ought* to have been captured by the bourgeoisie. In our country, too, there are still positions of this kind to be taken, but these we shall only get if the impulse comes from without, from a country where the amalgamation of the old forms—feudalism, bureaucracy and police—with more or less modern, civil institutions, has given such preponderance to the first as to produce a situation of impossible complexity. And that is the happy state in which you find yourselves, not to mention the even happier one of having a workers' movement big enough and strong enough to bring things to a head and thus, I hope, provide the impulse required by Germany, France and Italy if they are temporarily to disrupt the far too premature formation of the 'one reactionary mass',[214] and replace chronic reactionary oppression with a number of civil reforms such as freedom of movement for the masses. Not until you have fought for and won electoral reform—of no matter what kind—not until then will the agitation against the three-class electoral system in Prussia[291] have any significance. And even now the fact that there is going to be some sort of electoral reform in Austria has already averted the threat that hung over universal suffrage in Germany. So at this moment you people have a very important historical mission. It is you who will constitute the vanguard of the European proletariat, and initiate the general offensive which we can only hope will not falter again before we achieve victory all along the line—and it is you yourself who will be leading that vanguard; so unless you go out into the country forthwith and thoroughly recoup your strength, you will be neglecting what is your foremost duty.

And how serious that duty is becomes all the more apparent when you reflect that the only rivals whom you might have as a vanguard are the French. You wrote and told Louise that you would like me to report on the latter. I have put it off until today because 1. last week Tussy returned from the Glassworkers' Congress in Paris and 2. Bonnier came to see us the day before yesterday and I wanted to hear *their* side of the story first. WELL, so far as I can see, the position is this:

The last elections[208] brought some twenty-five 'Socialists'—Marxists, Broussists,[30] Allemanists,[21] Blanquists[20] and Independents—into the Chamber. At the same time they eliminated what had hitherto been the 'Radical group', also describing itself as *républicains socialistes*,[86] notably by excluding all its former leaders. Thereupon some thirty members of that group, who had been re-elected, combined under the leadership of Millerand and Jaures and suggested that they and the 'Socialists', should join forces.[169] It was a very safe move on their part for not only were they more numerous then the old Socialists, they were also united whereas the latter were fragmented into umpteen groups. In this way they once more formed in the Chamber a respectable group some fifty or sixty strong without having to offer the old Socialists anything more than a highly platonic socialist programme, the politically radical articles of which had already formed part of their earlier programme as had their general pro-working class attitude, while the *socialisation des moyens de production*ᵃ still remained an innocent chimera which might perhaps acquire practical significance three or four generations hence, but certainly not any sooner.

Our twenty-five old Socialists seized on the opportunity with both hands. They were not in a position to lay down conditions, being far too disunited for that. The intention was, it is true, that they should act in concert in the Chamber, as during the elections, but that, for the rest, all the separate organisations should continue to exist alongside one another; indeed, an attempt on the part of any one group to lay down specific conditions for the new Socialists would have brought it into conflict with the others. For that matter, they would not have been Frenchmen, had not the immediate prospect of swelling their numbers in the Chamber from twenty-five to fifty-five or sixty filled them with enthusiasm, and had not present victory, or a semblance thereof, blinded them to the dangers that lay ahead. Damn it all, aren't the Germans for ever crowing about their forty-four deputies? And at one fell swoop we've got fifty-five if not sixty! *La France reprend sa place à la tête du mouvement.*ᵇ

The thirty or thirty-five new Socialists have entered into a marriage of convenience with Socialism. They would just as soon not have done so, but taking the plunge was the shrewdest thing for them to do. Having realised that they would not, after all, be able to carry on without the workers, they have had to ally themselves with the latter for better or for worse. But for *no-one* was that alliance an altogether voluntary affair at first, as it certainly still is not for *many* today.

Of its leading representatives, Millerand is the shrewdest and, I believe, the most sincere, but I fear that some of his bourgeois-legal prejudices are more deep-seated than he himself realises. Politically he is the most capable of the whole bunch. Jaurès is an academic and doctrinaire who enjoys the sound of his own voice and whose voice the Chamber enjoys listening to more than to that of Guesde or Vaillant because he is more closely akin to the gentlemen of the majority. I believe it is his sincere intention to turn himself into a decent Socialist but, as you know, the zeal of such neophytes is in direct relation to their lack of practical knowledge which, in the case of Jaurès, is very great. Which explains how it was that

---

ᵃ the socialisation of the means of production – ᵇ France will once more resume her place at the head of the movement.

in Paris Jaures tabled as socialist the self-same motion as that put forward in Berlin by Count Kanitz in the interest of the Junkers—the nationalisation of the import of grain with a view to raising the price of corn.[356] And since the old Socialists in the Chamber evince a lack of practical knowledge in *oeconomicis*[a] hardly less extreme—Lafargue's defeat at Lille means there is no one on the spot who knows anything about the subject—Guesde could not abstain from supporting at least part of the motion as 'socialist' and directed against 'speculation'. To propose to do away with 'speculation' by handing over the grain trade to a government and a government party consisting of Panamite confidence tricksters[60] is indeed a splendidly socialist idea. I have, through Bonnier and Lafargue, conveyed to the gentlemen concerned my unvarnished opinion of this colossal blunder.

I further told them that, though fusion rather than a mere alliance with the new Socialists might be their inevitable fate, they should bear in mind the possibility of there being bourgeois elements amongst the latter and that this might involve them in a conflict over principles, in which case a split might become inevitable. They must, I went on, prepare for this so that in the event the transition to a simple alliance could proceed smoothly and not surprise them into making blunders. Above all, should the chaps in the joint group put forward anything they felt unable to endorse and they be outvoted, they should repudiate any obligation to take the floor in the Chamber in support of such measures, but rather reserve the right to justify their adverse opinion in their press even if, for the sake of unity, they had had to vote in favour of the said measures.

Well, we shall have to see if it does any good.

Thus, on the one hand there are the new Socialists who are imposing a certain unity on the most disparate groups of old Socialists. On the other, our chaps abroad, who find it puzzling that a group of some sixty men should suddenly have appeared 'out of thin air' and that its chief spokesmen, Millerand and Jaurès, should not hitherto have been known to be Socialists; hence the very natural doubts as to the authenticity of the aforementioned sixty, particularly after the brilliant impression left behind in Zurich by the French delegates.[250]

Beneath the surface, the intrigues and mutual recriminations of the various sects continue unchecked. In particular the Marxists complain about Vaillant who is constantly touring the provinces for propaganda

---

[a] economic matters

purposes and is alleged to be spreading all manner of false calumnies about the Marxists there. At one time Vaillant used almost always to act in concert with the Marxists but 1. He is a strictly Blanquist party man who carries out the party's resolutions no matter what the circumstances, and for two years there has been trouble between the Blanquists and the Marxists; and 2. There are a great many Possibilists[30] in his constituency; he needs these people and this is partly why he has gone over to them.

It is very possible that the new reactionary measures in France[383] will act as a spur to the new Socialists and that the group of sixty will gradually become a truly socialist group. But that is not yet the case and things might well turn out differently.

In this country life is proceeding in the usual English leisurely fashion. Economic and political developments alike are increasingly impelling the majority of English working men in our direction, but it may be years before these 'pragmatists', wholly unaccustomed to taking a theoretical view of things and incapable of seeing beyond their own noses, become conscious of their own feelings and requirements unless virtually forced to do so. In the meantime political intrigue of the bourgeois-parliamentary variety continues to flourish mightily amongst the 'leaders', and never a day goes by without one's hearing of some startling instance of this.

Ludwig is today sitting his examination for admission as MEMBER, (not merely LICENCIATE) OF THE ROYAL COLLEGE OF PHYSICIANS. The thing goes on for a fortnight. Soon after it is over we shall, with any luck, be able to go to the seaside—this year I shall be prevented from leaving England by domestic business.

Louise sends her love and says that there is no question of umbrage having been taken; you will shortly learn the reason for your not yet having had a reply.

Warm regards to your wife, Adelheid, Popp and all our friends.

Yours,

F. E.

First published in part
in *Arbeiter-Zeitung*, No. 327,
28 November, 1920 and
in full in: *Victor Adlers*
Aufsätze, Reden und Briefe.
Erstes Heft: *Victor Adler*

und Friedrich Engels,
Wien, 1922

Printed according to the original

Published in English for the first time

193

ENGELS TO JULIUS MOTTELER

IN LONDON

[London,] 21 July 1894

Dear Julius,

Herewith a letter from Siegel which I have been asked to pass on to you.[384] I have written to the Executive Committee about the 300 marks.[25] Should you be able to do something in the Club[62] here, or anything else for the chaps, it would be a good deed; in the meantime I have sent them a pound.

Kindest regards to your wife. Our house is in mourning, the canary hen having died while sitting on her four eggs—from a stroke, it would seem.

Yours,

F. E.

First published in Russian
in: Marx and Engels, *Works*,
Second Russian Edition,
Vol. 39, Moscow, 1966

Printed according to the original

Published in English for the first time

194

ENGELS TO KARL KAUTSKY[385]

IN STUTTGART

London, 28 July 1894
122 Regent's Park Road, N. W.

Dear Baron,

There is no hurry about printing the article.[a] Once I have seen to the proofs you can print it when you wish, in September, say, or even October. I have been mulling the thing ever ever since 1841 when I read a lecture

---

[a] F. Engels, *On the History of Early Christianity*.

by F. Benary on *Revelation*. Since then I have been in no doubt that here we have the earliest and most important book in the New Testament. After a gestation period of fifty-three years there is no great need to hasten its emergence into the world at large.

As to your questions.

1. If I have expressed myself correctly in other respects, I certainly would not describe serfs and small peasants[a] as being amongst the earliest *adherents* of Christianity; rather I should number them amongst those classes where it might expect to find adherents. And to these they quite certainly belonged—especially in the 2nd and 3rd centuries. There is no doubt that, from the time Christianity first spread from Judaea to Northern Syria and Asia Minor and Greece, Egypt and Italy, it was in the *towns* that it developed and found its earliest adherents.

2. You ask whether the millennium is of this world or of the next. That depends on how one interprets it. I call the next world that which *comes after death*. And on this point *Revelation* leaves one in absolutely no doubt whatever. The millennium is reserved only for the martyrs and at best for such Christians as happen to be still living when it comes about, and to that extent, for *the latter, it is of this world*, whereas *for the martyrs*, who are only then resurrected from the dead, it is of *the next*. So it's the old story: YOU PAYS YOUR MONEY AND YOU TAKES YOUR CHOICE. To my mind what decides the issue is the fact that it is impossible unless one has a concept of immortality and a belief in reward and punishment in the next world. Even less of this world is the New Jerusalem which is to come after the millennium and the Last Judgement.

But the so-called Pauline Epistles also have it that those believers still living at Christ's second coming are to be 'changed', i.e. transformed and magnified from mortals into immortals.

That the millennium was here depicted in *earthly colours* goes without saying. Even *Revelation* cannot rest content with such heavenly delights as sitting with a bare bottom on a damp cloud, twanging a harp with more or less gory hands and singing hymns to all eternity.

The preface to Volume III[b] has 1. not yet been written and 2. I cannot give it to you. This solution of the rate of profit and price question and of

---

[a] As can be judged from Kautsky's letter of 23 July 1894, to which Engels is replying, there is apparently a slip of the pen here: *Kleinbauern*. *Kleinbürger* (petty bourgeois) in the ms. – [b] of *Capital*

the distribution of price can only be given its due in the book itself.

Save for Sorge and Schlüter there are no intelligent correspondents to be found anywhere in America, because the Germans there stick obstinately to the same sectarian attitude towards the workers as is stubbornly adhered to by the Social Democratic Federation[44] over here. Instead of seeing in the movements of the Americans the propulsive element which, even though it may take wrong or circuitous paths, is bound in the end to lead to the same goal as the one they themselves brought with them from Europe, they see only the wrong paths, treat the blind, foolish Americans with arrogant condescension, boast of their own orthodox superiority, repel the Americans instead of attracting them and, as a result, have themselves remained a small, impotent sect. Hence it has come about that their writers have also relapsed into pure ideology and place a false and narrow interpretation on conditions as a whole. Little Hepner, for one, could always be said to have lived in a world of fantasy and when he gets sentimental his stuff beggars description. I once read a comedy of his—though the funny bits were pretty good, the serious love scenes contained so much gush that one became convulsed with laughter.

Kindest regards from one household to another.

Yours,

F. E.

First published in:
Aus der Frühzeit den Marxismus. Engels Briefwechsel mit Kautsky, Prag, 1935

Printed according to the original

Published in English in full for the first time

195

ENGELS TO LAURA LAFARGUE

AT LE PERREUX

London, 28 July 1894
122 Regent's Park Road, N. W.

My dear Löhr,

This morning I had a letter from Paul, but much obliged as I am to him for it, yours is older and claims attention first; and indeed I have been trying to find time to write, all the week, and have been stopped day after day by interruptions endless in number and variety. The fact is I am not sure of remaining much longer in 122; I ought to have settled that business last year, but was enjoying myself on the continent,[189] and now have to face the dilemma: either to get the whole house thoroughly overhauled or to look out for another. I have attended to both eventualities, and maybe in a few weeks may know where I am, or at least where I am to be in future.

You ask about Pumps. I have hardly heard from them for months past. Percy had lost, or given up, the agency for his brothers in the Isle of Wight; he had spent a lot of money (not his own) but induced me to become surety for him for a loan to enable him to look out for other agencies in the same line of business, where he said he could make it pay. All at once, in June, I am informed by him that, in consequence of some arrangement with his family, he is going to sell up his furniture and come back to London; on my remonstrating, I am told it is now too late and the plan must be carried out. Then I heard that they were at a school in Kent where their little boy is, and at last, last Monday, they turned up here. As far as I can learn, the family arrangement is all moonshine, at least it leaves him in the same shiftless position as before, After all I have done for them, I am not going to quietly submit to such treatment, and did not receive them very heartily. What Percy is going to do and how this is to end, is more than I know. The children are at schools. Lily at Herne Bay and is said to be getting on well; the boy is near Sittingbourne, very delicate, and ailing again while Pumps was there last week. The youngest girl is with them.

Thanks to you for the article of Jaurès in the *Revue Socialiste*;[a] it seems awfully shallow as far as I can see, but the man looks after all as if he was learning a bit, so we will not give up all hopes. The *Petite République* is indeed awful reading—the discursive matter as well as the *soi-disant*[b] reports of facts, and you will not be astonished to learn that I do no longer long for it, unless it given *real* news, real reports, or articles from Jaurès (whose evolution I should like to follow) and Millerand. *Les élucubrations de MM. Rouanet, Fournière, Viviani etc. ne me laissent que tro froid.*[c]

---

[a] J. Jaurès, 'Introduction à la *Morale Sociale* de Benoît Malon,' *La Revue Socialiste*, t. XIX, June 1894. – [b] so-called – [c] Disquisitions of Messieurs Rouanet, Fournière, Viviani etc. leave me indifferent.

I am really obliged to the *Ere Nouvelle* for giving you a chance to restore in the French *Manifeste*,[a] as published by the *Socialiste*, those passages where the Parisian text revisers, *dans l'intérêt et de la langue française et des auteurs du 'Manifeste',*[b] had considerably narrowed the horizon of certain expressions. Of course I shall be very glad to see it reprinted as often as you can get it done.

My congratulations to Paul on the Delagrave acquisition.[386] May this lead to further business!

Where do I go this summer? alas all hope of going to Le Perreux is knocked on the head by that beautiful new law![383] And the worst of it is that this time the old English lawyer's saying becomes applicable to France: the law is there, and *what the courts will make of it, is more than we know.* My impression is that the government will not lose much time before it sees that a precedent is established of the application of that law to Socialism, and to the inclusion of Socialism under the heading of anarchism. The *Cour de cassation*[c] is quite capable of that. The German Socialist law[15] kept me from Germany thirteen years, let us hope this new law will not last long enough to prevent me from coming to France once more in my life.

Paul is not quite so enthusiastic about the situation in in France as *ce cher* Bonnier who considers the whole debate—result and all—an unmitigated triumph for French Socialism; but still his way of looking at the subject seems to me rather *couleur de rose.* The main advantage I consider indeed to be the irrefutable proof that our party is the only real and serious opposition party in France as well as in Germany; and that the French Radicals[86] are no more serious in their pretended opposition than the German Richters & Co. From that, as Paul says, a real union of all Socialist elements must grow; and the persecution now initiated will hasten it; and if this unification, under the auspices of Jaurès, Millerand & Co, and their lot,[d] means a lowering of the standard of the official expression of the party, *un abaissement de niveau intellectuel et politique,*[e] this comes from the previous indulging in revolutionary phraseology, as Paul also sees very clearly, and is but the necessary consequence of it.

Love from Louise. Freyberger who sends his kind regards has just been re-

---

[a] K. Marx and F. Engels, *Manifesto of the Communist Party* – [b] in the interests of the French language and the authors of the Manifesto – [c] Court of appeal – [d] See this volume, p. 318 – [e] a lowering of theoretical and political level

ceived a member of the Royal College of Physicians, after examination.
Salut à Paul.

Ever yours
F. E.

First published in Russian
in: Marx and Engels, *Works*,
Second Russian Edition,
Vol. 39, Moscow, 1966

Reproduced from the original

Published in English for the first time

196

ENGELS TO FILIPPO TURATI[387]

IN MILAN

London, 31 July 1894
122 Regent's Park Road, N. W.

My dear Turati,

A certain Mr Pasquali has arrived here a couple of days ago saying that he has been banished for the Sicily business[388] and was obliged to leave Paris, where he was a correspondent for *Punto Nero* (and in possession of authorisation from the editorial board), but had been threatened by the police.

In Turin he was a preacher or missionary of the English sect of Baptists, and showed me the letter from his ecclesiastical superior in which he was removed from this post because of his socialism.

He will need assistance since, even if he seriously looked for work, he does not speak a word of English.

As in other countries we have had some curious experiences with ex-ecclesiastics of Christian, Jewish and other religions. I and my other friends here would be obliged to you if you could give us some information on this man, who claims to know you.

Has he indeed been banished from Italy?

Has he indeed been obliged to leave Paris to escape pursuit?

Has he indeed played a role, and if so, what, in the events in Sicily and in the socialist movement in Italy in general?

Greetings to you and Mme Anna from Louise Kautsky-Freyberger and myself,

Yours,

F. Engels

First published in the language of the original (French) in: *Annali*, an. I, Milano, 1958

Printed according to the original

Translated from the French

Published in English for the first time

197

ENGELS TO VICTOR ADLER

IN VIENNA

London, 4 August 1894

Dear Victor,

The encl. letter and also a parcel were handed in here along with the anonymous note[389] overleaf, addressed to me. Probably from the anarchist philologist Nettlau (...)[a] No doubt you will give instructions in due course as to what is to be done with the parcel.

I have asked Cerny to pass on to you people a renewed request from the Spanish National Council that you send them a brief congratulatory message in Spanish or French on the occasion of the congress they are holding on 29 August.[390] I am repeating this in order to be on the safe side. Address:

Pablo Iglesias, Hernán Cortès 8, pral. *Madrid*.

Warm regards to your wife and yourself.

Yours,

F. E.

Louise and Ludwig also send you their warmest regards.

---

[a] At this point there is a break in the text.

First published in:
Victor Adlers Aufsätze, Reden und Briefe,
Erstes Heft: *Victor Adlers und*
Friedrich Engels, Wien, 1922

Printed according to the book

Published in English for the first time

198

ENGELS TO PABLO IGLESIAS

IN MADRID

[*Draft*]

[London, between 9 and 14 August 1894]

Dear Iglesias,

I have received your letters of 8 June and 27 July. With regard to your congress[390] I have written to Berlin (the answer is affirmative) and to Vienna (no answer so far); also to the Social Democratic Federation[44] here (H. W. Lee, Secretary), the Independent Labor Party[114] (Tom Mann, Secretary) and the gas workers[391] (W. Thorne, Secretary; Comrade Aveling[a] is a member of the Executive Council)—they will all drop you a line. Further, to the Standing Parliamentary Committee of the Trades-Unions Congress[28] (Fenwick, Secretary, M. P.), the League for Eight Hours[197] (Sheridan, Secretary; they are certain to write to you) and the Fabian Society[43] (E. R. Pease, Secretary), from which I have received no reply.

The above list will give you an idea of the personal divisions, jealousies and quarrels adorning the labour movement here. Look: on Monday, the 6th instant, the S. D. F. held a conference. There it was proposed that in the coming parliamentary elections the S. D. F. should support the candidates of the Independent Party provided that they declared themselves socialists. The proposal was rejected. But if the 'independents' refuse to vote for the Federation's candidates and to support them, they will be seen as traitors! Further, the S. D. F. Conference resolved that because the London international congress in 1896[392] is not to be *exclusively socialist*, the Federation will convene an exclusively socialist international

---

[a] Eleanor Marx-Aveling

congress, to be opened three days before the general congress of workers!! What will the socialists of other nations say? While all that—and much else—has no practical importance, those are attempts by various groups to exploit in their particular interests the convocation and holding of an international congress. It is best not to discuss or attach too much importance to those things in the press until they have taken a more distinct form. For all that, the movement among the working masses is making headway, the idea of socialising the means of production is gaining ground, and the day will come when the class-conscious masses throw out all schemers and corrupt leaders.

Every week Comrade Eleanor Marx-Aveling publishes in *Workman's Times* a report on progress in the international movement. You would do well to send her *El Socialista* if possible, for she understands Spanish. Address: Eleanor Marx-Aveling, etc.

Take care of yourself. All the best from your old and faithful friend.

First published in Russian
in: K. Marx and F. Engels,
Works, First Edition,
Vol. XXIX, 1946

Printed according to the original

Translated from the Spanish

Published in English for the first time

199

ENGELS TO EDUARD BERNSTEIN

IN BROADSTAIRS

Eastbourne, 14 August 1894
4 Royal Parade

Dear Ede,

We are safely installed here and up till now, i.e. since 2.30, have been very pleased also with the way they have looked after us. Let's hope it will so continue.[393]

I shall be interested to hear whether and how Liebknecht has reacted to your promptings on the subject of Arndt. The matter ought not to be passed over in silence like this. We had better wait and see what transpires. A man who behaved as he did at Zurich has no place on the *Vorwärts*.[394]

I have returned your textile worker.[a] Dogmatism. If one wants to base oneself on that sort of dogma, one ought to secure one's allies in advance, otherwise one is likely to make an ass of oneself.[395]

As to the Social Democratic Federation[44] and its special congress, I have already advised Spain[b] of the matter and shall do the same in the case of Italy and Paris, but am asking the chaps not to make too much fuss about it for the time being. For either the Social Democratic Federation issues a circular to justify the resolution and get its own brand of agitation going or we scotch the whole thing simply by means of statements in the Continental press to the effect that not a single delegate would be sent to such a congress. If, however, the circular does appear, there will be official discussions about it on all sides and that would be far preferable.

The Social Democratic Federation must have got wind of the Parliamentary Committee's[28] S061 proposal (long bruited about) to change the 1896 Congress[392] into a TRADES UNION congress and to take the requisite steps to that end in Norwich.[396] Hence they obviously wanted to be first in the field. These little schemes might well result in the Continentals saying: Neither of the two congresses is the one you *ought* to convoke and, since you don't *want* to convoke the latter, we'll simply go somewhere else and leave you to settle your squabbles between you.

It is inconceivably stupid of the Social Democratic Federation to have passed at the same time the resolution in regard to the Independent Labour Party[114] candidates, whether Socialists or not. It's the old story: either you are a Socialist, in which case you belong to the Social Democratic Federation or else you are unwilling to join the Social Democratic Federation, in which case you are no Socialist. But what seems to have entirely escaped their minds is the fact that these two resolutions, set side by side, would be bound to make the Continentals feel disinclined to have anything to do with the Social Democratic Federation's congress.

All this, incidentally, has left me comparatively unmoved. Between now and the congress all kinds of water will flow down the Thames and neither the quantity nor the quality of that water can possibly be predicated today.

I am writing to August too about *all* these things, incl. Arndt.

Warm regards to Gine, Ernst, Käte[c] and you yourself from Louise,

---

[a] *Der Textil-Arbeiter* – [b] See previous letter. – [c] Ernst and Käte Schattner, Bernstein's adopted children.

Ludwig and

Yours,

F. E.

Are the Mendelsons also in Broadstairs?

First published, in Russian,   Printed according to the original
in *Marx-Engels Archives*,
Vol. I, 1924   Published in English for the first time

200

ENGELS TO THOMAS CLARKE[397]

IN LONDON

[*Draft*]

[London, not earlier than 15 August 1894]

That from long personal acquaintance I consider Mr. S. Mendelson a respectable and responsible person that in your place I should not hesitate in accepting him as a tenant for such a place as you mention.

First published, in Russian,   Reproduced from the original
in: Marx and Engels, *Works*,
Second Russian Edition,   Published in English for the first time
Vol. 39, Moscow, 1966

201

ENGELS TO FILIPPO TURATI

IN MILAN

Eastbourne, 16 August 1894

4 Royal Parade

My dear citizen Turati,

I am infinitely grateful for the trouble you have taken concerning

Pasquali.[a] Fortunately, the *'seccatore di prima sfera*[398] *ha cessato di seccare la nostra sfera.*[b] In my day they said in Milan[398] of those banished financiers who took the road to Switzerland *'L'è ànd à Varés'*[c]: Pasquali has gone to Edinburgh, where he is probably going to try his fortune. He announced his visit *'colla mia moglie e col mio piccolo Marx Guglielmo',*[d] but he never came, and when one of our friends went to his lodgings, he was told that Mr Pasquali had left, with his family, for Edinburgh. Probably some 'Christian socialists', of whom there are a large number here, and someone else from a religious sect, will become interested in this interesting character. Let us wish him *bon voyage!*

Your bust of Marx does not have many admirers here.[400] There is too little of Marx and too much of Garibaldi in the head. Moreover, even if the bust bore a resemblance, it would be difficult to sell it outside Italy. In Paris they have just struck a rather big medallion which they are trying to sell, and in Germany, Austria and Switzerland these Marxes in plaster have multiplied to the point of being unsaleable.

Your law on suspects[401] goes further than ours of 1878,[15] and the one passed in France in 1894.[383] It entails administrative exile as in Russia. I hope, however, that this is one of those instances which will illustrate the German proverb *'es wird nichts so heiss gegessen wie es gekocht wird.'*[e] What is certain is that, of all the countries of Europe, Italy is the one where all political ailments suffer acute inflammation: rebellion with the outright use of force on the one hand, and excessively violent reaction on the other. However, where Bismarck failed, Crispi will certainly not succeed: in the end persecution will strengthen socialism in Italy, and all that I desire is that this squall will pass without forcing you temporarily into either the hell of Eritrea or the purgatory of London.

Speaking of London, the Social Democratic Federation,[44] one of the five or six socialist sects here—it has a Marxist programme, but the tactics of an exclusive sect—has just held a congress at which two quite important resolutions were adopted.[f] The first is characteristic of this Federation: it was proposed that the Federation should support the candidates of the Independent Labour Party[114] in the coming parliamentary elections if these candidates proclaim themselves openly to be socialist—rejected

---

[a] See this volume, p. 333 – [b] The bore of the first degree has ceased to pester *our* circle. – [c] He went to Varés. – [d] "together with my wife and my little Marx Guglielmo" – [e] the devil is not so black as he is painted – [f] See this volume, p. 337

by a large majority. The Independent Party of Workers is a rival group which has also included 'the socialisation of the means of production' in its programme, and which consequently *is* socialist, although it does not publicise this fact, and has as its aim to secure the election of worker candidates independent from the Conservative and Liberal parties. Everyone had hoped that these two groups would join together for the elections, but no, says the Federation: either you are socialists, in which case you should join our ranks, or else you refuse to join us, and constitute a separate group, and then you are not socialists. So create a movement with such elements!

However, now for that which concerns us more nearly. After a debate in which it emphasised the fact that the congresses held in Paris,[227] Brussels[228] and Zurich[229] were not truly socialist congresses, and that it is time for the socialists to free themselves from the trade-union (corporative) element which is not socialist, the Federation has officially resolved to convene in London, in 1896, *a purely socialist congress which will begin three days before the general congress in London.*[392]

Note that the group which is calling on the socialist world to attend a special congress which has no mandate whatever, declared at the congress I have just referred to that it had 4,500 members; but according to the secretary,[a] last year they had 7,000 names on the membership list, so that they have lost almost as many as they have retained, and another member boasted that during the fourteen years that this organisation has existed, no less than a *million members* have joined and left (except for the 4,500 mentioned above).

An organisation possessing such an ability to attract (and repel), which rejects all socialist candidates save its own (note that the Independent Labour Party, in the provinces, exists in perfect harmony with the SDF!), and which also wishes to exclude the trade unions at a time when they (our largest and most promising terrain for propaganda) are probably going to declare themselves at Norwich[396] for the second time in favour of the socialisation of the means of production (adopted at Belfast in 1893)[402] and adopted again by the council of workers of London[197] in 1894—such an organisation is indeed well positioned to take the initiative on such a question.

The continental socialists, now united in all the countries, will have

---
[a] Henry Mayers Hyndman

to judge whether or not they should agree to the convocation of a congress at which they will have to pass resolutions which will bind them *in advance* as regards their actions at the general congress. This could not but annoy—and quite rightly—the delegates to the main congress sent by groups which are not quite socialist. And as we know by experience that these groups, by the very fact of attending our congresses, are unconsciously drawn into the socialist lap—the English trade unions are the best proof of this—are we going to be sufficiently narrow to close this door?

You have no idea of the intrigues afoot here as regards this congress. The parliamentary committee of the Trade Union Congress[28] wishes, so *it is said*, to take control of our congress in order to transform it into a trade union congress pure and simple, like the one held here in 1888,[403] and about which C. Lazzari could tell you certain things. Naturally, on the continent the response to this attempt will be bursts of laughter. However, the Social Democratic Federation would seem to have taken these rumours seriously, and wishes to take advantage of them so that it can take control of the congress and turn it into a separate event. As the resolution adopted by the SDF is official and has been published, one can discuss it in the press. However, it would be better not to lend it too much importance, as it is clearly an attempt to see which way the wind is blowing, and will become important only if there then come steps to carry it through, a circular letter of invitation, etc., etc.

Greetings to you and Mme Anna from Mme Freyberger and myself,

Yours,

F. E.

Please consider this letter as private and confidential.

First published in French
in: *Filippo Turati attraverso
le lettere di corrispondenti
(1880-1925)*, Bari, 1947

Printed according to the original

Translated from the French

Published in English for the first time

202

ENGELS TO PAUL LAFARGUE

AT LE PERREUX

Eastbourne, 22 August 1894
4 Royal Parade

My dear Lafargue,

Here we are at Eastbourne since the past week,[393] Louise, her husband and I. I needed it badly and the ozonised sea air is already taking effect. Unfortunately it has been raining more than necessary since yesterday.

Your cheque will arrive during the first days of next month as soon as I shall have had some payments.

I am very curious to see how they are going to administer the new law against suspects.[383] I am by no means sure that they will not use it against the Socialists as much as against the anarchists at a given moment. But though a few individuals may suffer by it, this law will certainly do for you what the '78 law did for the Germans[15]; you will defeat it and you will emerge from the struggle infinitely stronger than you went into it.

Here the Social Democratic Federation,[44] which for a time seemed to try to adopt a reasonable and tolerable line of conduct, has suddenly fallen back on the Hyndmanniads of yore. At the Congress which they held in London a fortnight or three weeks ago,[404] the Liverpool delegate moved that at the next general elections they should support the Independent Labour Party[114] candidates provided they publicly declared themselves Socialists. This, against all the rules of English procedure, was *turned down* in favour of a motion adopted by 42 to 12, that the duty of every Socialist was to belong to an openly revolutionary socialist organisation, such as the Social Democratic Federation (and as the S.D.F. claims that apart from itself there is no other, this meant: *belong to the S.D.F.*). As for electoral tactics, this was delegated to a committee which will report to the Executive Committee. You know of course that the nationalisation of the means of production is an integral part of the I.L.P. programme. Thus, the reciprocity which hitherto has existed in the North (particularly in Lancashire and Yorkshire) between the two groups, is to all intents and purposes rejected by the S.D.F. which proclaims the policy of the Caliph Omar in burning the Alexandria library: either these books are contrary to the Koran, in which case they are bad; or they contain the same thing, in which case they are superfluous—into the flames with them! And these people claim the leadership of the socialist movement in Britain!

But there is worse to come. Hyndman has stated that it was time for socialism to detach itself outright from trade unionism, and that instead of joint congresses of the two, there should be an out and out socialist congress. And, as it was realised at the same time that it is still too early to strike a direct blow against the 1896 Congress,[392] they resolved that the *S.D.F. should convene an exclusively socialist Congress to be held in London three days before the general Congress of 1896.*

What will the continentals say to that? Will they go to such a congress in order later to attend the large, *our* congress, tied hand and foot by the resolutions passed two or three days earlier[a] in a small committee? Will they provoke a split between the delegates who are thoroughgoing Socialists and those who are not yet that but are on the point of becoming so? Will they administer this slap in the face to the British trade unionists, who have made such progress since the New Unionism[405] has set them on the road towards socialism, who at Belfast in 1893[402] voted for the nationalisation of the means of production (adopted a few weeks ago in the political programme of even the recalcitrant London Trades Council[197]) and which, in a fortnight's time, at Norwich[396] will be stating its position in relation to us once again?

But do you know how the S.D.F. in its annual report and the speeches at a conference depicted the strength of that organisation which claims to change the Zurich resolutions[229] (for this is a palpable emendation which contradicts the Zurich resolution)? It has—4,500 members. Last year 7,000 names passed through its membership list, so it has lost 2,500! But what of it? asks Hyndman. In the 14 years of its existence the S.D.F. has seen a *million people* pass through its ranks. What organisation! Out of one million, 995,500 have hopped it, but—4,500 have stayed!

Now for the key to all these idiocies, inconceivable without that key. The 1896 Congress will not leave untouched any of the sects, fractions, groups, etc. which compose what one calls here Organised Labour. The Parliamentary Committee of the Trades Congress[28] would very much like

---

[a] A mistake in the manuscript: after [après].

TO BOSS THE Congress. There are already motions tabled on the agenda for the Trades Congress at Norwich (September) to confine admission of British delegates to the '96 Congress only to those qualified for the Trades Congress: bona fide workingmen, working or having worked at the trade they represent. And it is said that they are not a little desirous of extending this system to the continental delegates as well, which would cause explosions of laughter violent enough to shake all London to its foundations. Very well, the S.D.F., which, in its turn, thinks the opportunity has come for it to boss the Congress and, through Congress, the British movement, appears to have taken these rumours as an excuse to launch its little counter-plan.

So far it is only a feeler. But as soon as the S. D. F. issues an invitation circular or something of that kind, the matter will take on substance, and the continental parties will be called upon to come to a decision.

One question: Le Socialiste lebt or noch, oder aber ist er tot?[a] Since April we haven't seen a trace of it. If you have succeeded in killing it, do you count this as one of the Party's victories in France?

Whatever the case, the two months of September and October will be interesting. Towards the 5, the Trades Congress, at Norwich[396] (after the Spanish congress[390] next Sunday), then your congress at Nantes,[406] then the Germans at Frankfurt on 21 October.[418] The last two will be dealing with the question of peasants and farm workers. Overall, the views of the two national groups are the same, only that you intransigent revolutionaries of the bygone days are now inclining a little more towards opportunism than the Germans, who probably will not support any measure which might serve to maintain or conserve small property against the corrosive action of capitalism. On the other hand, they will agree with you that it is not *our* task to accelerate or intensify this corrosive action, and that a most important thing is to organise small property-holders into agricultural associations to cultivate land in common and on a large scale. I am curious to see which of the two congresses will show itself to be the more advanced in economic theory and propose the more effective practical measures.

Give my greetings to Laura and remind her that she owes me a letter. Greetings from the Freybergers.

Yours,

F. E.

---

[a] Is *Le Socialiste* still alive or is it dead?

In a couple of weeks the *Neue Zeit* will have an article from me on the origins of Christianity.[a] The 3ʳᵈ volume[b] is underway, 43 sheets are written; I am writing the Preface.

First published abridged in English, in the *Labour Monthly* No. 11, 1955 and, in French, in *Cahiers du Communisme*, No. 11, 1955 and in full in F. Engels, P. et L. Lafargue, *Correspondance*, t. III, Paris, 1959

Printed according to the original

Translated from the French

203

ENGELS TO EDUARD BERNSTEIN

IN LONDON

Eastbourne, 6 September 1894
4 Royal Parade

Dear Ede,

I shall write and tell Schlüter[25] that you haven't the time and that he can reprint the piece from the *Neue Zeit*.

The errata can wait until I return on 18 September.[393] The preface[c] won't be finished until later, but you can come and see it at my house before it goes off. You will find the part on the rate of profit in the book proper. There is nothing new on the subject in the preface, merely a critique of the attempts at solving it.[407]

As to Edwards, I would in your place first inquire from the Avelings as to *why* they refused and what they know about the man. In English the expression 'DON'T KNOW HIM' is not wholly unequivocal. If you are prepared to sacrifice the time, it would certainly be quite a good idea, if you prevent an Arndt, say, or a Hyndman, from writing the article. On the other hand contributing to an annual of this sort which has suddenly been brought into being by someone you don't know can involve you in some unpleasant experiences. The chap can't take it amiss if you ask him

[a] F. Engels, *On the History of Early Christianity*. – [b] K. Marx, *Capital*. - [c] Preface to Vol. III of *Capital*

for the names of the contributors he has already secured. After all, that would enable you to form a more definite opinion.[408]

Pinkau is welcome to a photo as soon as I myself have got another one. As you know, Inka's attempts miscarried and since then I have not been anywhere near a lens.

Many regards to Gine and the children[a] from Louise and

Yours,

F. E.

Freyberger is in London today doing hospital duty.

First published, in Russian,
in *Marx-Engels Archives*,
Vol. I, 1924

Printed according to the original

Published in English for the first time

204

ENGELS TO EDUARD BERNSTEIN

IN LONDON

[London,] Tuesday, 18 September 1894

We got back this evening.[393] The Baron wants me to let him have some 'unpublished stuff' on the International. I have now searched through my old papers and found something that might possibly do. Could you pick it up here so that it can be translated? Time is pressing, to judge by the Baron's letter. I shall be in town tomorrow between 10 and about 11 and shall then come back here, but Louise knows where the things are.

Regards to Gine and the children[a] from us all.

Yours,

F. E.

First published, in Russian,
in *Marx-Engels Archives*,
Vol. I, 1924

Printed according to the original

Published in English for the first time

---

[a] Bernstein's wife and adopted children

205

ENGELS TO LAURA LAFARGUE

AT LE PERREUX

[*Fragment*]

[London, second half of September 1894

Now to something else. The Trades Union Congress[396] marks a distinct progress against last year, and combined with the Leicester election and other symptoms, shows that things are on the move in England. Of course there is no progress here without a drawback: take the resolution against foreign working men immigration passed at Norwich; but such contradictions and inconsistencies one will have to put up with for some time yet 'in this free country'. The moment will come after all, when the masses, having attained a sufficient degree of consciousness, will break through the tangled web of the intrigues and sectarian squabbles of the 'leaders'.

The war between China and Japan[409] seems to me instigated by the Russian government, who use Japan as their tool. But whatever may be the proximate consequences of this war, it must lead to one thing: the total break-up of the whole traditional system in old China. There, an old-fashioned system of agriculture and domestic industry combined has been artificially kept going by rigid exclusion of all disturbing elements. That exclusion of everything foreign has been partially broken through by the wars with the English and French; this war with *Asiatics*, rivals living next door to the Chinese, must put a complete stop to it.

The Chinese, licked on land and on sea, will have to Europeanise themselves, open their ports generally to trade, establish railways and factories, and thus completely smash up that old system which made it possible to feed so many millions. There will be all of a sudden a constantly increasing surplus population, superseded peasants, who will flock to the coast to search for a living in foreign lands. Where up to now thousands emigrated, millions will want to go then. And then the Chinese Coolies will be everywhere, in Europe as well as America and Australia, and will try to reduce wages and the standard of living of our working men to the Chinese level. And then the time will come for our European workmen.

And the English will be the first to suffer from this invasion and *to fight*. I fully expect that this Japan-Chinese War will hasten our victory in Europe by five years at least, and facilitate it immensely, as it will drive all non-capitalist classes over to our side. Only the large landed proprietors and manufacturers will be *pro*-Chinese.

Paul's articles in the *Neue Zeit* are on the whole very good.[a] There are some historical views in them that do him great credit. The exposition of the causation and course of French history since 1871 is the best I have yet seen. I have learned a good deal from them.

But the considérant of the Nantes agricultural programme,[406] which declares it the duty of the Socialists to maintain and defend the peasants' property, and even the *fermiers* and *métayers* who *employ labourers*, is more than most people outside France will be able to swallow.

Kind remembrances from the Freybergers. Ever yours

F. Engels

First published, in Russian,   Reproduced from the original
in: Marx and Engels, *Works*,
Second Russian Edition,   Published in English for the first time
Vol. 39, Moscow, 1966

206

ENGELS TO KARL KAUTSKY[410]

IN STUTTGART

London, 23 September 1894
122 Regent's Park Road, N. W.

Dear Baron,

Your appeal for documents on the International[b] reached me while I was still in Eastbourne. Unfortunately I couldn't ask Ede to look out something for you, as I had brought the keys to my cupboards with me and he would have had to search through *several* of them—I myself

---

[a] P. Lafargue, 'Der Klassenkampf in Frankreich', *Die Neue Zeit*, Nos. 46, 479 48, 49, 1893-94, Vol. II – [b] See this volume, p. 346

hardly know where I am amidst the disorder of my old papers. Then, on our return the following day (Tuesday), I looked out something for Ede and we asked him to call that evening but he had to finish the article for the *Neue Zeit*.[a] On Wednesday morning the things were collected by Ernst,[b] but were brought back that same evening by Ede who said that it was now too late and that in any case you already had something. What I had found was in any case nothing out of the ordinary. It is difficult to find an *unknown* document of the Internationals that will, of itself, still have a telling effect today.

Many thanks for the *Entwicklung*[c] in Armenian. Luckily I can't read it.

As regards the fee for Marx's chapters, kindly deduct this from, or alternatively charge it against, the fee for my own article and remit it to me for the heirs. Should mine be insufficient, kindly set off the difference against future contributions.[411]

Needless to say copies of the *complete* issue will do just as well as off-prints of the article. I only need them for one or two quite specific incidental purposes.

The payment of fees to the Austrians remains in force until further notice.

The Italians are beginning to fill me with dread. Yesterday that blatherer Enrico Ferri sent me all his recent writings along with an over-cordial letter which only served to make me feel less cordial towards him than ever. And yet one is expected to send the chap a courteous reply! His book on Darwin-Spencer-Marx[d] is an atrocious hotchpotch of insipid rubbish. The Italians will long continue to suffer from this their younger generation of heddicated bourgeois. I shall doubtless soon have to do something to put an end to the ominous increase in my popularity (which the chaps are not fostering WITHOUT A CONSIDERABLE EYE TO BUSINESS). Meanwhile I shall make a bit of an example of Achille Loria in the preface to the 3rd volume.[e]

The war between China and Japan[409] signifies the end of the old China and with it the total if gradual revolution of the entire economic base until the old ties between agriculture and rural industry have been dissolved

[a] E. Bernstein, 'Der dritte Band des *Kapital*,' *Die Neue Zeit*, Nos, 11-14, 16, 17, 209 1894-95, Vol. I – [b] Schattner – [c] F. Engels, *Socialism: Utopian and Scientific* – [d] E. Ferri, *Socialismo e scienza positiva (Darwin, Spencer, Marx)*, Roma, 1894 – [e] P. Engels, *Preface* [to K. Marx's *Capital*, Vol. III]

by big industry, railways, etc., the result being a mass exodus of Chinese Coolies, to Europe included and hence, for ourselves, an acceleration of the débacle[a] and an intensification of the conflict to the point of crisis. Here we have another splendid quirk of history—China is all that is left for capitalist production to conquer, yet the latter, by the very fact of having finally conquered her, will itself be hopelessly compromised in its place of origin.

Many regards from one household to the other.

Yours,

F. E.

We shall shortly be moving to 41 Regent's Park Road, nearer to St Mark's Church; more details anon.

First published in:
Aus der Frühzeit des Marxismus.
Engels Briefwechsel mit
Kautsky, Prag, 1935

Printed according to the original

Published in English in full
for the first time

207

ENGELS TO EMILE VANDERVELDE

IN BRUSSELS

[*Draft*]

[London, after 21 October 1894]

Dear citizen Vandervelde,

Allow me to express my congratulations to you personally on your election, and also to our Belgian comrades in general on their splendid successes these last two Sundays.[412] This second victory of the Belgian proletariat is of great importance for us all.[b] Small countries such as Belgium and Switzerland are our modern political laboratories, the testing ground

---

[a] ruin – [b] The following phrase is crossed out by Engels: "If a small country like yours is not destined to resolve the great problems of our epoch on its own..."

where experiments are carried out which can be later applied to the large states. It is often from these small countries that there comes the first impulse of a movement destined to overturn Europe. Thus, before the February revolution,[a] there was the Swiss war of the Sonderbund.[273]

At the moment we are, it seems to me, in a period of high tide, a period which dates from the suffrage victory of the Belgian workers.[276] After Belgium, Austria joined the suffrage movement; following Austria, proletarian Germany has just requested that universal suffrage be extended from the Reichstag to the parliaments of the federal states. The repressive laws launched against the worker parties in France[383] and Italy,[401] similar laws being prepared in Germany, will have no more success than the violent measures of the Austrian government. Today the socialist movement everywhere is more powerful than the so-called public force.[b]

As for the Belgian workers, 14th October assures them an even stronger position. For the first time they have learned to know precisely their own forces and those of the enemy; thus henceforth they will be able to base their tactical decisions on knowledge of the situation; and you and the other socialist representatives will be able to raise your heads still higher, and will be listened to with considerably more attention following official recognition of the fact that you are the mouthpiece of 350,000 Belgian citizens. It is with you that the Belgian proletariat is making its 'joyous entry' into parliament, an entry that is joyous not only for you, but for the proletarians of the whole of Europe!

First published in Russian in:
Marx and Engels, *Works*,
First Russian Edition, Vol. XXIX,
Moscow, 1946

Printed according to the original

Translated from the French

Published in English for the first time

---

[a] of 1848 in France – [b] the following words are crossed out by Engels "This splendid victory of the Belgian socialists marks a new stage..."

208

ENGELS TO MARIA MENDELSON

IN LONDON

London, 26 October 1894
41 Regent's Park Road, N. W.

Dear Madame Mendelson,

At last we are able to receive our friends—even though the house still bears as it were the marks of seige and bombardment—we will have the pleasure of seeing both of you on Sunday evening.[a]

Louise and the doctor[b] send their greetings,

Yours sincerely,
F. Engels

First published in Russian
in: Marx and Engels, *Works*,
Second Russian Edition,
Vol. 39, Moscow, 1966

Printed according to the original

Translated from the French

Published in English for the first time

209

ENGELS TO GEORGI PLEKHANOV

IN LONDON

[London] 1 November 1894
41 Regent's Park Road, N. W.

My dear Plekhanov,

It goes without saying that I will do all I can to assist the examination of the *Neue Rheinisehe Zeitung*, etc.,[413] and I do not exactly see why you should be embarrassed to speak to me frankly on the subject. At the moment my books are still not in order; this work was interrupted by a

---

[a] 28 October – [b] Freyberger

number of other matters to be dealt with, trips into town, legal consultations, and other nuisances caused by the legal formalities and material difficulties without which it is impossible to rent a house in England, and particularly in London. Nor is it yet finished.

As my books are not organised, I can hardly begin, and therefore I must ask you to continue to have patience. However, rest assured that you will have all the books, newspapers, etc., that I am able to find on the subject that interests you. We shall discuss it on the first occasion that I have the pleasure to see you.

Yours,

F. Engels

I have just learned that a new oven range is being fitted in our kitchen, and that this will prevent us from cooking until after Sunday. We will not therefore be able to entertain you on Sunday evening,[a] since we will not be able to give you anything to eat. However, if you would like to call on any evening after eight o'clock, we can talk about the question of the books.

First published in Russian in: *Gruppa "Osvobozhdeniye Truda"*, No. 2, 1924

Printed according to the original

Translated from the French

Published in English for the first time

210

ENGELS TO CARL HIRSCH[414]

IN COLOGNE

[London,] 8 November 1894

Dear Hirsch,

While thanking you very much for your regular despatch of the *Rheinische Zeitung*, I would ask you to be so kind as to change the address from 122 to No. 41, Regent's Park Road, London, N. W. It is on the

---

[a] 4 November

other side of the road, but *at the bottom* of Primrose Hill and closer to the entrance to the Park. All well in other respects.

Yours,

F. E.

First published in:
Marx/Engels, *Werke*,
Bd. 39, Berlin, 1973

Printed according to the original

Published in English for the first time

211

ENGELS TO ELEANOR MARX-AVELING[415]

IN LONDON

[London, 10 November 1894,] Saturday

My dear Tussy,

Of course we expect you to-morrow to dinner—the hour is unchanged, 2.30 or a little later, as the capabilities of the new kitchen-range are not yet quite known.

Here everything goes on well.

Shall be glad to see Edward,[a] especially if he is a good deal better as I hope.

Look at to-day's *Vorwärts re Hyndman*.[416]

Ever yours

F. E.

First published, in the language
of the original, in: *Friedrich Engels
1820-1870. Referate. Diskussionen.
Dokumente*, Hannover, 1971

Reproduced from the original

Published in English for the first time

---

[a] Aveling

212

ENGELS TO FRIEDRICH ADOLPH SORGE[417]

IN HOBOKEN

London, 10 November 1894
41 Regent's Park Road, N. W.

Dear Sorge,

From the above address you will see that I have moved house. After Louise's marriage our old home had become rather too cramped and, since the consequences of that marriage soon manifested themselves, we could no longer make do. We therefore took a larger house which became available a little further down the road, close by the gates into Regent's Park and, after a great bother, moved in four weeks ago—bother with house agents, solicitors, contractors, furniture salesmen, etc., and it's not yet over, my books being still in great disarray. Downstairs we have our communal living-rooms, on the first floor my study and bedroom, on the second Louise, her husband, the baby daughter, born on Tuesday the 6th of this month, and nursery maid, on the third floor the two housemaids, lumber-room and visitor's room. My study is at the front, has three windows and is so big that I can accommodate nearly all my books (eight cases full) in it and yet, despite its size, very nice and easy to heat. In short, we are a lot better off. In the circumstances Louise and her baby are very well, and everything went off swimmingly.

Today, you will get two fat parcels, 3 copies of the (Berlin) *Sozialdemokrat*, 3 of the Pest *Volksstimme*, the rest of the proceedings of the Party Conference in the *Vorwärts*[418] and a *Critica Sociale* containing a letter by me.ᵃ Because of the removal, we have not been able to send things quite so regularly. The *Workman's Times* no longer exists, more's the pity. Tussy's articles in it were the only ones in which the truth about the Continental movement was neither withheld from the English workers nor falsified.

The movement in this country continues to resemble the American one except in being a *little* more advanced than yours, The instinct of the

---

ᵃ F. Engels, 'International Socialism and Italian Socialism'

masses which tells them that Labour must form a party of its own in opposition to the two official parties is growing ever stronger and was more
than ever in evidence at the municipal elections on 1 November. But old
traditional memories of various kinds, combined with a lack of people
who might be capable of translating that instinct into conscious action
and crystallising it throughout the land, are conducive to the prolonga-
tion of this preliminary stage—a stage at which thinking is ill-defined
and action isolated and localised. Anglo-Saxon sectarianism is also rife in
the Labour movement. The Social Democratic Federation.[44] just like your
German Socialist Labor Party,[367] has succeeded in turning our theory into
the rigid dogma of an orthodox sect and is not only narrowly exclusive
but, thanks to Hyndman, has a thoroughly rotten tradition where international politics is concerned, a tradition which, although shaken from
time to time, has nevertheless remained intact. The Independent Labor
Party[114] is excessively vague in the matter of tactics, while its leader, Keir
Hardie, is an over-canny Scot whose demagogic tricks one cannot trust
for a moment. Although a poor devil of a Scottish miner, he has started
a big weekly, *The Labour Leader*, something that could not have been
effected without a great deal of money, and this money he obtains from
a Tory or at any rate Liberal-Unionist,[206] i.e. anti-Gladstonian and anti-
Home Rule quarter[171]—of that there can be no doubt, as is confirmed not
only by first-hand information and his own political attitude, but also by
the literary connections he is known to possess in London. Consequently
he might—through the defection of the Irish and Radical voters—very
easily lose his parliamentary seat in the General Election of 1895[345] and
this would be fortunate, for at the moment the man is the greatest stum-
bling-block of all. He appears in Parliament only on demagogic occasions, so as to draw attention to himself by spouting hot air about the UN-
EMPLOYED to no effect whatever, or else to address inanities to the Queen[a]
on the birth of some prince[b] which, in this country, is cheap and trivial
to the utmost, etc. Otherwise, and particularly in the provinces, there
are some very good elements, both in the Social Democratic Federation
and in the Independent Labor Party —elements which, though scattered,
have at least succeeded in frustrating every attempt made by the leaders to
set the two organisations at each other's throats. John Burns is something
of a lone wolf politically; he is furiously attacked by both Hyndman and

---

[a] Queen Victoria – [b] Edward Albert, Prince of York

Keir Hardie and acts as though, having despaired of a political Labour organisation, he is now pinning his hopes solely on the Trades Unions. True, his experience with the former has not been altogether happy and he might starve if the Engineers Union did not pay his parliamentary salary. He is vain, having let himself be rather excessively soft-sawdered by the Liberals, i.e. by the 'social wing' of the Radicals, and definitely sets too much store by the many individual concessions he has obtained, but is for all that the only really honest man in the whole movement, i.e. among its leaders, and has a thoroughly proletarian instinct by which he will, or so I believe, be guided more surely at the crucial moment than will the others by their cunning and calculated self-interest.

On the Continent success has kindled an appetite for more success, and peasant-catching in the literal sense of the term[a] is coming to be all the rage. First the French declare at Nantes, through Lafargue,[419] not only that it is no business of ours (I had already written and told them as much[b]) to precipitate the ruin of the small peasant by direct intervention, a task that may safely be entrusted to capitalism, but also that it behoves us actually to *protect* the small peasant against taxation, usury and the big landowner. But we cannot go along with this, firstly because it is stupid and secondly because it is impossible. Next, Vollmar[418] goes to Frankfurt and actually proposes to bribe your *peasant as such*; nor is the peasant with whom he is concerned in Upper Bavaria, your small, debt-ridden Rhenish chap, but your middling if not big peasant who exploits his farmhands, male and female, and sells cattle and grain in quantity. And that would not be feasible unless one were to abandon the whole principle of the thing. We can only win over the Alpine peasants and the big peasants of Lower Saxony and Schleswig-Holstein at the cost of betraying their ploughboys and day labourers, and in so doing we should lose politically more than we should gain. The Frankfurt Party Conference failed to come to any decision on this question and that is a good thing, in as much as the matter will now be properly gone into; the people who attended it knew far too little about peasants, or rural conditions, which vary so greatly from province to province, to do anything more than form resolutions out of thin air. But the matter will have to be settled sooner or later.

---

[a] In German peasant-catching (*Bauernfängerei*) also means confidence trick. – [b] See this volume, p. 348

Here a question occurs to me about the Paris *Socialiste*; is it still alive or is it dead? No one seems to know, When Tussy was in Paris this summer it was not yet defunct, but anyone who wanted a copy had to go to the office and get one!! I haven't set eyes on it since February or March. Dereure has gone off his head. He was manager and, having got things into a mess, did nothing whatever about it. Typically French.

Following the electoral victories in Belgium,[412] the Belgians and French are making arrangements for the socialist parliamentarians in the various countries to keep in regular touch with each other and hold periodic conferences. Whether anything will come of this is questionable. At the moment the fifty French parliamentarians (among them some twenty-six Radical[86] converts of a somewhat dubious kind) are very pleased with themselves, but there are snags. Amongst the twenty-four old Socialists a fierce but silent struggle is going on between the Marxists on the one hand and the Blanquists[20] and Allemanists[21] (Possibilists[30]) on the other; whether it will result in an open breach is hard to say.

Besides other socialist papers, I am now also sent the Romanian one (*Munca*) and the Bulgarian (formerly *Rabotnik* (*Working Man*), now (*Socialist*), and am gradually familiarising myself with those languages, The Romanians are going to bring out a daily in Bucharest.[a]

More than any other world event, the death of the Russian Tsar is likely to bring about a change, either as a result of an internal movement or as a result of a financial crisis and the impossibility of obtaining money abroad. I cannot suppose that the existing system will continue to subsist if it brings to the throne an idiot whose health, both physical and mental, has been shattered by onanism. (This fact is notorious in all the faculties of medicine. Krause, a professor at Dorpat,[b] who attended Nicholas, informed Tsar Alexander at the latter's request that this—onanism—was the immediate cause of the illness, was boxed over the ears for his pains, resigned, returned the Order of Vladimir sent him after his departure, and went back to Germany where he related the story.) If the fun begins in Russia, however, young William, too, will become aware that something novel is afoot. For then a liberal wind will blow through Europe—a wind which *now* can only be of benefit to us.

The war in China[409] has given the coup de grâce to the old China. Isolation has become impossible, for the introduction of railroads, steam

---

[a] *Lumea noua*. – [b] Modern name: Tartu

engines, electricity and large-scale industry is essential if only for reasons of military defence. But this means the collapse of the old economic system of small farms, a system in which the family also manufactured its industrial products, and with it that of the whole of the old social system which admitted of a relatively dense population. Millions will be evicted and compelled to emigrate and those millions will find their way as far, even, as Europe, whither they will come in droves. But in your country as in ours, Chinese competition will, as soon as it attains massive proportions, quickly bring things to a head and thus the conquest of China by capitalism will at the same time provide the impulse for the overthrow of capitalism in Europe and America.

I hope you and your wife are feeling better than when you wrote last. Though I am not feeling at all bad myself, one does notice after a while how wide is the gap between 73 and 37.

Cordial regards to yourself and your wife,

Yours,

F. E.

First published abridged in:
Briefe und Auszüge aus Briefen von Joh. Phil. Becker, Jos. Dietzgen, Friedrich Engels, Karl Marx u.A. an F.A. Sorge und Andere, Stuttgart, 1906 and in full, in Russian, in: Marx and Engels, *Works*,

First Russian Edition, Vol. XXIX, Moscow, 1946

Printed according to the original

Published in English in full for the first time

213

ENGELS TO LAURA LAFARGUE

AT LE PERREUX

London, 12 November 1894
41 Regent's Park Road, N. W.

My dear Löhr,

Qui s'excuse s'accuse,[a] you began your letter of 24th October, and your

---

[a] one who offers excuses accuses oneself

last note of Saturday, received this morning, shows how little time it has taken you to pass from 'excusing' to 'decusing'. However you will have to come it considerably stronger before you upset my good humour, and so I will only just state that since 9ᵗʰ October we are in No. 41, that I have had no end of trouble with lawyers, house-agents, contractors etc, before I got the house put into tenantable condition, so much so that I only got yesterday the last heap of books from my study-floor into the book-cases, where they await sorting; that no sooner was the place something like ship-shape when last Tuesday Louise became the mother of a little girl (both doing very well); that to crown all, London is becoming flooded with *proscrits*:ᵃ Russian, Italian, Armenian etc. etc. who duly honour me with their visits; that at the same time I had to hurry off the very badly printed proofs of the last 5 or 6 sheets *Capital* (proofs and revision); and that in consequence of all this not only my correspondence but also your French Manifestoᵇ in the *Ere Nouvelle* got sadly neglected.

However this morning I hunted up the October and September Nos. of that revue from my higgledy-piggledy books and compared them with the original. *Je vous en fais mes compliments*ᶜ—this is better then even the *Feuerbach*![³¹⁰] It is the first French translation of the old *Manifest* I read with real and unbroken pleasure. Unfortunately the November No. which contains the Conclusion has not yet come to hand, so I cannot look them over. A few suggestions follow, they are very unimportant.

You may well say *trois déménagements valent un incendie*ᵈ more than once I felt inclined to throw all my books into the fire, and house and all, such a bother it was. But now I expect the worst is over—that is to say the *only* little evil to contend with now is a flooded coal cellar and a sweating wine cellar! But that, too, must at last be vanquished.

The Czarᵉ is dead, *vive lé Czar*,ᶠ and indeed the poor beggar does require all the encouragement the French bourgeoisie and press can give him by their shouts. He is next door to an idiot, weakly in mind and body, and promises just that vacillating reign of a man a mere playball of other people's cross-purpose-intrigues which is wanted to break up finally the Russian despotic system. Financial difficulties will help. Mother Crawford let it out the other day that France now holds not less than eight milliards of Russian *Rentes*ᵍ which accounts for the failure of the

---

ᵃ exiles – ᵇ K. Marx and F. Engels, *Manifesto of the Communist Party.* – ᶜ My compliments to you – ᵈ three removals amount to one fire – ᵉ Alexander III – ᶠ Nicholas II – ᵍ loans

last Russian loan[123] and makes very improbable the success, *in France*, of the impending one. Out of France Nicholas will get no cash. When 6 or 7 years ago an attempt was made to raise the wind in Berlin, the bankers replied unanimously: With the guarantee of a National Assembly, any amount; without it, not a farthing; could not that cry be raised now, when the opportunity offers, in the *Petite République*? To tell the French *gogos*[a] that a constitution *must* come in Russia and that therefore it will not be safe to entrust their money to a moribund absolutism? Or does *le patriotisme* render such a proceeding too dangerous?

Many thanks for your offer to translate my *Urchristentum*[420]; but do you really think that theological subject—especially II and III—attractive enough for French readers? I have my very strong misgivings. The I article might perhaps pass: *les Internationaux sous l'empire des Césars*[b] or something like it—however that I leave entirely to you.

Bebel confirms in a letter today that Vollmar had said in Frankfurt,[418] had expressly approved the new programme *agricole* of Nantes[406]; now the only thing I wrote to anybody about it was to you[c]: that I was afraid the French would stand alone with their appeal to support, in this present condition, the *petits propriétaires* and even *les fermiers qui sont obligés d'exploiter des ouvriers*.[d] So Vollmar's assertion is an invention of his own. Unfortunately it will compel me to reply in public[421] and in order to avoid provoking fresh misunderstandings, I shall be obliged to speak of the peasant question more fully, and then I cannot pass by the Nantes debates. I shall send it to the *Neue Zeit*,[e] perhaps you will find that more interesting than Christianity.[f]

This is how one gets always interrupted! This confounded peasant question will take me another week. And yet I have my hands full with work urgently needed, even before I come to start what I ought to do: the history of Mohr's part in the *International*. And that leads me to something: in the Berlin (anarchist) *Sozialist* they publish from the *Société Nouvelle* a letter of Bakounine—very long—in which he gives his version of the Hague affair[115] etc.[g] Is that to be had in Paris? Or does it appear in Brussels? The German text I have only received in fragments, possibly in

---

[a] simpletons – [b] the Internationals during the Caesars' empire – [c] See this volume, p. 348 – [d] small proprietors and even farmers who are obliged to exploit labourers – [e] F. Engels, *The Peasant Question in France and Germany* – [f] F. Engels, *On the History of Early Christianity* – [g] M. Bakunin, 'Ein unbekanntes Schreiben', *Der Sozialist*, Nos. 40, 41, 44, 45, 46, 48, 49, September 29, October 6, 27, November 3, 10, 24, December 1, 1894—

consequence of seizures by the police.

Paul says he wants to dedicate to me his *Evolution de la propriété*.[568] Very much obliged to him. In general I would rather remain undedicated, but I leave it entirely to him.

Praise no one happy before his death, said Solon. He must have foreseen the case of my *présidence d'honneur*[a] over the *présidence effective*[b] of Regnard! Who ever would have thought that! of all men, Regnard!

Ever yours
F. E.

September No.

Page 4 – alinéa 2, *Verkehrsmittel* is given *moyens de communication*.[c] *Verkehr* we used in the *Manifesto* generally in the sense of *Handelsverkehr*,[d] and later on it is always translated correctly *échange*. In this passage *échange* would be better, though it is of no importance.

Page 7 alinéa 1: La Bourgeoisie, the *e* left out in the text.

Page 10: alinéa 2: der *Hausbesitzer*,[e] der *Krämer*,[f] is rendered: *le petit propriétaire*[g]; would it not be more textual to say: *le propriétaire*,[g] *le boutiquier*,[f] *le prêteur sur gages*[h]?

Page 12, line 5: misprint: garantie *locale* for: *légale*.

Page 15, "   3: Courgeoisie instead of *Bourg*eoisie.

You see I must take refuge in common misprints in order to find fault! with the text in the October No. I cannot even manage to do that.

First published, in Russian,   Reproduced from the original
in *Istoriya* SSSR, No. 5, 1965

                                        Published in English for the first time

214

ENGELS TO AUGUST BEBEL AND PAUL SINGER

IN BERLIN

London, 14 November 1894

To August Bebel & Paul Singer

The thousand pounds I have bequeathed to you for 'electoral pur-

---

[a] honorary presidency – [b] actual presidency – [c] means of communication – [d] trade relations – [e] landlord - [f] shopkeeper – [g] small proprietor – [h] usurer

poses'—from which death duty will be deducted—had to be bequeathed in this form because I could not bequeath the money to the party in any other form if it was to be regarded as a legally valid legacy in this country. That was the only reason for the above proviso. So first of all make sure that you get the money and, when you have got it, that it does not fall into the hands of the Prussians. And while passing a resolution on these points mind you drink a bottle of good wine; do this is memory of me.

Friedrich Engels

First published in
the newspaper *Sächsisches.
Volksblatt*, No. 125,
22 October, 1895

Printed according to the original

Published in English for the first time

215

ENGELS TO EDUARD BERNSTEIN[422]

IN LONDON

[London,] 14 November 1894

Dear Ede,

Herewith two sheets,[a] nos. 21/22.

Meissner wants to know whether there are any more errata. If you have any to hand, please let me have them[407]; otherwise don't bother; for in that case I shall write to Meissner tomorrow, telling him to close the list.

Should you be writing to the Baron *today*, please let him know that I am sending him Ferri's *Socialismo e scienza positiva* with Labriola's notes and at Labriola's request. No hurry about this if your letter has already gone off.

Many regards; all well here.

Yours

F. E.

First published, in Russian,
in *Marx-Engels Archives*,
Vol. 1, 1924

Printed according to the original

Published in English for the first time

---

[a] K. Marx, *Capital*, Vol. III

216

ENGELS TO LAURA LAFARGUE AND ELEANOR MARX-AVELING

London, 14 November 1894

To Laura Lafargue and Eleanor Marx-Aveling
My dear girls,

I have to address to you a few words with regard to my will.

First you will find that I have taken the liberty of disposing of all my books, including those received from you after Mohr's death, in favour of the German party. The whole of these books constitute a library so unique, and so complete at the same time, for the history and the study of Modern Socialism and all the sciences on which it is dependent, that it would be a pity to disperse it again. To keep it together, and to place it at the same time at the disposal of those desirous to use it, has been a wish expressed to me long ago by Bebel and other leaders of the German Socialist Party, and as they do indeed seem to be the best people for that purpose, I have consented. I hope that under the circumstances you will pardon my action and give your consent too.

Second. I have had many a discussion with Sam Moore as to the possibility of providing, in my will, in some way for our dear Jenny's children. Unfortunately, English law stands in the way. It could only be done under almost impossible conditions, where the expense would more than eat up the funds to be taken care of. I therefore had to give it up. Instead, I have left each of you *three*-eighths of the residue of my estate after defraying legacies etc. Of these, *two*-eighths are intended for yourselves, and the third eighth is meant to be held by each of you in trust for Jenny's children, to be used as you and the children's guardian, Paul Lafargue, may think best. In this way you are freed from all responsibility with regard to English law and can act as your own moral sense and love for the children may dictate.

The money I owe to the children for shares of profits on Mohr's writings are put down in my ledger, and will be paid by my Executors to the party who, according to English law, will be the children's legal representative.

And now good bye, my dear, dear girls. May you live long and healthily in body and soul and enjoy it!

Frederick Engels

Tussy will have to inform Meissner, Dietz, and the *Vorwärts* Buchhandlung[a] of Berlin that they will henceforth have to pay to *her direct* any sums due to the heirs of Karl Marx for honorarium etc. As to Sonnenschein, that will have to be settled in some other manner, the agreement about *Capital*[b] being between him and me.

F. E.

First published in the language of the original (English) in: F. Engels, P. et L. Lafargue, *Correspondance*, t. III, Parts, 1959

Reproduced from the original

217

ENGELS TO KARL KAUTSKY

IN STUTTGART

[London,] 15 November 1894

Dear Baron,

I have just been going through Tussy's article[c] with her—at one point there is an amendment by which she rightly, or so it seems to me, sets store but which, because it was written on a sheet of paper, she failed to include. It belongs at the end of the preface, which should read: 'in general Mr Brentano's manner of writing history is distinguished by three characteristics: 1.' etc.

Will you still be able to add this?

By the time this arrives you may already have seen from the *Vorwärts*[421]

---

[a] book-shop – [b] about English translation of Vol. I – [c] E. Marx-Aveling, 'Wie Lujo Brentano zitirt,' *Die Neue Zeit*, No, 9, 1894-95, Vol. I

that I am being forced to write an agrarian article[a] upon which I am working at this moment and which I shall very shortly have the honour of placing at your disposal.

Yours,

F. E.

First published in:
Aus der Frühzeit des Marxismus.
Engels Briefwechsel mit Kautsky,
Prag, 1935

Printed according to the original

Published in English for the first time

218

ENGELS TO EDUARD BERNSTEIN

IN LONDON

[London,] 20 November 1894

Dear Ede,

The *Sozialdemokrat* (Berlin) contained a translation of Lafargue's report on the programme agraire.[419] Lafargue has drawn my attention to it since he has no copy of the original to hand. Now I cannot find my copy of the *Sozialdemokrat* (it was in the issue of 18 November and possibly an earlier one as well). Can you lend them to me for a day?

I have a bad cold but am getting better.

Yours,

F. E.

Many regards.

First published, in Russian,
in *Marx-Engels Archives,*
Vol. I, 1924

Printed according to the original

Published in English for the first time

---

[a] F. Engels, 'The Peasant Question in France and Germany'

219

ENGELS TO KARL KAUTSKY

IN STUTTGART

London, 22 November 1894
41 Regent's Park Road, N. W.

Dear Baron,
The agrarian article[a] goes off to you today by *registered* book post.
Since the handwriting is rotten, may I have the proofs? They will be
promptly attended to.
Am just reading Ledebour's reply to you.[424] The chap's trying to be too
clever by half. As though, two years ago, you could have foreseen what
Vollmar would be like today. And it really is a bit much to conclude,
merely because the small peasant has been told there is no intention of
forcibly evicting him, that the intention is to provide economic conditions such as will enable him to continue farming on his own account.
Obviously, as things are today, you would have worded this or that passage differently. But nobody is proof against verbal hair-splitting and my
article might suffer exactly the same fate.
I look forward to seeing how the polemic initiated by Bebel is going to
develop.[425] It was long overdue.
I simply have not got the time just now to go into the matter of the
International's attitude to the question of land ownership. Besides, it has
been a ticklish point so far as the International is concerned. Firstly because of the Proudhonists in France, Belgium, etc., and their enthusiasm
for parcels of land, and secondly because of Bakunin's hobby-horse, the
abolition of inheritance, which tended to obscure the issue.[426]
Needless to say, the *Vorwärts* has come down in favour of unity, i.e. of
hushing things up. Nothing can be done about this for the present. But
anyone who hushes things up can now only be of assistance to Vollmar
and will have to bear the consequences. The only correct thing for *me* to
do is, I think, to intervene in an absolutely objective way and leave personalities completely out of it. Otherwise it will again be said that I am

---

[a] F. Engels, 'The Peasant Question in France and Germany'

trying to influence the party from without, etc.

Apropos, could you, when convenient, insert the enclosed review[427] in such a way that people don't realise it emanates from me? I don't want to put a correction in the *Vorwärts*, or Liebknecht would again append some rigmarole or other, and yet I cannot allow the thing to pass. Congratulations on son no. III—as you will have heard, we have also had a lying-in here; Louise having born a strong girl, everything went off all right and the baby girl ought to be called 'tippling Amalie'!

Yours,

F. E.

First published in:
*Aus der Frühzeit des Marxismus
Engels Briefwechsel mit Kautsky*
Prag, 1935

Printed according to the original

Published in English for the first time

220

ENGELS TO PAUL LAFARGUE[35]

AT LE PERREUX

London, 22 November 1894

My dear Lafargue,

I have found your report in the *Sozialdemokrat*.[419] That was lucky, for it has allowed me to put the responsibility for quite a few things on a somewhat careless editorship and to conclude that, although I did not agree with what the Nantes resolution[406] said, I think I agree with what it tried to say. At the same time I have tried to be as friendly as possible; but in view of the way this resolution is being abused in Germany, it is no good remaining silent about it.

The fact is you allowed yourself to lean a bit too much towards the opportunist tendency. At Nantes you came near to sacrificing the future of the Party to a momentary triumph. There is still time to call a halt: if my article[a] can contribute towards this, I shall be happy. In Germany—

---

[a] F. Engels, 'The Peasant Question in France and Germany'

where Vollmar went so far as to suggest that the large peasants in Bavaria, each with the 10-30 hectares, should enjoy all the benefits that you had promised to the small French peasants[418]—in Germany Bebel took up the challenge, and the matter will be exhaustively discussed; it will not come off the agenda until it has been thrashed out. You will have seen in *Vorwärts* Bebel's speech in the 2nd electoral constituency of Berlin.[425] He complains with reason that the party is going bourgeois. That is the misfortune of all extreme parties when the time approaches for them to become 'possible'. But our Party cannot go beyond a certain limit in this respect without betraying itself, and it seems to me that in France as in Germany we have now reached that point. Fortunately there is still time to call a halt.

For some while I have not seen your letters in *Vorwärts*, and I thought there was some misunderstanding; last Wednesday I was happy to receive a number of 'Gallus'.[a] If there are difficulties with the editorial board, let me know, perhaps I could be of some use to you.

If the Russian Government is spending money to strengthen its currency, that is an infallible sign that a new loan is in the air; the French are the only ones who might be tempted; let's hope they aren't. But when Russia needs gold, she must naturally try to get it!

Loria will be even more pleased when he reads the preface,[b] he is treated there as he deserves and without the least regard for 'il primo economista dell' Italia'.[c]

Young William[d] is behaving admirably. He gets it into his head to combat 'subversive tendencies'[428] 'and starts by subverting his own government.[429] Ministers fall like lead soldiers. The poor young man had to keep quiet and lie low for over eight months; he can't stand it any longer, he blows up—and there you are! At a time when we are winning a quarter of Belgium,[412] when electoral reform in Austria is about to send our people into Parliament, when in Russia everything is in a state of uncertainty about the future—the young man gets it into his head to outdo Crispi and Casimir Périer! You can tell the effect this will have in Germany from the fact that at the Frankfurt Congress[418] the delegates, or at least many of them, called for a new repressive law as the best means for the Party to gain ground!

---

[a] [P. Lafargue] Gallus, 'Der landwirtschaftliche Kredit in Frankreich', *Vorwärts*, No. 259, 6 November 1894. – [b] F. Engels, – [d] Preface [to K. Marx's *Capital*, Vol. III] – [c] 'the foremost Italian economist' – [d] William II

The situation in Austria is interesting. Since the death of his son,[a] the Emperor[b] has been afraid of the fall of his dynasty in the near future. His heir presumptive[c] is an arrogant imbecile of the utmost unpopularity. The Hungarians are not likely to tolerate him, they are demanding personal union pure and simple to start with, to be followed by total separation and complete independence. To tie his successor's hands in advance, Francis Joseph is trying to strengthen Parliament and make it more genuinely representative. That is why he has agreed with his friend Taaffe on a fairly extensive electoral reform.[270] But Parliament, an assembly of privileged persons, a real States General of 1789[d] (elected by categories: large land-owners, commerce, towns, rural areas), turns it down, and Taaffe goes out. Thereupon the Emperor, like a true constitutional monarch, appoints a Minister from the majority,[e] a coalition of Liberals, Poles, etc., all arch-reac-tionaries. But he makes them promise that in return they will introduce an electoral reform of their own kind and that within a year. The year runs out with all kinds of abortive attempts. Thereupon the Emperor puts them in a position to keep their word—and that is why for the last 3 weeks Vienna has been talking of nothing but electoral reform. But the coalition is in-capable of producing anything; at the first positive proposition they start fighting among themselves. So that probably Taaffe will shortly replace them and re-table his Bill, and if Parliament turns it down he will dissolve it and grant the reform, which the Constitution allows him to do. So here you have 'fellow traveller' Francis Joseph pushing from one side and Victor Adler from the other! But what an irony of history that this Emperor, cre-ated in December 1848 deliberately to crush the Revolution, should be called upon to inaugurate a fresh one 46 years later!

Kiss Laura for me.

Ever yours,

F. E.

Louise and the child are well, she and Freyberger send their greetings.

First published in part in: Printed according to the original
Le Socialiste No. 115, 24 November,
1900 and in full in F. Engels,   Translated from the French
P. et L. Lafargue, *Correspondance*,
t. III, Paris, 1959

[a] Rudolf – [b] Francis Joseph – [c] Francis Ferdinand – [d] in France – [e] Alfred von Windischgrätz

221

ENGELS TO JOSSIF ATABEKJANZ

IN STUTTGART

London, 23 November 1894
41 Regent's Park Road, N. W.

Dear Comrade,

Many thanks for having translated my *Entwicklung des Sozialismus* and, recently, the *Communist Manifesto*,[a] into your Armenian mother tongue. Unfortunately I am not in a position to comply with your request that I send you a short introduction to the latter translation. I cannot very well write anything that is to be published in a language which I do not understand. Were I to do so as a favour to yourself, I could not refuse to oblige others, in which case it might happen that my words were ushered into the world in unintentionally, if not deliberately, garbled form, while I might not learn about it for years, if ever.

Then there is another reason—grateful though I am to you for your interesting exposé of the Armenian situation—namely, that I do not regard it as right or fair to try and express an opinion on matters of which I have not acquired a knowledge from *personal study*. Particularly in this instance when the people concerned belong to an oppressed nationality unfortunate enough to be trapped between the *Scylla* of Turkish and the *Charybdis* of Russian despotism, a situation in which Russian Tsarism speculates on playing the role of liberator and the servile Russian press never fails to make the most of every word uttered in favour of Armenian liberation by turning it to the advantage of a Tsarism bent on conquest.

If, however, I am to tell you honestly what I think, it is this—that Armenia's liberation from the Turks *and* Russians will become a possibility only on the day when Russian Tsarism is overthrown.

With best wishes for the welfare of your people,

Yours,

F. Engels

---

[a] F. Engels, *Socialism: Utopian and Scientific*; K. Marx and F. Engels, *Manifesto of the Communist Party*

First published in: *Dokumente des Sozialismus*, Bd. III, Heft 12, Stuttgart, 1903

Printed according to the original

Published in English for the first time

222

ENGELS TO NIKOLAI DANIELSON

IN ST. PETERSBURG

London, 24 November 1894
41 Regent's Park Road, N. W.

My dear Sir,

I am in possession of your kind letters 7 and 11 June, 15 October and 12 November.

Of Mr. Struve's works I have only seen the article in Braun's *Centralblatt*,[a] and cannot therefore speak as to what assertions he may have made. If in my letters you find any *facts* that may be useful to you in your reply, you are welcome to make use of them.[430] But as to any *opinions* of mine, I am afraid, your opponents—not perhaps Mr. Struve but the Russian press generally—would use them in a way they do not warrant. I am daily and weekly assailed by Russian friends to reply to Russian reviews and books in which the words of our author[b] are not only misinterpreted but misquoted and where they say my interference would suffice to set the matter right. I have constantly declined doing so, because I cannot, without giving up real and serious work, be dragged into controversies going on in a faraway country, in a language which I do not yet read with as much ease as the better known western languages, and in a literature whereof at best I but see occasional fragments and where it is utterly impossible for me to follow the debate closely and in all its phases and passages. There are people everywhere who, in order to defend a position once taken up by them, do not shrink from any distortion or unfair manoeuvre; and if this is the case with the writings of our author, I am afraid I should get no better treatment and be compelled, finally, to interfere in the debate, both for other people's sake and my own. In fact, if my

---

[a] P. Struve, 'Zur Beurtheilung der kapitalistischen Entwickelung Russlands', *Sozialpolitisches Centralblatt*, No. 1, 2 October 1893 – [b] Karl Marx

opinions as stated in private letters, did appear in the Russian press with my sanction, I should then have no defence *via-à-vis* my Russian friends here and on the Continent, who urge me actively to interfere in Russian debates and to set this or that man right on this and that point; I should not have any valid reason to decline, as they would be able to tell me: you *have* already once interfered in Russian debates; you must own that our present case is quite as important as that of Mr. D., so if you please, treat us as you have treated him. And then, my time would be no longer my own, and my interference in Russian debates would after all be extremely inefficacious and incomplete.

These are the reasons which compel me, to my very great regret, to request you, not to insist on quoting opinions of mine, at least not *as mine.*

I will try to forward to you some continuation of what you have already received.[a]

Yours very truly
L. K.[b]

First published, in Russian,
in *Minuvshiye godi*, No. 2,
1908

Reproduced from the original

Published in English for the first time

223

ENGELS TO WILHELM LIEBKNECHT

IN BERLIN

[London,] 24 November 1894
41 Regent's Park Road, N. W.

Dear Liebknecht,

I have written to Bebel,[25] suggesting that, in political debate, one should always consider things calmly and do nothing in haste or in the heat of the moment. I myself having often come a cropper in consequence. On the other hand, however, I also have a small bone to pick with yourself.

---

[a] proof-sheets of *Capital*, Vol. III – [b] Louise Kautsky's initials are used as Engels' penname in correspondence with Danielson.

Whether Bebel's conduct in the assembly was *inept* is open to question.[425] But in point of fact he was absolutely right. to As editor of the central organ you are, of course, bound to cast oil on troubled waters, to argue away even what are very real differences, TO MAKE THINGS PLEASANT ALL ROUND, and to promote unity in the party until the day the breach comes. Thus as *editor* you may have deplored Bebel's conduct. But what was displeasing to the *editor* should have been welcome to the *party leader*, namely the fact that there should be men who do not always have to sport an obligatory pair of editor's spectacles upon their noses, and who also remind the editor that, in his capacity as party leader, he would do well now and again to view the world with the naked eye rather than through rose-tinted spectacles.

On the very eve of the Frankfurt Party Conference the Bavarians formed what was tantamount to a *Sonderbund* at Nuremberg.[431] They arrived in Frankfurt with what was manifestly an *ultimatum*. To add insult to injury, Vollmar spoke of *marching separately*, while Grillo[a] declared: 'Resolve any thing you like; we *shall not conform*.' They claimed special rights for the Bavarians and dubbed their opponents in the party 'Prussians' and 'Berliners'. They demanded that the grant of supplies be approved, as also an agrarian policy which is actually further to the *right* than that of the petty bourgeoisie. Instead of promptly putting a spoke in their wheels, as had always been done before, the Party Conference did not venture to pass a resolution. So if that wasn't the time for Bebel to speak of the penetration of the party by petty-bourgeois elements then I'm at a loss to know when he should have done.

And what did the *Vorwärts* do? Fasten upon the form of Bebel's attack, say things weren't so bad after all and place itself in such 'diametrical opposition' to him that only the—in the event inevitable—'misunderstanding' of Bebel's opponents forced you to declare that your diametrical opposition referred simply to the *form* taken by Bebel's attack, but that, so far as its substance was concerned—the matter of supplies and the agrarian question—he had been right and you were on his side.[432] I should have thought that the mere fact of your having been *forced* to make this statement *after the event* would have proved to you that you had strayed much further to the right than Bebel could have strayed to the left.

And after all, the whole debate hinged solely upon the two points in which the action of the Bavarians culminated, namely, the opportunism

---

[a] Karl Grillenberger

of granting supplies in order to catch the petty bourgeoisie, and the opportunism of Vollmar's agrarian propaganda intended to catch the middle and big peasants. These, and the sectarian attitude of the Bavarians were the only practical questions under consideration, and if Bebel took them up at the point at which the Party Conference had left the Party in the lurch, you ought to be grateful to him. If he described the impossible position created by the Party Conference as attributable to the growing influence of philistinism in the party, he was merely placing a particular question in the general context in which it belongs, and that is also worthy of recognition. And if he forced a debate on all this, he was only doing what absolutely had to be done and ensuring that, when confronted by urgent questions, the next Party Conference should act in full knowledge of the facts instead of being left gaping, as at Frankfurt.

The danger of a split cannot be laid at the door of Bebel who called a spade a spade. It must be laid at the door of the Bavarians who presumed to act in a way hitherto unprecedented in the party, much to the glee of the vulgar democrats on the *Frankfurter Zeitung* who recognise in Vollmar and the Bavarians men of their own stamp, while the latter rejoice and become ever more audacious,

You say Vollmar is not a traitor. Maybe. Nor do I think he regards himself as such. But what would you call a man who asks of a proletarian party that it should oblige the Upper Bavarian big and middle peasants, owners of anything between ten and thirty hectares, by perpetuating a state of affairs based on the exploitation of farm servants and day labourers? A proletarian party, expressly founded for the perpetuation of wage slavery! The man may be an anti-Semite, a bourgeois democrat, a Bavarian particularist and anything else you care to name, but a Social Democrat? Come to that, in a *growing* workers' party, the accretion of petty-bourgeois elements is inevitable, nor does it do any harm. Any more than the accretion of 'academics',[a] failed students, etc. A few years ago they still constituted a danger. Now we are able to digest them. But the process of digestion must be allowed to run its course. And for this, hydrochloric acid is needed; if there is not enough of it (as Frankfurt went to show), we ought to be thankful to Bebel for giving us an extra dose, thereby enabling us properly to digest the non-proletarian elements.

For it is in this that the restoration of true harmony in the party con-

---

[a] persons with higher education

sists, not in seeking to do away with every question involving genuine internal controversy by ignoring or denying its existence.

According to you, what is at stake is 'the bringing about of effective action'. Very nice, too, but when exactly is the action going to start?[a]

First published, in Russian, abridged in the newspaper *Pravda*, No. 195, 17 July 1931 and in full in: Marx and Engels, *Works*. First Russian Edition, Vol. XXIX, Moscow, 1946

Printed according to a typewritten copy collated with the text in: W. Liebknecht, *Briefwechsel mit Karl Marx und Friedrich Engels*, The Hague, 1963

Published in English for the first time

224

ENGELS TO MRS KARPELES

IN VIENNA

[London,] 30 November 1894
41 Regent's Park Road, N. W.

Dear Madam,

May I tender my warmest thanks for the delightful present you were so kind as to send me for my birthday? I value it all the more highly, not only for being your own handiwork, but also and above all for your having found leisure to do it at a time when you already had enough and more than enough to do for the little one that is on its way. For during that self-same time I was again afforded an opportunity of seeing, here in my own house, what a multitude of cares and preoccupations the expectation of motherhood involves.[b] I have all the more reason to pride myself in a present made for me at such a time.

I put it to use at once, on my birthday, when I took a short siesta. One sleeps upon it as sweetly as the proverbial 'quiet conscience' upon a 'good pillow'. In fact I feel pretty sure that it would be able to cope without difficulty even with a pretty uneasy conscience.

---

[a] the end of this letter is not extant – [b] Engels is referring to Louise Freyberger's expectant child

I was glad to hear from Ludwig that you and your little one are still keeping well and trust that you will continue to do so.

Again, many thanks and kindest regards to you and to Dr Karpeles from

Yours very sincerely,
F. Engels

First published, in Russian, in: Marx and Engels, *Works*, Second Russian Edition, Vol. 39, Moscow, 1966

Printed according to the original

Published in English for the first time

225

ENGELS TO FRIEDRICH ADOLPH SORGE[113]

IN HOBOKEN

London, 4 December 1894

Dear Sorge,

Thank you and your wife for your good wishes. Between ourselves, my 75th year doesn't hold out quite so much promise as previous ones. True I am still nimble enough on my pins, besides having an appetite for work and a reasonable capacity for it, but nevertheless I find that stomach upsets and colds, which I could once afford to treat with supreme contempt, now demand the most respectful treatment. But that is nothing so long as it amounts to nothing more.

Yesterday I sent you three copies of the *Preface* to Volume III.ᵃ One for the luckless Stiebeling who has sent me several specimens of his stuff.ᵇ One for P. Fireman, D. Phil., if you know or can discover his address. Please give the third, after you have done with it, to Schlüter who might be able to put it to good use. In about a week's time at the most I hope to be able to send you a copy of the actual book, having been notified that this is on its way. In addition today, rolled up and sent Book Post;

1. *Sozialdemokrat*
2. *Justice*, which I shall again be sending you regularly because of the

---

ᵃ of *Capital* – ᵇ G. C. Stiebeling, *Das Werthgesetz und die Profit-Rate*, New York, [1890]

wrangling with the Germans, from which they can't desist.[433] Nearly everything the paper says about the triumphs of the Social Democratic Federation[44] is a lie; compared with other organisations, especially the Independent Labour Party,[114] the Social Democratic Federation is dwindling and, if things go on like this, it will soon dwindle into nothingness. Unfortunately the Independent Labour Party no longer has a proper paper.

3. *Glühlichter* from Vienna and *Wahrer Jakob* from Stuttgart, so that you may acquaint yourself with the 'wit' the party has at its disposal.

4. Bebel's speech in Berlin and his four articles attacking Grillenberger and Vollmar.[434]

The latter is the most interesting of the lot. The Bavarians, who have become very, very opportunistic and are already *almost* an ordinary People's Party (i.e. most of the leaders and many of the party's more recent recruits), had voted in favour of the general estimates in the Bavarian Landtag, while Vollmar, in particular, had begun to agitate on behalf of the peasants so as to catch the big peasants of Upper Bavaria—men with 25-80 ACRES of land (10-30 hectares) and thus *quite unable to manage without wage labour*—but *not their labourers*. Having no high hopes of the Frankfurt Party Conference[418] they organised, *a week before the latter*, a Bavarian Party Conference of their own in the course of which they constituted what amounted to a Sonderbund,[431] in as much as they agreed that at Frankfurt the Bavarian delegation should, on all questions relating to Bavaria, vote *as a body* and in accordance with the Bavarian resolutions previously settled upon. So, having arrived there, they declared that they had *had* to grant the general estimates in Bavaria, there having been no other alternative and that it was, furthermore a purely Bavarian question in which no one else had any business to poke his nose. In other words, if you resolve anything we Bavarians do not like, if you reject our ultimatum, then it will be your fault if there's a split!

Such was the claim, unprecedented in the annals of the party, with which they confronted the other delegates who were utterly unprepared for it. And to such extremes has the clamour for unity been taken in recent years that, having regard to the influx of as yet insufficiently trained elements during the same period, it is small wonder that this attitude, incompatible as it is with the party's continued existence, should have got by without the peremptory rebuff it deserved, and that no resolution should have been taken on the question of supplies.

Now let us suppose the Prussians, who are in the majority at the Party Conference, were also to hold a preliminary congress and were to pass resolutions there on, say, the attitude of the Bavarians—resolutions binding upon all the Prussian delegates so that the whole lot, both the majority and the minority, voted as a body for those resolutions at the General Party Conference, what would be the good of holding General Party Conferences at all? And what would the Bavarians say if the Prussians were to do exactly what they themselves have just done?

In short, the matter could not be allowed to rest at that, and it was now that Bebel stepped into the breach. He simply put the question back on the agenda and it is now being debated. Bebel is by far the most lucid and far-sighted man of the lot.

I have been corresponding with him regularly for some fifteen years and we see eye to eye about almost everything. Liebknecht, on the other hand, is very hidebound in his outlook and the old democrat of South German-federalist, particularist complexion in him is forever coming to the surface. Worse still, he cannot tolerate the fact that Bebel, who has long since outgrown him, refuses to submit to his guidance although he puts up willingly with his presence at his side. Furthermore, so badly has he managed the central organ, the *Vorwärts*—mainly because of the jealousy with which he guards his LEADERSHIP, wanting to direct everything and in fact directing nothing, i.e. placing obstacles everywhere—that the paper, which could be the best in Berlin, serves only to provide the party with profits amounting to 50,000 marks but no political influence whatsoever. Needless to say, Liebknecht is now intent on acting as mediator and pours scorn on Bebel, but in my view, it's the latter who will turn out to be right. In Berlin the Executive and the best of our chaps are already taking his side and I am convinced that, if he appeals to the party at large, he will get a big majority. Meanwhile we must wait and see. I would also send you the Vollmariad, etc., but have only got one copy of the same for my own use.

Louise and the baby both well.

Warm regards to you and your wife. I trust your eyes will soon be better again, as also your other infirmities.

Your old friend,
F. E.

First published abridged in:
Briefe und Auszüge aus Briefen

Printed according to the original

von Joh. Phil. Becker, Jos. Dietzgen,
Friedrich Engels. Karl Marx u. A. an
F. A. Sorge und Andere, Stuttgart, 1906
and in full, in Russian, in: Marx and
Engels, *Works*, First Russian Edition,
Vol. XXIX, Moscow, 1946

Published in English in full
for the first time

226

ENGELS TO FILIPPO TURATI

IN MILAN

[London,] 4 December 1894
41 Regent's Park Road

My dear Turati,

Where the deuce do you find the patience to keep writing to this dear *Monsieur E.*? But let's leave aside the bourgeois titles. As to your students, I regret infinitely that I am unable to come to their aid other than by giving them my best wishes.[435] My time is so occupied that I cannot get down even to the most urgent matters at hand. The same day as I receive your card, one addresses the same request to me on behalf of Berlin students; I am obliged to send them the same refusal as I do to your friends. These little things are but trifles if taken separately, yet when all this happens day after day with a desperate regularity, it all adds up to a considerable loss of time. Be so kind as to make my excuses to your young friends to whom, nevertheless, I wish complete success.

I enclose my preface to the 3d volume of *Capital* for the benefit of citizeness Anna—there are several lines in which one might become interested in Italy.

It was good of you to cite Bebel in the *Critica Sociale*.[425] Bebel has said bitter, but quite necessary truths. This was more opportune than the opportunism of his adversaries.

Yours truly,
F. E.

Please note the change of my address.

First published in the
language of the original (French)
in: *Annali*, an. I, Milano, 1958

Printed according to the original

Translated from the French

Published in English for the first time

227

ENGELS TO FRIEDRICH ADOLPH SORGE

IN HOBOKEN

London, 12 December 1894

Dear Sorge,

Today one copy of Marx's *Capital*, Vol. III, has gone off to you by registered Book Post. I trust you will get it.

'What has earned us such an undeserved stroke of luck as the 'lese-majestie' suit brought at little Willie's[a] behest against our chaps for having remained seated *in the Reichstag*, is beyond my comprehension.[436] No one could have done us a greater service. Little Willie and 'Mr von Köller, Whatever they do there's worse to foller' are a fine pair and as if cut out to get everything into a mess and us—out of it.

Bebel has emerged victorious. In the first place, after Bebel's articles Vollmar broke off the controversy,[434] in the second, his appeal to the Executive was most resolutely rejected and, in the third, he appealed to the parliamentary group but the latter, having been declared incompetent by Bebel, admitted its incompetence, which means that the matter will come up before the next Party Conference, when Bebel can be *certain* of a majority of two-thirds or three-quarters.

It is the third campaign Vollmar has fought for a leading position in the party outside of Bavaria. On the first occasion he demanded that we should actively support Caprivi and become government socialists.[437] On the second, that we should go in for state socialism and assist the present German Empire in its socialist experiments.[438] On both he got a flea in his ear. And now he has got another.

---

[a] William II

The act of staying seated in the Reichstag has impressed the French more than all the work the party has done over the past thirty years. Between ourselves, the Parisians—and I mean the Parisians, not the French—have gone *very much* to seed. Their love of fine phrases and their respect for the melodramatic are gradually becoming intolerable.

I hope you and your wife are well.

Warm regards to you both.

Yours,

F. E.

Out of gratitude to Schlüter for sending me the CENSUS REPORTS,[a] etc., I have also sent him a copy of Volume III[b] by *registered* BOOK POST. But since I do not know whether his address, 935 Washington, still holds good, I have sent it to him care of the *Volkszeitung*, P. 0. Box 1512, N. Y. City. Would you be so good as to let him know this?

First published abridged in:
*Briefe und Auszüge aus Briefen
von Joh. Phil. Becker, Jos. Dietzgen,
Friedrich Engels, Karl Marx u. A,
an F. A. Sorge und Andere*, Stuttgart,
1906 and In full, in Russian, in:
Marx and Engels, *Works*, First

Russian Edition, Vol. XXIX,
Moscow, 1946

Printed according to the original

Published in English for the first time

228

ENGELS TO VICTOR ADLER

IN VIENNA

London, 14 December 1894
41 Regent's Park Road, N. W.

Dear Victor,

Your letters of 12 and 26 safely received. So the K. Kautsky business has been settled. Best thanks for your good wishes for my birthday. I can assure you that it has been brought home to me and impressed upon my

---

[a] Department of the Interior, Census Office. *Compendium of the Eleventh Census: 1890*, Parts I-II, Washington, 1892-1894 – [b] of *Capital*

mind that I can no longer, in my seventy-fifth year, permit myself those imprudences you reprehend. On the contrary, I am on the strictest of diets, treat my alimentary canal like a grumpy bureaucratic chief whose every whim must be obeyed and, to ward off coughs, bronchial catarrh and the like, submit to being wrapped up, kept warm and generally maltreated in every conceivable way, as is only meet and right for a decrepit old man. But enough of that.

I need hardly tell you how pleased I was about the resolute stand Bebel adopted after the feeble Party Conference.[425] I was also pleased to have been indirectly compelled by Vollmar to throw in a word or two on this account.[a] We have in fact been victorious all along the line. First, Vollmar's exit from the lists after Bebel's four articles[434] in itself an unequivocal retreat, then the rebuff administered by the Executive; then the repudiation by the parliamentary group of the claim that it, rather than the Party Conference, should act as arbiter. I.e. Vollmar has suffered defeat after defeat in this, his third unsuccessful campaign. That should suffice even an erstwhile papal Zouave.[439] I have written Liebknecht two letters about this,[b] from which he will have derived little pleasure. The man is becoming ever more obstructive. He still claims to have the best nerves in the party—no great shakes, to go by his rotten speech in the Reichstag the day before yesterday.[440] Nor, it seems, has this gone unnoticed in government circles where an attempt is clearly being made to help him onto his legs again by accusing him of lesemajestie,[436] allegedly committed *a posteriori*.

That affair proves, by the way, either that William[c] and von Köller are completely crazy or that they are deliberately trying to engineer a coup d'état. Hohenlohe's speech has demonstrated that he is an utterly gormless,[d] feeble-minded, weak-willed old gentleman, and nothing but Mr von Köller's man of straw. Köller himself is a typical Junker—vain, forceful and narrow-minded, and is capable of presenting himself to Little Willie as the man who will put paid to 'subversion' and carry out to the very letter His Majesty's intentions with regard to the restoration of the royal prerogative. And William is capable of saying in reply: 'You are a man after my own heart!' If that's how matters stand—and every day brings fresh indications that it is—then *vogue la galère!*[e] We'll be in for a merry time.

---

[a] F. Engels, *The Peasant Question in France and Germany* – [b] See this volume, pp. 373-75; the editors do not possess the second letter. – [c] William II – [d] lacking awareness, dull, stupid, uncomprehending – [e] let the worst happen

But now for the most important thing. You express surprise at not having heard from Louise. In which case, might I suggest that you be so good as to answer the extremely urgent letters she has written to you, not only those about her acting as correspondent for you over here and whether you would also like articles from anyone else and, if so, who—but also and above all those about the offer of money.

Months ago, in September or early October, she wrote to you saying: 'There is now a group of people who, though not members of the party, nevertheless have confidence in you and in particular believe that you are the man to help the daily *Arbeiter-Zeitung*[377] along the road to financial success as well, always providing that you are *given the leading position*.' They are therefore prepared to assign to you a considerable sum for the daily *Arbeiter-Zeitung*—amounting, I understand, to some 5,000 fl., on condition that:

1. You accept the senior position on the paper.

2. The thing is treated purely as a business investment and interest is regularly paid.

3. All negotiations, payments, etc., are dealt with by you in Vienna and by Louise over here.

These, to the best of my recollection, were the conditions upon which the offer was made. 'Well, there has been no response of any kind from you, either to the above or to any of Louise's subsequent letters. Last week *she wrote again*, asking for an immediate reply which had to be here by Tuesday, the 11th, at the latest. In vain. Now this can only mean one of two things: Either you in your correspondence are so enmeshed in a web of postal and other kinds of intrigue that it is virtually impossible to get a letter to you, or your disinclination to answer letters is such that you would rather forego the money that has been offered you than write to Louise.

Either way we have got to know where we stand. *The chaps are pressing for a decision* for, if you refuse the money, they will invest it elsewhere. We have therefore been compelled to send this letter to Mrs Anna Pernerstorfer, with the request that she deliver it to you in person and to *no one else*. We would now ask you—*for the very last time*—if you would kindly let us know whether or not you wish to negotiate with us and or Louise regarding the money. If you do, you must tell her how letters are to be addressed to you, whereupon we shall send a reply by 'registered' mail.

Louise and her baby are both very well. The baby grows, flourishes and screams; she is suckling it herself and has plenty and to spare. She and Ludwig send their love, likewise

Yours,

F. E.

First published in: *Victor Adlers Aufsdtze, Reden und Briefe.* Erstes Heft: *Victor Adler und Friedrich Engels*, Vienna, 1922

Printed according to the original

Published in English for the first time

229

ENGELS TO WITOLD JODKO-NARKIEWICZ

IN LONDON

[London,] 14 December 1894
41 Regent's Park Road, N. W.

Dear Jodko,

I certainly would not have the least objection to your translating my article on the peasant question and should be glad if it could also prove helpful to your compatriots.[441]

Yours,

F. Engels

As you see, we have moved house.

First published, in the language of the original, in: *Z Pola walki*, No. 4 (12), 1960

Printed according to the original

Published in English for the first time

230

ENGELS TO LAURA LAFARGUE

AT LE PERREUX

[London,] 17 December 1894

My dear Löhr,

You say, after finishing the 3rd volume^a and before beginning with the 4th, I must long for a little rest. Now I will just tell you what my position is.

I have to follow the movement in five large and a lot of small European countries and the U. S. America. For that purpose I receive 3 German, 2 English, 1 Italian *dailies* and from January 1 the Vienna daily, 7 in all. Of *weeklies* I receive 2 from Germany, 7 Austria, 1 France, 3 America (2 English, 1 German), 2 Italian, and 1 each in Polish, Bulgarian, Spanish and Bohemian, three of which in languages I am still gradually acquiring. Besides that, calls of the most varied sorts of people (just now, a few minutes ago, Polak from Amsterdam sent me a German sculptor penniless and in want of employment) and an ever increasing crowd of correspondents, more than at the time of the International! many of whom expect long explanations and all of them taking away time. With all this and the 3rd volume, I have not, even during the proof-sheet-time, that is the whole of 1894, been able to read *more than one book*.

Now the next thing is the publication of Lassalle's letters to Mohr.[284] Tussy has typed them, they are in my desk, but—thanks to the removal—I have not been able to touch them. That means notes, references to facts long gone by as well as to my own old correspondence with Mohr—and a preface to be written diplomatically.

Then the heaps of arrears of my own. First the complete rewriting of the *Bauernkrieg*[235] which has been out of sale for years, and has been promised as my first work after Vol. III. That requires a considerable study; I hoped to do that along with the proof-sheets, But impossible. Anyhow I shall have to look myself up how to do it.

Then—not to speak of other little jobs hanging over me—I want to write at least the chief chapters out of Mohr's political life: 1842-1852,

---

^{a} of *Capital*

and the International. The latter is the most important and urgent, I intend to do it first. But that requires freedom from interruption, and when shall I get that?[316]

All these things are wanted from me, and moreover a re-edition of Mohr's and my own earlier smaller writings. For that I have been collecting; but have not succeeded in much—. Some more bits are in the *Parteiarchiv* in Berlin.[442] But a good deal is short yet, for instance a copy of the first *Rheinische Zeitung*. If I could get, say 2/3 of the old 1842-50 articles collected, I should start, as I am sure then that for a 2nd edition a lot more would come to light. But we are not so far advanced as yet.

And then Vol. 4.[443] Now of that there is a *very* rough manuscript, of which up to now it in impossible to say how much can be used. I myself cannot again undertake to unravel it and dictate the whole as I did Vol. 2 and 3. My eyesight would break down completely before I was half through. I found that out years ago and tried another dodge. I considered it would be useful to have one or two intelligent men of the younger generation broken in to read Mohr's handwriting. I thought of Kautsky and Bernstein. Kautsky was then still in London (some 6 or 7 years ago). I asked him and he assented; I said I would pay one hundred pounds for the complete 'fair copy' of what there is, and assist him where he could not decipher. He began. Then he left London, took one Heft[a] with him, and for years I heard no more, He was too busy with the *Neue Zeit*, so I had Manuscript and copy returned, as far as the latter went—perhaps 1/8 to 1/6 of the whole.[b] Bernstein too is not only very busy, but suffers from overwork, has not yet completely overcome his neurasthenia, and I hardly dare ask him. I shall see whether Tussy will; if he volunteers, all well; if not I do not intend to run the risk of having it said that I brought on a relapse of his illness by overloading him with work.

That is my position: 74 years the which I am beginning to feel, and work enough for two men of 40. Yes, if I could divide myself into the F. E. of 40 and the F. E. of 34, which would just be 74, then we should soon be all right. But as it is, all I can do is to work on with what is before me and get through it as far and as well as I can.

Now you know my position, and if you have now and then to wait for a letter from me, you will know the reason why.

Last night Bonnier came from Edinbro' and left to-day for Oxford. He

---

[a] notebook – [b] See this volume, p. 71

has cooled down considerably from his first anger over my *Bauernfrage*[a]— *vous nous traitez d'imbéciles*,[b] he wrote to me. Anyhow he was very pleasant and I think he is convinced that they have made a blunder at Nantes.[406] He really believed that it was not only possible but necessary to gain over the mass of the French peasants to Socialism between now and next general elections.

Post time. Must close. I owe you for your share of the
Sonnenschein account for *Capital* (English) £1.31.–
1/3 Share of £5.—received from *Neue Zeit* for the 2 chapters
from Vol. III[c] £1.13.4
And allow me to add as a remembrance that
Christmas is coming £5.–.–
Covered by cheque herewith .... £7.16.5.

Puddings could not be made this year, the little girl of Louise's (which is prosperous and gaining nearly a pound a week in weight) has stopped that. But Paul will have his cake.

Ever yours
F. Engels

First published abridged,
in German, in: *Die Neue Zeit*,
No. 11, 1905-069 Bd. I
and in full, in Russian, in:
Voprosi istorii KPSS, No. 1,1957;
first published in the language of

the original (English) in: F. Engels,
P. et L. Lafargue, *Correspondance*,
t. III, 1959

Reproduced from the original

231

ENGELS TO FYOTR LAVROV[444]

IN PARIS

London, 18 December 1894
41 Regent's Park Road, N. W.

My dear Lavrov,
Mme Lafargue has sent me your letter, and I hasten to assure you that

---

[a] F. Engels, *The Peasant Question in France and Germany* – [b] you call us imbeciles – [c] of *Capital*

I have not at all forgotten about you, But

1) *Dühring*,[a] 3rd edition—I had only 6 copies, which I sent to no one except Mme Lafargue and Mme Aveling. The rest have been taken, as always happens. I have found one more copy which I will send to you immediately.

2) *Capital*, 3rd volume. If it is on sale in Paris and elsewhere, this is because the editor has displayed exemplary avarice towards me. There were copies in *Rome* before I had received a single one! However, I am expecting another delivery in a few days, and then I will be able to send you the copy long since intended for you.

I hope you are keeping well—as for me, I cannot complain, but I am beginning to realise that 74 is not 47. However, events should help us to maintain our vital forces, the whole of Europe is warming up, crises are brewing everywhere, particularly in Russia. The situation cannot last much longer over there. So much the better.

Yours
F. Engels

Please note the change of address!

First published, in Russian,
in: K. Marx and F. Engels,
Works, First Russian Edition,
Vol. XXIX, Mosoow, 1946
Published in English for the first time

Printed according to the original

Translated from the French

232

ENGELS TO PAUL LAFARGUE[35]

AT LE PERREUX

London,18 December 1894
41 Regent's Park Road

My dear Lafargue,

I am returning Lavrov's letter to Laura. I replied to him at once to say

---

[a] F. Engels, *Anti-Dühring*

that he shall have the two books[a] as soon as I myself shall have copies.[b] Meissner supplied me, and still supplies me, after he has supplied everyone else. I am also sending you a copy for *Deville.*

As I said: the (Nantes) *programme*[406] itself has only one pointless clause: the reduction of LEGAL rates of interest, i.e., the revival of the ancient laws against usury whose total uselessness was demonstrated 2,000 years ago. You cannot effectively reduce the rates of interest paid by mortgaged peasants without turning all mortgages on property into debts against the State, in which case you are free to reduce the interest—except that you lose money yourself, when it falls due. And also the clause on hunting, as it is drafted, is self-contradictory.

Not only is young William[c] cracked, but this time he is pushing things to a crisis. The new chancellor[d] is simply a man of straw, the moving spirit in the new government is Köller (*der macht as immer döller,*[e] as *Kladderadatsch* said of him years ago). They are provoking a conflict with the Reichstag. They are going to prosecute Liebknecht for lese-majesty after the closure.[436] They are pressing for a dissolution which will mean a recalcitrant Reichstag in Berlin and then—a little coup d'état. We may look forward to some nice happenings in Germany if everything turns out as these gentlemen visualise.

In Italy, too, the monarchy is hard pressed. The Crown Prince[f] is involved in the Banca Romana to the tune of 300,000 francs, the King[g] in the name of various nominees, for very much larger amounts. All that is well known. Crispi is mortally wounded by Giolitti's sensational move[445]—the whole of Parliament as well as all the higher officials are compromised by it, and in simple-minded Italy they are still so Catholic, that is to say, *pagan,* that all this is done in broad daylight and there is no means of concealing the corruption, of which, on the contrary, they boast—until there is a crisis.

And then, Russia—the unknown, where only one thing is certain: that the present regime will not be able to stand a change of tsar, and there will be a crisis there too.

What you say about the effect produced by the little scene in the Reichstag goes for England as well. All the years of work, all the electoral and real victories count for nothing; a little melodramatic scene—that is

---

[a] K. Marx, *Capital*, Vol. III. – [b] See previous letter. – [c] William II – [d] Prince zu Hohenlohe – [e] Who lets himself go more and more. – [f] Vittorio Emmanuele – [g] Umberto I

the striking, the dazzling thing. How petty people are!

I shall write to Adler about your letters. But there, with the small working strength they have, it seems to me very unlikely that a regular correspondence would suit them, unless it were written in German and ready for the printer. So, strictly speaking, one ought to ask Frankel first. But we shall see.

Ever yours,
F. E.

Laura should have received my letter of yesterday.

First published in:
F. Engels, P. et L. Lafargue,
Correspondance, t. III. Paris,1959

Printed according to the original

Translated from the French

233

ENGELS TO GEORGE WILLIAM LAMPLUGH[446]

IN LONDON

[London] 21 December 1894
41 Regent's Park Road I, N. W.

We have moved to 41 Regent's Park Road. You'll see Dr. Freyberger's name on the door—and shall be glad to see you there whenever you find time to look in—in the meantime a merry Xmas you and your family.

Yours truly
F. Engels

21/12/94, the shortest day, and with a vengeance!

First published, in Russian,
in *Letopisi marksizma*, Book I,
1926

Reproduced from the original

Published in English for the first time

234

ENGELS TO VICTOR ADLER

IN VIENNA

London, 22 December 1894
41 Regent's Park Road, N. W.

Dear Victor,

So the offer of money[a] has at last reached the stage at which we can get down to business. Louise will be letting you have further details.

As regards correspondents over here, please give M. Beer a pseudonym that will so distinguish him from all the other correspondents as to obviate any possibility of confusion. The man is *very* green so far as England is concerned and sees things through Galician-Talmudic spectacles.—I hardly imagine that E. Bernstein will be able to send you a great deal; as it is, he seldom has much time to spare for articles for the *Vorwärts* and prefers to work for the *Neue Zeit.*

Lafargue has asked whether you could make use of him as a contributor. I told him that in the first instance you would have to consider Frankel but that I was unaware of all the circumstances and would write.[b] He—Lafargue—is a lively and interesting writer but his stuff, like the Gallus reports he sends to the *Vorwärts*, is *all in French.* His wife *does not write* German either and speaks it only on fairly rare occasions. Nor is she as fluent as Tussy. I don't know whether it would be convenient for you to do the translating over there yourselves. Lafargue would naturally have a fee in mind, since he has lost his deputy's salary. I couldn't tell him anything about that either.

Things are getting complicated on the Continent. In your country electoral reform is assured—and nowadays, when something like that gets under way, it is not so easy to stop—while Russia is seeing the beginning of the end of Tsarist omnipotence, for it is improbable that autocracy will survive this latest change of monarch; in Italy they are heading straight for a revolution that may cost the monarchy its head, and in the German Empire Little Willie[c] seems intent on crossing the Halys and destroying a great empire. You could hardly wish for a better moment at which to found a daily newspaper—material in plenty and what's more, of a kind

---

[a] See this volume, p. 384 – [b] See this volume, p. 391 – [c] William II

that the other parties are bound to distort and misconstrue, whereas our party is the only one that will construe it aright from the very start.

And now a Merry Christmas to you, your wife (to whom please convey my warm regards) and your children.

Yours,

F. E.

First published in: *Victor Adlers Aufsätze, Reden und Briefe.* Erstes Heft: *Victor Adler und Friedrich Engels*, Vienna, 1922

Printed according to the book

Published in English for the first time

235

ENGELS TO PAUL SINGER[447]

IN BERLIN

[*Excerpt*]

[London, between 26 and 29 December 1894]

...incidentally, your conditions are very favourable. The English workers would leap as high as St. Paul's Cathedral if they got a labour exchange that could force the bourgeois either to justify his refusal to employ a worker before a court of arbitration or take him, etc....

Published in *Vorwärts. Berliner Volksblatt*, No. 1, 1 January 1895 Published in English for the first time

Printed according to the newspaper

236

ENGELS TO VICTOR ADLER[448]

IN VIENNA

[*Draft*]

[London, 27 December 1894]

Dear Victor,

I would ask you to convey my congratulations to the Austrian workers on their daily paper.[377] Its first daily paper invariably signifies a tremendous step forward in the life of a party, especially of a workers' party. It is the first position from which it can tackle its opponents with the same weapons, at least in the field of the press. You have won this position; now the second is at stake: suffrage, parliament. And you are certain of this too, if you exploit the political situation—becoming ever more favourable to you as it is with the same skill as [you have done] in the past fifteen months; if you are determined to act at the right time, but also, as so often necessary, determined to wait at the right time; if you know how to let circumstances act on your behalf.

Good luck and success to the daily *Arbeiter-Zeitung*!

Yours

First published abridged in
the *Arbeiter-Zeitung*. No. 1,
1 January 1895 and in full,
in Russian, in: Marx and
Engels, *Works*, First Russian
Edition, Vol. XXIX, Moscow, 1946

Printed according to the original
collated with the newspaper

Published in English for the first time

237

ENGELS TO LAURA LAFARGUE

AT LE PERREUX

London, 29 December 1894
41 Regent's Park Road, N. W.

My dear Löhr,

Thanks for your news of the 23rd about the Allemanists[21] and their dissensions—this sets me up again as far as the *personalia* of the Parisian movement are concerned. I hope the whole set of Allemanists will soon be smashed up and whatever is decent among them joining our people who, if they wait patiently, seem to stand the best chance of absorbing gradually all the rest.

May the new dailies flourish[449] and soon bring forth a Parisian daily!

As to the preface to the French *Manifest*,[a] my proposal would be that

---

[a] K. Marx and F. Engels, *Manifesto of the Communist Party*

you work out some sort of preface out of the four German ones, giving such information about the fates of the work as may interest your readers, then send me the Manuscript for additions to be proposed by me (I have just received an Armenian translation[a]) to which I might add a few words in my own name.[450] Don't you think that would solve the difficulty?

Last Sunday Tussy being in Manchester sent me your letter to her about Vol. IV.[443] I am quite willing and shall be glad to assist her if she will undertake the work of writing out the original Manuscript.

As to what you say about Mohr's papers and their treatment in case of my death, the matter is simple enough. All these things I hold *in trust for you*, that you know; and consequently on my death they revert to you. In the last will I made (when Sam Moore was here last time but one) there is no special provision, but in the instructions to my executors accompanying it, there is a distinct direction to them, to hand over to Tussy, as the administrator of the will, the whole of Mohr's Manuscripts that are in his own handwriting, also all letters addressed to him with the sole exception of my own correspondence with him.[b] And as Tussy seems to have some doubt about the matter, I shall as soon as Sam Moore comes back in Summer ask him to draw up a new will in which this is distinctly and unmistakably declared. If you have any other wish please let me know.

Adler writes about Paul's correspondence for the daily *Arbeiter Zeitung*: 'was Lafargue anlangt so habe ich nichts gegen *französische* Korrespondenzen, ich werde viel übersetzen müssen. Natürlich wird Frankel regelmässig schreiben—Lafargue ist ein Korrespondent wie ich es für den *Vorwärts* bin, selten, aber dann lang. Nun wäre mir ja mit seinen geistsprühenden Artikeln sehr gedient, wenn ich nicht fürchtete dass er mir dieselben schickt wie an *Vorwärts* und *Echo*.[c] Kannst Du arrangieren dass er mir *etwa zweimal im Monat* oder bei besondern Anlässen schreibt, so wäre es mir ein grosser Gefallen, wir können nur nicht viel zahlen, 20 fr. für den Artikel müsste ihm genügen.'[d]

---

[a] See this volume, p. 371 – [b] See this volume, pp. 364 – [c] *Hamburger Echo* – [d] 'As regards Lafargue, I have nothing against *French* correspondence, I shall have a lot to translate. Naturally Frankel will write regularly—Lafargue is a correspondent of the kind that I am for *Vorwärts*, infrequent, but then long-writing. Of course his scintillating articles would be very welcome if I were not afraid that he would send me the same as those for *Vorwärts* and *Echo*. Can you arrange for him to write for me, *say twice a month* or on special occasions; that would be a great help to me, only we cannot pay much, he would have to make do with 20 francs an article.'

There. Paul might write to Vienna during the odd week when he does not write to Berlin, and on some other general subject.

We have not been able to see anything in the English papers about G. Richard's election.[451] Is he *en ballottage*? Your figures 1,802 votes do not look very encouraging.

In Germany we shall have a busy year. We drank the *Umsturz-Kaisers*[428] jolly good health on Christmas day so he will now perhaps be satisfied.

A very happy and pleasant New Year to you and Paul from all of us here!

Ever yours

F. Engels

First published, in the language
of the original (English), in:
F. Engels, P. et L. Lafargue,
Correspondance, t. III (1891-95),
Paris, 1959

Reproduced from the original

The seaside at Eastbourne

1895

238

ENGELS TO EMMA ADLER

IN VIENNA

London, 1 January 1895
41 Regent's Park Road, N. W.

Dear Mrs Adler,

I am most grateful for your kind good wishes as also for those of your husband and children which I wholeheartedly reciprocate. I trust that the New Year will be a thoroughly enjoyable one for you in every way. Today a new and promising field of activity has opened up for you and Victor and no doubt we shall frequently be able to detect your own hand in it. All of us over here wish this new enterprise, the daily *Arbeiter-Zeitung*,[377] the very best of success in the practical field.

Please tell Victor that I will answer his last letter within the next few days[a] and that I have sent him today, by 'registered' post, a copy of the 3rd volume of Marx's *Das Kapital*.[452] No doubt it will have already arrived by the time this reaches you; like this letter it is addressed to Windmühlgasse 30A.

Once again my best wishes and cordial regards to you all from
Yours,
F. Engels

First published in: *Victor Adlers Aufsätze, Reden und Briefe Erstes Heft: Victor Adler und Friedrich Engels*, Vienna, 1922

Printed according to the book

Published in English for the first time

---

[a] See this volume, pp. 408-11

239

ENGELS TO LUDWIG KUGELMANN

IN HANOVER

London, 1 January 1895
41 Regent's Park Road, N. W.

Dear Kugelmann,

I am most grateful to you, your wife and your daughter for your kind good wishes which I sincerely reciprocate. But now we had better get down to business straight away, as I am overwhelmed with correspondence, etc.[453]

If I understood you aright, the collection in America was mainly to do with Marx's articles in the *Tribune*. I have two collections of these over here, of which one *at any rate* is incomplete and probably both, since the *Tribune* also published Marx's articles as unsigned leaders. A third collection could therefore only be of use to me for the purpose of completing the set and that was why I suggested at the time that it should be temporarily housed in the archives where I could always have access to it when necessary.

But you now speak of *earlier* things, i.e. stuff from the period up till 1851, and that, of course, is quite a different matter and not what I had understood you to say in Berlin.[454] These things are in fact of the utmost value and it is only the lack of them that has prevented me from bringing out a complete edition of these lesser works as well as of the articles by Marx and myself that appeared between 1842 and 1852. It has long been my wish to publish these things, once I am in some sort of a position to do so and if, therefore, you can place as many of them as possible at my disposal, you will be making your own contribution towards that end. In which case I shall resume my search for a copy of the *Rheinische Zeitung* of 1842, chiefly with regard to Marx's articles.

Please tell me again where the collection originated and, if you cannot at once get hold of the things themselves, kindly procure for me, if possible, a list of the books, periodicals, etc., contained therein, but excluding the *Tribune* articles.[455]

Since the beginning of last year Mrs Kautsky has not been Mrs Kautsky but Mrs Freyberger. Her husband is an extremely able young Viennese doctor, formerly Nothnagel's assistant, who fell out with the faculty over there because he gave lectures on practical anatomy to working men and explained to them the social causes of their ailments. He is now addressing himself to the higher realms of applied medicine in this country and will, I do not doubt, soon make a success of it, for he is far more knowledgeable than most Englishmen. In order that my domestic arrangements should not be revolutionised more than necessary, we have taken a larger house in the same road where all three' or rather four, of us (there having been the addition of a little girl seven weeks ago) live together.

So once again a Happy New Year and kindest regards to you all from Louise and myself.

Yours,
F. Engels

As regards the misprint, which is itself a misprint, I shall look into the matter.[456]

<table>
<tr><td>First published in:
Marx and Engels, Works,
First Russian Edition,
Vol. XXIX, 1946</td><td>Printed according to the original

Published in English for the first time</td></tr>
</table>

240

ENGELS TO HERMANN SCHLÜTER[184]

IN HOBOKEN

London, 1 January 1895
41 Regent's Park Road, N. W.

Dear Schlüter,

Your letter of 11 August still remains unanswered, nor have I yet thanked you for the Census Compendium[a] which arrived safely. I have, however, been overwhelmed with all manner of work, while urgent party

---

[a] Department of the Interior. Census Office. *Compendium of the Eleventh Census: 1890.*

and business correspondence has virtually precluded my attending to my private correspondence, something from which Sorge has also had to suffer. You will have heard from him that Louise Kautsky is now Mrs Freyberger and the mother of a strong and healthy little girl and that we have all moved to 41, Regent's Park Road.

As Sorge will have told you, I have sent you a copy of Volume III of *Capital* addressed to the *Volkszeitung*, as I didn't know whether your Hoboken address still held good. At all events the *Volkszeitung* seemed safer to me. I could not, however, pass on your commission to Ede, he having long since been engaged for the same purpose by the *Neue Zeit*.[457] I ought really to have advised you of this—please accept my apologies.

Over here things are much the same as with you. Amongst the *masses* the socialist instinct is becoming ever stronger, but whenever it behoves them to translate their instinctive impulses into clear ideas and demands, the chaps at once go their several ways, some to the Social Democratic Federation,[44] others to the Independent Labor Party,[114] while the rest stay put in the Independent Labour Party, Trades Unions Organization etc., etc. In short, not a party but so many sects. The leaders are nearly all of them pretty unreliable fellows, while the candidates for the supreme leadership, though thick on the ground, are by no means eminently fitted for the post. At the same time we have the two big bourgeois parties who are standing by, purse in hand, to see whom they can buy. Moreover, what is known as 'democracy' over here is much restricted by *indirect* barriers. Periodicals are shockingly expensive, ditto candidatures for Parliament, ditto life as a Member of Parliament—if only on account of the vast correspondence this entails. To revise the deplorably kept registers of electors also costs a great deal of money and hitherto none but the two official parties have been able to defray that cost. Hence it is unlikely that anyone who does not support either of those parties will appear on the register. People over here are far behind the Continent in all these matters and, what's more, they are beginning to notice it; again, there is no second ballot, a relative majority or, as you Americans would say, PLURALITY, being enough. It is a situation in which everything is organised on the basis of *only two* parties and, until a third party is strong enough to be a match for them, the most it will be able to do is turn the scales. In the same way there is little likelihood of the Trades Unions over here bringing off something on the lines of the Berlin beer boycott[458]—a court of arbitration such as was secured over there is something that is still unattainable in this country.

On the other hand—as in the case of America—once the workers over here know what they want, the state, the land, industry and everything else will be theirs.

This is intended for you alone, not for the *Volkszeitung.*

Louise sends her kindest regards and both of us wish you a very Happy New Year.

Yours,

F. Engels

First published in: Marx and Engels, *Works*, First Russian Edition, Vol. XXIX, 1946

Printed according to the original

241

ENGELS TO KARL KAUTSKY

IN STUTTGART

London, 3 January 1895

Dear Baron,

Firstly, a very Happy New Year from one household to the other, and, secondly, my thanks for the amusing report of the MARE'S NEST discovered by Liebknecht. Hardly had I read the first couple of lines of your account than I realised that it could only refer to the old business with Schweitzer and for me that gave twice the savour to the humour of the situation.[459] Incidentally it will be sufficient if you make a note in your own copy of the variations of the original from the printed text and let me have them some time or other for insertion in mine. I would rather not enter into correspondence with Liebknecht about the copyright of the original ms., for it is improbable that it would get us anywhere.

Parts of Fireman's article[a] are, I agree, rendered so complex by his mis-

---

[a] P. Fireman, *Kritik der Marx'schen Werttheorie.* In *Jahrbücher für Nationalökonomie und Statistik.* 3. Folge, Bd. 3, 1892

guided incursions into other aspects of Marx's theory and by all manner of metaphysical, i.e. anti-dialectical divagations, as virtually to conceal the fact that, by a happy chance, he has been able to get closer than anyone else to the crux of the problem. Hence the total ineffectuality of the article. Only someone who gives his undivided attention to the specific problem under discussion will make the discovery that here is something which, if pursued, will lead to the solution of the whole problem.

It would seem that you will be having a thoroughly lively year in Germany. If Mr von Köller carries on in this way,[460] no thing is impossible—conflict, dissolution, granting concessions, coup d'état. Obviously he would also be content with less. The Junkers would be happy enough with more generous douceurs, but to obtain these he will have to appeal to certain cravings for personal domination and pander to them to the point at which elements of resistance are also brought into play, and it is here that chance—i.e. what is involuntary, incalculable—comes into play. And to secure those douceurs he will have to raise the spectre of conflict—if he goes a step further, the original aim, the douceur, will become of secondary importance and then it will be a case of Crown versus Reichstag, of bend or break, and that's when the fun may begin. At the moment I am reading Gardiner's *Personal Government of Charles I* in which the parallels with present-day Germany are so close as to be almost absurd. As, for instance, the arguments over immunity from the consequences of actions performed in Parliament. Were Germany a Latin country, a revolutionary conflict would be inevitable, but as it is, you can't be certain about nowt, as Jollymeier[a] used to say.

Meanwhile the business of the peasants has quietly fizzled out, though August's attack was most meritorious nevertheless and made good much of which had been omitted at Frankfurt.[425]

The worthy Bavarian socialists who favour reserved rights will be in no hurry to burn their fingers again.

Amongst the various small factions over here things are, for the moment, jogging along in the usual dilatory way. Though their mutual squabbles are no longer so heated, the intrigues behind the scenes are being conducted with proportionately greater zeal. The masses, on the other hand, who are being instinctively drawn towards socialism, are experiencing a growing urge for conscious and unified action. Though less

---

[a] Carl Schorlemmer

clear-sighted than individual leaders, the masses are certainly far better than the leaders as a whole, yet the process of acquiring consciousness is slower than elsewhere, since pretty well *all* the old leaders also have an interest in diverting this burgeoning consciousness into one specific channel or another, or, to put it crudely, in vitiating it. Well, one must just be patient.

So once again a Happy New Year and many regards.

Yours,

F. Engels

First published abridged in:
Die Neue Zeit, Jg. 27, Bd. I,
No. 1, Berlin, 1908 and in full
in: *Aus der Frühzeit des Marxismus.*
Engels Briefwechsel mit Kautsky,
Prag, 1935

Printed according to the original

Published in English for the first time

242

ENGELS TO LUDWIG SCHORLEMMER

IN DARMSTADT

London, 3 January 1895
41 Regent's Park Road, N. W.

Dear Schorlemmer,

I have not yet thanked you for your kind good wishes on my birthday and for your New Year's card, my response in each case being a resounding Happy New Year.

Here, too, all manner of changes have since taken place. At the beginning of last year Mrs Kautsky married Dr Freyberger, a young Viennese physician resident in this country, and we decided that, as we all wanted to remain together, we should take a larger house, one such being available close by. Hardly had we moved in and got things in order than Mrs Freyberger was delivered of a baby girl; mother and child are fit and well. Last summer Pumps and family also returned to London. Her husband's[a]

___

[a] Perry White Roscher

business in the Isle of Wight was not doing particularly well and he therefore wants to try his luck again here.

Carl's book *Rise and Progress*[313] was also sent to me not long ago. Volume I (re-edited by two young chemists[a]) of the big text-book published in collaboration with Roscoe has come out.[311] In view of the usual terms governing payment for such works, it is unlikely that Carl's heirs will receive much, if anything at all.

Even though the Party Conference in Frankfurt[418] proved a somewhat feeble affair by comparison with its predecessors, mainly because Vollmar and the Bavarians literally caught the other deputies napping with their Bavarian ultimatum,[b] while the latter, fearing the possibility of a split, failed to reach a decision on the most important issues, the stupidity of our opponents will nevertheless help us overcome all these little tribulations. Not content with the Subversion Bill,[428] those men of genius must needs institute proceedings against Liebknecht on account of a spot of bother in the Reichstag,[436] i.e. actually make us the champions of the constitutional rights of the Reichstag! And it was precisely this new conflict that provided us with the opportunity of bringing the Berlin beer boycott to a victorious conclusion,[458] a victory which has made a great impression abroad and especially here in England, For despite their seventy years of publicly organised trade clubs and considerable freedom of association, the workers over here are very far from securing the kind of court of arbitration that was successfully fought for in Berlin. In the words of one paper:

'Kaiser William would do well to reflect on the fact that the men who have got the better of a beer barrel will also get the better of a sceptre.'

And that was our doing. In Germany there are now only two people whose speeches command general attention—the Kaiser William and August Bebel. His last speech was brilliant, but it must be read in the original transcript.[461]

Though I am again in good health, I realise, of course, that 74 isn't 47 and that I can no longer make so free with food, drink, etc. Nor am I as hardy as in the past. But I am nevertheless still perfectly robust for my age and trust I shall live to see this and that, especially if, as seems distinctly probable, the gentlemen in Berlin decide to engage in a slight tussle with the Constitution.[462] The Prussian Junkers are quite capable of bringing

---

[a] Edvard Hjelt and Ossian Aschan – [b] See this volume, pp. 357, 374-75

about a situation in which the Social Democrats will be compelled to act as the defenders of the Imperial Constitution against a body of Junkers who not only infringe that Constitution but are intent on staging a coup d'état. That will suit us admirably. Let's have at 'em.

Many regards from

Yours

F. Engels

First published in: Marx and Engels, *Works*, First Russian Edition, Vol. XXIX, 1946

Printed according to the original

Published in English for the first time

243

ENGELS TO PAUL STUMPF

IN MAINZ

London, 3 January 1895
41 Regent's Park Road, N. W.

Dear Old Man,

As you see, I reciprocate your congratulations on the completion of my 74th year (you were kind enough to make me a year younger (than I am) with a resounding Happy New Year. Let us hope that, come the next one, we shall both of us still be hale and hearty; for I have a great desire just to take one peek into the new century, though by the first of January 1901 or thereabouts, I shall be a complete wreck, and then let happen what may.

I was not unduly disturbed about the row in the party.[463] It is much better that things of this kind should crop up from time to time and be properly thrashed out than that people should don their nightcaps. For the very fact that the party has steadily and inexorably grown and expanded has meant that the new elements are more difficult to absorb than their predecessors. The working men of the big cities, i.e. the most intelligent and wideawake, are already ours and what we are now getting are either the working men of the small towns and rural areas, or students, salesmen, etc., or again, those struggling to keep their heads above water, the petty bourgeois and such independent craftsmen as still own or rent a parcel of land, and now, into the bargain, the small peasant proper. And since our party is in fact the only really progressive party and, what is more, the only one strong enough to ensure that advances are made, it is obviously tempting to bring a little socialism to bear on the debt-ridden and near-rebellious middle and big peasants as well, particularly in districts where such people predominate on the land. That might well involve going beyond the limits of what is allowed on principle by our party, in which case there will be a bit of a fracas, but so sound is our party's constitution that no harm will have been done. No one is so stupid as seriously to envisage a break with the great majority of the party, nor is anyone so conceited as to believe himself able to set up, *alongside* our big party, a small private one, like the Swabian People's Party[464] which has actually succeeded in swelling its numbers from seven to eleven Swabians. All this quarrelling has served only to disappoint the bourgeois who, for twenty years now, have been regularly counting on there being a split, while at the same time ensuring that there should not be the slightest risk of one. Take, for instance, the present Subversion Bill[428] and Liebknecht's elevation to the status of representative of the rights of the Reichstag and of the Imperial Constitution,[436] likewise the threatened coup d'état and infringement of the law by the powers that be. Of course stupidities are committed on our side also, but to render it possible for opponents such as these to get the better of us, we should have to be of a stupidity so abysmal as to be without rival anywhere else in the world today. Otherwise your idea of giving the younger generation a chance to take the helm in the party and thus get itself into a fix would not be at all bad; but I believe that they will acquire experience and common sense even without an experiment of that kind.

As you can see from my address, I have, as we used to say, moved a few doors along. This house is much better and more convenient and is very close to the park entrance.

I hope that the 'Heilig Geist' where we downed a good few glasses in our time, is still flourishing.[465] I should like to cool off on some hot summer's day in its Gothic vaults. But who knows what may not happen? One should never say die.

Well, once again a Happy New Year and warm regards from

Yours

F. Engels

First published abridged in:
F. Engels, *Politisches Vermächtnis
aus unveröffentlichen Briefen,*
Berlin, 1920 and in full in:
Marx and Engels, *Works,*

First Russian Edition,
Vol. XXIX, 1946

Printed according to the original

Published in English for the first time

244

ENGELS TO PASQUALE MARTIGNETTI

IN BENEVENTO

London, 8 January 1895
41 Regent's Park Road, N. W.

Dear Friend,

I have had your various letters of 6 Sep., 16 Dec. and the 1st of this month and have passed on your message to Aveling.[466]

Many thanks for the trouble you have been to over the preface to the third volume of *Capital.* It in quite a good thing that it should come out in the *Rassegna*[467] since it will enable people in Italy to see that abroad Loria's spurious greatness is viewed in a very different light from what it is at home. On the other hand I can understand that at present Turati should consider it better tactics not to attack the man as vehemently as I do.[a] When we had the exceptional laws[15] to contend with in Germany, our tactics were different in many respects, and individual opponents whom we have since mercilessly attacked were temporarily spared for one reason or another. In cases such as these I must rely to a very large extent on the judgement of men who, like Turati, are in the thick of the fray; those men may not always do what I, from my standpoint over here, would consider best or most important, but nevertheless they are doing something, are doing their duty to the best of their knowledge, and are prepared to take the consequences. If the government didn't find Turati and his Milan friends exceedingly objectionable, it would not have put them under *domicilio coatto*[b] for three months or five.

---

[a] See present edition, Vol. 37, pp. 876-82 – [b] house arrest

Admittedly neither of the two chapters of the third volume of *Capital* solves the kind of question relating to the theory of value that might be raised by any old bourgeois economist. There is nothing of the sort in one chapter or the other of the book. But those aspects of the subject that could not be developed in Volume I are elucidated in Parts 1-4 of Volume III.

Two or three copies of your translation of the preface will amply suffice me.

I most sincerely reciprocate your good wishes for the New Year and remain

Yours,

F. Engels

First published abridged, in the language of the original (German), in: *Critica Sociale*, No. 10, 16 May 1895 and in full in *La Corrispondenza di Marx e Engels con Italiani. 1848-1895*, Milan, 1964

Printed according to the original

Published in English for the first time

245

ENGELS TO VICTOR ADLER

IN VIENNA

London, 9 January 1895
41 Regent's Park Road, N. W.

Dear Victor,

My only real reason for writing to you today is to advise you that on Sunday evening[a] Louise sent off in a wrapper a ms. containing three items addressed to the Editor, *Arbeiter-Zeitung*, 10 Schwarzspanierstrasse; these contain:

1. Something about the cotton industry.

---

[a] 6 January 1895

2. Something about the activities of the Parliamentary Committee of the Trades Union Congress[28] (already to some extent anticipated in the *Arbeiter-Zeitung*)

3. An extract from Mrs Crawford's Paris Correspondence.[469] As you have previously had trouble over manuscripts sent in a wrapper, I believe this notification to be pertinent.

Should another attempt be made to charge you excess postage after the event on the pretext that the package has been handled *as a letter*, it will be high time to lodge a complaint. According to the official excerpt (cited in inverted commas) in the English Post Office Guide, 'MANUSCRIPT OF BOOKS OR OTHER LITERARY PRODUCTIONS' may be sent in a wrapper at a cost of a ha'penny for two ounces anywhere within the area covered by the International Postal Union. It must surely be possible to get this enforced in Austria too, or is the *Arbeiter-Zeitung* prepared of its own free will to pay a surcharge at twenty times the proper rate ($2\frac{1}{2}$ for a $\frac{1}{2}$ oz)?

Another thing. From Russia we hear that the December issue of the *European Messenger* (*Vestnik Yevropy*)[a] contained an article on Alexander III of extreme and, indeed—censorship in that country being what it is—unprecedented acerbity. Since your wife[b] has a perfect command of Russian, might it not be worth your while to have a look at and, perhaps, make use of it? It really would be a capital joke if the *Arbeiter-Zeitung* were also to steal a march on the bourgeois press in this particular field.

Up till now, Nos 1 and 3-8 of the *Arbeiter-Zeitung* have arrived here, all of them addressed to Ludwig Freyberger, as well as a copy of No. 1 addressed in your hand to myself. So far as the arrangement of the material is concerned, the change-over from a twice-weekly to a daily paper[377] is not yet quite complete, but one can see that it is under way and that the Thursday evening and Sunday numbers are distinct from the others in that each has its own particular character to suit a particular reading public. That you should not at present have time to spare for leading articles is understandable; Marx fared likewise with the *Neue Rheinische Zeitung*[c]—in the entire first month only two were by him, and throughout the whole of the first quarter five, if that. At the outset the editor-in-chief is kept busy enough organising the thing, than which nothing is

---

[a] [name in Russian], Vol. VI, Book 12, December 1894, section [in Russian] (Internal Review). – [b] Emma Adler – [c] *Neue Rheinische Zeitung. Organ der Demokratie.*

more important, All in all, the paper has turned out very well considering this is its first week; such shortcomings as it has will all be overcome in the end.

We gave your message to Vandervelde on 1.1., when he called in here for a moment.[470]

I have passed on to Laura as much as was necessary of your letter[a] but have heard nothing about this since. Perhaps Lafargue has written to you direct.

I cannot supply you with very much material on 'Marx in Vienna in 1848'. Some time I shall search through the *Neue Rheinische Zeitung* for facts and also see if I can find anything more about Becher.[471] Our Vienna correspondent was one Müller-Tellering from Koblenz, like all Koblenzers, fanatical and an inveterate trouble-maker. After returning to Germany at the end of 1849, he first came to Cologne and picked a quarrel with red Becker.[b] His next port of call was London where he promptly fell out with us over a trifling personal matter (which, with a little less contrariness on his part, could have been settled in a few minutes' conversation) and instantly produced a pamphlet, *Vergeschmack der Diktatur von Marx und Engels*.[c] Next he went to America and tried to stir up trouble against us, but very soon disappeared from the scene. His reports from Vienna before the advent of Windischgrätz showed an undue bias towards violent revolution which, at a time when reaction was everywhere gathering strength, was not unwelcome to us. In those days we could not, from a distance, assess the value of his pronouncements on personalities, but he was doubtless strongly influenced by personal inclination. In such turbulent times we had to allow our correspondents a great deal of responsibility and a corresponding amount of latitude.

And now for another piece of political news which might be of use to you should such matters crop up again: On the evening before last we heard political rumours of a ministerial crisis here, according to which Harcourt, the Chancellor of the Exchequer, was proposing to resign. At the same time, however, he denied this, saying that the allegation, AS MADE, was completely unfounded. It was improbable that the Chancellor of the Exchequer *alone* should resign at a moment when he had a surplus of three million pounds and was thus in a position to present a first class

---

[a] See this volume, p. 395 – [b] Hermann Becker – [c] *A Foretaste of the Dictatorship of Marx and Engels.*

budget. But the real facts of the case are as follows: Harcourt *favours* the introduction of salaries for M.P.s *before* the dissolution and is encountering strong opposition in the Cabinet—and probably also from the Queen.[a] He had apparently threatened to resign, thus obtaining concessions in regard to the afore-said question. At all events everything has returned to normal for the time being. You can see how unstable things are in official circles over here.

All the necessary steps have been taken as regards the money. You will, I think, be hearing more about this in a few days' time when, I trust, you will also get the cash.[b]

Louise wishes to append a line or two. She and Ludwig send their regards, as do I, to you and your wife

Yours

F. Engels

On the 5th of this month we sent you three copies of the English Socialist papers, *Clarion*, *Justice* and *Labour Leader* (Keir Hardie) and shall be sending sundry other issues thereof from time to time to enable you to decide which you like best. Please take a look at them.

(Postscript from Louise Freyberger)

Dear Victor,

Now that the matter of finance is all but settled, the money should shortly arrive in Vienna. I have one further request to make, namely that you get a certificate of identification made out for Ludwig and myself. Ludwig is applying for temporary membership of the National Liberal Club, the leading club of its kind over here, close to the Houses of Parliament, and frequented by all the Liberal and Radical M.P.s and by journalists of all shades of political opinion. In this country, credentials have to be produced for everything, and it couldn't do you any harm. Much love from the three L.L.L.s.[c]

First published in:
Victor Adlers Aufsätze, Reden und Briefe, Erstes Heft: *Victor Adler und Friedrich Engels*, Vienna, 1922

Printed according to the book

Published in English for the first time

---

[a] Queen Victoria – [b] See this volume, p. 384 – [c] Louise, Ludwig and Lulu.

246

ENGELS TO NIKOLAI DANIELSON[472]

IN ST. PETERSBURG

London, 9 January 1895
41 Regent's Park Road, N. W.

My dear Sir,

I have duly received yours of the 1st December. What Mr. von Struve means by saying that Marx, *completes* but not *disproves* Malthus' theory of population I do not understand.[a] I think the note on Malthus in Vol. I, Note 75, to Chapter XXIII, 1[b] ought to have been explicit enough for anybody. Moreover, I do not see, how anybody can speak of *completing* Malthus' theory today, when that theory rests upon the assumption, that *population presses on the means of subsistence*, while corn in London is at 20/- the quarter, or less than half the average price from 1848 to 1870, and when it is universally acknowledged that *the means of subsistence now press upon the population* which is not large enough to consume them! As to Russia, if the peasant is compelled to sell the corn which he ought to eat, surely it is not pressure of [excess] population which compels him to do so, but pressure from the tax-gatherer, the landlord, the kulak[*] etc. etc. As far as I know, the low price of Argentinian wheat has more to do with agrarian distress all ever Europe, Russia included, than anything else.

We have just learned that a savant of your city has been informed that he can have Vol. III[c] passed free to him on applying specially for it at the office of the Censorship. I think it as well to communicate this fact to you because it may lead you to give me instructions how to forward to you the remaining sheets which I hold at your disposal,

Yours very truly
L. K.[d]

Please note change of house number.

---

[a] P. von Struve, *Critical Notes on the Development of Capitalism in Russia*, St. Petersburg, [in Russian], 1894(footnote[1] to p. 183). – [b] See present edition, Vol. 35, Chapter XXV, Section 1, pp. 611-13 – [c] of *Capital* – [d] Engels' pen-name consisting of Louise Kautsky's initials – [*] word in Russian

First published, in Russian,
in: *Minuvshiye gody*, No. 2, 1908

Reproduced from the original

Published in English in full
for the first time

247

ENGELS TO LUDWIG KUGELMANN[473]

IN HANOVER

[London.] 9 January 1895

Dear Kugelmann,

Please write at once to Livingston in Pittsburg and ask him for Meyer's list of *earlier* stuff;[455] to judge by your last letter there's unlikely to be very much, but there are also sundry items, some of them anonymous, in old newspapers and compendiums of the 1843-47 period. Ask him, too, if the collection of *Tribune*[a] articles is still in existence. At the same time I shall get other friends in America to search for such ancient tomes as may still be in existence there, so that the matter can be put in hand.

Many regards to your wife and daughter,

Yours

F. E.

Could you possibly supply me with a few of your red brass locks?

First published in: Marx and Engels,
Works, First Russian Edition,
Vol. XXIX, 1946

Printed according to the original

Published in English for the first time

---

a *New-York Daily Tribune*

248

ENGELS TO VICTOR ADLER

IN VIENNA

London, 12 January 1895

Dear Victor,

My last letter was sent to you at Schwarzspanier[a] on the 9th of this month. Today, simply as a precaution, I am again notifying you that yesterday Louise addressed a registered letter to you at Ferstelgasse 6,[b] containing a CHEQUE for 3,500 gulden drawn on the tenth of this month by the Anglo-Foreign Banking Company Ltd. on the Union Bank of Vienna to the order of Dr Victor Adler, *payable dans les huit jours*.[c]

If you have received this safely, would you please drop a line to Louise informing her of the fact so that she may pass on the information to the chaps over here and thus set their minds at rest. Then the formal document with its various signatures can follow.[d]

But if you have not received the CHEQUE, then hasten at once to the Union Bank and STOP PAYMENT. Unfortunately the international postal services do not admit of a declaration of value or insurance, hence a certain amount of anxiety prevails over here.

As regards Marx, I have searched through the *Neue Rheinische Zeitung*[e] and all I have found is this: The issue of 25 Aug. 1848 states that 'yesterday K. M. left for Vienna where he will be spending a few days'. (Not from Cologne, mind you; he had already gone away and it was, I think, from Hamburg that he arranged for the insertion of this notice.) And then there is a later piece of news, 31 August from Vienna, to the effect that Marx gave a lecture yesterday at the Vienna Workers' Association in Josefstadt on social conditions in Western Europe (*Stifft* spoke after him, at the same Association) (*Neue Rheinische Zeitung*, 6 Sept.) and, according to the issue of 8 Sept., Marx spoke on 2 Sept. 'at a meeting of the first Vienna Workers' Association on the subject of socio-economic conditions'.—That is all. Meanwhile in Berlin, on 7 September, a crucial vote

---

[a] See this volume, pp. 408-11 – [b] residence of the *Arbeiter-Zeitung* Editorial Office – [c] payable within eight days – [d] See this volume, p. 411 – [e] Ibid., p. 410

had been taken on Stein's motion,[474] Hansemann's Ministry had fallen and, conflict being inevitable, Marx returned hot-foot. On 12 Sept. he wrote another leading article[a] for the issue, which came out that same afternoon, of 12 Sept. 1848.

Yesterday evening Louise sent you two more items in a wrapper.

Yours,
F. E.

Clarion and *Labour Leader* have today gone off as before to the editorial office.

Very many thanks to you and your wife for the magnificent calendar.

First published in:
Victor Adlers Aufsätze, Reden und Briefe. Erstes Heft:
Victor Adler und Friedrich Engels, Vienna, 1922

Published according to the book

Published in English for the first time

249

ENGELS TO KARL KAUTSKY

IN STUTTGART

[London,] 12 January 1895
41 Regent's Park Road N. W.

Dear Baron,

Just now I received a registered letter from Mr Stiebeling containing a curious reply to my preface[b] and the even more curious request that I should arrange for it to be published in the *Neue Zeit*.[475] All I can tell the man is that the columns of the *Neue Zeit* are not at my disposal, but that I should be very glad if the editors were to disseminate *this*, his reply, as widely as possible. And with that I bid Mr Stiebeling a fond farewell and leave him to his fate.

---

[a] K. Marx, *The Crisis and the Counter-revolution*. – [b] to the third volume of *Capital*

As regards the subversion debate, Nazi[a] appears to have done a very good job.[476] Incidentally, we can thank our lucky stars that there should still be jackasses in Berlin!

Yours
F. E.

First published in: *Aus der Frühzeit des Marxismus. Engels Briefwechsel mit Kautsky*, Prag, 1935

Printed according to the original

Published in English for the first time

250

ENGELS TO HERMANN ENGELS

IN BARMEN

London, 12 January 1895
41 Regent's Park Road, N. W.

Dear Hermann,

At long last! But I haven't got the time to make excuses. First of all, my thanks for your news which has put me pretty well *au fait* again. I shall now repay the debt by telling you all manner of things in return. To begin with, you will see above a change of address. This came about as follows:

About a year ago Mrs Kautsky, my fellow-lodger, became engaged to a compatriot of hers, Dr Freyberger, a young and extremely able Viennese physician who settled in this country two years ago. Before long a desire manifested itself to clinch the engagement with a marriage but, since I had no desire to put myself at the mercy of strangers in my old age, it was arranged that we should all three set up house together, and thus the need arose for a larger place. In the meantime the young couple had got married early in February while we were still living at 122, but we soon found and took a very nice, large and exceptionally cheap house in a far better part of the same road. We moved in at the beginning of October and, at

---

[a] Ignaz Auer

the beginning of November, Louise, with—for her—unusual punctuality, presented her spouse with a baby girl.

The house is situated some five hundred paces closer to town, a hundred paces from Primrose Hill and rather less from the entrance to Regent's Park. Below stairs, in the BASEMENT, there is a cosy breakfast room in addition to the kitchen, etc., on the ground floor a drawing room and dining room which could seat twenty-four people in comfort, on the first floor at the front my study, with three windows facing the street and very easy to keep warm—at the back my bedroom, also large; 2nd floor: four rooms occupied by the Freyberger family; 3rd floor, likewise four rooms for maid servants, visitors, box rooms, etc. A small front garden and a larger and, for these parts, really quite pleasant one at the back. All this at a cost of £85 a year, as compared with the £60 I used to pay! The secret lies in the fact that the LANDLORD lives in Lancashire and doesn't want to spend money, but merely to take it. So I advanced round about £200 for repairs, in return for which I shall pay no rent for two and a half years and live on the advance. The last tenant, a doctor, used to pay £130, from which you will see how much the value of houses fluctuates here.

This rehousing business happened during the summer and, since I took the place on a seven year lease with the option to renew for another seven years, this and obtaining a guarantee for my advance have necessitated prolonged legal negotiations which have prevented me from going any distance away from London. Hence I only spent five weeks or so at Eastbourne on the south coast.[393] It is one of the nicest seaside places I know and is, in fact, already becoming a seaside suburb of London for people who don't have to come up to town more than a couple of times a week.

Please will you again convey my belated congratulations to Elsbeth[a] on her engagement, and to Walter[b] on having, or so I hope, successfully passed his examinations, Actually, I still owe Walter a letter but must, alas, continue in his debt, thus also owing him, no less than yourself, an apology. I trust he won't take it amiss.

Well, now for the sherry. *Less jours se suivent et ne se ressemblent pas,*[c] and the same thing applies to vintage years; getting hold of more of the *old*

---

[a] His niece, Elsbeth Engels – [b] His nephew, Walter Engels – [c] Though the days follow one another, they are not alike.

sherry is beyond our powers, What I had been waiting for was a visit from Brett, my supplier, but he came much later than usual. I have now asked him to let me have three sample bottles of sherry, as similar as possible to the first that was sent to you, and of three qualities. The little case has just arrived. On Monday I shall take it to the CONTINENTAL PARCELS EXPRESS and it will probably come to you by carrier; the weight exceeds the 7 lb. limit laid down by international postal regulations, Now, when you try them out, I would advise you to decant half a bottle of the variety you prefer and keep it there. The bottles are numbered 1, 2, 3 and, when you order, only the number need be given. The price of all three is 42/- a dozen, or 3/6d a bottle, carriage paid from London. Unless otherwise instructed, I shall arrange for them to be brought by steamer direct to Cologne or Düsseldorf.

One more thing. Since fewer payments now have to be debited to my account over there, the balance you hold for me is continually mounting. The removal has involved other expenses, aside from the advance to my LANDLORD, and I should be glad if, in the course of this month, you could let me have, say, £40.

Finally, I have a pleasant piece of news to impart, namely that I have at last become an old man. Last spring I had an attack of bronchitis which, though not at all severe, refused to budge for six weeks or more; and on top of that I suffered a great deal last year from stomach-ache, constipation, etc. So in the end I had perforce to believe Freyberger when he said I must no longer indulge in my former *Sparjitzen*.[a] And when the looking glass reflects an ever more abject image of encroaching baldness, I can no longer conceal from myself the realisation that there is very little in common between 74 and 47. Eating and drinking have both been considerably curtailed and I also have to submit to all kinds of unwonted protective measures against catching cold. Well, I shall have to put up with it, and at least it hasn't cost me my sense of humour.

So that's that, and my debt, I trust, is now repaid. My best love to Emma[b] and your children and grandchildren, also to Rudolph[c] and Hedwig[d] and their families.

Now, as always, your old
Friedrich

---

[a] antics – [b] His sister-in-law, Emma Engels – [c] His younger brother Rudolph Engels – [d] His sister, Hedwig Boelling

First published in *Deutsche Revue*, Jg. 46, Bd, III, 1921

Printed according to the original

Published in English for the first time

251

ENGELS TO PAUL LAFARGUE[35]

AT LE PERREUX

London, 13[-14] January 1895

My dear Lafargue,

I am glad to see that you have already arranged matters with Adler and have at last found a translator who does you justice.[477]

Things are going well. If the year '95 finishes as it has begun we may see some strange happenings. In Germany, young William[a] has fallen into the hands of the 'agrarians' (the big aristocratic landowners of the Eastern provinces, the *Junkern*)[b] who want to make sure of their control over this young ninny and who can only do so by compromising William to the point of no return. Thus they are hinting at a dissolution of the Reichstag, which will emerge from fresh elections more refractory than ever and then, his throne and his honour being at stake, there will be nothing for it but a coup d' état to give William the means of obtaining new soldiers and ships, and the Junkers new import duties on agricultural produce and subsidies on the export of sugar, spirits, etc. That seems to be these gentlemen's idea; impossible to say how far it will materialise. In the meantime, they are playing with fire—the War Minister[c] openly inviting our people in the Reichstag to come out on to the streets by jeering at them—they are absolutely determined to create an opportunity for firing on the people.[478]

And in your country there are the scandals of bourgeois corruption which go beyond anything and are driving towards a crisis: certainly if the Ministry threatens to bring the majority to court unless it votes against Gérault-Richard, matters cannot go on much longer.[479] The

---

[a] William II – [b] Junkers – [c] Bronsart von Schellendorf

victory of the bourgeois, who have succeeded in electing a model bour-geois[a] President of the Republic, may well bring about the collapse of the whole bourgeois régime; the climax is approaching when they will be overthrown. As I see it, it is the bourgeoisie itself which, in your country, takes responsibility for doing socialist propaganda amongst the peasants. It is a long and wearisome task to enlighten peasants on political matters, but they will not be so stupid as not to realise at this juncture that they are being robbed. But once they have spotted that, there is nothing for them but to turn to the Socialists, the only party which is not involved in the thefts; for the Radicals[86] are well and truly done for.

So you see we can jolly well shout: *Prosit Neujahr*[b]!

Speaking of the new year: your credit account of sixty pounds has been opened, if you want a cheque for twenty pounds, you have only to let me know.

I have sent Laura some working-class papers from here, Blatchford's (alias Nunquam) *Clarion* and Keir Hardie's *Labour Leader*. Since the end of the *Workman's Times*, this is the only literature of the Independent Labour Party.[114] Sad but true.

A fortnight ago I received a letter from Vaillant enclosing some of his Bills.[480] I promised I would examine them critically as soon as I had the time.[c] Meanwhile I told him[25] that Wroblewski, in Nice, has written asking me for money, that he has had an accident, broken his arm, has been in hospital and is in great distress; that I have given him as much help as I could but that it is beyond my means and that in my view the Communards and the socialist deputies owe it to their honour not to let him die of starvation. He replied that they had tried to get up a *public subscription* for Wroblewski but that he, W., was against this and that there is nothing to be done.

Do you know anything about this? Wroblewski as a true Pole does not understand the handling of money, he spends it lavishly when he has it; perhaps he has done similar things in relation to Vaillant and others who would have been able to help him. What he needs is a little regular pension, paid out once a month in small amounts. But in my view it is a matter of the honour of French socialism which cannot claim credit for the Commune of 1871 if they allow the last general of the Commune to die of hunger. What do you and the others—Guesde, the National

---

[a] Gean Casimir-Périer – [b] Happy New Year! – [c] See this volume, pp. 453-5

Council—think? Is there no way of making these former Communeux feel some shame?[481]

Kiss Laura for me.

Ever yours,

F. E.

Monday [14 January 1895][a]: received *Le Temps* and copies of *Petite République*. Thanks. First Gérault-Richard and now Rouanet, that's nice[482]! What luck if this leads to a crisis, to a dissolution and a more and more revolutionary situation in your country and in Germany!

Monday: Aveling told us yesterday that the *Labour Leader* is on its last legs, the chief backer (said to be Passnevre Edwards, a rich Liberal Unionist) will not put up any more money.

Louise asks me to thank you for the charming card of congratulation which you and Laura sent her.

<table>
<tr><td>

First published in:
F. Engels, P. et L. Lafargue,
Correspondance, t. III, Paris, 1959
</td><td>

Printed according to the original

Translated from the French
</td></tr>
</table>

252

ENGELS TO FRIEDRICH ADOLPH SORGE[113]

IN HOBOKEN

London, 16 January 1895
41 Regent's Park Road, N. W.

Dear Sorge,

Have received card of 6th and letters of 19th and 31st Dec. Many thanks. And may I again heartily reciprocate your and your wife's good wishes for the New Year.

By way of a New Year's greeting Stiebeling sent me his grotesque riposte[475] together with the suggestion that *I* should get the *Neue Zeit* to print it!! I replied[25] to the effect that its columns were not at my disposal

---

[a] These last three paragraphs are written in the margin of this letter.

but that I had told K. Kautsky (which is true) he would be doing me a special favour were he to ensure that the thing was disseminated as widely as possible.[a] The man is a blockhead.

I cannot understand how it was that you should have failed to receive Volume III[b] until five days after Schlüter had got his. I posted both at the same time on 12 Dec. and the receipts for both *are still joined together*. I enclose them herewith in case you should wish to lodge a complaint,

I have for some time been aware of the temporary decline of the movement in America and it is not the German socialists who will stem it. Though America is the *youngest* it is also the *oldest* country in the world. In the same way as you have, over there, the most antiquated furniture designs alongside your own vernacular ones or, in Boston, cabs such as I last saw in London in 1838 and, in the mountains, seventeenth century STAGE COACHES, alongside PULLMAN CARS, so too you continue to sport all the old mental trappings which Europe has already discarded. Everything that is outmoded here may persist in America for another generation or two. Karl Heinzen, for instance, not to mention religious and spiritualist superstition. Thus you still have old Lassalleans amongst you, while a man like Sanial, who would now seem passé in France, is still able to play a role over there. This may be attributed on the one hand to the fact that, over and above its concern for material production and the accumulation of wealth, America is only now beginning to find time for untramelled intellectual work and the preliminary training this demands; on the other hand, it may also be attributed to the dual nature of America's development, still engaged as it is on the one hand in the *primary* task of reclaiming the vast area of untamed country, while being already compelled on the other to compete for first place in industrial production. Hence the UPS AND DOWNS of the movement, according to which point of view takes precedence in the average person's mind—that of the urban working man or that of the peasant engaged in reclamation. In a couple of years' time all this will change and then we shall witness a great step forward. The evolution of the Anglo-Saxon RACE with its ancient Teutonic freedom happens to be quite exceptionally slow, pursuing as it does a zig-zag course (small zig-zags here in England, colossal ones on your side of the Atlantic) and tacking against the wind, but making headway none the less.

---

[a] See this volume, p. 415 – [b] *Capital*

Here in Europe the New Year will bring with it a very complex state of affairs. In Germany the peasant question has been pushed into the background by the Subversion Bill[428] and the latter—by young William (his *Song to Aegir*,[483] the lord of the waves, owes its inspiration solely to the seasickness from which he invariably suffers, which is why he and his Fleet always make for the calm waters of the Norwegian fjords). The young man has thrown Germany into complete disorder, no one knows where he stands or what the morrow will bring, the confusion in governmental circles, as in the ruling classes generally, grows worse from day to day and, during the debate on the Subversion Bill, the only people with cheerful expressions were our chaps. But it really is too marvellous! At the head of the anti-subversionists stands a man who is unable to desist from subversion for five minutes on end. And the aforementioned young William has now fallen into the clutches of the Junkers who, in order to keep him in a frame of mind in which he is prepared to give them extra help with their bankrupt estates, are presently dangling before him the carrot of more taxation and more troops and warships by their ostentatious advocacy of *regis voluntas suprema lex*,[a] and are egging him on to dissolve the Reichstag and stage a coup d'état. At the same time, however, these gentlemen, Köller & Co., despite their ostentatious catchwords, are so poorly endowed with courage that they are already prey to all manner of forebodings, and it may well be asked whether they will not take fright when the moment for action comes.

And as for France! There, as in Italy, the bourgeoisie precipitated itself head first into corruption in a manner that would put America to shame. For the past three years all efforts in both countries have been directed towards finding a bourgeois government—admittedly not free from corruption—but whose *immediate* involvement in *public* scandal is nevertheless so slight that a parliament could support it without unduly violating the commonest decencies. In Italy Crispi will hang on for a little while longer only because the King[b] and the Crown Prince[c] are as deeply implicated in the banking scandals as he is himself.[d] In France, our forty-five or fifty socialist deputies have just toppled their third Ministry on the count of actual corruption, and Casimir-Périer has gone tumbling after.[484] Presumably his intention is to pose as the one and only saviour of

---

[a] the King's will is supreme law. – [b] Umberto I – [c] Victor Emmanuel – [d] See this volume, p. 390

society, get himself re-elected with an immense majority, and thus consolidate his position, But it's a risky game. At all events there is nothing stable about France either, and this year may see new elections, not only in England, but also in Germany and France, which will be of *crucial importance* this time. On top of that a crisis of the first water in Italy and, in Austria, the certainty of electoral reform[270]—in short, things are growing critical throughout the whole of Europe.

I was very pleased to hear that you and your wife are feeling better. Let us hope the improvement continues.

Many regards to you and your wife from the Freybergers and

Yours
F. Engels

First published abridged in:
*Briefe und Auszüge aus Briefen
von Joh. Phil. Becker, Jos. Dietzgen,
Friedrich Engels, Karl Marx u. A.
an F. A. Sorge und Andere*,
Stuttgart, 1906 and, in full, in:
Marx and Engels, *Works*,

First Russian Edition, Vol. XXIX,
1946

Printed according to the original

Published in English
in full for the first time

253

ENGELS TO LAURA LAFARGUE

AT LE PERREUX

London, 19 January 1895
41 Regent's Park Road N. W.

My dear Löhr,

Your last letter has indeed startled me.[485] I have tried, not very successfully, to recollect the terms used in my letter to you of December 29th[a]; still, in what I do remember there is not a word which ought to offend you. And indeed, if there is anything in the tone of that letter which you think strange, it is there entirely against my will and intention.

It never could occur, nor has it ever occurred to me for a moment to

---

[a] See this volume, pp. 394-96

doubt the right or the propriety, on your part, of inquiring at any time what steps I had taken or intended to take in order to secure the return, at the time of my death, to you, the rightful owners, of those papers of Mohr's which you have entrusted to me. Nor have I ever found anything to object to in the terms in which you spoke of that subject to Tussy. It seems, therefore, so exceedingly strange to me that I should have written to you in a tone that ought to give you reason to complain.

I did indeed feel nettled at the *way* Tussy caused the question to be submitted to me, and, under the circumstances, thought I was bound to speak to her about it. When I did, I told her, *not once, but three or four times over*, that I had not one word to say against your letter, neither as to the subject matter, nor as to the terms used. Anyhow, Tussy and I had an explanation, which as far as I know, settled everything connected with that subject, and left us as good friends as before; and I should regret very much if, through any unguarded words of mine, or through some other circumstance, that little incident had thrown its shadow as far as Le Perreux.

In the meantime things have come to a crisis in your neighbourhood. I intended to write at some length about that, but Bebel all at once asked me for historical materials as to the various and pretty frequent riots here in England which are settled without ever attempting to encumber the Statute Book with increased penal laws or exceptional legislation. He is in the Committee on the *Umsturzvorlage*[428] and wants it for them, so I had to leave everything else alone and get it off by this day's post before the usual Sunday delays in postal communication retard it.

Anyhow our 50 French Socialist members are in luck. In less than 18 months they have upset three ministries and one president.[484] That shows what a Socialist minority can do in a parliament which, like the French or English, is the really supreme power in the country. A similar power our men in Germany can get by a revolution only; still, the break-up of the Centre party[71] would make them the arbiters of the house and give them the balance of power.

What a miserable retreat is that of Casimir's[a]! After the brag with which he came in, to skedaddle at the first serious difficulty[486]! It looks as if our bourgeois heroes had individually degenerated quite as much as their class has done collectively.

---

[a] Casimir-Périer

In Germany it looks as if the same principle was prevailing; Bebel does not seem to think von Köller and Co. the men likely to carry through a coup d'état to the end; it seems everywhere the story of Béranger's old fool who courted Babette and found out too late that his courting days were past and gone.[a]

The greatest success, however, seems to me to be this, that the scandalous affairs of the opportunist majority have been again exposed, that Raynal has been nailed down, and that it seems impossible to have the subject burked again.[487] The evidence of the corruption of all other parties must work wonders in favour of ours, especially in France, and ought to secure us immense and unhoped for successes at the next general election which cannot be very distant now, for who can govern with the present Chamber?

Ça chauffe![b] and neither Félix Faure nor young William[c] will be able to put out the fire.

I shall write to Paul as soon as ever I get a moment's time. Thanks for the papers which I have sent on to Tussy after using them.

Ever yours,

F. Engels

First published, in the language
of the original (English), in:
F. Engels, P. et L. Lafargue,

Correspondance, t. III, 1959

Reproduced from the original

254

ENGELS TO PAUL LAFARGUE[35]

AT LE PERREUX

London, 22 January 1895

My dear Lafargue,

How lucky you are, you French! You bring down a Minister[d]; then the whole Cabinet follows him and by way of aftereffect the President of

---

[a] Reference to Pierre-Jean de Béranger's *Le vieux Célibataire* – [b] It's getting hot! – [c] William II – [d] Charles Dupuy

the Republic is involved in the general collapse.[a] Three Cabinets and one President finished off[484]—that's not doing too badly. The socialist group seems to have succeeded to the role of the late Clemenceau[488]—and will play it better, I hope. It is now established that no ministry can exist without at least the help of the extreme Left. That will lead to the dissolution, to which the growing stench of the opportunists' corruption is also leading.[87] In which case you will be returned in greater strength, both numerically and morally; that can lead to the formation of Lassalle's 'great reactionary mass',[214] the coalition of all the bourgeois parties against socialism, a mass which is always formed at a time of danger, afterwards to be dissolved again into its various and mutually opposed groups of interests; large landowners, large manufacturers, high finance, small and middling bourgeoisie, peasants, etc. But, each time it is reformed, it gains solidity until the day of crisis, when we shall have a compact mass confronting us. We have had this process of continual concentration and dissolution in Germany ever since our Party numbered more than 20 members in the Reichstag; but in your case, it will go faster because decisive power is in the hands of your Chamber of Deputies.

Mr Faure may do what he likes, he cannot halt this process of forming into two opposing camps, nor the confusion which is necessarily born of this interplay of opposing forces, attraction and repulsion, within the milieu of the bourgeois parties. That is precisely the milieu we need, and which the existence of a socialist group creates everywhere, however little power it may have in Parliament. You will race ahead; it is the Party's progress itself that will first subdue and then eliminate the intestine and traditional quarrels.

The addition of 30 Radicals has brought you luck, without them the group would not have had cohesion. Without Millerand you would not have been able to take advantage of the political situations as you have done. And Jaurès, indeed, seems full of goodwill—if he develops rather slowly it is perhaps a good thing for him and for us. Though frankly, in economic matters he needs further schooling. His Bills for immediate reforms in the *Petite République*[489] article are not quite as wild as his Bill for a corn monopoly,[b] but they are calling on the bourgeois for sacrifices incompatible with the advance of capitalist industry, so that in their eyes they are tantamount to immediate expropriation; whereas, on the other

---

[a] Gean Casimir-Périer – [b] See this volume, p. 275

hand, he proposes improvement of the soil at the nation's expense, of the soil which would remain private property, and under conditions perpetuating the small peasant and which would create a new Panama[60] for the big landowners who would laugh at the 'obligation' etc. with which the Bill saddled them. This is to see as a complete abstraction the environment in which one lives and *in* which these reforms would be carried out. So long as the air is not cleansed by the removal of all the parliamentary and financial rogues, this improvement of individual landed property at everyone's expense would end as a colossal theft; and when we have got rid of these gentlemen, we shall be strong enough to do better than that.

The presidential crisis furthermore will have a capital effect on European politics. The Franco-Russian alliance is becoming more and more lenitive, insofar as the Russian hope of seeing the restoration of the monarchy emerge from the presidential crisis suffers repeated disillusionment. At the same time the Triple Alliance[126] has ceased to exist except on paper; bankrupt Italy slips through its fingers, Austria is only retained: by fear of war with Russia, for which she would foot the bill; this danger vanishes as Russia loses the chance of using the French army when she sees fit; young William[a] has made himself far more disagreeable to his friends than to his enemies. So that, with the complete revolution in weapons since 1870 and, in consequence, of tactics, there is a total uncertainty about the outcome of a war where so many imponderables are involved and regarding which all the calculations made in advance are based on fictitious quantities. In these circumstances we seem to be assured of peace and even the most frenzied bourgeois chauvinists of the Déroulède type can keep calm: the Prussians have taken over responsibility in Alsace for maintaining and nourishing French patriotism.

Herewith cheque for twenty pounds; if that can do you until the beginning of April, I should be glad; at that time I shall have certain payments coming in which will allow me to be more liberal. But, if needs be, I could perhaps, after all, send you ten pounds in March—we'll see.

Greetings from the Freybergers. Kiss Laura very warmly for me.

Ever yours,
F. E.

I am sending you a report of the Norwich Trades Union Congress.[396]

---

[a] William II

First published in;   Printed according to the original
F. Engels, P. et L. Lafargue,
Correspondance, t. III,   Translated from the French
Paris, 1959

255

ENGELS TO FERDINAND TONNIES

IN KIEL

London, 24 January 1895
41 Regent's Park Road, N. W.

Dear Sir,

I still have to thank you for your kindness in sending me your critique of Barth's book and your interesting article on Pestalozzi.[490] I would beg you to excuse the delay which was occasioned by an excess of work, the latter being aggravated by my having moved house (please note the change of address).

I should say that you have let Mr Barth off rather lightly; he would, at any rate, have fared far worse at my hands. However, in literary debate one has to get used to the fact that, lawyer-fashion, one's opponent suppresses what doesn't suit his book and introduces extraneous matter if he thinks this will enable him to pull the wool over his reader's eyes. But in Mr Barth's case this is done in a manner and to an extent that cannot but lead one to ask whether what we have here is simple ignorance and boneheadedness or deliberate, wilful distortion. To take only his chapter on Marx—how does one explain the horrendous misinterpretations, nearly all of which are incomprehensible in a man who does, after all, claim to have read my *Anti-Dühring* and *Feuerbach*[a] which should have constituted a perfectly adequate antidote? And what can one say about the absurd causal nexus attributed to me on p. 135.

'In France Calvinism had been conquered, *which is why* in the eighteenth century, Christianity had become incapable of serving as an ideo-

---
[a] F. Engels, *Ludwig Feuerbach and the End of Classical German Philosophy*.

logical cloak for any sort of progressive class'? When I compare it with the original, *Feuerbach*, p. 65,[a] find it virtually impossible to believe that this is not deliberate distortion.

I am interested by what you have to say about August Comte. So far as this 'philosopher' is concerned, there still remains, in my opinion, a fair amount of work to be done. For five years Comte was secretary and confidant of Saint-Simon. The latter positively suffered from an over-fertile intellect; he was at once a genius and a mystic. Lucid analysis, classification, systematisation, none of this was his cup of tea. Thus in Comte he got hold of a man intended, perhaps, to present this proliferation of ideas to the world in orderly fashion after the Master's death; Comte's mathematical training and mode of thought may have made him seem peculiarly suited to the purpose as compared with the other, visionary disciples. But then Comte suddenly broke with the 'Master' and withdrew from the school. After quite a while he re-emerged with his 'positive philosophy'.[b] In this system there are three characteristic elements; 1. A series of brilliant ideas nearly all of which, however, suffer to a greater or lesser extent from inadequate development; 2. A correspondingly narrow, philistine outlook in stark contrast to that brilliance; 3. A religious system of undoubtedly Saint-Simonian origin but stripped of all mysticism, hierarchically organised and utterly flat—with, at its head, a pope, no less. Thus Huxley was able to say of Comtism[491] that it was catholicism without christianity.[c]

Now I am willing to bet that No. 3 supplies the key to the otherwise incomprehensible inconsistency of Nos 1 and 2; namely, that Comte derived all his brilliant ideas from Saint-Simon but he assembled them in a manner peculiar to himself and by so doing bowdlerised them. By stripping them of the mysticism with which they were imbued, he simultaneously degraded them to a lower level, giving them a philistine slant in accordance with his own lights. A great many of them can be easily traced back to their Saint-Simonian source and I feel sure that certain others would admit of the same treatment if only someone could be found who would seriously apply himself to the task. This fact would assuredly have been discovered long since had not Saint-Simon's own writings been

---

[a] F. Engels, *Ludwig Feuerbach and the End of Classical German Philosophy.*[a] See present edition, Vol. 26, p. 396 – [b] A. Comte, *Cours de philosophie Positive* – [c] See Th. Henry Huxley, *On the Physical Basis of Life.* In *The Fortnightly Review*, No. XXVI, Vol. V, 1 February 1869

completely overwhelmed after 1830 by the clamour of the *école et religion saint-simmoniennes*ᵃ which emphasised individual aspects of the Master's teaching and elaborated it at the cost of the grand design. There is one further point I should like to put right, namely the note on p. 513.⁴⁹² Marx was never Secretary General to the International but merely Secretary for Germany and Russia. And none of the Comtists in London participated in the founding of the International. At the time of the Commune, Professor E. Beesly did yeoman service in defending the International in the press against the violent attacks then being made upon it, and Frederic Harrison also publicly defended the Commune.⁴⁹³ But a few years later the Comtists' attitude towards the labour movement grew perceptibly cooler; Labour was becoming too powerful and, if a proper balance was to be maintained between capitalists and workers (both being, of course, *producteur*ᵇ in the sense understood by Saint-Simon⁴⁹⁴), the former should again, it was felt, be given support, since which time the Comtists have kept quite mum on the subject of the labour question.

Yours sincerely,
F. Engels

First published abridged in;
G. Mayer, *Eine Biographie*,
Bd. II, The Hague, 1934 and,
in full, in Russian, in
Bolsheviks, No. 14, 1935

Printed according to the original

Published in English
in full for the first time

256

ENGELS TO LUDWIG KUGELMANN⁴⁷³

IN HANOVER

[London,] 25 January 1895

Dear Kugelmann,

I cannot yet give you an indication of the compendiums,⁴⁹⁵ etc., in which the articles in question may be found, for 1. I shall first have to

---

ᵃ Saint-Simonian school and religion. – ᵇ producers

know what we have already got (some being in Germany, about which I shall shortly be hearing, and some in America, which I am waiting for), aside from my own things; 2. Because I myself cannot say exactly, though all sorts of things recur to me whenever any new stuff arrives; 3. Because, as soon as No, 1 has been attended to, we must so arrange matters that neither of us competes with the other, and thus puts the price up. In the meantime it would be a good thing if you were to keep an eye open for specifically *Westphalian* literature of 1845-47: *Dampfboot*ᵃ and compendiums as well as other stuff written by those people at that time.

I believe I *have* got Meyer's collection of *Tribune* articles here; it will be the more comprehensive of the two collections, Marx having obtained various things from over there shortly after Meyer's death.[455]

Kindest regards to all,

Yours
F. E.

Frankfurter Zeitung received with thanks.

First published in: Marx
and Engels, *Works*,
First Russian Edition,
Vol. XXIX, 1946

Printed according to the original

Published in English for the first time

257

ENGELS TO VICTOR ADLER

IN VIENNA

London, 28 January 1895

Dear Victor,

Many congratulations from myself and everyone else here on the rapid success achieved by the *Arbeiter-Zeitung*[496] It was no more than I expected, but to see it confirmed in actual fact is, of course, also worth a great deal.

ᵃ *Das Westphälische Dampfboot*

There is no need at all for you to worry about the editorial side. During the early weeks you, as organiser, are infinitely more important than you would be as actual editor. Once everything is going smoothly, you should have no difficulty in striking the right note in the paper. You are quite right about it's being a mite too serious. A bit more humour, particularly on the front page, *which* used always to be very funny in the twiceweekly edition, would do no harm at all. However, that will come.

A direct telegraph service from foreign capitals would be of absolutely no use to you, That would mean your having a properly organised office in every city with a chief correspondent to run it professionally, and solely on your account; here in London this would cost between six hundred and a thousand pounds a year, and even so you wouldn't be getting the best news from ministerial or opposition circles, for the simple reason that you are only accorded priority and given news of this sort *ahead of* everyone else and before it has become common property if you are able to reciprocate by giving your informants your support and publishing the ready-made puffs they send you. But that is just what our press cannot do. So, where news from official circles is concerned, you will never be able to compete with the big bourgeois papers who not only monopolise the sources but can also organise news-gathering services on a footing similar to that of big industry.

It's hard luck, your having to content yourselves during the first few weeks with the little provincial assemblies, but the Diet will soon be meeting again and then you will have plenty of material, whereupon your personal intervention will again become necessary,

The differences in the Ministry here are of no great account so far as their practical consequences are concerned. The Liberal government contains as many shades of opinion as it has members. Now that the big bourgeoisie together with Whig aristocrats[497] and the university ideologues have gone over to the Conservative camp (a process which began after 1848, gained impetus after the Reform Bill of 1867[498] and became very marked after the HOME RULE BILL[171]). Liberalism has been largely an omnium gatherum of all the sects and sectarian crotchets in this sect-ridden country. And since each individual sect considers its own particular crotchet to be the one and only panacea, the result is constant strife.

But of greater moment than that strife is the certain knowledge that only cohesion vis-à-vis the outside world can keep them in power for a few months longer. Consequently it is a matter of pure chance which tendency may gain the upper hand.

I have been sending you in rotation copies of the three labour newspapers which still survive here. Since you get the *Clarion* by way of exchange I shall spare you this in future. There is nothing much in any of the three but nevertheless it's advisable that you should take a look at one or the other from time to time. The *Labour Leader* is an institution for the idolisation of Keir Hardie; he is a cunning, crafty Scot, a Pecksniff and arch-intriguer, but too cunning, perhaps, and too vain. The financial sources he draws upon to keep the paper going are of a dubious kind, which might cause unpleasantness when the new elections are held.

Apropos. *Not a single* copy of Thursday evening's issue[a] (confiscated) arrived here. But nevertheless I should like to read the article, *K. M. in Wien*[471] Could you get hold of another copy for me? That was an astounding piece of cheek, by the way your announcing the confiscation to have been so extraordinarily effective that it enabled you to save yourselves the expense of another, quite unnecessary, edition.[499] You people are lucky in Austria—if you were to say something like that in Prussia they would promptly chuck three Subversion Bills[428] at your head.

We shall be sending you extracts from *la* Crawford's Paris letters whenever they contain something of interest. I would specially call your attention to them. She has been in Paris for over forty years, knows every mouse in the place by name, possesses dossiers on the career of every politician and is a good judge of character. No one in Paris can equal her knowledge of personalities and you would therefore be well-advised to file away for future reference even those articles for which you have no present use. Over and over again she has seen all her Radical and Republican friends plunge into the mire of corruption and has thus, bourgeois though she is, acquired a remarkable sympathy for Socialists. She has one unshakeable conviction, however, and that is that J. Guesde is Marx's son-in-law.

Yesterday I sent you another excerpt from one of her articles.[500]

Louise has been especially gratified by the unequivocal rejection of the petitions of the Women's Union—see Clara Zetkin's article in the supplement to Thursday's *Vorwärts*.[501] Clara is right and did after all manage to get the article accepted in the teeth of long and determined opposition. Bravo Clara!

---

[a] of the *Arbeiter-Zeitung*

Love from Louise and Ludwig and the baby who always yells with glee whenever the *Arbeiter-Zeitung* arrives, and from

Yours,
F. E.

First published abridged in
Arbeiter-Zeitung, No. 327,
28 November 1920 and in full
in: *Victor Adlers Aufsätze,
Reden und Briefe.* Erstes Heft:
Victor Adler und Friedrich Engels,
Vienna, 1922

Printed according to the book

Published in English in full
for the first time

258

ENGELS TO WILHELM ELLENBOGEN[502]

IN VIENNA

London, 28 January 1895
41 Regent's Park Road, N. W.

Esteemed Comrade,

Unfortunately for somewhat over a year I have been forced to make it my duty politely but firmly to decline all invitations to contribute to festive messages, etc., in particular periodically recurring ones, or to send messages of greetings on holidays (18 March, May Day, etc.), the only deviation from this rule being certain exceptional occasions, which promise an immediate specific effect. When you were bringing out the first issue of the daily in Vienna, I believed congratulations to be indicated.[a] If I sent you two lines for the May Day address, I would be compelled to do the same for the Czechs, Hungarians, Italians, Germans, Romanians and who knows what other nations and, moreover, probably send in addresses for the various May Day meetings, leave alone anniversaries like the 13th[b] and 18th of March.

---

[a] F. Engels, 'Message of Greetings to the Austrian Workers on the Daily Publication of the *Arbeiter-Zeitung*'. – [b] Probably a slip of the pen. Should be 14 March, the day of Karl Marx's death.

If I am to have time for work, I am obliged to leave the demonstrating to younger forces.

Much as I would like to do a favour precisely to the Austrian comrades, I trust the above will help them realise that this time I must refuse.

Yours faithfully,
F. Engels

First published in: Marx and Engels, *Works*, Second Russian Edition, Vol. 50, Moscow, 1981

Printed according to the original

Published in English for the first time

259

ENGELS TO VERA ZASULICH[503]

IN LONDON

London, 30 January 1895

Dear citizeness Vera,

I shall certainly be at home either tomorrow between 3 and 5, or Friday[a] from 3 to 4 in the afternoon, when I shall be happy to see you.

The book by G. Plekhanov[b] is quite to the purpose; today the newspapers announce that Nicholas has just declared to the Zemstvos[504] he abides as firmly as his father[c] by tsarist autocracy.[d] There is no remedy against the folly of princes.[505] So much the better if Georgi has made a furore.[e]

Always yours,
F. E.

First published, in Russian, in: *Gruppa 'Osvobozhdeniye Truda'*, No. 1, 1924

Printed according to the original

Translated from the French

Published in English for the first time

---

[a] 1 February – [b] [name in Russian] *The Development of the Monist View of History*, put out in St. Petersburg under the pen-name of N. Beltov [name in Russian]. – [c] Alexander III – [d] [word in Russian] – [e] [phrase in Russian]

260

ENGELS TO WITOLD JODKO-NARKIEWICZ

IN LONDON

[London,] 2 February 1895
41 Regent's Park Road, N. W.

Dear Comrade,

Unfortunately I can give you absolutely no hint as to how the German comrades might view the proposal regarding the addition to the name of the next congress.[506] So far as I myself am concerned, I think that *on this occasion* one might oblige the Trades Unions, since the congress will be held on English soil where the Trades Unions have, after all, always got the bulk of organised labour behind them, so that a congress in which they played *no* part would create a bad impression. At the same time it cannot but be of importance to us to encourage the trend that is driving Trades Unions more and more into the socialist camp.

Kindest regards.

Yours,
F. Engels

Dr and Mrs Freyberger also send you their kindest regards.

First published, in the language of the original (German), in: *Z pola walki*, No. 4 (12), 1960

Printed according to the original

Published in English for the first time

261

ENGELS TO RICHARD FISCHER

IN BERLIN

London, 2 February 1895
41 Regent's Park Road, N. W.

Dear Fischer,

You and the others have an odd way of holding a pistol to a fellow's head. Having made your plans for Marx's articles, you really might have told me about them a bit sooner rather then at the very last moment.[507] In a case such as this, where I am the administrator of other people's property, I *cannot* rush things in the same way as I could if the matter simply concerned myself. Added to that, I am at this moment getting Lassalle's letters[284] ready for you and these are far more likely to fall foul of the Subversion Bill[428] than Marx's articles—the *latter*, then, is the work I ought to put on one side!

So tell me first of all what format and type you are using and how large the edition is to be, also the selling price, for on this occasion I shall, for various reasons, only sell you the right to *one* edition of a *specific size*. Meanwhile I shall have a word with Tussy; as soon as I get your reply, I shall let you know for certain.

If you cannot advise me of the exact selling price, it will be sufficient if you say how much you propose to charge per printed sheet.

I assume that you have a copy of the *Neue Rheinische Zeitung—Revue* from which to reprint. For I myself do not possess one of my own and if I did I couldn't let it out of my hands.

Now for another matter. When the *Vorwärts* set up its bookselling side, August[a] wrote to say that I would be sent *two copies* of all your publications. Of late, however, that has been very far from the case. For instance, I have *not* received your latest edition of the *Manifesto*, or indeed either of the Berlin editions.[508] I am still short of sundry lesser pieces and am listing those that immediately spring to mind. You would greatly oblige me by sending them to me, namely your *reprint of the Subversion Debate* in two parts[b] and a *couple* of copies of the most recent edition of the *Communist Manifesto*.—As regards the other things I am short of, I have just seen from your list that you are not to blame, since you were not the publisher. Apart from the above I am still short of

Minutes of the *Wyden*[c] Congress, 1880[343]
      ”   ”   *Brussels*[d]   ”   1891[228]
and one on *Zurich*[229] if it was you who published it.[509]

---

[a] Bebel – [b] *Umsturz und Sozialdemokratie. Verhandlungen des Deutschen Reichstags am 17. Dezember 1894 und 8-12. Januar 1895 nach dem offiziellen stenographischen* Bericht. – [c] *Protokoll des Kongresses zu Wyden 1880.* Berlin, 1893. – d *Verhandlungen und Beschlüsse des Internationalen Arbeiter-Kongresses zu Brüssel* (16-22. August 1891). Berlin, 1893 – e *Protokoll des Internationalen Sozialistischen Arbeiterkongresses in der Tornhalle Zürich vom. 6. bis 12. August* 1893.

The list I used for comparison was issued in 1893 and it is therefore possible that one thing or another may still be missing.

So please let me have the information by return and I shall send you a definite answer as promptly as possible.

Give my kindest regards to your wife and children and all my friends.

Yours

F. E.

First published in: Marx and Engels, *Works*, First Russian Edition, Vol. XXIX, 1946

Printed according to the original

Published in English for the first time

262

ENGELS TO GEORGI PLEKHANOV

IN ZURICH

London, 8 February 1895

My dear Plekhanov,

Freyberger will happily undertake to give Vera[a] an examination, but how shall we make it seem plausible to her? Naturally, Freyberger cannot go to her and say: George Plekhanov has asked me to take a look at you. You will have to speak to her about it first, and obtain her consent, and then the best would be for her to talk to me, and I will take care of the rest. Or else she can talk to Louise Freyberger if she prefers, and Louise will see to everything. That is my suggestion, but if you think you have another idea on how to achieve your aim, tell me about it, and we can discuss it.

Vera has given me your book,[b] for which my thanks. I have begun to read it, but it will take time. However, it is a great success to have managed to have it published in *your country*. That is a step forward, and even if we cannot retain the new position we have just gained, a precedent has

---

[a] Vera Zasulich – [b] The reference is to G. V. Plekhanov [name in Russian], *The Development of the Monist View of History* [in Russian], published in St. Petersburg under the pen-name of N. Beltov [name in Russian]

been established, the ice is broken. The suppression of the *Russkaya Zhizn* (Russian Life)[a] would seem to mark the beginning of reaction. Nikolai would seem to want to prepare his moujiks[b] for liberty by compulsory education, so that only the next generation will be ripe for the constitution; it is still just another formula for the old: *après nous le déluge!*[510] However the deluge is like the devil in Faust!

> den Teufel spürt das Völkchen nie,
> und wenn er sie beim Kragen hätte—[c]

And when the Devil of the revolution has someone at his collar, then he has Nicholas II.

As for my health, it is better than it has been for a long time. My digestion is good, my respiratory system working perfectly, I sleep my seven hours per night, and work with pleasure—happy to be able, at last! to recommence my own work after an interruption of almost a year: proofs of the 3rd volume, correspondence, moving house, intestinal trouble, etc., etc.

Greetings to Mme Plekhanov and to Axelrod from myself, and also from Ludwig and Louise Freyberger.

Yours,

F. Engels

You did not give me any special address, and therefore I am using the old one.

First published, in Russian, in: *Gruppa 'Osvobozhdeniye Truda'* No. 2, 1924

Printed according to the original

Translated from the French

Published in English for the first time

---

[a] [the name of the newspaper is written in Russian] – [b] This Russian word meaning "peasants" is written by Engels in Latin letters – [c] Goethe, *Faust*, Part I, Scene 5; this quotation and the following paragraph are written in German.

263

ENGELS TO HERMANN ENGELS

IN BARMEN

London, 8 February 1895

Dear Hermann,

The arrival of your letter of the 23rd coincided with a spell of fine, frosty weather which has been playing Old Harry with consignments of wine. I have nevertheless ordered your sherry from Dublin but with the proviso that I shall not give instructions for it to be despatched until such time as the Rhine is open again and there is no longer any danger of the wine freezing en route. Indeed, I myself had a mild fright when five cases!—fifteen dozen of port and claret en route to me from Dublin were exposed for about forty-eight hours to an unexpected frost. It would seem, however, that everything has turned out all right, for the stuff I have sampled so far has not suffered, while a period of repose in my splendid wine cellar—an even temperature and space for nearly one hundred dozen in eight brick-walled bins—will see to the rest.

For the first time in many years we are again having a real Continental winter over here. Warm, almost spring-like up till the New Year with the shrubs all coming into bud, then cold and, for the past three weeks, constant sharp frost (80-100 Centigrade—60-80 Réamur of frost at night) and snow. When the north-easter blows it is bitterly cold but when, like yesterday and today, there is little wind, it is glorious. Fortunately there is always enough wind to disperse the fog, the result being a marvellous blue sky.

I can well imagine your tribulations as a result of wining, dining and dancing to the accompaniment of serenades from a cavalry band. Over here we call it THE SOCIAL TREADMILL which, however diverting it may often have been in one's younger days, is a pretty ghastly business when one gets older. I fight tooth and nail to keep out of it, but in this country, too, the likes of us cannot escape it entirely at Christmastime.

The £40 from Wilhelm Pf. duly and gratefully received.

Incidentally, on this occasion I survived the treadmill of the festive season in better shape than usual because I took proper care of myself and just now, what with icy weather so similar to that at home, I feel better than I have done for a long time. I have also been able to put the heating properties of my new study to the supreme test, for not only is there the extraordinary cold to contend with, but, added to that, the two neighbouring houses are both empty, i.e. unheated, and my room abuts on the two party walls. And I have nevertheless managed to keep it warm. It was not until yesterday that I felt a bit chilly, but whenever one's need is greatest, help is always close at hand. On this occasion Rudolf's[a] nightshirt stepped into the breech, whereupon I smartly stepped into it.

You can learn about my fellow occupants[b] from Oscar Jaeger who met them both at my house when he last visited us here. Freyberger was courting at that particular time and spent the evening with us.

I have just received a deputation from the local rating authority. The gentlemen wished to satisfy themselves that I was not in fact paying more than, £85 for the house, the reason being that the last tenant had paid £130, while the rates for the house are based on an annual rental of £110. Needless to say I protested. I showed the gentlemen all the documents and shall now see what they do. Out of the eight houses close by, four are empty and so I hope they will deal mercifully with me.

Well then, I have ordered $1^1/_2$ dozen No. 1 and $1^1/_2$ dozen No. 2 sherry as per samples.

As you have said nothing further about it, I assume that Walter[c] has passed his exam and I send him my congratulations. Even heartier congratulations to Elsbeth[d] on her forthcoming marriage. But she must also tell me the day, so that we over here can also indulge ourselves in her and her bridegroom's[e] honour.

Much love, then, to Emma[f] and all your children, your sons and daughters-in-law and your children's children.

Your old

Friedrich

I shall pay for the sherry in May and debit it on delivery.

First published in
Deutsche Revue, Jg. 46,
Bd. III, 1921

Printed according to the original

Published in English for the first time

---

[a] Rudolf Engels, Engels' brother – [b] Louise and Ludwig Freyberger – [c] Walter Engels— Engels' nephew – [d] Elsbeth Engels—Engels' niece – [e] Arthur Schuchard – [f] Emma Engels— Engels' sister-in-law

264

ENGELS TO RICHARD FISCHER

IN BERLIN

London, 12 February 1895
41 Regent's Park Road, N. W.

Dear Fischer,

If you yourself are of the opinion that the difference in price as between 60 Pfennigs and 1 Mark will make little difference so far as sales are concerned, I am, of course, in favour of selling the edition for 1 Mark. In return for a fee of 400 Marks I therefore assign you the right to bring out an edition of up to 3,000 copies and you may start printing straight away.[507] I shall get down to the *Introduction* forthwith and let you have it very shortly. The copy I have of the *Neue Rheinische Zeitungs-Revue* came into my possession on the strict understanding that it would not leave this house, besides which it is most necessary to me for the correction of proofs, since the relevant text was corrected in *Hamburg* and contains a mass of misprints—it was copied from Marx's manuscript. It is equally necessary to me for purposes of comparison in respect of the *Introduction*. So please send me the first proofs in *galley* form and I can then insert the necessary explanatory notes.[511]

N. B., thirty-six free copies should be reserved for myself; a considerable number of them have to be passed on to the heirs.

So for the time being I shall leave Lassalle's letters[284] on one side. The explanatory introduction and notes call for a good deal of rummaging about amongst my papers and I cannot therefore say in advance when it will be done.

When printing Marx's articles, please note that, in the original, *Konstitution, Klasse, Kollision*, etc. are generally spelt with a 'C' but also probably with a 'K'. *Please put 'K' throughout*; that will save a great deal of Korrigiererei.[a]

Congratulations on your maiden speech[512]; it will have made the bourgeois pretty furious!

---

[a] correction

Many regards from everyone.

Yours,

F. Engels

The various pamphlets—two lots—arrived safely. Very many thanks.

First published in: Marx and Engels, *Works*, First Russian Edition, Vol. XXIX, 1946

Printed according to the original

Published in English for the first time

265

ENGELS TO RICHARD FISCHER

IN BERLIN

London, 13 February 1895

Dear Fischer,

I enclose the titles for the pamphlet[a] as well as for the chapters. In order to complete the three articles it will be necessary to add the passages on France from the 5th and 6th (double) issue as a 4th chapter.[513] Arranged, that is, as set out on the encl. sheet; first (in square brackets) my few introductory words, then the passage on pp. 150/153[b] as shown, then a line of dots indicating the omission and, by way of conclusion, the main passage on pp. 160-171.[c] That will provide a perfectly respectable chapter and, with the abolition of universal suffrage which served Bonaparte as a pretext in Dec. 1851, round off the whole with a pertinent conclusion without which it would remain a fragment.

Tomorrow I shall get on with the introduction to the whole.[d]

In Germany matters are really coming to a head quite nicely. I can hardly imagine that the Centre[71] would deliberately saw off the branch it was sitting on. But the foolishness of our opponents increases from day

---

[a] K. Marx, *The Class Struggles in France, 1848 to 1850*. – [b] See present edition, Vol. 10, pp. 507-10, 132-35. – [c] See present edition, Vol. 10, pp. 516-25, 135-45. – [d] F. Engels, *Introduction to Karl Marx's 'The Class Struggles in France, 1848 to 1850'*, 1895 – See present edition, Vol.27, pp. 506-524.

to day and in this respect nothing is really impossible. If the gentlemen's defection is consummated, that will mean making over the whole of the Rheinland and Westphalia to us.

Regards.

Yours,

F.E.

(The title should include: Reprinted from the *Neue Rheinische Zeitung. Politisch-ökonomische Revue, Hamburg, 1850)*

First published in: Marx and Engels, *Works*, First Russian Edition, Vol. XXIX, 1946

Printed according to the original

Published in English for the first time

266

ENGELS TO JULIUS MOTTELER[515]

IN LONDON

[London,] 23 February 1895
41 Regent's Park Road, N. W.

Dear Julius,

One Theodor Barlen,[a] the bearer of a card from the Dortmund club, has called on me seeking assistance. He is a deserter, having decamped from Spandau, and alleges that he was previously a very active party member in Hörde, Dortmund, etc. I referred him to the Society.[62] He came back today to say that the Society refused to recommend him to me, since they did not know whether the papers he produced were his own. As I should like to have some information on the man so as to know whether I ought not to send him packing once and for all, I would ask you to tell me whether this accords with the facts and, once his case has been investigated, what view they take of him at the Society.[516]

Many regards to your wife and yourself from

---

[a] Hermann Barlen in the ms.

Yours,

F. Engels

First published in: Marx and Engels, *Works*, First Russian Edition, Vol. XXIX, 1946

Printed according to the original

Published in English for the first time

267

ENGELS TO PAUL LAFARGUE

AT LE PERREUX

[London,] 26 February 1895
41 Regent's Park Road, N. W.

My dear Lafargue,

I am sending the Manuscript to you by registered post with a few comments—as always the translation is excellent.[517] There has been a delay of a few days, and this is why; in Berlin they want to reprint the three articles by Marx on the events in France in 1848-49 (published in 1850 in the *Revue de la Nouvelle Gazette Rhénane*[a] and this cannot be done without an introduction[507]; this introduction has become quite long, since besides a general review of the events since that date, it would be necessary to explain why we were right to expect the imminent and definitive victory of the proletariat, why that has not come about, and to what point events have modified the way we saw things then. This is important because of the new laws which are threatening us in Germany.[428] A Reichstag Commission is attempting to transform all the articles of the penal code into rubber articles which are applicable or not, depending on the political party to which the defendant belongs. Arguments in favour of an act declared criminal, etc. will be punished if they are made in circumstances which could justify the opinion that the accused wished to provoke or incite imitation! etc., etc. that is, you who are socialist will be punished for having said something which any conservative, liberal or

---

[a] *Neue Rheinische Zeitung. Politisch-ökonomische Revue.*

clerical may say with impunity. The clericals in the commission are worse than the government itself. Just imagine, they are requesting two years in prison for anyone who denies in public or in the press the existence of god or the immortality of the soul.

This is a fury of reaction wholly without purpose, and absolutely inexplicable except on the supposition that all these gentlemen are threatened by a *coup d'état*. This coup d'état is openly preached by *top-ranking officials*. Constantin Rössler, ministerial counsellor, has called for it in a brochure.[a] Boguslawski, a retired general, has just done the same thing.[b] The liberals and clericals know that, faced with such determination on the part of the government, there is nothing left for them but to submit. In the presence of 2 million socialist electors, these gentlemen do not have the courage to resist a coup d'état openly—the government uses this threat to disarm them, and they will vote just to 'save' the constitution and domestic peace! Wait and see, they will vote for all the taxes, all the battleships, all the new regiments requested by William[c]—if the electors do not become involved. For our bourgeois deputies are so cowardly that even the courage of cowardice may prove lacking.

In any case, we are striding towards a crisis, if there can be a crisis in this Germany of the Bourgeoisie, where everything is blunted. What is certain is that there will be a new age of persecution for our friends. As for us, our policy should be not to let ourselves be provoked at this point; we would be fighting without the least chance of success, and we would be bled like Paris in 1871, whereas in two or three years our forces may have doubled, as under the exceptional law.[15] Today our Party would be fighting alone against all the others, rallied around the government under the banner of social order; in two or three years we will have on our side the peasants and the petty-bourgeois crushed by taxation. The battle corps does not engage in frontline battles but reserves itself for the critical moment.

Anyway, we shall see how it ends.

How ironical that you, one of the most French writers of our age, should be doomed to be published almost always in German! And what German! The translators of Berlin and Stuttgart display a truly Germanic heaviness. There is only Adler who does you justice, and he will not al-

---

[a] C. Rößler, *Die Sozialdemokratie*. – [b] A. Boguslawski, *Vollkampf—nicht Scheinkampf. Ein Wort zur politischen Lage imInnern.* – [c] William II

ways have the time to translate you himself. The only consolation I can offer is to tell you that I myself always breathe a little of the French spirit when I retranslate mentally your translator; sometimes I succeed.

We have been without water for 15 days, the pipe beneath our road is frozen; otherwise everything at home is going well. For one week we had almost no gas, as paraffins containing C_4, C_5 and C_6, and more of carbon are precipitated in the pipes by the cold. It was one of those periods when London relapses into barbarity. And the *Standard* tells you that, this is the proof that England has reached the summit of civilisation!

Thank Laura for her fine translation; I still have not received the letter you promised I would receive from her, but I hope that she has received the copy of the 3rd volume[a] for Deville that I sent to her on 1st January.

Greetings from the Freybergers.

Yours,

F. E.

The preface to the 3rd volume has been published in Italian in *La Rassegna*[467] translated by Martignetti, and reviewed by Labriola, who has rendered the passages on Loria with a voluptuousness which bursts through each line. On the other hand, Loria has written a critique of the 3rd volume in the *Nuova Antologia* which is of unequalled superficiality.[b] 1st volume: Napoleon I, 2nd: the king of Rome, tubercular, 3rd: Louis Bonaparte III. In Germany, Werner Sombart, a Berlin professor and a rather eclectic Marxist, has written a good article on the 3rd volume.[c] How are things progressing for 1st May? People are talking only of the Allemanists.[21] And how is the unity, or disunity, of the groups progressing, particularly as regards your own? Vaillant has written to me again, he wants my opinion on his draft laws.[d] I have still not found the time to read Jaurès on materio-idealism.[518]

Engels' Comments on the French translation of his *On the History of Early Christianity:*

---

[a] of *Capital* – [b] A. Loria, '*L'opera postuma di Carlo Marx*'. In: *Nuova Antologia*, Anno XXX, fascicolo III - 1 febbraio 1895. – [c] W. Sombart, 'Zur Kritik des ökonomischen Systems von Karl Marx'. In: *Archiv für Soziale Gesetzgebung und Statistik*. Bd. 7, H. 4, [1894] – [d] See this volume, pp. 420, 453

p. 17[*]
The Philonic school of Alexandria and Greco-Roman vulgar philosophy—Platonic and especially Stoic—played an important role in the development of Christianity as the state religion under Constantine. This role is far from being established in detail etc. etc.

p. 34[**]
What holy indignation was provoked after 1830 in the pious nursery that was Germany at the time by, as Heine called it, Saint Simon's reinstatement of the flesh! The most shocked were the aristocratic estates who dominated at the time (I'm not speaking of the aristocratic class, given that in 1830 classes did not yet exist in our country) who, etc.

––––––––––

same page, last word conception—doesn't this word lend itself too well to a play on words here?

First published, abridged,
in *Voprosy philosophii* No. 5,
Moscow, 1965 and in full in:
Marx and Engels, *Works*,
Second Russian Edition, Vol. 39,
Moscow, 1966

Printed according to the original

Translated from the French

Published in English for the first time

268

ENGELS TO GEORGI PLEKHANOV[119]

IN GENEVA

London, 26 February, 1895
41 Regent's Park Road, N. W.

My dear Plekhanov,
Everything was arranged eight days ago, Vera[a] wrote to me and said that she would be delighted to be treated by Freyberger. He went to see her eight days ago yesterday, and has since been twice. He discovered that she had a severe case of bronchitis, and has prescribed the necessary medicines. However, he says that what she needs most is a different diet.

––––––––––
[a] Zasulich – [*] See p. 453, Vol. 27 – [**] See p. 459, Vol. 27

She should eat meat instead of fruit jellies and other vegetable foods. Freyberger is out at the moment, so I will return to the question of her health before finishing this letter.

Now, since you have made me more or less responsible for the state of her health, you must tell me if she has need of money. If she has, I would ask you to permit me to offer you some for her, however little, at least during her illness, I will send you, say, five pounds to begin with, that you can persuade her to accept as *coming from you*, so that I do not come into it at all. You could tell her that you have sent her this money to remove any excuse for refusing to change her diet, and that Freyberger has said that she must do so. Or perhaps you can find another excuse.

I will not have the time to read the critical review of my book[a] in *Russian Heritage.*[b] I have already seen enough on this subject in the issue for January 1894.[520] As for Danielson, I fear that there is nothing to be done with him. I sent him *by letter post*[25] the Russian material from *Internationales aus dem Volketaat*, and in particular the 1894 appendix, which was written, *in part*, directly with him in view.[522] He has received it but, as you see, it is useless. There is no way of discussing with this generation of Russians to which he belongs, and which still believes in the spontaneous-communist mission which distinguishes Russia, the true Holy Russ,[c] from other profane peoples.

As for the rest, in a country such as yours, where largescale modern industry is grafted onto the primitive peasant commune, and where all the intermediary stages of civilisation are represented simultaneously, in a country which, in addition, is surrounded more or less effectively by an intellectual wall of China erected by despotism, it is scarcely surprising if the most bizarre and impossible combinations of ideas are produced. Take the poor devil Flerovsky, who imagines that tables and beds think, but have no memory. It is a phase the country must pass through. Little by little, with the growth of the towns, the isolation of men of talent will disappear, and with it these mental aberrations caused by loneliness, the inconsistency of the patchy knowledge of these curious thinkers, and also a little, in the Narodniki,[d] by the despair of seeing their hopes evaporate. Indeed, one ex-terrorist Narodnik[d] would end quite appropriately by becoming a tsarist.

---

[a] F. Engels, *The Origin of the Family, Private Property and the State.* – [b] The magazine title is written by Engels in Russian. – [c] [in Russian] – [d] [in Russian]

To join in these polemics I would have to read a vast literature, keep up to date, and reply. This would then take up all my time for a whole year, and the only useful result would be that I would probably know Russian considerably better than I do now, but I am asked to do the same for Italy on the question of l'illustre[a] Loria. And I am already overwhelmed with work!

Jaurès is on the right road. He is *learning* Marxism, and he should not be hurried too much. However, he has already made good progress, much more than I had dared hope.[518] As for the rest, let us not require too much orthodoxy! The party is too large, and the theory of Marx has become too widespread for relatively isolated muddle headed persons to do too much harm in the West. In your part of the world it is different, as it was with us in 1845-59.

I share your opinion as regards Nicholas.[b] The 'Zemsky Sobor'[c] will come despite this little gentleman.[523]

Freyberger has just returned, and tells me that Vera is a great deal better, and that up to the present he has discovered nothing more than chronic and neglected bronchial catarrh.

Yours,

F. E.

First published, in Russian, in:
Gruppa 'Osvobozhdeniye truda',
No, 2, 1924
Published in English in full
for the first time

Printed according to the original

Translated from the French

269

ENGELS TO JULIUS MOTTELER[515]

IN LONDON

[London,] 2 March 1895
41 Regent's Park Road, N. W.

Dear Julius,

I am returning Meyer's[d] letter herewith, also one written to me by

---

[a] famous – [b] Nicholas II – [c] [in Russian] – [d] Johann Meyer

Lütgenau of Dortmund on the same subject,[a] which I should like to have back. The man is the right Barlen, Barlwin being, presumably, merely a misnomer by people who have never seen the name in writing. He *was able* to give the name of the confidential agent Bochum, and also confirmed what Meyer had written concerning Kritzler and the money—although that money, ten marks, he said, had fallen into the hands of the police. On the first occasion I gave him three shillings and, when he came back today, ten shillings, but he said he would have to give it all to his *landlord* and would then be penniless, so I gave him another five shillings, eighteen shillings in all, but even that will leave him in dire straits—he's living in a robber's den in the seamen's quarter, and is suffering from laryngitis and can't talk, so that I wasn't able to subject him to a long interrogation.

Even if the Society[62] is unable to do anything else, it could at least take care of the poor devil to the extent of getting him out of the seamen's district and helping him to find lodgings in which he wouldn't be so exploited and from which he could look around for work; and surely the chaps could give him a modicum of assistance. He should, at any rate, have an address to which letters could be sent. Anything that goes to his present diggings probably falls into the clutches of the landlord. In view of your illness and the Coheniad,[524] I would have come to see you myself about this business, but I am again suffering from one of those attacks I get in the spring and which temporarily prevent me from walking.

Apropos of which, I should like to say how very sorry I am that you and your wife should be ill. I wish you a speedy recovery and congratulate you on the merciless thrashing you inflicted on the great anarchist.[b] Let him take to his bed again alongside Kropotkin.

Many regards to you and your wife from

Yours,

F. Engels

First published in: Marx and Engels, *Works*, First Russian Edition, Vol. XXIX, 1946

Printed according to the original

Published in English for the first time

---

[a] See this volume, p. 445 – [b] Alexander Cohen

270

ENGELS TO EDUARD VAILLANT

IN PARIS

London, 5 March 1895
41 Regent's Park Road, N. W.

Dear citizen Vaillant,

I was unable to reply sooner to your letter of 8th January—at the moment our friends in Germany are having to hurry as much as possible with the publication of all works, brochures, articles, etc., now in preparation before the new reactionary legislation which is now threatening them is enforced.[428] That has kept me, and is still keeping me, busy from morning to night with both literary work and the accompanying correspondence.

To return to your draft laws,[480] the first, No. 384, agricultural delegates, deals with an institution of indisputable importance; as a means of propaganda among farm workers it will have a very favourable effect; but it has no chance of becoming law, particularly in France, where the inspection of factories is still so neglected.

No. 928, communal agricultural land. This draft goes into too much detail for me to pass knowledgeable judgement on it. First of all one would need to know whether, in the great majority of cases, this communal land does not consist of forests, moorland, heath or, at very most, land suitable only for grazing, and where agriculture proper cannot be practiced to advantage. Such is the case in Germany and, if I am not mistaken, in a large part of northern France. In these cases, farming such land, unless kept within very narrow territorial confines, would risk falling into the errors of the National Workshops of 1848.[525] However, as I have just said, one needs very specialised knowledge to form an opinion on this subject.

No. 933, an eight-hour working day and a minimum wage for workers, etc., employed by the state, corresponds more or less to what has been instituted here by the County Council, and in part also by the ministries of war and the navy. A measure very useful both as an example for the capitalists, and as a means of propaganda; however, the day before yesterday the workers abandoned the County Council *Progressives* who had introduced these measures. Three of these progressives have been black-balled because tiny minorities (50 to 300 votes) were cast for 'socialist' candidates who are more or less 'revolutionary', but these minorities were sufficient to ensure the election of reactionary 'moderates'.[526]

No. 939, ministry of labour, etc. This subdivision of work, which would remove some of the functions of the ministry of the interior and unite them with new functions hitherto neglected seems to me to be very useful. As for the details of the attributes of the new ministry, we can discuss this at greater length when the idea becomes feasible in practice.

I see these proposals simply as a means of propaganda, since with the present house there is no chance of seeing them accepted. From this point of view, we would first have to assure ourselves of their efficacy, and then determine whether or not they might be of interest for future action by the party when we are in a position to proceed to positive legislative activity. It is from this angle that I have formulated my criticism, and here I find just one point that seems to me to be dubious; whether it is wise to promise 40 million annually to the peasants in a form and for a purpose so clearly defined. The peasants could one day present us with this promissory note, and at a time when we might have better uses for such a sum.

Thank you for your comments concerning Wroblewski[a]. I have calculated that the roughly 45 socialist deputies receive a total of 400,000 fr. annually from the state, and that it would not perhaps be wholly impossible to provide on the basis of this sum, an annual income of, say, 1,200 francs to the sole surviving general of the Commune. I am perfectly well aware that the requests made by electoral constituencies on the funds of their deputies are not very reasonable, but here it seems to me to be a question of the honour of the whole of revolutionary France. It will be difficult to make the world understand that the survivors of and successors to the Commune are represented in the house by 45 deputies, and that a party of this size is not, however, capable of guaranteeing its most senior general against the most extreme poverty. And indeed, I still dare to hope that it will be found possible to use this means of enabling him to live out his life, without exposing him to the humiliation of a public subscription.

Here socialist sentiment (it is far more a sentiment than a clear idea) is continuing to make progress among the masses, but the existing organisations and their leaders are also continuing with the disputes and

----

[a] See this volume, p. 420

rivalries that keep them powerless. It is a matter for despair for those who do not know the English character; in any case the European continent would seem about to give the English the impetus it so needs. That band of swindlers who govern and exploit France shamelessly will not retain support much longer. The same is true for Italy, where bribery and corruption is even more shameless. In Germany, everything is leading to a crisis, generals and high-ranking officials are openly calling for a coup d'état. The end of the century is taking a decidedly revolutionary turn. In France, the socialists are the only serious and honourable party, in Germany they are the only real opposition party; if a crisis comes, there will be no other party to turn to except this. In Austria, everyone agrees that the socialists will enter parliament, and it only remains to decide through which door. And in Russia, little Nicholas[a] has done us the service of making revolution absolutely inevitable.

Yours sincerely,

F. Engels

First published in:
Marx and Engels, *Works*,
First Russian Edition,
Vol. XXIX, 1946
Published in English for the first time

Printed according to the original

Translated from the French

271

ENGELS TO NIKOLAI DANIELSON

IN ST. PETERSBURG

London, 5 March 1895
41 Regent's Park Road, N. W.

My dear Sir,

I am very sorry, in reply to your kind letter of Jan. 29th, to inform you that our author[b] has not left any manuscripts relating to his views upon, and deductions from the state of landed property in Russia such as might be useful to the Russian translator.[527] All I have been able to find

---

[a] Nicholas II – [b] Karl Marx

are simple and very voluminous extracts from Russian sources statistical and generally economical, but, and this more or less *against* his habit, not interspersed with observations of his own.

I enclose you a letter received from Berlin for you, and am requested by the Mr. Engels mentioned in it to complete it by the following bits of information. Mr. Engels received some time ago an inquiry from a Dr. Lux who writes on economic subjects: whether the *Essays*[a] were worth translating, and if so, would he do something to assist the publication of a German translation? to which he replied, that he was very desirous of seeing a German translation brought out, and that not only would he recommend the same for publication to Dietz, but also very gladly write an article upon it, when brought out, in the *Neue Zeit*, pointing out the importance of the results of your inquiries, but at the same time also stating that he differed from some of the conclusions arrived at by you. At the same time he stated, that he, Engels, had no right whatever to authorise a translation, but that the translator, a friend of Dr. Lux, had better apply to you direct for your permission. To avoid indiscretion, he insisted that the letter to you should be sent through him.

The translator, a young Russian[b] in Berlin, was said to be capable of undertaking the work (Dr. Lux's wife is a Russian lady), and Dr. Lux has promised to revise the German text in order to insure correctness. The translator is also said to have occupied himself with economical subjects, so as to be no stranger to the contents of your book.

The letter enclosed seems to *assume* that your consent has already been given, at least I cannot find in it any trace of a formal request to you to that effect. I know that *some* young Russians abroad[c] are of opinion that such is an unnecessary formality, but such is not my opinion, and if you feel inclined to entertain at all Mr. Konov's proposal, I think a hint in that direction might do the young man good.

As to myself I know nothing at all of the intended translation.

If you will kindly send me your reply to Mr Konov, I will see that it is forwarded at once.[528]

Yours very sincerely
L. K.[d]

---

[a] Nikolai-on. [Danielson N. Fr.], *Essays* (see FN p. 308) – [b] Andrei Konov – [c] [word in Russian] – [d] Engels used Louise Kautsky's initials for his pen-name.

First published, in Russian,
in *Minuvshiye gody,* No. 2,
1908

Reproduced from the original

Published in English for the first time

272

ENGELS TO RICHARD FISCHER

IN BERLIN

[London,] 8 March 1895
41 Regent's Park Road, N. W.

Dear Fischer,

I have taken as much account as possible of your grave objections although I cannot for the life of me see what is objectionable about, say, half of the instances you cite.[529] For I cannot after all assume that you intend to subscribe heart and soul to absolute legality, legality under any circumstances, legality even vis-à-vis laws infringed by their promulgators, in short, to the policy of turning the left cheek to him, who has struck you on the right. True, the *Vorwärts* sometimes expends almost as much energy on repudiating revolution as once it did—and may soon do again—on advocating the same. But I cannot regard that as a criterion.

My view is that you have nothing to gain by advocating complete abstention from force. Nobody would believe you, *nor* would *any* party in any country go so far as to forfeit the right to resist illegality by force of arms.

I also have to take account of the fact that my stuff is read by foreigners as well—Frenchmen, Englishmen, Swiss, Austrians, Italians, etc.—and I simply cannot compromise myself to that extent in their eyes.

I have therefore accepted your amendments with the following exceptions: 1. Slip 9, re the masses, now reads: 'they must have realised what they are coming out for'.[a]—2. next paragraph: the whole sentence about going into battle deleted; your suggestion contained an outright mistake. The *slogan* 'going into battle' is used daily by the French, Italians, etc., if

---

[a] Cf. present edition, Vol. 27, p. 520

with less serious intent.—3. Slip 10: 'Social Democratic subversion which *presently* owes its existence to'; you wish to remove the *'presently'*, thus changing present into permanent, and relatively into absolutely valid, tactics. This I will not and cannot do without making an eternal ass of myself. I shall therefore avoid the contradiction of terms and say: 'Social Democratic subversion to which *it is of very great benefit* just now to abide by the law.'[a]

Why you should see anything dangerous in the allusion to Bismarck's procedure in 1866, when the constitution was infringed, I find utterly incomprehensible. If ever there was an *argumentum ad hominem*,[b] I should say that this was it. However, I bow to your wishes.

Well, I can go so far and *no further*. I have done everything in my power to spare you embarrassment in debate. But you would be better advised to adhere to the standpoint that the obligation to abide by the law is a legal, not a moral one, as indeed, has been so nicely demonstrated to you by Boguslawski[c] (who has got the pip); and that it ceases absolutely when those in power break the law. But you people—one or two of you at any rate—have been weak enough not to oppose your adversaries' pretensions as you ought to have done, and to accept the obligation to abide by the law as being also a *moral* one and binding under all circumstances, instead of telling them: 'You are in power, it is you who make the laws; if we infringe them, you can deal with us in accordance with those laws and we must put up with it, that and nothing more—we have no further obligations, and you no further rights.' That's how the Catholics behaved in the face of the May Laws,[530] likewise the Old Lutherans in Meissen and likewise that Mennonite[531] soldier who figures in all the newspapers, and it's a standpoint you people must not betray. The Subversion Bill[428] is in any case doomed; a thing of that sort cannot even be formulated, let alone put into practice and, given the power to do so, the chaps will manage to muzzle you and harass you in any case.

If, however, your intention is to make the chaps in the government see that we only want to bide our time because we are not yet strong enough to help ourselves and because the army is not yet thoroughly disaffected—if such is your intention, my dear fellows, then why the eternal bragging in your press about the party's victories and the enormous strides it is

---

[a] Cf. present edition, Vol. 27, p. 523 – [b] a biased argument – [c] A. Boguslawski, *Vollkampf—nicht Scheinkampf. Ein Wort zur politischen Lage in Innern.*

making? Those chaps know as well as we do that victory is almost within our grasp and that in a few years' time there will be no stopping us, and that is why they are already anxious to get us by the scruff, though unfortunately they don't know how. Nothing we say can alter that fact, and they know all this as well as we do; they likewise know that, once power is *ours*, we shall use it for our own purposes, not theirs.

So when next there's a general debate in plenary session, mind you uphold the right of resistance to as good effect as did Boguslawski on our behalf, and do not forget that your audience also comprises old revolutionaries—French, Italian, Spanish, Hungarian, and English—and that the time may again come—how soon, no one can tell—when the deletion of the word 'legal', effected donkey's years ago at Wyden,[343] will really be consummated. Take a look at the Austrians whose threat to use force, should suffrage not soon be forthcoming, could hardly be plainer![523] Think of your own unlawful actions at the time of the Anti-Socialist Law,[15] a law they would like to foist upon you again. Legality for so long as and to the extent that it suits your book, but not legality at any price, not even as a manner of speech!

Yours,

F. E.

Too late now to put quotations into German (most already *have been* in the text[a]) already made up into pages.

The proofs are being sent to Hamburg from here.

First published, in the language of the original (German), in the *International Review of Social History*, Vol. XII, Part 2, Amsterdam, 1967

Printed according to a type-written copy

Published in English for the first time

---

[a] of K. Marx's *The Class Struggles in France, 1848 to 1850*

273

ENGELS TO WERNER SOMBART

IN BRESLAU

London, 11 March 1895
41 Regent's Park Road, N. W.

Dear Sir,

In replying to your note of the 14th of last month, I should like to thank you for so kindly sending me your book on Marx[a]; I had already read it with great interest in the volume of the *Archiv*[b] which Dr H. Braun was good enough to send me and was glad at long last to find such appreciation of *Capital*[c] at a German university. Needless to say, I cannot identify myself with all the expressions into which you have transposed Marx's exposition. In particular, it seems to me that the definitions of the concept of value, given by you on pp. 576 and [5]77, are rather too generalised; for one thing, I should delimit them historically by expressly confining them to the economic phase in which alone there has and could have been any question of value hitherto—to the social forms in which exchange of *commodities* and production of commodities exist; primitive communism was innocent of value. And in the second place the proposition would also seem to me to be susceptible of a conceptually narrower formulation. But this would take us too far afield and on the whole you are certainly right in what you say.

On p. 586, however, you appeal directly to me and I could not but laugh at the unconcerned way in which you hold a pistol to my head. But you need not worry—I am not going to 'contradict you flat'. The conceptual transitions whereby Marx arrives at the general and equal rate of profit from the various values produced in individual capitalist concerns, namely $s/c = s/(c+v)$, are wholly foreign to the consciousness of the individual capitalist. In so far as they have any historical parallel or any reality outside our own heads, this consists in, say the fact that the individual constituents of the amount of surplus value produced by capitalist

---

[a] W. Sombart, '*Zur Kritik des ökonomischen Systems von Karl Marx*' – [b] *Archiv für soziale Gesetzgebung und Statistik.* – [c] Volume III

A., over and above the rate of profit or his share of the total surplus value, pass into the pocket of capitalist B. whose own output of surplus value is normally less than the dividend accruing to him. But this process takes place objectively and unconsciously, in the nature of things, and only now, when we have attained to a proper consciousness of that process, can we judge how much labour it has cost. Had the creation of the average rate of profit demanded the *conscious* collaboration of the individual capitalists, and had the individual capitalist *known* that he was producing surplus value and how much, and that in many cases he would have to surrender part of his surplus value, the connection between surplus value and profit would, of course, have been more or less clear from the start, and would certainly be found in Adam Smith if not already in Petty.

As Marx sees it, the whole of past history, so far as major events are concerned, is an unconscious process, i.e. those events and the consequences thereof are not deliberate; either the supernumeraries of history have wanted something that was the diametrical opposite of what was achieved, or else that achievement entailed consequences quite other than those that had been foreseen. If we apply this to political economy, we find that each individual capitalist is in pursuit of *bigger* profits for himself. Bourgeois economics reveals that this pursuit of *bigger* profits on the part of each individual capitalist results in a general and *equal* rate of profit, an approximately *equal* rate of profit for all. But neither capitalists nor bourgeois economists are aware that the real purpose of that pursuit is the equal percentual distribution of the total surplus value over capital as a whole.

But how did this process of equalisation really come about? That is a very interesting point about which Marx himself has little to say. But Marx's whole way of thinking [Auffassungsweise] is not so much a doctrine as a method. It provides, not so much ready-made dogmas, as aids to further investigation and the method *for* such investigation. Here, then, is a piece of work to be done which Marx himself did not attempt in his first draft. Here, for a start, we have the statements on pp. 153-156, III, I[a] which also have some bearing on your rendering of the concept of value and prove that that concept has, or had, more reality than you ascribe to it. In the early days of exchange when products gradually changed into commodities, exchanges were made *in proportion to value*. For the labour

---

[a] See present edition, Vol. 37, pp.174-76; see also, pp. 882-84

expended on two articles was the sole criterion of quantitative comparison. At that time, then, value *existed in an immediate and real sense.* That this immediate realisation of value ceased in exchange, that it now no longer exists, we know. And I do not suppose you will have any particular difficulty in tracing the intermediate stages, at any rate in broad outline, that led from the above-mentioned real and immediate value to value as represented in the capitalist mode of production, value which is so thoroughly well-concealed that our economists can happily deny its existence. A genuinely historical exposition of this process—which, though admittedly requiring a great deal of research, holds out the prospect of correspondingly rewarding results—would be a most valuable pendant to *Capital*.[534]

Finally, I must again thank you for the high esteem in which you must hold me if you take the view that I could have turned Volume III into something better than it is. But I am unable to share that opinion and believe I have done my duty by presenting Marx in Marx's own words, even at the risk of expecting the reader to do rather more thinking for himself.

Yours very truly,
F. Engels

First published in:
*Beiträge zur Geschichte
der deutschen Arbeiterbewegung,*
No. 3, 1961

Printed according to the original

274

ENGELS TO CONRAD SCHMIDT[417]

IN ZURICH

London, 12 March 1895
41 Regent's Park Road, N. W.

Dear Schmidt,

I have before me your two letters of the 13th of November last and of the lst of this month. Let me begin with the most recent, No. 2.

So far as Fireman is concerned, you had better leave well alone.[535] Lexis had simply posed the question[536] as you did in $\sum s/\sum(c+v)$. He is the only one to have gone *a step further* along the right road in as much as he *classified* the progression s'/(c'+v') + s"/(c"+v") + s"'/(c"'+v"') ... etc., set out by you and divided it, according to the *varying composition* of capital, into groups of the branches of production between which equalisation only comes about as a result of competition. The fact that this was the next important step will be evident to you from Marx's own text in which, up to that point, the process is exactly the same. Fireman's mistake was to break off here and rest on his laurels, which is why he necessarily remained unnoticed until the book[a] itself came out.—But there's no need for you to worry. You have every reason to be content. After all, you discovered for yourself why it is that the rate of profit tends to fall and how commercial profit is created—and discovered, not just two thirds as did Fireman the rate of profit, but the whole bally thing.

Your letter, I think, sheds some light on why you allowed yourself to be side-tracked when it came to the rate of profit. In it I find you lapsing into detail in just the same way, and for this I blame the eclectic method of philosophising endemic at German universities since 1848, a method which loses sight of the whole, and all too often goes astray by indulging in almost endless and unprofitable speculation on minutiae. Now it so happens that your earlier studies of classical philosophy revolved primarily around Kant, and Kant was more or less compelled by the then state of philosophising in Germany and by his own antipathy to Wolf's pedantic Leibnizianism to make what appeared to be formal concessions to Wolfian speculation. It is thus I explain your tendency, also apparent from your epistolatory digression on the law of value, to become engrossed in minutiae; hence your occasional failure, or so it seems to me, to see the wood for the trees, which is why you reduce the law of value to a fiction, a necessary fiction, in much the same way as Kant reduced the existence of God to a postulate of practical reason.

Your objections to the law of value apply to *all* concepts regarded from the standpoint of reality. The identity of thinking and being, to use a Hegelian expression, corresponds in all respects to your example of the circle and the polygon. In other words, the concept of an object and its reality run side by side like two asymptotes which, though constantly

---

[a] Vol. III of *Capital*

converging, will never meet. The difference between the two is the self-same difference which is responsible for the fact that the concept is not immediately and ipso facto reality and reality is not immediately its own concept. Because a concept is by its nature essentially a concept, hence does not ipso facto and *prima facie*[a] correspond to the reality from which it has had first to be abstracted, that concept is always something more than a fiction, unless you declare all reasoned conclusions to be fictive on the grounds that they correspond to reality only in a very circuitous way and even then only approximately, like converging asymptotes.

Is it otherwise with the general rate of profit? At no time is it more than an approximation. Should it ever prove to be absolutely identical in two separate undertakings and should both achieve *exactly the same rate of profit* in a given year, it would be purely fortuitous; in reality rates of profit vary from business to business and year to year, according to circumstances, while the general rate exists only as the average achieved by a large number of businesses over a succession of years. If, however, we were to insist that the rate of profit—say, 14.876934... be exactly the same down to the last decimal point in every business every year, on pain of being reduced to a fiction, we should be grossly mistaking the nature of the rate of profit and of economic laws generally—they none of them have any reality save as an approximation, a tendency, an average, but not as *immediate* reality. This is due partly to the fact that their action is frustrated by the simultaneous action of other laws, but also to some extent by their nature as concepts.

Or take the law of wages, the realisation of the value of the power of labour, a value which is only, and even then not always, realised as an average and varies from locality to locality, indeed from branch to branch, according to the standard of living customary in each. Or ground rent, which represents the surplus profit, in excess of the general rate, arising from a monopolisation of a natural force. Here, too, real surplus profit and real rent do not by any means automatically correspond, but do so only approximately and on an average.

Exactly the same thing applies to the law of value and the distribution of surplus value through the rate of profit.

1. Both come closest to full realisation only in as much as capitalist production has everywhere been fully implemented, i.e. society has been

---

[a] self-evidently

reduced to modern classes of landowners, capitalists (industrialists and traders) and workers, all intermediate stages having been eliminated. That has not yet happened even in England nor will it ever happen—we shouldn't let things get to that pitch.

2. Profit, including rent, has a number of constituents:

a) profit from sharp practice which you discount in your algebraic sum;

b) profit from an increase in value of stocks (e.g. what is left of the previous harvest when the next one fails). In theory this *ought* also to equalise out, so long as it has not already been discounted by a fall in the value of other commodities, for either the capitalist buyer's contribution must be equal to the seller's gain, or else, where means of subsistence for workers are concerned, wages must eventually rise. The most significant of these rises in value are, however, not *lasting ones*, hence equalisation takes place only over an average of years and in very incomplete form and, as is well known, at the expense of the workers; they produce more surplus value because their labour power is not paid for in full;

c) the total amount of surplus value from which, however, we must again deduct that portion that is *presented to the buyer*, especially at times of crisis when overproduction is reduced to its true content of socially necessary labour.

From this it necessarily follows that the total profit and the total surplus value can correspond only approximately. If, however, you also consider that neither the total surplus value nor the total capital are constant quantities but variables which change from day to day, then any correspondence between the rate of profit and $\Sigma s / \Sigma (c+v)$, other than an approximate progression, and any coincidence of the total price and total value other than one which constantly tends towards, and yet as constantly tends away from, unity, will be seen to be a sheer impossibility. In other words, the unity of concept and phenomenon turns out to be an essentially endless process, and so indeed it is, in this case as in every other.

Has feudalism, then, ever corresponded to its concept? Having begun in the Kingdom of the Western Franks,[537] been further developed in Normandy by the Norwegian invaders, and taken a stage further in England and the south of Italy by the Norman French, it came closest to its concept—in the ephemeral Kingdom of Jerusalem, a relic of which, the *Assises de Jérusalem*,[538] the most classical expression of the feudal order. Was that order a fiction merely because it was in Palestine alone that it achieved a short-lived existence in fully classical form—and even then largely on paper?

Or are the concepts that prevail in the natural sciences fictive because they by no means always correspond to reality? From the moment we accept the theory of evolution, all our concepts of organic life correspond only approximately to reality. Otherwise there would be no change; if the day should ever come when concept and reality coincide completely in the organic world, evolution will cease. The concept 'fish' embraces life under water and breathing through gills; how is it possible to evolve from fish to amphibian without infringing that concept? And infringed it has been; we know of a whole number of fish whose air-bladders have evolved into lungs and which are thus able to breathe air. How is it possible to evolve from oviparous reptile to viviparous mammal without bringing one or both concepts into conflict with reality? And in fact we have, in the monotremata, an entire sub-class of oviparous mammals—in Manchester in 1843, I saw the eggs of a duck-billed platypus and, in my narrow-minded arrogance, cast scorn on the folly of supposing that a mammal could lay eggs, and now it has been proven! So do not treat the concept of value in the same manner as has obliged me to proffer my belated apologies to the duck-billed platypus!

In Sombart's otherwise excellent article on Volume III[a] I have also found a similar tendency to emasculate the theory of value; evidently he, too, had hoped to find a rather different solution.[b]

Your article in the *Centralblatt*, however, is first-rate,[c] and your demonstration—by quantitative determination—of the specific differences between Marx's theory of the rate of profit and that of the earliest political economists, is very well done. In his wisdom, the illustrious Loria sees Volume III as nothing less than an abandonment of the theory of value,[d] and thus your article is a cut-and-dried reply. There are now two more interested parties, Labriola in Rome, and Lafargue, the latter having joined battle with Loria in the *Critica Sociale*.[539] If, therefore, you could send a copy to Prof. Antonio Labriola, Corso Vittorio Emmanuele 251, Rome, he would do his best to get an Italian translation of it published; and a second copy to Paul Lafargue, Le Perreux, Seine, France, would give the

[a] W. Sombart, 'Zur Kritik der ökonomischen Systems von Karl Marx'. In: *Archiv für soziale Gesetzgebung und Statistik*, Bd. 7, H. 4. – [b] See this volume, p. 461 – [c] C. Schmidt, 'Der dritte Band des *Kapital*'. In: *Sozialpolitisches Centralblatt*, 25. Februar 1895 – [d] A. Loria, 'L'opera postuma di Carlo Marx.' In: *Nuova Antologia*, Anno XXX, fascicolo III, 1 febbraio 1895

latter the support he needs; he would also mention your name. I have written to both of them about this,[540] saying that your article supplies a ready-made answer on the main issue. Please let me know if you are unable to supply the copies.

With this, however, I must close, for otherwise I shall never be done.

Kindest regards,

Yours,

F. Engels

First published in
Sozialistische Monatshefte,
No. 24, 1920

Printed according to the original

Published in English in full
for the first time

275

ENGELS TO KARL KAUTSKY

IN STUTTGART

[London,] 13 March 1895

Dear Baron,

Just to inform you in all haste that Plekhanov has misread or misunderstood my letter. I *have no intention whatsoever* of concerning myself with Loria, and have written to tell Plekhanov[25] that he should not allow himself to be put off. Loria has written a reply to the preface[a] and only if *absolutely necessary* shall I write a few words in return, but that is all. Everything the chap has published has been sent me from Rome.

I should be grateful if you were to send me Platter's thing[541]—I have already got W. Sombart's—it is good.[b] I'm glad you should have used it as an excuse to stave off Enrico Ferri since the man's quite incapable of writing about Volume III.

---

[a] Loria, 'L' opera postuma di Carlo Marx'. In: *Nuova Antologia,* Anno XXX, fascicolo III —1 febbraio 1895 – [b] W. Sombart, 'Zur Kritik des ökonomischen Systems von Karl Marx'. In: *Archiv für soziale Gesetzgebung und Statistik.* Bd. 7, H. 4

My preface has come out in Italian and is said to have made quite an impact.[467]

Yours,

F. E.

First published in: *Aus der Frühzeit des Marxismus. Engels Briefwechsel mit Kautsky*, Prag, 1935

Printed according to the original

Published in English for the first time

276

ENGELS TO VICTOR ADLER[417]

IN VIENNA

London, 16 March 1895

Dear Victor,

Herewith by return the information you request. Sombart's article is very good,[a] except that his view of the law of value is impaired by some disappointment over the solution to the rate of profit question. He clearly expected a miracle, instead of which he merely found what was rational and that is anything but miraculous. Hence his reduction of the significance of the law of value to the domination of the productive force of labour as the determining economic power. This is all much too generalised and imprecise.—Little Conrad Schmidt's article in the *Sozial politisches Centralblatt* is very good.[b] Eduard Bernstein's articles were very muddle-headed[c]; the man is still neurasthenic and, what is more, scandalously over-worked. Having too many other things on hand, he left the article on one side and then was suddenly dunned for it by K. Kautsky.

Since you want to swot away at *Capital* II and III while you're in quod,[542] let me give you a few hints to lighten your task.

---

[a] W. Sombart, 'Zur Kritik des ökonomischen Systeme von Karl Marx,' In: *Archiv für soziale Gesetzgebung und Statistik*, Bd. 7, Heft 4 – [b] C. Schmidt, 'Der dritte Band des *Kapital*'. In: *Sozialpolitisches Centralblatt*, 25 Februar 1895 – [c] E. Bernstein, 'Der dritte Band des *Kapital*'. In: *Neue Zeit*, 1 Bd., Nr. 11-149 16, 17 und 20, 13 Jg. 1894/95

Book II. Part I. Read Chap. I carefully, after which you can more or less skim through Chaps 2 and 3; pay closer attention to Chap. 4, it being a résumé; 5 and 6 are easy, 6 in particular being concerned with incidental matters.

Part II. Chaps 7-9 are important. 10 and 11 exceptionally so. Likewise 12, 13 and 14. On the other hand 15, 16 and 17 need only be read cursorily to begin with.

Part III. Is an absolutely first-rate exposé of a subject which has not been dealt with since the days of the physiocrats, namely the entire circulation of commodities and money in capitalist society—brilliant as to content, but terribly ponderous as to form, firstly because put together from two versions using two different methods and, secondly, because version 2 was completed under duress, namely an illness involving chronic insomnia. If I were you, I should keep that *to the very last, after an initial* reading of Volume III. Also, it is the one you can most easily dispense with so far as your work is concerned.

Now for Volume III.

Important in Part I are Chaps 1-4; on the other hand, Chaps 5, 6 and 7 are less important so far as the *general* context is concerned, so not very much time should be spent on them to start off with.

Part II. *Most important* are Chaps 8, 9, 10. 11 and 12 to be treated cursorily.

Part III. *Most important*, the whole of it, 13-15.

Part IV. Likewise most important, though 16-20 also easy to read.

Part V. Most important, Chaps 21-27. Less so, Chap 28. Chap. 29 important. Chaps 30-32 not, on the whole, important for your purposes, but Chaps 22 and 34 important as soon as they turn to paper money, etc., 35 important as regards international rates of exchanges; 36 of great *interest to you*, and also easy to read.

Part VI. Ground Rent. 37 and 38 important. 39 and 40 less so, but nevertheless not to be skipped. 41-43 demand rather less attention. (Differential rent II, individual cases.) 44-47 are again important and also, on the whole, easy to read.

Part VII very fine; unfortunately truncated and, moreover, strongly symptomatic of insomnia.

So if you make a thorough study of the essentials by following the above, and devote less attention initially to what is of lesser importance (preferably having first reread the essential bits of Vol. I), you will get a general view of the whole and will afterwards find it easier to digest the passages to which you have devoted less attention.

Your news about the paper[a] pleased us very much. The main thing is *political* efficacity; financial efficacity is bound to follow, and will be achieved far more easily and quickly once the former is assured. It is with pleasure I detect your hand in the notes on electoral reform on the front page[532]—there you have the FULCRUM for the efficacity you need.

As a result of the old trouble which comes to plague me periodically, especially in springtime, I am again somewhat lame but less so than usual, the attack being milder and, in about a fortnight I should, I think, be rid of it without any need for sea air as in 1893 and 1894.

The movement over here may be summed up as follows: Amongst the masses, progress is steady if instinctive, and the *tendency* is adhered to; the moment it comes to giving conscious expression to that instinct and to that impulsive tendency, however, their sectarian leaders set about it in so stupid and narrow-minded a way as to make one feel like hitting out left, right and centre. But I suppose it's just the typical Anglo-Saxon way of going about things.

Many regards,

Yours,

F. E.

First published in
Der Kampf, Jg. I, Heft 6,
1 March 1908

Printed according to the magazine

Published in English in full
for the first time

277

ENGELS TO CARL HACKENBERG[543]

IN BARMEN

London, 16 March 1895
41 Regent's Park Road, N. W.

Dear Sir,

Following are my brief answers to your questions:

---

[a] *Arbeiter-Zeitung*

1) Becker[a] was in Cologne when we came there in May 1848[544]; I had heard nothing of him previously.

2) 1 know-nothing about this.[545]

3) ditto.[546]

4) We got to know Becker as belonging to the more moderate trend in the democratic party.

5) I believe Becker also gave talks in the Democratic Association[547] (the Eiser Hall) from time to time, but I hardly ever went there. W. Wolff, F. Wolff and Dronke attended more frequently on behalf of our editorial board[b] than did Marx or I.

6) I do not know what associations you mean. On the whole, the Workers' Union[548] and the Democratic Association worked hand in hand in Cologne, although the former was more radical than the latter. As for what had been going on *before* our arrival, at the time when the Workers' Union had been led by Dr. Gottschalk, I can say nothing definite about it.

7) If by the Central Association[549] you mean the central section of democratic associations, led by the Frankfurt Left, I must say the Rhenish democrats soon lost trust in it and made themselves independent.

8) We were on the same good terms with Becker as with the other bourgeois democratic leaders in Cologne, without making a secret of the fact that we were going considerably further than they and without expecting them to unconditionally support the stance taken by the *Neue Rheinische Zeitung.* The majority of them, Becker included, were not contributors to the paper, except, at the most, for publishing short, usually signed, articles from time to time in the local news section (then printed 'under the line'). You will often come across the initials H. B.[550] there. After the onset of reaction, in the autumn of 1848, democracy became more radical and Becker also drew closer to us. But he did not work more for the paper then either.

9) I've no knowledge of this at all.[551] I was already gone by then, we left Cologne in May.

10) After we had gone, Becker and Heinrich Burgers founded the *Westdeutsche Zeitung*, one might say on the inheritance of the *Neue Rheinische Zeitung.*[552]

11) I have no further material on the Communist trial[553] concerning

---

[a] Hermann Heinrich Becker – [b] of the *Neue Rheinische Zeitung*

Becker specifically. Becker had joined the Communist League, which was set up anew on the Continent at the end of 1849 or the beginning of 1850, and sat on the *Cologne* district authority, which was entrusted with the functions of central authority after the split in London.

12) I know of no attempts to free Becker while he was on remand. If anything of the kind was contemplated, certainly good care was taken not to mention it in letters to London, for it would hardly have escaped the notice of the Prussian postal service.

For the rest, I regret to be unable to give you any further information. I hope you have the latest edition (Zurich 1885) of Marx's revelations concerning the Cologne trial,[a] with my introduction.[b] If not, you may obtain a copy from the bookshop of *Vorwärts*, 2 Beuthstrasse, Berlin; the earlier editions are incomplete.

Incidentally, Becker's involvement with the League was only an episode in his life, caused by the then rampant reaction. With the return of calmer times he again became what he had been previously, a bourgeois democrat, and, as you will know, went through all the changes undergone by German, and particularly Prussian, bourgeois democracy. This attitude stemmed from his whole nature, so I am far removed from seeing any sort of careerism in it; on the contrary, if he had tried to remain more radical and carry the communist episode on, he would have missed his calling. In this he differed, very favourably, from Miquel.

I hope these notes will be of use to you.

F. Engels

First published in
*Beiträge Zur Geschichte
der Arbeiterbewegung*, No. 5, 1973

Printed according to the original

Published in English for the first time

---

[a] K. Marx, *Revelations Concerning the Communist Trial in Cologne* – [b] F. Engels, *On the History of the Communist League*

278

ENGELS TO PABLO IGLESIAS

IN MADRID

[*Draft*]

London, 16 March 1895

Dear friend Iglesias,

I could not answer your letter of 19 October 1894 earlier because I did not know whether or not you had come out of Malaga prison[554]; nor could I answer your letter of 1 February, being busy finishing some publications[a] for our people in Berlin which had to be circulated before the new repressive draft laws[428] became law.

Before I got your letter of 19 October, friends in Barcelona had asked Comrade Eleanor Marx-Aveling to inform the British Trades-Unions of the Malaga strikers' situation, and she had done all she could, so that nothing more is left for me to do. And as you know, some of the Trades-Unions helped.

As regards really socialist organisations in England, they are so disunited and so poor that no help can be expected from them.

I have been following the progress of this strike with great interest, admiring the workers' tenacity and courage. Marquis de Larios' name reminds me of an episode that occurred about 1850.

At that time there was a firm of Larios Bros. (Jews) in Gibraltar. A British merchant used to send his goods to the firm on commission to be *smuggled* to other merchants on Spanish territory. Those goods were constantly seized by Spanish Customs, and Larios Bros. would pay the Englishman the guaranteed sum in insurance, as is customary in this kind of business. But that did not suit the Englishman, for he lost his customers in Spain and a substantial amount of profit. He arrived in Gibraltar to see for himself why those accidents always befell his goods but never those of others. However, he could not find out the reason. One day as he was taking a walk in the city, he saw a cart lose a wheel and some boxes with goods fall to the ground and burst open. The boxes were

---

[a] See this volume, p. 444

his—they bore his trade-mark—but he saw that, instead of goods, they contained, yes, sand. The mystery was solved. It became clear that Larios Bros. had always notified Spanish Customs of the dispatch of the boxes of sand, which had been seized, the Englishman being paid insurance; thereupon Larios Bros. had dispatched the goods on their own behalf by a safe route to their Spanish correspondents, thus pocketing without risk the whole profit derived from the operation.

The enraged Englishman descended on Larios. 'I'll disclose all that, I'll make a scandal, I'll have you put on trial!' 'Why get excited, sir? We will pay you for your goods and make the amends you want.' After much argument, the Englishman was paid a definite sum, and Larios Bros. signed the following statement:

'We, Larios Bros., are the greatest swindlers there are here in the city of Gibraltar, and we advise everybody against doing business with us, for they can rest assured that we would cheat them.

'Gibraltar, (date).

'Larios Bros.'

The statement was posted for general information in the Bourse of Gibraltar, where old Larios continued for another twenty years to buy and sell goods.

Would the marquis be a relative of the Larios of Gibraltar?

First published, in Russian, in: K. Marx and F. Engels, *Works*, First Russian Edition, Vol. XXIX, 1946

Printed according to the original

Translated from the Spanish

Published in English for the first time

279

ENGELS TO CARL HIRSCH

IN COLOGNE

London, 19 March 1895
41 Regent's Park Road, N. W.

Dear Hirsch,

I am willing to oblige you,[555] but only on two conditions: 1. that the matter remains *strictly between ourselves*, for otherwise I shall get a hundred such requests for advance criticism; and what I do for one person I cannot refuse to do for others—in which case I might as well throw up the sponge. 2. That this is the last time you ask me to do anything of this kind. I get more things sent to me in a week than I can read in a month, but if I am to criticise them into the bargain, I shall be in even worse case.

P. 4. *One-sided!* This is far less the case in big industry than in *manufacture*. On the contrary, big industry does to a large extent *eliminate* the disabling effect of manufacture, although it produces a similar effect of *its own*, which last may be exacerbated by the intensification of labour. From what I know of big industry, I should say that in your case this point is given *more* emphasis than is justified by the circumstances. The division of labour is, and will continue to be, the chief cause of the disablement of labour.

P. 6. – 'in every case overproduction, crises'. *May*, has a tendency to—realisation by no means inevitable. 'Spiral movement'—seems to me too general a term. What mode of production have you in mind here? 'The minimum of socially necessary labour time'—if this is supposed to be the time needed to produce the gross social product, it is meaningless so far as capitalist society is concerned, since in its apportionment among individual workers, the industrial reserve army is wholly left out of account.

P. 15. 'Everywhere' (etc., up till the end of the sentence)—this is expressed very obscurely, to say the least and, as it stands, is a contradiction. First, the increase in the products of labour is said to give rise to 'a gain as such' and then to a 'loss of value, which is at least a possibility'. This will not do unless explanatory and delimiting intermediate links are provided.

P. 18. 'The capital of the working man is his own person.' That sounds very nice, but in this context the word capital loses every vestige of meaning. Why the devil must you go and translate things that are sensible into nonsensical philistine cliches? What you say here is quite beyond my comprehension. Similarly on p. 18, no. 2. The concentration of labour resulting from improvements in machinery is all of a sudden supposed to be unhealthy. It may be so, and very often is, in the capitalist system but of itself it is no more unhealthy than is eating and digesting on the following page. Not only will it not cease, but we shall be able to augment it considerably because, with it, we shall get compensation for the workers. Other incidental comments—should there ever be a second edition, I would advise you to substantiate what are, after all, very generalised arguments by providing specific examples, citing facts relating to various branches of industry and, in general, indicating which industries you are referring to. E.g., your propositions are true of the highly developed English textile industry only in a very limited sense. On the other hand, they may be far more true of Germany where big industry is still in its infancy and is only just coming into its own in a whole number of branches of production in which old methods are being superseded and the intensity of labour suddenly augmented. However, these are merely transitional stages. The main thing, when dealing with economic and, more especially industrial matters of this kind, is not to succumb to parochialism. Seen for what they are, these transitional phases are of undeniable importance, but one must also recognise and say that *that* is what they are and nothing else. And your immediate surroundings provide you with the most splendid opportunity for presenting all your propositions as having been deduced from real life, while you yourself will learn something in the process.

Now, do your best in the Cologne by-election[556] so that we may at least win here. And if by chance you should be writing to me again, let me know if the old house, behind Hutmacher, where the *Neue Rheinische Zeitung* used to be, is still no. 17 and whether the owner of the sweatshop who now lives there is called Salomon or Lewi—I have forgotten.

So far you have been conducting your battle with the Centre[71] quite nicely, but it seems to me that you might castigate the conduct of the Liebers et al in the Reichstag rather more often in your leading articles.[557]

Many regards,

Yours,

F. E.

First published in: Printed according to a
Marx and Engels, *Works*,   typewritten copy
First Russian Edition,
Vol. XXIX, 1946   Published in English
                                       for the first time

280

ENGELS TO LUDWIG KUGELMANN

IN HANOVER

London, 19 March 1895
41 Regent's Park Road, N. W.

Dear Kugelmann,

The *eachets crampons*[a] have arrived here safely and have already been put to use. The machine presents no difficulty to the doer-up of letters—whether it does to the opener thereof is something that could be elucidated for us by the German and Austrian postal authorities to whom we have already most humbly submitted several samples. Many thanks. Köller will, I hope, be obliged to introduce a Subversion Bill[428] for the subversion of these staples in the face of which the best intentions of the *cabinets noirs*[b] fail so ignominiously.

Thanks for your endeavours in the Bielefeld district. If there is anything of mine or, indeed of Marx's in the *Dampfboot*, it is likely to be anonymous.[558]

No news from Livingston.[559]

The cold suited me very well; it acted on me like a powerful tonic while it lasted, and I felt twenty years younger. On the other hand, it precipitated London as always back into an age of barbarism. The water pipes froze; we went on having water until the Company shut off supplies, whereupon the water froze in the mains. Ours was about four and a half to five feet down and when uncovered a fortnight after the thaw, was still completely frozen up. Then we had to wait another two days until our connecting pipe thawed out. At eight o'clock in the evening, a week ago today, the water at last came on again. We then discovered that the drains were blocked because of the inadequate flow of water. By the end of last week everything was back to normal again, after four weeks during which we had to have forty buckets of water a day carried up to the attic on the

---

[a] A type of staple for closing letters – [b] The name given in France to the office where letters of suspect persons were opened and examined before being forwarded to the addressees. (*Trans.*)

fourth floor in order to keep the house supplied with water and prevent the boiler exploding every time the range was lit in the kitchen.

There was no need for you to worry and take so much trouble over the duty on the staples; in this country all industrial products are duty-free.

Many regards to you and your family from Louise and

Yours,

F. Engels

First published in:
Marx and Engels, *Works*,
First Russian Edition,
Vol. XXIX, 1946

Printed according to the original

Published in English for the first time

281

ENGELS TO HERMANN ENGELS

IN BARMEN

London, 20 March 1895
41 Regent's Park Road, N. W.

Dear Hermann,

Many thanks for the kind wedding invitation which I am unfortunately unable to accept. Apart from other obstacles, I have again fallen prey to the springtime complaint which, for the past four or five years, has regularly crippled me for some weeks at this season. A little rest will no doubt suffice to put paid to the thing, thus enabling me, a week tomorrow, to drink a glass of the best to Elsbeth's[a] and her bridegroom's[b] health, as will be conscientiously done.

Otherwise I am well and have grown more or less accustomed to the domestic and dietary regulations befitting an elderly gentleman—so much so, in fact, that any deviation therefrom becomes instantly apparent to me from all manner of little upsets and I get given the well-meant but earnest advice to desist from the same in future. I had never imagined

---

[a] Elsbeth Engels, F. Engels' niece – [b] Arthur Schuchard

that pedantry could again be imposed upon me as a rule of life and a moral duty.

Well, I hope that, even in my absence, you will all have a very happy day, and wish Elsbeth the best of luck in her new status as a married woman; also offspring more distinguished by their health than by their numbers.

Much love to Emma[a] and all the children,

Your old

Friedrich

First published in
Deutsche Revue, Jg. 46,
Bd. III, 1921

Printed according to the original

Published in English for the first time

282

ENGELS TO VERA ZASULICH

IN LONDON

[London,] Friday 22 March 1895
41 Regent's Park Road, N. W.

Dear citizen Vera,

On Sunday evening we will be without a maid and without a cook. They are both leaving us tomorrow, and therefore the house will be upside down, and in a state which will scarcely permit us to receive our friends—you will therefore, I hope, excuse us for that evening.

Cordial greetings from the Freybergers—we hope that the fine weather will cure you completely.

Sincere good wishes,

F. Engels

First published in:
Marx and Engels, *Works*,
Second Russian Edition,
Vol. 39, Moscow, 1966

Printed according to the original

Translated from the French

Published in English for the first time

---

[a] Emma Engels, F. Engels' sister-in-law.

283

ENGELS TO KARL KAUTSKY

IN STUTTGART

London, 25 March 1895
41 Regent's Park Road, N. W.

Dear Baron,

No difficulty about a reply to your telegramm—'with pleasure'. The text will follow by book-post. It is in proof form and is entitled *Introduction to Karl Marx's 'The Class Struggles in France, 1848 to 1850'* by F. Engels. The text explains that the contents are a reprint of the old articles from the *Neue Rheinische Zeitung, Revue.* My text has suffered to some extent from the apprehensive objections, inspired by the Subversion Bill,[428] of our friends in Berlin—objections of which, in the circumstances, I could not but take account.[529]

I at once wrote to Plekhanov to clear up the misunderstanding.[a] It was very right of you to stave off Ferri; the chap is a belletrist and sensation-monger in no matter what field and, like most Italians, holds Loria to be a giant in the field of economics, an opinion the illustrious one has implanted in them by dint of 'reiterated appearances' (to use Ruge's expression) and by a refined system of camaraderie.

I have not read the stenographic version of Liebknecht's militia speech[560] and one cannot go by the newspaper reports. A long dissertation might be written on the subject of militia and the standing army. If France and Germany were to agree gradually to turn their armies into militias, each with the same period of training, that would be that; Russia could be left to her own devices and Austria and Italy would be delighted to follow suit. But because of domestic circumstances France and Germany cannot afford to do this and, even if they could, it would not be feasible because of Alsace-Lorraine. And that will prove the undoing of the whole of the militia business.

Unfortunately your *Early History of Socialism*[561] hasn't reached me yet; I look forward keenly to seeing it, and specially, if not exclusively, to your

---

[a] See also this volume, pp. 439-40, 449-50, 467

account of the Anabaptists[562]; in the earlier movements, too, there is still a good deal to be elucidated. It is a great pity that you have not been able to have recourse to Czech sources on the Taborites,[563] but that would have been quite out of the question unless you had spent a long time in Bohemia and been given special access to mss. No doubt you could find someone on the spot, a young Czech, who would be able to help you.

What I have seen of Ede's[a] work has pleased me very much, particularly as regards the material and the perspectives it opens out. On the other hand, I should say that he planned it in rather too much of a hurry, but that is something one can only judge when one has the whole thing in front of one.

So far as you people are concerned, there would be considerable snags to a history of the International. First of all, you would have to collect the material from the individual countries. So far as Spain is concerned, Mora is now bringing it out—very much by dribs and drabs—in the feuilleton of the *Socialista*. I myself possess quite a lot on Italy up till the time of the Hague Congress,[115] where, however, a great deal went on behind the scenes. Frankel and Lafargue could probably lay hands on a fair amount of stuff on France up till 1870 and, so far as Switzerland is concerned, you would have the *Tagwacht*, the *Vorbote*, the *Égalité* and the *Bulletin jurassien*.[b] (Héritier's articles in the *Berliner Volks-Tribüne* should be treated with the greatest circumspection; they are all written in unconscious extenuation of the Bakuninists[49]; so unaware was the man of what he was doing that he didn't realise, until told by *me*, after the event, what a slap in the face they had been to his spiritual foster-father, Becker[c]). The other countries don't really matter.

For years past I have been intending to make use of the material in my possession for a biography of Marx and, in fact, it is this, as it happens to be *quite the most important part, that I shall do first*. A number of circumstances make this necessary. Firstly, I was personally involved during the crucial period, 1870-72, and can fill out the material from my own experience. Secondly, it is at one and the same time the most important episode in Marx's public life and that least amenable to accurate portrayal from printed sources. Thirdly, the calumnies to be disposed of belong for the most part to this period. Fourthly, I am seventy-four years old

---

[a] Eduard Bernstein – [b] *Bulletin de la Fédération jurassienne de l'Association internationale des travailleurs.* – [c] Johann Philipp Becker (See this volume, pp. 82, 85, 141)

and shall have to make haste. And, fifthly, the other period during which Marx was publicly active (1842-62) can perfectly well wait until later and even, if necessary, be depicted by someone other than myself, since public controversy up to the time of *Herr Vogt* throws light on most of it and Marx had so emphatically lived down the calumnies of the then vulgar democrats that these no longer call for individual refutation.

I shall apply myself to this task, to which I have long been looking forward, as soon as I possibly can,—indeed I only have one or two small jobs to do in the mean time, in effect merely the revision of the introduction to the new edition of the *Peasant War*[235] (for which I need your book too). Then I shall turn my back on all my correspondence (which is enormously time-consuming) and on all incidental work (no doubt with the help of the Subversion Bill[428]?!), when I should be able to manage it all right.

Your news about the *Arbeiter-Zeitung* is indeed very gloomy; however, I believe it will come through all right. Maybe the chaps planned things on rather too lavish a scale at the start[377] and will now have to cut down a bit. But its *political* success seems assured and, that being so, it would be very strange if it didn't eventually prove a financial success also. Electoral reforms[270] that would enable us to get into parliament are, I consider, a virtual certainty in Austria, unless a period of general reaction were suddenly to set in. In Berlin they would seem to be making determined efforts in that direction, but unfortunately no one there knows his own mind from one day to the next. So they may find themselves in the same boat as the recruit from Lancashire who, while training, was ordered by his N.C.O. to 'slope arms—order arms—slope arms—order—slope—order'. 'I WINNOT,' cried the recruit. 'YOU WON'T?' 'NO, I WINNOT', 'YOU REFUSE TO OBEY YOUR SUPERIOR OFFICER?' 'I WINNOT!' 'AND WHY NOT?' 'BECAUSE YOU DUNNOT KNOW YOUR OWN MIND FOR TWO MINUTES TOGETHER!'

Many regards from one household to the other.

Yours,

F. E.

Please keep to yourself what I have said above about my plans; there are so many indiscreet men of letters in the party!

First published abridged in: *Neue Zeit*, Bd. II, Nr. 47,   Printed according to the original

1894-95 and in full in:
Aus der Frühzeit des Marxismus.
Engels Briefwechsel mit
Kautsky, Prag, 1935

Published in English for the first time

284

ENGELS TO LAURA LAFARGUE

AT LE PERREUX

London, 28 March 1895
41 Regent's Park Road, N. W.

My dear Löhr,

If you were in danger of being flooded, it was just the reverse with us—four weeks without water, and at the end of the frost the canalisation blocked up as the result. A fine mess it was. London was thrown back into barbarism by this month of hard frost, and the *Standard* with truly British Conservatism congratulated us on the fact that the non-supply of water was a proof of the high civilisation attained here, while it pitied the uncivilised cities of the Continent where the water-pipes had not frozen. Well, thank goodness, it's over.

You grumble at the mythical union and real squabbles of the French Socialists—they are babies at that game, compared to the English. They are especially interesting—the English Socialists I mean—since Social Democratic Federation[44] and Independent Labour Party[114] fight each other under the cloak of a pretended harmony. This harmony goes exactly as far as their common hatred of John Burns, and allows the Social Democratic Federation to invite Keir Hardie to speak at their Commune meeting; at which meeting Keir Hardie (read his speech in the *Labour Leader*[a]) directs hidden attacks against the Social Democratic Federation to which that body replies in *Justice*.[b] The Social Democratic Federation says the Independent Labour Party has no right to exist, the Social Democratic Federation being the

---

[a] No. 51, 23 March 1895 – [b] No. 584, 23 March 1895: *Topical Tattle*

only true orthodox church; and the Independent Labour Party says the Social Democratic Federation ought to allow itself to be absorbed in the Independent Labour Party. Their latest exploit was at the County Council Election where both of these organisations put up candidates, and only against 'Progressives'[526]; the result was: 1,300 votes *in all* out of 486,000, and the election of 4 Moderates (Conservatives) for seats held formerly by Progressives, and the cry of triumph in both *Justice*[a] and *Labour Leader*[b] that *they* had beaten the Progressives. Imagine the Paris Socialists voting *with* Clericals, Monarchists and Opportunists[87] *against* the parties claiming municipal autonomy for Paris, and you have the exact counterpart of the Socialist vote in London. But—to support the Progressives would have been to acknowledge that John Burns had behaved well in the County Council, and to endorse the policy of Sidney Webb and the Fabians[43] who, muffs though they be as *Socialists*, are really doing very good work municipally, and fighting energetically and cleverly for an autonomous London. And so the 'Socialists' prefer to support the party which refuses to allow London its self-government and fights hard to keep the County Council powerless. Now the County Council is the next and best and easiest-to-be-conquered piece of governmental machinery—the working class could have it tomorrow if they were united. And what would Parliament be with a Socialist autonomous Council for London!

The Berlin people are republishing Mohr's articles in the *Revue der Neuen Rheinischen Zeitung* on France 1848-50 and I have written an introduction which will probably first appear in the *Neue Zeit*. It has suffered somewhat from the, as I think, exaggerated desires of our Berlin friends not to say anything which might be used as a means to assist in the passing of the Umsturzvorlage in the Reichstag.[428] Under the circumstances I had to give way.[529] But this Umsturzvorlage and the absolutely uncertain state of things in Germany—splendid though it be for the general progress of our party—upsets a good deal of my calculations. I was, I believe you know, getting ready the Lassalle correspondence[284]; for that I have to compare a lot of old papers, letters, etc. But if the new bill passes, neither the letters nor my notes and introduction will be printable in Germany. And a reprint of our old articles of 1843-52 will be equally impossible. So I am compelled to neglect all this until we can see somewhat clearer *wie*

---

[a] *Justice*, No 582, 9 March 1895: 'A Pill for Palmer' and H. W. Lee, 'A Much-Needed Lesson for Progressives and Social-Democrats' – [b] *The Labour Leader*, No. 49, 9 March 1895: 'The L.C.C. Elections' and 'The L.C.C. and the I.L.P.'

der Hase läuft.[a] In the meantime I am taking up Vol. IV of the *Capital*,[102] reading and correcting the parts already copied out by Karl Kautsky and shall then arrange with Tussy about her continuing the work.

Things in Germany are decidedly becoming critical. The latest escapade of young William[b]—his *tiefste Entrüstung*[c] at the Reichstag's anti-Bismarck vote[564] is big with serious eventualities. First as a symptom; it shows that he has now not only 'a slate off' but that the whole of his slate roof is getting out of order. Then as a *défi.*[d] I have no doubt our party will reply to that in the Reichstag, and although the thing may appear to be buried for the moment, the *conflict is there* and will crop up again. There is no doubt, we are *facing* in Germany a modern Charles I, a man possessed by *Cäsarenwahnsinn.*[e]

Then look at the confusion the fellow creates in the ranks of the bourgeois parties. The Conservative Junker he in turns cajoles and repels; their clamour for state-secured rents he cannot satisfy; the alliance between landed aristocracy and large manufacturers, founded by Bismarck [in] 1878 by means of his protective tariff,[565] has gone to pot over conflicting economic interests; the Catholic party,[566] who hold the balance of power in the Reichstag with their 100 members, was on the best way of being bribed into voting for the Umsturzvorlage, when the Bismarck vote and the *Entrüstunskaiser*[f] throw them at once back into opposition—and that means furthering the splitting up of the Catholic Centre into an aristocratic-bourgeois wing and a democratic, peasant and working men's wing. Everywhere confusion and disunion, pushing William to a coup d'état to assert his divine right to absolute power and to get rid of universal suffrage, and on the other side the silent and resistless advance of our party manifesting itself at every election for any post accessible to working men's votes. This does look critical—*qui vivra verra*[g]!

In a day or two I shall write to Paul about his half of his double-bedded book.[h] He has got a strange bed-fellow![567]

Ever yours

F. Engels

First published, in the
language of the original
(English), in: F. Engels, P. et
L. Lafargue, *Correspondance*,

t. III, Paris, 1959

Reproduced from the original

---

[a] how the cat jumps – [b] William II – [c] profound indignation – [d] challenge – [e] Caesaristic mania – [f] the indignation of the Kaiser – [g] time will show – [h] See this volume, pp. 487-90

285

ENGELS TO KARL KAUTSKY[568]

IN STUTTGART

London, 1 April 1895

Dear Baron,

Postcard received. I was amazed to see today in the *Vorwärts* an excerpt from my 'Introduction' that had been *printed without my prior knowledge* and tricked out in such a way as to present me as a peace-loving proponent of legality *quand même*.[a][569] Which is all the more reason why I should like it to appear in its entirety in the *Neue Zeit* in order that this disgraceful impression may be erased. I shall leave Liebknecht in no doubt as to what I think about it and the same applies to those who, irrespective of who they may be, gave him this opportunity of perverting my views and, what's more, without so much as a word to me about it.

Platter received with thanks.[541] Of very minor importance, though the man is coming increasingly into line. If things go on like this, we soon shan't be able to stir for all these professors. It is absolutely capital that J. Wolf should also have replied.[570] I shall lay him alongside the others, together with Stiebeling and Loria. Sic transit gloria mundi.[b]

Kindest regards from one household to the other.

Yours

F. E.

We get two copies of *Deutsche Worte*, one for Freyberger and one for myself.

First published abridged in:
Neue Zeit, Bd. I, No. 11 1908
and in full in: *Aus der Frühzeit
des Marxismus. Engels Briefwechsel
mit Kautsky*, Prag, 1935

Printed according to the original

Published in English in full
for the first time

---

[a] come what may – [b] Thus passes away the glory of the world (words from the ritual of the Pope's inauguration.)

286

ENGELS TO HARRY QUELCH[571]

IN LONDON

[Draft]

[London,] 2 April 1895

Dear Comrade,

I have been compelled to decline, at least for this year, all demands for contributions to extra numbers of periodicals both for 18 March and 1st May, and am therefore unable to make an exception in the shape of an 'winterview' for *Justice*. This, however, does not mean that I should not be quite willing, if you should wish it, to discuss with you *privately* and in a friendly way the progress and the present position of the movement, in England and out of England.

If this should meet your views and you will be good enough to propose a day and hour when you could call, I will try to arrange to be at home.

Yours faithfully

First published in:
Marx and Engels, *Works*,
First Russian Edition,
Vol. XXIX, 1946

Reproduced from the original

Published in English for the first time

287

ENGELS TO PAUL LAFARGUE[572]

AT LE PERREUX

London, 3 April 1895
41, Regent's Park Road, N. W.

My dear Lafargue,

I had not yet finished reading your half-book[567] when I received Vol. I of the *History of Socialism* by Kautsky,[561] various Italian reviews concerning Loria (from Labriola) and a heap of Russian journals (from Nikolai Danielson). I am overwhelmed with post. Well, I read yours to the end nevertheless. It has a brilliant style, some very striking flashes of historical insight, there is truth in it and originality and, what is more important, it is not like the German professor's book where what was true was not original and what was original was not true. Its principal fault is that apparently you were in too great a hurry to be done with it; the arrangement, in particular of the sections on feudal and capitalist property, could have been more careful, especially for a Paris public, accustomed to easy reading and, moreover, adapted for lazy readers; the Parisian, too, asserts his right to be lazy.[573] Many very good passages may possibly lose some of their effect because they are written as though in parentheses, or because you have left the trouble of drawing conclusions and results too much to the reader.

As for the material itself, the main point of criticism is in the chapter on tribal communism.[574] There you lay too much emphasis, I think, on the form in which that phase has been maintained up to our own times, *in France*, and on the form of its dissolution in that country. The form of coparcenary under which the consanguineous community has gone on so long in France is already in itself a *subdivision* of the *large* family community, continued to our day in the *zádruga* of the Serbians and Bulgarians. This form, it appears certain, preceded the *peasant commune* in Russia, in Germany, etc.; in breaking up, the Slav *zádruga*, the German *Hausgenossenschaft* (genealogy of *lex Alamannorum*[575]) passed over to the commune of separate families (or, quite often at first, and still today in Russia, to coparcenaries), with *separately cultivated* fields though *subject to periodic redistribution*—that is to say, what emerged from it was the Russian *mir*[a] and the German *Markgenossenschaft*. The more restricted community of several families which was kept up in France was no more, as I see it, than an integral part of the *Markgenossenschaft*, at any rate in the North (the *Frankish* region); in the South (former Aquitaine) it may perhaps have formed a unity holding its land under the superior ownership of the *lord of the manor* alone, without being subject to the control of the village *commune*. It is only this special French form which, on breaking up, could pass in one leap to the individual ownership of the land.[b]

This is a point on which there are still many things to study. It is from

---

[a] This Russian word meaning 'peace', 'world' and 'community' is written by Engels in Latin letters. – [b] Cf. F. Engels, *The Origin of the Family, Private Property and the State*, present edition, Vol. 26, pp. 250-55

you that I learn of this special character of tribal communism in France, and since you are already in it heart and soul, you could not do better than to pursue this study, which holds out great promise.*

Small errata:

p. 338, you make the water of the Peruvian aqueducts *flow upwards*; as there is scarcely any natural water in Peru save in 'the heart of the mountains', and as your aqueducts are expressly built to carry water to them, it must, I suppose, be sea-water?

p. 354. Terra salica.ᵃ Guérard is making a huge mistake with his derivation of *Sala* house.ᵇ So the Salian Franks were Franks living in houses? They were called Salians, Salio, after the small region of Holland, Salland, where the group which conquered Belgium and France between Ardennes and Loire was formed for the conquest; the name still exists today. At the time when the Salic Law was drafted (about 400),⁵⁷⁶ the *Sala* was still, as you have observed yourself, a *personal estate* among the Germans.

p. 386 'another likes to set the snares or prepare *grass-hoppers*' [sauterelles]. Did they eat grasshoppers in Berry in 1787? I look in my dictionary and I find saute*rolle*, bird-trap.

p. 393. Black redistribution—in Russia tchornoi,ᶜ black, is used for *dirty*, and in a secondary sense popular, common, vulgar. Tchornoi narod,ᶜ the black people—the common people, the people as a whole. Tchornoi perediel,ᶜ black redistribution, means rather therefore the general, universal distribution, where everyone has his share, including the poorest. And in this sense a Narodnik (friend of the peasants) journal in Switzerland was called *Tchornoi perediel*,ᶜ which was meant to signify the distribution of *aristocratic estates* amongst the peasants.

That is all that I have noted and you will have had enough. As for Yves Guyot, I wash my hands of it.

Liebknecht has just played me a fine trick.⁵⁶⁹ He has taken from my introduction to Marx's articles on France 1848-50 everything that could serve his purpose in support of peaceful and anti-violent tactics at any

---

* You must note the tripartition of France: France proper, to the Loire, strong Germanic influence; Burgundian area, to the East of Saône and Rhône, less Germanic; Aquitaine, between sea, Loire and Rhône, minimal Germanic influence. (Note by F. Engels.)
– ᵃ Salian land – ᵇ B. E. Guérard, *La terre salique*. Bibliotèque de l'École des chartes, November-December 1841. – ᶜ These Russian words meaning black redistribution are written in Latin letters.

price, which he has chosen to preach for some time now, particularly at this juncture when coercive laws are being drawn up in Berlin.[428] But I preach those-tactics only for the *Germany of today* and even then with many *reservations*. For France, Belgium, Italy, Austria, such tactics could not be followed as a whole and, for Germany, they could become inapplicable tomorrow. So please wait for the complete article before judging it—it will probably appear in *Neue Zeit*, and I expect copies of the pamphlet any day now. It's a pity that Liebknecht can see only black and white. Shades don't exist for him.

However, things are warming up in Germany, it promises a splendid end to the century. Young William's[a] 'indignation'[564] is highly amusing. You may be sure our people will answer him in the Reichstag where there is no lese-majesty.

I intended to say a lot of other things to you as well, but I cannot bring them to mind at the moment when I need them. I am gradually aging. So, as I must write a few lines still to Laura before the post goes, goodbye! Greetings from the Freybergers (whose little girl gets on wonderfully well) and from your

F. Engels

First published abridged in:
Socialiste, No. 115, 24 novembre
1900 and in full in: F. Engels,
P. et L. Lafargue, *Correspondance*,
t. III, Paris, 1959

Printed according to the original

Translated from the French

288

ENGELS TO RICHARD FISCHER

IN BERLIN

Londont 5 April 1895
41 Regent's Park Road, N. W.

Dear Fischer,

You will have got my letter of the 3rd.[25] Your postcard arrived this morning. So another snag has cropped up.[577] I would ask you to seek legal

---

[a] William II

advice straight away *as to the extent to which the copyright owned by Marx's heirs still applies to his articles in the 'Rheinische Zeitung' of 1842.* The articles appeared anonymously. As anonymous articles, however, they are of no value to Mr Baake. So far as he is concerned they only acquire value through Marx's name. And if he publishes them under Marx's name, is he not thereby acknowledging that we have the copyright in so far as this might perhaps have been compromised by the fact of their having first appeared anonymously?

If there is no recourse to law—which would first have to be established so that we can act accordingly—it would be best if you were to get copies made of all the articles—three—in the library and send me duplicates, so that I could look through them quickly and write an introduction. There are three articles.

1. On the proceedings of the Rhine Province Assembly,
2. On thefts of wood,
3. On the condition of the wine growers on the Mosel.[578]

You would then have to issue an announcement straight away to the effect that they would be brought out *by you* and edited *by me*, along with an introduction and notes (if any).

So far as the Russians are concerned, it is normal practice to encroach upon an author's rights without so much as your leave 'in the interests of propaganda', not to speak of the interests, as is frequently the case, of their own private printing-shop and publishing house, as opposed to those of others.[579] Up till now, however, I have not been accustomed to that kind of thing when dealing with Germans.

Had I only known what I had merely *suspected*, namely that the old *Rheinische Zeitung* is in the Berlin Library, I should have gone there back in 1893[580] and looked it out, in which case we should have made a good deal more progress in regard to other matters too.

Is Baake a brother of Kurt Baake's?

Regards to everyone.

Yours,

F. E.

First published in: Marx and Engels, *Works*, First Russian Edition, Vol. XXIX, 1946

Printed according to the original

Published in English for the first time

289

ENGELS TO CONRAD SCHMIDT[139]

IN ZURICH

London, 6 April 1895
41 Regent's Park Road, N. W.

Dear Schmidt,

I am most indebted to you for your tenacity over the 'fiction'.[a] (There is in fact a difficulty here which I only mastered as a result of your insistence upon the 'fiction'. The solution may be found in III, 1, pp. 154-157[b] though it has not been elaborated or emphasised with sufficient exactitude, a circumstance that has persuaded me to enlarge briefly on the above point in the *Neue Zeit* with reference to Sombart's[c] and your objections. In any case there is a further point regarding which I should like to make an addition to Volume III and bring it into line with the situation today by taking account of certain changes in economic conditions since 1865.[534]

But if I am to develop that point concerning the effectiveness and validity of the law of value, it would make thing easier for me if you would permit me to make mention, not only of the 'hypothesis' of your *Centralblatt* article,[d] but also of the 'fiction' you discuss in your two letters and to quote one or two passages from them for the purpose of defining more precisely what you mean by the hypothesis of the article. So would you kindly reread the passage alluded to above and then tell me whether I may say that the aforesaid quotations were extracted from letters by Dr C. Schmidt to myself. Should you be convinced by Marx' passage that, where the production of commodities is concerned, the law of value is, after all, rather more than a necessary fiction, we should then see eye to eye, and in that case I should of course be glad to dispense with this.

Mrs Freyberger, formerly Louise Kautsky I, along with her little girl, sends you her best compliments in the same way as I would ask you to remember me very kindly to your wife.

---

[a] See this volume, pp. 462-66 – [b] See present edition, Vol. 37 – [c] Sombart, 'Zur Kritik des Ukonomischen Systems von Karl Marx'. In: *Archiv für soziale Gesetzgebung und Statistik*, Bd.7, H. 4 – [d] C. Schmidt, 'Der dritte Band des *Kapital*'. In: *Sozialpolitisches Centralblatt*, 25 Februar 1895

Yours,
F. Engels

First published in: Printed according to the original
Sozialistische Monatshefte
No. 24, 19 20   Published in English in full
                                        for the first time

290

ENGELS TO STEPHAN BAUER[581]

IN BRNO

London, 10 April 1895
41 Regent's Park Road, N. W.

Dear Sir,

May I say how very grateful I am to you for so kindly sending me the facsimile of Quesnay's *Tableau* as well as your monograph on it[a] which I am just reading with much interest. You are right to stress the point that, after Baudeau, no one understood this important piece of work on political economy[582] until Marx who was, in fact, the first to raise the physiocrats from the obscurity whither they had been consigned by the subsequent successes of the English school. Should it be granted me to edit Book IV of *Capital* as well, you will find there a further, more exhaustive tribute to the services rendered by Quesnay and his pupils.[b]

I am, Sir,

Yours very truly,
F. Engels

First published in: Printed according to the original
Marx and Engels, *Works*,
First Russian Edition,
Vol. XXIX, 1946

---

[a] S. Bauer, 'Zur Entstehung der Physiokratie. Auf Grund ungedruckter Schriften François Quesnays', In: *Jahrbücher für Nationalökonomie und Statistik.* 21 Bd., 1890, S. 113-158 – [b] See present edition, Vol. 31, pp. 204-40 and Vol. 34, pp. 195-96, 289-90.

291

ENGELS TO HERMANN ENGELS

IN BARMEN

London, 12 April 1895
41 Regent's Park Road, N. W.

Dear Hermann,

I have heard nothing further about the sherry since it was despatched.[a] All I know is that immediately after the hard weather the two Cologne steamers *Energie* and *Industrie* were reported as having arrived here—departures are difficult to keep track of in the newspapers and I don't therefore know whether both have sailed—and if so when. If the wine doesn't turn up in the course of next week, please send me a postcard and I shall then make inquiries.

The news that the wedding had gone off so merrily and that the loving couple[b] had enjoyed their honeymoon pleased me enormously. It is all right about the 80 marks. I hope that by now you have quite shaken off your influenza. Luckily I have recovered from mine and am gradually beginning to get out and about again.

Very many thanks for the information re the Schaaffhausens. I shall be glad to take up the allotment of 1000 marks—*à* 120%. The initial payment of 700 marks will be amply covered by my balance as at 30.4.94, even after deduction of the £40 (...)[c] per P.P. & Co., while accrued interest and the last Schaaffhausen dividend ought to be just about enough for the remaining payment of 500 marks. Should a few more marks be needed, you might be so good as to advance them to me pending the next dividend—i.e. assuming that I have not overlooked anything in the above calculation, in which case kindly advise me.

The conversion into bonds *à* 1,000 marks would also be perfectly acceptable to me if it could be done without leaving a tiresome or unproductive balance, something that can't be managed just now when all bonds must be in denominations of 1,000 or 450. So if the thing is impossible it

---

[a] See this volume, pp. 416, 441, 478 – [b] Arthur Schuchard and Elsbeth Schuchard (née Engels) – [c] Ms. damaged

would best be forgotten. But there might after all be some solution.

Well, you now have the prompt answer you wanted. For the past four days we have been having wonderful spring weather; overnight everything began sprouting and burgeoning and the warm sun in the day time is quite untypical of a normal English April with its grey skies and biting north-easters.

For the first time in my life I paid a dentist 10/6d last Monday[a] for pulling out a couple of old stumps. Now I only have seventeen teeth left, all of them in front and all of them so far complete, but nothing at the back, so I may have to be fitted with a set of false teeth!

Love to you all.

Yours,

Friedrich

First published in:
Deutsche Revue, Jg. 46,
Bd. III, 192

Printed according to the original

Published in English for the first time

292

ENGELS TO KRYSTJU RAKOWSKI

IN NANCY

London, 13 April 1895
41 Regent's Park Road, N. W.

Dear citizen,

I am answering at once your request to drop a line to the Bulgarian comrades. Being overburdened with work, I answered in the negative the requests directed to me by the comrades both on the occasion of 18 March and on that of May Day. I also sent a negative reply last week[b] to the British Social-Democratic Federation.[44] You will see that if I were to comply with your request, I should have to comply with the requests of roughly forty groups from ten to twenty different countries, which is

---

[a] 8 April – [b] See this volume, p. 487

more than I can do. Please be so kind as to give the Bulgarian comrades my excuses and to tell them that I regret not being able to render them the service they are asking for and that in a different situation I should have been glad to write something specially for the Bulgarians as the youngest followers of socialism.

Sincerely yours,

F. Engels

First published, in Bulgarian, in *Sotsialist*, Nos. 54 and 55, 19 April 1895

Printed according to the newspaper text

Translated from the Bulgarian

Published in English for the first time

293

ENGELS TO RICHARD FISCHER[139]

IN BERLIN

London, 15 April 1895
41 Regent's Park Road, N. W.

Dear Fischer,

The 400 marks received with thanks. I shall change them tomorrow and distribute them to the heirs.[583]

So the position as regards the essays in the old *Rheinische Zeitung* is as I feared.[a] The copyright has lapsed and only by acting swiftly can we restore our title to it. It will therefore be perfectly in order if you at once announce that the articles will be published by you and edited and annotated by me. Possibly under the title:

Karl Marx's Early Writings. Three Essays from the (First) 'Rheinische Zeitung' of 1842. I. The Rhine Province Assembly on Freedom of the Press. II. The Same on the Law relating to Thefts of Wood. III. The Condition of the Wine-Growers on the Mosel. Edited and with an Introduction by F. Engels.[578]

---

[a] See this volume, pp. 490-91

I am not quite happy about the title and should like you if possible to refrain from giving it a definite title until we have found one that is more suitable. As to the Mosel article,[584] I am sure of the facts in as much as Marx always used to tell me that it was precisely his preoccupation with the law on thefts of wood and the condition of the Mosel wine-growers that led him from politics pure and simple to economic conditions and thus to socialism. And during our conversations we always treated the Mosel article as having emanated from him. I didn't read it, as I was already in England at the time. It is so long ago since we spoke of the matter that I cannot entirely rule out the eventuality of a misunderstanding. Once I have the article in front of me, I cannot possibly go wrong.

Now as to your great scheme,[585] I think you would do best to shelve it until the fate of the Subversion Bill[428] has been decided. A library which re-issues historical documents and writings from earlier periods cannot tolerate any kind of censorship—quite literally or not at all. Still less could I consent to Marx's and my own early works being subjected to a process of emasculation, however wild, in order to conform to the conditions temporarily obtaining in the press. But in view of the fact that we used to write in a very unrestrained way and were forever justifying things which, in the territories of the German Empire, are regarded either as a crime or an offence, a re-issue in Berlin after the passing of that exemplary Bill would be quite impossible without numerous deletions.

Secondly, however, I have a scheme for again presenting Marx's and my lesser writings to the public in a *complete edition*—not, that is to say, by instalments but all at one go, in whole volumes. I have already been in correspondence with August[a] on the subject and we are still discussing it. So you might have a word with him when he gets back. I am by no means certain that an enterprise like this is really your cup of tea, nor do I know whether you, i.e. the publishing side of the *Vorwärts*, are the best people for the job—quite aside from the harassment of the press which has already inclined me to believe that we may be forced to have recourse to a publisher outside the German Empire.

Marx would *never* have consented to the issue of a work by instalments. In the case of the 2nd Ed. of *Capital I* he once allowed Meissner to bring out seven *big* instalments, each of some seven sheets, but that was as much as he could stomach.[586] To chop up books such as *The Holy Family*, *Herr*

---

[a] Bebel

Vogt, etc., into instalments of two sheets or so would certainly not do. In such cases people derive absolutely nothing from their reading and to read a work in this way, piecemeal, is conducive only to incomprehension.

The *Tribune* articles exist only in *English*.[587]

We survived the holiday without too many mishaps and the weather was really beautiful. Otherwise no news. As soon as you have a copy of one of the three articles from the *Rheinische Zeitung*[a], please send it to me straight away so that I can set to work. By registered book post or, if not, in some other manner with adequate regard for safety precautions.

Many regards to everyone.

Yours

F. E.

First published abridged in:
Marx and Engels, *Works*,
First Russian Edition, Vol. I,
Preface, 1928 and in full:
ibid., Vol. XXIX, 1946

Printed according to the original

Published in English in full
for the first time

294

ENGELS TO LAURA LAFARGUE

AT LE PERREUX

London, 17 April 1895
41 Regent's Park Road, N. W.

My dear Löhr,

Yesterday I sent you cheque for £6.9.9., your share of honorarium for the *Klassenkämpfe*.[b] To-day I return *registered*, book post, your translation with thanks and suggestions.[517] In one passage I had to make an alteration, you yourself had marked it as unintelligible, which indeed it was owing to omission of a word in the German text. The alteration is at the back of the page and requires a little frenchifying at your hands. I hope all your trouble will be rewarded by the French reading public!

---

[a] See this volume, p. 491 – [b] See this volume, pp. n421, 517

I have at last succeeded in hunting up the old *Rheinische Zeitung* of 1842. It was all this time in the Berlin Bibliothek, and our friends in Berlin, who might have known that long ago, only found it out now. Someone in Berlin[a] had a sharper way of doing things than they, and intended publishing *Mohrs* articles therefrom[578]; we have no right to stop this, as according to German law all anonymous or pseudonymous works become public property after 30 years from date of publication, unless copyright has been previously registered by the author or other *qui de droit*.[b] However this threatened competition roused our friends all at once; Fischer who manages now the publishing department of the *Vorwärts* book-selling firm, has at once, at my suggestion,[c] set some one to copy Mohrs chief articles, and will announce that I am going to edit them with introduction, etc. This will probably stop competition. Financially we can hardly expect much, if anything, therefrom, but at all events the articles are safe.

For the Lassalle letters[284] and ulterior plans of republication of old affairs, we shall have to await the fate of the Coercion Bill[428] before the Reichstag; if that passes, I do not see how we can safely proceed to work, at least in Berlin. Maybe Stuttgart may remain more favourable—anyhow *qui vivra verra*.[d]

I hope you send the *Devenir social* also to Madrid—our friends there are almost entirely dependent, for foreign reading, on French literature, and it strikes me they get to see more from other sects' publications than from ours. For if the management of the *Socialiste* is to serve as a pattern, woe be unto us! The *Vorwärts* announces the complete reorganisation of that illustrious paper, published '*mit Ausschluss der Oeffentlichkeit*',[e] and that Chauvin has remodelled the publishing department[588]—if so, *il est tellement chauvin*[f] that nobody here has seen a trace of it. But then, the *Vorwärts* seems to know of France only the Boulevard *Bonne Nouvelle*, and if the *nouvelles ne sont pas assez bonnes, il les fabrique lui-même*.[g]

Many thanks for your news about Sganarelle, they are quite sufficient for the *éclairage de ma tête*[h] upon the subject.[589]

I had in my head only the Sganarelle of the *Médecin volant* and *Don Juan*.

---

[a] Hans Baake – [b] authorised person – [c] See this volume, p. 497 – [d] wait and see – [e] in camera – [f] he is so chauvinist – [g] news is not interesting enough, he invents it himself – [h] enlightenment of my mind

Please tell Paul that if he is in want of a draught composed of L, s, and d (in which case the British philistine spells it draft) he is quite welcome to one.

Kind regards from Louise

Ever yours

F. E.

First published, in the language of the original (English), in F. Engels, P. et L. Lafargue, *Correspondance*, t. III, Paris, 1959

Reproduced from the original

295

ENGELS TO LUDWIG KUGELMANN

IN HANOVER

London, 18 April 1895
41 Regent's Park Road, N. W.

Dear Kugelmann,

I apologise for having overlooked your request that I should at once write to you about Livingston, though his letter as such hardly seemed to call for any special reply.[559] I don't imagine that Jacobi or M. Becker will have anything useful. If Livingston writes to them, we shall find that out. We have been regularly corresponding with Sorge for many many years.

Apart from that I am most grateful to you for your information. I, too, am at a loss to know how to trace anything that may have appeared anonymously in the *Westphälisches Dampfboot*.[558] It is possible that when I get down to work one thing or another will refresh my memory. Besides, *should* there be anything in it, it would be of little consequence and serve at most as proof of our lack of agreement with the Bielefeld sentimental socialism of the day.[590]

Lastly, I shall doubtless have to do as you say.[591] I, too, having long been of the opinion that this was how we should proceed if the worst came to the worst. Meanwhile one thing and another continues to turn up as, recently, the old *Rheinische Zeitung* in the Berlin Library. What might badly upset our calculations, however, is the Subversion Bill.[428] Until that has been decided there can be no thought of devising a plan of action.

Many regards from the Freybergers and myself to you and yours.

Yours

F. E.

You will be getting one by post.[592]

First published in: Marx and Engels, *Works*, First Russian Edition, Vol. XXIX, 1946

Printed according to the original

Published in English for the first time

296

ENGELS TO RICHARD FISCHER

IN BERLIN

London, 18 April 1895
41 Regent's Park Road, N. W.

Dear Fischer,

One further matter: Would you please take another look at the old *Rheinische Zeitung* with regard to the Mosel articles[584] to find out whether some sort of polemic may not have arisen over the things and if so whether there are also articles under Marx's usual pseudonym and written in his own style—short, antithetically expressed sentences—as well as any *other* shorter articles under the same pseudonym and stylistically the same. If there are, let me know.

I can no longer remember my own articles—the best of them fell foul of the censor—or even my pseudonym; most of the longer ones, i.e. those that are not merely day to day reports, are in the supplement or the feuilleton.

In addition to the articles in the *Rheinische Zeitung*,[578] I have discovered another one by Marx dating from the same period and also dealing with the machinations of the censor.[a] This can be printed with the remainder but no one must get wind of it since it, too, appeared *anonymously*. It will run to between 1 1/2 and 2 sheets. I may possibly discover some other shorter pieces, in which case we shall have collected all the main items from Marx's *pre*-socialist period. Meanwhile see to it that a copy is sent off to me quickly and we can then agree upon our next move.

Yours

F. E.

First published in: Marx and Engels, *Works*, First Russian Edition, Vol. XXIX, 1946

Printed according to the original

Published in English for the first time

297

ENGELS TO STANISLAW MENDELSON

IN LONDON

[London,] 23 April 1895
41 Regent's Park Road, N. W.

My dear Mendelson,

If it is convenient, I will call to see you tomorrow, on Wednesday, between 3 and 4 in the afternoon—*weather permitting*.

My best wishes to Mme M. and yourself,

From yours

F. Engels

First published in:
Marx and Engels,
Works, Second Russian
Edition, Vol. 39, Moscow,
1966

Printed according to the original

Translated from the French

Published in English for the first time

---

[a] K. Marx *Comments on the Latest Prussian Censorship Instruction*.

298

ENGELS TO FRANZ MEHRING

IN BERLIN

London, [End of April 1895]
41 Regent's Park Road, N.

Dear Mr Mehring,

May I say how very grateful I am for your offer, which is gladly accepted, to help me hunt out Marx's early writings for republication. The first difficulty to confront me was the *Rheinische Zeitung* of 1842, which I had imagined to be in the Berlin Library. Despite numerous inquiries, I was unable to ascertain whether it was actually there, but now that that point has been cleared up, we can make a start.

Marx was in Bonn up till October 1842. When I passed through at the end of September or the beginning of October on my return from Berlin, the editorial board consisted, so far as I recall, only of M. Hess and Dr Rave, a former editor of the *Elberfelder Zeitung* (which was, I believe, known by another name at the time). Rutenberg had, I believe, already been expelled, though I am not sure about that. When I dropped in again towards the end of November on my way to England, I ran into Marx there and that was the occasion of our first, distinctly chilly meeting. Marx had meanwhile taken a stand against the Bauers, i.e. he had said he was opposed not only to the *Rheinische Zeitung* becoming predominantly a vehicle for *theological* propaganda, atheism, etc., rather than for political discussion and action, but also to Edgar Bauer's hot air brand of communism, which was based on a sheer love of 'going to extremes' and was soon after replaced by Edgar with other kinds of extremist hot air. Since I corresponded with the Bauers, I was regarded as their ally, whereas they caused me to view Marx with suspicion.

To the best of my recollection Marx resigned—at any rate officially—from the post of editor *en chef* on 1 January 1843. That, however, did not prevent him from surreptitiously contributing to the paper up to and including February. I think I am equally right in saying that the ukase requiring the paper to close down on 31 March 1843 was served on it no later than 31 December. Negotiations then began, the result of which proved negative, hence the delay in publishing the ukase until 28 January and likewise in appointing the chief censor who had, in fact, already been functioning for some time. At one period there were no less than three censors: 1. the usual censor, 2. assessor von Saint-Paul who had been sent from Berlin, 3. the District President. Saint-Paul was still there at the time of the paper's funeral feast. The vacillations between 12 and 18 February would pretty well coincide with Marx's departure from Cologne.[593]

If, by comparing these data with the paper itself, you could discover more details or rectify inaccuracies, it would be of great benefit both to your work and to mine.

As regards the Mosel articles,[584] it will doubtless turn out to be as you say. Marx was tied to Cologne at the time and could not possibly have collected material of that kind in person.

The article I mentioned to Fischer[a] is in fact the one about the censorship instruction which appeared in Ruge's *Anekdota*.[b]

One of the best pieces in the *Rheinische Zeitung*, again in the feuilleton, is a long critique of Leo's *History of the French Revolution*. It is my Marx's friend C. F. Köppen[c] (who also wrote about old Fritz[d] and Norse mythology[e]) and (for the first time in any language) gives a correct explanation for the reign of terror.

Certain quotations and retrospective insights in your articles in the *Neue Zeit* have already shown me that you have made a thorough study of the period previous to 1848. 1 am glad that it has fallen to you to deal with this, as well as with the later period in respect of Germany.

There might possibly be one or two more things of Marx's in the supplement for the period prior to October 1842; it would hardly be worth your while to search out smaller items from Bonn in the main part of the paper.

My heartfelt condolences on the destruction of the *Freie Volksbühne*.[594] Subversion from above could not possibly have passed that institution by.

Once again my best thanks.

Yours faithfully

F. Engels

---

[a] See this volume, p. 502 – [b] K. Marx, *Comments on the Latest Prussian Censorship Instruction*. – [c] C. F. Köppen, *Leo's Geschichte der Revolution*. In: *Rheinische Zeitung*, 1921, 22 May 1842 – [d] Frederick II – [e] C. F. Köppen, *Friedrich der Grosse und seine Widersacher* and *Literarische Einleitung in die Nordische Mythologie*.

First published in: Marx and Engels,
Works, First Russian Edition,
Vol. XXIX, 1946

Printed according to the original

Published in English for the first time

299

ENGELS TO FRANZ MEHRING

IN BERLIN

London, 9 May 1895
41 Regent's Park Road, N. W.

Dear Mr Mehring,

Very many thanks for your long and informative letter plus enclosures, which I shall reply to at length as soon as my cranium permits. Unfortunately for the past week a rheumatic condition of the scalp has been encircling and compressing it as though with a band of iron. I hope to have got over it by next week along with the attendant insomnia. Meanwhile I agree to your proposal that the only articles from the *Rheinische Zeitung* that should be published in their entirety are the two long ones and those on Communism[a] (as also the article from the *Anekdota*[b]). It would only be necessary to copy from the remainder such passages as you might be so good as to indicate as being the most pregnant (along with particulars of the context). As regards the Mosel articles,[584] it would be desirable if my introduction included a brief outline both of the course of the debate and of the contents.

Would you be kind enough to acquaint Fischer with the foregoing?

Once again my best thanks and until my next, which has to do with one minor detail,

I remain
Yours sincerely
F. Engels

---

[a] K. Marx, *Proceedings of the Sixth Rhine Province Assembly. First Article. Debates on Freedom of the Press and Publication of the Proceedings of the Assembly of the Estates; Proceedings of the Sixth Rhine Province Assembly. Third Article. Debates on the Law on Thefts of Wood* and *Communismus and the Augsburg 'Allgemeine Zeitung'.* – [b] K. Marx, *Comments on the Latest Prussian Censorship Instruction.*

First published in: Marx and Engels, *Works*, First Russian Edition, Vol. XXIX, 1946

Printed according to the original

Published in English for the first time

300

ENGELS TO RICHARD FISCHER

IN BERLIN

London, 9 May 1895
41 Regent's Park Road, N. W.

Dear Fischer,

At the moment I feel so run down as a result of rheumatic pains in the scalp and the insomnia associated therewith that I am incapable of any kind of work. I hope to be all right again by next week. In the meantime, however, seeing that you and Mehring can both take a look at the copy of the *Rheinische Zeitung*, I think it would be best if you yourselves were to arrange what should be done with the shorter and Mosel[584] articles and to provide me with a copy just of the most important bits. I am also sending Mehring a line or two about it.[a]

Ms. just arrived.[595]

Yours,

F. E.

First published in:
Marx and Engels, *Works*,
First Russian Edition,
Vol. XXIX, 1946

Printed according to the original

Published in English for the first time

---

[a] See previous letter

301

ENGELS TO LAURA LAFARGUE

IN LE PERREUX

London, 14 May 1895
41 Regent's Park Road, N. W.

My dear Löhr

I was extremely glad, and indeed so were Louise and Ludwig to learn that both you and Paul were ready and willing to come over here for a bit, and I should have written at once in reply, had it not been for those confounded pains which for a week nearly drove me mad and even now have not left me, anything but painless, but extremely stupid and unfit for anything. The fact is this. Some time ago I got a swelling on the right side of the neck, which after some time resolved itself into a bunch of deep-seated glands infiltrated by some cause or other. The pains arose from direct pressure of that lump on the nerve and will of course only give way when that pressure disappears. At present a process of resorption is going on very satisfactorily, but a couple of these glands are suppurating and will have to be cut; and as they are so deep-seated and slow in coming to the surface, and we old people being such slow coaches, the time for the operation cannot be exactly fixed, but it is hoped will come off this week. That once performed I am ordered to the sea-side; but the uncertainty is still about the time.

Now as things are situated, would it not be the best thing for you to come over say in the course of next week, and then as soon as possible you and I could bundle off to Eastbourne[596] and settle down in comfortable quarters and prepare for visitors from London. I say you and I, because I intend to keep you here a good bit longer than very likely Paul would care to separate himself from his studies and your animals and the garden work; so he perhaps would prefer to do as you say and come tumbling after.

When I shall have cleared out from here, Louise intends giving my two rooms a good cleaning down and after that she might come and join us with her baby for a week or so; after that Tussy and Edward might come, and then Paul who by that time is sure to be tired of his solitude, and then we might bethink ourselves of returning all of us to London and show Paul our new establishment too.

This is such a sort of rough prospectus as a man with neuralgic pains in the head after a series of sleepless nights has been able to excogitate under the present indefinite conditions, and therefore subject to alterations as novel circumstances and novel ideas may command. It is humbly submitted to you for approval or improvement as may be.

The heat is insupportable, 22°C in the room all day long—no wind, clouds and impending thunder which unfortunately *keeps* impending. And that 2 months after that hard frost!

Kind regards from the Freybergers to both of you. Amitiés à Paul et au revoir.

I enclose cheque £10—for your journey hither and any little additions you may like to make to your outfit.

So please say when we may expect you.

Ever yours,

F. Engels

302

ENGELS TO IGNAZ BRAND[597]

IN VIENNA

Londong 20 May [18]95
41 Regent's Park Road, N. W.

Esteemed Comrade, many thanks for kindly sending the two copies of *Námezdni Prace a Kapital*,[a] a one of which I have given to Mrs Eleanor Marx Aveling. If she does not learn Czech now, I am not to blame. Please give my thanks to the translator[b] with the assurance that my progress in Czech, though slow, is, I hope, none the less steady for it.

Yours,

F. Engels

---

[a] K. Marx, *Wage Labour and Capital* – [b] J. K. Náchodsky

Friendly greetings to Mr Heller.

First published in:
Marx and Engels, *Works*,
Second Russian Edition,
Vol. 50, Moscow, 1981

Printed according to the original

Published in English for the first time

303

ENGELS TO CARL HIRSCH

IN COLOGNE

London, 20 May 1895
41 Regent's Park Road, N. W.

Dear (...)[a]

You have set us a difficult task. We are to seek out 'the journalist Tollitt[b] England' as also those 'English papers' containing the relevant details about Brauweiler.[598] In the first place, the English daily press does not even mention the name *Braunweiler* in its accounts of the case. The report of a Parliamentary Committee is not, however, published until its work has been completed. So the item must doubtless have emanated from some obscure trade paper and will therefore be impossible to trace in this country. In the second place, no one here knows the journalist Tollitt, who according to some is called Pollitt. Dr Freyberger tried in vain to track him down at the NATIONAL LIBERAL CLUB which has a vast number of journalists amongst its members. We have now taken further steps in order to discover the man if possible—it seems quite clear that he does not live in London or work for the *political* press; more likely he is in some trade branch—though that will take time. But it is very naïve of you to expect that he would appear over there as witness on your behalf. After all, he himself says that he got into the prisons by stealth, and consequently be would at once be thrown into jug in Cologne for bribery of officials or something of the kind, and put on trial. Hofrichter's

---

[a] Ms. damaged – [b] reference is to James Pollitt

suggestion that he should submit to a judicial examination here is also impracticable. If, however, *he is willing*, he can swear an affidavit (a statement made on oath which, if false, carries with it all the consequences arising from perjury) before a Justice of the Peace in which he attests the statements he made before the committee. Once the document had been ratified by the German Consul, it would also be legally valid over there.

Bernstein was away from London during that week and Beer has no connections whatever in the circles in which Tollitt must be sought.

As soon as we discover anything further we shall let you know.[a] But time is damned short. *Where* did you get the item *from*? Keep on inquiring over there until you have found out *how and through whom* it got into the German press. That would provide a clue.

Many regards.

Yours,

F. Engels

First published in: Marx and Engels, *Works*, First Russian Edition, Vol. XXIX, 1946

Printed according to the original

Published in English for the first time

304

ENGELS TO KARL KAUTSKY[599]

IN STUTTGART

London, 21 May 1895
41 Regent's Park Road, N. W.

Dear Baron,

I should have replied at once to your letter of the 6th had not a nasty inflammation of the glands in my neck, accompanied by much pain and inevitable loss of sleep, rendered me almost wholly incapable of work during the past two weeks. But now you are to be kept waiting no longer.

At the time in question you took it upon yourselves to produce a

---

[a] See this volume, p. 514

History of Socialism.[561] Of all the people then living there was only one, I think I may say, whose collaboration was absolutely necessary, and that person was myself. I might even say that, without my help, a work of this nature cannot today be anything but incomplete and inadequate. And this you knew as well as I did. But of all those who might have been of use to you, I and I alone was the only one who was *not* invited to collaborate. So you must have had very pertinent reasons for choosing to exclude me. I am not complaining—far from it. You had a perfect right to act as you did. I merely remark on the fact.

What did pique me, however, if only for a moment, was the strange secretiveness with which you withheld from me a matter about which all the rest of the world was talking. It was only from third persons that I learned of the whole enterprise, and it was only from the printed prospectus that I learned of the general outline of the scheme, Not a word either from you or from Ede; it was as though you had a guilty conscience. At the same time all manner of people kept surreptitiously inquiring what connection I had with the thing, whether I had refused to collaborate, etc. And then at length, when silence could no longer be maintained, the good Ede got round to mentioning the subject with a sheepishness and embarrassment that would have been worthy of a worse cause—though nothing wrong had been done save for this absurd play-acting which, in the meantime, as Louise can testify, has enlivened many a dull hour for me.

Well and good. You have presented me with a fait accompli; a *History of Socialism* on which I have not collaborated. I have accepted the fact without complaint from the very start. But that fact is of your own making, nor can you do away with or ignore it, should this ever happen to suit your purpose. And neither can I do away with it. If, on mature reflection, you chose to slam the front door in my face at a time when my advice and help might have been of material use to you, please do not expect of me that I should now slink in through some little back door in order to help you out of a quandary. I must admit that, had the roles been reversed, I should have reflected for a very, very long time before coming to you with a request such as this one.[600] Is it really so terribly difficult to see that everyone must bear the consequences of his own actions? As YOU MADE YOUR BED SO YOU MUST LIE IN IT. If there is no room for me here, it is only because you wanted it so.

Well, that settles that. And now you would oblige me by considering this reply as irrevocable. Let us both regard the whole incident as finished and done with.[601] Nor shall I mention it to Ede again unless he is the first to broach it.

Meanwhile I am engaged in producing another piece for the *Neue Zeit* which should gladden your heart—*Ergänzungen und Nachtäge zum* 'Kapital', *Buch III*, No. 1: *Law of Value and Rate of Profit. Reply to the Objections of Sombart and C. Schmidt.* No. 2—the role of the Stock Exchange which has changed very considerably since Marx wrote about it in 1865—will follow later.[534] A sequel will follow if required and should time permit. The first article would have been finished had I had nothing else on my mind.

Of your book,[a] I can say that it improves the further into it one gets. To judge by the original plan, your treatment of Plato and early Christianity still leaves something to be desired. You do very much better on the medieval sects, after which you go from strength to strength; and are at your beat on the Taborites,[563] Münzer and then the Anabaptists.[562] Alongside a great many more important economic analyses of political events there are also some commonplaces which would seem to indicate a gap in your studies. I have learnt a great deal from your book which is indispensible preliminary reading for my new edition of *The Peasant War*.[235] It would seem to me to have two main faults—1. Very inadequate research into the development and role of the déclassé, almost pariah-like elements who had no place whatever in the feudal system and who were the inevitable outcome of urban development,, It is they who in all cases formed the lowest stratum of urban population in the Middle Ages—devoid of rights and set apart from village communities, craft guilds and feudal dependence. Though difficult, this should serve as your *main basis*, for by degrees, with the dissolution of the feudal bonds, these elements became the *pre*-proletariat which, in 1789, was responsible for the revolution in the faubourgs[b] of Paris and absorbed all the outcasts of feudal and guild society. You talk of proletarians—a term which is inapt—amongst whom you comprise weavers whose importance you quite rightly stress—but you can count them among your 'proletariat' only *after*, and *in so far as*, déclassé journeymen weavers came into existence outside of the guilds. There is still much room for improvement here.

2. You have not fully grasped the position of Germany—her international economic position in so far as it is possible to speak of any such

---

[a] Kautsky, *Von Plato bis zu den Wiedertaufern* – [b] suburbs

thing—in the world market at the end of the fifteenth century. That posi-tion *alone* explains why the bourgeois-plebeian movement, disguised as religion, which failed in England, the Netherlands and Bohemia should, in sixteenth century Germany, have enjoyed a *certain* success—the suc-cess of its *religious trappings*—whereas the success of its bourgeois sub-stance was reserved for the next century and for the countries, Holland and England, which had meanwhile evinced a new tendency in interna-tional trade. It is a lengthy subject which I hope to deal with *in extenso* in *The Peasant War*—would I had got to that stage!

In an attempt to remain popular your style is now that of the leader writer, now that of the dominie. This you should be able to avoid. Again, is it for Janssen's sake that you still refuse to see the pun in which Ulrich von Hutten is indulging with his *obscuri viri*? The joke lies in the fact of its meaning both—obscure or obscurantist—and that is what Hutten was *trying* to say.[602]

But that is all by the way. You and Ede have both been working on a completely new subject, and you cannot expect to attain perfection straight away. You should be glad to have produced a book that is pre-sentable, even at this stages when it is, as it were, in its initial draft form. Now, however, you are both honour-bound not to allow the ground you have broken to lie fallow but to continue with your researches so that, in a few years' time, you will be able to bring out a new edition capable of meeting every requirement.

Someone in St Petersburg has sent me a Russian translation of your old piece on marriage and the family[a] (*Kosmos*).[b] I don't know who did it. I shall send it to you.

Many regards from one household to the other,

Yours,

F. Engels

One more thing. I have suggested to Sorge that, when he has finished his articles on the American movement, these should be published as an off-print.[603] He is agreeable but says there will have to be a great deal of revision and many corrections and additions, for which he is unlikely

---

[a] K. Kautsky, *Die Entstehung der Ehe und der Familie*. In *Kosmos*, 6. Jg. 12 Bd. – [b] [Kautsky—title of work in Russan]

to have time until his summer holidays. He accepted my proposal that the thing be suggested to Dietz. Perhaps you would be so good as to ask Dietz if he would care to take it on and, if so, on what terms. The articles are the best, and the *only authentic*, stuff we have got on the American movement, and I think it most desirable that they should be preserved for readers as a consecutive whole in an off-print.

First published abridged in:
Neue Zeit, Bd. II, Nr. 47, 1894-95
and in full, in Russian, in:
Istorik-Marksist, No. 2, 1936

Printed according to the original

Published in English in full
for the first time

305

ENGELS TO THE EDITORS OF THE *RHEINISCHE ZEITUNG*[598]

IN COLOGNE

London, 22 May 1895
41 Regent's Park Road, N. W.

Dear Editors,

The man has been found, is called James Pollitt, and is ready to do anything within reason. Has already supplied us with all the material to be had. The articles are in *The Hardwareman*, 11 and 18 May—stenographic reports of the sessions of the BOARD OF TRADE COMMITTEE on convict labour abroad, at which his statements were made. These are being sent to you in the original with translations of the passages relating to Braunweiler. He will further supply us with samples of the commodities produced in Braunweiler and sold over here, and also an affidavit as to the accuracy both of his statements before the Committee and of the excerpts quoted by you.

But since the material is very ample and would not lend itself to being paraphrased in a letter in such a way as to put you in a position to make full use of it in court, a personal discussion is urgently called for. This morning I therefore telegraphed Hirsch, 37 Hämergasse, Cologne: 'Most important that Hirsch, Hofrichter or lawyer come over here forthwith Engels'.[133]

It is to be hoped that someone has set off at once and will, on arrival, present himself at 41 Regent's Park Road, where he will find accommodation and thus be able to get down to work forthwith. The whole thing should be settled in twelve hours, after which he could, if necessary, leave for home.

I enclose a note of the expenses that have arisen so far and shall later let you have a full account of them.

The man who gets his London agent, S. A. Rothschild, to sell the Braunweiler products for him in this country is called Christian Abner and lives in Cologne. He would be your most important witness. He would have to be asked to declare on oath what commodities he obtains from Braunweiler and exports to England. Pollitt followed the fully laden waggons from the institution in Braunweiler to his place of business in Cologne. Abner has, in fact, had statements printed in English to the effect that he does not sell the products of convict labour, for he maintains that Braunweiler is not a prison but merely a house of correction. But such distinctions cut no ice over here.

More tomorrow, if no one has turned up by then.

Kindest regards from

Yours,
F. Engels

First published in: Marx and Engels, *Works*, First Russian Edition, Vol. XXIX, 1946

Printed according to the original

Published in English for the first time

306

ENGELS TO RICHARD FISCHER

IN BERLIN

[London,] 29 May 1895

Dear Fischer,

Thanks for the package. Am not yet in a fit state to deal with it. In the meantime I would ask you to send me in addition a copy of all the articles on the Mosel wine-growers.[584] For Hofrichter of Cologne has been here and would like to have them so as to make use of them at home.[605] He and I have therefore agreed that I should send for them and that, if unable to use all or any of them, I should let him have them, in which case he will repay you, at the *Rheinische Zeitung*, the cost of having them copied. So you are covered either way.

Kindest regards.

Yours,

F. E.

First published in: Marx and Engels, *Works*, First Russian Edition, Vol. XXIX, 1946

Printed according to the original

Published in English for the first time

307

ENGELS TO NIKOLAI DANIELSON

IN ST. PETERSBURG

London, 4 June 1895
41 Regent's Park Road, N. W.

My dear Sir,

I am rather unwell at present (though not seriously) and must confine myself to what is absolutely necessary.

I have sent to Mr. Konow the additions and alterations[606] forwarded by you and requested him to correspond direct with you, giving him your address. His address is

Andrej Konow
Augsburgerstr.37 *III*
Berlin

Hoping soon to be able to give you better news I remain

Yours faithfully
L. K.[a]

---

[a] Engels' pen-name made up of Louise Kautsky's initials

First published, in Russian,
in *Minuvshiye gody*, No. 2. 1908
Published in English for the first time

Reproduced from the original

308

ENGELS TO EDUARD BERNSTEIN

IN LONDON

Eastbourne,[596] 18 June 1895
4 Royal Parade

Dear Ede,

Thank you for your letter—there is some improvement but, in accordance with the principles of dialectics, the positive and the negative aspects are both showing a cumulative tendency. I am stronger, eat more and with a better appetite and look very well, or so I am told; thus my general condition has improved. On the other hand, the disease as such has also shown a cumulative tendency—more tumours and hence more pain and greater difficulty in getting to sleep. etc. The thing is taking a course that is normal, if more critical and not quite so sluggish as in London. Consequently my duly acquired pathological stupidity has tended to grow worse, as has my inability to work. Today I have had another particularly bad day but now, at 5 p.m., my mind is just beginning to grow a little more lucid.

Louise, Ludwig and their little girl came down on Saturday.[a] Ludwig has to be back on duty at his London hospital on Sunday but will probably return here on the Friday or Saturday.

The Avelings are coming down on Saturday or Sunday and, perhaps, Sam Moore also. Unfortunately they will have to provide their own entertainment since, subjectively and objectively, I am a bore.

Love to Gine and the children.[b] My visitors have all gone out and I have been trying to get a little sleep.

Yours,

F. E.

---

[a] 15 June – [b] Bernstein's wife and her children

First published in:
Marx and Engels, *Works*,
First Russian Edition,
Vol. XXIX, 1946

Printed according to the original

Published in English for the first time

309

ENGELS TO BOLESLAW ANTONI JEDRZEJOWSKI

IN LONDON

Eastbourne, 28 June 1895
4 Royal Parade

Dear Comrade,
In reply to your inquiry of the 25th of this month, which has been forwarded to me here, I beg to inform you that I should have no objection at all to your translating my article in the *Commonwealth* and publishing it in the way you suggest.[607]

Yours faithfully,
F. Engels

B. A. Jedrzejowski,
Editor, *Przedswit*

First published, in the
language of the original
(German), in: *Z pola walki*,
No. 4 (12), 1960

Printed according to the original

Published in English for the first time

310

ENGELS TO FILIPPO TURATI[139]

IN MILAN[608]

[Draft]

Eastbourne, 28 June 1895
4 Royal Parade

Dear citizen Turati,
To write a summary of the three volumes of *Capital* is one of the most

difficult tasks a writer could set himself.[609] In the whole of Europe there are, in my opinion, no more than half a dozen men capable of undertaking it. Among other prerequisites one must have a profound knowledge of bourgeois political economy, and also complete mastery of the German language. Now you say that your Labriolino[a] is not very strong in the second, while his articles in *Critica Sociale*[b] prove to me that he would do better to begin by understanding the 1st volume before wishing to produce his own work on all three volumes. I do not have the legal right to prevent him from doing this, but I must wash my hands of the affair completely.

As for the other Labriola,[c] the malicious tongue which you attribute to him may have a certain justification in a country such as Italy, where the socialist party,[340] like all the other parties, has been invaded, like a plague of locusts, by that 'declassed bourgeois youth', of which Bakunin was so proud.

Result: rampant literary dilettantism which only too often lapses into sensationalism and is inevitably followed by a spirit of camaraderie dominating the press. It is not our fault that this is the state of affairs, but you are subjected to this environment, as is everyone else. I would speak at greater length about Labriola but when I find that bits and pieces from my private letters have been reproduced in the *Critica Sociale* without my knowledge,[610] you must agree that it is better if I remain silent. For the rest, after all the quarrels and controversies, the party would seem to have behaved in general at the last elections as the situation required: independent confirmation at the 1st round when that did not help the Crispinis, support for the radicals and republicans at elections where our candidates had no chance of winning.[611] Warmest greetings from Dr and Mme Aveling, who are here with me, and also from myself, to you and citizen Anna Kulishov.

Yours,

F.

Please continue to address my letters to London.

---

[a] Arturo Labriola – [b] Arturo Labriola, *La teoria marxista del valore e il saggio medio del profitto* and *La conclusioni postume di Marx sulla teoria del valore*, in: *Critica Sociale*, Nos. 3 and 5, February I and March 1, 1895 – [c] Antonio Labriola

First published in the
language of the original,
French, in: *Lo stato operaio*,
No. 3, 1933

Printed according to the original

Translated from the French

Published in English in full
for the first time

311

ENGELS TO PAUL LAFARGUE[612]

AT LE PERREUX

[Eastbourne, 29 June 1895]

If the mountain will not come to Mohammed, Mohammed must go to the mountain. If Paul will not come to Eastbourne, Eastbourne must go to him. Thus what Mohammed could not accomplish, Paul accomplishes in the twinking of an eye. Witnessed the 29th June, 1895, by the undersigned

F. Engels
Tussy
Edward
Laura

First published in: Marx
and Engels, *Works*, Second
Russian Edition, Vol. 39,
Moscow, 1966
Published in English for the first time

Printed according to the original

Translated from the French

312

ENGELS TO RICHARD FISCHER[613]

IN BERLIN

Eastbourne, 29 June 1895
4 Royal Parade

Dear Fischer,

The Mosel articles[584] have arrived safely in London.[a] Thank you.

Unfortunately I can say nothing definite about completing the ms. or about the introduction which can only be done in London, since I am in no condition to do any work, nor do I know how long I shall continue to be held up by these processes which, while they may be normal at my age, are hideously slow.

The weather has been finer here than the farmers would like; at this place, in particular, there's a positive drought.

Regards to your wife and children.

Yours,

F. E.

First published in:
Marx and Engels, *Works*,
First Russian Edition,
Vol. XXIX, 1946

Printed according to the original

Published in English for the first time

313

ENGELS TO LOUISE FREYBERGER

IN LONDON

[Eastbourne,] 1 July 1895

Dear Louise,

Will you also please bring me a small bottleful of the carbolic acid solution in my bedroom? My nose is again suffering from hallucinations.

---

[a] See this volume, p. 515

You would also be well-advised to rig yourself and the baby out for rather chilly weather. Yesterday it was certainly not above 12 or 13 degrees Centigrade here.

With regard to E. Aveling's article[614] on the Independet Labour Party,[114] which I left in your keeping on my departure, would you please forward it to him at Green Street, Green NEAR Chislehurst, Kent. Edward and Tussy left this morning. Laura, too, intends to take the day boat from Newhaven on Wednesday morning so as to be home that same evening. So you won't be seeing her again. She sends her love. This morning it was fine, then wet, and now it's sunny again. I slept very well last night, but on Saturday evening the powders didn't have much effect, whereas yesterday they acted all the more effectively—in consequence am somewhat muzzy today, Regards to Ludwig. Love and a kiss to the little one and to yourself from

Yours
F. E.

First published in *Die Volksstimme*, No. 35, 1 September 1935

Printed according to the original

Published in English for the first time

314

ENGELS TO EDUARD BERNSTEIN[615]

IN LONDON

Eastbourne, 4 July 1895
4 Royal Parade

Dear Ede,

Letter received. Thanks. So far the same as always, i.e. my mood changes constantly, according to my physical condition. No question of being able to work or even deal with the most urgent correspondence. Laura left yesterday and Louise is back. Like me, she sends her love to you, the children and Gine.[a]

---

[a] Bernstein's wife and her children

Yours,

F. E.

First published, in Russian,
in *Marx-Engels Archives,*
Book I, 1924

Printed according to the original

Published in English for the first time

315

ENGELS TO ELEANOR MARX-AVELING[616]

IN LONDON

Eastbourne, 4 July 1895
4 Royal Parade

My dear Tussy,

The Glasgow affair[617] might be a trap—maybe something else, as the people hardly will be in a position to follow the offerings seriously.

As for your translation,[618] there indeed I do pity you. Where is the poor girl to have picked up the necessary knowledge for such work!

Here everything 'as you were', as the military command says. Louise and baby and nurse came yesterday. I am much as usual, that is to say subject to all sorts of variations of temper and spirits. That will last for some time yet to come. Either Louise or myself will keep you informed of how I go on. Love to you both.

F. E.

Laura left yesterday morning as arranged.

First published, in the
language of the original
(English), in: *Friedrich
Engels 1820-1970. Referate
Diskussionen, Dokumenten,*
Hanover, 1971

Reproduced from the original

316

ENGELS TO FILIPPO TURATI[619]

IN MILAN

Eastbourne, 4 July 1895
4 Royal Parade

Letter received.
All the best.
Goodbye.

F. Engels

First published, in the language
of the original (Italian), in:
*Filippo Turati attraverso le let-
tere di corrispondenti* (1880-1925),
Bari, 1947

Printed according to the original

Translated from the Italian

Published in English for the first time

317

ENGELS TO ANTONIO LABRIOLA

IN ROME

[Eastbourne,] before 8 July 1895

It's all of it very good, just a few small factual errors and, at the beginning, a somewhat too erudite style. I look forward keenly to seeing the
rest of it.[620]

First published, in the language
of the original (German), in:
*La Critica. Rivista di Letteratura,
Storia e Filosofia*, an XXVI,
Napoli, 20 January 1938

Printed according to the magazine

Published in English for the first time

318

ENGELS TO ELEANOR MARX-AVELING

IN LONDON

Eastbourne, 9 July 1895
4 Royal Parade

My dear Tussy,

Thanks for Johnnie's[a] letter returned herewith. Of course the boy is right in sticking to the house. Edgar[b] seems a downright Normand, looking after momentary advantage. More's the pity.

Edward's reply to Glasgow is all right.[617] The solution is to be found *Labor Leader*, 6 July page 2, Keir Hardie against Edward Aveling in the *Jeunesse Socialiste*.[614] Now the noble nature of Keir Hardie shines out brilliant. While E. Aveling attacks him, Keir Hardie generously finds him a candidature, which if E. Aveling accepted, Keir Hardie could on general grounds get cancelled by the Executive Council.

I was pretty fairly going on till Sunday night, since then had two bad nights and days, maybe partly from the acceleration, by the sea air, of the processus of elimination going on in my neck, but chiefly from the decreasing effects of the anaesthetics which I now have been using daily and in increasing quantities for about eight weeks. On the other hand I have found out several weak sides of my capricious appetite and take *lait de poule*[c] with brandy, custards with stewed fruits, oysters up to nine a day etc.

Love to you both
F. E.

First published in:
Marx and Engels, *Works*,
Second Russian Edition,
Vol. 39, Moscow, 1966

Printed according to the original

Published in English for the first time

---

[a] Jean Longuet – [b] Longuet – [c] milk egg-flip

319

ENGELS TO LAURA LAFARGUE

AT LE PERREUX

Eastbourne, 23 July 1895

My dear Löhr,

To-morrow we return to London. There seems to be at last a crisis approaching in my potato field on my neck, so that the swellings may be opened and relief secured. At last! so there is hope of this long lane coming to a turning. And high time it is for with my deficient appetite, etc. I have been pulled down considerably.

The elections here have come off as I said: a large Tory majority, the Liberals hopelessly beaten and I hope in full dissolution.[345] The brag of Independent Labour Party[114] and Social Democratic Federation[44] face to face with a reality of some 82,000 votes for Labour Candidates up to now (hardly any yet to come) and the loss of K. Hardie's seat. Still that was more than they had a right to expect.

Victor Adler is here. Have you or Paul any questions to ask him about Paul's arrangement with the *Arbeiter-Zeitung*[a] or can I be of any use in any way to you with him?

I am not in strength to write long letters, so good bye. Here's your good health in a bumper of *lait de poule*[b] fortified by a dose of cognac vieux.[c]

Amitiés à Paul[d]

Ever yours
F. Engels

First published, in the language of the original (English), in: F. Engels, P. et L. Lafargue, *Correspondance*, t. III, Paris, 1959

Reproduced from the original

---

[a] See this volume, pp. 419 – [b] milk egg-flip – [c] old brandy – [d] Regards to Paul

SUPPLEMENT

LETTERS

WILL AND CODICIL OF ENGELS

Supplementary Letters

1

ENGELS TO ARNOLD RUGE[621]

IN DRESDEN

Berlin, 19 April 1842

Dear Sir,

When, during your stay in Berlin, I had the honour of making your personal acquaintance at the Wallmüller Inn, I believe to have mentioned, in the course of our conversation about Schelling, a pamphlet on him written by me,[a] which was then being printed. I am taking leave to enclose a copy of this little work, just off the press, with the request of kindly contributing to its circulation by mentioning it in the *Jahrbücher*[622] When an occasion offers itself. I need hardly say that it is calculated for a public with roughly the educational level of a student.

Perhaps I will take the liberty of soon sending you an article for the *Jahrbücher* which, without reference to any particular recently published work, deals with the Christian poetry of the Middle Ages, notably with its central figure, Dante. This is done in the context of the perspectives opened up by Feuerbach.[623] Meanwhile I am sending you my regards and best wishes for the success of the *Jahrbücher*.

Yours faithfully,
F. Oswald[b]

First published in *Marx-Engels-Jahrbuch* 3, Berlin, 1980
Published in English for the first time

Printed according to the original

---

[a] F. Engels, *Schelling and Revelation* – [b] Engels' pen-name

2

MARX TO WILHELM SAINT-PAUL

IN COLOGNE

[Cologne, February 1843]

Your Honour,

I am sending you this pamphlet[624] with the request to grant permission for its publication as a supplement to our newspaper.[a]

Yours faithfully,

Dr. Marx

First published in *Marx-Engels-Jahrbuch* 1, Berlin, 1978
Published in English for the first time

Printed according to the original

3

MARX TO FRIEDRICH KAPP[625]

IN PARIS[626]

Cologne, 9 December [1848]

My dear Kapp,

I have exhausted all means of making the wretched dispatch office pay up. Now I would advise you to draw, in common with Dronke, and perhaps in his name, a bill for 35 thaler on the dispatch office of the *Neue Rheinische Zeitung* here. It will be forced to pay then. I would have sent you money long ago had I not been bled white by the shareholders lately—they knew I would pay, up to the last penny, under the present circumstances. You have no idea of the meanness of these bourgeois. Tell Dronke I appeared at the editorial office for the first time, and only for a

---

[a] *Rheinische Zeitung für Politik, Handel und Gewerbe*

few minutes, in three or four days today, for a serious indisposition had kept me at home. But for this, I would already have written to him. Give him and Rosanis my warm regards.

Yours,

K. Marx

Published for the first time   Printed according to the original
                                                          Published in English for the first time

4

MARX TO GEORG FRIEDRICH RHEINLÄNDER[627]

IN LONDON

London, 4 March 1859
9 Grafton Terrace, Maitland Park,
Haverstock Hill

Dear Sir,

I am sorry you did not find me at home. I would have sought you out one of these days, had my brother-in-law from the Cape of Good Hope not been visiting with me.[a]

You will oblige me greatly by coming to have lunch with us the day after tomorrow (Sunday, 6 March) at 1 p. m. This will give us the best opportunity to talk without disturbance.

With friendly greetings,

Karl Marx

First published in facsimile in   Published from a xerox of
Catalogue de la vente à l'Hôtel   a facsimile off-print
Drouot le 16 novembre 1983 and in
Schriften aus dem Karl-Marx-Haus.   Published in English for the first time
Unbekanntes von Friedrich Engels
und Karl Marx, No. 33, Treves, 1986

---

[a] Johann Carl Juta

5

MARX TO PHILIP STEPHEN KING[628]

IN LONDON

London, 7 July 1869

Dear Sir,

Please send me 1) The *Report on Emigration*, just issued, 2) ditto: *On Water Supply*

Yours truly
K. Marx

First published, in Russian, in:
*Marksism i rabocheye dvizheniye
XIX veka. Nekotoriye aktualniye
problemy teorii i istorii,*
Moscow, 1988

Reproduced from the original

Published in English for the first time

1

TO AN UNKNOWN CORRESPONDENT[632]

[London, end of December 1892]

Hail to eighteen
      ninety three!
Hope and joy dawn
      with it newly.
Bright and happy
      may it be
To the end, prays
      yours most truly

F. E.

First published in:
Marx and Engels, *Works*,
Second Russian Edition,
Vol. 38, Moscow, 1965

Reproduced from the original

2

TO NATALIE LIEBKNECHT[633]

IN BERLIN

London, 1 July 1894]

Dear Mrs Liebknecht,

We are all at 122, Regent's Park Road, drinking German beer and waiting for a telegram about the elections.

F. Lessner	Ed. Bernstein	F. Demuth
W. Thorne	Wilhelm[a]	F. Engels
Marie Mendelson		L. Freyberger

---

[a] Wilhelm Liebknecht

Otto Wittelshöfer Gine Bernstein
Stanislaw Mendelson Julius[a] Louise Freyberger

First published in:
Marx and Engels, *Works*,
Second Russian Edition,
Vol. 39, Moscow, 1966

Printed according to the original

Published in English for the first time

3

LAURA LAFARGUE TO ISAAK HOURWICH

IN CHICAGO

[Draft]

Eastbourne, 2 July 1895
Mr. I. A. Hourwich. Chicago

Sir,

In reply to your letter dated May 18,[634] addressed to Mr. Frederick Engels, I beg to inform you that Mr. Engels has been out of health and is still at the present moment abstaining from literary work.

I am commissioned by Frederick Engels to say that he does not consider himself authorised to hand over for publication to third partner any MSS. or fragments of MSS. left by my father, Karl Marx.

I am, Sir,

Yours truly
Laura Lafargue

First published in:
Marx and Engels, *Works*,
Second Russian Edition,
Vol. 39, Moscow, 1966

Reproduced from the original

Published in English for the first time

---

[a] Julius Motteler

4

SAMUEL MOORE TO ELEANOR MARX-AVELING

IN LONDON

[London,] 21 July 1895[a]
2 Stone Buildings
Lincoln's Inn, W. C.

My dear Tussy,

I felt very anxious to know how the General was getting on, so went down to Victoria to meet the 7:15 p.m. from Eastbourne this evening by what train Dr. Freyberger generally returns.

I met him and I am sorry to say that his report is anything but cheering; he says that the disease has attained such a hold that, considering the General's age, his state is precarious. Apart from the diseased glands of the neck there is danger either from weakness of the heart or from pneumonia—and in either of these two cases the end would be sudden. He may go on for some weeks if pneumonia does not intervene, but if it does then it will be a question of a few hours. In spite of all, however, the General is quite hopeful and is certain that he will recover—he intends, and has arranged with the 2 doctors, to return to London on Wednesday evening[b] so that if you want to see him you had better go to 41 R.P.R. on Thursday.

This is sad news and I trust the doctors may be mistaken. There is so much work to be done which the General alone is capable of doing, that his loss will be irreparable from a public point of view—to his friends it will be a calamity.

I have just time to write this in haste.

Yours very sincerely
S. Moore

First published in:
Marx and Engels, *Works*,
Second Russian Edition,
Vol. 39, Moscow, 1966

Reproduced from the original

Published in English for the first time

---

[a] the original erroneously has: '1891' – [b] 24 July

5

HERMANN ENGELS TO LUDWIG SIEBOLD[635]

IN SALE (CHESHIRE)

[Draft]

[London, 28 July 1895]

To L. Siebold, Esq.,
Sale, Cheshire

Dear Sir,

At the request of Mr F. Engels who is at present prevented by illness from writing in person, I am returning the enclosed letter to you.[636]

These fragments will certainly not pass muster as a *History of Chemistry*,[312] according to Mr Engels. But were you to entitle them *Researches in Magnetism* (or *Contributions to the History of Early Chemistry, Fragments by the late C. Schorlemmer,* or something of that kind) you would not have to get anyone to edit or finish off the work. If the worst comes to the worst, you will have to have recourse to a journal which specialises in the history of chemistry.

In sending you these views of Mr Engels at the latter's behest, I remain, etc.

First published in:
Marx and Engels, *Works*,
First Russian Edition,
Vol. XXIX, 1946

Printed according to the original

Published in English for the first time

Will and Codicil
of FREDERICK ENGELS

1

ENGELS' WILL

29 JULY 1893

I *Frederick Engels* of 122 Regent's Park Road, London, hereby revoke all former Wills[629] made by me and declare this to be my last Will. I appoint my friends Samuel Moore of Lincolns Inn,[630] Barrister at Law, Edward Bernstein of 50 Highgate Road, London, journalist, and Louise Kautsky who now resides with me at 122 Regent's Park Road Executors of this my Will and I bequeath to each of them the sum of £250=(two hundred and fifty pounds) for his or her trouble. *I bequeath* to my brother Hermann the oil portrait of my Father[a] now in my possession and in case my said brother should predecease me I bequeath the same to his son Hermann. *I bequeath* all the furniture and other effects in or about or appropriated for my dwelling-house at the time of my death other than money or securities for money and except what I otherwise dispose of by this my Will or by any Codicil thereto to the said Louise Kautsky. *I bequeath* to August Bebel of Berlin in the German Empire, Member of the German Reichstag, and Paul Singer of Berlin, aforesaid Member of the German Reichstag, jointly the sum of £1000 upon trust to be applied by them and the survivor of them in furthering the election to the German Reichstag of such persons at such time or times and in such place or places as the said August Bebel and Paul Singer or the survivor of them shall in their or his absolute discretion think fit. *I bequeath* to my Niece Mary Ellen Rosher, Wife of Percy White Rosher of The Firs Brading Road, Ryde, Agent and Accountant, the sum of £3000. *I direct* that all manuscripts of a literary nature in the handwriting of my deceased friend Karl Marx and all family letters written by or addressed to him which shall be in my possession or control at the time of my death shall be given

---

[a] Friedrich Engels

by my Executors to Eleanor Marx-Aveling of 7 Gray's Inn Square W. C., the younger daughter of the said Karl Marx. *I bequeath* all books in my possession or control at the time of my death and all my copyrights to the said August Bebel and Paul Singer. *I bequeath* all manuscripts in my possession or control at the time of my death (except the said literary manuscripts of Karl Marx) and all letters (except the said family letters of Karl Marx) to the said August Bebel and Edward Bernstein. As to the residue of my estate *I direct* it to be divided into eight equal parts. *I bequeath* three of such parts to Laura Lafargue of Le Perreux near Paris France, the elder daughter of the said Karl Marx and the Wife of Paul Lafargue, Member of the Chamber of Deputies of France. *I bequeath* other three of such parts to the said Eleanor Marx-Aveling and the remaining two parts of the said residue I bequeath to the said Louise Kautsky. I authorise my Executors at any time or times at their discretion to allot and transfer any part of my Estate in its then actual state of investment or condition in or towards satisfaction of any legacy or any share in the said residue of my Estate with power for that purpose conclusively to determine the value of my said Estate or any part or parts thereof in such manner as they shall think fit. In *WITNESS* whereof I the said Frederick Engels, have to this my Will set my hand this 29th day of July 1893.

Frederick Engels

Signed by the said Testator as his last Will in the presence of us present at the same time who in his presence and in the presence of each other have hereunto subscribed our names as witnesses.

Frederick Lessner, 12, Fitzroy Street, Fitzroy Sq. W. C.

Ludwig Freyberger M.D.L.R.C.P. 11, Gower Street, Bedford Sq. W.C.

2

ENGELS' LETTER TO THE EXECUTORS OF HIS WILL

14 November 1894[631]

To the Executors named in my Will

1) The following lines are supplementary and explanatory to my will. They express merely what are my wishes and are in no way *legally* binding upon my Executors. On the contrary, wherever they should be found to clash with the legal meaning of my will, they are to be disregarded.

2) My distinct wish is that my body be cremated and my ashes thrown into the sea at the first opportunity.

3) Immediately after my death I desire a copy of my will to be forwarded to my brother Hermann Engels, Barmen, or in case of his death to Hermann Engels junior, Engelskirchen, near Cologne.

4) Unless Sam Moore is in England at the time of my death, and can attend at once to his executorship, Bernstein and Louise will have to act without his assistance. In that case and even if Sam Moore should not be in London but somewhere in England, I recommend them to make a copy of my will *for their own use* and hand the original to Crosse and Sons solicitors, 7 Lancaster Place, Strand, to get it proved and to legally assist my executors. These latters will have to attend at once to the following points:

a) To ascertain from Mess. Cross what steps they must take to obtain as soon as possible the full control of my balance at the Union Bank of London Limited Regent Street Branch and the right to dispose of such parts of my investments as may have to be sold to defray current expenses.

b) To ascertain the value of my estate. My furniture, books etc. will have to be valued. Mess. Cross will attend to that. The value of my investments in stocks, shares etc. at the time of my death can be calculated from the official stock and Share List with which my Stockbrokers Mess. Clayton and Aston, 4 Tarnhouse buildings, Tolmhouse Yard, E. C., will supply my executors.

a) As Messrs Cross will tell my executors, the various legacies in money made in my will are not to be paid in the full nominal amount but are subject to deduction of the share of death duties appertaining to each of them.

5) There will be found in my books various sums of money paid for a good many years back by me to Laura and Paul Lafargue, Percy and Ellen Rosher, Edward and Eleanor Marx-Aveling. These sums, as I wish to state expressly, do not represent loans owing to me, but are *and always were free gift, on my part.* They are therefore not to be claimed in any shape or form.

6) In part-payment of the legacy left by me to Ellen Rosher, there is to be used by my executors the Reversion of certain funds payable to Percy Rosher after the death of his father and mother and which I bought from the said Percy Rosher. I desire it to be charged to Ellen Rosher at what it cost me, namely £250 paid to Percy Rosher and £30—solicitors' expenses incurred on account of this transaction, in all £280-.

7) I desire to supplement my will by the following details as to the disposal of papers left by me, viz;

a) All papers in Karl Marx's handwriting (except his letters to me) and all letters addressed to him (except those written by me to him) are to be restored to Eleanor Marx-Aveling as the legal representative of Karl Marx's heirs.

b) All letters written to me by Percy and Ellen Rosher, Laura and Paul Lafargue, Edward and Eleanor Marx-Aveling, or by my relations in Barmen and Engelskirchen, or by the Beust family in Zürich are to be restored to the writers thereof.

That is all, I believe, I have to say.

London 14 November 1894

Frederick Engels

P. S. It is understood that the honorarium or royalties paid by Sonnenshein for *Capital* and for my *Condition of the Working Class* are to be paid as heretofore the first to the heirs of Marx and the translators (1/5 to Laura, 1/5 to Tussy, 1/5 to Jenny's children, 6/25 to Sam Moore, 4/25 to Ed. Aveling) and the second in full to Florence Kelley.

CODICIL OF 26 JULY 1895

I Frederick Engels of 41 Regent's Park Road London formerly of 122 Regent's Park Road aforesaid declare this to be a first Codicil which I make this 26th day of July 1895 to my Will which is dated the 29th day of July 1893. I revoke the bequest made in my said Will of the sum of £3,000 to my Niece Mary Ellen Rosher the Wife of Percy White Rosher and in lieu thereof I bequeath to her the sum of £2,230. And I also bequeath to her the Reversionary Interest of the said Percy White Rosher in certain monies to which he is or was entitled expectant on the death of his parents under their Marriage Settlement which said Reversionary Interest I have bought from him for the sum of £240 and which also cost me £30 for legal expenses making £270 in all. I direct that all money payments made by me without receiving a consideration for the same to Percy White Rosher, Mary Ellen Rosher his Wife, Paul Lafargue, Laura Lafargue his Wife, Doctor Edward Aveling, Eleanor Marx his Wife, Eugene Oswald and Frederick Lessner or to any of them shall be considered as free gifts to them respectively. And I bequeath the same accordingly. I bequeath to Doctor Ludwig Freyberger of 41 Regent's Park Road London as an acknowledgment and in consideration of the unremitting care with which he has for years professionally attended me without ever accepting any remuneration the sum of £80 for every complete year elapsed from the 1st day of July 1893 down to the date of my death and also the sum of £50 for the fraction of a year however small which may have elapsed from the 1st day of July preceding my death down to the day of my death and I make this bequest conditional on his making no claim against me or my Estate for his professional Services.

I empower and direct my Executors before they dispose in open market of the Lease of my house No. 41 Regent's Park Road aforesaid to give to Louise Freyberger referred to in my said Will as Louise Kautsky and who is now the Wife of the said Doctor Freyberger the option of taking an assignment of the said Lease subject to the payment of the rent and the performance of the Covenants therein, she indemnifying my Estate and Executors against all claims by the Lessor under the said Lease the said option to be exercised by Notice in writing to any of my Executors other than the said Louise Freyberger within one month of my death. Whereas by my said Will I have directed that all family letters written by or addressed to Karl Marx which shall be in my possession or control at the time of my death shall be given by my Executors to Eleanor Marx Aveling, now I hereby revoke the said direction as to family letters, and in lieu, thereof I direct that all letters written by or addressed to the said Karl Marx (except my letters to him and his letters to me) which shall be, in my possession or control at the time of my death shall be given by my Executors to the said Eleanor Marx Aveling who is the legal personal Representative of the said Karl Marx and I further direct by this Codicil that all letters in my possession at the time of my death written by my relatives in Barmen and Engelskirchen by Percy W. Rosher or Ellen his Wife, by Paul Lafargue or Laura his Wife, by Doctor Edward Aveling or Eleanor Marx his Wife, by Doctor Ludwig Freyberger or Louise his Wife and by the Beust family in Zurich be returned by my Executors to the respective writers thereof and accordingly I hereby revoke the bequest in my said Will to August Bebel and Edward Bernstein of all letters (except the said family letters of Karl Marx) and in lieu thereof I bequeath to the said August Bebel and Edward Bernstein all letters (except those directed to be given by this Codicil to the said Eleanor Marx Aveling and except those otherwise disposed of by this Codicil). And subject as aforesaid I confirm my said Will. In witness whereof I have hereunto set my hand the day and year first above written.

Signed and Declared by the
above named Frederick Engels
as a Codicil to his last Will   Frederick Engels
in the presence of us both present
at the same time who in his
presence and in the presence
of each other have hereunto
set our hands as witnesses

Ada Pearce Nurse 41 Regents Park Road
S. Nichols Nichols 41 Regents Park Road Cook

First published in German   Printed according to the original
in *Der Abend* No. 438,
18 September 1929   Published in English for the first time

NOTES

1. Probably another part of a Gobelin tapestry from the study of Gottfried Wilhelm von Leibniz. Ludwig Kugelmann had sent two parts of this tapestry to Karl Marx on his birthday, 8 May 1870.

2. In his letter of 28 September 1892 Ludwig Kugelmann informed Engels he had three copies of *Herr Vogt* which had been sent to him for custody on a commission from Karl Marx. Kugelmann expressed the desire to have them sent to Engels so that the latter could dispose of them at his discretion.

3. The rough copy of this letter written in Engels' own hand is still available. Louise Kautsky copied the rough notes of the letter. Engels wrote in the word '*hochachtungsvoll*' (with kind respects) and added his signature. The texts of the original letter and of the rough notes are identical.

4. Working on the book *Handbuch des socialismus*, Hugo Lindemann and Carl Stegmann requested Engels in their letter to clarify 'certain moot points' and, if possible, grant them some journals not available in the British Museum.

5. Addressing the 10th Congress of the French Workers' Party on 25 September 1892 in Marseille (see Note 11) as a representative of German Social-Democracy, Wilhelm Liebknecht said the following, partly on the outcome of the Franco-Prussian War of 1870-71 and partly on the seizure of Alsace-Lorraine by Germany: '... the matter would be settled without any trouble once the social and democratic Republic was established on both sides of the Rhine.' This statement triggered rabid attacks in the French bourgeois press against the Socialists. Thus, in its editorial note of September 28 titled 'Herr Liebknecht', the newspaper *La France* urged his immediate expulsion from France. Meanwhile, Lucien Millevoye, deputy for the Nord in the Chamber of Deputies, asked the Minister of the Interior: 'Following the example of Mr. Liebknecht, does the government of the Republic intend to tolerate that foreigners should come to France in order to arouse hatred and contempt for the French nation?'

6. *Boulangism*—a movement that emerged in France in the mid-1880s; named so after its leader, General Georges Boulanger, the War Minister in 1886-87. This movement

expressed the views of reactionary chauvinism. Appealing to the injured national pride of the French in connection with the loss of Alsace-Lorraine in the Franco-Prussian War of 1870-71, the Boulangists succeeded for some time in enlisting significant popular support in their cause and in influencing the army rank and file. Capitalising on popular discontent with the domestic policies of the bourgeois Republicans, the Boulangists were preparing a coup d'etat to restore the monarchy in France. Yet the Boulangist movement suffered a fiasco due to steps taken by the Republican government with the backing of progressive forces, and its leaders fled from France.

7. On 9 September 1870 the Prussian authorities arrested members of the Brunswick-based Committee of the Social-Democratic Workers' Party of Germany which was its steering body (Wilhelm Bracke, Leonhard von Bonhorst, Samuel Spier, Hermann August Kühn and Heinrich Gralle). These men were deported to the fortress of Boyen (Lötzen) in East Prussia. The arrest came as a result of the promulgation of the Party's Manifesto on 5 September 1870 (*Manifest des Ausschusses der Sozial-demokratischen Arbeiterpartei. An alle deutschen Arbeiter !*—Brunswick, den 5. September 1870) calling for protest meetings against the plans of the Prussian ruling circles to annex Alsace-Lorraine. Included in the text of the Manifesto were excerpts from the letter by Marx and Engels to the Committee in reply to its request to clarify their opinion on the attitude of the German proletariat to the Franco-Prussian War that had just begun (see present edition, Vol. 22, pp. 260-262). However, the names of the authors were not indicated therein—it was said in the Manifesto that the text was written by 'one of our oldest and most respected comrades in London'. On 23 November 1871 the Committee members appeared before the district court on charges of breaking the public order laws and affiliation with the International Working Men's Association. The court sentenced the accused to prison terms ranging from 5 to 16 months. The sentence was commuted on appeal to 3 months, including the period of preliminary detention; it meant that they were virtually acquitted.

8. Addressing a Reichstag session on 27 July 1870, August Bebel supported the Reichstag's refusal to vote for credits to finance the war against France. On 26 November 1870, when the German Reichstag took up this issue again, Bebel and Liebknecht demanded that credits be refused and peace with the French Republic promptly concluded without annexations. On 28 November the entire Social-Democratic group in the Reichstag, together with Bebel and Liebknecht, voted against the granting of war credits. After the Reichstag session closed on 17 December Bebel, Liebknecht and Hepner were arrested and charged with high treason.

9. All the required materials mentioned in the letter were handed over to Paul Lafargue through Engels. But since Lafargue's planned statement in the Chamber of Deputies never took place, Lafargue used them subsequently in his pamphlet *La Démocratie Socialiste Allemande devant l'histoire* which came from the press in Lille in 1893. It bore the following imprint (after the Preface and the Afterword): *Conseil national du Parti ouvrier:* J. Guesde, P. Lafargue.

10. The miners' strike at Carmaux (Southern France) which continued from mid-August to early November 1892. The strike action was caused by the dismissal of one of the miners, Calvignac, the head of the local union, who had been elected to the post of town mayor. The workers demanded that the managers of the mine revoke their decision and, this demand having been refused, went on strike. This stoppage became political in character. The government's arbitration actually sanctioned the decision of the mine management. The French Workers' Party came out in support of the strike action; a country-wide fund-

raising campaign was launched. Eventually the strikers succeeded in getting Calvignac and other participants in the action reinstated.

11. Marseille was the venue of the 10th Congress of the French Workers' Party which continued in session from 24 to 28 September 1892. The Congress considered the party's situation and its activities, its work in country districts, the celebration of May Day, its participation in the International Socialist Congress of 1893 at Zurich, its participation in the forthcoming parliamentary election, among other issues. The Congress worked out an agrarian programme—its critical analysis is contained in Engels' work *The Peasant Question in France and Germany* (see present edition, Vol. 27, pp. 481-502). The Congress also passed a decision not to participate in the International Congress on an Eight-Hour Working Day convened by the British Trades-Unions but to invite their representatives to the International Socialist Working Men's Congress at Zurich.

The French Workers' Party (*Le Parti ouvrier français*) was set up by Marx's followers— Jules Guesde and his supporters—by the decision of the Workers' Congress held in Marseille in 1879; this Congress endorsed the Party Rules. In 1880 Jules Guesde and Paul Lafargue drew up the Workers' Party Programme, with Karl Marx taking part in framing its theoretical chapter. In November 1880 a Workers' Congress in Le Havre adopted the Party Programme by a majority vote whereby the French Workers' Party took shape.

12. A reference to August Bebel's article 'Ein internationaler Kongress für den Achtstundentag' carried by *Die Neue Zeit*, Bd. 1, Nr. 2, Stuttgart, 1892-93. In his letter to A. Bebel of 26 September 1892, Engels requested 12 copies of the article for circulation in British newspapers (see present edition, Vol. 49, pp. 485-89).

13. Late in 1884 Bismarck, in a bid to intensify Germany's colonial policies, urged the Reichstag to approve annual subsidies for steamship companies with the aim of organising regular voyages to East Asia, Australia and Africa. This demand caused a split within the Social-Democratic faction in the Reichstag. The Left wing with August Bebel and Wilhelm Liebknecht at the head spoke out against support for the government's demand. The Right-wing majority in the faction (J.H.W. Dietz, P. Frohme, G. Grillenberger) intended to vote for the subsidies on the pretext of furthering international ties.

The Right-wing stand was condemned by the party's rank and file and its central organ, the newspaper *Der Sozialdemokrat*. As a result, the majority of the faction was compelled to modify their attitude to the government motion during Reichstag debates in March 1885 by making its 'yes' votes conditional on passage by the Reichstag of some of the proposals of the faction (in particular, the demand that ships for these lines be built only at German yards). Only after these demands had been turned down by the Reichstag did all the members of the Social-Democratic faction vote against.

14. In his book *Der Klassenkampf in der deutschen Sozialdemokratie* (Zurich, 1892, p. 48), Hans Müller, representing *Die Jungen* (see Note 129) cited W. Liebknecht's speech in the Reichstag on 31 May 1881.

15. The *Anti-Socialist Law* (*The Exceptional Law Against the Socialists*) was introduced by the Bismarck government on a majority vote cast in the Reichstag, on 21 October 1878 to combat the socialist and workers' movement. It banned all party and mass workers' organisations, and the socialist and workers' press, and sanctioned confiscation of socialist literature and persecution of Social-Democrats. Nevertheless, the Social-Democratic Party, in accordance with Constitution preserved its group in the Reichstag. Assisted by Marx and Engels, the Party was able to overcome both the reformist and anarchist tendencies within its ranks and expand its base among the popular masses by a skilful combination of legal and illegal methods of work. Under pressure from the mass workers' movement, the Anti-

Socialist Law was abrogated on 1 October 1890. For Engels' assessment of the Law, see his article 'Bismarck and the German Working Men's Party' (Vol. 24, pp. 407-09).

16. The Independent Socialists Union was founded in Berlin on 8 November 1891 by representatives of a semi-anarchist opposition group better known as The Young (*Die Jungen*) that was formed within the Social-Democratic Party of Germany in 1890 (see Note 129). Separate groups of 'Independent Socialists' sprung up also in other towns—in Magdeburg, Wiesbaden, Fürth, and Freiburg (Baden-Würtemberg). The newspaper *Der Sozialist*, published from 1891 to 1899, was the Union's mouthpiece. The 'Independents' opposed any participation of Socialists in the parliament (Reichstag) and other institutions of the bourgeois state; they scoffed at the political struggle of the working class and overrated the significance of direct action so-called, or 'revolutionary mass action'. By the latter they meant work stoppages, boycotts and sabotage, as well as work at the grass-roots level in trade union locals. There was a good deal of infighting between the 'Independent Socialists' and the Anarchists—mainly for the newspaper *Der Sozialist*. The controversy between the two factions concerned above all the model of a society of the future and ways of achieving it. Eventually the anarchists got the upper hand in the summer of 1893, a victory that caused the Union's disintegration and demise in the spring of 1894.

17. Engels wrote this letter on a postcard. It also has the address in Engels' handwriting: Herrn Dr. L. Kugelmann, Warmbüchenstr. 20.I. Hannover, Germany.

18. The letter of Karl Marx and Frederick Engels to the Committee of the German Social-Democratic Workers' Party. Only a fragment of it is preserved, one included in the text of the Brunswick Committee Manifesto (see Note 7).

19. In his first speech in the Chamber of Deputies on 8 December 1891 P. Lafargue validated the substance of his motion to grant a general pardon for political prisoners. His speech was repeatedly interrupted by hecklers from among the bourgeois deputies. The Chamber defeated Lafargue's motion.

20. Blanquists (*les blanquistes*)—supporters of Louis A. Blanqui who, after leaving the Workers' Party (*Le Parti français ouvrier*, see Note 11), set up an organisation of their own, the Central Revolutionary Committee (*Comité Revolutionnaire Central*) in 1880. After Blanqui's death in 1881, E. Vaillant, E. Eudes and E. Granger came into the Committee's leadership. The Blanquists upheld the slogan of a general strike and advocated the independence of labour unions from the party. They opted for political struggle at the expense of economic struggle. During Boulangism (see Note 6) the Blanquists broke into two factions; one with Édouard Vaillant at the head came out against General Boulanger and thus made common cause with the Workers' Party, while the other (E. Granger, E. Roche), having cooperated with the Boulangists, walked out of the Central Revolutionary Committee and fell apart soon after.

21. *Allemanists* (*les allemanistes*)—supporters of the French socialist Jean Allemane. After a split in the Possibilist Party (see Note 30), the Allemanists formed a Revolutionary-Socialist Workers' Party (*Le Parti ouvrier socialiste-révolutionnaire*) in October 1890; this party existed up to 1905. Considering economic struggle above the political one and opposing excessive parliamentarism, the Allemanists concentrated their efforts on propaganda work in labour unions (*les syndicats*) and assigned the political party of the proletariat but a secondary role. A significant part of their activity was devoted to campaigns to win seats at municipal councils.

22. Engels alludes to W. Liebknecht's speeches at rallies in Mannheim, Karlsruhe, Frankfurt a.M. and Offenbach on 2-4 October 1892 in which he reported on his trip as a represen-

tative of the German Social-Democracy to the Congress of the French Workers' Party in Marseille (see Note 11).

23. The Congress of the National Federation of Labour Unions (*Congrés national des syndicats*) was held in Marseille on 19-23 September 1892. Besides other issues (the organisational set-up of the labour-union movement, a general strike, May Day celebrations, female and child labour in industry), it discussed the decision of the Glasgow-held congress of the British trades-unions to convene an international congress on 1 May 1893 on the issue of an eight-hour working day (see Note 24).

The French syndicats, meeting in Marseille, decided not to take part in the congress convened by the British trades-unions; instead, it was decided to invite their representatives to the International Socialist Congress in Zurich.

24. Engels means British Trades-Union Congress which was in session in Glasgow on 5-10 September 1892. The Congress considered worker representation in Parliament, cooperation, factory inspection, among other issues, and came out for an eight-hour working day. The British trades-unions refused to accept the invitation to the International Socialist Congress which was to be convened in Zurich in the summer of 1893 but decided to hold a parallel international congress in London on the struggle for an eight-hour working day. Qualifying this decision as an attempt to split the international working-class movement, Engels sent letters to German and French socialists and asked them to speak out against the plan of the British trades-unions. Engels also addressed the socialist parties of Spain and Austria.

25. This letter has never been found.

26. Engels refers to Ludwig Schorlemmer's letter of 9 October 1892 in which he told Engels about the intention of Richard Anschütz to write Carl Schorlemmer's biography and asked what Engels thought of that.

27. In keeping with the decision of the Second International Socialist Working Men's Congress held in Brussels on 16-22 August 1891 (see Note 228), the worker and socialist organisations of Switzerland, beginning January 1892, launched preparations for the next congress due in Zurich in the summer of 1893. They set up an Organising Committee which included representatives of the Social-Democratic Party, of the Grütli Union (founded in 1838 as an enlightenment alliance of artisans and workmen, it adhered to reformist positions) and of the trade-union amalgamation. In February 1892, the Organising Committee issued an appeal to the working men of all lands saying that it began its activities and urging them to send in suggestions concerning the congress agenda.

28. The Parliamentary Committee—the executive body of the Trades Union Congress of Great Britain that met in Manchester in 1868 and united the country's unions. As of 1871 the Parliamentary Committee was elected at annual congresses of the British trades-unions and, in fact, was their steering body in between the congresses. It nominated candidates to Parliament, supported draft bills tabled in the interests of the trades unions and worked to prepare regular trades-union congresses.

29. Labour bourses (*bourses du travail*) was the name given in France to worker associations set up beginning with the latter half of the 1880s largely at the municipal councils of major towns and comprising representatives of various syndicats (labour unions). Such *bourses du travail* were initially supported by government bodies and subsidised by them; thereby the government hoped to use these bourses as a 'tool of social appeasement'. Yet the activity of the labour bourses (labour exchanges) engaged in job placement of the unemployed (each bourse had a special department in charge of that), in the organising of new *syndicats* in the

professional training of workers, and in strike action soon caused apprehension among the government, and it started combatting their further proliferation. The Saint-Étienne Congress of 1892 formed a federation of *bourses du travail* in which the Possibilists soon came to play a leading part (see Note 30). The Paris *Bourse du travail* was opened on 3 February 1887. Using armed force, the French government seized the Paris Bourse on 7 July 1892 and expelled labour union representatives. It closed the Bourse on the pretext that this body had ostensibly been prohibited by the law. The Bourse remained closed until 1896.

30. Possibilists, or Broussists—a reformist trend in the French Socialist movement which, in the 1880s through the early 20th century, was headed by P. Brousse and B. Malon who caused a split in the French Workers' Party (1882) and formed an independent party, The Workers' Party of Socialist-Revolutionaries (*Le Parti ouvrier socialiste-revolutionnaire*). It abided by the theory of municipal socialism as the mainstream idea. The Possibilists proclaimed a 'policy of possibilities' (*la politique des possibilitées*) as their principle. At the turn of the 20th century they joined the French Socialist Party.

31. In his letter of 10 October 1892 Victor Adler told Engels that the Austrian trades unions would 'undoubtedly' adopt a decision to stay away from the International Congress convened by the British trades unions. The text of the resolution, he said, 'had already been prepared'. In this connection he asked Engels to give him the address of the Parliamentary Committee to which he intended to send the text of the resolution.

32. Engels refers to V. Adler's German translation of the first volume of the book by Sergei Kravchinsky (alias Stepniak) *The Russian Peasantry. Their Agrarian Condition, Social Life and Religion* that was published in English in 1888 by Swan Sonnenschein & Co. In his letter of 22 September 1892 Adler asked Engels to approach Stepniak so as to obtain formal permission from S. Sonnenschein to publish the German translation of the book, and pay the royalties due to the author and the publisher. Stepniak read the German edition and wrote a brief preface. The book appeared in Stuttgart in 1893 under the title *Der Russische Bauer* (Dietz Publishers).

33. In his preface to Volume III of *Das Kapital* (written in October 1894), Engels noted that Part V presented 'the chief obstacle in preparing it for the press' (Division of profit into interest and entrepreneural income. Capital yielding interest). Engels completed the bulk of this work in the spring of 1893 (see present edition, Vol. 37. pp. 8-9).

34. Engels alludes to the issue of militarism discussed at the Second International Socialist Working Men's Congress in Brussels in 1891 (see Note 228).

35. The full text of this letter was first published in English in: F. Engels and Paul and Laura Lafargue, *Correspondence*, Vol. 3, 1891-1895. Moscow, 1963.

36. Engels refers to L. Millevoye's statement in the Chamber of Deputies on 29 October 1892 with a question concerning W. Liebknecht's speech of 25 September 1892 in Marseille (see Note 5). P. Lafargue did not attend that session. Millevoye thus broke his promise to Lafargue not to speak up before his (Lafargue's) return from Carmaux.

37. The French Workers' Party (see Note 11) was not in a position to send its delegate to the Berlin congress of the German Social-Democratic Party (see Note 51). Instead, it sent a message of greetings signed by Guesde and Lafargue.

38. Engels means the colonial war unleashed by France against the West African state of Dahomey in 1890. In the latter half of November 1892 French troops captured the country's capital. In 1893 Dahomey became a French colony ruled by a governor-general. In the

course of this colonial expedition the French forces were the first to use artillery shells containing the powerful explosive, melinite.

39. On 2 November 1892 the newspaper *Le Figaro* (No. 307) carried an interview with John Burns, an activist in the British working-class movement and an MP. His interviewer was Jules Huret, a French journalist who, from 1 August 1892, had published a series of articles under the general heading 'La question sociale—theoriciens et chefs de sectes'. J. Burns was reported as saying that as an adherent of gradual reforms, he could not agree with the continental Socialists in their idea of a violent revolution; in his opinion, Britain had less of the antagonism between working men and capitalists than France.

40. Engels wrote this letter on a postcard which likewise bears the address inscribed with his own hand: F.A. Sorge, Esq., *Hoboken, N.J., U.S. America.*

41. In that letter Sergei Kravchinsky (alias, Stepniak) said he had sent to V. Adler the materials for the German edition of his book *The Russian Peasantry. Their Agrarian Condition, Social Life and Religion* (see Note 32).

42. Engels probably means the proposal of the Solingen party organisation to the Berlin congress of the Social-Democratic Party of Germany (see Note 51) to limit the mandates of Social-Democratic deputies to the Reichstag to 2 or 3 years in order to secure a rotation of elected deputies. Besides, the party local proposed to expel Georg Schumacher from the Reichstag's Social-Democratic parliamentary group. These proposals, together with amendments to the agenda tabled by other party locals, were published by the *Berliner Volksblatt Vorwärts* (No. 259) on 4 November 1892.

43. *Fabians*—members of the Fabian Society founded in 1884 by democratic-minded intellectuals. It was named after the Roman general of 3d century B.C., Quintus Fabias Maximus, surnamed Cunctator ('the delayer') because of his cautious tactics in the war against Hannibal. The Fabian Society included such prominent members as Sidney and Beatrice Webb, Bernard Shaw, H. Bland, among others. Its local organisations drew support from industrial workers who were attracted by a sharp critique of the capitalist order contained in Fabian publications. However, except in 1892, when it attracted a number of otherwise 'homeless' working-class socialists, the number of actual 'practising' workers (i.e., non-official trade-union members) never exceeded 10 per cent of the identifiable membership, and perhaps even less if the total numbers were counted. Rejecting the possibility of a revolutionary transformation of bourgeois society, the Fabians thought it was possible to shift from capitalism to socialism by implementing reforms within the framework of so-called municipal socialism. In 1900 the Fabian Society joined the Labour Party.

44. *Social Democratic Federation*—a British socialist organisation set up in August 1884 on the basis of the bourgeois-radical Democratic Federation; it united heterogeneous socialist elements, predominantly intellectuals and a section of politically active workers. The Federation stated in its programme that the entire wealth of the nation should belong to Labour, its only source. It also set as its aim a socialisation of the means of production, distribution and exchange, and came out for a society of 'emancipated labour'. That was Britain's first socialist programme based mainly on Marxist ideas. The leadership of the Federation was in the hands of Henry Hyndman, prone to authoritarian methods of guidance, and his supporters who did not deem it necessary to conduct work in the trades unions, a stance that inevitably led to isolation of the organisation from the working-class masses. A group of Socialists within the Federation (Eleanor Marx-Aveling, Edward Aveling, William Morris, Tom Mann and others) opposed Hyndman and championed closer ties with the working-class movement. The differences on tactical issues and interna-

tional cooperation resulted in a split and the formation of an independent organisation—The Socialist League (see Note 136).

45. Apparently a reference to K. Kautsky's article 'Der Parteitag und der Staatssozialismus' published by the journal *Die Neue Zeit*, Bd. I, No. 7, 1892-93, S. 210-221, immediately after G. Vollmar's article 'Zur Streitfrage über den Staatssozialismus'.

46. In his letter dated 18 October 1892, A. Bebel told Engels about his suggestion of having a new central Party weekly, *Der Sozialdemokrat*, instead of the unprofitable *Die Berliner Volks-Tribüne*. This issue was resolved in 1893 at a party congress in Cologne. The weekly was being published from 3 February 1894 to December 1895 under the name *Der Sozialdemokrat. Wochenblatt der Sozialdemokratischen Partei Deutschlands*; its editor was M. Schippel.

47. Engels paraphrases the epigram *C'est magnifique, mais ce n'est pas la guerre* ('It's magnificent, but it's not warfare') ascribed to the French general (subsequently, marshal) Pierre Bosquet. He was said to have uttered this phrase during the Crimean War of 1853-56. The words applied to the reckless bravery of the English 'Charge of Light Brigade' at the Battle of Balaklava.

48. *Le Socialiste. Organe Central du Parti Ouvrier*—it was planned to make this French Workers' weekly a daily publication. Engels was watching closely the course of negotiations of which he had learned from Laura and Paul Lafargue. Yet this plan did not come off.

49. From 6 August to 24 December 1892 the German Social-Democratic newspaper *Die Berliner Volks-Tribüne* was publishing (in its supplement) a series of articles by the Swiss Socialist Louis Héritier under the general title 'Die Juraföderation und Michael Bakunin'; the author's name was indicated only in the final article. Proceeding from Bakuninist principles, the author gave a slanted picture of the history of the First International in Switzerland and vindicated the divisive activities of the Bakuninists in particular, of the anarchist Jura Federation which, at its congress in La Chaux-de-Fonds held between 4 and 6 April 1870, had broken away from the International sections in Roman Switzerland. In addition, the articles contained numerous innuendoes about the activity of the General Council, Marx and his associates, specifically, about Johann Philipp Becker. Thus, it was claimed without any ground whatever that the London Conference of the First International (1871) had been held in Marx's house. The tenth article, published on 12 November 1892, contained particularly numerous distortions. Engels therefore decided to speak out and refute the insinuations without waiting for the end of the series. He sent his statement, together with the present letter, to August Bebel for delivery to the editorial board of *Die Berliner Volks-Tribüne*. The newspaper published Engels' statement on 19 November 1892 (see present edition, Vol. 27, pp. 344-46). On 24 December 1892 L. Héritier offered his reply, which was published together with his final article. As in his letter to Engels of 15 December 1892, Héritier tried to rebut the accusations. See also Engels' letters: to Héritier of 20 January 1893 and to Kautsky of 25 March 1895 (see this volume, pp. 85-6, 481).

50. On 14 November 1892 British Socialists held a rally in London's Trafalgar Square to commemorate the fifth anniversary of the 'Bloody Sunday' of 13 November 1887, when a socialist meeting culminated in clashes with the police. Several hundred demonstrators received injuries (three, fatal injuries), and some organisers were arrested.

    Louise Kautsky's account, which Engels mentions in his letter, was published without any title by *Die Arbeiter Zeitung* (no. 49) on 2 December 1892.

51. The Berlin Congress of the Social-Democratic Party of Germany took place on 14-21 November 1892. It heard the reports of the Party's Executive and of its Reichstag group, and discussed issues related to May Day celebrations in 1893, as well as the economic crisis and its consequences, the boycott tactics, the attitude to anti-Semitism, etc. After lengthy debates the Congress adopted a resolution that contained a negative attitude to state socialism (see Note 84). The delegates also rejected the invitation to an International Congress that was to be convened in Glasgow by decision of the British Trades-Union congress (see Note 24) and came out for participation in the International Socialist Working-Men's Congress in Zurich in 1893.

52. The Berlin Congress of the German Social-Democratic Party (see Note 51) also discussed the issue of the newspaper *Vorwärts*, the Party's central organ, whose editor was Wilhelm Liebknecht. He became the target of sharp criticism by Party members who objected to the allegedly high salary he was receiving for editing the *Vorwärts* and for his nonchalance, as it was claimed, in discharging that responsibility.

53. Engels refers to the proposal of the Executive of the German Social-Democratic Party and of the Party's parliamentary group in the Reichstag to the Berlin Party Congress (see Note 51) to purchase all the newly established Social-Democratic newspapers and turn them into official organs of the Party. The Congress turned down this proposal.

54. The International Socialist Working-Men's Congress held in Brussels in 1891 (see Note 228) adopted a resolution which recommended, wherever it was possible, to combine May Day celebrations with work stoppages. All the delegates, including those from Germany, voted for this resolution, even though during the discussion on this issue the British and the German delegations had insisted on this action being held on the first Sunday of May. The Berlin Congress of the German Social-Democratic Party (see Note 51) passed a decision to celebrate May Day 1893 on the evening of May 1 and refrain from general work stoppages owing to the bad economic situation in the country.

55. In his address to the Berlin congress of the German Social-Democratic Party on 17 November 1892, A. Bebel vindicated the proposal to hold 1893 May Day celebrations in Germany without staging work stoppages on May 1. V. Adler, who was attending the Congress as a representative of the Austrian socialists, opposed this proposal in a speech he made the same day.

56. Engels means the Third International Socialist Working-Men's Congress due at Zurich in 1893 (see Note 229).

57. At the bottom of this letter was a hand-drawn picture of a theatre stage. Engels signed his name just where the proscenium was depicted.

58. Engels refers to the characters of the Grimm brothers' fairy-tale *Sieben Schwaben*.

59. An allusion to George Bernard Shaw's letter to A. Bebel of 29 May 1892 which Engels had copied. This letter was published in a supplement to Volume 49 of the present edition, p. 563; in it Shaw pointed to the need of an alliance between the Socialists and the Liberals in the election campaign. The only chance for the Socialists to win the election, he wrote to Bebel, was 'to force the Liberals to accept our men as their party candidates'. According to Shaw, the Fabians were 'compelled' to force their candidates on the Liberals, or otherwise 'at every election' they would 'suffer defeat and disgrace'.
    In his letter to Kautsky on 4 September 1892, Engels analysed the Fabian electoral tactics and the causes of the defeat of the Fabian candidates on the Liberal list during the 1892 elections. (see present edition, Vol. 49, p. 514).

60. The Panama affair—a shady transaction connected with the bribery of French statesmen, government officials and the press by the Panama Canal joint-stock company set up in France in 1880 at the at the initiative of Ferdinand de Lesseps for building a canal across of the isthmus of Panama. In December 1888 the company declared its insolvency which caused the ruin of small-time shareholders and numerous bankruptcies. This scandal compelled the French authorities to start an investigation. On 19 November 1892 the Monarchists tabled three questions on the Panama crash in the Chamber of Deputies which on 21 November elected a Commission of Inquiry of 33 with M. Henri Brisson, a Radical, as chairman. The Commission obtained irrefutable evidence implicating a number of high-ranking officials, e.g., the former French premier C.L. de Freycinet and others who had been bribed by the Lesseps company which wanted to conceal its true financial situation and embezzlements. French justice hushed up the affair by going no further than condemning F. Lesseps and a number of his cat's-paws (see Note 157). 'Panama' became a byword for major dealings in which government officials were implicated.

61. Engels means the pronouncements of Émile de Girardin, a French bourgeois journalist and editor of the newspaper *La Presse*, in 1846-47 with sensational charges levelled at some figures of the July monarchy and the Guizot ministry whom he accused of corruption (the selling of peerage, bribery of the press, etc.); these statements fomented a crisis which culminated in the Revolution of 1848. For details, see Engels' article *The Decline and Approaching Fall of Guizot.—Position of the French Bourgeoisie* (see present edition, Vol. 6, pp. 213-19).

62. This refers to the London German Workers' Educational Society. Founded in 1840 by Karl Schapper, Joseph Moll, Heinrich Bauer and other activists of the League of the Just. In 1847 and 1849-50 Marx and Engels took part in the work of the Society. With the foundation of the First International it joined the International Working-Men's Association. The London Educational Society continued in existence under different names until 1918 when it was closed by the British government.

63. A reference to the soirée arranged on 17 November 1892 by the Social-Democrats of Berlin for delegates of the Party Congress (see Note 51).

64. Engels wrote this letter in two languages, English and Spanish.

65. The envelope of this letter exists on which Engels wrote the address: An das sozialdemokratische Parteisekretariat, Katzbachstr. 9, *Berlin S.W.*, Germany.

66. Engels wrote this facetious letter in reply to the birthday greetings sent to him on behalf of the Secretariat of the Social-Democratic Party of Germany by Ignaz Auer and Richard Fischer on 27 November 1892. Jakob Bamberger made a postscript to the message and joined in the greetings on Engels' 72nd birthday.

67. Apparently an allusion to Louise Kautsky's cooperation with the Vienna-published newspaper *Arbeiterinnen-Zeitung*.
    In his letter to Laura Lafargue of 2 October 1891 (see present edition, Vol. 49, p. 251) on the forthcoming release of the newspaper's first number, Engels described it 'a hyaena paper'. The epithet 'hyaena' is from Schiller's poem *The Song of the Bell* in which the poet compares revolutionary women to hyenas.

68. *Ultramontanes*—the Italian party of the Roman Catholic Church favouring the doctrine of papal supremacy and the Pope's right to interfere in the secular affairs of any state.

69. On 21 November 1892 Paul Stumpf greeted Engels on his 72nd birthday and three days later, on 24 November, sent him as a birthday gift a special issue of the newspaper *Mainzer*

Journal which came from the press on 23 November 1892; it had the following dedication: 'Unserem Papa zum 72sten Geburtstage' ('To our Papa on his 72nd birthday'). The number dealt with the returns of an election to the municipal council of Mainz which brought a significant victory for the Social-Democrats.

70. Engels refers to events in Mainz during its occupation by the French revolutionary army in October 1792 - July 1793 when the French military authorities set up a provisional administration there. The Mainz democrats formed a *Society of Equality and Freedom Friends* (*The Mainz Club*). The Rhineland-German National Convent elected in February 1793 deposed the Kurfürst (Elector) and proclaimed Mainz and adjacent districts a republic which joined France in March 1793. The decree of the French National Convent of 15 December 1792 abolished feudal dependence privileges of the nobility and clergy; also, the Mainz Republic was to pay an indemnity to France. In July 1793, after a siege of many months, Mainz was overrun by Prussian troops which restored the Kurfürst back in power and the old body politic.

71. Centre—a political party of German Roman Catholics formed in 1870-71 as a result of unification between the Catholic factions in the Prussian Landtag and the German Reichstag (the seats of their deputies used to be in the centre of the assembly hall). The Centre Party would take an intermediate stand, as a rule, by manoeuvering between the parties that backed the government and the Left-wing opposition groups of the Reichstag. It rallied under the banner of Catholicism the socially heterogenous strata of the clergy, the landed aristocracy, the bourgeoisie, that part of the peasantry predominantly in small and medium-sized states, as well as Roman Catholic working men in Western and South-Western Germany. The Centrists, while being in opposition to the Bismarck government, voted nonetheless for its anti-labour and anti-Socialist enactments. Engels gave a detailed analysis of the Centre in his work *The Role of Force in History* (see present edition, Vol. 26, pp. 453-511) and in the article *What's Next?* (see present edition, Vol. 27, pp. 7-11). Since in 1893 the Centre Party had 196 seats in the Reichstag out of 397, it could play a decisive role in the event of differences among other parties.

72. *The Brimstone Gang* (*Die Schwefelbande*)—the name of a student's association at Jena University in the 1770s; its members were notorious for their brawls. In his work *Mein Prozess gegen die Allgemeine Zeitung. Stenographischer Bericht, Dokumente und Erläunterungen*, Geneva, 1859, K. Vogt, a German petty-bourgeois democrat, called Marx and his supporters "The Brimstone Gang". Marx responded with the lampoon *Herr Vogt* which came out in London in December 1860 (see present edition, Vol. 17).

73. In October 1890 Karl Liebknecht began a course in law at Berlin University. He completed this course in March 1893 and, after passing an examination in October 1893, obtained the rank of a *Referender* (a low-rank official in Germany, usually a lawyer, on probation at court of law or government office).

74. 'In Geldfragen hört die Gemütlichkeit auf' (literally, 'In money matters there is no room for sentiments'—'Where money begins, benevolence ends'). Engels cites the phrase from a statement from one of the leaders of the Rhineland liberal bourgeoisie and Prussian Finance Minister David Hansemann at a session of the first United Landtag of Prussia on 8 June 1847.

75. The Ems dispatch—a report on the results of negotiations held between the Prussian King William I and the French Ambassador M. Benedetti in the town of Ems concerning the candidacy of Prince Leopold Hohenzollern to the Spanish throne; this dispatch was sent to Bismarck on 13 July 1870. William I declined the demand of the French side that Prussia

desist from Hohenzollern's claim to the Spanish throne. Being in receipt of this epistle, Bismarck abridged the text in such a way that it acquired a stridently insulting connotation for France and, then and there, passed it on for publication in all German news agencies. The promulgation of the Ems dispatch in that form was a public insult to France and served as an immediate pretext for the Franco-Prussian War. The fraud came to light only many years after the event.

In the summer of 1891 W. Liebknecht published the pamphlet *Die Emser Depesche oder wie Kriege gemacht werden* in Nuremberg, in which he collected sundry documents on this episode and exposed Bismarck's bellicose policies. In October 1892 Bismarck actually admitted the deception. 'It is so easy... completely to alter the meaning of a speech, without forgery, but by simple omission', he said in an interview. 'I once tried this myself, as editor of the Ems telegram... The King sent it to me with the order to publish it either in whole or in part, and after I had edited it to my taste, by cancelling and condensation, Moltke, who was with me, exclaimed, "A few minutes ago it was a *charade*; now it is a fanfare."'

76. An allusion to the draft law tabled in the Reichstag on 23 November 1892 by the War Minister Werd and the General Staff Chief Waldersee providing for an increase in the numerical strength of the German armed forces within the next seven years. The mean annual strength of this army was fixed at 492,068; it was proposed to introduce a two-year term of service in the Infantry, which could increase the war machine's throughput by 30 per cent. The planned increase in the strength of the land forces exceeded all the previous increments, as of 1874, combined. It was planned to compensate the significant growth in the war expenditures by raising taxes on consumer goods. This elicited widespread discontent among the popular masses and with some bourgeois political parties as well. On 6 May 1893 the Reichstag majority rejected the draft bill of the government. The same day the Kaiser dissolved the Reichstag two years ahead of time. After a new election, in June 1893, a similar draft law was endorsed by the Reichstag.

77. Engels probably means the intention of W. Gladstone's Liberal Government in Britain to grant Home Rule for Ireland (see Note 171). The decision to table a draft bill to this effect was largely due to conditions attending the formation of the Gladstone cabinet after parliamentary elections in the summer of 1892 when the Liberals could form the government only with the the backing of the Irish deputies. The Home Rule Bill was introduced in February 1893 and, after heated debates and agitation throughout the spring and summer, was adopted by the Commons but turned down by the House of Lords, as had been the case in 1886.

78. This is in reply to Charles Bonnier's letter to Engels of 2 December 1892 in which he protested against the decision of the Berlin Congress of the German Social-Democratic Party (see Note 51) to refrain from work stoppages on 1 May 1893 and have May Day celebrations on the evening of the same day.

79. In a letter addressed to Engels on 2 December 1892 Charles Bonnier agreed that in Britain May Day celebrations were to be held on the first Sunday of May, as it had been in 1890 and 1891 (see also Engels' article *May 4 in London*; present edition. Vol. 27, pp. 61-67).

80. A. Bebel's article 'Die Maifeier und ihre Bedeutung' published by the journal *Die Neue Zeit*, Bd. 1, No. 14, Stuttgart, 1892-93.

81. The attitude to the Austrian Social-Democrats which Engels expressed in this letter was further elaborated in his message of greetings to Austrian working men on May Day 1893 (see present edition, Vol. 27).

82. In his letter of 22 November 1892 A. Bebel wrote the following about what Engels had thought of the Social-Democratic party press: 'If you mean the nationalisation (*Verstaatlichung*) of our press, you must be utterly misinformed. All the newspapers without exception are independent, including those that are getting money from us. We never sought to exert pressure even in cases when it was absolutely necessary in the Party's interests.'

83. A. Bebel's article 'Der Parteitag der deutschen Sozialdemokratie' published by the journal *Die Neue Zeit*, Bd. 1, No. 10, Stuttgart, 1892-93. It dealt with the work of the Berlin Congress (see Note 51) and stressed, in particular, the significance of the decision to hold 1893 May Day celebrations in Germany on the evening of May 1.

84. The reference is to the resolution of the Berlin Congress of the German Social-Democratic Party (see Note 51) condemning state socialism. Proposed by W. Liebknect and G. Vollmar, the resolution was adopted by the Congress on 18 November 1892.

85. Because of the drop in circulation of the journal *Die Neue Zeit*, J.H.W. Dietz suggested certain changes in its content and periodicity. Thus, the arts and current politics sections were to be expanded at the expense of the theoretical part.

86. *Radicals*—in the 1880s-1890s, a parliamentary group in France that used to belong to the party of moderate Republicans (the 'Opportunists'). The Radicals relied chiefly on the petty bourgeoisie and, to some extent, on the middle bourgeoisie; they supported certain bourgeois-democratic demands like a unicameral parliament, separation of the Church from the state, a progressive income tax, limitation of the working day and other social issues. The Radicals were led by G. Clemenceau. Officially the group became known as the Republican Radical and Radical-Socialist Party (Parti républicain radical et radical-socialiste), formed in 1901.

87. *Opportunists*—a party of moderate bourgeois Republicans which emerged after the 1881 split in the Republican Party and the formation of the left-wing Radical Party with Georges Clemenceau as its head (see Note 86). This name was introduced in 1877 by the journalist Henri Rochefort who coined it from the words of L. Gambetta, the leader of the 'Moderates', that reforms should be implemented 'at an opportune time' ('*en temps opportun*').

88. An extract from P. Lafargue's letter to Engels was published by the newspaper *Vorwärts* (No. 286) on 6 December 1892 without the author's name being indicated. Appended to the text was an editor's note: 'Man schreibt uns aus Paris über den Panama-Skandal'.

89. The Fourth International Glass Workers' Congress took place in London on 5-9 July 1892. An account of its proceedings was released in a separate edition the same year: *The Fourth Report of the International Union of Glass Workers and Report of the Third International Congress*, London, 1892.

90. On 27 November 1892 the Social-Democratic group in the Reichstag cabled a message of greetings to Engels on the occasion of his birthday. On behalf of the group the telegram was signed by August Bebel, Heinrich Meister and Paul Singer.

91. A reference to a journal on the issues of social and economic history—*Die Zeitschrift für Sozial- und Wirtschaftsgeschichte* published by S. Bauer, C. Grünberg, L.M. Hartmann and E. Szanto. The journal appeared from 1893 to 1900 in Leipzig, Freiburg and Weimar.

92. Engels sent Kautsky his article 'A Newly-Discovered Case of Group Marriage' (see present edition, Vol. 27) for publication in the journal *Die Neue Zeit*. Its subject-matter drew on a

publication in the Russian-language newspaper *Pycckue Begomocmu* (No. 284, 14 October 1892) dealing with findings of the Russian ethnographer L. Sternberg who had been studying the life and society of the Sakhalin *Gilyaki*, a small ethnic group otherwise known as the *Nivkhi* (Nivkhs). In his article Engels cited the text of the original almost verbatim, with only a few deviations.

93. On 24 November 1892 P. Lafargue wrote to Engels: 'From the international standpoint Bebel behaves himself but very poorly by permitting Liebknecht, to put himself right. Their alliance is impossible for the German party'.

94. An allusion to the 'Free Theatres' trend in the *fin-de-siècle* West European art. The 'Free Theatres' expressed the protest of progressive actors and playwrights against the conservatism of the state-run stage, its isolation from life and the contemporary art, against censorship, etc. Such theatres appeared in major European cities in the late 1880s and early 1890s.

95. This letter, written by Louise Kautsky at the request of Engels, was in reply to Ellenbogen's letter of 2 December 1892 in which he said he had sent Engels his pamphlet on the history of the Workers' Educational Society in one of Vienna's districts. Ellenbogen added he was sending a copy from the first edition that had been confiscated by the Austrian police.

The envelope of the former letter has the address inscribed on it: '*Dr. W. Ellenbogen*. IX Bergstrasse 18. *Vienna*. Austria' ....

96. The envelope of this letter has likewise been preserved, with the inscription written by Engels: 'Monsieur Pierre Lavroff, 328, rue St. Jacques, *Paris*, France'.

97. In his letter of 12 December 1892 P. Lavrov asked for permission to publish H. Lopatin's letter of 20 September 1883 to M. Oshanina, member of the Executive of the illegal Russian Revolutionary organisation ('People's Freedom'). In it Lopatin gave the gist of his talk with Engels in London on 19 September 1883 concerning the prospects of a revolution in Russia.

An excerpt from this letter was published in Geneva in March 1893 in the book *Foundations of Theoretical Socialism as Applied to Russia*; see also present edition, Vol. 26, pp. 591-93.

98. Engels described these events in his letters to P. Lafargue of 31 January and 6 February 1891, and to F. Sorge of 11 February 1891 and 4 March 1891; see present edition, Vol. 49, pp. 115, 121, 125, 137.

99. On 13 December 1892 A. Bebel made a long speech in the Reichstag criticising the draft military law tabled by the government (see Note 76).

The Heinze Law—a package of laws against prostitution, drafted in the wake of the 1891-92 trial of a Heinze, a pimp, accused of murder and burglary. The Heinze Law, tabled in the Reichstag in 1891 and envisaging heavier penalties for pandering, pimping and propagation of pornographic literature, was adopted after long debates only in 1900.

Speaking during the Heinze Law debates in the Reichstag on 15 December 1892, A. Bebel attacked the bigotry and hypocrisy of the then acting German laws on prostitution. The Bebel speech was published in a supplement to *Vorwärts* (No. 295) on 16 December 1892.

100. In 1888 the Panama Canal Company (see Note 60), assisted by the bribed Chamber deputies and acting in circumvention of the French laws forbidding lotteries, gained permission to issue lottery-loan bonds.

101. Engels sent this letter to A. Bebel (together with a letter addressed to Bebel personally, not available today) who, at Engels' request, sent it to K. Kautsky.

102. Engels refers to *The Theories of Surplus Value* which were a component part of the 1861-63 manuscript of the second preliminary variant of *Das Kapital* (see present edition, Vols. 30-34). In 1889-90 Engels gave a part of *The Theories of Surplus Value* to Kautsky for deciphering. He thus hoped to get assistance in preparing the MS for the press and in coaching expert editors and publishers of the Marxian manuscripts. Engels did not live to see the publication of *The Theories of Surplus Value* as Volume IV of *Das Kapital*. It was K. Kautsky who published them in 1905-10. *The Theories of Surplus Value* were also published in *The Complete Works of Marx and Engels* in the languages of the original (MEGA, Abteilung II, Bd. 3, Teile 2-4, Berlin).

103. A fragment of this letter was first published in English in: *The Labour Monthly*, L., 1934, No. 10.

104. Engels refers to a scandal that broke out in 1892 over the bankruptcy of the building society 'Liberator' and its affiliated banks and building societies. It was stated that upwards of seven million sterling had been invested in these undertakings, chiefly by the working and poorer trades classes.

105. L. Baare, a German industrialist and director of the Bochum Steel Company, was taken to court for tax evasion and other machinations. The issue of rifles (nearly half a million) supplied to the German army by the Jewish firm Löwe & Co. was on the Reichstag agenda in 1892. That same year Hermann Ahlwardt's anti-Semitic pamphlet *Neue Enthüllungen. Judenflingen* came off the press in Dresden. It accused Isidor Löwe, an arms manufacturer, of supplying faulty rifles to the German army. The owners of the firm sued the author for libel. In December 1892 Ahlwardt was found guilty on libel charges and sentenced to five months in prison.

106. Engels means flagrant abuses in the activity of the Banca Romana which came to light during debates held in the Italian Parliament in December 1892-January 1893. Implicated in these shady dealings were statesmen, MPs, lawyers, journalists and private individuals. The scandalous affair came to be known as *Panamino*, a hint at the Panama Company fraud. The debates were sparked off by a statement of one of the deputies, Napoleone Colajanni. Engels responded by the article 'The Italian Panama' (see present edition, Vol. 27, pp. 356-60) published in the newspaper *Vorwärts* in February 1893. For more detail about the Panama sobriquet, see Note 60.

107. The editors of the present edition do not have at their disposal the original of Engels' letter to Karl Henckell. The phrase quoted here came from the notes on the poem 'The Steam-King' by E.P. Mead, an English workman and poet; these verses were published in a collection of revolutionary poetry, *Das Buch der Freiheit*, published in Berlin in December 1893. This edition was sponsored by the Social-Democratic group in the Reichstag. In the course of his work K. Henckell asked Engels on 2 November 1892 for verses and songs that could be included into the collection and also for the texts of his letters to be sent to the English poets Swinburne and W. Morris. Engels must have responded favourably to Henckell's request. Besides the verses of Swinburne, Morris, Goethe, Heine, Schiller, Byron, Mickiewicz and the Russian poets Pushkin, Ryleyev and Nekrasov, the anthology included the poem 'The Steam-King' which Engels had translated into German (see present edition, Vol. 6, pp. 474-77) and the old Danish folk song 'Herr Tidman', also translated by Engels (see present edition, Vol. 20 pp. 34-35).

108. A. Labriola's translation of *The Manifesto of the Communist Party* into Italian was not published at that time; the Italian edition of this work in Pompeo Bettini's translation was released in Milan in 1893 by the journal *Critica Sociale* Publishers. Engels wrote a special preface to that edition—'To the Italian Reader', translated by Turati (see present edition, Vol. 27). The booklet also included the prefaces published in the fourth German edition of *The Manifesto* that came out in London in 1890—the publication that Engels mentions in his letter. At Turati's request, Engels sent it to him in January 1893.

109. August Bebel was visiting Engels in London as guest on 3-10 January 1893.

110. Engels wrote the following lines on a postcard. He also wrote the address: Mrs. Mendelson 27, Stonor Road, West Kensington, W.

111. Maria Mendelson, a Polish socialist, told Engels about the arrest in France on 7 January 1893 of Polish emigrés accused of plotting to assassinate the Russian Czar Alexander III. Engels' article exposing the collaboration of the French and Russian police 'On the Latest Caper of the Paris Police' (see present edition, Vol. 27), was published anonymously by the newspaper Vorwärts (No. 11) on 13 January 1893 in the section *Politische Übersicht*. The following editorial note was attached to the article: 'We are getting word from most competent quarters about the escapade of the Paris police that we reported yesterday'.

112. After Carl Schorlemmer's death on 27 June 1892 his friends and associates intended to set up a Schorlemmer laboratory at Victoria University in Manchester. Their plans were realised.

113. An abridged version of this letter in English was first published in: *The Labour Monthly*, L., 1934, No. 12.

114. *The Independent Labour Party* was founded by leaders of the new trades unions at the Bradford Conference on 13-14 January 1893 in a situation characterised by the mounting strike action and the movement for a greater say of the British working class in politics. This party was headed by Keir Hardie. In its programme the Independent Labour Party championed collective ownership of the means of production, an eight-hour day, prohibition of child labour, social insurance, unemployment allowances, among other demands. The party leadership focused on parliamentary forms of struggle in its practical activities. In 1900 the Independent Labour Party joined the Labour Party.

115. The Hague (Fifth) Congress of the First International held on 2-7 September 1872. It was in fact the last congress of the First International. Its work was directed by Marx and Engels.

116. Engels means the Left Wing of the British Conservative Party in which the industrial bourgeoisie and intellectuals (men-of-letters, lawyers, etc.) were represented. The Conservative Left-Wingers came forward with a demagogic programme of social reforms in a bid to win working men's votes during election campaigns.

117. In this letter Sorge wrote to Engels that a few days before, the editor of *Die New Yorker Volkszeitung*, Friedrich Schlüter, had been visited by a group of Polish emigrés who wished to learn about the newspaper's stand on an uprising which allegedly was to take place in Poland.

There was a welcome ceremony at Kronstadt in July 1891 for a French naval squadron to demonstrate a rapprochement between tsarist Russia and France. The two countries, meanwhile, were holding diplomatic negotiations which, in August 1891, terminated in the signing of an agreement whereby France and Russia undertook the commitment to consult each other on foreign policy issues and to come to terms on steps which both governments were to take in case of the threat of an attack on either. Further talks led to the signing of a Franco-Russian military convention in August 1892 which envisaged joint military operations if either side was attacked. This convention was an important landmark toward a Franco-Riussian alliance which was sealed with the ratification of the convention by both governments on 27 December 1893—4 January 1894. Seeking to enlist Poland's support in the event of a war with Russia, the German ruling quarters took steps in the early 1890s to soften the German policies in the western Polish lands under German jurisdiction, specifically by relaxing the police surveillance over Polish national societies, by making concessions in teaching the Polish language at school, and so on.

118. A reference to the London Conference of the First International on 17-23 September 1871. Convened under the conditions of vicious reprisals on the International and its members after the defeat of the Paris Commune of 1871, this forum had a relatively narrow representation; taking part were 22 delegates with casting votes and 10 with consultative voices. Countries that were unable to send their delegates were represented by correspondent secretaries. Marx represented Germany, and Engels Italy. Nine closed sessions were held all in all. No communiqués were released on the proceedings. The resolutions of the Conference were published only in November and December 1871. One of the resolutions, 'On the Political Action of the Working Class', outlined the fundamental principle of the international working-class movement—the need for setting up an independent proletarian party. The keynote of the Conference was the struggle of Marx, Engels and their followers against the Bakunin trend as epitomised by the Jura Federation (see present edition, Vol. 22, pp. 423-31).

119. An excerpt from this letter was first published in English in: Marx, K., Engels, F. *Selected Correspondence*. M., F.L.P.H., 1955.

120. In the 1885 parliamentary debates on the budget, the Irish MPs headed by Ch. S. Parnell, who were dissatisfied with the policy of the Gladstone cabinet toward Ireland, joined hands with the Conservatives and forced the Gladstone government to resign. The Salisbury Conservative Cabinet that came to power lasted only six months. The parliamentary election of December 1885 gave no decisive margin to any of the contesting parties. With the Liberals gaining a few more seats in Parliament, Gladstone was able to form a new cabinet, this time with the backing of the Irish deputies. As the new cabinet head, Gladstone tabled two bills in 1886—on the Irish agrarian legislation and on Home Rule (see Note 171), both favourable to Ireland. In the 1892 election Gladstone formed an alliance with the Irish MPs again and, in 1893, tabled a second draft of the Home Rule; but neither the first nor the second bill succeeded.

121. This addendum to Article 69 of the Criminal Code was suggested by Victor Rintelen, a centrist deputy, in Reichstag debates (15 December 1892) on its amendment.

122. Reptiles, the reptilian press—an expression that gained wide currency after Bismarck's speech in the Prussian Chamber of Deputies on 30 January 1869, when he used the word 'reptiles' to denigrate opponents of the government. The Left-Wing press, taking up this epithet, applied it to the semi-official press bribed by the Bismarck government and to journalists working for it.

123. Engels alludes to a three percent interest loan which France agreed to grant Russia in September 1891 to a sum of 125 million gold roubles (or 500 million francs). The loan was a great success initially, with the sum of 125 million being surpassed seven-and-a-half-fold during the subscription. But then, because of the dramatic fall in the rate of Russian securities at European exchanges as a result of the 1891 famine in Russia and the country's worsening economic situation, subscribers refused to accept the bonds. In a bid to prevent a

total crash, the Russian government was compelled to buy up a portion of the bonds. As a consequence, bonds worth only 96 million roubles were sold.

124. Engels uttered this idea in his article 'The Foreign Policy of Russian Tsardom' (see present edition, Vol. 27, pp. 11-49).

125. After the death in January 1892 of the Turkish Viceroy (Khedive) of Egypt, Tewfik, his successor Khedive Abbas Hilmi II made an attempt to steer a policy independent of Great Britain. However, in January 1893 the British Consul General in Egypt, Lord Cromer, intervened after Abbas Hilmi II had replaced his prime-minister and, though the French government demanded the Khedive's independence, forced the viceroy to discard the first candidate and appoint another person in his stead. This move strengthened British dominion over Egypt.

126. *The Triple Alliance*—a military and political bloc of Germany, Austria-Hungary and Italy against France and Russia. This alliance took its final shape in 1882 after Italy had acceded to the Austro-German military alliance concluded in 1879. The Triple Alliance Treaty was signed for a term of five years; it was prolonged in 1887 and 1891 and then automatically extended (in 1902 and in 1912). The Triple Alliance set the stage for division of Europe into two major groups of states hostile to one another and ultimately led to the World War of 1914-18.

127. Engels refers to the outcome of the Russo-Turkish War of 1877-78 sealed by the decisions of the Berlin International Congress (13 June - 13 July 1878) which involved representatives of Russia, Britain, Austria-Hungary, Turkey, Germany as well as France and Italy. The Congress made significant changes in the terms of the preliminary San Stefano Peace Treaty (of 3 March 1878) between Russia and Turkey which fortified Russia's positions in the Balkans.

128. Engels means the speech of Franz Tutzauer, a Social-Democrat, in the Reichstag on 21 January 1893 during the first reading of the draft law on enterprises selling their merchandise on an instalment plan (the text of the speech was published by the newspaper *Vorwärts* on 22 January 1893). The speaker, who owned a small furniture-dealing shop, defended the rights of shop owners; in particular, their right to recover debts from defaulters, the working people as a rule.

129. *Die Jungen* (The Young Ones)—a semi-anarchist opposition group in German Social-Democracy formed in the spring and summer of 1890. It was led by former university students: young literati and editors of party newspapers (hence the name), as well as trade-union and party leaders from local organisations. The opposition drew support from Social-Democratic Party members among industrial workers and craftsmen. The leaders of the Young Ones were Paul Ernst, Paul Kampffmeyer, Hans Müller, Bruno Wille, Wilhelm Werner, Carl Wildberger and others. Ignoring the new realities obtained for the Party's activity with the abrogation of the Anti-Socialist Law (see Note 15), the Young Ones opposed the Party's parliamentary activities as not radical enough and were making demagogic attacks on the Party and its Executive Board (*der Vorstand*); thus, they accused it of political corruption, opportunism and violation of the Party democracy. In October 1891 the leaders of the Young Ones were expelled from the Party.

130. In his letter to Engels on 5 January 1893 K. Kautsky said he was going to write a detailed biography of Karl Marx for the forthcoming tenth anniversary of Marx's death. He was to proceed from the materials at his disposal—the article of Engels 'Karl Marx' (see present edition, Vol. 24, pp. 183-95; pp. 463-81), W. Liebknecht's article about Karl Marx and G.

Gross' book *Karl Marx* (Liepzig, 1885); Kautsky asked Engels for advice about additonal materials for the biography. Evidently Kautsky was unable to carry out the work.

131. In this letter, dated 5 January 1893, Kautsky approached Eleanor Marx-Aveling through Engels with a request to write reminiscences about Marx for the journal *Die Neue Zeit.* This request was apparently not granted.

132. In his letter to Engels on 5 January 1893 K. Kautsky enclosed a Rio de Janeiro-published newspaper with an article on the Brazilian Workers' Party and its programme; the name of this newspaper has not been determined.

133. The whereabouts of the cable is unkown.

134. Applying the German word '*Gründungen*' to Menotti Garibaldi, Engels hints at his entrepreneurial activities in the early 1870s.*Gründertum,* a period of 'prosperity' in Germany in 1871-73. It was made possible to a large extent by the war reparations of five thousand million francs and the annexation of Alsace and Lorraine under the terms of the Frankfurt Peace Treaty (1871) which concluded the Franco-Prussian War of 1870-71.

135. Engels wrote this letter on a postcard to the following address penned with his own hand: Sig. Filippo Turati, Portici Galleria V.E. 23, *Milano,* Italy.

136. Engels means The Socialist League's programme document—*The Manifesto of the Socialist League* (see *The Commonweal* No. 1, February 1885). This organisation was founded in Britain in December 1885 by a group of Socialists who had left the Social Democratic Federation (see Note 44). *The Manifesto* proclaimed in part that its members '… seek a change in the basis of Society… which would destroy the distinction of classes and nationalities'. The Socialist League pursued the following objectives: setting up a national and international socialist party; gaining political power by electing Socialists to local government bodies; assisting the trade-union and cooperative movements. In the inital years of its existence the League was actively involved in the working-class movement, However, after 1887 its leadership split into several factions, and there surfaced strong sectarian tendencies, with many members leaving the ranks. In 1895 the Socialist League actually ceased to exist.

137. The *Gazeta Robotnicza,* which Maria Mendelson sent to Engels, carried a statement of Polish Social-Democrats about Marcin Kasprzak's expulsion from the Party for the embezzlement of Party funds, abuse of trust and suspicious links with the police. Besides, the newspaper published a statement of Berlin Socialists who urged breaking off ties with Kasprzak. Subsequently Marcin Kasprzak proved the slanderous nature of such accusations and took an active part in the revolutionary movement. In 1905 the Central Committee of the Polish Social-Democratic Party adopted an official decision clearing him from imputation.

138. In her letter to Engels on 5 February 1893 Maria Mendelson spoke about the anti-Semitic and anti-Polish sentiments among Russian university students and army officers in Moscow and St. Petersburg.

139. An abridged version of this letter was first published in English in the book: Marx, K., Engels, F., *Letters on 'Capital'.* London: New Park Publications, 1983.

140. Vladimir Shmuilov, a Russian émigré and Socialist, told Engels in his letter of 4 February 1893 that acting on the request of Pavlenkov, the St. Petersburg publisher of the series *Biographies of Illustrious Men,* he intended to write a detailed biography of K. Marx, from 6 to 8 signatures large. Shmuilov asked Engels for assitance in collecting materials on three

subjects: 1) biography proper, 2) the practical activities of Marx, specifically, in 1847-49 and in the period of the First International, and 3) the genesis of Marxism. Shmuilov asked Engels to send him a copy of *The Holy Family*, written jointly by Marx and Engels, or recapitulate its substance and send excerpts from its most essential parts. Shmuilov said that if he did not succeed in having this book published in Russia, he would have it printed abroad. However, Shmuilov apparently did not succeed in his undertaking.

141. Beginning with 1845 Marx and Engels propagated their views among German workmen resident in Brussels. For this purpose they set up a German Workers' Society in August 1847, where Marx read his lecture on political economy (*Wage Labour and Capital*, see present edition, Vol. 9, pp. 197-228). The Society remained active until the Revolution of 1848.

  The Communist League—the first German and international communist organisation of the proletariat formed under the leadership of Marx and Engels in London early in June 1847. Concerning the history of this organisation, see Engels' article 'On the History of the Communist League' (present edition, Vol. 26, pp. 312-330).

142. Marx undertook his first systematic study into the surplus value problem in his MS of 1857-58: *Grundrisse der Kritik der politischen Ökonomie* (Rohentwurf) which consituted the basis of the 1859-published *A Contribution to the Critique of Political Economy* (first instalment). His further studies in this field are contained in the 1861-63 MS conceived as a second instalment of the *Outlines* (see present edition, vols. 28-29 and 30-34).

143. In the course of the Reichstag deliberations in late January 1893 on the state budget for 1893-94, the bourgeois deputies hurled accusation at the Social-Democrats to the effect that they allegedly wanted no more than foment popular discontent but were unable to say how they envisioned a socialist state of the future. Responding in his two parliamentary speeches on 3 and 6 February 1893, August Bebel laid down the fundamental socialist principles. He sought to capitalise on the widespread discontent and the inability of the imperial government to combat the gathering economic depression. For several days this issue was the subject of debates in the Reichstag, an occasion which the Social-Democratic deputies used to articulate their ideas. Speaking on 7 February, A. Stoecker, representing the Right Wing, said that after W. Liebknecht's speech he would make no statement as he had originally intended and suggested that the debates be terminated. The discussion ended therewith.

144. Speaking in the Reichstag on 4 February 1893, with a critique of the Centrist Catholic Party, K. Frohme, a Social-Democratic deputy, cited the medieval scholastic philosopher Thomas Aquinas so as to prove that the Church had always encouraged serfdom. In his reply speech F. Hitze, a deputy representing the Centre Party, said the quoted passage did not belong to Thomas Aquinas but was taken from Aristotle's treatise *Politics* to which Thomas Aquinas had written a commentary.

145. The personages from the pamphlet of E. Richter, the leader of the German Party of 'Free-Thinkers': *Sozialdemokratische Zukunftsbilder. Frei nach Bebel*, Berlin 1891. This lampoon was directed against German Social-Democracy.

146. Writing to Engels on 31 January 1893, A. Bebel suggested that tsarist Russia, by entering into an alliance with France, pursued the aim of a joint war against Germany without, however, involving other European states and Turkey into it. In the case of Germany's defeat, he said, France would obtain the left bank of the Rhine, while Russia would be able to consolidate its influence in the Balkans.

147. The reference is to the annexation by Prussia after its victory in the war against Austria (1866), of the Hesse-Cassel (Kurhesse) Kurfürstentum which had sided with Austria. In that war, Prussia annexed other lands as well.

148. In the Battle of *Spichern* (Lorraine), one of the first major engagements in the Franco-Prussian War of 1870-71, Prussian troops defeated French forces. This battle was fought on 6 August 1870.

149. *The German Party of Free Thinkers (Die Deutsche Freisinnige Partei)* was formed in 1884 with the merger of the progressist *Fortschrittspartei* and the National-Liberal Left Wing. One of the Freisinnige's leaders was Eugen Richter, a Reichstag deputy. Expressing the interests of the petty and middle bourgeoisie, the Party was in opposition to the Bismarck government. In 1893 the Party split into two factions (see Note 223).

150. Below Engels cites the (German) translation of the article 'Lomza janvier 1893' (from the French) which appeared in the February issue of the newspaper *Przedswit* of the Polish Socialist Party, in its feature *Z Kraju i o Kraju*; the original heading of the article was 'Z Lomzynskiego w Styczniu 1893, Russo-Boruska przujazn'.

151. The amendment that censured the government for taking no steps to alleviate the plight of the jobless was rejected by 276 votes against 109. A detailed analysis of the programme of the Gladstone cabinet in the context of this amendment was published by Eduard Bernstein in the newspaper *Vorwärts*, No. 35, on 10 February 1893.

152. In a reference to Liberal Radicals, Engels meant the Radicals within the Left Wing of the Liberal Party who represented broad strata of the industrial and commercial bourgeoisie, bourgeois intellectuals and the trades-union leadership. In Britain the Radicals did not make up an organisation in its own right.

153. The constituent conference of the Independent Labour Party held in Bradford on 13-14 January 1893. Keir Hardie, who chaired at this conference, played the chief role in founding the Party and in its leadership (see note 114).

154. About the origin of the sobriquet *Panamites*, see Note 60.

155. Engels intimates that since the beginning of the debates in the French Chamber of Deputies on the Panama scandal (see Note 60) the Socialists have not spoken on the issue.

156. The forthcoming elections in August and September 1893 to the French Chamber of Deputies (see Note 208) housed in the Bourbon Palace in Quai d'Orsay in Paris.

157. On 11 February 1893 the British newspaper *The Daily News* published the article of its Paris correspondent Emily Crawford: 'The Sentence on the Panama Directors. Sympathy for Mr. de Lesseps'.
    The French government had to bring to trial some of the men implicated in the Panama scandal (see Note 60). On 9 February 1893, the court found Ferdinand-Marie Lesseps, the 88-year-old head of the company, guilty, and his son Charles Lesseps, together with the other defendants, Fontacem Cottu and Fiffel. F. Lesseps and Ch. Lesseps were sentenced to 5 years in prison and a fine of 3,000 francs each, while the other defendants received 2 years in jail and fines. However, on 15 June 1893 the Court of Cassation reversed the sentence and acquitted the defendants of all the charges. Yet Ch. Lesseps had to remain in custody pending the payment of the fine imposed on him.

158. A. Bebel's speech in the Reichstag on 3 February 1893 (abridged) as well as excerpts from W. Liebknecht's speech on 7 February 1893 (see Note 143) were published by the newspaper *Le Socialiste* (No. 126) on 19 February 1893.

159. A reference to deliberations in the German Reichstag in mid-January 1893 in connection with inquiry of the Social-Democratic parliamentary group on 31 December 1892 concerning the dire economic situation in the country, a sequel to the world economic crisis of the early 1890s. This crisis caused a fresh upsurge in strike action in 1892 and 1893.

160. The work *Can Europe Disarm?* was inspired by A. Bebel's letter to Engels of 11 February 1893 with a request to air his views as to what stand the Social-Democratic group in the Reichstag was to take on the draft military law tabled by the government (see Note 76). Having done so, Engels sent the MS to Berlin on 23 February 1893; in keeping with his wishes, the work was published in the newspaper *Vorwärts* in eight instalments (on 1-5, 7,9 and 10 March 1893). Late in March 1893 it came out in a separate edition to which Engels wrote a preface.

161. On 18 February 1893 the newspaper *Workman's Times* (No. 144), in its section *International Working-Class Movement*, published a review of the debates in the German Reichstag on a state of the future (see this volume, pp. 99-100).

162. In the parliamentary elections in the summer of 1892 the Socialist organisations nominated a considerable number of independent candidates; of these, three—Keir Hardie, John Burns and John Havelock Wilson—were elected as MPs.

    At the House of Commons on 20 February 1893, a First Reading was given to two Bills dealing with modifications of the electoral law. Amongst other things they contemplated the abolition of all property qualifications; the introduction of returning officers, nominated and paid by municipal councils, to be responsible for drawing up the electoral register; and the establishment of a single register of voters for all elections (parliamentary, municipal, etc.). This draft legislation was turned down by the House of Lords.

163. *The Parish Councils Bill* was tabled in Parliament by the Gladstone cabinet in 1893 and approved on 1 March 1894. The entire system of local self-government was reorganised with this Bill. The Parish councils, which had been performing the functions of church and secular government in rural districts, now retained their prerogatives only in ecclesiastical affairs, while secular government was turned over to Parish Assemblies elected by local tax-payers. In larger rural communities such assemblies elected Parish Councils from their midst.

164. An excerpt from this letter was first published in English in the book: Marx, K., and Engels, F. *Correspondence 1846-1895. A Selection with Commentary and Notes.* Translated and edited by Dona Torr. Martin Lawrence (1934).

    The envelope of this letter has the following address which Engels wrote with his own hand: Monsieur N.F. Danielson, 8 grande rue de Ecuries, logis No. 7, *Saint-Petersbourg,* Russia.

165. See the letters which Engels wrote to Danielson on 29-31 October 1891, and on 15 March, 18 June and 22 September 1892 (present edition, Vol. 49, pp. 278, 382, 440, 535).

166. Engels alludes to Russia's defeat in the Crimean War of 1853-56.

167. Engels alludes to a pseudonym used during his correspondence with N. Danielson in the 1880s and in 1891-92; Engels used the surname of the husband of his wife's niece—Percy White Rocher.

168. On 16 February 1893, in the Panama case debates (see Note 60), P. Lafargue spoke in the Chamber of Deputies; his speech was published by the newspaper *Le Socialiste* (No. 126) on 19 February 1893. In his letter to Engels on 23 February, Lafargue said that all the bourgeois newspapers had ignored that speech.

169. In his letter to Engels on 23 February 1893 Lafargue wrote in part that the French Workers' Party (see Note 11) and the Radical Socialists (the Radical Left Wing, see Note 86), who were led by Étienne Millerand and Jean Jaurés, had agreed on cooperation in the August-September 1893 elections to the Chamber of Deputies and that they planned to launch an agitation campaign in Northern France on 5 March.

170. At the municipal elections of 1 and 8 May 1892 the French Workers' Party polled over 100,000 votes, with 635 Socialists being elected to municipal bodies. They gained a majority in the local councils of 26 cities.

171. *Home Rule*—the demand for Irish self-government within the British Empire, as put forward by the Irish liberal bourgeoisie in the 1870s. Home Rule provided for an independent Irish parliament and national bodies of government. However, the British government was to retain the key positions in Ireland.

172. The conference held by representatives of European socialist parties in preparation for the forthcoming Third International Socialist Working-Men's Congress in Zurich (see Note 229). At the initiative of the Organizing Committee (see Note 27) this conference met in Brussels on 26 March 1893; it involved representatives of 6 European countries. Its decisions urged the delegates of the forthcoming Congress to recognise the need of the political struggle of the working class. One of the aims of this demand was to keep the Anarchists from taking part in the Congress.

173. This letter was first published in English in F. Engels—P. et L. Lafargue. *Correspondence.* T.3. (1891-1895), Paris, Ed. Sociales, 1959.

174. The full text of this letter is in reply to the inquiry of the London firm Thomas Cook & Son which asked Engels for a letter of recommendation for L. Freyberger who wanted to open an account with this firm.

175. Engels was taking a rest at Eastbourne from March 1 to March 17 1893 or thereabouts.

176. This letter was written on a postcard with the following address penned by Engels: W. Liebknecht Esq., 160, Kantstrasse, *Charlottenburg-Berlin*, Germany.

177. This letter was written on a postcard, with the address inscribed by Engels: Sigr. avv. Filippo Turati, Portici Galleria V.E. 23, *Milano*, Italy.

178. On 7 March 1893 F. Turati sent the proofs of the Italian translation of *The Manifesto of the Communist Party* (see Note 108) and asked Engels to return them as soon as possible, for it was to be published the following week. Turati did not succeed in his plans to include the programme documents of the International in the supplement, as had been done in the 1882 Russian edition of the *Manifesto.*

   Of the two brochures mentioned in the text, the name of only one has been determined: Pasquale di Fratta, *La socializzazione della terra*, Milano, 1893.

179. This letter was first published in English in full in: *Science and Society*, N.Y., 1938. Vol. 11, No. 3.

180. The rough notes of this letter jotted down by Engels are extant, together with the copy he made for F. Sorge; Engels sent it to Sorge with his letter of 18 March 1893 (see this volume, pp. 124-126). The different reading of the copy compared with the original is marked in the footnotes. As is clear from these three documents, the letter is indicated to have been written in London, though at that time Engels was recuperating in Eastbourne (see Note 175).

Engels wrote the following address on the envelope: Mr. F. Wiesen, Baird, Texas, U.S. America.

181. *The Bloomsbury Socialist Society*, which sprung from the Bloomsbury Branch of the Socialist League (see Notes 44, 136), became an independent organisation in August 1888, soon after the Bloomsbury branch had left the League. In its activities the Society was guided by E. Marx-Aveling, E. Aveling, John L. Mahon, James Macdonald, among others.Taking an active part in its work were such veterans of the working-class movement as F. Lessner and A. Weiler. The Society received significant support from F. Engels.

The Bloomsbury Socialist society proclaimed as its aim the propaganda of socialist ideas amongst the working class and the struggle for a worker political organisation. In subsequent years it often organised meetings to commemorate the epic days of the Paris Commune of 1871; it also arranged lectures on various topics related to acute social and political issues. Its members were doing active propaganda work in other Socialist and Radical clubs and societies, as well as in 'new trades unions'.

182. The International Socialist Working-Men's Congress, in session in Brussels in August 1891 (see Note 228), entrusted the convocation of the next congress to Swiss Social-Democrats who set up an Organising Committee in Zurich (see Note 27), with Robert Seidel as secretary.

183. Bebel was visiting Engels in London from 28 March to 4 April 1893 or thereabouts.

184. The full text of this letter in English was first published in Marx K., Engels F., *Letters to Americans*. 1848-1895. A Selection. New York, International Publishers, 1953.

185. In his letters to Engels on 3 February and 9 March 1893 H.D. Lloyd, an American journalist and the author of books on social issues, asked him to take part in worker congresses scheduled for late August-early September 1893 in Chicago during an international exhibition that was to be held to commemorate the four hundredth anniversary of America's discovery. Lloyd requested that Engels read lectures on the following two subjects: 'The Working-Class Movement in Britain from a Socialist Standpoint' and 'International Labour Congresses', and also speak on other related topics at his discretion.

186. An excerpt from this letter was first published in English in: *The Labour Monthly*, L., 1934, No. 12; the full text in English appeared in: *Science and Society*, N.Y., 1938, Vol. 11, No. 3.

187. A reference to the tug of war in the United States between the advocates of bimetallism and those of a single gold standard. In 1890, under the Sherman Silver Purchase Act, the West's demands for more and more coinage of the metal were heeded. But as predicted, gold was hoarded and driven out of circulation, and the silver-to-gold ration became 26.5 : 1 in 1893. In the summer of that year, under President Cleveland's Administration, Congress had to repeal the Sherman Act to keep gold from vanishing altogether. By the end of the 19th century gold was fully restored as a single currency standard in the United States. Engels gave his assessment of these developments in his letter to Sorge of 2 December 1893 (see this volume, pp. 235-36).

188. In a letter sent to Engels on 18 March 1893 August Radimsky said that the editor of the *Delnické Listy*, the organ of the Czech Workers' Party, which appeared in Austria, intended to publish *The Manifesto of the Communist Party*, translated into Czech, in a separate edition. Yet fearing a possible confiscation of the booklet by the authorities, the editor published the *Manifesto* (in instalments), as a series of articles in the above newspaper. Radimsky had sent the initial numbers of the newspaper and asked if Engels wanted the rest.

189. From 1 August to 29 September 1893 Engels made a tour of Germany, Switzerland and Austria-Hungary; he visited Cologne and then, together with A. Bebel, went to Zurich via Mainz and Strassburg; thence he went to the Canton of Graubünden for several days to meet his brother Hermann. Upon his return to Zurich on 12 August, Engels attended the final session of the International Socialist Working-Men's Congress in Zurich (see Note 229), where he made a short speech in English, French and German (see present edition, Vol. 27, pp. 404-05) and, on behalf of the Bureau, closed the session. After a fortnight's sojourn in Switzerland, Engels left for Vienna through München and Salzburg; in Vienna, on 14 September, he addressed a meeting of Social-Democrats (see present edition, Vol. 27, pp.406-07). Then, via Prague and Karlsbad (Karlovy Vary), he went to Berlin and stayed there from 16 September to 28 September; on 22 September he spoke at a Social-Democratic meeting (see present edition, Vol. 27, pp. 409-10). Thereupon Engels returned to London by way of Rotterdam.

190. *Bank holiday*—in Great Britain, any of six legal holidays on which banks are closed. Introduced in 1871, bank holiday is celebrated on Monday as a rule: after Easter Sunday, after Whitsunday, and on the first Monday in August; also all banks are closed on 26 December.

191. Engels wrote the draft of his reply on an empty page of M.R. Cotar's letter of 21 March 1893. Cotar asked for permission to translate Volume II of *Das Kapital* into French and requested assistance in this undertaking.

192. On the envelope of this letter Engels wrote the following address: G.W. Lamplugh Esq., Ballafurt, Port Erin, Isle of Man.
    The full text of this letter was first published in English in *Marx, Engels, Lenin, Stalin. Facsimiles*. M., 1939.

193. An excerpt from this letter was first published in English in: Marx K., Engels F., *On Literature and Art*, Moscow, Progress Publishers, 1976.

194. This part of Engels' letter of 28 September 1892 to Franz Mehring (see present edition, Vol. 49) was published in Mehring's article 'Über den historischen Materialismus' appended to the first separate edition of his work: *Die Lessing-Legende. Eine Rettung von Franz Mehring*, Stuttgart, 1893. Engels also mentions the book by Lavergne-Peguilhen: *Grundzüge der Gesellschaftswissenschaft*. Erster Theil. *Die Bewegungs-und Productionsgesetze*, First Part. Königsberg, 1838.

195. A reference to the publication of Engels' work *The Origin of the Family, Private Property and the State* translated into French by Henri Ravé; this translation was edited by Laura Lafargue who did a stupendous amount of work to correct the numerous deficiencies contained in it. Having read the thus revised translation, Engels had a high opinion of the work done. The book was published in October 1893 under the title *L'Origine de la famille, de la propriété privée et de l'état*.

196. On 30 April 1892, *L'Illustration* published two pages of the portraits of personalities prominent in the international socialist movement.

197. Engels means *The Legal Eight Hours and International Labour League* founded in 1890 by a group of English Socialists with Engels' participation on the basis of a Committee which had organised Britain's first ever May Day demonstration in London in 1890. The League set as its aim the struggle for the liberation of the working class and action on the decisions of the Paris Congress of the Second International (see Note 227). In 1893 League representatives took part in setting up The Independent Labour Party (see Note 114).

London Trades Council was established at a conference of delegates representing London's trades-unions (May 1860). Among its members were the leaders of major trades-unions and men from the so-called worker aristocracy. In the early 1860s the Council led the action of the British workers against intervention in the American Civil War, in defence of Poland and Italy, and later, for legalisation of trades-unions. Early in the 1890s the Council, which embraced predominantly the old trades-unions, took a negative stand on the movement for new trades-unions and for the legal eight hours. Yet the mass character of this movement compelled the Council to join in the May demonstrations of the 1890s.

198. The Hull dockers went on strike on 8 April 1893. This strike, which continued until 19 May, was caused by the decision of the Shipowners' Federation to give employment preferences to non-unionised job-seekers. Thousands of strikebreakers were brought to Hull under armed force protection. Two gunboats entered the port. Hull became an arena of fierce confrontation and looked like a military camp all through the strike action. Even though the strike drew support from miners, railwaymen and other trades-unions, the dockers did not succeed in winning a victory. The conflict ended in an *agreement* which both sides reached in keeping with the *reciprocal freedom* principle.

199. Concerning the publication of Carl Schorlemmer's literary heritage; he died on 27 June 1892. Ludwig Siebold and Philipp Klepsch took charge of this job as the executors of Carl Schorlemmer's will.

200. Adolf Spiegel, manager of a paraffin-making factory, wrote a brief biography of Carl Schorlemmer and had it published in the journal *Berichten der Deutschen Chemischen Gesellschaft*, Jg. 25, Bd. III, 1892.

201. In his letter of 28 April 1893 F. Sorge asked Engels if Abraham Lincoln had replied to a message of greetings sent to him in 1864 by the General Council of the International Working-Men's Association on the occasion of his election for a second term as President of the United States (see present edition, Vol. 20, pp. 19-21). This message, which Marx had written late in November 1864, was sent to Lincoln through the American Ambassador in London, Charles Francis Adams. On 28 January 1865 the General Council received a reply sent on Lincoln's behalf which was read out at the Council's meeting of January 31 and then published by *The Times* (No. 25101) on 6 February 1865, under the heading: 'Mr. Lincoln and the International Working-Men's Association'.

202. *Conservatives*—a political party expressing the interests of the Prussian Junkers, army circles, top bureaucracy and Lutheran clergy. With the formation of the North German Union and in the initial years of the German Empire, the Conservatives made a strong right-wing opposition to the Bismarck government; they came out against bourgeois reforms and broader powers conceded to the Reich authorities. In 1866 there was a split in their ranks which gave rise to the Free Conservative Party (*Die Freikonservative Partei*, or *Reichspartei*) representing the interests of big landed proprietors and of a segment of the industrial magnates. The Free Conservatives took a stand of unequivocal support for the Bismarck government.

In 1876 the Conservatives made common cause with other right-wing groups and formed a German Conservative Party (*Die Deutschkonservative Partei*) which continued up to the year 1918.

203. *National Liberals*—a Prussian (and from 1871, an all-German) bourgeois political party active between 1867 and 1918 as a bulwark of the Junkers and industrial magnates. This party expressed the interests of a larger part of the big industrial and commercial bourgeoisie, and also of the financiers—the strata that supported the domestic and foreign pol-

icy steered by Bismarck and by subsequent reactionary governments of the German Empire. In the early 1890s the National Liberals came forward with the idea of 'suspending' any kind of social legislation and mounted a crusade for unrestricted entrepreneurial powers.

204. At the Reichstag election of 15 June 1893 the German Social-Democrats gained a major victory: they polled 1,787,000 votes. All in all, 44 Social-Democratic deputies were elected to the Reichstag, among them, W. Liebknecht, A. Bebel and P. Singer. Of the six deputies elected in Berlin, five were Social-Democrats. Engels commented on these election returns in his interview for a correspondent of *Daily Chronicle* (see present edition, Vol. 27, p. 549).

205. During the May Day demonstration held in London's Hyde Park on 7 May 1893, the Legal Eight Hours and International Labour League (see Note 197) organised an international rostrum from which socialists of many countries spoke, among them, Alfred Delcluze, Louise Kautsky, Friedrich Lessner, Eleanor Marx-Aveling, S.M. Kravchinsky (Stepniak).

206. *Liberal Unionists*—a group led by Joseph Chamberlain which, in 1886, broke away from the Liberal Party because of the differences over Home Rule for Ireland (see Note 171). The Liberal Unionists were advocating continued Union with Ireland (1801). They leagued themselves with the Conservative Party and, a few years later, joined its ranks.

207. Hastings—a resort on the English Channel.

208. At the elections to the French Chamber of Deputies on 20 August and 3 September 1893 the Socialists of various trends gained 700,000 votes and 30 seats (among the elected deputies 12 were from the Workers' Party—J. Guesde, J. Juarés, E. Vaillant and others).

The deputies representing the Workers' Party agreed to form a united socialist group in the new Chamber; this group comprised 20 deputies who belonged to the bourgeois Left Wing, Radicals for the most part (also known as 'independent socialists') and other socialists. All in all the Socialist group in the Chamber of Deputies numbered 50 deputies.

Engels more than once criticised the leadership of the Workers' Party for concessions it had made to the Radicals in the matter of Programme and organisational principles for the sake of forming a joint Socialist parliamentary group. See, e.g., Engels' letters to V. Adler of 17 July 1894 and to F. Sorge of 30 December 1893 (see this volume, pp. 249, 324-25).

209. Hermann Lopatin was imprisoned in the Schlüsselburg fortress at the time.

210. Together with this book Isaak Hourwich had sent a number of articles on the revolutionary movement in Russia and asked Engels what he thought of them. Hourwich intended to have these articles published in *The Progress* along with Engels' commentary.

211. The second edition of Henry Lloyd's book *A Strike of Millionaires against Miners* saw print in Chicago in 1891 (the first edition being published there in 1890).

This book looks into the history of a major lockout staged by the owners of Illinois coal mines. At the end of 1888 and in early 1889 the company fired a third of its coal miners and declared a general lockout; it closed stores selling foodstuffs on credit. For nearly six months about five thousand miners were involved in a struggle to defend their rights. Yet this standoff ended in a victory of the entrepreneurs who succeeded in imposing the lowest pay rates for miners in the United States by slashing the old ones 1/3. The author had twice visited the scene and published a number of articles in the press, urging assistance to the jobless coal miners and their families. H. Lloyd's book became very popular in the United States.

212. K. Kautsky wrote to Engels in his letter of 19 May 1893 that the journal *Die Zeitschrift für Social- und Wirtschaftsgeschichte*, Bd.I., Ausgabe I, Freiburg in Breisgau Leipzig, 1893) had published the article by Lujo Brentano, a Katheder Socialist: 'Die Volksvirtschaft und ihre

konkreten Grundbedingungen' which permitted attacks on Engels' work *The Origin of the Family, Private Property and the State* (see present edition, Vol. 26).

213. By the old *Concordia* business Engels means L. Brentano's articles published anonymously by the journal *Concordia* in 1872 in which he attempted to discredit Marx as a scientist. Thus, Brentano accused Marx of incompetence and falsifications; Marx responded by two articles in the newspaper *Volksstaat*: 'A Reply to the Brentano Article' and 'A Reply to the Second Brentano Article' (see present edition, Vol. 23, pp. 164-67, 190-97). In 1890, continuing his campaign of slander against Marx, L. Brentano published the pamphlet *Meine Polemik mit Karl Marx* which elicited a response from Engels, the pamphlet *Marx contra Brentano* (see present edition, Vol. 27, pp. 97-154).

   Engels criticised the views of A. Mülberger, a German Proudhonist, in his work *The Housing Question* which he wrote in 1872-73, in Parts I and III (see present edition, Vol. 23, p. 317-391).

214. Engels hints at the thesis of 'one reactionary mass' which entered into the Programme of the German Social-Democratic Party adopted at its Gotha Congress in 1875. Thus, the Programme said this in part: 'Emancipation of labour ought to be the cause of the working class in relation to which all the other classes consititute but one reactionary mass'. Marx censured this tenet in his *Critique of the Gotha Programme* (see present edition, Vol. 24, pp.75-99).

215. An allusion to E.B. Bax's articles 'Der Fluch der Zivilisation' and 'Menschenthum und Klasseninstinkt' published by the journal *Die Neue Zeit*, 11 Jg. 1892/93, Bd. 2, Nos. 45 & 47; this worked was translated from English by V. Adler.

216. In his letter of 31 May 1899 Hermann Bahr, an Austrian journalist, asked Engels to explain his stand on anti-Semitism and the Jewish problem; he intended to have this material, along with the pronouncements of other persons on this subject, published in the Vienna newspaper *Die Deutsche Zeitung*.

217. By anti-Semitic candidates, Engels means representatives of *Die Christlich-soziale Arbeiterpartei* (The Christian Social Worker Party) founded in 1878 by Adolf Stoecker, a reactionary German political figure and advocate of anti-Semitism. This party saw its aim in combatting the socialist movement; subsequently it used the slogan of anti-Semitism to mount a demagogic campaign against financial capital. Its members succeeded in winning support among the backward strata of the peasantry and artisans in some districts of Germany; this success had a part to play in the setup of the poll. In 1895 A. Stoecker transformed his organisation into *Die Christlich-soziale Partei* .

   About the election to the German Reichstag, see Note 204.

218. In his letter of June 1893 F. Turati told Engels about the plans of G. Domanico, an Italian anarchist, to publish the Italian translation of *Das Kapital*, beginning with Vol. 1, in 50 installments at low price; writing to Engels on 2 June 1893, G. Domanico expressed his confidence that Engels would approve of this initiative and asked for a letter that might be used as a preface. G. Domanico also asked Engels to him know about corrections in the text, remarks and amendments. This undertaking never came off.

219. About the middle of May 1841 Engels, in his father's company, made a tour of southern Germany, Switzerland and Northern Italy (Lombardy). See also his travel notes in *Wanderings in Lombardy* (present edition, Vol. 2, p. 170).

220. As F. Turati wrote to Engels, the Italian Socialist E. Guindani was undertaking the Italian edition of G. Déville's book *Le Capital de Karl Marx. Résumé et accompagné d'un aperçu sur le socialisme scientifique.* The book was published in Cremona in 1893.

    Engels commented on G. Déville's work in his letters to K. Kautsky of 9 January and to P. Lavrov of 5 February 1884 (see present edition, Vol. 47).

221. On the envelope of this letter Engels inscribed the following address: Monsieur Stojan Nokoff, Chemin de la Roseraie 8, Genève, Switzerland.

222. Engels made a mistake by identifying two different towns. Philippopolis was the Greek name of the present Bulgarian city Plovdiv.

223. On 6 May 1893 there was a split within *Die Deutsche Freisinnige Partei* (see Note 149) due to the differences over the draft military legislation tabled by the Bismarck government (see Note 76). The pro-government faction of this party in the Reichstag formed an Alliance of Free-Thinkers (*Die Freisinnige Vereinigung*) led by Ludwig Bamberger; the other faction, opposing the higher war budget, starting calling itself a Free-Thinking People's Party (*Die Freisinnige Volkspartei*), with Eugen Richter as its leader.

224. In his *Interview* J. Guesde elucidated the principle of internationalism in the working-class and socialist movement. It was published by the newspaper *Le Figaro* on 17 June 1893 under the heading 'Les Socialistes et la Patrie', and also by *Le Socialiste* (No. 144) on 17 June 1894.

225. The reactionary French politicians P. Déroulède and L. Millevoye mounted a campaign against G. Clemenceau, the leader of the Radical Party (see Note 86) in June 1893; they accused him of links with one of those implicated in the Panama affair (see Note 60) and of his being in the pay of the British government. The monarchist press started printing documents stolen from the British embassy which indicated breach of allegiance on Clemenceau's part. Yet these documents proved false upon their promulgation in the Chamber of Deputies.

226. In the spring of 1893 the monarchist quarters of France, backed by the anarchists, launched a slanderous campaign against the Socialists; they branded as anti-patriotic the Socialist principle of internationalism. In this connection J. Geusde and P. Lafargue organised meetings in towns of northern France on June 17 and 18 at which they read out an appeal to the working people of France ('Le Conseil national du Parti ouvrier aux travailleurs de France'). The appeal was published inthe newspaper *Le Socialiste* (No. 144) on 17 June 1893 on behalf of the National Council of the French Workers' Party. Its full text reads as follows:

    TO THE WORKING PEOPLE OF FRANCE
    Comrades!
    In their impotent fury over the onward march of the Workers' Party our class enemies have resorted to the only weapon left in their arsenal, slander. They are distorting our internationalism the way they have tried to distort our socialism. And albeit those who seek to present us as having no Motherland are the selfsame people who, all through this century, have been but abetting incursions into Motherland's territory and dismemberment, a Motherland whom their class gave up to sack and plunder by the banditry of cosmopolitan financiers and whom it had been exploiting without stopping at bloodshed at Ricamari and Fourmi, we, far from permitting them to confuse a collectivist solution to the question with anarchy, this mockery of bourgeois individualism, shall never allow them to translate our glorious motto 'Long Live the International!' as the preposterous ventriloquy 'Down with France!'

No, internationalism means no humiliation of our Motherland, nor does it mean its immolation. When *patries* came into being, they were the first and essential stage toward the unity of humankind, a goal that we are pursuing; and internationalism, begotten by the entire course of the new civilisation, is likewise an essential stage along this path. Just as the French *Patrie* was taking form not in opposition to various provinces which she wrested from the state of defunct antagonism with the aim of bringing them together, but in the interests of their freedom and prosperity, so the *Patrie* of humankind—which requires social organisation of production, exchanges and science—is not and cannot be formed to the detriment of the now extant nations, it is formed for their good and consummate progress.

He who embarks upon the path of internationalism leading to an absolute flourishing of humanity does not cease to be a patriot just as we, becoming French at the end of the last century, continued to remain Provençals, Flemish or Bretons.

Contrariwise, internationalists may well call themselves the only patriots because they are only ones to be aware to what extent conditions must improve under which the future and the grandeur of their *Patrie* can and should be secure—in fact, of all the *patries* who will have turned from antagonistic to solid ones.

By proclaiming 'Long Live the International!' they proclaim: 'Long live the France of labour! Long live the historic mission of the French proletariat that will be able to liberate itself only by assisting in the liberation of the proletariat of all countries!'

French Socialists are patriots also from another standpoint and from other considerations: because France was in the past, and she is destined already now to evolve into one of the most significant factors of social advancement, as we understand it.

So, we want—and we cannot but want—to have a great and strong France capable of defending the republic against united monarchies, and also of protecting her new year of 1789 which is to come against the coalition, at least against a possible coalition, of the capitalist states of Europe.

It is France who by the works of Babeuf, Fourier and Saint-Simon has made a beginning in the development of the socialist ideas to which Marx and Engels have imparted scientific consummation.

It is France, the country of the first bourgeois revolution, which is the inevitable precursor of a proletarian revolution, who became an epic battlefield of the classes and who sacrificed to the cause of emancipated labour a countless number of her heroic rebels in Lyon in 1832 and Paris in 1848 and 1871.

It is France who, in spite of her sons having been butchered in the Versailles massacre, raised in 1889, at her immortal Congress in Paris, the banner of the International—a banner crimson with her own blood—and made a beginning in the celebration of May Day; she is the first to have hoisted the red banner of the proletariat, marching on toward winning political power, on the town halls seized by means of ballots.

And since her revolutionary past is the earnest of her socialist future, 23 years ago, as she faced danger, the internationalists of Italy, Spain and other countries rushed under the tricolor to her rescue, while the nascent German Social-Democracy, risking its freedom, did everything to prevent her dismemberment, just as absurd as criminal.

But this is why we, patriots, do not want a war which, be it victorious or not, would equally result in unspeakable calamities, leaving in the battlefield millions of people and the engines of death they will have been armed with.

We do not want a war which, whatever its outcome, would be but a game of Asiatic cruelty in the person of the Russian czar for the exhausted West.

We want peace, a lasting peace, because it is to our benefit but, is against the domination of the capitalists and governments, a domination we are out to destroy—for they can prolong their despicable and pernicious existence only by dividing and exterminating the nations.

We want peace because the bourgeois order is foredoomed.

And now that we know that patriotism and internationalism, far from excluding one another, are the two mutually complimentary forms of human amity, we repeat it loud and clear to the face of our calumniators:

Yes, the French Workers' Party constitutes one whole with the German Social-Democracy against the German Empire.

Yes, the French Workers' Party constitutes one whole with the Belgian Workers' Party against the bourgeois Koburg monarchy.

Yes, the French Workers' Party constitutes one whole with the toilers and Socialists of Italy against the Savoy monarchy.

Yes, the French Workers' Party constitutes one whole with the young but already so strong Labour Party on the other side of the Channel against the oligarchic and capitalist constitutionalism of Britain.

Yes, we do and shall constitute one whole with the proletariat of both hemispheres against the ruling and propertied classes everywhere.

And we hope that our French comrades, the people of the workshops and fields, will join their voices to the Party National Council in a double call which, in substance, constitutes but one whole:

Long Live the International!

Long Live France!

National Council:

Joseph Crepin, Simon Dereure, Ferroul, deputy;

Jules Geusde, Paul Lafargue, deputy;

Prevost, Kennel.

227. *The International Socialist Working-Men's Congress in Paris*, which was actually the constituent congress of the Second International, opened on 14 July 1889, the centennial of the storming of the Bastille. About 400 delegates from 20 countries of Europe and America attended. The Congress heard the reports of Socialist representatives on the condition of the working-class movement in their respective countries, outlined fundamental principles of the international labour legislation by approving demands for the legal eight hours, prohibition of child labour and for labour protection of working women and adolescents. The Congress stressed the need of a political organisation of the proletariat and of a struggle for the implementation of workers' democratic demands; it spoke out for a dissolution of regular armies which were to be replaced by a people's militia. The most significant decision of the Congress was its resolution on holding demonstrations and meetings in all countries on 1 May 1890 in support of an eight-hour working day and of a fair-labour code. The anarchists, who opposed the congress resolutions, failed to enlist support from the absolute majority of the delegates.

228. The International Socialist Working-Men's Congress in Brussels was held on 16-22 August 1891. It was attended by 370 delegates from 16 European countries and the United States who represented, by and large, the Marxist trend in the working-class movement. Most of the delegates voted against anarchists participating in the Congress (who had sent their delegates). Attending the Congress were also representatives of the British trades unions, a rather positive factor according to Engels. Such issues were on its agenda as the labour code, work stoppage and boycott, and militarism. In its resolution on labour legislation the Congress called on workers of the world to join forces in the struggle against the capitalist rule; it urged workers, wherever they had political rights, to use these rights for their eman-

cipation from wage servitude. The resolution on work stoppage and boycott recommended that workmen use both forms of the struggle. It emphasised the absolute need of trade unions for the workers.

The attitude of the working class to militarism was the central issue on the agenda. The reports delivered by W. Liebknecht and E. Vaillant, as well as the resolution proposed by Liebknecht characterized militarism as an inevitable follow-up of the capitalist system; they stressed that a socialist system alone would be able to put an end to militarism and establish peace among the nations; that Socialists were a genuine party of peace. Yet these documents did not define specific tasks and ways of the struggle against the war threat.

The resolution proposed by Liebknecht was attacked by the leader of the Dutch Socialists D. Nieuwenhuis, a man of anarchist leanings. He tabled a resolution urging the Socialists of all countries to appeal in the event of a war to their peoples to stage a general strike, but it failed to win support among the delegates. The overwhelming majority of votes was cast for the W. Liebknecht resolution (see also F. Engels 'The Brussels Congress. The Situation in Europe'; present edition, vol. 27).

229. *The Third International Socialist Working-Men's Congress* was held in Zurich on 6-12 August 1893. Attending were over 400 delegates from 18 countries. The British delegation had a much broader representation than at the previous two congresses. The following issues were on the agenda: the legal eight hours, May Day celebration, the political tactics of Social-Democrats and the position of Social-Democracy in the event of a war. Since participation in the Congress was conditional on one's recognition of political activity (something that the anarchists denied), the Congress began its work by considering the legitimacy of the mandates of the anarchist delegates. Following a heated debate a resolution was carried by a majority of votes. It interpreted the notion of political activity as the use of political rights and law-making institutions by working-class parties in the interests of the proletariat and for gaining political power. Upon the adoption of this amendment the anarchists, including the representatives of The Young (see Note 129), had to leave the Congress.

On the issue of May Day festivities the Congress rejected by a majority of votes the proposal of the German Social-Democrats to have the celebrations as late as the first Sunday of the month; it stressed the major political significance of a demonstration on May 1 as the day of proletarian solidarity. On the third issue of the agenda (the political tactics of Social-Democrats) the Congress adopted a resolution which recognised the need of combining the parliamentary and non-parliamentary forms of struggle depending on specific conditions in this or that country.

Concerning the attitude of Social-Democrats to war, the Congress turned down the Nieuwenhuis proposal for a general strike to be declared in case of a war and reaffirmed the basic provisions of the Brussels Congress resolution on this issue (see Note 228); it added a clause urging workers to wage a disarmament struggle and obliging the Socialist MPs to vote against war credits.

230. *The Belgian Workers' Party* was founded in Brussels on 5 April 1885 on the basis of the Belgian Socialist Party formed in 1879. The Workers' Party likewise comprised other workers' organisations—trade unions, cooperatives, etc. The Party crusaded for economic demands of the working class and for universal suffrage; it led the strike action of the proletariat.

231. Charles Verecque, a French Socialist, was sentenced to a term in prison and public penance according to Article 226 of the French Criminal Code which had been in abeyance for about 100 years. With the consent of a group of Socialists of the town of Amiens, Verecque (accused of saying to the prosecuting attorney, 'One ought to stick Mr. Viviani's plea onto the prosecutor's back') wrote a letter to the prosecuting attorney which concluded by

saying: 'I plead guilty and declare it in a written deposition, as it ensues from Article 226, that I am guilty of momentarily mistaking the back of a magistrate for one of the machines on which, in a few weeks' time, we shall have the honour of sticking the programme—a victorious programme—of Socialism'; Verecque's statement contained a pun: magistrate ('magistrat') as a justice and as a municipal officer.

232. in his letter of 28 June 1893 P. Lafargue told Engels that the National Council of the French Workers' Party had appealed to the Organising Committee of the Zurich International Congress (see Note 182) with a request to adjourn the convocation of the Congress from August to November in view of the election to the Chamber of Deputies due on 20 August 1893. Lafargue asked Engels to write to Bebel to get the Germans to second this request.

233. Engels visited Como during his tour of Germany, Switzerland and Italy in August-September 1865.

234. This letter was first published in English with deletions in: K. Marx and F. Engels, *Correspondence 1846-1895. A Selection with Commentary and Notes*. London, Martin Lawrence, 1934; and in full in: K. Marx and F. Engels, *Selected Correspondence*, F.L.P.H. Moscow, 1955.

235. Engels never realised this intention. For the available fragments and outlines, see present edition, Vol. 26, pp. 554-56.

236. The Duchy of *Burgundy*, formed in eastern France in the 9th century, became an independent feudal state in the 14th and 15th centuries; it attained maximum might under Duke Charles the Bold in the latter half of the 15th century. In a bid to expand its dominions the Duchy of Burgundy worked against the centralist policy of the French King Louis XI and waged a war of conquest against the Swiss and Lorraine. Finally Louis XI succeeded in having the Swiss and Lorrainians form a coalition against Burgundy. In a war against this coalition (1474-77) the troops of Charles the Bold were defeated, and the Duke was killed in the Battle of Nancy (1477). His dominion was divided between Louis XI and Maximilian Habsburg, the German Emperor's son.

237. R. Meyer gave a 'truncated version' of this letter for publication; the end of the letter is missing.

238. In his letter of F. Engels of 22 June 1893 R. Meyer recapitulated a conversation he had with a lawyer who, in his political views, was close to the Conservatives (see Note 202). The lawyer had told Meyer about the opinion current among the Conservatives to the effect that Reichskanzler Caprivi 'would use all his powers as Chancellor for suppressing Social-Democracy which had won "too great a victory" in the last election'.

239. The reference is to Engels' interview to a correspondent of the British newspaper *Daily Chronicle*, published on 1 July 1893. The interview was granted on the occasion of the June-held elections to the German Reichstag and the good returns for German Social-Democrats (see Note 204). The text of this interview was carried in an abridged form by *Le Socialiste* (No. 148), 15 July 1893, in P. Lafargue's translation and under the heading 'F. Engels et las élections allemandes' (see present edition, Vol. 27, pp. 549-53).

240. The first issue of *L'Ere nouvelle* on 1 July 1893 carried the final chapter of Engels' book *The Origin of Family, Private Property and the State*. In light of the Researches by Lewis H. Morgan (see present edition, Vol. 26), 'Barbarism and Civilisation'. The second issue of the journal, which came out on 2 August, had chapter V of the above work—'The Emergence of the Athenian State'.

241. In 1882-83 France, pushing ahead with the colonialist thrust in Southeast Asia, ran into stiff resistance in the Kingdom of Siam. Several military clashes occurred as a result. In July 1883 French naval ships invested Siam's capital city, Bangkok. The Siamese government had to yield and it signed a treaty with France, ceding the vassal Siamese territories on the left bank of the Mekong to France.

In 1882 the French government began a colonial war in North Vietnam (Tongking) which developed into a war with China. Although France established its protectorate over Vietnam, the hostilities continued with French troops suffering setbacks in 1885; this caused the fall of the Ferry government.

242. On the envelope of this letter Engels wrote the following address: 'Sigr. Filippo Turati, Portici Galleria V.E. 23, *Milano*, Italy'. Turati made this note on the envelope; 'Engels, Proprietà. opere Marx': the few words that followed are illegible.

243. The Printing-and-Publishing Union (la Unione tipografica-editrice) of Turin filed a declaration of protest against the intention of E. Guindani, an Italian Socialist from Cremona, to publish the Italian edition of G. Déville's work *Le Capital de Karl Marx, Résumé et accompagné d'un aperçu sur le socialisme scientifique* (see note 220); the Union claimed it allegedly purchased the copyright on all the works of Marx from his heirs.

244. On 24 July 1893 Natalie Liebknecht sent Engels a photograph of the house where he was born, in Bruch, a suburb of Barmen. The photograph had been ordered by W. Liebknecht during one of his propaganda tours of Germany.

245. On 21-28 July 1893 Engels was on holiday in Eastbourne.

246. In her letter of 24 July 1893 Natalie Liebknecht told Engels that her son Karl had not been accepted into military service in Berlin because of his being a Saxon subject.

247. A reference to the annexation of the larger part of Alsace and East Lorraine by Germany in 1871 as a result of the French defeat in the Franco-Prussian War of 1870-71. France regained this territory in 1919.

248. Engels means the rule of the French Emperor Napoleon III (2 December 1852—4 September 1870). The Second Empire collapsed in the wake of the September Revolution of 1870.

249. In the first round J. Guesde won a victory by polling 6,887 votes: Deschamps, a moderate Republican, got 2,138 votes and Vienne, a Roman Catholic Worker—4,403. Paul Lafargue, who had been running in Lisle's second electoral district, polled 4,745 votes.

250. Since the International Socialist Working-Men's Congress in Zurich was being held on the eve of the election to the French Chamber of Deputies, the leaders of the French Workers' Party were unable to attend. The French delegation comprised 41 men of whom only two (Bonnet and Bonnier) represented the Party. The other delegates were from non-Marxist parties and political groups: the Possibilists (see Note 30), the Independent Socialists (Jaclard), the Blanquists (see Note 20) [Degay and Rémy], etc. The French delegation distinguished itself by its inconsistent voting and its opposition to Bebel's theses and to the majority at the Congress.

251. The text of this letter was written on a post card. Engels indicated his whereabouts: Frau Hermann Engels aus Barmen (Engelskirchen), Hotel Bellevue, *St. Moritz Bad* Engadin.

252. The hope that Paul Lafargue would be elected to the French Chamber of Deputies did not materialise. In order to defeat his opponent, Lafargue (as well as Gustave Dron, an opportunist candidate) had to receive 3,000 votes in his constituency. During the election cam-

paign Lafargue and Dron reached an agreement whereby Socialists in Dron's constituency were to cast their votes for him, Gustave Dron, while pro-opportunist candidates in Lafargue's constituency were to vote for his candidacy. While the Socialists secured a victory for Dron, the opportunist electorate cast their votes for Lafargue's opponent.

253. Engels wrote this letter on a form that had A. Bebel's address printed on it.

254. Prior to his trip to Europe in 1893 (see Note 189) Engels had last visited Germany in the latter half of June 1876 as he went to Heidelberg for domestic reasons.

255. Engels was in Berlin from September 1841 to October 1842 after he had joined as a volunteer to do his tour of military duty.

256. *Die Freie Volksbühne* ('Free Popular Stage')—a theatrical society founded in Berlin in 1890. It staged theater shows for the populace and championed classical authors like Goethe, Schiller, Hauptmann, Ibsen as well as Gogol and Tolstoy. It was not a commercial enterprise; it put on performances in circumvention of official censorship.

257. Returning together with A. Bebel from the Zurich Working-Men's Congress (see Note 229), Engels stayed for a few days in Vienna. On 11 September 1893 Austrian Social-Democrats organised a reception which, according to the Vienna newspaper *Die Arbeiter-Zeitung* of 15 September 1893, was attended by about 600 people. There was another rally on 14 September, at which about 2,000 took part, on the results of the Zurich Congress. The speakers included V. Adler, A. Bebel and other delegates to the Congress. Engels spoke at the end of the meeting (see present edition, Vol. 27, pp. 406-07).

258. After the stormy anti-Austrian demonstrations of the summer of 1893 at which the protesters demanded universal suffrage, the Taafe government imposed a state of emergency in the Prague district on 12 September 1893. It banned all Radical-Progressist and Social-Democratic publications.

259. P. Lafargue's article 'Die politischen Parteien in Frankreich und die letzten Wahlen' published by *Die Neue Zeit* (12. Jg., 1893/1894, Nos. 3, 4 and 5), and also his letter to Engels on 5 September 1893 about the results of the election to the French Chamber of Deputies. V. Adler's article 'Die Wahlen in Frankreich', published in *Die Arbeiter-Zeitung* (No. 37) on 15 September 1893, was based on this information.

260. Engels is answering Karl Kautsky's letter of 20 September 1893 asking permission to publish Heinrich Heine's letter to Marx of 21 September 1844 in *Die Neue Zeit*. This letter was in the possession of Eleanor Marx-Aveling. Kautsky asked Engels to write an introduction to the intended publication, but Engels did not do so. The Heine letter was published in *Die Neue Zeit* (No. 1, 1895-96, Vol. 1) only after Engels' death; Kautsky supplied a commentary and a facsimile of Engels' letter.

261. A reference to the royalties paid by the publishers of *Das Kapital* to Marx's heirs.

262. On his way back from the International Socialist Working-Men's Congress in Zurich (he was accompanied by A. Bebel, see Note 229), Engels stopped in Berlin, staying from 16 to 28 September 1893, where he received a warm reception. A rally was held in the *Concordia Hall* on 22 September in which about 4,000 took part. Wilhelm Liebknecht made a speech on the role of Engels in the German working-class movement. Engels spoke in reply (see present edition, Vol. 27, pp. 409-10).

263. *Norici*—a group of Illyrian-Celtic tribes that used to live in the ancient Roman Province of Noricum situated south of the Danube in what is now Austria.

264. The whereabouts of this postcard is unknown.

265. In 1893 William Reeves, a London publisher, printed the English translation of A. Bebel's book *Die Frau und der Sozialismus* ('*Woman and Socialism*'), without any prior consultations either with the author or with the translator, Mrs. Adams Walter, who had prepared the first English edition, published in London in 1885 by The Modern Press. The book's title (*Die Frau in der Vergangenheit, Gegenwart und Zukunft*) was Bebel's own and was retained in the German editions, from the Second to the Eighth (1883-90). The same name—*Women in the Past, Present and Future*—was used in all the English translations.

266. Hermann Blocher, a Swiss Social-Democrat, approached Engels with a request to help him in selecting the literature in connection with a work on Bruno Bauer he was going to write.

267. An allusion to the warm reception given to Engels at the concluding session of the International Socialist Working-Men's Congress in Zurich (see Note 229).

268. The French Chamber of Deputies, elected in August-September 1893 (see Note 208) was to open its sessions in November 1893.

269. Victor Adler made his speech at a rally in one of Vienna's largest halls, the Schwender Colisuem, on 2 October 1893; more than 4,000 were in attendance. He spoke against the state of emergency declared in the Prague district on 12 September (see Note 258). Adler's speech was published by *Die Arbeiter-Zeitung* (No. 40) on 6 October 1893.

270. A reference to the draft electoral reform tabled in the Austrian Reichskrat on 10 October 1893 by Ministerpräsident (Premier) Eduard Taaffe whose government represented the conservative bloc of the big landed proprietors and top bureaucracy. He was supported by the Polish, Czech and Slovenian feudal-clerical interests, A broad campaign for a reform of the country's electoral system began in the early 1890s. On 9 July 1893 Social-Democrats organised a mammoth demonstration of Vienna's workers for universal suffrage. Similar demonstrations and rallies were held countrywide. Under the circumstances the Taaffe government proposed a draft electoral reform which provided for a considerably wider range of prospective voters, but preserved the old curial system and the privileges for the landlords and the bourgeoisie. The reactionary political parties, however, opposed the draft law, and the Taaffe cabinet had to resign in October 1893. The country's electoral system was reformed as late as 1896.

271. *Phoenicians*—a tribe of seafarers described by Homer in *The Odyssey*. According to Homer, they inhabited the island of Scheria north of Ithaca, the island of Odysseus.

272. The Social-Democratic Workers' Party of Austria was founded at a unification congress that was in session at Heinfeld (Low Austria) on 30 December 1888—1 January 1889. This congress adopted a programme ('Declaration of Principles') which was based on the fundamental tenets of Marxism. In its Declaration the Party defined as its objective a political organisation of the proletariat; it pledged to promote the class-consciousness of the proletariat. Its other targets included socialisation of the means of production, emancipation of Labour, political rights for working people and their education.

273. *Der Sonderbund*—a separatist union of the seven economicallly backward Catholic cantons formed in 1843 to resist progressive bourgeois reforms and to defend the privileges of the Church and the Jesuits. The decree of the Swiss Diet of 1847 dissolving the Sonderbund served as a pretext for the latter to start hostilities against other cantons early in November. On 23 November 1847, the Sonderbund forces, consisting largely of milita detachments, were defeated by the federalist army.

274. Pius IX, who succeeded to the Holy See in 1846 under the conditions of an imminent revolution in Italy, announced a restricted political amnesty and embarked on moderate reforms, thus gaining popularity as a 'liberal Pope'. The demonstrations of 1846, 1847 and early 1848 held under the motto 'Long Live Pius IX', turned into a powerful revolutionary catalyst. But with the outbreak of the 1848 Revolution, the Pope appealed to the Catholic powers to intervene against the Italian Republic and, after the defeat of the Revolution, followed overtly reactionary policies.

275. In January 1848, the Neapolitan troops of King Ferdinand II, subsequently named King Bomba for his savage bombardment of Messina in the autumn of that year, ordered a shelling of Palermo in an effort to suppress a popular uprising, a move that sparked off the bourgeois revolution of 1848-49 in the Italian states.

276. The years 1890-93 saw a mass campaign for universal suffrage in Belgium. In April 1893 the General Council of the Belgian Workers' Party (see Note 230) declared a general political strike for a revision of the acting electoral law. Under the pressure of mass actions and work stoppages the Chamber of Deputies was compelled, on 18 April 1893, to adopt a law on universal suffrage (with certain reservations, however); the franchise was granted to men over 25 on the condition they had been resident in the country for no less than a year (residential qualification). On the other hand, this law introduced a system of multiple voting whereby some categories of voters were eligible for an additional 1-2 ballots depending on their property status, education and government service record.

277. The *Young Czechs*—a bourgeois-liberal party which championed the interests of the Czech bourgeoisie.

The *Old Czechs*—the Right Wing of the national movement in Bohemia, Moravia And Silesia; they expressed the interests of the nobility.

278. In view of the Socialists' success at the elections to the French Chamber of Deputies in August-September 1893 (see Note 208), the reactionary press mounted a campaign of slander accusing them of being German agents on the pretext that German Social-Democrats had donated 2,500 francs to the election fund. In this connection P. Lafargue wrote to Engels on 5 September 1893 that French Socialists had better not receive money from Germany in the future.

279. Engels means a congress held by the Social-Democratic Party of Germany in Cologne on 22-28 October 1893. The congress heard the reports of the Party Executive of the Social-Democratic group in the Reichstag, and discussed the Party press, the labour union movement and its support by the Social-Democrats, May Day celebrations in 1894, as well as August Bebel's report 'Antisemitismus und sozialdemokratie'. The delegates came out against Social-Democrats taking part in the election to the Prussian Landtag and against any compromises with the bourgeois parties.

280. On 10 October 1893 P. Lafargue wrote to Engels about the plan to start a newspaper that could enable the Workers' Party to rise to a leading position in the French Socialist press. Here Engels recalls that in 1892 *Le Socialiste* had announced that it would be a daily newspaper as of October 1892; the announcement began with the words '*pour paraître en Octobre*' ('to appear in October'). In actual fact, *Le Socialiste* continued as a weekly.

281. The present letter was first published in English in K. Marx and F. Engels, *Correspondence 1846-1895. A Selection with Commentary and Notes.* London, Martin Lawrence, 1934.

282. Engels had the fee for his works printed by the Dietz Publishers in Stuttgart sent to V. Adler for the needs of Austrian Social-Democracy.

283. The Second Congress of the French Workers' Party that took place in Paris on 7-9 October 1893. The Congress was attended by 92 delegates representing 499 trade-union and Party organisations. Already at its first meeting the Congress adopted a Declaration urging internationalist actions of the proletariat; the Party voiced solidarity with the striking miners of France, Britain and Belgium and with militant Socialists in other countries. On the domestic scene, the Declaration warned against the mounting wave of chauvinism.

The Congress also considered the returns of the elections to the French Chamber of Deputies (see Note 208), the tasks of Socialist deputies, Socialist propaganda, etc. The Party Congress stressed the need of unity among all Socialists and spoke out for the Socialist deputies forming a parliamentary group in the Chamber of Deputies; it also recommended that, whenever it was possible, they donate their deputy's fees for propaganda.

A report on the Congress was published by the newspaper *Vorwärts* (no. 240) on 12 October 1893 under the headline 'Der Kongress der Französischen Arbeiterpartei'.

284. The letter of Ferdinand Lassalle to Marx and Engels which Engels wanted published with his notes and a preface; this was done by Franz Mehring in 1902.

285. In the latter half of September 1893 French miners in the departments of Nord and Pas de Calais went on strike; the strikers demanded higher wages and a ban on dismissing workers older than forty. The stoppage lasted some two months and ended in a defeat.

At about the same time there was a strike of Belgian miners who demanded a 10 per cent wage rise. This strike, which ended in mid-October, also fell short of its objectives.

286. In the summer of 1893, after the announcement of a lockout in the British mining industry (see this volume, pp. 204-05), the employers tried to use strikebreakers. On 7 September 1893, as there was unrest among the miners of Featherstone (Yorkshire), the mine owners called in troops who opened fire, wounding several people. Thereupon nearly all the coal districts were overrun by government troops, a move that caused outrage countrywide. As a result, the employers had to refrain from introducing lower pay rates for the time being.

287. Engels sketched the draft of his reply to Ferdinand Wolff on the reverse side of Wolff's letter received late in October 1893 and containing innuendoes and threats against Engels. Ignorant as he was of Wolff's mental illness, Engels wrote a letter of reply, but it is not known whether it was ever sent. Visiting Wolff shortly afterwards, Engels could see at first hand his grave condition. See this volume, pp.222-23, 243.

288. Victor Adler made a German translation of the first volume of Stepniak-Kravchinsky's book *The Russian Peasantry. Their Agrarian Condition, Social Life, and Religion*; it was published in English by Sonnenschein in 1888. In his letter of 22 September 1892 Adler asked Engels to secure, through Stepniak's mediation, W. Sonnenschein's formal permission for the publication of the German translation and for paying the royalties due to the author and the publisher. Stepniak read Adler's translation and wrote a brief preface to it. The book was published by J.H.W. Dietz in Stuttgart in 1893 under the title *Der russische Bauer*.

289. Karl Kautsky, then in Stuttgart, told Engels in his letter of 1 November 1893 about his plans to move to Austria. In his letter of 25 November 1893, Kautsky explained that, while living in Stuttgart, he felt isolated from the Austrian working-class movement.

290. Karl Kautsky asked Eduard Bernstein to write an article on the general strike for publication in *Die Neue Zeit*; he hoped this would start a discussion on the subject. Engels' advice to Bernstein was apparently not taken into account, for in February 1894 *Die Neue Zeit* published Bernstein's article 'Der Streik als politische Kampfmittel'.

291. *The three-class electoral system* (*Dreiklassenwahl*) was introduced in Prussia in keeping with the electoral law of 30 May 1849, after the defeat of the 1848-49 Revolution. This system provided for high property qualifications and, consequently, contributed to unequal representation.

292. The reference is to the Croatian border regiments stationed in the Military Border Area, a special military region of the Austrian Empire along the frontier with Turkey.

    Ruthenes (*Ruthenians*)—the name given in the nineteenth-century West-European ethnographical and historical works to the Ukrainian population of Galicia, Bukovina and the Eastern Carpathians, who were separated at the time from the rest of the Ukrainian people.

293. A reference to *Karl Marx. 'Le Capital'. Extraits faits par M. Paul Lafargue*, Vilfredo Pareto wrote the introduction. This book was published by Guillaumin in Paris in 1893.

294. Joseph Baernreither, a Liberal deputy, tabled a draft electoral reform on 13 October 1893; it granted voting rights in parliamentary elections only to workers eligible for health insurance. They were to form a special curia. The draft law restricted to twenty the number of worker deputies elected in this way.

295. On 3 November 1893 opponents of the electoral reform assembled in Vienna's Ronacher Hall. This meeting sparked a protest among Social-Democrat workers who responded by a demonstration which resulted in clashes with the police.

296. Engels sent this letter with the cheque to F. Sorge's address in Hoboken; see this volume, pp. 229.

297. Engels indicated the following address on the envelope: Frau Liebknecht, Kantstr. 160, Charlotenburg/Berlin (Germany).

298. Karl Liebknecht, who together with his brother Theodor was doing his tour of duty in the Guards Corps of Engineers (Gardenpionieren) sought a court referendar's job (Gerichtsreferendar) at Hamm. Eventually he was offered to choose between Arnsberg and Paderborn (Westphalia).

299. *Bimetallism* (double currency)—a monetary system based on two metals (chiefly, gold and silver) with a fixed ratio to each other as legal tender.

300. In 594-593 B.C., Solon, an Athenian statesman and lawgiver, brought in a number of reforms so as to remodel the state and economic system of Athens. The situation was characterised by an acute struggle between the aristocracy and the people. The most important of Solon's reforms was one that abolished the land tenure debts of the Athenian peasants and prohibited bondage for defaulters, etc. Solon and his laws solidified Athens as a slave-owning city-state and laid the keystones of Athenian democracy.

301. A reference to the controversy over the McKinley protectionist tariff adopted in November 1890 (William McKinley was one of the leaders of the Republican Party [and President of the United States in 1897-1901]). The new tariff provided for a dramatic rise in duties on merchandise imported to the United States and, as a consequence, sent consumer prices up. The situation of the worrking class deteriorated as a result. The tariff bill invested the President with the right to increase import duties in the future as well. Engels commented on this legislation in his article 'The American Presidential Election' (see present edition, Vol. 27, pp. 329-31).

302. This letter was written on a postcard. Engels indicated the following address: H. Schlüter Esq., 936 Washington St., Hoboken, N.J., US America.

303. *The Berne Copyright Convention* was signed on 9 September 1886 by Great Britain, Germany, France, Italy and other countries.

304. *Humpty Dumpty*—egg-shaped figure of a well-known nursery rhyme:
    Humpty Dumpty sat on a wall,
    Humpty Dumpty had a great fall.
    All the king's horses
    And all the king's men
    Couldn't put Humpty together again.

305. In 1867 Benjamin Disraeli, then Chancellor of the Exchequer, played a crucial role in carrying out the Second Reform Act of 1867.

306. Engels wrote the draft of the reply on the reverse side of the letter which Paul Arndt had sent on 4 December 1893.

307. On 20 August 1893 Jules Guesde was elected to the French Chamber of Deputies from the town of Roubaix (see this volume, p. 182).

308. The Dupuy cabinet fell on 25 November 1893 after three-day debates on the government declaration in which Charles Dupuy leveled sharp attacks at socialism. The united socialist group in the Chamber took a firm stand against the course of the government majority and championed social reforms. The new cabinet, headed by Jean Casimir-Périer, ran into major difficulties at the very outset as Jean Juarès, speaking in a debate on the tax reform, tabled a motion whereby small farms were to be tax exempt. This proposal, made on behalf of the socialist parliamentary group, was carried by a majority of votes; however, Casimir-Périer annulled the results of voting to prevent a fall of the new cabinet.

309. In 1893 the anarchists committed a number of terrorist acts in Paris. Thus, on 9 December 1893 Auguste Vaillant threw a bomb into the hall where the French Chamber of Deputies was in session. The government retaliated by the laws against the anarchists (see Note 383) and by increasing the police budget.

310. Laura Lafargue was at the time translating into French Engels' *Ludwig Feuerbach and the End of Classical German Philosophy* (see present edition, Vol. 26); the translation was published in the journal *L'Ere nouvelle* (No.4 and No. 5, 1894); Engels had read the MS of the translation.

311. Sir Henry Roscoe's and Carl Schorlemmer's work appeared in English under the title *A Treatise on Chemistry*. Volumes I-III. London-New York, 1877-92; the whole edition comprised 9 books.
    The German name of the work was *Ausführliches Lehrbuch der Chemie*. Bände I-IV. Braunschweig, 1877-89. Julius Wilhelm Brühl continued the series beginning with Volume V; after C. Schorlemmer's death the nine-volume edition was completed in 1901.

312. Carl Schorlemmer's manuscript on the early history of chemistry, as mentioned by Adolf Spiegel in the obituary *Carl Schorlemmer*, was never published. This MS, written in German and 650 pages long, is in Manchester University library.

313. A reference to the English edition of Carl Schorlemmer's *The Rise and Development of Organic Chemistry* which came out in Manchester and London in 1879. The German text was published in 1889 as *Der Ursprung und die Entwicklung der organischen Chemie* in Brunswick. Arthur Smithells prepared a new English edition which was published in London and New York in 1894 under the same title as the 1879 edition.

314. A. Dworzak wrote a letter to Engels on 24-28 November 1893 in which she congratulated him on his 73d birthday.

315. A reference to the so-called 'original minute-book' fabricated by Prussian police spies and presented at the Cologne trial of Communists in 1852 as the chief evidence for the prosecution against members of the Communist League. See present edition, Vol. 11, pp. 420-43.

316. Engels never realised this intention.

317. Edouard Vaillant framed a draft law on abolishing the regular army and replacing it with a national milita; all the Socialist deputies put their signatures to it.

318. At the trial of Spanish anarchists in Madrid in 1890 it came out that one of them, Muñoz, was a police agent. All the defendants were sentenced to 7 years of forced labour.

319. Speaking of the harmony between Carnot and the Russian tsar, Engels implied the Franco-Russian alliance sealed in those days (see Note 177). About the anarchist police bombs, see Note 309.

320. Engels sketched out a version of his reply on the reverse side of Giuseppe Cànepa's letter of 3 January 1894. Cànepa asked Engels to find an epigraph to the weekly L'Era nuova due to appear in Geneva as of March 1894 'which in a few words could synthesise the Socialist ideal and set off the new era against the old era that is epitomised in the Dantesque words: one people rules, and the other languishes'. For the quote given by Engels, see present edition, Vol. 6, p. 506.

321. On 5 January 1894 Die Arbeiter-Zeitung (No. 9) carried the article 'Das allgemeine Wahlrecht eine "konservative Maßregel"'; cited in this article was a passage from K. Kautsky's article 'Ein sozialdemokratischer Katechismus' published in December 1893 by Die Neue Zeit (Bd. I, NN12 and 13, 1893-1894). The publication in Die Arbeiter-Zeitung proved the inadequacy and harm of a general political strike in the struggle for electoral reform.

322. The first congress of the Austrian trade unions, held in Vienna from 24 to 27 December 1893, set up a single centralised organisation and endorsed a single strike statute for all the unions. The congress spoke out against a general strike as a tool in the struggle for universal suffrage.

The Czech Social-Democrats held their congress on 24-26 December 1893 in Budweis (the present name, Ceské Budejovice). It passed a decision on forming a Czechoslavonian Social-Democratic Party [Ceskoslovanská Sociálne domekratická strana] on the basis of the principles proclaimed by the Unification Congress of the Austrian Social-Democrats at Heinfeld in 1888 (see Note 272).

The proceedings of the congresses held by the Austrian trade unions and the Czech Social-Democrats were covered by Die Arbeiter-Zeitung (NN 1 and 2) on 2 and 5 January 1894.

323. The fourth Congress of the Social-Democratic Party of Austria was held in Vienna on 25-31 March 1894. The Congress passed a resolution stating that the Austrian workers intended to campaign for universal suffrage using all available means, including a general strike. The congress also adopted new Party Rules and resolved to continue with the annual May Day celebrations by holding demonstrations for an 8-hour day, universal suffrage and in support of international brotherhood among all working people.

324. Engels wrote the following address on the envelope: G.W. Lamplugh Esq., Geological Survey, 28 Jermyn St., S.W.

325. Robert Burton's *The Anatomy of Melancholy* was first published under the pen name Democritus Junior in 1621. George William Lamplugh sent a copy of the ninth edition published in London in 1800.

326. Engels wrote the draft of his reply on the reverse side of Henri Ravé's letter of 1 January 1894.

327. Engels alludes to Karl Höger's speech at the congress of the Austrian trade unions (see Note 322).

328. Engels wrote these lines in the left margin of Albert Delon's letter of 19 January 1894 in which the sender asked for permission to translate Volume II of *Das Kapital* into French. The whereabouts of Engels' letter to A. Delon is not known.

329. Engels replies to W. Borgius' letter of 19 January 1894. The journal *Der sozialistische Akedemiker* (No. 20, 1895) published this reply for the first time together with the addressee's name; the subsequent publications gave the wrong name, Heinz Starkenburg.

     The condensed English version of the letter was first published in: K. Marx, F. Engels, V.I. Lenin, *On the Theory of Marxism*, International Publishers, New York, [1948].

330. On 26 January 1894 the newspaper *Vorwärts* published a lengthy article entitled 'Ein edles Brüderpaar' which claimed that Theodor Reuß and Heinrich Oberwinder had, beginning in 1886, been publicly exposed by the press as police spies.

     As R. Fischer wrote in his letter of 27 January 1894, Reuß had voiced protest over this article and denied any connection between his departure from *The Daily Chronicle* and the exposures in *Vorwärts*. On 14 January 1894, Fischer also asked Engels if he remembered a second publication on Reuß in *Vorwärts* .

331. The Erfurt Congress of the German Social-Democratic Party took place on 14 to 20 October 1891. Among the other issues, the Congress discussed and adopted a new Party Programme which, despite some shortcomings, was essentially based on Marxist principles. The criticism of the original draft of the Programme, which Engels made in his work 'A Critique of the Draft of the Social-Democratic Programme of 1891' (see present edition, Vol. 27), applies in part to the adopted Programme. The decisions of the Erfurt Congress sealed the Marxist trend in Germany's working-class movement.

332. Apparently a reference to the fee for the Engels pamphlet *Internationales aus dem 'Volksstaat'* *(1871-75)* published in Berlin by the *Vorwärts* Editorial Board.

333. Engels left for Eastbourne on 9 February or thereabouts because of poor health; he stayed there until 1 March 1894.

334. The reference is to the Engels article 'The Future Italian Revolution and the Socialist Party' (see present edition, Vol. 27, pp. 437-40) published by *Critica Sociale* (No. 3) on 1 February 1894; Victor Adler probably did not finish the translation of this article for *Die Arbeiter-Zeitung*; however, it appeared in *Der Sozialdemokrat* on 12 July 1894 under the heading 'Friedrich Engels über die Lage in Italien'.

335. Engels probably means the violent repression by the crew of the German cruiser *Die Hyäne* of a mutiny of native soldiers in the Cameroons on 21 December 1893.

336. Eduard Bernstein, Karl Kautsky and other authors were preparing a series of works on the history of socialism. In this connection Kautsky asked Engels in his letter of 7 February

1894 whether it would not be better to call it *History of Communism*. The book appeared in Stuttgart in 1895 under the title *Die Geschichte des Sozialismus in Einzeldarstellungen*.

337. Engels jotted down the draft of his reply on the reverse side of the letter from Professor Gizycki of Berlin, dated 14 February 1894; Georg von Gizycki asked Engels to contribute an article to the weekly *Ethische Kultur* on the ethical designation of the woman.

338. This letter was written on a postcard. Engels indicated the following address: Ed. Bernstein Esq., 50 Highgate Road, London, N.W.

339. Eduard Bernstein advised Engels to read Giordano Bruno's book *Del'Infinito, Universo e Mondi* which appeared in 1893 in Berlin; the title of the German translation was *Von Unendlichen, dem All und den Welten*.

340. Pertaining to the Socialist Party of the Italian Working People [Il Partito socialista dei lavoratori italiani] founded in 1892 at a congress in Genoa. The Party took a resolute stand in distancing itself from the anarchists; in 1895 it changed its name and came to be known as The Italian Socialist Party [Il Partito socialista italiano].

341. Engels congratulated Adelheid Dworzak and Julius Popp on their marriage which took place early in February 1894.

342. In February 1894 the French Chamber of Deputies debated the issue of corn tariffs. Jean Juarès proposed a law which provided for a state monopoly on grain imports. Jules Guesde supported this motion.

343. The Congress of the Socialist Workers' Party of Germany in Wyden (Switzerland) was held in August 1890. That was the first illegal congress of the German Social-Democrats following the introduction of the Anti-Socialist Law of 1878 (see Note 15). The Congress criticised the anarchist stand of Johann Most and Wilhelm Hasselmann, who rejected all legal means of struggle, advocated individual terror and launched an open campaign against the Party leadership; it expelled them from the Party.

The Congress unanimously decided to strike out the word 'legal' from the statement contained in Part II of the Gotha Programme of 1875 to the effect that the Party was working to attain its goals 'with all legal means'. The Congress confirmed the status of *Der Sozialdemokrat* as the Party's official organ.

344. As August Momberger wrote to Engels on 26 February 1894, he wanted to take part in disseminating socialist ideas among foreigners resident in Wiesbaden, the English in the first place. He asked Engels to recommend the significant socialist, socio-political and natural science works, as well as some English journal similar to the German *Die Neue Zeit*.

345. On 12-29 July 1894 Britain had a parliamentary election which gave the Conservatives a majority of over 150 votes in the Commons. Many candidates from the Independent Labour Party, among them Keir Hardie, were blackballed.

346. Speaking in the Commons on 19 March 1894, Randolph Churchill proposed a bill banning members of the Liberal cabinet from interfering in the course of future parliamentary elections and from speaking in the constituencies.

347. Engels means the articles published anonymously by *Der Arbeiter-Zeitung* (Nos. 19-22) on 6, 13 and 16 March 1894; apparently they were written by Victor Adler. The article that Engels refers to appeared on 6 March 1894, likewise without a signature; it was entitled 'Die Wahlreform Stadnicki'. It criticised the draft of an electoral reform suggested by the coalition government of Alfred von Windischgrätz. The bill envisaged only an insignificant increase in the Reichstag representation by setting up a fifth curia.

348. The draft of this letter, which Engels wrote on the back side of Panait Musoiu's letter of 24 February 1894, is extant. The texts of the draft and the letter are identical.

   Musoiu told Engels he had translated into Roumanian *Socialism: Utopian and Scientific* and *The Manifesto of the Communist Party*. He asked Engels to write a preface to a second edition of these works.

349. In the summer of 1894 Victor Adler had to serve a prison term of 2.5 months on several counts: 14 days for a public insult to the district commissioner of the town of Ceska-Lipa, one month for his speech at a public rally in Vienna's Schwender Coliseum on 30 October 1893 and yet another month for his speech in the same 'coliseum' on 28 January 1894.

350. By using the conventional symbols adopted in biology (for the male sex and for the female sex), Engels meant *Die Arbeiter-Zeitung*, and *Die Arbeiterinnen-Zeitung*, a newspaper for the working women. Both were published in Vienna.

351. An excerpt from this letter was first published in English in K. Marx, F. Engels, V.I. Lenin, *Anarchism and Anarcho-Syndicalism*. International Publishers, New York, 1972.

352. *Carlism*—onslaughts of the feudal reactionaries who unleashed two civil wars in Spain, in 1833-40 and in 1872-76, in the form of dynastic feuds between two lines of the Spanish Bourbons. Defeated in these wars were the Carlists, supporters of Don Carlos the Elder, whom they had proclaimed king in 1833. The Carlists relied on the backward strata of the peasantry and opposed forces interested in Spain's capitalist development. The two Carlist wars resulted in a weakening of the feudal-clerical strata and a strengthening of the positions of the bourgeoisie.

353. The Spanish anarchists had been perpetrating acts of terrorism since the late 1880s (in 1889 they bombed the royal palace).

354. Benno Karpeles sent Engels his book *Der Arbeiter des mährisch-schlesischen Steinkohlen-Reviers*. In his letter of 19 March 1894 he praised Engels as a scientist and author of the work *The Condition of the Working-Class in England* and as an outstanding socialist.

355. In her letter of 11 April 1894 Laura Lafargue told Engels that the French anarchists (libertaires) were out to publish one of the works of Eugen Dühring. In this connection Bonnet, the secretary of the Editorial Board of the journal *L'Ere nouvelle*, suggested that a translation into French of Engels' work *Anti-Dühring* should be begun without delay so as to have it ready before the appearance of Dühring's book. Such a translation did not materialise at the time.

356. Speaking in the Reichstag on 7 April 1894, Earl von Kanitz proposed a state monopoly of grain imports and exports; the state was likewise to fix grain prices. The Social-Democrats voted against; on 14 July 1894 the motion was rejected by 159 votes against 49.

357. Marx's *Speech on the Question of Free Trade* was published by *L'Ère nouvelle* (no. 6, 1894) and by *Le Socialiste* (No. 194-196, on 23, 30 June and 7 July 1894).

358. The English translation of Marx's *Speech on the Question of Free Trade* was published in Boston in 1888; it was prefaced by an introduction (*Free Trade*) written by Engels; it was published in Boston and London in 1889. The Italian translation of Marx's speech was published in *La Critica Sociale* (Nos. 7 and 8) on 1 and 16 April 1894; the same periodical carried Engels' introduction on 1 and 16 May and 1 June 1894 (Nos. 9, 10 and 11) [see also this volume, p. 297]; both works then appeared in a booklet published in Milan in 1894.

359. Engels wrote the following address on the envelope that still remains: Sig. avv° Filippo Turati, Portici Galleria V.E. 23, Milano, Italy.

360. Engels means A. Loria's article 'Karl Marx' published in *La Nuova antologia di scienze, lettere ed arti* on 1 April 1883 (see present edition, Vol. 47) as well as the preface to Volume III of *Capital* (see present edition, Vol. 37).

361. Henry William Lee, writing to Engels on 13 April 1894, asked him to give a lecture to members of the Social-Democratic Federation.

362. Probably a reference to the newspaper *La Réveil Ouvrier*, the organ of the local organisation of the French Workers' Party in Calais.

363. The reference is to the proof sheets of the French edition of Marx's *Speech on the Question of Free Trade* (see note 357).

364. The Italian translation of Marx's *Speech on the Question of Free Trade*, put out in *La Critica Sociale*, was made from the Russian text published as a supplement to Marx's work *Misère de la philosophie* (*Poverty of Philosophy*) and translated from the German edition of 1885 by Georgi Plekhanov.

365. Engels wrote the following address on the envelope: Sig. avv° Filippo Turati, Portici Galeria V.E. 23, Milano, Italy. The MS has the mark made by Turati: R 17/5.

366. First published in English in: *The Socialist Review* (London), 1908, III-VIII, p. 32 (abridged).

367. This is how Engels referred to members of the Socialist Labour Party of North America founded in 1876, in which German emigrés continued to figure prominently.

368. Boris Krichevsky, a Russian emigré Socialist, had sent Engels the Russian translations of Marx's works *The Eighteenth Brumaire of Louis Bonaparte* and *Wage Labour and Capital* with Engels' introduction to the 1891 edition (see present edition, Vols. 11,9,26); both works, published in Geneva in 1894 in the series *Social-Democratic Library*, were translated into Russian by Krichevsky. He told Engels in his letter that the same publishers undertook the printing of Engels' article 'On Social Relations in Russia' (in the series of his articles *Refugee Literature*) [see present edition, Vol. 24]. Krichevsky asked Engels to write a preface to the Russian edition of the above article. However, the printing was stopped because of protest from Engels who had earlier given Vera Zasulich the copyright. This article appeared in V. Zasulich's translation in *The Library of Contemporary Socialism* (Geneva, 1894) under the title 'Friedrich Engels on Russia. 1) A Reply to P.N. Tkachev (1875), 2) The Afterword (1894)'.

369. First published in English in: K. Marx and F. Engels, *On Britain*. Moscow, Foreign Languages Publishing House, 1953 (abridged).

370. Some of the works written by Engels in 1871-75 were republished in Berlin in 1894 in a separate edition entitled *Internationales aus dem 'Volksstaat' (1871-75)*.

371. On 7 June 1894 Nikolai Danielson told Engels he had not recieved the next sheets of Volume III of *Das Kapital*. He recommended a translator for the German edition of his *Essays on Our Post-Reform Social Economy*.

372. The Russian edition of Engels' work *The Origin of the Family, Private Property and the State* appeared in St. Petersburg in 1894. It was published with deletions made by the censor, in particular relating to Marx and his works.

373. N. Danielson had sent Engels the first two volumes of statistical data filed by the Department of Trade and Manufactories of the Russian Finance Ministry for the 1893 World Columbian Exhibition in Chicago: *The Industries of Russia. Manufactures and Trade:*

with a General Industrial Map, St. Petersburg, 1893. Russia was among the countries participating in the exhibition sponsored by the U.S. Congress to commemorate the quadricennial of America's discovery and its discoverer, Columbus.

374. Eugéne Turpin, a French chemist who in 1885 invented melinite, a powerful explosive, was accused of trying to sell his invention to a foreign power; he was cleared of this charge. However, he was nevertheless sentenced to five years in prison for publishing in 1889 a pamphlet on this episode. Turpin was pardoned on 10 April 1893. The newspaper *Le Temps* said on 2 June 1894 that the aim of the whole affair was publicity for the firm exploiting the Turpin invention.

375. An allusion to the case of the Building Society whose director, Spender Jabez Balfour, had fled overseas. Anthony John Mundells, an MP from Sheffield, President of the Board of Trade and, until 1892, Director of the New Zealand Loan Company, had to resign on 12 May 1894. Acting together with James Fergusson and John Gorst, he in 1893 closed down the company that had become the target of a public investigation.

376. Stanislaw Zablocki in his letter of 3 June 1894 asked for permission to publish the Polish translation of Engels' article 'The Polish Proklamation'.

377. The central organ of the Austrian Social-Democratic Workers' Party *Die Arbeiter-Zeitung* was a weekly newspaper in 1893; it became a semiweekly in 1894 and a daily as of January 1895.

378. The French President S. Carnot was assassinated by Santo Caserio, an Italian anarchist, on 24 June 1894. On 17 August 1893, the Aiguesmortes salt mines in Southern France were the scene of bloody clashes between French and Italian workers; the cause of the conflict was that the employers were paying higher wages to the French workers than to their Italian mates.

379. Apparently Engels wrote this letter after Hellmut von Gerlach had visited him late in June 1893 on Major Otto Wachs' recommendation.

380. *Der Sozialdemokrat* (Zurich) on 24 December 1887 promulgated a list of Berlin police agents. Among the agents exposed by Swiss Socialists was Heinrich Oberwinder, formerly a member of the First International (see also Engels' letter to Paul Lafargue of 29 December 1887, present edition, Vol. 48).

381. For cited passages see present edition, Vol. 37, Part I, K. Marx, *Capital*, Vol. III, present edition, pp. 374, 378, 382.

382. In connection with a third German edition of *Anti-Dühring* due for publication, Engels revised somewhat the Marx-written Chapter X of the second part of this work; the title of the chapter was *From 'Critical History'* (see present edition, Vol. 25, pp. 211-43, and also p. 15); the third edition of *Anti-Dühring* was off in Stuttgart in 1894.

383. Using the anarchist acts of terror as a pretext, the French government enacted laws against anarchists, the vague wording of which made it possible to apply them against Socialists as well. The first enactment was endorsed in December 1893 after August Vaillant had thrown a bomb in the French Chamber of Deputies (see Note 309); the second enactment was approved at the end of July 1894 after the assassination of President Carnot by the Italian anarchist Caserio (see Note 378), against heavy resistance from the Socialists and some of the Radicals. These two bills imposed restrictions on freedom of the press and provided for special courts to handle cases of violation of the laws on the press.

384. Twenty-two German emigrés took part in the Scotch miners' strike being held at the time. In their latter of 19 July 1894 signed by August Siegel and other German miners, they asked Engels to send their message to the Executive of the German Social-Democratic Party in which they requested a loan of 300 marks; they also asked Engels to approach Julius Motteler and other comrades in London with a request for material assistance.

385. First published in English in K. Marx and F. Engels, *On the United States*, Progress Publishers, Moscow, 1979 (abridged).

386. Concerning Paul Lafargue's negotiations with the Paris publisher Charles Marie Delagrave about the publication of his work *Origine et évolution de la propriété* (see Note 567).

387. F. Turati wrote, on this letter with his own hand: 'Scritto a Treves. R[isposto] 2./8./94. Tornato a rispondere 6./8./94/ ('Written in Treves. Replied 2./8./94./. In receipt of reply a new letter was written 6./8./94.')

388. In 1893-94 Sicily was the stage of sporadic peasant revolts caused by the aftermath of an economic crisis and abuses of the local administration. The revolts were crushed by brute force.

389. It was stated on the reverse side of the letter that the parcel and the letter with it were for Victor Adler; the parcel contained newspapers that could not be sent to Austria, while enclosed in the letter was about two pounds sterling. Engels was asked to get this letter to the addressee; the signature was illegible.

390. At the request of Pablo Iglesias, Engels wrote the appeal 'To the English Socialist and Working Men's Organisations' (see present edition, Vol. 27) in which he gave notice of the forthcoming 4th annual Congress of the Spanish Socialist Workers' Party. He sent similar appeals also to the Social-Democrats of Austria and Germany.

The Fourth Congress of the Spanish Socialist Workers' Party took place in Madrid from 29 August to 1 September 1894. The Congress heard reports of the Party's National Council and of a delegate who had attended the International Socialist Working-Men's Congress in Zurich (held in 1893, see Note 229); it discussed the issue of the Party press and adopted the new Party Rules. The Congress received numerous messages of greeting from the British organisations to which Engels had appealed, as well as from the Socialists of Britain, Austria, Germany and other countries.

391. A reference to the Gas Workers' and General Labourers' Union, the first union of unskilled workers in the history of the British labour movement. It was formed in late March-early April 1889 under the conditions of a mounting strike movement. A major contribution to the foundation and work of the union was made by Eleanor Marx-Aveling and Edward Aveling. The Union campaigned for the legal eight hours. It gained considerable influence within a short span of time; as many as 100,000 gas works employees joined it within a year.

392. A reference to the Fourth International Socialist Working-Men's Congress (Second International) which met in London in July 1896.

393. Engels was taking a rest in Eastbourne from 14 August to 18 September 1894.

394. Engels probably refers to the speeches made at the Zurich International Socialist Working-Men's Congress (see Note 229) by some members of the French delegation who leveled sharp criticism at the parliamentary activity of Socialists and put forward the idea of social revolution by means of a general strike. Among the members of the French delegation was Paul Arndt, a Paris correspondent of the newspaper *Vorwärts*.

395. In his letter to Engels on 12 August 1894 Eduard Bernstein wrote about the International Congress of Textile Workers held in Manchester in July 1894; in his opinion, it was an attempt to divorce trades-union congresses from socialist congresses. In this context Bernstein also mentioned Paul Arndt's article about the Manchester Congress, which appeared in *Vorwärts* on 2 August 1894. (Subsequently Engels received the issue of the newspaper *Der Textil-Arbeiter* with commentaries on the Congress.) Bernstein asked Engels what he thought of the Manchester Congress and of the decision of the conference of the Social-Democratic Federation (see Note 44) to convene an exclusively socialist congress prior to the congress of 1896 (see this volume, pp. 340-41, 343). The present letter contains Engels' reply to Bernstein's questions.

396. The 27th Annual Congress of the British Trades-Unions was held in Norwich on 3-8 September 1894. The Trades-Union Congress spoke out for the legal eight hours and for the nationalisation of all means of production, distribution and exchange; for Engels' assessment of this congress, see this volume, pp. 341, 343-44, 347.

397. In his letter of 15 August 1894, Thomas Clark asked Engels if he could vouch for Stanislaw Mendelson 'as a yearly tenant'.

398. Filippo Turati wrote to Engels in his letters of 2 and 6 August 1894 he had made inquiries about Felice Pasquali, an Italian emigré in London (see this volume, pp. 333, 338-39) and received contradictory references; thus, some called him 'seccatore di prima sfera' ('a burr of the first water').

399. Engels had stayed in Milan for three months in 1841.

400. Together with his letter of 2 August 1894 Filippo Turati sent Engels a photograph of a mold cast in Florence from the bust of K. Marx and asked him as well as Eleanor Marx-Aveling to confirm the likeness of the replica before it was cast.

401. Engels means the Exceptional Law on Public Security passed by the Italian Parliament on 14 July 1894. This law, enacted with the aim of combatting the anarchists, was used by the Crispi government against the working-class movement and Socialists as well. It banned the Socialist Party of the Italian Working People (*Il Partito Socialista dei lavoratori italiani*), closed worker organisations and worker periodicals; arbitrary arrests, searches and trials assumed mass proportions. All this notwithstanding, the Italian Socialists kept up their struggle and, in January 1895, they convened in Parma illegally for a third congress of their party.

402. Belfast was the venue of the Twenty-Sixth Annual Trades-Union Congress. It recognised the principle of collective ownership of the means of production and distribution and supported the demand for the legal eight hours.

403. The International Congress of Trade Unions, convened in London in November 1888 at the initiative of the British trades unions, involved delegates from Belgium, the Netherlands, Denmark, Italy as well as representatives of the the trade-union organisations in France. However, Germany and Austria were not represented—trade unions were illegal there and could not send their delegates. The Congress called on the working people to wage a struggle for labour protection laws and for the legal eight hours; it adopted a decision on convening an International Working-Men's Congress in Paris in 1889 (see Note 227).

404. A reference to the 14th Annual Conference of the Social Democratic Federation, held in London on 5 and 6 August 1894.

405. *New Unionism*—a development in the British trade-union movement at the end of the 1880s in the shape of the 'new' trades unions. Unlike the old craft unions—admitting craft workers exclusively—the new unions were open to labourers as well. The new labour organisations were formed by the various trades employed in a given industry (general unions). British Socialists, in particular Eleanor Marx-Aveling and Tom Mann, played a major part in setting up the new trades unions. Engels made an appraisal of New Unionism in his article 'May 4 in London' and in the Preface to the 1892 English Edition of *The Condition of the Working Class in England* (see present edition, Vol. 27).

406. The 12th Congress of the French Workers' Party (*Le Parti ouvrier français*) took place in Nantes on 14-16 September 1894 in a situation characterised by a mounting peasant movement, reactionary onslaughts and growing differences in the French Socialist movement. The Congress pointed to the heavier commitment of the French working people against the anti-Socialist laws of 1893-94 (see Note 383) and distanced itself from the anarchists who, by their terrorist acts, provided a pretext for adoption of these laws. In one of its major decisions the Congress adopted the motivational part of the Party's agrarian programme and incorporated a number of specific demands into it. For Engels' critique of the Nantes agrarian programme see *The Peasant Question in France and Germany* (see present edition, Vol. 27).

407. This and the preceding paragraph deal with an article on Volume III of *Das Kapital* which E. Bernstein intended to write for *Die Neue Zeit* (see Note 542); having read the proof sheets of Volume III, he told Engels in his letter of 5 September 1894 about the errata he had found. Bernstein refused to fulfill H. Schlüter's request to contribute an article on the same subject for *New Yorker Volkszeitung*.

408. As Eduard Bernstein wrote to Engels on 5 September 1894, Joseph Edwards invited him to write a series of articles on the situation of the German Social-Democratic Workers' Party and its plans for the future; the proposed materials were intended for *The Labour Annual*, a publication that J. Edwards was editing. Bernstein also told Engels that Edward Aveling had advised him not to take part in that publication.

409. An allusion to the Chino-Japanese War of 1894-95 which ended in China's defeat. By the Peace Treaty of Shimonoseki, Korea, overrun by Japan, received nominal independence. China ceded a number of its islands (including Taiwan) to Japan. China was also to pay a war indemnity of 200,000,000 taels.

410. First published in English in K. Marx and F. Engels, *On Colonialism.* Progress Publishers, Moscow, 1959 (abridged).

411. The fees for the articles which Engels wrote for *Die Neue Zeit* were being sent, according to his instructions, to V. Adler for the Austrian Social-Democrats. However, since the royalties due for the chapters for *Das Kapital*, published in the same periodical, had been remitted by mistake to V. Adler's account, Engels asked for the reimbursement of the sum to Marx's heirs at the expense of his article 'On the History of Early Christianity' (see present edition, Vol. 27).

412. On 14 and 21 October 1894 Belgium had its first elections in accordance with the new electoral law adopted on 18 April 1893 (see Note 276). The Belgian Workers' Party succeeded in having 30 of its representatives elected to the Chamber of Deputies.

By calling the Belgian elections a second victory, Engels meant to say that the first victory was won in April 1893 when the Belgians gained universal suffrage.

413. Georgi Plekhanov in his letter of 30 October 1894 asked Engels for permission to look through the files of the newspaper *Die Neue Rheinische Zeitung* and the journal *Die Neue Rheinische Zeitung. Politisch-ökonomische Revue* which Engels had in his custody.

414. This letter was written on a postcard on which Engels indicated the following address: 'Herrn Carl Hirsch, Red. der *Rheinischen Zeitung*, Hämmergasse 37, Köln, Germany.'

415. This letter was written on a postcard on which Engels indicated the address: 'Mrs. Aveling, 7 Gray's Inn Square, W.C.'

416. The reference is to the anonymous note 'Die Verleumderischen Hetzereien Hyndman's carried by the newspaper *Vorwärts* (No. 262) on 9 November 1894. It said Hyndman's attacks on the German Social-Democrats elicited disapproval among the British Socialists and workmen.

417. First published in English in an abridged form in K. Marx and F. Engels, *Correspondence. 1846-1895*. A Selection with Commentary and Notes. London, Lawrence, 1934.

418. Engels refers to a congress of the Social-Democratic Party of Germany held in Frankfurt am Main on 21-27 October 1894. The co-report on the main issue on the agenda—the agrarian question—was made by Georg von Vollmar, the leader of the Bavarian Social-Democrats; he insisted on augmenting the agrarian programme by clauses expressing the interests of all the peasantry, including the affluent strata. Some of the delegates, August Bebel among them, voiced objections. The congress elected a commission that was to draft the final text of the Party's agrarian programme as a supplement to the general programme. In addition, delegates heard the reports of the Party Executive Board and the Party group in the Reichstag; it considered such issues as the role of trusts and other major capitalist amalgamations, May Day celebrations, etc.

The final account of the proceedings of the Frankfurt Congress of the German Social-Democratic Party was published by the newspaper *Vorwärts* (No. 254) on 31 October 1894.

419. A reference to P. Lafargue's report 'La propriété paysanne et l'évolution économique', presented on behalf of the National Council of the French Workers' Party to its Nantes congress (see Note 406). Lafargue's report was also published by *Der Sozialdemokrat* (No. 38, supplement) on 18 October 1894.

420. Engels' work *On the History of Early Christianity* (see present edition, Vol. 27), translated into French by Laura Lafargue, appeared in the journal *Le Devenir social* (nos. 1 and 2, 1895) under the title *Contribution a l'Histoire du Christianisme primitif.*

421. In his *Letter to the Editors of 'Vorwärts'* (see present edition, Vol. 27) Engels refuted the statement made by Georg von Vollmar at the Frankfurt Congress of the German Social-Democratic Party.

422. This letter was written on a postcard on which Engels indicated the following address: Ed. Bernstein Esq., 50, Highgate Road, N.W.

423. Engels wrote this letter on a postcard on which he indicated the following address: Ed. Bernstein Esq., 29, Red Lion Square, W.C.

424. A reference to the polemics between Karl Kautsky and Georg Ledebour in the newspaper *Vorwärts* in a discussion after the Frankfurt Congress of the German Social-Democratic Party (see Note 418). On 20 November 1894 *Vorwärts* carried Kautsky's protest against Ledebour's contention to the effect that Kautsky—in his article on the Erfurt Programme—and Georg von Vollmar and others—in the debates on the agrarian question

at the Party Congress—had said there would be only petty peasant property in a socialist society. *Vorwärts* published Ledebour's objections on 21 November 1894.

425. On 14 November 1894 August Bebel spoke at a party meeting in Berlin's second constituency with a critique of the stand taken by Georg von Vollmar and other Bavarian Social-Democrats at the Frankfurt Congress of the German Social-Democratic Party (see Note 418) and of the resolution adopted by the Congress on the agrarian question. Bebel's speech was published by the newspaper *Vorwärts* (No. 268) on 16 November and reprinted in *La Critica Sociale* (No. 23) on 1 December 1894.

426. The agrarian programme sparked great controversy within the International Working-Men's Association (First International). It was hammered out in an acute struggle against the Proudhonists, who were insisting on the immutability of petty private ownership of land, and the Bakuninists, out to prove that with the abolition of inheritance, private property—including private ownership of land—would wither away. After prolonged debates the Brussels Congress of the First International (1868) and then its Basel Congress (1869) recognised the abolition of private ownership of land and its transformation into public ownership as a necessary condition.

427. The anonymous note 'On the Fourth Volume of Karl Marx's Capital' (see present edition, Vol. 27) was written by Engels in reply to an editorial carried by the newspaper *Vorwärts* (No. 266) on 14 November 1894 about the publication of Volume III of *Capital.* The editorial contained false data on the nature of the manuscript of Volume IV; in addition, the editors wrongly assumed Engels had given up his intention to have it published. Engels' refutation was published by Karl Kautsky in *Die Neue Zeit* (No. 9), 1894-95, Vol. 1.

428. Engels refers to the Draft of a Law on amendments and addenda to the Criminal Code, the Military Criminal Code and the legislation on the press ('Der Entwurf eines Gesetzes, betreffend Änderungen und Ergänzungen des Strafgesetzbuchs, des Militärstrafgesetzbuchs und des Gesetzes über die Presse'), known for short as the *Subversion Bill* ('Umsturzvollage'). It envisaged harsh punishment for 'the intention to effect an overthrow of the existing state system' even in the absence of a criminal act, and also for an encroachment on religion, monarchy, matrimony and property. The government tabled the draft law in the Reichstag in December 1894, but the top German legislature rejected it in May 1895.

429. On 26 October 1894 Reichskanzler Leo von Caprivi was forced to resign; he was succeeded by Fürst (Prince) zu Hohenlohe-Schillings.

430. In his letter of 12 November 1894 Nikolai Danielson told Engels about the publication of Pyotr Struve's book *Critical Notes on the Question of the Economic Development of Russia* and asked permission to quote passages from Engels' letters to him in his comments on the above book.

431. A reference to the second congress held by the Bavarian Social-Democratic organisation on 30 September 1894 in Munich. It was attended by 160 delegates. Two questions were on the agenda: 1) the activity of Social-Democratic Deputies in the Bavarian Landtag and 2) agitation among the peasants. Georg von Vollmar and Karl Grillenberger drew support from the majority of the congress which approved the activity of the Social-Democratic parliamentary group and adopted a decision on setting up a special organisation of the Bavarian Social-Democratics under the central guidance of the Landtag deputies—von Vollmar, Karl Grillenberger and others.

Sonderbund—an ironic analogy with the separatist union of reactionary Catholic cantons in Switzerland in the 1840s (see Note 273); here Engels means the separatist leanings of the Bavarian Social-Democrats.

432. Engels means the two editorial materials probably written by Wilhelm Liebknecht: the leading article in the newspaper *Vorwärts* (No. 273, 23 November 1894) under the title 'In eigener Sache' and a note under the same name carried by *Vorwärts* (No. 274, 24 November 1894) in the section *Zur Diskussion über den Frankfurter Parteitag*. The editors said in the former article they were 'diametrically opposed' to what Bebel had said at the meeting in the second constituency of Berlin (see Note 425). In the latter publication the editors said that in the leading article in *Vorwärts* on 23 November 1894 they had meant only 'Bebel's pessimistic appraisal of the entire course of the proceedings at the Party Congress and its spiritual level' (about the Frankfurt Congress see Note 418).

433. Engels means the anonymous article 'The Movement in Germany' published in *Justice* (No. 568) on 1 December 1894. The author of that article reproached the editors of *Vorwärts* for their silence about the differences among the German Social-Democrats over the agrarian issue and the attacks on *Justice* and Hyndman. A reply to that article appeared in the next issue of *Justice* (No. 569) on 8 December 1894; it was E. Bernstein's statement 'The *Vorwärts* and *Justice*. To the Editor of *Justice*' in which he rebutted the accusations.

434. A reference to A. Bebel's speech in the second constituency of Berlin on 14 November 1894 (see Note 425).
      Georg von Vollmar and Karl Grillenberger replied with a press polemic. Thus, on 17 and 21 November 1894 Grillenberger published notes in his newspaper *Frankische Tagespost* in which he commented on the above speech and which were reprinted by the newspaper *Vorwärts* (Nos. 271 and 274); on 20 and 24 November 1894 von Vollmar burst into print in the newspaper *Münchener Post* with a series of articles entitled *Bebel's Fahnenerhebung* which soon after were reprinted by the newspaper *Vorwärts* (Nos. 273, 274 and 276) on 23, 24 and 27 November 1894. A.Bebel responded by two statements and four articles under the general title *Zur Diskussion über den Frankfurter Parteitag. Zur Entgegnung* which were published by *Vorwärts* in November-December 1894.

435. Filippo Turati wrote to tell Engels on 28 November 1894 that a Socialist group of Italian university students was planning to release an *Almanocco socialista per l'anno 1895* and would like to have a short note from him.

436. On 6 December 1894 the members of the Social-Democratic faction in the Reichstag did not rise but remained seated as the Reichstag President von Levetzow had proposed the health of Emperor William II, and the other deputies had stood up to shout three 'hurrahs!' Such behaviour of the Social-Democratic group was qualified as *lèse-majesté*, thereupon the district court of Berlin decided to start criminal proceedings against Liebknecht. On 11 December the Reichskanzler, Prince zu Hohenlohe, demanded that the Reichstag approve the court decision. But on 15 December the Reichstag rejected this demand by 168 votes against 58.

437. A reference to the speech made by Georg von Vollmar at an open Social-Democratic meeting in Munich on 1 June 1891 on the targets and tactics of the Party under the conditions of the 'new course' so-called proclaimed by the Caprivi government. He attempted to get the Social-Democratic Party to cooperate with the ruling classes in matters of both domestic and foreign policy, especially in the event of a war within Russia. Von Vollmar's speech, which received approval from the bourgeois press, was condemned at Party meetings, by most of the Party's newspapers and then at the Erfurt Congress which took place on 14-20 October 1891.

438. Engels refers to the polemics of the newspaper *Vorwärts* with Georg von Vollmar, which was touched off by his article 'Le socialisme de M. Bismarck et le socialisme de l'empereur

Guillaume' published by the French journal *Revue bleue. Revue politique et littéraire* in June 1892. Von Vollmar claimed that some of the planks of the Erfurt Programme of the German Social-Democratic Party were akin to the state socialism of Bismarck and Emperor William II. This article sparked off a wide discussion in the Social-Democratic press. The newspaper *Vorwärts*, in its editorials on 6,12,21 and 22 July 1892 (Nos. 155,160,168,169) censured von Vollmar's views.

439. In 1867 Georg von Vollmar served as a volunteer in a detachment in the employ of the Papal States.

440. On 12 December 1894 Wilhelm Liebknecht spoke in the Reichstag in debates on the state budget for 1895-96 and other bills. Liebknecht devoted most of his speech to the Subversion Bill (see Note 428) and to the issue of *lèse-majesté* (see Note 436).

441. On 13 December 1894 Witold Jodko-Narkiewicz asked Engels for permission to translate his work *The Peasant Question in France and Germany* (present edition, Vol. 27) for the Polish journal *Przedsmit*. The translation was published in No. 12 of this journal for 1894.

442. The archives of German Social-Democracy were set up in 1882 to preserve for posterity the manuscripts of figures prominent in the German working-class movement (including those of Marx and Engels), the literature on German history and the international working-class movement as well as related press publications. With the abrogation of the Anti-Socialist Law (see Note 15) these archives were moved from Zurich to Berlin.

443. Marx died before completing the MS of his *Theories of Surplus Value* for publication; this work constituted a relatively independent part of a larger manuscipt dated 1861-63 (see present edition, Vols. 30-34). Nor could Engels realize in his lifetime the intention of publishing the Marxian manuscript as Volume IV of *Capital*. It was K. Kautsky who had *The Theories of Surplus Value* published in 1905-10.

444. This letter was written on a postcard, with the following address: Monsieur Pierre Lavroff, 328, rue Saint Jacques, Paris - France.

445. On 11 December 1894 the Italian Prime-Minister Giovanni Giolitti had to hand to the Parliament the documents on abuses in *La Banca Romana* (Roman Bank); (see Engels' article 'The Italian Panama', present edition, Vol. 27) whereupon a commission of inquiry was set up.

446. Engels indicated the following address on the postcard on which the letter was written: G.W. Lamplugh Esq., 28 Jermin St., S.W.

447. Only an excerpt from this letter to Paul Singer has come down; it was quoted in the article 'Berlin Bierboykott' published in the newspaper *Vorwärts* (No. 1) on 1 January 1895.

448. The text of this letter without the opening greeting. The initial phrase is published in the present edition, Vol. 27, under the title 'Message of Greetings to the Austrian Workers on the Daily Publication of the *Arbeiter-Zeitung*'.

449. On 23 December 1894 Laura Lafargue told Engels that the newspapers *Le Peuple* (Lyon) and *Réveil du Nord* (Lille) of the French Workers' Party would thereforth be daily publications.

450. *The Manifesto of the Communist Party* was published in the monthly *L'Ère nouvelle* (Nos. 9-11) in September-December 1894. Laura Lafargue, who wanted to have it published as a separate pamphlet, asked Engels on 23 December 1894 for advice about the preface. The

pamphlet that appeared in 1895 with the *L'Ère nouvelle* Publishers had the short prefatory note which had preceded the text of the first publication.

By referring to the 'four prefaces' to the *Manifesto* Engels meant one, to the London German-language edition of 1890; those to the German editions of 1872, 1883 and 1890, and probably the preface to the Russian edition of 1882 included into the preface of 1890.

451. Alfred-Léon Gérault-Richard, a Blanquist, was the first to be convicted in keeping with the French law of July 1894 against the anarchists (see Note 383); he received the maximum punishment—one year in prison and a fine of 3,000 francs for his article in the newspaper *Le Chambard* in which he attacked President Jean Casimir-Périer. Thereupon, on 6 January 1895, Blanquists nominated his candidacy in the 13th constituency of Paris. Gérault-Richard was elected to the Chamber of Deputies and set free.

452. Engels wrote the following dedication to Victor Adler on the title page of Volume III of *Das Kapital*: 'Seinem Victor Adler, London. 1/1.95 ('To my Victor Adler, London. 1.1.95').

453. After the publication of Volume III of *Das Kapital* in December 1894 Engels began preparations for republishing the earlier works written by Marx and himself, including those published by the *New-York Daily Tribune* in the 1850s. Therefore in January 1895 he resumed his correspondence with Ludwig Kugelmann who for many years had been collecting the works of Marx and Engels for his library.

454. In September 1893, during his trip to the European continent, Engels had two meetings with L. Kugelmann in Berlin to discuss the planned publication of the works of Marx and Engels.

455. As L. Kugelmann wrote to Engels on 7 January 1895, Hermann Meyer, who emigrated to America after the 1848 Revolution, had been collecting Marx's works. After Meyer's death in a shipwreck in 1875, the books and other documents that still remained in his collection fell into the hands of his nephew, Max Livingston of Pittsburgh, Pennsylvania. Having learned of this, Kugelmann asked Lvingston to send on Marx's works in his possession. Livingston replied in his letter on 21 March 1876 that he had only the articles and reports written by Marx for the *New-York Daily Tribune* in 1851-58 (see also Note 559).

456. On 28 December 1894 L. Kugelmann wrote this to Engels: 'Indicated in the list of 'errata' for Volume III is also "page 352, line 13 from top", but I have found none.—Will you not give the correct place in the *Neue Zeit* and *Vorwärts?*'

457. In his letter to 11 August 1894 Hermann Schlüter asked Engels to approach Eduard Bernstein with an invitation to contribute a series of articles on Volume III of *Das Kapital* for the newspaper *New-Yorker Volkszeitung* (see also this volume, p. 345).

E. Bernstein's articles under the general title *Der dritte Band des 'Kapital'* appeared in *Die Neue Zeit* (13.Jahrgang, 1. Band, Nr. 11-14, 16, 17) in 1894-95.

458. On 3 May 1894 the workers of Berlin breweries declared a 'beer boycott' to protest against the firing of about 300 coopers of the Ricksford Union of Brewers who had taken part in the May Day demonstrations of 1894. The brewery workers pressed their demands for having May 1 as a day off, for reducing the working day to 9 hours, a legal status for the trade-union organisations of brewers, an independent court of arbitration, and for the reinstatement of the sacked workers with compensation for damages. The owners of large breweries responded by a mass lockout. However, since the beer boycott attained a wide scope, in September 1894 the employers had to enter into negotiations with the workers and meet their demands by and large. An arbitration court, comprising representatives of employers and workers, was likewise set up. The beer boycott was stopped on 26 December 1894.

459. As Karl Kautsky wrote to Engels on 29 December 1894, Wilhelm Liebknecht had found the original of the letter Marx had written to Johann Baptist Schweitzer; he also said that Liebknecht was going to offer it to Dietz Publishers for publication. However, Liebknecht did not know that this letter had been published as an article—under the name 'On Proudhon'—by the newspaper *Der Sozial-demokrat* in February 1865 (see present edition, Vol. 20). Kautsky also told Engels he had found certain differences between the manuscript and the printed text of the article.

460. Probably a reference to Ernst von Köller's speech in the Reichstag on 15 December 1894. Speaking in the debates on court proceedings against W. Liebknecht (see Note 436), von Köller advocated stiffer disciplinary liability for Reichstag deputies.

461. Engels mentioned A. Bebel's speech in the Reichstag on 15 December 1894 in the debates on bringing W. Liebknecht to court trial (see Note 436). Bebel drew attention to the violation of Article 30 of the Constitution which prohibited court prosecution of deputies for statements made in the Reichstag.

462. A reference to the constitutional conflict of February 1860 in Prussia between the Prussian government supported by the Junkertum, on the one hand, and the bourgeois majority of the lower house of the Prussian Landtag, on the other, over appropriations for army reorganisation.

463. Writing to Engels on 26 November 1894, Paul Stumpf voiced his apprehensions about the differences at the Congress of the German Social-Democratic Party in Frankfurt am Main in October 1894 (see Note 418) which, in his view, showed the inadequate theoretical grounding of the young party members.

464. A reference to the *German People's Party* (*Deutsche Volkspartei*) founded in 1865; it comprised democratic elements of the petty bourgeoisie and to some extent those of some other strata of the bourgeoisie—for the most part from the southern German states. The German People's Party opposed the Prussian hegemony in Germany and championed a Great German Reich, so-called, which was to include Prussia and Austria. Although it steered anti-Prussian policies and put forward democratic slogans, the People's Party expressed at the same time the particularist aspirations of the individual German states. It was against Germany's unification into unified democratic republic.

465. An allusion to the stay of Marx and Engels in Mainz on 7-9 April 1848 en route from Paris to Cologne. While in Mainz, they met local members of the Communist League, including Paul Stumpf, to discuss the unification of workers' associations for participation in the German revolution of 1848.

466. In his letter of 6 September 1894 Pasquale Martignetti asked Engels to tell Edward Aveling that the attempt to publish in Italian his work *The Student's Marx* had not come off.

467. Martignetti's Italian translation of the preface which Engels had written to Volume III of *Capital* was published in the journal *Le Rassegna agraria, industriale, commerciale, letteraria, politica, artistica* No.1/2 for January 1895.

468. A reference to the note written by Louise Freyberger (Kautsky)—'Aus den Trades-Unions'—and published by *Die Arbeiter-Zeitung* (No. 15, 15 January 1895; signed: K.L.); also, to the anonymous report *England,* published by the same newspaper on 5 January 1895 (No. 5) in the feature *Aus den Organisationen.*

469. This dispatch by Louise Freyberger (Kautsky) about the report of Mrs. Crawford to the newspaper *Weekly Dispatch* on 6 January 1895 was published by *Die Arbeiter-Zeitung* (No. 10) on 10 January 1895 (signed: K.L.).

470. In his letter to Engels on 27 December 1894 Victor Adler asked him to invite Émile Vandervelde as a correspondent for the Vienna newspaper *Arbeiter-Zeitung*. A similar request was uttered with respect to Paul Lafargue as well (see Note 477).

471. On 27 December 1894 Victor Adler wrote in his letter to Engels about his plans to have the *Arbeiter-Zeitung* publish the article 'Karl Marx in Wien' and asked if Engels could help him with the material for it. He also said he had found some of the data in the newspaper *Der Radikale* published in 1848 by Alfred Julius Becher.

On 24 January 1895, the *Arbeiter-Zeitung* published Max Bach's article 'Karl Marx in Wien" which drew upon the facts supplied by Engels (see also this volume, p. 434).

472. An English excerpt from this letter was first published in *Marx and Engels on Malthus*. Edited by Ronald L. Meek, Lawrence and Wishart, London, 1953.

473. Engels wrote this letter on a postcard with the following address: Herrn Dr. L. Kugelmann, 20 BI Warmbüchenstr., Hannover, Germany.

474. On 9 August 1848 the Prussian National Assembly approved the motion of one of the deputies, Julius Stein, whereby the War Minister Schreckenstein was to issue an order providing for a voluntary discharge of army officers opposing the constitutional aspirations of the people. Yet no such order was issued. On 7 September 1848 Stein tabled his motion again and demanded an immediate vote on it. The proposal was adopted by 219 votes against 143; as a result, the Auerswald-Hansemann government had to tender its resignation. The Pfuel cabinet that succeeded did finally issue the order on 26 September 1848, but it remained on paper only.

475. In the preface to Volume III of *Capital* Engels took a critical view of certain tenets of George Stiebeling's work *Das Werthgesetz und die Profit-Rate. Leichtfaßliche Auseinandersetzung einiger wissenschaftlicher Fragen*. Stiebeling's letter was published in *Die Neue Zeit*, 13. Jg.1894-95, 1 Bd., No. 18.

476. Speaking on 7 January 1895 in the Reichstag debates on the proposed Subversion Bill (see Note 428), Ignaz Auer argued there were no valid motives for its introduction.

477. P. Lafargue began to cooperate with the *Arbeiter-Zeitung*. His first article "Der 'Panama Bazillus'" was published by this newspaper on 8 January 1895.

478. A hint at the Reichstag speech on 10 January 1895 by the German War Minister General Bronsart von Schellendorff in the debates on the Subversion Bill (*Die Umsturzvorlage*, see Note 428). He tried to validate the necessity of this legislation by pointing to the activity of 'instigators' who had to be combatted with the aid of law and right.

479. Speaking in the Chamber of Deputies on 10 January 1895, Étienne Millerand proposed that Gérault-Richard be released from prison (see Note 451) and demanded a broad discussion on the issue. But the Chairman of the Council of Ministers Charles Dupuy opposed the Millerand proposal and put a vote of confidence on the agenda. The Millerand proposal was turned down by 294 votes against 205. Gérault-Richard was pardoned only after the resignation of President Casimir-Périer.

480. On 24 December 1894 Édouard Vaillant sent Engels a number of draft laws on labour legislation and agrarian issues which Socialist deputies had tabled in the Chamber of

Deputies. He asked Engels to pay particular attention to the draft law on agricultural communal holdings.

481. Engels hints at a group of French Blanquist emigrés (É. Vaillant, Fr.-É. Cournet et al.) who, in June 1874, published in London the pamphlet *Aux Communeux* (*On Communal Property*).

482. The daily *La Petite République* (before 1893, *La Petite Republique Francaise*) on 12 January 1895 published an article by A.G. Rouanet; like the article of A.L. Gérault-Richard in *Le Chambart* (see Note 451) it was directed against the President of the French Republic, Casimir-Périer.

On 12 January 1895 Amand Rouanet, a Socialist deputy, made a proposal in the Chamber of Deputies providing for a cut in the pensions paid to the holder of the *Legion d'honneur* order; such pensions were not to exceed 1000 francs. The aim of this motion was to prevent arbitrary decorations being conferred on all kinds of parvenus. Rouanet intimated, however, he had no hope for an unbiased voting on his proposal (Rouanet recalled the deputies had rejected the proposal on Gérault-Richard's liberation). At this point the President of the Chamber of Deputies demanded that Rouanet leave the assembly hall, which he had to do in spite of protests from some of the deputies.

483. *Sang an Ägir*—a musical composition by Emperor William II.

484. Three successive French governments had to resign since November 1893: the Dupuy cabinet (November 1893), the Casimir-Périer cabinet (May 1894) and then the Dupuy cabinet again (January 1895). Thereupon, on 15 January 1895, President Casimir-Périer tendered his resignation; he was resolutely opposed by the Socialist faction in Parliament enjoining the French to defend the Republic 'in jeopardy'. On 17 January 1895 François Félix Faure was elected President of the French Republic.

485. The reference is to Laura Lafargue's letter of 12-13 January 1895 about the testamentary dispositions which Engels had made concerning Marx's literary heritage.

486. The French President Jean Casimir-Périer resigned on 15 January 1895. The day before, the Chamber of Deputies had declined his proposal on the order of proceedings in the inquiry into the government's involvement in major financial speculations (see Note 487).

487. Late in 1894 the French Chamber of Deputies raised the issue of the agreements concluded in 1883 by the government and the railroad company. These agreements gave the company virtually a free hand in speculation for as long as ten years; but the government refused to revise them. Then, on 14 January 1895, Étienne Millerand proposed to look into the matter and exposed the role *David Raynal*, the then Minister of Public Works, had played in that deal. The Chamber approved this motion by 263 votes against 241. A parliamentary commission of inquiry in 1896 found Raynal not guilty.

488. The leader of the Radical Party (see Note 86) Georges Benjamin Clemenceau had gained the reputation of a 'government toppler' for, as a result of his incessant interpellations in the Chamber of Deputies, the following cabinets had to resign: of Gambetta (1882), Freycinet (1882), Ferry (1885) and Brisson (1885). By calling Clemenceau 'the late', Engels intimated that the Radical Party had lost some of its former influence.

489. A reference to the article *La Situation* by Jean Juarès which was published by the newspaper *La Petite République* (No. 6855) on 20 January 1895. Juarès proposed a package of the following reforms: pensions for industrial and agricultural workers at the expense of factory and land owners; new shop regulations providing for worker participation in decision-making; an institution of labour protection inspectors; worker profit-sharing at the enterprise

level; steps to improve soil fertility. In February 1894 he tabled a motion in the Chamber of Deputies for a state monopoly of grain imports with the aim of raising the grain prices.

490. A reference to the following works of Ferdinand Tönnies: 'Neuere Philosophie der Geschichte: Hegel, Marx, Comte' (*Archiv für Geschichte der Philosophie*, Bd. 7 for 1894) which disputed the tenets of P. Barth's book *Die Geschichtsphilosophie Hegels und der Hegelianer bis auf Marx und Hartmann*; and *Pestalozzi als Sozialpädagog* (*Sozialpolitisches Centralblatt*, 3 December 1894).

491. *Comtism* or *positivism*—a trend in philosophy, sociology and historiography that surfaced in the 1830s; its leading exponent was Auguste Comte, a French philosopher and sociologist. The positivists extended the methods of natural science to social studies. They viewed the historical process as slow evolutionary changes and denied the role of revolutions.

492. This note to F. Tönnies' article 'Neuere Philosophie der Geschichte: Hegel, Marx, Comte' (see Note 490) says this in part: 'Hervorragende englische Comtisten gehörten zu den Mitbegründern der "Internationale", deren General-Sekretär K. Marx war...' ('Illustrious English Comtists were among the founders of the "International" the Secretary-General of which was K. Marx').

493. The reference is to the statements in defense of the Paris Commune made in the press by positivists Edward Beesly and Frederick Harrison between March and September 1871. Thus, from March to June 1871 *The Bee-Hive Newspaper* carried a series of articles by Professor Beesly; the opening article was entitled 'On the Paris Revolution'. In May and August 1871 *The Fortnightly Review* published two big articles by Harrison in support of the Commune.

494. The idea that besides working men, factory-owners and merchants were also among the industrialists so-called *producteurs* was formulated by Saint-Simon in his *Catéchisme des industriels*, published in Paris in 1823-24.

495. In his letter of 12 January 1895 Ludwig Kugelmann asked Engels for the names of German publications in which works by Marx and Engels had been published, signed or unsigned (see also this volume, p. 500).

496. On 23 January 1895 Victor Adler wrote to Engels that the publication of the *Arbeiter-Zeitung* 'was making very good progress': as many as 14,000 copies were being printed daily instead of the planned 10,000, while on Sundays the circulation reached 22,000 copies.

497. Engels means the Liberal Party's Right Wing akin to the Conservatives and expressing the interests of big industrial, commercial and financial bourgeoisie.

In 1893 the Gladstone cabinet tabled a second edition of the draft Home Rule Bill (see Note 77) which riled the Liberal Party's Right Wing. Having declared themselves 'independent', the Right-Wingers actually sided with the Conservatives.

498. A reference to the second electoral reform of 1867 in Britain. Town residents—house-owners and tenants who had been resident for not less than a year and whose annual rent was not under £10—received voting rights. In counties the property qualification was reduced to £12 of rent per annum. As a result, the number of eligible voters increased more than twofold (with voting rights being granted to part of industrial workers).

499. Engels refers to an article in the *Arbeiter-Zeitung* (No. 26) on 26 January 1895 in which the editors reported the confiscation of the paper's evening issue of 24 January and stated that since a larger part of the confiscated circulation had nevertheless reached the subscribers, a repeated publication of the issue was not necessary.

500. This excerpt from Emily Crawford's report in *The Weekly Dispatch* of 27 January 1895 was published by the *Arbeiter-Zeitung* (No. 32) on 1 February 1895 in Louise Freyberger's article 'Zur Charakteristik des neuen Präsidenten'.

501. On 9 January 1895 the newspaper *Vorwärts* published an appeal of the Union of Women's Societies to the German women 'of all classes and all parties' urging them to sign a petition to the Reichstag and Landtags to concede women the right of association and assembly in those German lands where they had not yet this right. Writing in *Vorwärts* on 24 January 1895, Clara Zetkin ran a sharp critique of this appeal on the grounds that it lacked a class approach. She stressed that 'the women's question ought to be considered only in the context of the total social question' and called on the proletarian women not to put their signatures on the petition.

502. Engels indicated the following address on the envelope of this letter: Herren Dr. W. Ellenbogen. IX Wasagasse 22. Wien.

503. Engels wrote these lines on a paper chit, and he gave the following address: Madame Beldinsky, 2, Regent's Square, W.C.

504. *Zemstvo*—elective district councils instituted in some provinces of European Russia in keeping with the local government reform of 1864.

505. Engels means the statement made by the Russian Tsar Nicholas II on 29 (17) January 1895 at a reception for deputations of the Russian nobility, *zemstvos* (see Note 504) and town communities on the occasion of the royal marriage. The tsar dismissed as 'idle dreams' the desire of some *zemstvo* representatives to participate 'in the affairs of domestic government' and gave it to understand he would 'safeguard the autocracy principle as firmly and steadfastly as had his lamented parent'.

506. The Committee, set up to prepare the International Socialist Working-Men's Congress due in London in 1896, suggested that henceforth it be named as an International Congress of Socialist Working Men and Trade Unions. In this connection Tomasz Jodko-Narkiewicz, a Polish Socialist emigré, asked Engels in his letter of 31 January 1895 what he and German Social-Democrats thought of the suggestion.

507. In his letter of 30 January 1895 Richard Fischer told Engels about the plans of *Vorwärts* to release in a separate edition a series of articles which Marx had written for *Neue Rheinische Zeitung. Politische-ökonomische Revue* in 1850 on the 1848-49 Revolution in France (see present edition, Vol. 10, pp. 47-131) and asked for his agreement to the proposed publication. He also asked him to write an introduction (see also Note 529).

508. A reference to the fifth and sixth authorized editions of *The Manifesto of the Communist Party* published in Berlin in 1891 and 1894, respectively.

509. The protocols of the Zurich Congress were never issued by *Vorwärts*. They appeared in Zurich in 1894 under the title: *Protokoll des Internationalen Sozialistischen Arbeiterkongresses in der Tonhalle Zürich vom 6. bis 12.August 1893*.

510. *Après nous le déluge* ['After us, the deluge']—a saying attributed to Madame de Pompadour and addressed to King Louis XV of France.

511. The final version of the text of the *Introduction to Karl Marx's The Class Struggles in France, 1848 to 1850* (1895) contained no explanatory notes from Engels in it.

512. The reference is to Richard Fischer's speech in the Reichstag on 6 February 1895 during the debates on worker representation in settling moot issues among workmen and employers.

Fischer criticised the social policies of the Centre Party (see Note 71) which did not go beyond demands for minor social concessions (like, for instance, granting recognition to working-men's alliances), while leaving aside the workers' vital interests: shorter working hours, social insurance and guarantees for freedom of association.

513. Appended to this letter were the titles of the first three chapters of Marx's work *The Class Struggles in France, 1848 to 1850* (see Note 507). Engels suggested changing the original titles 'The Defeat of June 1848', 'June 13, 1849' and 'Consequences of June 13, 1849' (as given by Marx in *Neue Rheinische Zeitung. Politische-ökonomische Revue*) for: I. 'From February to June 1848', II. 'From June 1848 to June 13, 1849', and III. 'From June 14, 1849 to March 10, 1850', respectively. As Chapter IV Engels suggested materials on the revolutionary events in France from 'The Third International Review' published by the *Neue Rheinische Zeitung. Politische-ökonomische Revue*(No. 5-6) for 1850; he entitled this chapter 'The Abolition of Universal Suffrage in 1850' (see present edition, Vol. 10, pp. 47-145). The above work—*The Class Struggles in France*—was to be published as a separate booklet.

514. Louis Napoleon Bonaparte used the decision by the French National Assembly in May 1850 to abrogate universal suffrage, to seize power and impose dictatorial rule. Following the coup d'état of December 1851 he re-instituted universal suffrage in an election to the Legislative Corps.

515. Engels indicated the following address on the envelope: Julius Motteler Esq., 30, Hugo Road, Tufnell Park, N.

516. Acting on Engels' request, J. Motteler had made inquiries in Germany and, having received a letter from a Johann Meyer in which Theodor Barlen's person was confirmed, sent it to Engels (see this volume, p. 452).

517. Concerning the French translation of Engels' work *On the History of Early Christianity* (see present edition, Vol. 27) made by Laura Lafargue (see also Note 420).

518. A reference to the lecture *L'Idéalisme de l'histoire* which Jean Juarès delivered in Paris early in 1895.

519. *Stoicism*—a philosophical system founded by Zeno and current in Ancient Greece between the late fourth century B.C. and the sixth century B.C. The Stoics believed that all events were the result of divine will and that therefore man should be calmly accepting and free from passion, grief or joy.

520. Engels refers to Y. Zack's article 'Historical Materialism', published in the first issue of the journal *Russian Heritage* for 1895, and also to N.Mikhailovsky's review 'Literature and Life', published by the above journal in 1894 (No. 1).

521. In his letter to Engels on 20 February 1895, G. Plekhanov called N. Danielson a 'reactionary and utopian, all in one'.

522. Refers to Engels' fifth article 'On Social Relations in Russia' (see present edition, Vol. 24, pp. 39-50) in the series *Refugee Literature* which, alongside the first and second articles, he included in the collection *Internationales aus dem Volksstaat (1871-75)*, as well as to the *Afterword* (1894) which Engels had written for this collection (see present edition, Vol. 27, pp. 421-33).

523. Writing to Engels on 20 February 1895, G. Plekhanov described Tsar Nicholas II as 'the young idiot of the Winter Palace' whose speech of 29 January 1895 'has done a great service to the revolutionary party'.

524. J. Motteler told Engels in his letter of 28 February 1895 that on 18 February he had been attacked in his house by two anarchists who had identified themselves by false names— Alexander Cohen and Zimmer.

525. *National workshops* were set up by the Provisional Government of France immediately after the February Revolution of 1848 for jobless workers, artisans, office employees, school teachers as well as petty entrepreneurs who were given menial jobs at miserable wages.

526. According to the local government reform on 1888, the *London County Council* could be elected by all male citizens who were eligible to vote in parliamentary elections, as well as by women 30 years and older. *The London County Council*, which controlled taxation, local budgets, etc., was elected every three years. The 1889 and 1892 elections brought victory to the *Progressists*, a group comprising bourgeois Liberals, members of the Fabian Society (see Note 43) and Socialists; it defeated the group of *Moderates* that united the Liberal Unionists (see Note 206) and the Conservatives. At the elections of 2 March 1895, the *Moderates* gained a few new seats in the *London County Council* because of the refusal of the Socialists to vote in a bloc with the *Progressists*.

527. Nikolai Danielson wrote in this letter that the passage in Engels' preface to Volume III of *Capital* about Marx's research on Russian land ownership made him want to find out if there were any notes written by Marx on this topic.

528. In his letter to Engels of 10 March 1895 N. Danielson enclosed a message to Andrei Konov, a Russian emigré in Berlin who undertook the translation. N. Danielson's book *Essays on Our Post-Reform Social Economy* was translated by G. Polonsky and came out in Munich in 1899.

529. On 6 March 1895 Engels received a letter from Richard Fischer, the Executive Secretary of the German Social-Democratic Party, who requested him to soften what appeared to be the stridently revolutionary tenor of the manuscript of the *Introduction to Karl Marx's The Class Struggles in France, 1848 to 1850* (1895); R. Fischer feared the moot points would be taken advantage of by the enemies of Social-Democracy, a making it easier for the government to push through the Subversion Bill (see Note 428). Being obliged to fulfill the request of the Party's Executive Board, Engels agreed to make some amendments in the text and omit some of the passages, e.g., ones dealing with the armed struggle which the proletariat was to wage against the bourgeoisie. Engels admitted that the original text of the *Introduction* 'suffered somewhat' as a result of such deletions (see this volume, p. 480).

530. *May laws*—the four laws adopted at Bismarck's initiative in May 1873; they provided for strict state control over the activity of the Catholic Church. These laws marked the culmination of the *Kulturkampf* ('Struggle for Culture') policy.

531. *Mennonites*—an evangelical Protestant Christian sect founded in the 1530s-1540s in Friesland by Anabaptists who, after the defeat of the Peasant War of 1524-26 and the Münster Commune of 1534-35, abandoned their revolutionary aspirations. Named after Menno Simons, the founder of this sect, Mennonites oppose the taking of oaths, infant baptism, military service, and the acceptance of public office; they favour plain dress and plain living.

532. The movement for universal suffrage organised by the Social-Democrats gained new momentum in Austria in 1895 (see Note 270). There were 12 mass rallies in Vienna on 19 February 1895, in support of this demand. The newspaper *Arbeiter-Zeitung* carried regular reports by V. Adler on this matter.

533. The English text of this letter was first published in K. Marx and F. Engels, *Selected Correspondence*, Progress Publishers, Moscow, 1965.

534. In May 1895 Engels wrote the article 'Law of Value and Rate of Profit' conceived as an addendum to Volume III of *Capital*. It was published shortly after his death by *Die Neue Zeit* (14.Jg., 1. Bd., Nos. 1,2 for 1895/96) under the heading: 'Fr. Engels' letzte Arbeit: Ergänzung und Nachtrag zum dritten Buch des 'Kapitals'' (see present edition, Vol. 37).

Engels intended to write yet another article, 'The Stock Exchange', but could not go further than the general outline (see present edition, Vol. 37).

535. The reference is to Peter Fireman's article 'Kritik der Marx'schen Werttheorie' published in the economic and statistical yearbook *Jahrbücher fur Nationalökonomie und Statistik* for 1892 (3. Folge, Bd. 3). Engels gave a positive appraisal of this article in his preface to Volume III of *Capital*. However, Conrad Schmidt took exception to this assessment: writing to Engels on 1 March 1895, he said Fireman had only repeated what Professor Wilhelm Lexis had found before him.

536. A reference to W. Lexis' article 'Die Marx'sche Kapitaltheorie' published in the yearbook *Jahrbücher fur Nationalökonomie und Statistik* (11 Bd.) for 1885, and C. Schmidt's book *Die Durchschnittsprofitrate auf Grundlage des Marx'schen Wertgesetzes* published in Stuttgart in 1889.

537. *The West Frankish Kingdom* came into being after the disintegration of the Frankish Empire of Charlemagne (Charles the Great). According to the Verdun Treaty of 843, it was divided among Charlemagne's three grandsons. The West Frankish Kingdom occupied a territory of roughly what is now France.

538. *Assises of Jerusalem* (Assises de Iérusalem)—a code of laws for courts in the Kingdom of Jerusalem established by the medieval crusaders after the First Crusade; this kingdom was in existence from the end of the eleventh to the late thirteenth century.

539. A reference ot the two articles by Paul Lafargue: 'Breve risposta - domanda ai critici di Marx circa la teoria de valore' and *Replica di Lafargue* published by *Critica Sociale*, Nos. 20 and 22 on 16 October and 16 November 1894.

540. The letters to P. Lafargue and A. Labriola have not been found.

541. In his letter of 5 March 1895 K. Kautsky told Engels about J. Platter's critique of Volume III of *Capital* in the Swiss journal on economic and social policy—*Schweizerische Blätter für Wirtschafts- und Sozialpolitik* (1. Märzheft, 1895)—under the title 'Die Lösung'. Kautsky added he had declined E. Ferri's offer for publication of his article in defence of the Marxian theory of value.

542. In March 1895 Victor Adler, the editor of the *Arbeiter-Zeitung*, was sentenced to a seven-week term in prison for the paper's criticisms of the Austrian government. He was incarcerated in the Vienna prison Rudolfsheim from 18 May to 18 June 1895.

543. This is in reply to Carl Hackenberg's letter to Engels of 8 March 1895 in which he asked for more information about the activities of Hermann Becker, a German lawyer and journalist, in 1848-50; C. Hackenberg planned to write a biography of H. Becker. Probably unable to verify data on the events 45 years ago, Engels allowed himself some inaccuracies in his reply.

544. With the outbreak of the 1848 Revolution in Germany Marx and Engels moved from Paris to Cologne where they arrived on 11 April 1848. On 15 April or thereabouts Engels set off on a tour of German towns and returned to Cologne on 20 May 1848. In 1848-49 H. Becker was one of the leaders of *The Cologne Democratic Association* (see Note 547).

545. C. Hackenberg had asked Engels if H. Becker had stayed put in Cologne in the spring of 1848 or he had undertaken trips to other towns to propagandise his ideas.

546. C. Hackenberg had inquired about H. Becker's attitude to the Schleswig-Holstein issue.
This issue, concerning the Danish duchies of Schleswig and Holstein, became particularly acute during the Revolution of 1848-49. Backed by Prussia, the German population of these regions in March 1848 had begun a war of national liberation against the Danish monarchy.

547. *The Cologne Democratic Association*—formed in Cologne in April 1848; until April 1849 Marx and Engels had been among its leadership.

548. *Der Kölner Arbeiterverein* (*The Cologne Workers' Union*)—a working-men's assocation founded on 13 April 1848. Owing to the influence of Marx and Engels, it became a major centre of revolutionary activity involving working men and peasants.

549. Engels means *The Central March Association*, named after the March 1848 Revolution in Germany. Founded in Frankfurt am Main at the end of November 1848 by Left-Wing deputies to the Frankfurt National Assembly, it had branches in various German towns.

550. The *Neue Rheinische Zeitung* never published any articles signed by H.B.

551. Engels answers C. Hackenberg's question whether he knew of the book *Ungarns Fall*, allegedly by H. Becker.

552. The *Westdeutsche Zeitung*, published by H. Becker in Cologne, was launched on 25 May 1849 immediately after the termination of the publication of the *Neue Rheinische Zeitung*. Heinrich Bürgers did not take part in setting up the *Westdeutsche Zeitung*.

553. The reference is to the *Cologne Communist Trial* when members of the Communist League were framed on the basis of forged evidence and perjury; they were accused of 'conspiring' against the Prussian state. The trial took place in Cologne from 4 October to 12 November 1852. Hermann Becker was among the defendants; he was sentenced to five years' imprisonment in a fortress (see this edition, Vol. 11: Marx, 'Revelations Concerning the Communist Trial in Cologne').

554. In October 1894 Pablo Iglesias was sentenced to a forty-day term in prison for leading a strike action of Málaga textile workers.
This strike broke out in the first half of October 1894 at the textile mills of Marquis Larios in protest over the decision of the entrepreneurs to disband the Textile Workers' Union and punish 19 workers active in it. The four thousand strikers were joined by workers in other cities, Madrid included. The Spanish Socialist Workers' Party, led by P. Iglesias, captained the movement of Spanish workers in support of the Málaga strike. Despite the intervention of the government which sided with the factory-owners, the 80-day strike action ended in a workers' victory. P. Iglesias appealed to Engels with a request to help in rallying British working men and Socialist organisations to support of the striking Spanish workers.

555. Writing to Engels on 16 March 1895, Carl Hirsch asked to review the four articles he had written for *Das sozialpolitisches Centralblatt*: i) 'Intensifikation der Arbeit und Verkürzung der Arbeitszeit', published on 8 January 1894—No. 15; ii) 'Intensifikation der Arbeit und ihr Widerstand', published on 19 February 1894—No. 21; iii) 'Die ökonomische und die sozialpolitische Schätzung der Arbeitskraft', published on 14 January 1895—No. 16; and iv) 'Die Verdichtung der Arbeit unter sozial-politischem Gesichtspunkt,' published on 18 February 1895—No. 21. C. Hirsch wanted to have these articles published as a separate booklet.

556. Refers to the by-election to the Reichstag in Cologne, due on 13 May 1895. It was between Franz Lütgenau, a Social-Democrat, and Adolf Greiß, representing the Centre Party. A. Greiß won.

557. The Cologne-published newspaper *Rheinische Zeitung* which, in 1894-95, was edited by Carl Hirsch.

558. Ludwig Kugelmann had been looking for the earlier writings by Marx and Engels for the publication of a complete collection of their works (see Note 453). In July 1846 the journal *Das Westphälische Dampfboot* had published, anonymously, Marx's and Engels' *Circular Against Kriege* (see present edition, Vol. 6, pp. 35-51); and in August and September 1847 it had published Chapter 4 of the second volume of *The German Ideology:* 'Karl Grün: *Die Soziale Bewegung in Frankreich und Belgien*' (Darmstadt, 1845) or 'The Historiography of True Socialism' (see present edition, Vol. 5, pp. 484-531).

559. L. Kugelmann, acting on Engels' request in connection with the preparation of a complete collection of Marx's works for the press (see this volume, p. 504), got in touch with Max Livingston. On 21 March 1895 Kugelmann informed Engels of Livingston's reply: 18 years before he had commissioned Friedrich Sorge to send Hermann Meyer's heritage (see Note 455) to London.

560. Wilhelm Liebknecht's speech in the Reichstag on 2 March 1895 during the debates on the budget committee's report on appropriations for the maintenance of the army. Liebknecht spoke out for a dissolution of the regular army and setting up instead militia-type forces after the Swiss model.

561. A reference to the book *Die Vorläufer des Neuren Sozialismus* which appeared in 1895 as the first volume of *Die Geschichte des Sozialismus in Einzeldarstellungen* published in Stuttgart by K. Kautsky, E. Bernstein, P. Lafargue, F. Mehring and others. The first part of Volume I—*Von Plato bis zu den Wiedertäufern*—was written by K. Kautsky; the second part includes contributions by K. Kautsky, P. Lafargue, C. Hugo as well as E. Bernstein's *Kommunistische und demokratisch-sozialistische Strömungen während der englischen Revolution des 17. Jahrhunderts.*

562. The *Anabaptists* (lit., those baptised again) belonged to one of the most radical and democratic religious-philosophical trends in Switzerland, Germany and the Netherlands during the Reformation. This sect denied the vaildity of infant baptism and practised baptism of adults.

563. *Die Taboriten*—the title of the sixth chapter of Part III of the Kautsky work *Von Plato bis zu den Wiedertäufern.* The *Taborites* (so called after their camp in the town of Tabor in Bohemia)—a radical trend in the Hussite movement. In contrast to the Calixtines, they formed a revolutionary, democratic wing of the Hussites; their demands reflected the striving of the peasantry and the urban lower classes to put an end to feudal oppression and all manifestations of social and political injustice.

564. The Reichstag at its session on 23 March 1895 rejected, by 163 votes against 146, the proposal to send a message of greetings to Bismarck on the occasion of his 80th birthday. Voting against were Social-Democrats, deputies of the Free-Thinking Party, the Centre Party, those representing the Polish lands, and others. This decision aroused the anger of Emperor William II who sent a cable to Bismarck expressing his profound indignation over the incident; he said the Reichstag decision was 'in gross contradiction to the feelings of all German princes and their peoples'.

565. In December 1878 Bismarck proposed a draft reform of customs tariffs to a Reichstag commission set up for the purpose. Following debates in the Reichstag, this bill was adopted on 12 July 1879. It provided for a substantial increase in the customs duties on imports of iron, machinery, textiles, grain, cattle, fats, flax, timber, etc.

566. The Centre Party (see Note 71).

567. A reference to P. Lafargue's work *Origine et évolution de la propriété* which came off the press in Paris in 1895. At the publisher's suggestion, it appeared under the same cover as Ives Gugot's work *Réfutation de l'essai sur l'origine de la propriété* which refuted P. Lafargue's conclusions.

568. An excerpt from this letter was first published in English in K. Marx, *Selected Works*. In two volumes. Vol. 2, International Publishers, New York, 1936.

569. On 30 March 1895 the newspaper *Vorwärts* carried the leading article 'Wie man heute Revolutionen macht' which cited, without prior consent from Engels, selected excerpts from his 'Introduction' to Marx's work *The Class Struggles in France, 1848 to 1850*. The aim was to represent Engels as a protagonist of an exclusively peaceful takeover of political power by the working class.

   Shortly before the appearance of this work in a separate edition, the 'Introduction' had been published in the journal *Die Neue Zeit* (13. Jg., 1894/95, 2. Bd., Nr. 27, 28) in the same form as in the separate edition (see Note 529). The original version did not see print even after the threat of a new Anti-Socialist Law in Germany had been over.

570. Engels means *Ein Wort des 'Adressaten'*—the introduction which Julius Wolf wrote to F. Bertheau's book *Fünf Brief über Marx an Herrn Dr. Julius Wolf*, published in Jena in 1895. In his Introduction J. Wolf replied to Engels' critical remarks on his address in the preface to Volume III of *Capital* (see present edition, Vol. 37).

571. The draft of this letter was written on the blank part of a page of Harry Quelch's letter to Engels of 1 April 1895. H. Quelch asked Engels for an interview about the contemporary condition of the working class in the May issue of the newspaper *Justice*.

572. An English excerpt from this letter was first published in: K. Marx, *Selected Works*. In two volumes. Vol. 2, New York, 1936. The full English text of the letter appeared in Frederick Engels, Paul and Laura Lafargue. *Correspondence*, Vol. 3, 1891-95, Moscow, [1963].

573. An allusion to P. Lafargue's book *Le droit à la paresse. Réfutation du 'Droit au travail' de 1848*, published in Paris in 1883.

574. This chapter of P. Lafargue's work *Origine et évolution de la propriété* bore the title 'Collectivisme consanguin'.

575. *Lex Alamannorum* (The Law of the Alamanni)—part of the *Leges Alamannorum*, or the records of the common law code of the Alamanni (Alemanni), the Germanic tribes which invaded and settled in Alsace and part of Switzerland in the early 5th century A.D. The Alamannic laws, dating from the 6th to 8th centuries A.D., reflected the transition from the primitive tribal system to early feudal society.

576. *Lex Salica* (Salic Law)—a code of laws of Germanic tribes, including the Salian Franks. Recorded in the early 6th century A.D., this code reproduces various stages of archaic court proceedings and is regarded as an important historical document illustrative of the evolution of Frankish society from the primitive communal system to nascent feudal society. The Salians were a tribe of Franks who settled along the Ijssel River, in the Netherlands, in the 4th century A.D.

577. On 3 April 1895 Richard Fischer told Engels—who had begun preparing for publication of the early works of Marx from the newspaper *Rheinische Zeitung*—that Hans Baake, a German Socialist, was planning a similar edition. Baake's plans never materialised.

578. A reference to the following articles written by Marx and published by the *Rheinische Zeitung* in 1842-early 1843: *Proceedings of the Sixth Rhine Province Assembly. First Article. Debates on Freedom of the Press and Publication of the Proceedings of the Assembly of the Estates; Proceedings of the Sixth Rhine Assembly. Third Article. Debates on the Law on Thefts of Wood; Justification of the Correspondent from the Mosel* (present edition, Vol. I, pp. 132-81, 224-63, 332-58). Engels never realised his intention to have these articles published in a separate edition.

579. Engels alludes to Boris Krichevsky, a Russian Socialist, who, without his consent, had published in 1894 the Russian translation of Marx's works *The Eighteenth Brumaire of Louis Bonaparte* and *Wage Labour and Capital* (see note 368). This publication was undertaken in the series 'Social-Democratic Library' (original in Russian).

580. Engels had stayed in Berlin on 16-28 September 1893 (see Note 262).

581. This letter was first published in English in: K. Marx, F. Engels, *Letters on 'Capital'*, London, 1983.

582. N. Baudeau's work *Explication du tableau économique* published in 1846 in the book *Physiocrates. Avec une introduction sur la doctrine des physiocrates, des commentaires et des notices historiques*, par E. Daire.

583. Refers to the royalties for Marx's *The Class Struggles in France, 1848 to 1850*, published in Berlin in 1895. Engels had written an introduction to this edition (see Note 507).

584. By the Mosel article (subsequently, the Mosel articles) Engels means the Marx article 'Justification of the Correspondent from the Mosel' published in January 1843 in five numbers of *Rheinische Zeitung*. Marx had planned five parts of this article (see present edition, vol. I, p. 334); however, only two parts had been written and published (ibid., pp. 334-58).

585. In his letter to Engels on 27 January 1894 R. Fischer proposed that works by Marx and Engels should be published in installments. In his opinion, this did not exclude the possibility of a complete collection of works, as Engels had contemplated.

586. The second German edition of volume I of *Das Kapital* was published in 1872-73 in nine installments. Marx wrote an afterword to the entire edition.

587. Marx had been writing articles for *New-York Daily Tribune* from August 1851 to 1862 at the suggestion of the paper's editor Charles Dana. A significant number of contributions, especially on military matters, were written by Engels at Marx's request. Some of the dispatches were co-authored by Marx and Engels. The articles which Marx and Engels wrote for *New-York Daily Tribune* have been published in volumes 11-17 of the present edition.

588. On 14 April 1895 *Vorwärts* published a note entitled 'Parteipresse' informing readers about the changes in *Le Socialiste*: the larger format of this periodical, the appointment of A. Zévaés as editor-in-chief and of René-Auguste Chauvin as managing editor.

589. At Engels' request Laura Lafargue told him in detail about the characters in Molière's plays in her letter of 6 April 1895. Engels showed an interest in Sganarelle in view of Achille Loria's theory that he personified vulgar common sense.

590. The reference is to 'true socialism', a trend that gained wide currency in Germany in the 1840s, chiefly amongst the petty bourgeois intellectuals. Critical of capitalism, True

Socialists idealised the pre-capitalist way of life (medieval guilds, etc.) and believed Germany could reach socialism without passing through the stage of capitalist industry. True Socialists would hold forth on friendship and solidarity, and preach against participation in political activity and the struggle for democracy; they denied the necessity of a bourgeois-democratic revolution in Germany. The views of 'True Socialists' were sharply criticised by Marx and Engels.

591. Writing to Engels on 21 March 1895, Ludwig Kugelmann suggested publishing a complete collection of works by Marx and Engels, beginning with articles published in *Deutsch-Französische Jahrbücher* and *The Manifesto of the Communist Party* .

592. Probably a reference to the copy of Marx's *The Class Struggles in France, 1848 to 1850* the receipt of which L. Kugelmann acknowledged in his reply letter to Engels on 14 July 1895.

593. Some of the data given by Engels in this and in the preceding paragraph and referring to his *curriculum vitae* are erroneous: he was in Bonn after 8 October 1842, the day when he had completed his military service in Berlin; Marx left the editorial board of the *Rheinische Zeitung* on 17 March 1843, and his statement to this effect was published in the newspaper on 18 March 1843. The ban on *Rheinische Zeitung* of 1 April 1843 was issued on 21 January 1843 with the adoption, on 19 January of the same year, of the decision by the Prussian government to close down the newspaper; this decision was published in the *Kölnische Zeitung* on 26 January and in the *Düsseldorfer Zeitung* on 27 January 1843. Marx left Cologne for Bad-Kreuznach in May 1843.

594. On 18 April 1895 the Berlin Polizei-Präsidium imposed censorship over theatrical performances of *Die Freie Volksbühne Gesellschaft* (see Note 256). Its steering committee replied by stopping performances altogether, while its president, Franz Mehring, appealed to the court and demanded the defence of the right of free expression. Since the court had rejected this plea, the Free Popular Stage Society disbanded in March 1896, but it was reinstituted in the spring of 1897 with a new charter.

595. Engels refers to the copies of the two articles written by Marx for the *Rheinische Zeitung* in 1842: 'Debates on Freedom of the Press and Publication of the Proceedings of the Assembly of the Estates', and 'Debates on the Law on Thefts of Wood'—the copies which R. Fischer sent him on 6 May 1895.

596. Engels stayed at Eastbourne from early June to 24 July 1895.

597. This is in reply to the message from Hugo Heller, a bookseller in Vienna, in which he informed Engels that a Vienna publisher, Ignaz Brand, had sent him the Czech translation of Marx's *Wage Labour and Capital.*
Engels wrote this letter on a postcard, indicating the following address: Herrn Ignaz Brand Exped. Wiener Volksbuchhandlung VI, Gumpendorferstraße 8. *Wien, Austria.*

598. On 15 May 1895 Carl Hirsch, then cooperating with the *Rheinische Zeitung*, told Engels about criminal charges being brought against A. Hofrichter, the managing editor of that newspaper. The criminal proceedings had been instituted by Schellmann, the superintendent of a reformatory at Braunweiler, since the newspaper had accused him of intensifying the inmates' work. The editors asked Engels to find James Politt, a British journalist who had, at the request of British factory-owners, visited a number of German prisons, including one at Braunweiler, and had described his impressions in the newspaper *The Hardwareman.* The *Rheinische Zeitung* editors wanted Politt as a witness at the trial.

599. Engels had written the rough copy of this letter somewhat earlier, on 12 May 1895.

600. In his letter of 6 May 1895 to Engels, K. Kautsky asked him to write a section on the First International for Volume IV of *Die Geschichte des Sozialismus in Einzeldarstellungen*; this volume was to come out in 1897.

601. In his reply to Engels on 25 May 1895 K. Kautsky wrote that he and E. Bernstein had not asked Engels for contributions to *Die Geschichte des Sozialismus* only because in the winter of 1893-94 he, Engels, had been busy preparing the manuscript of Volume III of *Capital* for the press.

602. In his work *Von Plato bis zu den Wiederstäufern* K. Kautsky had translated Ulrich von Hutten's *Epistolae obscurorum virorum* as *Briefe unberühmter Männer*; like Johannes Janssen, the author of *Die Geschichte des deutchen Volkes set dem Ausgang des Mittelalters*, Kautsky believed the accepted translation of the *Epistolae*'s name was not clear enough.

603. In 1890-95 Friedrich Adolf Sorge had written a series of articles for the journal *Die Neue Zeit* on the labour movement in the United States in a period from the 1830s to 1892: 'Die Arbeiterbewegung in den Vereinigten Staaten'. As far back as 21 November 1891 Engels had suggested that these articles should be published in a separate edition and had promised to find a publisher (see present edition, vol. 46). However, this publication did not materialise at the time. A book of his articles in Russian translation appeared in St. Petersburg only in 1907, i.e., after Sorge's death (1906).

604. Engels wrote this letter on a postcard and gave the following address: Herrn Richard Fischer, Buchhandlung des *Vorwärts*, Beuthstr. 2, Berlin, Germany.

605. A. Hofrichter probably intended to have these articles reprinted in the *Rheinische Zeitung*.

606. Concerning the additions and alterations for the revised German translation of Nikolai Danielson's book *Essays on Our Post-Reform Social Economy* (original in Russian). The author had sent these corrections enclosed in his letter to Engels of 1 June 1895 for A. Konov, the translator.

   The German edition of this book appeared only in 1899 in G. Polonsky's translation.

607. The reference is to Engels' work *What Have the Working Classes to Do with Poland* (present edition, Vol. 20) which, translated into Polish, was published by the journal *Przedswit* (No. 7) in July 1895 under the title: *Klasa robotnicza a rwestya polska*.

608. Engels wrote the following address on the envelope of the letter: Sig. avv° Filippo Turati, 23, Portici Galleria V.E. Milano, Italy. The first page of the letter has the note written by F. Turati: 'Riferito al Arturo Labriola. 1.7.95' ('Told Arturo Labriola, 1.07.95').

609. On 19 June 1895 F. Turati asked Engels for permission to allow Arturo Labriola to make a précis of *Capital* for publication in Italian.

610. In the article 'Un fatto personale che infolge una questione generale', published under the pseudonym Noi ('We') in the *Critica Sociale* (No. 10) on 16 May 1895. F. Turati reproduced a passage from the letter which Engels had written on 8 January 1895 to Pasquale Martignetti (see this volume, pp. 407). Writing to Engels on 1 July 1895, F. Turati apologised for not having indicated the author of the passage quoted.

   F. Turati wrote the above article in reply to A. Labriola's articles on the situation in Italy, which were published anonymously on 3 and 7 May 1895 by the *Liepziger Volkszeitung*. In them Labriola had criticised the stand of the Italian Socialist Party at a parliamentary election (see Note 611).

611. At the election to the Italian Parliament on 26 May and 2 June 1895, the Italian Socialist Party, which had joined in a coalition with the Radicals and Republicans against the Crispi government and its supporters, gained 17 seats in the Parliament.

612. Engels wrote these lines on a postcard showing a view of the Eastbourne beach. Laura Lafargue wrote the following address on this card: Monsieur Paul Lafargue, Le Perreux, Siene, *France*.

613. Engels wrote this letter on a postcard to the following address which he indicated on it: Herrn Richard Fischer, Buchhdlg. des *Vorwärts*, Beuthstr. 2, Berlin S.W. 19; Germany.

614. In April 1895 the Paris monthly journal *Le devenir social* carried Edward Aveling's article 'Les sans-travail en Engleterre' in which he claimed that Keir Hardie, the leader of the Independent Labour Party, denied the fact of unemployment in Britain. In June 1895 the French youth monthly *La jeunesse socialiste* reprinted excerpts from this article. On 6 July 1895 the journal *Labour Leader* carried a refutation from K. Hardie.

615. Engels wrote these lines on a postcard and indicated the following address: Ed. Bernstein, Esq., 29, Red Lion Square, W.C. London.

616. Engels wrote this letter on a postcard to the following address: Mrs. Aveling, Greenstreet Green, near *Chislehurst, Kent.*

617. Apparently a reference to the proposal made to E. Aveling in June 1895 by the Glasgow organisation of the Independent Labour Party (see Note 114) to nominate his candidacy at the forthcoming parliamentary election. Aveling declined for reason of poor health. This was reported in *The Labour Leader* (No. 67) on 13 July 1895 (see Note 614).

618. A reference to the work of Eleanor Marx-Aveling translating into English the French edition of G. Plekhanov's pamphlet 'Anarchism and Socialism' (original in Russian). The English edition, to which Eleanor wrote a preface, was published in London in 1895.

619. This letter was written on a postcard with a view of Eastbourne. Engels gave the following address: Sig. Filippo Turati, Portici Galleria V.E. 23, Milano, Italy.

620. A reference to the first part of A. Labriola's article 'En memoire du Manifeste du parti communiste' published by *Le Devenir social* (No. 3) in June 1895; the second part of this article appeared in the next, July issue of the journal.

621. This letter, discovered in the late 1970s in the National Archives of Classic German Literature at Weimar, opens the correspondence of Engels with Arnold Ruge, a German journalist. Their first meeting took place in late March 1842 in Berlin where Engels was doing his military service. The present letter sheds additional light on Engels' little-known article on Dante which Engels mentioned in his second letter to Ruge on 15 June 1842 (see present edition, Vol. 2, p. 543), an article which has not survived.

622. A. Ruge complied with this request. In a review published by the *Deutsche Jahrbücher fur Wissenschaft und Kunst* (Nos. 126-128) on 28, 30 and 31 May 1842 he praised Engels' work *Schelling and Revelation*. Ruge stressed in particular the author's clarity in his exposition and critique of the Schelling philosophy.

623. Engels means Ludwig Feuerbach's *Das Wesen ses Christenthums.*

624. Marx refers to the brochure written by A. Ruge and O. Wigand: *An die Hohe Zweite Kammer der Sächsischen Ständeversammlung*. 'Complaint against the suppression of the journal Deutsche Jahrbücher fur Wissenschaft und Kunst, as ordered by the High Ministry for the Interior and carried out on 3 January 1843'). The *Rheinische Zeitung* did not publish

this pamphlet; however, the supplements to No. 71 and 73 and 12 and 14 March, 1843, respectively, carried Pfützer's review (Pfützer was the paper's Dresden correspondent): *Über die Broschüre an die Hohe Zweite Kammer der Sächsischen Ständeversammlung.*

625. Marx—at the time editor of the *Neue Rheinische Zeitung*—wrote this letter in reply to Friedrich Kapp, a German National-Liberal, who was cooperating with the newspaper, about the delay in the payment of royalties that were due to him. Acting on Marx's advice, on 11 December 1848 Kapp presented a promissory note to the newspaper, but it was not paid. Later Marx reimbursed the required sum to him.

626. Marx wrote the address on the envelope: M. Fr. *Kapp. Paris.* Avenue Breutell 28.

627. This letter was first published in the *Catalogue de la vente a l'Hotel Drouot le 16 novembre 1893* with a note attached to it that Marx had addressed the letter to *'son collaborateur et secrétaire Reinländer'.* It must have been George Friedrich Rheinländer, a German salesman in 1850s-1860s, who then emigrated to London.

628. The present letter was addressed to Philip Stephen King, the owner of a London book-selling firm that dealt in official government publications, draft bills, statistical reports and communications from academic and state institutions overseas. In the 1860s, 1870s and 1880s Marx approached King on several occasions with a request to send reference litera-ture to him (see also present edition, Vols. 42, 43).

629. Engels made his will already in Marx's lifetime, bequeathing all his property to Marx. After Marx's death Engels drew up another will according to which all his property was divided in equal shares among Marx's daughters Laura and Eleanor, the children of Jenny (the deceased daughter of Marx) and Helene Demuth, Marx's housemaid.

630. *Lincoln's Inn (Inn of Court)*—one of the four London legal societies with the exclusive right to admit persons to practice at the bar.

631. This document is reproduced from the copy made by E. Bernstein and Louise Freyberger (Mrs. Kautsky), with the following postscript which A. Bebel wrote on the envelope: 'The letter with codicils, dated 14 November 1894, to Engels' Testament. Lay in the drawer of Engels' desk'.

632. This letter is a limerick jotted down by an unknown person. Engels signed his name with a pencil. First published in English in the German edition of the works of Marx and Engels: K. Marx, F. Engels, *Werke*, Bd. 38. Berlin, 1968.

633. These lines were written by Louise Kautsky (Freyberger) on a postcard. Engels wrote the following address: Mrs. Natalie Liebknecht, 160, Kantstraße, Charlottenburg Berlin.

634. In that letter Isaak Hourwich, a Russian economist living in the United States, told Engels about the forthcoming Russian-language publication of his work *The Economics of the Russian Village* and asked him to supplement it with an appendix of the notes which Marx had made from Russian statisical books.

635. Hermann Engels wrote this draft with a pencil on the back of L. Siebold's letter to F. Engels of 22 July 1895.
      This letter must have been rewritten in a fair copy by Louise Freyberger (Mrs. Kautsky) and sent to L. Siebold.

636. The reference is to L. Siebold's letter of 22 April 1895 in which he asked for Engels' opinion concerning the publication of sketches on the history of chemistry from C. Schorlemmer's literary remains (see Note 312).

NAME INDEX

A

of Comité Révolutionnaire Central.—11, 209, 242, 336-7, 345, 354

Arnold, Sir Alfred (1835-1908)—Tory candidate during by-elections in Halifax in 1893, M. P. (from 1896).—103

Aschan, Ossian—chemist, professor Edvard Hjelt's assistant at Helsinki University.—404

Aston—stock-exchange broker in London.—539

Atabekjanz, Jossif Nersessovich (1870-1916)—Armenian Social-Democrat; agronomist by profession; translated several works by Marx and Engels into Armenian.—371

Auer, Ignaz (1846-1907)—German Social-Democrat; saddler by trade; a leader of the Social-Democratic Party; was elected deputy to the Reichstag several times.—41, 416

August—see *Bebel, August.*

Augustus (*Gaius Julius Caesar Octavianus*) (63 B. C.-A. D. 14)—Roman Emperor (27 B. C.-A. D. 14).—266

Aveling, Edward Bibbins (1851-1898)—English journalist, one of the translators into English of Marx's *Capital*, Volume One; member of the Social-Democratic Federation from 1884; subsequently one of the founders of the Socialist League; an organiser of a mass movement of unskilled workers and unemployed in the late 1880s and early 1890s; husband of Marx's daughter Eleanor.—12, 18, 26, 34, 37, 74, 82, 95, 108, 123, 124, 137, 153, 176, 192, 220, 224, 268, 277, 314, 335, 345, 354, 407, 421, 517, 519, 520, 522, 525, 540-41-42

Aveling, Mrs—see *Marx-Aveling, Eleanor.*

Axelrod, Pavel Borisovich (1850-1928)—Russian Social-Democrat, member of the Emancipation of Labour group from 1883, author of a few works on the history and theory of Marxism.—305, 440

B

Baake, Hans—German publisher, Social-Democrat, Kurt Baake's brother.—491, 499

Baake, Kurt (1864-1938)—German Social-Democrat, journalist, one of the founders and masters of the Social-Democratic theatrical society Freien Volksbühne (1890). —491

Baare, Louis (1821-1897)—German industrialist, manager, of a steelworks company in Bochum; was sued for shirking taxes and for other machinations.—75

Bachem, Karl Joseph Emil (1858-1945)—German politician, historian and lawyer, a Centrist, member of the Reichstag from 1889.—100

Baernreither, Joseph Maria (1845-1925)—Austrian politician, lawyer and journalist, member of the Bohemian Landtag and Austrian Reichsrat (from 1885).—149

Bahr, Hermann (1863-1934)—Austrian journalist, critic, novelist and playwright.—149

Bakunin, Mikhail Alexandrovich (1814-1876)—Russian revolutionary and journalist, participant in the 1848-49 revolution in Germany; an ideologist of Narodism and anarchism; opposed Marxism in the First International; was expelled from the International at the Hague Congress in 1872 for his splitting activity.—31, 82, 98, 317, 361, 367, 519

Balfour, Jabez Spencer (1843-1916)—English politician and financist; Liberal M. P. (1880-92), manager of the Building Society; after its bankruptcy in 1892, fled to Argentina; was extradited in 1895 and sentenced to 14 years of hard labour.—64, 311

Barlen, Theodor—German Social-Democrat, emigrant in London.—445, 452

Baron—see *Kautsky, Karl*

Barry, Maltman (1842-1909)—English journalist, member of the First International, of the General Council (1872) and of the

returned to France after the amnesty; member of the Chamber of Deputies from 1888, sided with the socialists.—72

Cohen, Alexander.—452

Colajanni, Napoleone (1847-1921)—Italian politician, sociologist and journalist, Republican; took part in the national-liberation movement in Italy; close to the socialists in the 1880s and 1890s; deputy to the Parliament from 1890.—96

Columbus, Christopher (1451-1506)— Genoese-born navigator, discoverer of America.—198

Comte, Auguste (1798-1857)—French philosopher, founder of positivism.—430

Constans, Jean Antoine Ernest (1833-1913)— French statesman, moderate republican; Minister of the Interior (1880-81 and 1889-92).—68, 75

Constantine I, the Great (c. 285-337)—Roman Emperor (306-37).—449

Cotar, M. P.—French socialist.—132

Crawford, Emily (née *Johnson*) (1831-1915)— British journalist, Paris correspondent of several English papers.—64, 106, 380, 409, 434

Crispi, Francesco (1819-1901)—Italian statesman, initially a bourgeois republican, participant in the national-liberation movement in Italy; champion of constitutional monarchy from the late 1860s; a leader of the so-called bourgeois Left, Prime Minister (1887-91 and 1893-96).—369, 390, 423, 519

Croesus—last King of Lydia (560-546 B. C.).—168

Cromwell, Oliver (1599-1658)—leader of the English Revolution, Lord Protector of England, Scotland and Ireland from 1653.—266

Croon, Berta—sister-in-law of Hermann Engels, Frederick Engels' brother.—179

Crosland, Sir Joseph (1826-1904)—English manufacturer, conservative, M. P. (1893-95).—103

Cross—chief of the solicitors' office Cross & Sons in London.—539

Cunow, Heinrich Wilhelm Karl (1862-1936) —German Social-Democrat, historian, sociologist and ethnographer.—257

D

Dakyns—English geologist, member of the First International since 1869, an acquaintance of Marx and Engels.—259

Dalziel, Davison Alexander (1854-1928)—one of the founders of a British information agency, Conservative, M. P.—89

Danielson, Nikolai Frantsevich (pseudonym; *Nikolai-on* (1844-1918)—Russian economist and writer; an ideologist of Narodism in the 1880s-90s; translated into Russian volumes I (together with Hermann Lopatin and N. N. Lybavin), II and III of Marx's *Capital*, corresponded with Marx and Engels for several years.—109, 143, 212, 255, 280, 372-3, 412, 450, 455, 488, 516

Dante Alighieri (1265-1321)—Italian poet.— 256, 529

Darwin, Charles Robert (1809-1882)—English naturalist, founder of the theory of evolution by natural selection.—349

Debski, Aleksander (1857-1935)—Polish socialist, a founder of the Proletariat Party and the Polish Socialist Party (1892); an editor of the *Przedświt* in 1893; later withdrew from the working-class movement. —312

Delagrave, Charles Marie Eugène (1842-1934) —French publisher.—332

Delecluze, Mark Louis Alfred (1857-1923)— French socialist, formed a section of the Workers' Party in Calais (1882).—184

De Leon, Daniel (1852-1914)—prominent figure in the labour and socialist movement

Hyndman, Henry Mayers (1842-1921)—English socialist, founder (1881) and leader of the London Democratic Federation, which became Social-Democratic Federation in 1884; later a leader of the British Socialist Party.—120, 125, 277, 340, 342-3, 345, 354, 356

I

Iglesias, Posse Pablo (1850-1925)—prominent figure in the Spanish working-class and socialist movement; printer, journalist, member of the Spanish Federal Council of the First International (1871-72), opponent of anarchists; one of the founders of the Socialist Workers' Party of Spain (1879), later a leader of its reformist wing.—286-87, 334-5, 473-4

Ignatiyev—see *Helfand, Alexander Lazarevich*

J

Jaclard, Charles Victor (1843-1903)—French socialist, Blanquist, journalist, member of the First International, a Communard; after the suppression of the Commune emigrated to Switzerland and later to Russia; returned to France after amnesty in 1880 and continued his activity in the socialist movement.—182

Jacobi, Abraham (1830-1919)—German physician, member of the Communist League, defendant at the Cologne Communist trial (1852), acquitted by the jury; later emigrated to the USA, professor at and president of a few U.S. medical institutions.—500

Jaeger, Oscar (b. 1856)—husband of Hermann Engels' daughter Anna.—442

Janssen, Johannes (1829-1891)—German historian and theologian, author of numerous works on the history of Germany.—513

Jaurés, Jean Léon (1859-1914)—prominent figure in the international and French socialist movement, historian; leader of the reformist wing of the French Socialist Party; member of the Chamber of Deputies (1885-89, 1893-98); took part in all congresses of the Second International.—121, 155, 156, 185, 245, 249, 262, 269, 272, 274-75, 276, 291, 318, 325-26, 331-32, 448, 451

Jaworski, Apollinar, knight von (1825-1904)—Austrian statesman, Polish noble, member of the Chamber of Deputies (from 1887); minister without portfolio in the Windischgrätz Coalition Cabinet.—228

Jedrzejowski, Boleslaw Antoni (1867-1914)—Polish socialist, journalist; a founder and leader of the Prolétariat Party and the Polish Socialist Party; refugee in Berlin in 1891, later in Paris, and in London from 1893; an editor of the *Przedświt*.—518

Jodko-Narkiewicz, Tomasz Witold (Rabin) (1864-1924)—Polish journalist, a founder of the Polish Socialist Party and a leader of its revolutionary wing, member of the Prolétariat Party in the 1880s; contributed to the *Przedświt* in the 1890s, its editor (1893-1906).—311, 385, 437

Jogiches—see *Tyszka, Jan.*

Jollymeier—see *Schorlemmer, Carl.*

Jourde, Antoine (1848-1923)—French trade employee, socialist; delegate to several congresses of the French Workers' Party; later sided with the Boulangists; member of the Chamber of Deputies (from 1889).—183

Julius—see *Motteler, Julius.*

Juta, Johann Carel (1824-1886)—Dutch bookseller in Cape Town; husband of Marx's sister Louise.—531

K

Kanitz, Hans Wilhelm Alexander, Earl von (1841-1913)—German politician, a leader of the Conservative Party, deputy to the Prussian Landtag and to the German Reichstag.—326

Mora, Francisco (1842-1924)—a leader of the Spanish working-class and socialist movement, shoemaker, an organiser of the International's sections in Spain and Portugal, member of the Spanish Federal Council of the International (1870-72); fought anarchistic influence; an organiser of the Spanish Socialist Workers' Party (1879).—481

Morgan, Lewis Henry (1818-1881)—American ethnographer, archaeologist and historian of primitive society.—266

Morris, William (1834-1896)—English poet, writer and artist; took an active part in the labour and socialist movement in the 1880s and 1890s, a leader of the Socialist League (1884-89).—277, 299

Motteler, Emilie—Julius Motteler's wife.—37, 282, 452

Motteler, Julius (1838-1907)—German Social-Democrat; deputy to the Reichstag in 1874-78; an émigré in Zurich and later in London at the time of the Anti-Socialist Law; was responsible for the transportation of *Der Sozialdemokrat* and illegal Social-Democratic literature to Germany.—37, 38, 207, 282, 313, 328, 445, 451-2, 534

Mülberger, Arthur (1847-1907)—German physician, journalist, Social-Democrat.—146

Müller, Hans (1867-1950)—German journalist and writer; studied in Zurich; sided with the German Social-Democrats in the late 1880s, a leader of "The Young" in the early 1890s, contributed to a number of Social-Democratic newspapers.—8, 15, 17, 26

Müller-Tellering, Eduard von (born c. 1808)—German lawyer and writer, petty-bourgeois democrat; contributed to the *Neue Rheinische Zeitung* (1848-49); emigrated to England after the defeat of the revolution; libeled Marx and Engels in the press; emigrated to the USA in 1852.—410

Mundella, Anthony John (1825-1897)—British statesman and manufacturer, MP (from 1868), held several ministerial posts.—311

Muñoz—Spanish anarchist, agent provocateur.—254

Münzer, Thomas (c. 1490-1525)—leader of the urban plebeians and poor peasants during the Reformation and Peasant War of 1525 in Germany; advocated ideas of egalitarian utopian communism.—512

Musoiu, Panait (1864-1944)—Romanian socialist, an editor of *Munca* and contributor to several other Romanian socialist newspapers; translated into Romanian the *Manifesto of the Communist Party* and other works by Marx and Engels.—281

N

Nachodsky, Joseph Klapka—translator of Marx's *Wage-Labour and Capital* into Czech.—508

Napoleon I Bonaparte (1769-1821)—Emperor of the French (1804-14 and 1815).—157, 266

Napoleon III (Charles Louis Napoleon Bonaparte) (1808-1873)—Napoleon I's nephew, President of the Second Republic (1848-51), Emperor of the French (1852-70).—51, 58

Nechayev (Netschajeff), Sergei Gennadyevich (1847-1882)—Russian revolutionary, conspirator, representative of the extremely adventurist trend in anarchism; was connected with Bakunin in 1869-71; was extradited by the Swiss authorities to the Russian government in 1872; sentenced to twenty years' imprisonment, died in the Peter and Paul Fortress in St Petersburg.—307, 317

Nettlau, Max (1865-1944)—Austrian historian, phylologist; anarchist; author of a few works on the history of anarchism.—334

Nicholas II (1868-1918)—Emperor of Russia (1894-1917).—360, 436, 440, 451, 455

Nichols, Sarah Nichols—Frederick Engels' cook.—542

Nieuwenhuis, Ferdinand Domela (1846-1919) —prominent figure in the Dutch working-class movement; a founder of the Dutch Social-Democracy (1881); went over to anarchists in the 1890s.—20

Nokov (Nokoff), Stojan (1872-1959)—Bulgarian Social-Democrat, lived in Geneva in 1889-94; a founder and leader of the Bulgarian Social-Democratic students' organisation in Switzerland; returned to Bulgaria in 1894; village teacher.—152

Nothnagel, Hermann (1841-1905)—German and Austrian clinicain, director of a clinic in Vienna (from 1882).—21, 399

O

Oberwinder, Heinrich (1846-1914)—prominent figure in the Austrian and German working-class movement, journalist; a Lassallean in the early 1860s, later joined Eisenachers, delegate to the Basle Congress of the First International (1869), editor of the *Volksstimme* and *Volkswille*; withdrew from the working-class movement in the late 1870s; exposed as a Prussian police spy in the late 1880s; editor of *Das Volk* from 1890.—316

Omar I, Omar ibn-al-Chattab (born c. 580-644)—Arab Caliph (634-644).—343

Orléans—royal dynasty in France (1830-48).—68, 75

Oswald, Eugen (1826-1912)—German journalist, democrat; took part in the revolutionary movement in Baden in 1848-49; emigrated to England after the defeat of the revolution.—541

P

Pareto, Vilfredo (1848-1923)—Swiss-born Italian economist and sociologist, member of the so-called mathematical school of economics, professor at Lausanne University (from 1894).—226

Parnell, Charles Stewart (1846-1891)—Irish politician and statesman, Liberal, MP

(from 1875), leader of the Home Rule League (1877-90); President of the Irish Land League (from 1880).—87

Pasquali, Felice (real name *Nicolo Giolotti*)—Italian refugee in England.—333, 339

Paul—see *Lafargue, Paul*.

Pauli, Ida—Philipp Viktor Pauli's wife.—80

Pauli, Philipp Viktor (1836-d. after 1916)—German chemist, friend of Marx and Engels.—79

Pearce, Ada—medical nurse.—542

Pease, Edward Reynolds (1857-1955)—English socialist, a founder and leader of the Fabian Society, its secretary.—335

Percy—see *Rosher, Percy White*

Perkin, Sir William Henry (1838-1907)—English chemist, discoverer of aniline dyes, professor of organic chemistry in Manchester.—79

Pernerstorfer, Anna—Engelbert Pernerstorfer's wife.—384

Pernerstorfer, Engelbert (1850-1918)—Austrian politician, democrat, an editor of *Deutsche Worte* and *Arbeiter-Zeitung*, member of the Chamber of Deputies from 1885, joined the Social-Democratic Party of Austria in 1896.—117, 262

Pestalozzi, Johann Heinrich (1746-1827)—Swiss educator and writer, notable for his reforms in the methods of education.—429

Petersen, Nicolas Lorenzo (1854-c. 1916)—prominent figure in the Danish working-class movement, a leader of the left-wing of the Social-Democratic Party of Denmark.—177

Petty, Sir William (1623-1687)—English economist and statistician, founder of the classical school of bourgeois political economy in Britain.—461

Pflüger, Eduard Friedrich Wilhelm (1828-1940)—German physiologist, professor at Bonn University (from 1859).—45, 46

W

INDEX OF LITERARY AND MYTHOLOGICAL NAMES

INDEX OF PERIODICALS

La Justice—a daily newspaper of the Radical Party; published in Paris from 1880 to 1930; the organ of the Radical Party's left wing in 1880-96.—182

Kladderadatsch—an illustrated satirical weekly of a liberal trend published in Berlin from 1848.—390

Kosmos Zeitschrift für Entwickelungslehre und einheitliche Weltschauung—a natural scientific monthly expounding Darwinism, published in Leipzig from 1877 to 1880 and in Stuttgart from 1881 to 1886.—513

The Labour Elector—a socialist weekly published in London from June 1888 to July 1894 under the editorship of Henry Hyde Champion.—84, 142

The Labour Leader—a monthly published from 1882, initially under the title *The Miner*, and under this title from 1889 as the journal of the Scottish Labor Party, and of the Independent Labour Party from 1893; became a weekly in 1894. Its editor until 1904 was James Keir Hardie.—356, 411, 415, 420, 421, 434, 483, 484, 525

Lotta di Classe—an Italian socialist weekly, the central organ of the Italian Workers' Party; published in Milan from 1892 to 1898.—78

Lumea nouă—a newspaper of the Social-Democratic Party of Romania, appeared in Bucharest as a sequence of the Munca. It was published daily in 1894-98 and weekly 1898-1900.—358

Munca—a Romanian Social-Democratic weekly published in Bucharest in 1890-94.—17, 358

La Nation—a radical daily published in Paris from 1884.—49

Nature. A Weekly Illustrated Journal of Science—a British journal published in London since 1869.—80

Neue Rheinische Zeitung. Organ der Demokratie—a daily newspaper of the German revolutionary proletarian democrats during the German revolution of 1848-49; it was published in Cologne under Marx's editorship from 1 June 1848 to 19 May 1849, with an interval between 27 September and 12 October 1848; Engels was also one of the editors.—3, 352, 398, 409, 410, 414, 471, 530

Neue Rheinische Zeitung. Politisch-okonomische Revue—a theoretical journal of the Communist League; founded by Marx and Engels in December 1849 and published until November 1859.—3, 9, 127, 352, 438, 443, 445, 446, 480, 484, 496, 498, 499, 501, 502

Neue Rheinische Zeitungs-Revue—see *Neue Rheinische Zeitung. Politische-okonomische Revue.*

Die Neue Welt. Illustriertes Unterhaltungsblatt fur das Volk—a German socialist fortnightly published in Leipzig from 1876-1883, then in Stuttgart and Hamburg until 1919; Wilhelm Liebknecht was its editor in 1876-80.—297

Die Neue Zeit—a theoretical journal of the German Social-Democrats; published in Stuttgart monthly from 1883 to October 1890 and then weekly till autumn 1923. It was edited by Karl Kautsky from 1883 to October 1917 and by Heinrich Cunow from October 1917 to autumn 1923.—Engels contributed a few articles to it in 1885-94.—7, 26, 28, 48, 49, 50, 53, 54, 67, 91, 166, 193, 225, 227, 241, 243-44, 257, 279, 314, 320, 321, 345, 348, 365, 387, 388, 392, 400, 415, 421, 456, 484, 486, 490, 504

El Socialista—a weekly of the Socialist Workers' Party of Spain published in Madrid from 1885.—139, 287, 336

Le Socialiste, Organe Central du Parti Oubrier—a weekly founded by Jules Guesde in Paris in 1885; appeared with intervals until September 1890; press organ of the Socialist Party of France from 1902-1905 and of the French Socialist Party from 1905.—6, 7, 12, 30, 124, 135, 185, 209, 210, 277, 315, 332, 344, 358, 370, 499

La Société Nouvelle—a French monthly dealing with problems of sociology, art, science and literature; appeared in Brussels and Paris from 1884-1914 with intervals.—361

Der Sozialdemokrat—a Social-Democratic daily published in Berlin in 1894-95.—355, 366, 368, 377

Der Sozialdemokrat. Organ de Sozialdemokratic deutscher Zunge—a daily press organ of the Socialist Workers' Party of Germany, published in Zurich from September 1879 to September 1888, and in London from October 1888 to 27 September 1890. Its editor in 1878-80 was Georg Heinrich von Vollmar and in 1881-90 Eduard Bernstein. Marx and Engels were among its contributors.—28, 226

Der Sozialist—a weekly published in Berlin from 1891 to 1899; it was a newspaper of "independent" socialists from 1891 to 1893.—361

Sozialpolitisches Centralblatt—a Social-Democratic weekly, published under this title in Berlin in 1892-95; its editor was Heinrich Braun.—After a merger with the *Blatter fur sociale Praxis* in 1895, it appeared as *Soziale Praxis*.—213, 372, 466, 468, 492

The Standard—a conservative daily, founded in London in 1827.—and published to 1916; it emerged from *The Evening Standard*.—448, 483

Die Tagwacht—a German-language Swiss Social-Democratic newspaper published in Zurich from 1869-1880; press organ of the International's German sections in Switzerland in 1869-73 and then of the Swiss Workers' Union of the Social-Democratic Party of Switzerland.—481

Le Temps—a conservative daily published in Paris from 1861 to 1943.—421

Der Textil-Arbeiter—a weekly of the Textile Workers' Trade Union, published in Berlin from 1889.—337

Tribune—see *New York Daily Tribune*

Das Volk—a weekly of the Christian Social Party, published in Berlin from 1889.—316

Volks-Anwalt—a German-language weekly of the Socialist Labor Party of North America published in 1889-98 in Cincinnati, then Baltimore, Buffalo and Cleveland.—315

Der Volksstaat—central organ of the Social-Democratic Workers' Party published in Leipzig from 2 October 1869 to 29 September 1876 (twice a week until July 1873, then three times a week). General direction was in the hands of Wilhelm Liebknecht. An important part was played by August Bebel, who was in charge of the *Volksstaat* Publishing House.—The paper regularly carried articles by Marx and Engels.—6, 68

Volkstimme. Organ der Sozialdemokratischen Partei Ungarns—a German language weekly published in Budapest from 1872.—355

PERIODICAL NAMES IN RUSSIAN IN TEXT

SUBJECT INDEX

Heterick Memorial Library
Ohio Northern University

	DUE	RETURNED		DUE	RETURNED
1.			13.		
2.			14.		
3.			15.		
4.			16.		
5.			17.		
6.			18.		
7.			19.		
8.			20.		
9.			21.		
10.			22.		
11.			23.		
12.			24.